CODE OF CRIMINAL JUSTICE

A Practical Guide to the Penal Statutes

Kenneth Del Vecchio

PEARSON

Prentice
Hall

Upper Saddle River, New Jersey 07458

Library of Congress Cataloging-in-Publication Data

Del Vecchio, Kenneth.
    Code of criminal justice : a practical guide to the penal statutes / Kenneth Del Vecchio.
        p. cm.
    Includes index.
    ISBN 0-13-157829-4
    1. Criminal law—United States.   2. Criminal procedure—United States.   I. Title.

KF9219.D35 2008
345.73—dc22   2006052543

Editor-in-Chief: Vernon R. Anthony
Senior Editor: Tim Peyton
Editorial Assistant: Jillian Allison
Marketing Manager: Adam Kloza
Managing Editor: Mary Carnis
Production Liaison: Ann Pulido
Production Editor: Janet Bolton
Manufacturing Manager: Ilene Sanford
Manufacturing Buyer: Cathleen Petersen
Senior Design Coordinator: Miguel Ortiz
Cover Design: Jill Little, iDesign
Copy Editor/Proofreader: Maine Proofreading Services
Composition: Integra
Printing/Binding: Hamilton Printing
Cover Printer: Phoenix Color

Pearson Education LTD.   Pearson Educación de Mexico, S.A. de C.V.
Pearson Education Australia PTY, Limited   Pearson Education—Japan
Pearson Education Singapore, Pte. Ltd.   Pearson Education Malaysia, Pte. Ltd.
Pearson Education North Asia Ltd.   Pearson Education, Upper Saddle River, New Jersey
Pearson Education Canada, Ltd.

10 9 8 7 6 5 4 3 2 1
ISBN-13: 978-0-13-157829-6
ISBN-10:   0-13-157829-4

This book is dedicated to Chief Mary F. Rabadeau (Ret.),
the first woman police chief in New Jersey history
and my good friend.

Contents

PREFACE

Code of Criminal Justice: A Practical Guide to the Penal Statutes serves as a comprehensive and detailed work to assist those who are attempting to understand and apply United States criminal statutes. This codebook is written to decipher and explain the statutes for students studying criminal law, to educate trainees at the police academies, to aid police officers in their daily charging duties and to interpret the statutes' meanings for lawyers and judges. The book is designed to generally make the penal code a more interesting and educational tool.

This book contains, in complete verbatim text, hundreds of criminal statutes, ranging from the well-known basic offenses to the uncommon criminal laws that are rarely invoked. The statutes are primarily drawn from the New Jersey criminal code, though other states' statutes are also utilized.

Preceding each statutory chapter or group of chapters is a fictional fact pattern. Following each statute that defines a felony or misdemeanor is a Practical Application section. These sections draw on the fact patterns to explain the statutes. Readers can utilize the fact patterns and Practical Application Sections to understand the language of the statutes and thereafter determine how to appropriately charge pursuant to them.

While *Code of Criminal Justice: A Practical Guide to the Penal Statutes* primarily tackles the substantive statutes defining felonies and misdemeanors, it also explains many of the other related statutes, such as defenses and general provisions. Statutory language defining the offenses, the elements pertaining to them and the differences among the offenses are addressed in detail. In sum total, nearly every type of statute that defines a felony or misdemeanor has a Practical Application section that explains it; several other statutes are afforded Practical Application sections as well. Sentencing and administrative statutes are not the focus of this book, though they are discussed at times.

Code of Criminal Justice: A Practical Guide to the Penal Statutes provides valuable multiple-choice and essay questions at the end of each chapter. An answer guide at the end of the text, with bullet point summaries, provides possible answers to the end of chapter questions.

This text is practical and necessary for college and law students attempting to learn the actual criminal statutes enacted in the United States, and it is equally important for trainees at the police academies who must learn the nuances of criminal laws and be able to apply them once they graduate and hit the streets. Similarly, it is an essential tool for law enforcement officers who are presented daily with real-life criminal circumstances and need to know how to correctly charge pursuant to each peculiar and unique situation. This book is also a valuable instrument for lawyers and judges who are looking for mechanisms to better understand the often confusing and convoluted statutory language.

ACKNOWLEDGMENTS

Countless hours of typing, grammatical proofreading and research-related work were dedicated by my wife, Francine, to this book. As each chapter of the manuscript was completed, she read and examined it with me. Her honest excitement for my writing holds an intangible quality that I can't quite describe in this acknowledgment. Francine's unyielding efforts were modestly provided in face of the challenges and rigors she herself endured as an Ivy League doctoral student (Teachers College, Columbia University), as a professor at this prestigious university and as a full-time public school teacher. I thank her, with all my heart, for her loyalty and stamina.

I thank Prentice Hall and Pearson Education for giving me the opportunity to be their author of this important book, as well as a number of other books that I have written for them. I owe special thanks to the following individuals at Prentice Hall who shine in their efforts to make my books successful: Vern Anthony, Janet Bolton, Mayda Bosco, Angie Doyle, LeeAnne Fisher, Dianne Fortier, Gene O'Connor and Tim Peyton. In addition, I want to thank Margaret Lannamann from O'Donnell and Associates and Maine Proofreading Services. I also want to thank Kim Davies, for believing in me and getting me started with Prentice Hall, and Frank Mortimer, for continuing to believe in my work. Finally, I thank Sarah Hayday for introducing me to Prentice Hall and Pearson Education.

ABOUT THE AUTHOR

Often headlined as "Renaissance Man," Kenneth Del Vecchio has been the subject of hundreds of national magazine and newspaper articles. He has been called "Jack of All Trades, Master of All," "The Triple Threat: Attorney, Author, Filmmaker" and "The Next John Grisham" by print and television media.

Del Vecchio is the author of a number of criminal law books for Prentice Hall, a published novelist, the owner of a criminal law learning center, an attorney who has tried over 400 cases, the founder of New Jersey's largest film festival and a critically acclaimed filmmaker and actor.

In 1995, Kenneth Del Vecchio became one of the youngest attorneys in state history to try and win a criminal jury trial when he successfully defended a wrongfully accused man against firearms charges in Newark, New Jersey. A year later, Del Vecchio had his first novel published and traveled the East Coast on a book-signing tour. After a successful freshman novel publication, Del Vecchio expanded to filmmaking in 1998. Since then, he has written, directed and produced five feature films that star multiple Academy Award and Emmy winners and nominees; these critically acclaimed films also feature Del Vecchio himself in lead and supporting roles. During all this time, he has handled thousands of criminal cases, serving as both a defense attorney and a prosecutor. In 2004, Prentice Hall published Del Vecchio's *New Jersey Code of Criminal Justice,* followed in 2006 by *Test Prep Guide to Accompany New Jersey Code of Criminal Justice.*

As founder and chairman of the Hoboken International Film Festival, Del Vecchio has created the largest film festival ever to hit New Jersey. The festival, held in New Jersey's artistic capital, features a celebrity jury, with cash prizes being awarded to the winning filmmakers and writers.

Kenneth Del Vecchio's films, primarily focusing on matters of criminal law, include *Polycarp, Pride & Loyalty, The Drum Beats Twice, Tinsel Town* and *Rules for Men.* His crime suspense novels are *Revelation in the Wilderness* and *Pride & Loyalty.*

In addition to his film and writing projects, Del Vecchio is currently the Prosecutor of the Borough of Bogota and formerly served as the Prosecutor for the Borough of Hawthorne and the City of Clifton. He maintains a criminal defense practice and is a member of the New Jersey and Pennsylvania bars. Several times a year, Del Vecchio, via his criminal law learning center, instructs at intensive seminars for police officers and attorneys throughout New Jersey and surrounding states. He is also a frequent television and radio legal analyst.

Kenneth Del Vecchio resides in North Haledon, New Jersey, with his wife, Francine. His website may be visited at www.justiceforallproductions.com.

1

CRIMINAL HOMICIDE

FACT PATTERN

The State Attorney General called a special meeting at his East Side office to discuss four seemingly unrelated homicides. Invited were the detectives leading the investigations in the separate cases—a state trooper, a Jefferson lieutenant, an Adams detective and a Monroe County Prosecutor's Office investigator. Each officer provided a short summary of his or her investigation to the state's top law enforcement official.

While on patrol during a late evening winter shift, Trooper Gene Knollwood responded to a radio report that a toll collector on the state turnpike had just been robbed at gunpoint by a male traveling in a black SUV with a dented rear bumper. The felony occurred at Exit 16W, and the assailant fled toward Route 45 West.

Minutes after the felony, Knollwood located an SUV matching the description and activated his overhead lights and sirens, ordering the automobile to stop; instead, the suspect accelerated and a pursuit followed. The chase ended abruptly, however, when the driver made a sudden erratic turn, crossing from the left lane to the right, attempting to exit onto the off-ramp leading to Route 7. At this location, the vehicle struck a stranded motorist, killing him on impact. The suspect, Jeff Weiss, was arrested on the scene.

Weeks earlier in Alexander, the county seat of Monroe County, a fight broke out between two strangers in an upscale bar/restaurant directly after the bartender had announced "last call." When Alexander patrol officers arrived at the location, they found a male in his late twenties, later identified as George Carmichael, dead in a pool of blood. Witnesses advised that he was physically beaten by an unknown man in his late twenties after the two argued over who was next in line for a drink. According to the witnesses, the assailant had thrown the first punch and then had fled when he saw Carmichael fall to the ground. No weapons were used during the altercation. During the following week, an investigation led by Sheila Talamico of the Monroe County Prosecutor's Office resulted in the arrest of Larry Kelleher. Kelleher, under interrogation, admitted that he had struck Carmichael at the bar but was unaware that his blows had resulted in the man's demise.

Across the state, near the Spartan River, the Adams Police Department investigated the disappearance of a middle-aged lawyer for nearly three weeks. The search ended when his body was located in a wooded area under a pile of rocks and tree branches. The makeshift grave confirmed Detective Sergeant Nicholas Sane's fears that the man had been murdered. But by what means?

The lawyer's physical body, except for decomposition, was not harmed. An autopsy, however, revealed that the man had ingested an alarming amount of arsenic over time and had died several weeks after his final ingestion. A subsequent investigation, involving a joint task force of the U.S. Drug Enforcement Agency (DEA), Corona County Prosecutor's Office investigators, and Adams police personnel, led to the attorney's sister, Brigitte Madison, who was the beneficiary of his lucrative life insurance policy and all of his assets. Although she denied any wrongdoing, the investigators found traces of rodent poison in her garbage can; the poison's key ingredient was arsenic. Also, a forensic analysis of hair strands found on the decedent's body matched Madison's hair. Similarly, her fingerprints were found on her brother's watch, which was on his wrist when he was uncovered at his nature deathbed. Finally, passages in Madison's diary mentioned jealousy of her brother's wealth and her desire to see him dead. She even had described a fantasy plot to murder the barrister, which was to be carried out by poisoning him.

On the same day that the Adams police arrested Brigitte Madison, the Jefferson Police Department found Cindy Lemon, a woman in her early thirties, shot to death in her newly built townhouse. Immediately, the police suspected her live-in boyfriend to be the perpetrator, given reports of a tumultuous relationship. Lieutenant Mario Axel headed a manhunt for her missing boyfriend. However, his search was unwarranted, as the man arrived by his own volition at the Jefferson Police Department, hysterical after learning that his girlfriend was dead. He had been in Europe on business; airline personnel and other witnesses verified his out-of-the-country alibi, and accordingly, the investigation turned to Lemon's former roommate, Maggie Harkins.

Harkins had filed a lawsuit against Lemon, alleging that she had fraudulently duped her out of $30,000, which was later used as a down payment for the townhouse. Harkins' case subsequently was dismissed by a Superior Court judge; the dismissal occurred just hours before Lemon was found riddled with bullets in her home. Axel learned, through a neighbor's account, that Harkins was seen arriving at the townhouse that afternoon but couldn't advise when she departed. With this information, Axel asked Harkins to voluntarily come to police headquarters to discuss the matter with him. She complied and there admitted to shooting Lemon in a "blind rage."

After Axel completed explaining the Harkins case, the four officers sat silent with Attorney General Christian Taylor, confused as to any possible connection among their cases. There were no similarities in victims; the fact patterns were totally unrelated; the causes of death in each case were unique; the homicide locales were in different parts of the state; there appeared to be a definitive, distinct rationale for all four killings.

The relationship, Taylor ultimately advised, was that all four perpetrators—Jeff Weiss, Larry Kelleher, Brigitte Madison and Maggie Harkins—were part of a violent underground antisocial group, RS, which was purportedly planning a massive bombing of an unknown public building. These homicides were unrelated to their activities in RS, but the Attorney General's Office and the FBI were obviously greatly concerned about the pending massacre and wanted to capitalize on these fortuitous arrests, perhaps enticing one (if not all) of the defendants to "flip" on the bombing's masterminds.

Taylor explained that deals could be offered, amending each of their charges to lesser included offenses, if they cooperated and provided integral details. Accordingly, it was important for him to learn as much as possible about these individuals—who is the type to cooperate, who has a motive to cooperate and who may need to cooperate. The investigating officers could provide this insight. The first necessary factor to analyze was under what homicide statute each defendant was charged. With that information, Attorney General Taylor could determine what lower charges, if any, could ultimately be offered upon a suspect's cooperation. The state's homicide statutes were then reviewed.

1-1.   Definitions

The following definitions apply in this Criminal Code, unless a different meaning plainly is required:

  a. "Bodily injury" means physical pain, illness or any impairment of physical condition.
  b. "Serious bodily injury" means bodily injury which creates a substantial risk of death or which causes serious, permanent disfigurement or protracted loss or impairment of the function of any bodily member or organ.
  c. "Deadly weapon" means any firearm or other weapon, device, instrument, material or substance, whether animate or inanimate, which in the manner it is used or is intended to be used, is known to be capable of producing death or serious bodily injury or which in the manner it is fashioned would lead the victim reasonably to believe it to be capable of producing death or serious bodily injury.
  d. "Significant bodily injury" means bodily injury which creates a temporary loss of the function of any bodily member or organ or temporary loss of any one of the five senses.
  e. "Abortional act" means an act committed upon or with respect to a female, whether by another person or by the female herself, whether she is pregnant or not, whether directly upon her body or by the administering, taking or prescription of drugs or in any other manner, with intent to cause a miscarriage of such female.
  f. "Justifiable abortional act" means an abortional act that is committed upon a female with her consent by a duly licensed physician acting (a) under a reasonable belief that such is necessary to preserve her life, or (b) within 24 weeks from the commencement of her pregnancy. A pregnant female's commission of an abortional act upon herself is justifiable when she acts upon the advice of a duly licensed physician (1) that such act is necessary to preserve her life, or (2) within 24 weeks from the commencement of her pregnancy. The submission by a female to an abortional act is justifiable when she believes that it is being committed by a duly licensed physician, acting under a reasonable belief that such act is necessary to preserve her life or within 24 weeks from the commencement of her pregnancy.

1-2.   Criminal homicide

  a. A person is guilty of criminal homicide if he purposely, knowingly, recklessly or under the circumstances set forth in section 1-5 causes the death of another human being.
  b. Criminal homicide is murder, aggravated manslaughter, manslaughter or death by auto.

1-3.   Murder

  a. Except as provided in 1-4, criminal homicide constitutes murder when:
    (1) The actor purposely causes death or serious bodily injury resulting in death; or
    (2) The actor knowingly causes death or serious bodily injury resulting in death; or
    (3) It is committed when the actor, acting either alone or with one or more other persons, is engaged in the commission of, or an attempt to commit, or flight after committing or attempting to commit robbery, sexual assault, arson, burglary, kidnapping, carjacking, criminal escape or terrorism, and in the course of such felony or of

immediate flight therefrom, any person causes the death of a person other than one of the participants; except that in any prosecution under this subsection, in which the defendant was not the only participant in the underlying felony, it is an affirmative defense that the defendant:

   (a) Did not commit the homicidal act or in any way solicit, request, command, importune, cause or aid the commission thereof; and

   (b) Was not armed with a deadly weapon, or any instrument, article or substance readily capable of causing death or serious physical injury and of a sort not ordinarily carried in public places by law-abiding persons; and

   (c) Had no reasonable ground to believe that any other participant was armed with such a weapon, instrument, article or substance; and

   (d) Had no reasonable ground to believe that any other participant intended to engage in conduct likely to result in death or serious physical injury.

b. (1) Murder is a felony of the first degree but a person convicted of murder shall be sentenced, except as provided in subsection c. of this section, by the court to a term of 30 years, during which the person shall not be eligible for parole, or be sentenced to a specific term of years which shall be between 30 years and life imprisonment of which the person shall serve 30 years before being eligible for parole.

   (2) If the victim was a law enforcement officer and was murdered while performing his official duties or was murdered because of his status as a law enforcement officer, the person convicted of that murder shall be sentenced, except as otherwise provided in subsection c. of this section, by the court to a term of life imprisonment, during which the person shall not be eligible for parole.

   (3) A person convicted of murder and who is not sentenced to death under this section shall be sentenced to a term of life imprisonment without eligibility for parole if the murder was committed under all of the following circumstances:

     (a) The victim is less than 14 years old; and

     (b) The act is committed in the course of the commission of an aggravated sexual assault or sexual assault, whether alone or with one or more persons.

   (4) If the defendant was subject to sentencing pursuant to subsection c. and the jury or court found the existence of one or more aggravating factors, but that such factors did not outweigh the mitigating factors found to exist by the jury or court or the jury was unable to reach a unanimous verdict as to the weight of the factors, the defendant shall be sentenced by the court to a term of life imprisonment during which the defendant shall not be eligible for parole. With respect to a sentence imposed pursuant to this subsection, the defendant shall not be entitled to a deduction of commutation and work credits from that sentence.

c. Any person convicted under subsection a.(1) or (2) who committed the homicidal act by his own conduct; or who as an accomplice procured the commission of the offense by payment or promise of payment of anything of pecuniary value; or who, as a leader of a narcotics trafficking network and in furtherance of a conspiracy as part of a narcotics trafficking network, commanded or by threat or promise solicited the commission of the offense, or if the murder occurred during the commission of the felony of terrorism, any person who committed the felony of terrorism, shall be sentenced as provided hereinafter:

   (1) The court shall conduct a separate sentencing proceeding to determine whether the defendant should be sentenced to death or pursuant to the provisions of subsection b. of this section.

Where the defendant has been tried by a jury, the proceeding shall be conducted by the judge who presided at the trial and before the jury which determined the defendant's guilt, except that, for good cause, the court may discharge that jury and conduct the proceeding before a jury impaneled for the purpose of the proceeding. Where the defendant has entered a plea of guilty or has been tried without a jury, the proceeding shall be conducted by the judge who accepted the defendant's plea or who determined the defendant's guilt and before a jury impaneled for the purpose of the proceeding. On motion of the defendant and with consent of the prosecuting attorney the court may conduct a proceeding without a jury. Nothing in this subsection shall be construed to prevent the participation of an alternate juror in the sentencing proceeding if one of the jurors who rendered the guilty verdict becomes ill or is otherwise unable to proceed before or during the sentencing proceeding.

(2)   (a)   At the proceeding, the State shall have the burden of establishing beyond a reasonable doubt the existence of any aggravating factors set forth in paragraph (4) of this subsection. The defendant shall have the burden of producing evidence of the existence of any mitigating factors set forth in paragraph (5) of this subsection but shall not have a burden with regard to the establishment of a mitigating factor.

    (b)   The admissibility of evidence offered by the State to establish any of the aggravating factors shall be governed by the rules governing the admission of evidence at criminal trials. The defendant may offer, without regard to the rules governing the admission of evidence at criminal trials, reliable evidence relevant to any of the mitigating factors. If the defendant produces evidence in mitigation which would not be admissible under the rules governing the admission of evidence at criminal trials, the State may rebut that evidence without regard to the rules governing the admission of evidence at criminal trials.

    (c)   Evidence admitted at the trial, which is relevant to the aggravating and mitigating factors set forth in paragraphs (4) and (5) of this subsection, shall be considered without the necessity of reintroducing that evidence at the sentencing proceeding; provided that the fact finder at the sentencing proceeding was present as either the fact finder or the judge at the trial.

    (d)   The State and the defendant shall be permitted to rebut any evidence presented by the other party at the sentencing proceeding and to present argument as to the adequacy of the evidence to establish the existence of any aggravating or mitigating factor.

    (e)   Prior to the commencement of the sentencing proceeding, or at such time as he has knowledge of the existence of an aggravating factor, the prosecuting attorney shall give notice to the defendant of the aggravating factors which he intends to prove in the proceeding.

    (f)   Evidence offered by the State with regard to the establishment of a prior homicide conviction pursuant to paragraph (4) (a) of this subsection may include the identity and age of the victim, the manner of death and the relationship, if any, of the victim to the defendant.

(3)   The jury, or if there is no jury, the court shall return a special verdict setting forth in writing the existence or nonexistence of each of the aggravating and mitigating factors set forth in paragraphs (4) and (5) of this subsection. If any aggravating

factor is found to exist, the verdict shall also state whether it outweighs beyond a reasonable doubt any one or more mitigating factors:

(a) If the jury or the court finds that any aggravating factors exist and that all of the aggravating factors outweigh beyond a reasonable doubt all of the mitigating factors, the court shall sentence the defendant to death;

(b) If the jury or the court finds that no aggravating factors exist, or that all of the aggravating factors which exist do not outweigh all of the mitigating factors, the court shall sentence the defendant pursuant to subsection b; or

(c) If the jury is unable to reach a unanimous verdict, the court shall sentence the defendant pursuant to subsection b.

(4) The aggravating factors which may be found by the jury or the court are:

(a) The defendant has been convicted, at any time, of another murder. For purposes of this section, a conviction shall be deemed final when sentence is imposed and may be used as an aggravating factor regardless of whether it is on appeal;

(b) In the commission of the murder, the defendant purposely or knowingly created a grave risk of death to another person in addition to the victim;

(c) The murder was outrageously or wantonly vile, horrible or inhuman in that it involved torture, depravity of mind or an aggravated assault to the victim;

(d) The defendant committed the murder as consideration for the receipt, or in expectation of the receipt of any thing of pecuniary value;

(e) The defendant procured the commission of the murder by payment or promise of payment of anything of pecuniary value;

(f) The murder was committed for the purpose of escaping detection, apprehension, trial, punishment or confinement for another offense committed by the defendant or another;

(g) The murder was committed while the defendant was engaged in the commission of, or an attempt to commit, or flight after committing or attempting to commit murder, robbery, sexual assault, arson, burglary, kidnapping, carjacking or the felony of contempt;

(h) The defendant murdered a public servant, while the victim was engaged in the performance of his official duties, or because of the victim's status as a public servant;

(i) The defendant: (i) as a leader of a narcotics trafficking network and in furtherance of a conspiracy as part of a narcotics trafficking network, committed, commanded or by threat or promise solicited the commission of the murder or (ii) committed the murder at the direction of a leader of a narcotics trafficking network in furtherance of a conspiracy as part of a narcotics trafficking network;

(j) The homicidal act that the defendant committed or procured was during the course of an act of aggravated arson;

(k) The victim was less than 14 years old; or

(l) The murder was committed during the commission of, or an attempt to commit, or flight after committing or attempting to commit, terrorism.

(5) The mitigating factors which may be found by the jury or the court are:

(a) The defendant was under the influence of extreme mental or emotional disturbance insufficient to constitute a defense to prosecution;

      (b) The victim solicited, participated in or consented to the conduct which resulted in his death;

      (c) The age of the defendant at the time of the murder;

      (d) The defendant's capacity to appreciate the wrongfulness of his conduct or to conform his conduct to the requirements of the law was significantly impaired as the result of mental disease or defect or intoxication, but not to a degree sufficient to constitute a defense to prosecution;

      (e) The defendant was under unusual and substantial duress insufficient to constitute a defense to prosecution;

      (f) The defendant has no significant history of prior criminal activity;

      (g) The defendant rendered substantial assistance to the State in the prosecution of another person for the felony of murder; or

      (h) Any other factor which is relevant to the defendant's character or record or to the circumstances of the offense.

    (6) When a defendant at a sentencing proceeding presents evidence of the defendant's character or record pursuant to subparagraph (h) of paragraph (5) of this subsection, the State may present evidence of the murder victim's character and background and of the impact of the murder on the victim's survivors. If the jury finds that the State has proven at least one aggravating factor beyond a reasonable doubt and the jury finds the existence of a mitigating factor pursuant to subparagraph (h) of paragraph (5) of this subsection, the jury may consider the victim and survivor evidence presented by the State pursuant to this paragraph in determining the appropriate weight to give mitigating evidence presented pursuant to subparagraph (h) of paragraph (5) of this subsection. As used in this paragraph "victim and survivor evidence" may include the display of a photograph of the victim taken before the homicide.

d. The sentencing proceeding set forth in subsection c. of this section shall not be waived by the prosecuting attorney.

e. Every judgment of conviction which results in a sentence of death under this section shall be appealed, pursuant to the Rules of Court, to the Supreme Court. Upon the request of the defendant, the Supreme Court shall also determine whether the sentence is disproportionate to the penalty imposed in similar cases, considering both the felony and the defendant. Proportionality review under this section shall be limited to a comparison of similar cases in which a sentence of death has been imposed under subsection c. of this section. In any instance in which the defendant fails, or refuses to appeal, the appeal shall be taken by the Office of the Public Defender or other counsel appointed by the Supreme Court for that purpose.

f. Prior to the jury's sentencing deliberations, the trial court shall inform the jury of the sentences which may be imposed pursuant to subsection b. of this section or the defendant if the defendant is not sentenced to death. The jury shall also be informed that a failure to reach a unanimous verdict shall result in sentencing by the court pursuant to subsection b.

g. A juvenile who has been tried as an adult and convicted of murder shall not be sentenced pursuant to the provisions of subsection c. but shall be sentenced pursuant to the provisions of subsection b. of this section.

h. In a sentencing proceeding conducted pursuant to this section, no evidence shall be admissible concerning the method or manner of execution which would be imposed on a defendant sentenced to death.

i. For purposes of this section the term "homicidal act" shall mean conduct that causes death or serious bodily injury resulting in death.

j. In a sentencing proceeding conducted pursuant to this section, the display of a photograph of the victim taken before the homicide shall be permitted.

PRACTICAL APPLICATION OF STATUTE

The Intent to Kill

Brigitte Madison could appropriately be charged with murder under subsection a.(1) or a.(2) of the statute. This is a felony of the first degree, wherein she would face life in prison or even death if convicted. But why should she face this type of punishment? What is it about her actions that makes her susceptible to a murder conviction? As in most criminal statutes, the key element of the offense is the actor's criminal intent, or *mens rea*. Here she must manifest a criminal intent of either "purpose" or "knowledge"—the intent to kill. If the prosecution can prove that Madison poisoned her brother "purposely" intending to cause his death or "purposely" intending to cause him serious bodily injury that resulted in his death, then she will be convicted of murder. Similarly, if the prosecution can prove the lesser intent of "knowledge"—that she poisoned her brother "knowing" her actions would cause his death or his serious bodily injury that resulted in his death—then she will be convicted of murder.

Assuming the prosecution can prove that Madison did indeed poison her brother—through the evidence of her hair strands, fingerprints, diary entries, etc.—it is almost guaranteed that she will be convicted of murder, and not under a lesser homicide statute. Why? Because common sense dictates that she had to, at minimum, "know" that her act of poisoning her brother with cyanide would result in his death. More likely, however, she acted "purposely" to cause his death—remember, she was the beneficiary of his huge life insurance policy and the recipient of all his assets. Accordingly, murder is the correct statute to charge Brigitte Madison under. This gives the Attorney General a lot of room to downgrade to a lesser homicide statute such as aggravated manslaughter, though it is most likely the best deal she would be offered is a plea to murder with a stipulation that the state would not seek the death penalty.

Felony Murder

Jeff Weiss was indicted for murder, even though the prosecution would be unable to prove that he "purposely" or "knowingly" intended to kill the stranded motorist. How? He would be charged under subsection a.(3) of the statute, which is commonly known as the "felony murder statute."

In order to secure this first degree conviction, the state must prove that two criminal actions occurred—the killing of another individual and an "underlying" felony. Simply for the charge to be valid, a defendant must cause a person's death while committing a felony or during his flight after committing a felony. Only certain felonies apply, however: robbery, sexual assault, arson, burglary, kidnapping, criminal escape and terrorism.

Since Weiss first stole money from the toll collector at gunpoint, one of the requisite underlying felony offenses, robbery, exists. Immediately thereafter, during his flight from the robbery, he caused the stranded motorist's death by striking the man with his vehicle. With these two elements met, Weiss is ripe to be charged with murder.

It is interesting to note that if Weiss had an accomplice who was killed during the automobile accident, he would not be charged with that person's murder. The statute provides an exception for deaths of other participants of the felonies. It is even more interesting that the statute provides an "affirmative defense" to a charge of felony murder, under subsections a.(3)(a) through a.(3)(d).

This defense only applies where the defendant is "not the only participant" involved in the felony act. Further, the elements are extremely difficult to meet for the defendant, given that four prongs must necessarily be present:

1. The defendant did not actually commit the homicidal act or solicit it in any way;
2. The defendant was not armed with a deadly weapon;
3. The defendant had no reason to believe that another participant in the felony was armed with a deadly weapon; and
4. The defendant had no reason to believe that another participant intended to act in a way that would likely cause death.

Changing the facts in Jeff Weiss' case will provide an example where a defendant should not be charged with murder even though a death occurred during a felony such as robbery. Weiss and a second man, Sanford Lennox, plan to rob the tollbooth. They approach the money collector on foot and pass him a note demanding the monetary funds. The toll collector refuses to turn over the money. This angers Weiss and he reaches into the booth, grabbing two rolls of quarters, smashing them repeatedly across the man's head and screaming, "Die. Die. I want you dead." Lennox stands motionless, horrified at what has occurred. The toll collector crumbles to the ground, dead, as the two men flee.

Here, Weiss clearly should be charged with murder, but not Sanford Lennox. Lennox not only did not commit the homicidal act, but he stood silently to the side, not soliciting it in any way. He was not armed with a deadly weapon. Further, he did not have any reason to believe Weiss was armed with a deadly weapon or that Weiss intended to engage in an act likely to cause death—they planned to use a note to illegally obtain the toll money. With all these elements present, Lennox has an affirmative defense under the murder statute.

Court challenges to the "felony murder" component of the statute occur frequently. However, the subsection has been upheld as legal. An individual, therefore, can be convicted of a first degree charge of murder in cases where he does not manifest the specific intent to kill. Simply, if a person is killed during the commission of one of the enumerated felonies or flight therefrom, an individual in many cases will be charged and convicted of murder—even though he may not have intended to kill anyone.

1-4. Manslaughter

   a. Criminal homicide constitutes aggravated manslaughter when:

      (1) The actor recklessly causes death under circumstances manifesting extreme indifference to human life; or

      (2) The actor causes the death of another person while fleeing or attempting to elude a law enforcement officer. Notwithstanding the provision of any other law to the contrary, the actor shall be strictly liable for a violation of this paragraph upon proof that the actor did in fact elude or attempt to elude a law enforcement officer which

resulted in the death of another person. As used in this paragraph, "actor" shall not include a passenger in a motor vehicle.

b. Criminal homicide constitutes manslaughter when:

   (1) It is committed recklessly; or

   (2) A homicide which would otherwise be murder under section 1-3 is committed in the heat of passion resulting from a reasonable provocation.

c. Aggravated manslaughter under paragraph (1) of subsection a. of this section is a felony of the first degree and upon conviction thereof a person may be sentenced to an ordinary term of imprisonment between ten and 30 years. Aggravated manslaughter under paragraph (2) of subsection a. of this section is a felony of the first degree. Manslaughter is a felony of the second degree.

PRACTICAL APPLICATION OF STATUTE

Aggravated Manslaughter

Under 1-4a., a defendant is guilty of aggravated manslaughter, a first degree felony, when he "recklessly" causes death "under circumstances manifesting extreme indifference to human life." What exactly does that mean?

First, the statute does not require the "intent to kill" as does murder under 1-3. The defendant does not need to act "purposely" or "knowing" that his actions will result in death. The requisite *mens rea,* or mental state, here falls just short of that high level of intent.

For example, Maggie Harkins could be charged with aggravated manslaughter if the facts showed that she intended to fire her gun "only in the vicinity" of Cindy Lemon and not directly at her. In that scenario, she did not intend to kill Lemon, perhaps only seeking to frighten her. However, pointing a firearm, a deadly weapon, and firing it near someone certainly is "reckless" behavior that "manifests extreme indifference to human life." While Harkins may not have acted with purpose or knowledge that her actions would cause Lemon's death, could anything be more callous or uncaring toward another's life—especially when the result was that the bullets not only struck Lemon but did indeed kill her?

If the facts showed, however, that she purposely fired the gun at Lemon, then she would be ripe for a murder conviction. Ironically, though, under the circumstances of her case, the most appropriate charge may be an offense lower than both murder and aggravated manslaughter—manslaughter.

Manslaughter

While aggravated manslaughter is a felony of the first degree, manslaughter is a second degree felony wherein the prison term upon conviction can be significantly less. The reason is again predicated on the actor's intent or mental state.

The difference between aggravated manslaughter and manslaughter primarily rests in the omission of the language "under circumstances manifesting extreme indifference to human life." Manslaughter simply requires that the defendant cause a death while acting "recklessly." Manslaughter is the correct statute for the Monroe County Prosecutor's Office to seek an indictment against Larry Kelleher. An indictment of aggravated manslaughter in his case would be overreaching.

Kelleher did not cause George Carmichael's death "under circumstances manifesting extreme indifference to human life." He didn't repeatedly strike him on the head with a baseball bat or fire a gun in his direction. Kelleher, rather, just acted "recklessly": a drunkard in a bar fight, lacking any intent to kill but seeking to cause some bodily injury to his adversary. Unfortunately, his reckless fighting behavior resulted in Carmichael's death; therefore, he is facing the criminal homicide charge of manslaughter. The Attorney General, with broad sentencing range, could fairly offer Kelleher a minimal prison term if he cooperated and supplied information about the pending RS bombing. Conversely, if Kelleher didn't cooperate, the AG could seek the maximum term. However, as noted above, it would be inappropriate for the state to threaten a greater charge, such as aggravated manslaughter or murder, as the facts of the case don't meet the elements of those offenses. Please note that in some states, there is a "criminally negligent homicide" statute. In such states, the death caused by Kelleher's barroom brawl could appropriately be considered a "criminally negligent" act, which is something less than a "reckless" act. Accordingly, a charge of "criminally negligent homicide" would be valid in those states.

Manslaughter—Heat of Passion

Maggie Harkins' matter, however, provides more charging options. As discussed earlier, she could be indicted for aggravated manslaughter if the facts proved she only intended to fire near Cindy Lemon. Conversely, if the facts showed she fired directly at her victim, then Harkins could be indicted for murder because she acted purposely or knew that her actions would result in death. But under these latter facts, even with the intent to kill present, Harkins could avoid a murder charge and face only manslaughter—under 1-4b.(2), the "heat of passion" provision. The following facts could substantiate a manslaughter charge.

Maggie Harkins and Cindy Lemon were former roommates. Their relationship apparently had gone awry, to the extent that Harkins filed a lawsuit against Lemon alleging that Lemon had fraudulently duped her out of $30,000. Harkins' lawsuit quickly gets dismissed, and she confronts Lemon at her townhouse, the property Lemon bought with the money she heisted from her old friend. Harkins brings a gun with her but doesn't intend to use it. However, an argument immediately ensues between the two, where Harkins learns not only that her accusations of theft were true but also that Lemon had engaged in a sexual relationship with Harkins' boyfriend. In a "blind rage," she shoots Lemon.

The statute provides that in order for this act to be manslaughter, and not murder, the homicide must occur in the "heat of passion resulting from reasonable provocation." Would Harkins' "blind rage" shooting equate to an act perpetrated in the heat of passion? Probably.

From the mouth of Lemon, Harkins learned that she did indeed steal from her and, even more, that she had sexual relations with Harkins' boyfriend in the townhouse that was partially bought with the stolen funds. Given their previous friendship and the nature of the information abruptly learned by Harkins, her actions would likely be viewed as occurring in the heat of passion—and with reasonable provocation. Accordingly, Attorney General Taylor could downgrade Harkins' charge from murder to manslaughter in order to obtain the information and testimony he wants about RS and its bombing masterminds. This would be quite advantageous to Harkins, who could avoid a potential death sentence or life in prison and instead face a more moderate term of incarceration.

Aggravated Manslaughter—Death Caused While Eluding Police

Section 1-4a.(2) is distinguished from the felony murder statute under 1-3a.(3) in that it involves flight from a law enforcement officer in all matters other than robbery, sexual assault, arson, burglary, kidnapping, carjacking, criminal escape and terrorism. In other words, if a defendant causes another person's death while eluding the police after committing a simple assault or running a red light, he is guilty of aggravated manslaughter. Simply, if the state can prove the defendant committed the underlying offense of eluding and that another person's death is caused during the defendant's eluding of police, then that defendant is strictly liable for aggravated manslaughter.

1-5.   **Death by auto or vessel**

    a. Criminal homicide constitutes vehicular homicide when it is caused by driving a vehicle or vessel recklessly.

        Proof that the defendant fell asleep while driving or was driving after having been without sleep for a period in excess of 24 consecutive hours may give rise to an inference that the defendant was driving recklessly. Proof that the defendant was driving while intoxicated or was operating a vessel under the influence of alcohol or drugs shall give rise to an inference that the defendant was driving recklessly. Nothing in this section shall be construed to in any way limit the conduct or conditions that may be found to constitute driving a vehicle or vessel recklessly.

    b. Except as provided in paragraph (3) of this subsection, vehicular homicide is a felony of the second degree:

        (1) If the defendant was operating the auto or vessel while under the influence of any intoxicating liquor, narcotic, hallucinogenic or habit-producing drug, or with a blood alcohol concentration at or above the prohibited level of .08%, or if the defendant was operating the auto or vessel while his driver's license or reciprocity privilege was suspended or revoked for any violation of driving while intoxicated by the court for a violation of reckless driving, the defendant shall be sentenced to a term of imprisonment by the court. The term of imprisonment shall include the imposition of a minimum term. The minimum term shall be fixed at, or between, one-third and one-half of the sentence imposed by the court or three years, whichever is greater, during which the defendant shall be ineligible for parole.

        (2) The court shall not impose a mandatory sentence pursuant to paragraph (1) of this subsection unless the grounds therefore have been established at a hearing. At the hearing, which may occur at the time of sentencing, the prosecutor shall establish by a preponderance of the evidence that the defendant was operating the auto or vessel while under the influence of any intoxicating liquor, narcotic, hallucinogenic or habit-producing drug, or with a blood alcohol concentration at or above the level of .08% or that the defendant was operating the auto or vessel while his driver's license or reciprocity privilege was suspended or revoked for any violation of driving while intoxicated by the court for a violation of reckless driving. In making its findings, the court shall take judicial notice of any evidence, testimony or information adduced at the trial, plea hearing or other court proceedings and shall also consider the presentence report and any other relevant information;

    (3) Vehicular homicide is a felony of the first degree if the defendant was operating the auto or vessel while committing the offense of driving while intoxicated:

        (a) On any school property used for school purposes which is owned by or leased to any elementary or secondary school or school board, or within 1,000 feet of such school property;

        (b) Driving through a school crossing if the municipality, by ordinance or resolution, has designated the school crossing as such; or

        (c) Driving through a school crossing knowing that juveniles are present if the municipality has not designated the school crossing as such by ordinance or resolution.

            A map or true copy of a map depicting the location and boundaries of the area on or within 1,000 feet of any property used for school purposes which is owned by or leased to any elementary or secondary school or school board produced may be used in a prosecution under subparagraph (a) of this paragraph.

            It shall be no defense to a prosecution for a violation of subparagraphs (a) or (b) of this paragraph that the defendant was unaware that the prohibited conduct took place while on or within 1,000 feet of any school property or while driving through a school crossing. Nor shall it be a defense to a prosecution under subparagraphs (a) or (b) of this paragraph that no juveniles were present on the school property or crossing zone at the time of the offense or that the school was not in session.

    (4) If the defendant was operating the auto or vessel while committing the offense of driving while intoxicated, the defendant's license to operate a motor vehicle shall be suspended for a period of between five years and life, which period shall commence upon completion of any prison sentence imposed upon that person.

c. For good cause shown, the court may, in accepting a plea of guilty under this section, order that such plea not be evidential in any civil proceeding.

d. Nothing herein shall be deemed to preclude, if the evidence so warrants, an indictment and conviction for aggravated manslaughter under the provisions of subsection a. of 1-4.

    As used in this section, "auto or vessel" means all means of conveyance propelled otherwise than by muscular power.

e. Any person who violates paragraph (3) of subsection b. of this section shall forfeit the auto or vessel used in the commission of the offense, unless the defendant can establish at a hearing, which may occur at the time of sentencing, by a preponderance of the evidence that such forfeiture would constitute a serious hardship to the family of the defendant that outweighs the need to deter such conduct by the defendant and others. In making its findings, the court shall take judicial notice of any evidence, testimony or information adduced at the trial, plea hearing or other court proceedings and shall also consider the presentence report and any other relevant information. Forfeiture pursuant to this subsection shall be in addition to, and not in lieu of, civil forfeiture.

PRACTICAL APPLICATION OF STATUTE

Notwithstanding the robbery element of Jeff Weiss' case, he committed vehicular homicide, a second degree offense. Weiss raced from the left lane to the right on Route 45 in an attempt to exit onto Route 7. He did this even though a stranded motorist stood near the off-ramp. His "reckless" driving resulted in death; therefore, under 1-5a., he is guilty of vehicular homicide.

Under subsection b. of the statute, the punishment becomes more severe if the defendant commits vehicular homicide while also violating one of two motor vehicle violations—driving while intoxicated, commonly known as DWI, or driving while on the revoked list. It is interesting to note that the penalties are only enhanced for driving on the revoked list where the defendant is on the revoked list because of a DWI conviction or because of a conviction of reckless driving. Accordingly, Jeff Weiss would be charged under subsection b., rather than subsection a., if his vehicular homicide occurred in conjunction with a DWI or a violation of driving on the revoked list as discussed above.

The punishment becomes even harsher, with the offense growing to a felony of the first degree under paragraph (3) of subsection b. Weiss would be charged here if he commits a vehicular homicide while intoxicated (DWI) and if it occurs on school property or within 1,000 feet of school property or while he is driving through a school crossing. Law enforcement officers are to ignore whether the defendant was aware that he was in a school zone or school crossing when charging under this statute.

Additionally, the statute provides that the state is not precluded from also charging a defendant with aggravated manslaughter if the evidence so warrants. Accordingly, Attorney General Taylor has a wide range of possible plea offers to make to Jeff Weiss—murder, aggravated manslaughter and different degrees of vehicular homicide—depending on his sobriety, his motor vehicle standing and the location of the incident.

1-5.1.   **Knowingly leaving scene of motor vehicle accident resulting in death, third degree felony; sentencing**

A motor vehicle operator who knows he is involved in an accident and knowingly leaves the scene of that accident under circumstances that violate the provisions of the underlying motor vehicle offense of leaving the scene of an accident shall be guilty of a felony of the third degree if the accident results in the death of another person. The presumption of nonimprisonment shall not apply to persons convicted under the provisions of this section.

If the evidence so warrants, nothing in this section shall be deemed to preclude an indictment and conviction for aggravated manslaughter under the provisions of 1-4 or for vehicular homicide under the provisions of 1-5.

A conviction arising under this section shall not merge with a conviction for aggravated manslaughter under the provisions of 1-4 or for vehicular homicide under the provisions of 1-5 and a separate sentence shall be imposed upon each such conviction.

For the purposes of this section, neither knowledge of the death nor the knowledge of the violation is an element of the offense and it shall not be a defense that the operator of the motor vehicle was unaware of the death or of the provisions underlying the motor vehicle offense of leaving the scene of an accident.

PRACTICAL APPLICATION OF STATUTE

This third degree felony is primarily predicated on a motor vehicle statute, leaving the scene of an accident. Quite clearly, if Jeff Weiss left the scene of the accident after he struck and killed the stranded motorist, he would be convicted under this criminal homicide statute.

This offense, like the motor vehicle offense, requires the mental state of knowledge. The defendant must "know" that he was involved in a motor vehicle accident and "know" that he left the motor vehicle accident after it occurred. It is not an element of the offense, however, that the defendant knew that he killed someone—the state just needs to prove that the defendant knew that he was in an accident and that he knowingly left the accident.

In Jeff Weiss' case, obviously, he knew he was in a motor vehicle accident; such a fatal impact could not be missed. In fact, the motor vehicle statute imputes knowledge of the accident to any individual involved in a motor vehicle accident where death occurs. The motor vehicle statute, leaving the scene of the accident, provides "The driver of any motor vehicle involved in an accident resulting in injury or death to any person or damage in the amount of $250.00 or more to any vehicle or property shall be presumed to have knowledge that he was involved in such accident, and such presumption shall be rebuttable in nature."

Given Weiss' "knowledge," he is guilty of violating 1-5.1.

1-6.   ### Aiding suicide

A person who purposely aids another to commit suicide is guilty of a felony of the second degree if his conduct causes such suicide or an attempted suicide, and otherwise of a felony of the fourth degree.

PRACTICAL APPLICATION OF STATUTE

With the facts slightly changed, Brigitte Madison could be charged with aiding suicide rather than murder. If instead of purposely poisoning her brother with arsenic in an attempt to gain his monetary wealth, she "purposely" aided him to commit suicide, then she would be guilty of this lesser homicide statute. This would be a felony of the second degree because her conduct caused the suicide.

Section 1-6 is a rarely invoked statute given the minimal occurrences where individuals assist others in suicide. However, it is a viable statute and will be upheld where the facts are proven and meet the elements of the offense.

1-7.   ### Abortion

A person is guilty of abortion when he purposely commits an abortional act upon a female, unless such abortional act is justifiable pursuant to subsection f. of 1-1. Abortion is a felony of the third degree if the abortional act results in a miscarriage; otherwise it is a felony of the fourth degree.

PRACTICAL APPLICATION OF STATUTE

Libby, 28, has a one-night stand with Jeff. Conception occurs and she's pregnant with a girl she tentatively names Kim. At 20 weeks into the pregnancy, Libby decides that she doesn't want to give birth to Kim because it would be inconvenient to her lifestyle. Accordingly, she heads to the local abortion clinic, meets with Dr. Conkielty and aborts the child. Under 1-7, neither Libby nor Dr. Conkielty has done anything illegal.

As defined in 1-1, abortion is lawful when performed with the consent of the pregnant woman within 24 weeks of conception or when necessary to save her life. Outside of these circumstances, an abortional act is illegal.

Pursuant to the provisions of 1-7, there is no requirement that the female actually be pregnant or that a miscarriage actually occur in order for a defendant to be convicted of abortion. However, the illicit abortional act must be committed with the *intent* that a miscarriage results. Also, please note that the felony is elevated from a fourth degree felony to a third degree felony "if the abortional act results in a miscarriage."

1-8.   ### Self-abortion

A female is guilty of self-abortion when, being pregnant, she commits or submits to an abortional act upon herself which causes her miscarriage, unless such abortional act is justifiable pursuant to subsection f. of 1-1. Self-abortion is a class A misdemeanor.

PRACTICAL APPLICATION OF STATUTE

Self-abortion is not a felony; it is a class A misdemeanor. The female must be pregnant and either submits to or commits an unjustifiable abortional act upon herself—which actually causes a miscarriage. The crux of the charge is that the abortional act is not performed or directed by a duly licensed physician.

END OF CHAPTER REVIEW

Multiple-Choice Questions

1. In an Alexander bar, Larry Kelleher argued with George Carmichael over who was next in line for a drink. A fight ensued, which ended with Kelleher physically beating Carmichael to death. Witnesses told police that Kelleher threw the first punch. What would be the most appropriate offense to charge Kelleher with?

   a. murder

   b. aggravated manslaughter

   c. manslaughter

   d. aggravated assault

   e. no offense, because Kelleher probably didn't intend to kill Carmichael

2. Let's assume the above facts were modified to the following extent. Kelleher, instead of punching Carmichael, went home. After stewing about the bar argument for three days, Kelleher planned a knife attack against Carmichael. On the fourth day, Kelleher waited outside Carmichael's house and then stabbed the man to death as he tried to enter his car. What is the most appropriate offense to charge Kelleher with under these circumstances?

   a. murder

   b. aggravated manslaughter

   c. manslaughter

   d. aggravated assault

   e. no offense, because Carmichael cut into the line

3. The primary difference between aggravated manslaughter and manslaughter is:
   a. manslaughter simply requires that the defendant cause a death while acting recklessly, while aggravated manslaughter requires that the reckless actions occur under circumstances manifesting extreme indifference to human life
   b. manslaughter requires that the defendant act with the *mens rea* of negligence, while aggravated manslaughter requires that the defendant act with the *mens rea* of recklessness
   c. the maximum term of imprisonment for manslaughter is five years, whereas the maximum term of imprisonment for aggravated manslaughter is ten years
   d. a and c
   e. b and c

4. Which of the following circumstances best describes a felony murder?
   a. William breaks into Beth's house with the intent to kill her. Once inside, he shoots her to death.
   b. Michael keeps a baseball bat in his car. During a road rage incident, he stops at a red light, exits his car and proceeds to the car in front of him. Once there, he pulls the other driver from his vehicle and beats him to death with the baseball bat.
   c. Jeff Weiss points a pistol at a toll collector in an attempt to rob the man. The toll collector complies and turns over the funds to him. Weiss then flees the scene, with a state trooper chasing him. Attempting to cross from the left lane into the right lane, Weiss loses control of his vehicle and crashes his vehicle into a stranded motorist, killing him instantly.
   d. Barbara shakes her child, ultimately killing the infant.
   e. A corrections officer shot an inmate who was attempting to escape from the jail. The inmate died at the scene.

5. Which of the following best describes a first degree "vehicular homicide" offense?
   a. Jeff, angry at his sister, rushes out of his house completely sober. Not paying attention, he drives the wrong way down a one-way street. Aware that he is driving in the wrong direction, he determines not to stop because he believes no other automobiles will come his way. Suddenly, a pickup truck turns into his path. The crash results in the other driver's death.
   b. Driving on the revoked list and while intoxicated, Jeff races on Route 80 West at over 100 m.p.h. He strikes another vehicle, causing the death of Wilma.
   c. Driving while intoxicated, Jeff accidentally crosses onto a horse farm and kills Bobberino, an animal lover, who was petting his horse, Carmella.
   d. After smoking pot, Jeff drove his 1990 Honda Accord into a factory wall, instantly killing the passenger in his car, Moses.
   e. Driving while intoxicated, Jeff drove the wrong way down a one-way street through a school zone. There, he crashed into a cucumber stand located on the sidewalk. The cucumber salesman, Malanga, was instantly killed by the impact.

6. In order to be convicted of a criminal offense for leaving the scene of a motor vehicle accident that results in death, the actor must:

   a. negligently cause the accident

   b. recklessly leave the scene of the accident

   c. knowingly leave the scene of the accident

   d. purposely cause the accident

   e. none of the above

7. Which of the following offenses *cannot* give rise to a felony murder charge?

   a. criminal escape

   b. criminal sexual contact

   c. burglary

   d. kidnapping

   e. carjacking

Essay Questions

1. Elliot Rodman and Beef Norton determine to rob a Hamilton liquor store. Both men, armed with shotguns, enter the liquor store and immediately proceed to the clerk. Elliot and Beef point their shotguns at the clerk's head and demand all of the store's cash. Suddenly, a patron, holding a knife, begins to charge Elliot and Beef in an effort to thwart the robbery. Elliot points his gun at the patron and shoots and kills him. A moment later, the clerk grabs a pistol he had hidden in his pocket and shoots and kills Elliot. At that point, Hamilton police burst through the front door and arrest Beef, who does not put up a struggle. Could Beef be charged with murder for the shooting death of the patron? Why or why not? Could Beef be charged with murder for the shooting death of his partner, Elliot? Why or why not? In your answers, cite the relevant statutes, including the specific subsections that apply and the necessary statutory language.

2. Big Ed shoplifted 25 packs of batteries from a supermarket in Jackson. He fled on a motorcycle but was immediately spotted by police. A chase ensued, with Big Ed attempting to elude the police for over a mile. It ended abruptly, however, when Big Ed crashed into a pedestrian, instantly killing the man. For the pedestrian's death, what is the most appropriate homicide offense to charge Big Ed with? Why? What is the degree of this offense? If Big Ed wasn't fleeing the police but instead killed the pedestrian while driving while intoxicated, what is the best offense to charge him with? Degree of this offense? Be sure to explain the elements of these offenses, including the requisite *mens rea,* if any, for each.

2

ASSAULT; RECKLESS ENDANGERING; THREATS

FACT PATTERN

In Frisco City, Police Sergeant Samuel Paterson recently arrested two brothers in connection with the beating of a 50-year-old grocer. While on routine patrol, Paterson waited at a red light in a long line of traffic. As the automobiles ahead of him slowly started to move, he heard a low rumble of commotion through his cruiser's closed window. Turning to his left, he witnessed two men, later identified as Lance and Stanley Jones, violently beating another individual with golf clubs in front of a grocery store. They repeatedly struck the man in the body and face with the clubs.

Paterson, in full uniform, immediately exited his vehicle in an effort to stop the trauma. As he approached, however, Lance Jones reached into his coat pocket and produced a pistol. He aimed the weapon at Paterson; as he did so, a red laser beam raced from the gun's barrel toward the police officer. At the same time, Stanley Jones ran at Paterson and struck him in the head with a closed fist. Then Stanley turned around and pointed his own gun at a group of bystanders. He nodded to his brother and said, "Let's go, bro."

The two brothers, still pointing their guns, walked backwards to a nearby Ford Mustang, entered the vehicle and fled—Stanley was the driver. Sergeant Paterson radioed for assistance immediately and pursued them in his cruiser, keeping a safe distance from the felons, with his sirens blaring and lights flashing. Stanley weaved in and out of traffic, driving in excess of 80 m.p.h. down the busy Frisco City streets. After only a few minutes, however, the Jones brothers crashed their speeding vehicle into a parked car while attempting to avoid a maroon minivan that had crossed the double yellow line. Inside the parked vehicle was an elderly woman. The jolt of the crash caused her to lunge forward, and she smashed her forehead into her car's windshield. The minivan similarly struck a parked vehicle; the impact of this crash caused the unoperated car to jump the curb and hit a pedestrian.

The Jones brothers, uninjured, exited their vehicle and fled on foot. Fortunately, however, they were apprehended only two blocks from the motor vehicle accident. Backup officers caught up with them as they were attempting to mount a fence. They were handcuffed and transported to the closest precinct for processing. Also arrested at the site of the accident was Pedro Munoz, the driver of the minivan that crossed the double yellow line. Field sobriety tests and a strong odor of alcohol led Sergeant Paterson to believe that Munoz was driving while intoxicated.

All victims of the Jones brothers' rampage, including Sergeant Paterson, were rushed to the hospital for medical treatment. A tally of their injuries resulted in the following. The man beaten outside the grocery store turned out to be the store's owner. The strikes from the golf clubs were so severe that he was rendered unconscious and required over 40 stitches to his head; he also suffered several broken ribs. The elderly woman injured by the Jones' vehicle cracked her skull so hard that she went into a coma, which she remained in for two weeks. Fortunately, she recovered afterward; her injuries, though, required a metal plate as well as numerous staples to be placed in her head. The pedestrian struck via Pedro Munoz's accident suffered scrapes and bruises. Sergeant Paterson likewise only suffered a bruise to his face.

Once at police headquarters, Sergeant Paterson ran the criminal histories of both Jones brothers. He found that there was an open warrant against Stanley Jones involving a woman whom Jones had once dated. The woman alleged that Jones had slipped a drug in a beverage that she was consuming and that the drink tranquilized her, causing her to become disoriented. Thereafter, in the same evening, she stated that Jones sexually assaulted her.

She also claimed that Jones appeared in front of her house on five subsequent occasions and followed her when she drove to and from work. On each occasion, he verbally advised her not to report the sexual assault and twice threatened to kill her, her mother and her sister. Appropriate charges were filed against Stanley Jones, which were now the subject of this warrant. Sergeant Paterson also found that Jones had over 20 prior convictions, including convictions for arson, aggravated assault and burglary. At the time of the arrest, he was on parole for an arson conviction.

Lance Jones had ten prior convictions, including burglary and theft offenses. He also was once convicted of taking a pistol from a uniformed police officer's person. The officer was attempting to arrest Jones but was thwarted in his efforts when Jones wrangled the gun from him and discharged the weapon in the process.

2-1.   **Assault**

    a. Simple assault. A person is guilty of assault if he:

        (1) Attempts to cause or purposely, knowingly or recklessly causes bodily injury to another; or

        (2) Negligently causes bodily injury to another with a deadly weapon; or

        (3) Attempts by physical menace to put another in fear of imminent serious bodily injury. Simple assault is a misdemeanor A unless committed in a fight or scuffle entered into by mutual consent, in which case it is a misdemeanor B.

    b. Aggravated assault. A person is guilty of aggravated assault if he:

        (1) Attempts to cause serious bodily injury to another, or causes such injury purposely or knowingly or under circumstances manifesting extreme indifference to the value of human life recklessly causes such injury; or

        (2) Attempts to cause or purposely or knowingly causes bodily injury to another with a deadly weapon; or

        (3) Recklessly causes bodily injury to another with a deadly weapon; or

        (4) Knowingly under circumstances manifesting extreme indifference to the value of human life points a firearm at or in the direction of another, whether or not the actor believes it to be loaded; or

(5) Commits a simple assault as defined in subsection a. (1), (2) or (3) of this section upon:

    (a) Any law enforcement officer acting in the performance of his duties while in uniform or exhibiting evidence of his authority or because of his status as a law enforcement officer; or

    (b) Any paid or volunteer fireman acting in the performance of his duties while in uniform or otherwise clearly identifiable as being engaged in the performance of the duties of a fireman; or

    (c) Any person engaged in emergency first-aid or medical services acting in the performance of his duties while in uniform or otherwise clearly identifiable as being engaged in the performance of emergency first-aid or medical services; or

    (d) Any school board member, school administrator, teacher, school bus driver or other employee of a school board while clearly identifiable as being engaged in the performance of his duties or because of his status as a member or employee of a school board or any school bus driver employed by an operator under contract to a school board while clearly identifiable as being engaged in the performance of his duties or because of his status as a school bus driver; or

    (e) Any employee of the Division of Youth and Family Services while clearly identifiable as being engaged in the performance of his duties or because of his status as an employee of the division; or

    (f) Any justice of the Supreme Court, judge of the Superior Court, judge of the Tax Court or municipal judge while clearly identifiable as being engaged in the performance of judicial duties or because of his status as a member of the judiciary; or

    (g) Any operator of a motorbus or the operator's supervisor or any employee of a rail passenger service while clearly identifiable as being engaged in the performance of his duties or because of his status as an operator of a motorbus or as the operator's supervisor or as an employee of a rail passenger service.

(6) Causes bodily injury to another person while fleeing or attempting to elude a law enforcement officer or while operating a motor vehicle which has been unlawfully taken. Notwithstanding any other provision of law to the contrary, a person shall be strictly liable for a violation of this subsection upon proof of a violation of the offense of eluding or while operating in a risky manner a motor vehicle which has been unlawfully taken and which resulted in bodily injury to another person; or

(7) Attempts to cause significant bodily injury to another or causes significant bodily injury purposely or knowingly or under circumstances manifesting extreme indifference to the value of human life recklessly causes such significant bodily injury; or

(8) Causes bodily injury by knowingly or purposely starting a fire or causing an explosion which results in bodily injury to any emergency services personnel involved in fire suppression activities, rendering emergency medical services resulting from the fire or explosion or rescue operations or rendering any necessary assistance at the scene of the fire or explosion, including any bodily injury sustained while responding to the scene of a reported fire or explosion. For purposes of this subsection, "emergency services personnel" shall include, but not be limited to, any paid or volunteer fireman, any person engaged in emergency first-aid or medical services and any law enforcement officer. Notwithstanding any other provision of law to the contrary, a person shall be strictly liable for a violation of this paragraph upon proof of a violation of the arson statute which resulted in bodily injury to any emergency services personnel; or

(9) Knowingly, under circumstances manifesting extreme indifference to the value of human life, points or displays a firearm at or in the direction of a law enforcement officer; or

(10) Knowingly points, displays or uses an imitation firearm, at or in the direction of a law enforcement officer, with the purpose to intimidate, threaten or attempt to put the officer in fear of bodily injury or for any unlawful purpose; or

(11) Uses or activates a laser sighting system or device, or a system or device which, in the manner used, would cause a reasonable person to believe that it is a laser sighting system or device, against a law enforcement officer acting in the performance of his duties while in uniform or exhibiting evidence of his authority. As used in this paragraph, "laser sighting system or device" means any system or device that is integrated with or affixed to a firearm and emits a laser light beam that is used to assist in the sight alignment or aiming of the firearm.

Aggravated assault under subsections b.(1) and b.(6) is a felony of the second degree; under subsections b.(2), b.(7), b.(9) and b.(10) is a felony of the third degree; under subsections b.(3) and b.(4) is a felony of the fourth degree; and under subsection b.(5) is a felony of the third degree if the victim suffers bodily injury, but otherwise it is a felony of the fourth degree. Aggravated assault under subsection b.(8) is a felony of the third degree if the victim suffers bodily injury; if the victim suffers significant bodily injury or serious bodily injury it is a felony of the second degree. Aggravated assault under subsection b.(11) is a felony of the third degree.

c. (1) A person is guilty of assault by auto or vessel when the person drives a vehicle or vessel recklessly and causes either serious bodily injury or bodily injury to another. Assault by auto or vessel is a felony of the fourth degree if serious bodily injury results and is a misdemeanor A if bodily injury results.

(2) Assault by auto or vessel is a felony of the third degree if the person drives the vehicle while intoxicated and serious bodily injury results and is a felony of the fourth degree if the person drives the vehicle while intoxicated and bodily injury results.

(3) Assault by auto or vessel is a felony of the second degree if serious bodily injury results from the defendant operating the auto or vessel while intoxicated while:

(a) On any school property used for school purposes which is owned by or leased to any elementary or secondary school or school board, or within 1,000 feet of such school property;

(b) Driving through a school crossing if the municipality, by ordinance or resolution, has designated the school crossing as such; or

(c) Driving through a school crossing knowing that juveniles are present if the municipality has not designated the school crossing as such by ordinance or resolution.

Assault by auto or vessel is a felony of the third degree if bodily injury results from the defendant operating the auto or vessel in violation of this paragraph.

A map or true copy of a map depicting the location and boundaries of the area on or within 1,000 feet of any property used for school purposes which is owned by or leased to any elementary or secondary school or school board may be used in a prosecution under subparagraph (a) of paragraph (3) of this section.

It shall be no defense to a prosecution for a violation of subparagraph (a) or (b) of paragraph (3) of this subsection that the defendant was unaware that the prohibited conduct took place while on or within 1,000 feet of any school property or while driving through a school crossing. Nor shall it be a defense to a prosecution under subparagraph (a) or (b) of paragraph (3) of this subsection that no juveniles were present on the school property or crossing zone at the time of the offense or that the school was not in session.

As used in this section, "vessel" means a means of conveyance for travel on water and propelled otherwise than by muscular power.

d. A person who is employed by a hospital, nursing home or other institution that houses and/or provides care for elderly persons who commits a simple assault as defined in paragraph (1) or (2) of subsection a. of this section upon an institutionalized elderly person is guilty of a felony of the fourth degree. As used in this section, "elderly person" is defined as a person 60 years of age or older.

e. A person who commits a simple assault as defined in paragraph (1), (2) or (3) of subsection a. of this section in the presence of a child under 16 years of age at a school- or community-sponsored youth sports event is guilty of a felony of the fourth degree. The defendant shall be strictly liable upon proof that the offense occurred, in fact, in the presence of a child under 16 years of age. It shall not be a defense that the defendant did not know that the child was present or reasonably believed that the child was 16 years of age or older. The provisions of this subsection shall not be construed to create any liability on the part of a participant in a youth sports event or to abrogate any immunity or defense available to a participant in a youth sports event. As used in this act, "school- or community-sponsored youth sports event" means a competition, practice or instructional event involving one or more interscholastic sports teams or youth sports teams organized pursuant to a nonprofit or similar charter or which are member teams in a youth league organized by or affiliated with a county or municipal recreation department and shall not include collegiate, semi-professional or professional sporting events.

PRACTICAL APPLICATION OF STATUTE

Simple Assault

If the Jones brothers had merely punched or slapped the grocer in the face, they would be guilty of simple assault. Similarly, if they had merely waved their golf clubs at the grocer's head instead of striking him, they would be guilty of simple assault. Per the actual facts, however, they are guilty of an aggravated assault of the grocer. As will be discussed later, the defining factors that elevate their offense to aggravated assault are that they used a deadly weapon to actually beat the man and the fact that they caused *serious* bodily injury.

Under 2-1a.(1), a person is guilty of simple assault if he "attempts to cause or purposely, knowingly or recklessly causes bodily injury to another." The Jones brothers would be guilty of simple assault under this provision if they had punched or slapped the grocer in the face. Why? Because their actions would have only resulted in *bodily injury* to the man, not serious bodily injury.

Per subsection a.(3), a person is guilty of simple assault if he "attempts by physical menace to put another in fear of imminent serious bodily injury." The Jones brothers would be convicted of simple assault under this subsection if they had just waved the golf clubs at the grocer but never actually struck him. Please note that this subsection has a *serious* bodily injury component, as opposed to just bodily injury. Here, their physical menace of waving deadly weapons at him would have put the man in imminent fear of *serious* bodily injury. A person having golf clubs swung in front of his face would reasonably not just fear bodily injury but fear *serious* bodily injury. Accordingly, such actions would render the Jones brothers guilty of simple assault—even though no actual injury occurred.

Aggravated Assault—Generally

The aggravated assault statute is a complicated and diverse statute providing for numerous situations where an individual may be convicted of aggravated assault. The statute, in its various subsections, often differentiates among "bodily injury," "significant bodily injury" and "serious bodily injury," as well as the various mental states (i.e., "purposely," "knowingly" and "recklessly") that must be present for a conviction. It is also important to note that aggravated assaults range from fourth degree felonies to second degree felonies and many times are differentiated by the victim's occupational status. Each subsection has its own unique requirements. All of this, and more, will be examined in the following Practical Application sections.

Second Degree Aggravated Assault—Causing Serious Bodily Injury

The Jones brothers could be convicted of multiple counts of aggravated assault for their violent tirade in Frisco City. Their first count of aggravated assault arises out of their using golf clubs to beat the grocer.

Section 2-1b.(1) provides that an individual is guilty of aggravated assault if he "attempts to cause serious bodily injury to another, or causes such injury purposely or knowingly." An actor may also be convicted under this subsection of the statute if he acted "recklessly" in causing serious bodily injury. The reckless mental state requirement, though, necessitates that the defendant must act "under circumstances manifesting extreme indifference to the value of human life." Whatever the mental state—purposely, knowingly or recklessly—the actor must cause (or attempt to cause) *serious* bodily injury, not just bodily injury, in order to be convicted under this subsection of the statute.

Lance and Stanley Jones repeatedly swung golf clubs at the grocer's body and head. The strikes were so severe that their victim was rendered unconscious, suffered broken ribs and required over 40 stitches to his head. This is "*serious* bodily injury." Not only is it clear, by their actions, that they attempted to cause serious bodily injury to the grocer, but it is equally evident that they purposely intended to cause these serious injuries. Any person knows that repeatedly striking another in the body and head with golf clubs will result in serious bodily injury. Accordingly, the Jones brothers should be charged with aggravated assault, under 2-1b.(1), for their beating of the grocer. This is a felony of the second degree.

Now, what does acting "under circumstances manifesting extreme indifference to the value of human life" mean? Where would this "reckless" mental state fit in? Perhaps if the Jones brothers only struck the grocer in the body but not the head, then it may be difficult to prove that they purposely or knowingly caused serious bodily injury. However, in repeatedly hitting the man in the body with golf clubs, they could have killed him by rupturing an internal organ. Accordingly, this behavior would surely be deemed as acting with "extreme indifference to the value of human life," so any serious bodily injury resulting therefrom would certainly have been, at minimum, recklessly caused. Under these circumstances, the Joneses would still appropriately be charged under 2-1b.(1).

It is interesting to note that under 2-1b.(7), an individual is guilty of a felony of the *third* degree if he "purposely or knowingly or under circumstances manifesting extreme indifference to the value of human life recklessly causes" *significant* bodily injury to another. This subsection provides for an offense that falls between simple assault and second degree aggravated assault under 2-1b.(1). The differential factor is *significant* bodily injury, which is something less than *serious* bodily injury but something more than just bodily injury. Law enforcement officers determining under which statute to charge simply must use their judgment.

Bodily Injury Caused by a Deadly Weapon —Third or Fourth Degree Felony Depending on Mental State

An individual who causes bodily injury, but not serious bodily injury, with a deadly weapon is guilty of a third degree felony if he causes this bodily injury "purposely" or "knowingly." He is guilty of a lesser fourth degree felony if such bodily injury is "recklessly" caused via the use of a deadly weapon. A modification of the grocer's golf club beating can exemplify how these statutes should be implemented.

Instead of repeatedly beating the grocer with the golf clubs, Stanley Jones strikes him once in the arm, breaking the man's wrist. Here, a deadly weapon—a golf club—was utilized to purposely cause bodily injury. Therefore, under 2-1b.(2), Stanley Jones would appropriately be charged with aggravated assault, which is a felony of the third degree.

In a similar vein, if Stanley Jones simply intended to scare the grocer by swinging the clubs wildly in the air but accidentally struck him in the wrist, he should still be charged with aggravated assault. But why? If he didn't intend to hit the man, why should he be charged with aggravated assault? Because all three elements of 2-1b.(3) have been met in this scenario. The golf club, a deadly metal weapon, was utilized by Jones in a manner that was clearly reckless. Wildly swinging the instrument in the air posed a dangerous situation to any individual in its close proximity. Indeed, the net result was bodily injury to the grocer—the golf club struck him in the wrist. For his reckless assault with a deadly weapon, Stanley Jones would be charged with a fourth degree felony under 2-1b.(3).

Simple Assault of Law Enforcement Officers and Other Public Officials Automatically Becomes a Third Degree Aggravated Assault

Stanley Jones' punch to Sergeant Paterson's face is not a misdemeanor A. It is not a simple assault as it would be if Paterson was just some person whom Jones happened to hit in a street fight. But how is this so?

Subsection b.(5) of the aggravated assault statute enumerates multiple scenarios where a simple assault automatically is elevated to the status of a third degree aggravated assault. One of the scenarios is where a defendant commits a simple assault on "any law enforcement officer acting in the performance of his duties." Since Jones punched Paterson in the face while Paterson was performing his duties as a Frisco City police officer, Jones simply could be convicted of third degree aggravated assault. The reality, though, is that many times these charges will be downgraded to simple assault and resolved in the municipal court. Often where an officer only suffers bodily injury, such as bumps and bruises, the case will be remanded and handled as a simple assault just like other similar matters involving minor injuries.

Other situations under subsection b.(5) where a simple assault automatically becomes an aggravated assault include simple assaults of firefighters, first-aid workers, school board members, teachers, Division of Youth and Family Services employees, judges and even bus drivers and rail service operators. Of special note, though, is that the position alone does not necessitate the elevated charge to aggravated assault. The victim must be assaulted either during the performance of his position (e.g., a police officer doing his job, a teacher instructing a class) or because of his position (e.g., a police officer is assaulted because of his status as a police officer). In other words, a person who punches an off-duty police officer or a teacher during a bar fight will only be charged with simple assault—as long as the basis for the simple assault was other than the officer's or teacher's occupational status.

Pointing Firearm at Law Enforcement Officer— Third Degree Felony; Pointing Firearm at Other Persons—Fourth Degree Felony

Lance Jones is guilty of third degree aggravated assault for pointing his pistol at Sergeant Paterson—this per the provisions of 2-1b.(9). Interestingly, though, the Jones brothers are guilty of a fourth degree aggravated assault for pointing their guns at the crowd of bystanders under 2-1b.(4). Again, the Code makes an assault offense more serious in degree if the intended victim is a law enforcement officer rather than a layperson.

Pointing Imitation Firearm at Law Enforcement Officer— Third Degree Felony

It is also interesting to note that even if the gun pointed at Sergeant Paterson was an *imitation,* Lance Jones could be convicted of a third degree aggravated assault. Section 2-1b.(10) provides that an individual who knowingly points an imitation firearm at a law enforcement officer "with the purpose to intimidate, threaten or attempt to put the officer in fear of bodily injury or for any unlawful purpose" is guilty of a third degree aggravated assault.

Obviously, Lance Jones pointed his pistol at Sergeant Paterson in an effort to intimidate and threaten him. His goal, of course, was an unlawful purpose—to put the officer in fear of bodily injury and to be able to flee from arrest. Accordingly, even if the gun turned out to be fake, Lance Jones should be charged with a third degree felony under 2-1b.(10).

Firearm Laser System Activated upon Law Enforcement Officer— Third Degree Aggravated Assault

Lance Jones should be charged with an additional count of third degree aggravated assault for the red laser beam that ran from his gun at Sergeant Paterson. Section 2-1b.(11) defines a separate and distinct count of aggravated assault to cover situations where a person activates a laser sighting system, which is affixed to a firearm, at a law enforcement officer. Once again, this subsection only pertains to individuals performing their duties as law enforcement officers.

Lance Jones emitted a red laser beam at Sergeant Paterson, who was working as a police officer at the time, and the red beam flowed from a device affixed to his pistol. Accordingly, Jones is ripe to be charged with a third degree aggravated assault under subsection b.(11) of the aggravated assault statute.

Bodily Injury Caused While Fleeing/Eluding Law Enforcement Officer—Second Degree Aggravated Assault

Stanley Jones (if not both Jones brothers) should be charged with second degree aggravated assault, under 2-1b.(6), for the injuries he caused to the elderly woman when he struck her vehicle. This charge should be levied even though the automobile crash was not purposeful and actually was probably just accidental.

Section 2-1b.(6) provides that a defendant who "causes bodily injury to another person while fleeing or attempting to elude a law enforcement officer" is guilty of second degree aggravated assault. The eluding statute sets forth that an individual is guilty of the same where he knowingly eludes a law enforcement officer in a motor vehicle after having received a signal to stop his vehicle.

Sergeant Paterson attempted to arrest the Jones brothers while they were beating the grocer. Instead of submitting to the officer's demands, the brothers fled. Even more so, they entered a motor vehicle and refused to stop in spite of the officer's signals of a blaring siren and flashing lights. Their automobile only halted because it crashed into the parked car where the elderly woman was sitting. The impact of this crash caused the woman serious bodily injury, including a lapse into a coma.

The elderly woman's injuries were caused while the Jones brothers were fleeing and attempting to elude Sergeant Paterson. They knowingly eluded the officer, aware that he was signaling them to stop their motor vehicle. With these elements met, Stanley Jones should be charged with second degree aggravated assault under 2-1b.(6). His brother, Lance, probably should similarly be charged under this subsection, because he is an accomplice and because the injuries occurred during his flight (as well as Stanley's) from Sergeant Paterson.

It is important to note here that, under this subsection, it is irrelevant that the elderly woman's injuries were so serious. Simple "bodily injury" is sufficient for an individual to face charges of this second degree felony. Therefore, if the woman had only suffered a broken finger or even a black-and-blue eye, the Jones brothers could still face a count of second degree aggravated assault. Also interesting to note is that this subsection does not require intention to injure—the actor does not have to purposely, knowingly or even recklessly cause injury. The actor simply is "strictly liable" under this subsection; he is guilty of the second degree aggravated assault just as long as bodily injury is caused while he is fleeing or attempting to elude a law enforcement officer.

Assault by Auto

Pedro Munoz should be charged with fourth degree assault by auto for striking the pedestrian with his car. Section 2-1c.(2) provides that assault by auto is a felony of the fourth degree if the "person drives the vehicle while intoxicated and *bodily injury* occurs." It is a felony of the third degree if *serious* bodily injury occurs while the person drives the vehicle while intoxicated.

As is clear from the above, the degree of this offense becomes more serious as the injuries increase—bodily injury earns a fourth degree offense; serious bodily injury merits a third degree offense. The other defining element of subsection c.(2) is the person driving in violation of driving while intoxicated. Subsection c.(1) does not have the DWI requirement. This subsection simply sets forth that if an individual is caused bodily injury due to another's reckless driving, it is a misdemeanor A; if serious bodily injury is caused due to reckless driving, it is a fourth degree felony.

Pedro Munoz should be charged under subsection c.(2), and not c.(1), because he was operating his motor vehicle while intoxicated. His charge should only be a fourth degree offense because, fortunately, the pedestrian who was struck only suffered bodily injury—scrapes and bruises.

It is important to note that in certain circumstances assault by auto automatically becomes a second degree offense. Under subsection c.(3), if an intoxicated motor vehicle operator drives on property connected to schools or school crossings and *serious* bodily injury is caused by him, then he is guilty of second degree assault by auto. He is guilty of third degree assault by auto if only bodily injury results pursuant to the circumstances described in this paragraph.

Simple Assault Upgraded to Aggravated Assault at Youth Sports Events

Section 2-1f. is a provision that basically just upgrades a simple assault to a fourth degree aggravated assault where a person commits a simple assault in the presence of a child under 16 at a youth sports event. For example, Stanley Jones is sitting in the stands of a high school football game, watching his nephew return punts and play free safety. He gets upset when the referee penalizes his nephew's team for an apparent personal foul committed by his nephew. Jones, enraged, runs onto the field and punches the referee in the stomach. Ordinarily, this action would constitute a simple assault. Now, however, the assault would be elevated from its usual misdemeanor A status to a fourth degree felony. Why? Because at this high school football game, both in the stands and on the field, would be children under age 16. Committing the simple assault in their presence automatically makes this a fourth degree aggravated assault under this newly added section.

But what if an 18-year-old senior linebacker punches a 17-year-old junior halfback while they are walking to the stands after the game ended? There is a provision in the statute that says "this subsection shall not be construed to create any liability on the part of a participant in a youth sports event." So it seems to say that "participants" are exempt and therefore would not be eligible to have their assaults upgraded to fourth degree felonies.

But *after the game,* is this 18-year-old senior linebacker still a "participant"? If not, should the high school linebacker be charged with aggravated assault because his otherwise simple assault was in the presence of the same children under age 16 as mentioned above? Is that what the legislators intended when they enacted the provision? Technically, it appears that the appropriate charge would be a fourth degree aggravated assault—but in practice, this kind of case would probably be downgraded to a simple assault and remanded to the municipal court for handling.

2-1.1.   **Knowingly leaving scene of motor vehicle accident resulting in serious bodily injury, fourth degree felony; sentencing**

A motor vehicle operator who knows he is involved in an accident and knowingly leaves the scene of that accident under circumstances that violate the provisions of the motor vehicle statute for leaving the scene of an accident shall be guilty of a felony of the fourth degree if the accident results in serious bodily injury to another person.

If the evidence so warrants, nothing in this section shall be deemed to preclude an indictment and conviction for aggravated assault or assault by auto under the provisions of 2-1.

A conviction arising under this section shall not merge with a conviction for aggravated assault or assault by auto under the provisions of 2-1 and a separate sentence shall be imposed upon each conviction.

Whenever in the case of such multiple convictions the court imposes multiple sentences of imprisonment for more than one offense, those sentences shall run consecutively.

For the purposes of this section, neither knowledge of the serious bodily injury nor knowledge of the violation is an element of the offense and it shall not be a defense that the driver of the motor vehicle was unaware of the serious bodily injury or provisions of the motor vehicle statute for leaving the scene of an accident.

PRACTICAL APPLICATION OF STATUTE

This statute is a criminal counterpart to the motor vehicle statute for leaving the scene of an accident. The Jones brothers should be charged under this criminal statute, which is a fourth degree felony. Simply, the brothers *knew* they were involved in an accident—they crashed into a parked car; immediately thereafter, they *knowingly* fled the scene. An elderly victim inside the parked car suffered *serious* bodily injury (she fell into a coma and required dozens of stitches), which is the type of injury necessary for conviction under the statute. Accordingly, with all of the aforesaid elements met, the Joneses would be found guilty of violating this statute.

It is interesting to note that even if the brothers had no knowledge of the woman's serious injuries, they would still be convicted under this statute. Their actions being the cause of her injuries, coupled with their knowledge of the accident and their knowing flight of the scene, is sufficient for a guilty verdict.

2-1.2.

Endangering an injured victim

a. A person is guilty of endangering an injured victim if he causes bodily injury to any person or solicits, aids, encourages or attempts or agrees to aid another, who causes bodily injury to any person, and leaves the scene of the injury knowing or reasonably believing that the injured person is physically helpless, mentally incapacitated or otherwise unable to care for himself.

b. As used in this section, the following definitions shall apply:
   (1) "Physically helpless" means the condition in which a person is unconscious, unable to flee or physically unable to summon assistance;
   (2) "Mentally incapacitated" means that condition in which a person is rendered temporarily or permanently incapable of understanding or controlling one's conduct, or of appraising or controlling one's condition, which incapacity shall include but is not limited to an inability to comprehend one's own peril;
   (3) "Bodily injury" shall have the meaning set forth in 1-1.

c. It is an affirmative defense to prosecution for a violation of this section that the defendant summoned medical treatment for the victim, or knew that medical treatment had been summoned by another person, and protected the victim from further injury or harm until emergency assistance personnel arrived. This affirmative defense shall be proved by the defendant by a preponderance of the evidence.

d. A person who violates the provisions of this section shall be guilty of a felony of the third degree. A conviction arising under this subsection shall not merge with a conviction of the offense that rendered the person physically helpless or mentally incapacitated, nor shall such other conviction merge with a conviction under this section. The sentence imposed pursuant to this section shall be ordered to be served consecutively to that imposed for any conviction of the felony that rendered the person physically helpless or mentally incapacitated.

e. Nothing herein shall be deemed to preclude, if the evidence so warrants, an indictment and conviction for murder, manslaughter, assault or any other offense.

PRACTICAL APPLICATION OF STATUTE

The Jones brothers are guilty of endangering an injured victim after they left the grocer to flee police capture. This is a third degree felony.

A felony has been committed under 2-1.2 where three elements are met. First, the defendant must cause bodily injury to a person or aid, solicit or encourage another in causing bodily injury to a person. Next, the defendant must leave the scene of the injury. Finally, he must leave the injury scene "knowing" or "reasonably believing" that the injured person is physically helpless, mentally incapacitated or otherwise unable to care for himself.

The Jones brothers caused bodily injury—in fact, serious bodily injury—to the grocer by beating him in the face and body with golf clubs. The grocer was rendered unconscious by their beating and required 40 stitches to his head. Nonetheless, the brothers left the scene of the injury when Sergeant Paterson arrived. Given the extent of the grocer's injuries, the brothers obviously had to "know" (or at least "reasonably believe") that the grocer was physically helpless and unable to care for himself—the man was unconscious and in a pool of blood. Accordingly, the Joneses are guilty of the third degree felony of endangering an injured victim.

2-2.   Reckless endangerment

a. A person who purposely or knowingly does any act, including putting up a false light, which results in the loss or destruction of a vessel commits a felony of the third degree.

b. A person commits a felony of the fourth degree if he:

(1) Manufactures or sells a golf ball containing acid or corrosive fluid substance; or

(2) Purposely or knowingly offers, gives or entices any person to take or accept any treat, candy, gift, food, drink or other substance that is intended to be consumed which is poisonous, intoxicating, anesthetizing, tranquilizing, disorienting, deleterious or harmful to the health or welfare of such person, without the knowledge of the other person as to the identity and effect of the substance, except that it is a felony of the third degree if the actor violates the provisions of this paragraph with the purpose to commit or facilitate the commission of another criminal offense.

If a person is convicted of a felony of the fourth degree under paragraph (2) of this subsection, the sentence imposed shall include a fixed minimum sentence of not less than six months during which the defendant shall not be eligible for parole. If a person is convicted of a felony of the third degree under paragraph (2) of this subsection, the sentence imposed shall include a fixed minimum sentence of not less than 18 months during which the defendant shall not be eligible for parole. The court may not suspend or make any other noncustodial disposition of that person. A conviction arising under this subsection shall not merge with a conviction for any offense that the defendant intended to commit or facilitate, when the defendant violated the provisions of this section, nor shall any such other conviction merge with a conviction under this section. The sentence for a felony of the third degree imposed pursuant to this paragraph shall be ordered to be served consecutively to that imposed for a conviction of the offense that the defendant intended to commit or facilitate when the defendant violated the provisions of this subsection.

PRACTICAL APPLICATION OF STATUTE

Based on the allegations made by Stanley Jones' ex-girlfriend, he should be charged with reckless endangerment under 2-2b.(2). According to this woman, Jones laced her beverage with an intoxicating drug that caused her to become tranquilized and disoriented; thereafter, he sexually assaulted her.

Section 2-2b.(2) states that when an individual purposely or knowingly gives another person food or drink which is "poisonous, intoxicating, anesthetizing, tranquilizing, disorienting, deleterious or harmful" to the health of such person, then he is guilty of fourth degree reckless endangerment. He is guilty of third degree reckless endangerment if he performs the aforesaid actions "with the purpose to commit or facilitate the commission of another criminal offense."

If the state can prove that Jones "purposely" or "knowingly" slipped an "intoxicating, anesthetizing tranquilizing [or] disorienting" substance in his ex-girlfriend's drink, then he will be convicted of fourth degree reckless endangerment. If the state can further prove that Jones dropped in the substance in an effort to sexually assault the woman, then his felony will be elevated to third degree reckless endangerment.

Golf Balls and False Lights

Why does this statute have special subsections for "golf balls" and "destruction to vessels" where "false lights" are put up? There is no rhyme or reason for this. Simply put, individual states will have their own peculiar provisions, probably generated by some special-interest groups that lobbied the state legislators or by an unusual circumstance that occurred which motivated legislators, at a particular time in history, to enact statutes with bizarre elements.

2-3.   **Terroristic threats**

a. A person is guilty of a felony of the third degree if he threatens to commit any felony of violence with the purpose to terrorize another or to cause evacuation of a building, place of assembly or facility of public transportation, or otherwise to cause serious public inconvenience, or in reckless disregard of the risk of causing such terror or inconvenience. A violation of this subsection is a felony of the second degree if it occurs during a declared period of national, State or county emergency. The actor shall be strictly liable upon proof that the felony occurred, in fact, during a declared period of national, State or county emergency. It shall not be a defense that the actor did not know that there was a declared period of emergency at the time the felony occurred.

b. A person is guilty of a felony of the third degree if he threatens to kill another with the purpose to put him in imminent fear of death under circumstances reasonably causing the victim to believe the immediacy of the threat and the likelihood that it will be carried out.

PRACTICAL APPLICATION OF STATUTE

Stanley Jones is ripe for a conviction of terroristic threats per the language of 2-3b. This subsection provides that a person is guilty of a third degree offense "if he threatens to kill another with the purpose to put him in imminent fear of death." The statute also sets forth a "reasonableness" requirement—that the victim reasonably believes the immediacy of the threat and that it will likely be carried out.

Jones' ex-girlfriend had already been drugged by him and sexually assaulted. Subsequent to this, he continually appeared at her home and followed her; he even verbally threatened to kill her. Given these circumstances, it would be reasonable for this woman to believe that his threat to kill was serious and that he could immediately carry it out. Accordingly, Jones should be charged with the third degree felony of terroristic threats.

It is interesting to note that under subsection a. of this statute, an individual can be convicted of terroristic threats if he threatens to commit "any felony of violence with the purpose to terrorize another or to cause evacuation of a building" or places of assembly. Therefore, one who threatens to blow up a building—even if he is fabricating—is guilty of this third degree felony.

2-4.   **Definitions; stalking designated a felony; degrees**

   a. As used in this act:

      (1) "Course of conduct" means repeatedly maintaining a visual or physical proximity to a person or repeatedly conveying, or causing to be conveyed, verbal or written threats or threats conveyed by any other means of communication or threats implied by conduct or a combination thereof directed at or toward a person.

      (2) "Repeatedly" means on two or more occasions.

      (3) "Immediate family" means a spouse, parent, child, sibling or any other person who regularly resides in the household or who within the prior six months regularly resided in the household.

   b. A person is guilty of stalking, a felony of the fourth degree, if he purposefully or knowingly engages in a course of conduct directed at a specific person that would cause a reasonable person to fear bodily injury to himself or a member of his immediate family or to fear the death of himself or a member of his immediate family.

   c. A person is guilty of a felony of the third degree if he commits the felony of stalking in violation of an existing court order prohibiting the behavior.

   d. A person who commits a second or subsequent offense of stalking against the same victim is guilty of a felony of the third degree.

   e. A person is guilty of a felony of the third degree if he commits the felony of stalking while serving a term of imprisonment or while on parole or probation as the result of a conviction for any indictable offense under the laws of this State, any other state or the United States.

   f. This act shall not apply to conduct which occurs during organized group picketing.

PRACTICAL APPLICATION OF STATUTE

Three phrases of language are important to a conviction under the stalking statute—"course of conduct," "repeatedly" and "immediate family." A person is guilty of stalking if he engages in a "course of conduct" that consists of his "repeatedly" maintaining close visual or physical proximity to another, which in turn causes that other individual to *reasonably* fear bodily injury to himself or a member of his "immediate family." Similarly, an accused is guilty of stalking if the "course of conduct" consists of "repeatedly" conveying threats ("repeatedly" is defined as two or more occasions).

As the statute indicates, however, repeated close proximity to another or repeated threats are not, alone, sufficient for a conviction—these courses of conduct must be so severe that they would cause a *reasonable* person to fear bodily injury to himself or a member of his immediate family. An immediate family member is defined as a spouse, parent, child, sibling or any other person who has regularly resided in the household within the prior six months.

Stanley Jones is guilty of stalking his ex-girlfriend. First, he engaged in a "course of conduct" that violates the statute. He "repeatedly" maintained close physical and visual proximity to her by appearing in front of her house five times. Even more so, he twice threatened to kill her, her mother and her sister—and remember, Jones had previously drugged and sexually assaulted the woman. This course of conduct certainly would make any *reasonable* person fear bodily injury to herself and her "immediate family" members (her mother and sister). With these facts existing, Stanley Jones would normally be convicted of a fourth degree stalking charge; Jones' charge, however, should be elevated to a third degree offense under subsection e. of this statute.

Per subsection e., a person is guilty of third degree stalking if he commits the felony "while serving a term of imprisonment or while on parole or probation as the result of a conviction for any indictable offense." Since Stanley Jones was on parole from an arson conviction (an indictable offense) at the time he stalked his ex-girlfriend, his charge should be elevated to a third degree offense pursuant to the requirements of subsection e. of this statute.

It is important to note here that stalking also becomes a third degree offense under subsections c. and d. as well. If a person stalks in violation of an existing court order (i.e., a restraining order), he is guilty of a third degree felony. Likewise, if he commits a second or subsequent stalking offense, he is guilty of a third degree felony.

2-5.

Disarming a law enforcement or corrections officer; felony; degrees

a. A person who knowingly takes or attempts to exercise unlawful control over a firearm or other weapon in the possession of a law enforcement or corrections officer when that officer is acting in the performance of his duties, and either is in uniform or exhibits evidence of his authority, is guilty of a felony of the second degree.

b. A person violating the provisions of subsection a. of this section shall be guilty of a felony of the first degree if:

(1) The person fires or discharges the firearm;

(2) The person uses or threatens to use the firearm or weapon against the officer or any other person; or

(3) The officer or another person suffers serious bodily injury.

PRACTICAL APPLICATION OF STATUTE

Lance Jones' actions in disarming a uniformed police officer, and thereafter firing his gun, constitute a felony of the first degree pursuant to the language of 2-5b.(1). Under the basic requirements of this statute, however, disarming a law enforcement officer (or corrections officer) makes a person guilty of a second degree felony. The charge becomes a first degree offense under subsection b. (as in Jones' case) if the person discharges the firearm or threatens to use it against someone or if another suffers serious bodily injury as a result of the person's disarming activities.

As a special note, a conviction under this statute does not necessitate the taking of a firearm—other weapons such as a knife or even a nightstick may suffice. Also, the officer need not be in uniform when disarmed; the officer simply must be acting in the performance of his duties and exhibiting evidence of his authority.

2-6.

Throwing bodily fluid at certain law enforcement officers deemed aggravated assault; grading, sentence

As used in this act:

"Bodily fluid" means saliva, blood, urine, feces, seminal fluid or any other bodily fluid. "Department of Corrections employee" means any corrections officer, parole officer or other employee of the Department of Corrections and any person under contract to provide services to the department.

A person who throws a bodily fluid at a Department of Corrections employee, county corrections officer, juvenile corrections officer, State juvenile facility employee, juvenile detention staff member, probation officer, any sheriff, undersheriff or sheriff's officer or any municipal, county or State law enforcement officer while in the performance of his duties or otherwise purposely subjects such employee to contact with a bodily fluid commits an aggravated assault. If the victim suffers bodily injury, this shall be a felony of the third degree. Otherwise, this shall be a felony of the fourth degree. A term of imprisonment imposed for this offense shall run consecutively to any term of imprisonment currently being served and to any other term imposed for another offense committed at the time of the assault. Nothing herein shall be deemed to preclude, if the evidence so warrants, an indictment and conviction for a violation or attempted violation of chapter 1 of the state statutes or subsection b. of 2-1 or any other provision of the criminal laws.

PRACTICAL APPLICATION OF STATUTE

Simply said, one who throws bodily fluid at a law enforcement officer while he is performing his duties is guilty of aggravated assault. It is a third degree felony if the officer suffers bodily injury; otherwise, it is a fourth degree felony. One item of note—the bodily fluid does not necessarily need to be "thrown" for conviction—it is sufficient if the actor just "subjects such employee to contact with a bodily fluid."

END OF CHAPTER REVIEW

Multiple-Choice Questions

The following fact pattern pertains to questions 1–3.

Lance Jones and his brother, Stanley, physically beat a grocer with a set of golf clubs, knocking him unconscious. The grocer's injuries necessitated 40 stitches to his head, and he also suffered broken ribs. Frisco City Police Sergeant Samuel Paterson arrived at the scene, and immediately Lance Jones aimed a pistol at the officer. As he did so, a red laser beam raced from the gun's barrel toward the sergeant's head. The two Jones brothers then fled the scene, with Sergeant Paterson following them.

1. For pointing a firearm at Frisco City Police Sergeant Samuel Paterson, Lance Jones is guilty of:
   a. disorderly conduct
   b. simple assault
   c. third degree aggravated assault
   d. fourth degree aggravated assault
   e. nothing, as no harm was done to the officer

2. If Samuel Paterson was *not* a police officer but instead a regular citizen, Lance Jones would be guilty of what offense for pointing a firearm at him?
   a. disorderly conduct
   b. simple assault
   c. third degree aggravated assault
   d. fourth degree aggravated assault
   e. nothing, as no harm was done to the person

3. For pointing a firearm at Sergeant Paterson that activated a red laser beam that ran to the officer's head, what should Lance Jones be charged with?
   a. an additional charge of simple assault
   b. an additional charge of harassment
   c. an additional charge of disorderly conduct
   d. an additional charge of aggravated assault
   e. nothing, because Jones would already be charged with an offense for pointing the firearm at Sergeant Paterson

4. Disarming a law enforcement officer is:
   a. a felony of the first degree if the defendant discharges the firearm
   b. a felony of the second degree if the defendant doesn't discharge the firearm
   c. a felony of the first degree if the defendant threatens to use the firearm against the officer
   d. a felony of the first degree if the officer suffers serious bodily injury once the firearm is disarmed from the officer
   e. all of the above

5. The Hawthorne Bears battle it out in a close game with Queen of Peace's Golden Griffiths. Just after Queen of Peace's tight end Nick Bender scores a touchdown, 40-year-old Hawthorne Bears dad Terry Timly punches Queen of Peace dad Eddie Kole in the gut. They scuffle, and then the Hawthorne police intervene. What is the most serious offense that Terry Timly could be convicted of?
   a. harassment
   b. disorderly conduct
   c. riot
   d. simple assault
   e. fourth degree aggravated assault

6. Stanley Jones repeatedly sat in front of his ex-girlfriend's house, calling her each time she appeared; on each occasion, he threatened to physically beat her. On three of the events, he waved a baseball bat at her as she looked out the window. Stanley Jones could appropriately be charged with which offense?

    a. attempted murder

    b. stalking

    c. reckless endangerment

    d. endangering a victim

    e. all of the above

7. The use of terroristic threats is:

    a. a felony of the third degree

    b. a felony of the fourth degree

    c. a misdemeanor A

    d. a misdemeanor B

    e. all of the above

Essay Questions

1. Eduardo is the "front man" of an up-and-coming rock band based in the artistic city of Teasale. Sara thinks Eduardo is the hottest guy in the world, and she goes to all of Eduardo's gigs. Twice she obtained Eduardo's autograph, once kissing him after he signed a paper plate for her. Recently, though, she has started to annoy Eduardo, coming up to him at seven consecutive events and asking for a "date." She even offered sexual favors; she also snuck backstage at one of the band's concerts. Eduardo, through his agent, told Sara that she is no longer permitted to come to the band's concerts. Sara ignored the agent and showed up at the last gig, once again begging Eduardo for an autograph. Should Teasale police charge Sara with stalking? Why or why not? What elements of the stalking statute are present in Sara's case that would justify—or not justify—a stalking charge?

2. Beef doesn't like police. He also doesn't like his neighbor, Carl, and one of his town's first-aid workers, McMichael. After getting drunk one Friday night, Beef decided to have some fun. His first order of business was to throw a rock through Carl's sliding glass door on the back porch. Carl, hearing the crash, rushed to the back of his house. Beef, from across the street, called Carl on a cell phone and said, "I'm going to kill you because I hate you." Carl, frightened, called the police.

    Minutes later Officer Geronimo arrived. As the officer exited his patrol cruiser, Beef pointed a pistol at him and ordered him to the ground. Beef then cracked Officer Geronimo in the kneecap with a baseball bat, an injury that ultimately shattered the officer's knee and caused him to retire from the police force.

    At this point, another neighbor, Charles, came out of his house. Beef pointed his pistol at him and ordered him back inside. Moments later, McMichael, the first-aid worker, arrived. Beef ran up to McMichael and punched him square in the face, causing McMichael's lip to bleed. Then, noticing that Charles was outside again, Beef punched Charles in the face, causing a black eye. Beef was ultimately apprehended at a tanning salon and appropriately charged for his "night of fun."

What varied offenses should Beef be charged with for his acts against Carl, Officer Geronimo, Charles and McMichael? Are these offenses felonies or misdemeanors? For felonies, what degree are they—first, second, third or fourth? Are they misdemeanor A or B? Explain all of your answers.

3

KIDNAPPING AND RELATED OFFENSES: COERCION

In Maple County, the Oak Glen Police Department, working in conjunction with the County Prosecutor's Office, recently arrested Mercury Anderson for a variety of serious criminal offenses. Anderson's arrest resulted from an 18-month investigation predicated on an anonymous tip delivered to Oak Glen Lieutenant Sanford Stokes. The high-ranking police official had been advised that Anderson was taking women and children by force, committing various sexual offenses upon them and then turning his victims back into the community. Although none of the victims was able to identify Anderson because of an array of disguises and professional makeup he wore, an exhaustive investigation finally netted overwhelming physical evidence and taped conversations where Anderson made several incriminating admissions. The cases included the following victims and facts.

Candice Wesley. Ms. Wesley, 29, was Anderson's first victim. Anderson snatched Wesley from her automobile and forcibly brought her to an apartment located in East Pinedale. There, Anderson contacted Wesley's family and advised that she would be returned to them for a fee of $50,000. Six hours later, Anderson apparently got nervous and released Wesley, unharmed, at a local diner. He never received the payment he demanded.

Jerri Sloane. Just the same as with Candice Wesley, Ms. Sloane, 15, was abducted from an automobile and brought to the East Pinedale apartment; however, once there, Anderson engaged in nonconsensual sexual intercourse with her and beat her violently, breaking her nose with the butt of a handgun. Thereafter, he brought Sloane to a park and left her there.

Eric Mesos. Anderson invaded Mesos' car, advising him that if he left the vehicle, Mesos' mother would be killed. Mesos remained in the car with Anderson for 15 minutes. During this time period, Anderson twice exposed his genitals to Mesos. Then Anderson left the vehicle. Mesos was 20 at the time of the incident.

Frank Pileggi. Anderson lured Pileggi, age ten, into a pickup truck by offering Pileggi a set of baseball cards. Once Pileggi was inside the truck, Anderson rubbed his hands over Pileggi's buttocks and groin area. Pileggi was then told to leave the vehicle.

Samantha Cora. Anderson met Cora, 12 years old, at a carnival. He bought her cotton candy and ice cream and then asked if she would join him at his apartment. Cora agreed, and at the apartment she consensually engaged in sexual intercourse with him.

Kami Subron. In a department store, Anderson set up a hidden camera in the women's dressing room. There he videotaped Subron, 26, naked as she changed into various articles of lingerie. Anderson thereafter sold copies of the videotapes to numerous individuals. The following week, Anderson followed Subron to the law office where she worked. Inside, Anderson hid in the closet of Subron's private office. There Anderson consumed beer and secretly watched Subron engage in sexual relations with her lover, Suave.

After Anderson was arrested, the police also learned that, three years earlier, he had taken his own ten-year-old daughter from the child's mother. She had sole legal and physical custody of the minor and was never advised of her child's whereabouts. Authorities had been unable to solve the child's disappearance due to their inability to locate Anderson. Now Mercury Anderson, 52, was criminally charged for this abduction as well as for repeated sexual assaults on his daughter immediately upon her taking.

After probing further, police discovered that Anderson had been convicted of sexual assault 30 years earlier under the alias "Roger Ponot." Anderson/Ponot had never registered as a sex offender in the municipality where he resided. Anderson was charged for this failure to register, along with multiple other offenses for his string of violent unlawful activities.

Once Lieutenant Stokes processed Anderson, bail was set at $1 million. Although Anderson was unable to post the bail and be released, he contacted Stokes, via phone, at his private home. During their phone conversation, he threatened to kill Stokes if he testified at trial or furthered his case in any way. Anderson also threatened to reveal to the public a private secret of Stokes—that the lieutenant had schizophrenia and was treated multiple times at a local hospital for the disease. In addition, Anderson threatened to publicly accuse Stokes of beating him while in he was in custody. Lieutenant Stokes did not suffer from schizophrenia, nor had he beaten Anderson while he was in custody.

3-1.   **Kidnapping**

a. Holding for ransom, reward or as a hostage. A person is guilty of kidnapping if he unlawfully removes another from the place where he is found or if he unlawfully confines another with the purpose of holding that person for ransom or reward or as a shield or hostage.

b. Holding for other purposes. A person is guilty of kidnapping if he unlawfully removes another from his place of residence or business, or a substantial distance from the vicinity where he is found, or if he unlawfully confines another for a substantial period, with any of the following purposes:

   (1) To facilitate commission of any felony or flight thereafter;

   (2) To inflict bodily injury on or to terrorize the victim or another;

   (3) To interfere with the performance of any governmental or political function; or

   (4) To permanently deprive a parent, guardian or other lawful custodian of custody of the victim.

c. Grading of kidnapping.

   (1) Except as provided in paragraph (2) of this subsection, kidnapping is a felony of the first degree and upon conviction thereof, a person may be sentenced to an ordinary term of imprisonment between 15 and 30 years. If the actor releases the victim unharmed and in a safe place prior to apprehension, it is a felony of the second degree.

(2) Kidnapping is a felony of the first degree and upon conviction thereof, an actor shall be sentenced to a term of imprisonment by the court if the victim of the kidnapping is less than 16 years of age and if during the kidnapping:

(a) A felony of aggravated sexual assault, sexual assault or aggravated criminal sexual contact is committed against the victim;

(b) A felony of endangering the welfare of a child is committed against the victim; or

(c) The actor sells or delivers the victim to another person for pecuniary gain other than in circumstances which lead to the return of the victim to a parent, guardian or other person responsible for the general supervision of the victim.

The term of imprisonment imposed under this paragraph shall be either a term of 25 years during which the actor shall not be eligible for parole or a specific term between 25 years and life imprisonment, of which the actor shall serve 25 years before being eligible for parole; provided, however, that the felony of kidnapping under this paragraph and underlying aggravating felonies listed in subparagraph (a), (b) or (c) of this paragraph shall merge for purposes of sentencing. If the actor is convicted of the criminal homicide of a victim of a kidnapping under the provisions of chapter 1, any sentence imposed under provisions of this paragraph shall be served consecutively to any sentence imposed pursuant to the provisions of chapter 1.

d. "Unlawful" removal or confinement. A removal or confinement is unlawful within the meaning of this section and of sections 3-2 and 3-3 if it is accomplished by force, threat or deception, or in the case of a person who is under the age of 14 or is incompetent, if it is accomplished without the consent of a parent, guardian or other person responsible for general supervision of his welfare.

e. It is an affirmative defense to a prosecution under paragraph (4) of subsection b. of this section, which must be proved by clear and convincing evidence, that:

(1) The actor reasonably believed that the action was necessary to preserve the victim from imminent danger to his welfare. However, no defense shall be available pursuant to this subsection if the actor does not, as soon as reasonably practicable but in no event more than 24 hours after taking a victim under his protection, give notice of the victim's location to the police department of the municipality where the victim resided, the office of the county prosecutor in the county where the victim resided or the Division of Youth and Family Services in the Department of Human Services;

(2) The actor reasonably believed that the taking or detaining of the victim was consented to by a parent or by an authorized State agency; or

(3) The victim, being at the time of the taking or concealment not less than 14 years old, was taken away at his own volition by his parent and without the purpose to commit a criminal offense with or against the victim.

f. It is an affirmative defense to a prosecution under paragraph (4) of subsection b. of this section that a parent having the right of custody reasonably believed he was fleeing from imminent physical danger from the other parent, provided that the parent having custody, as soon as reasonably practicable:

(1) Gives notice of the victim's location to the police department of the municipality where the victim resided, the office of the county prosecutor in the county where the

victim resided or the Division of Youth and Family Services in the Department of Human Services; or

(2) Commences an action effecting custody in an appropriate court.

g. As used in subsections e. and f. of this section, "parent" means a parent, guardian or other lawful custodian of a victim.

PRACTICAL APPLICATION OF STATUTE

Kidnapping—First and Second Degree Offenses

Section 3-1 contains an array of circumstances that permit a charge of kidnapping. The offense generally is a felony of the first degree but may be lowered to a second degree offense if the defendant "releases the victim unharmed in a safe place prior to apprehension." Per this exception, which can be found in subsection c. of the statute, Mercury Anderson should be charged with second degree kidnapping for his felony involving Candice Wesley.

Ms. Wesley, an adult, was taken from her automobile against her will. She was brought to an apartment, and a ransom of $50,000 was demanded. For some reason, Anderson released her at a diner six hours later, unharmed. Under subsection a. of the statute, a person is guilty of kidnapping if he "unlawfully removes another from the place where he is found," confines this person unlawfully and demands a ransom. Since Anderson unlawfully removed Wesley from her car, confined her in his apartment and then demanded a $50,000 ransom, he is guilty of kidnapping. The felony is a second degree offense because he released her, unharmed, at the safe location of a diner.

It is important to note that Anderson could be convicted of kidnapping even if his felony was predicated on purposes other than obtaining a ransom. Subsection a. also provides that if Anderson removed and held his victim to be utilized as a "shield" (i.e., from gunfire by law enforcement) or as a "hostage," he could be convicted of kidnapping.

Under subsection b. he is guilty of kidnapping if he confines someone for a "substantial" period of time (or takes someone to another location and confines him) for a number of reasons, including facilitating a felony, inflicting bodily injury on the victim, interfering with a government function or intending to permanently deprive a parent of lawful custody. Accordingly, if Anderson had taken Wesley to his apartment to beat her rather than to demand a ransom, he would still be convicted of kidnapping. Similarly, if his purpose in removing her from her car and confining her was to stop the state assembly from legislating for a day, he is guilty of kidnapping. Finally, if Anderson had not actually taken Wesley to his apartment but instead had simply confined her in a car while he beat her, he is guilty of kidnapping as long as the confinement was for a "substantial" period of time. But what is a "substantial" period of time? Courts have ruled it can be as little as 30 minutes.

Permanently Depriving Lawful Custodian of Custody

Mercury Anderson also should be charged with kidnapping under subsection b. for the abduction of his own daughter. The child's mother had sole physical and legal custody of this juvenile. Anderson took the child from her and kept the minor in his custody for three years, never advising the mother of her child's whereabouts. This obviously was an effort to permanently deprive the mother of her lawful custody. Since Anderson did not release the child prior to his apprehension, he is guilty of first degree kidnapping of his daughter.

Under subsection e., it is an affirmative defense to the above form of kidnapping if the actor "reasonably believed that the action was necessary to preserve the victim from imminent danger." This defense is not available, though, if the actor does not notify the police, or other appropriate authorities, of the victim's location within 24 hours of the taking. It is also an affirmative defense if the actor reasonably believed that the child's parent, or an authorized state agency, consented to the taking or if the child is 14 years (or older) and consents to his own taking.

The above-listed defenses are not available to Mercury Anderson, however. He had no reason to believe his daughter was in imminent danger, and he never notified anyone of her location. Moreover, neither the child's mother nor any state agency consented to her taking. Also, the child was under 14 at the time of the taking, and there is no evidence that she joined Anderson on her own volition.

It should further be noted that even if Anderson's daughter were 14 or older and consented to going with him, he still would not have an affirmative defense to kidnapping. Subsection e.(3) sets forth that this type of affirmative defense is only available if the taking is "without the purpose to commit a criminal offense with or against the victim." Given that Anderson repeatedly sexually assaulted his daughter, he certainly acted with the purpose to commit a criminal offense upon the taking of his child. Therefore, even if his daughter were 14 or older and consented to his taking of her, Anderson would still be guilty of kidnapping. His failure to notify the child's mother (or any appropriate state agency) of her whereabouts for three years, in and of itself, may also be a felony sufficient to vitiate such a defense—even in the face of a child being 14 or older and consenting to the taking.

Special First Degree Kidnapping Provisions When Victim Is Under 16

Kidnapping is always a felony of the first degree, per subsection c.(2) of this statute, when the victim is under 16 years of age *and* one of the following felonies occurs during the kidnapping: aggravated sexual assault or sexual assault, aggravated criminal sexual contact, child pornography offenses, selling the child for monetary gain. A defendant who commits any of the aforesaid felonies during a kidnapping will receive an enhanced prison term—above and beyond the ordinary term of imprisonment for first degree offenses.

Mercury Anderson's kidnapping of Jerri Sloane is violative of subsection c.(2). Sloane was 15 at the time of her abduction. During the kidnapping, Anderson forced her to engage in nonconsensual sexual intercourse. Accordingly, he should be charged with this first degree kidnapping and be sentenced to the enhanced incarceration.

3-2.   **Criminal restraint**

A person commits a felony of the third degree if he knowingly:

  a. Restrains another unlawfully in circumstances exposing the other to risk of serious bodily injury; or
  b. Holds another in a condition of involuntary servitude.

The creation by the actor of circumstances resulting in a belief by another that he must remain in a particular location shall for purposes of this section be deemed to be a holding in a condition of involuntary servitude.

In any prosecution under subsection b., it is an affirmative defense that the person held was a child less than 18 years old and the actor was a relative or legal guardian of such child and his sole purpose was to assume control of such child.

Practical Application of Statute

Mercury Anderson's actions against Eric Mesos constitute a criminal restraint, a third degree felony. An individual is guilty of criminal restraint if he restrains another unlawfully, thereby exposing that person to serious bodily injury (subsection a.) or if he holds another in "involuntary servitude" (subsection b.). Creating a set of circumstances that makes someone believe that he must remain in a particular location is an "involuntary servitude" under this statute.

Anderson invaded Mesos' automobile, advising him that if he left the vehicle, his mother would be killed. These threats levied by Anderson made Mesos believe that he couldn't leave the automobile. Mesos remained in the car for 20 minutes until Anderson vacated. Accordingly, Anderson held Mesos in an involuntary servitude and therefore violated subsection b. of this statute.

If the facts were tweaked to the extent that Anderson duct-taped Mesos' mouth and stuffed him in the trunk of the car for 15 minutes—in an effort to restrain him—Anderson would still be convicted of criminal restraint. As subsection a. of the statute provides, a person is guilty of this offense if he restrains "another unlawfully in circumstances exposing the other to risk of serious bodily injury." Thus, Anderson's suffocating actions, which could cause serious bodily injury to Mesos, would make him guilty of criminal restraint. It should be noted, though, that if Anderson kept Mesos in this confined condition for much longer, he could be charged with kidnapping instead of criminal restraint.

3-3.   ### False imprisonment

A person commits a misdemeanor A if he knowingly restrains another unlawfully so as to interfere substantially with his liberty. In any prosecution under this section, it is an affirmative defense that the person restrained was a child less than 18 years old and that the actor was a relative or legal guardian of such child and that his sole purpose was to assume control of such child.

Practical Application of Statute

False imprisonment is a misdemeanor A, as it is basically a lesser form of criminal restraint. The statute requires that an actor knowingly restrain someone unlawfully so as to interfere substantially with his liberty. A modification of Mercury Anderson's restraint of Eric Mesos can exemplify this offense.

If Anderson entered Mesos' car and locked the doors, refusing to allow Mesos to exit, he would be ripe for a false imprisonment conviction. Here, Anderson's restraint would be substantially interfering with Mesos' liberty to move about freely. As long as the restraint did not subject Mesos to the risk of serious bodily injury, Anderson's actions would constitute a false imprisonment offense rather than criminal restraint.

3-4.   **Interference with custody**

a. Custody of children. A person, including a parent, guardian or other lawful custodian, is guilty of interference with custody if he:

   (1) Takes or detains a minor child with the purpose of concealing the minor child and thereby depriving the child's other parent of custody or parenting time with the minor child;

   (2) After being served with process or having actual knowledge of an action affecting marriage or custody but prior to the issuance of a temporary or final order determining custody and parenting time rights to a minor child, takes, detains, entices or conceals the child within or outside the State for the purpose of depriving the child's other parent of custody or parenting time, or to evade the jurisdiction of the courts of this State;

   (3) After being served with process or having actual knowledge of an action affecting the protective services needs of a child in an action affecting custody, but prior to the issuance of a temporary or final order determining custody rights of a minor child, takes, detains, entices or conceals the child within or outside the State for the purpose of evading the jurisdiction of the courts of this State; or

   (4) After the issuance of a temporary or final order specifying custody, joint custody rights or parenting time, takes, detains, entices or conceals a minor child from the other parent in violation of the custody or parenting time order.

Interference with custody is a felony of the second degree if the child is taken, detained, enticed or concealed: (i) outside the United States or (ii) for more than 24 hours. Otherwise, interference with custody is a felony of the third degree but the presumption of non-imprisonment for a first offense of a felony of the third degree shall not apply.

b. Custody of committed persons. A person is guilty of a felony of the fourth degree if he knowingly takes or entices any committed person away from lawful custody when he is not privileged to do so. "Committed person" means, in addition to anyone committed under judicial warrant, any orphan, neglected or delinquent child, mentally defective or insane person or other dependent or incompetent person entrusted to another's custody by or through a recognized social agency or otherwise by authority of law.

c. It is an affirmative defense to a prosecution under subsection a. of this section, which must be proved by clear and convincing evidence, that:

   (1) The actor reasonably believed that the action was necessary to preserve the child from imminent danger to his welfare. However, no defense shall be available pursuant to this subsection if the actor does not, as soon as reasonably practicable but in no event more than 24 hours after taking a child under his protection, give notice of the child's location to the police department of the municipality where the child resided, the office of the county prosecutor in the county where the child resided or the Division of Youth and Family Services in the Department of Human Services;

   (2) The actor reasonably believed that the taking or detaining of the minor child was consented to by the other parent or by an authorized State agency; or

   (3) The child, being at the time of the taking or concealment not less than 14 years old, was taken away at his own volition and without the purpose to commit a criminal offense with or against the child.

d. It is an affirmative defense to a prosecution under subsection a. of this section that a parent having the right of custody reasonably believed he was fleeing from imminent physical danger from the other parent, provided that the parent having custody, as soon as reasonably practicable:

  (1) Gives notice of the child's location to the police department of the municipality where the child resided, the office of the county prosecutor in the county where the child resided or the Division of Youth and Family Services in the Department of Human Services; or

  (2) Commences an action effecting custody in an appropriate court.

e. The offenses enumerated in this section are continuous in nature and continue for so long as the child is concealed or detained.

f. (1) In addition to any other disposition provided by law, a person convicted under subsection a. of this section shall make restitution of all reasonable expenses and costs, including reasonable counsel fees, incurred by the other parent in securing the child's return.

  (2) In imposing sentence under subsection a. of this section the court shall consider:

    (a) Whether the person returned the child voluntarily; and

    (b) The length of time the child was concealed or detained.

g. As used in this section, "parent" means a parent, guardian or other lawful custodian of a minor child.

PRACTICAL APPLICATION OF STATUTE

Interference with custody is a charge often filed during child custody battles occurring in the family courts. Many times, law enforcement personnel appropriately find that parents' complaints involving the taking or concealing of their children do not meet the elements of kidnapping but rather are offenses under 3-4. Other times, actions appearing to amount to interference with custody may not be felonies at all, and this should be noted. A review of family court proceedings and related orders is integral when charging under this statute.

Mercury Anderson is guilty of kidnapping his own daughter because he took the girl from her mother, *permanently* depriving the woman of her lawful custody. Anderson kept the child concealed from the mother for three years, never revealing her location. However, if the facts were changed slightly, he would be guilty of interference with custody, a third degree offense, instead of kidnapping.

The interference with custody charge would be proper if Anderson's taking of the child did not result in a permanent loss of custody or parenting by the mother. This charge would be valid just if the taking and concealing of the daughter resulted in any significant depriving of the woman's custody or parenting time.

Interference with custody is generally a third degree felony. It becomes a felony of the second degree if the child is taken outside the United States or taken for more than 24 hours. If a child is taken for more than 24 hours, though, and a law enforcement officer considers it serious enough to warrant a second degree interference with custody charge, then perhaps the true felony is kidnapping. In other words, does it sound right that a parent who takes his child for 25 (or 48 or 72) hours should be charged with a second degree offense? For such a serious charge, circumstances of a more illicit nature probably should be occurring, and therefore kidnapping may be the correct charge.

3-5.   Criminal coercion

   a. Offense defined. A person is guilty of criminal coercion if, with the purpose unlawfully to restrict another's freedom of action to engage or refrain from engaging in conduct, he threatens to:

   (1) Inflict bodily injury on anyone or commit any other offense;

   (2) Accuse anyone of an offense;

   (3) Expose any secret which would tend to subject any person to hatred, contempt or ridicule, or to impair his credit or business repute;

   (4) Take or withhold action as an official, or cause an official to take or withhold action;

   (5) Bring about or continue a strike, boycott or other collective action, except that such a threat shall not be deemed coercive when the restriction compelled is demanded in the course of negotiation for the benefit of the group in whose interest the actor acts;

   (6) Testify or provide information or withhold testimony or information with respect to another's legal claim or defense; or

   (7) Perform any other act which would not in itself substantially benefit the actor but which is calculated to substantially harm another person with respect to his health, safety, business, calling, career, financial condition, reputation or personal relationships.

   It is an affirmative defense to prosecution based on paragraphs (2), (3), (4), (6) and (7) that the actor believed the accusation or secret to be true or the proposed official action justified and that his purpose was limited to compelling the other to behave in a way reasonably related to the circumstances which were the subject of the accusation, exposure or proposed official action, as by desisting from further misbehavior, making good a wrong done or refraining from taking any action or responsibility for which the actor believes the other disqualified.

   b. Grading. Criminal coercion is a felony of the fourth degree unless the threat is to commit a felony more serious than one of the fourth degree or the actor's purpose is criminal, in which cases the offense is a felony of the third degree.

PRACTICAL APPLICATION OF STATUTE

The Oak Glen Police Department should charge Mercury Anderson with criminal coercion for his threats to falsely accuse Lieutenant Stokes of beating him while in custody and to expose the lieutenant to possible ridicule by revealing to the public that Stokes has schizophrenia. Anderson's threats are felonies of criminal coercion as they were levied in an effort to prevent Stokes from testifying at his trial. Ordinarily, criminal coercion is a felony of the fourth degree; Anderson's aforesaid actions amount to this grading level.

   Mercury Anderson should also be charged with a third degree criminal coercion for his threat to kill Stokes if the officer testified against him or furthered his case in any way. Under subsection b. of the statute, criminal coercion is elevated from a fourth degree offense to a third degree offense where "the threat is to commit a felony more serious than one of the fourth degree." Since Anderson threatened to kill Stokes (murdering someone is a first degree felony), he threatened to commit a felony more serious than a fourth degree offense. Accordingly, Anderson is here guilty of a third degree criminal coercion.

Generally, a threat to kill will simply fall under the terroristic threats statute. Indeed, Anderson's threat to kill Lieutenant Stokes is a terroristic threat; however, it is also an act of criminal coercion. Subsection a. of this statute defines criminal coercion as an unlawful purposeful action intended "to restrict another's freedom of action to engage or refrain from engaging in conduct." Because Anderson's intent in threatening to kill Stokes was to prevent him from testifying—"to restrict his freedom of action"—he is guilty of criminal coercion. This same rationale holds true as to why Anderson should face criminal coercion charges for his threats to publicly expose Stokes' schizophrenia and his in-custody beating—the threats were made for the unlawful purpose of preventing Stokes from testifying. Anderson should also be charged with witness tampering, which is a separate and distinct felony that will be discussed later in this book.

3-6.   **Luring, enticing child by various means, attempts; felony of second degree; subsequent offense, mandatory imprisonment**

A person commits a felony of the second degree if he attempts, via electronic or any other means, to lure or entice a child or one who he reasonably believes to be a child into a motor vehicle, structure or isolated area, or to meet or appear at any other place, with the purpose to commit a criminal offense with or against the child.

a. "Child" as used in this act means a person less than 18 years old.

b. "Electronic means" as used in this section includes, but is not limited to, the Internet.

c. "Structure" as used in this act means any building, room, ship, vessel or airplane and also means any place adapted for overnight accommodation of persons, or for carrying on business therein, whether or not a person is actually present. Nothing herein shall be deemed to preclude, if the evidence so warrants, an indictment and conviction for attempted kidnapping under the provisions of 3-1.

A person convicted of a second or subsequent offense under this section or a person convicted under this section who has previously been convicted of a violation of aggravated sexual assault, sexual assault, aggravated criminal sexual contact or endangering the welfare of a child shall be sentenced to a term of imprisonment. The term of imprisonment shall include, unless the person is sentenced pursuant to extended term provisions, a mandatory minimum term of one-third to one-half of the sentence imposed or three years, whichever is greater, during which time the defendant shall not be eligible for parole. If the person is sentenced pursuant to extended term provisions, the court shall impose a minimum term of one-third to one-half of the sentence imposed or five years, whichever is greater. The court may not suspend or make any other non-custodial disposition of any person sentenced as a second or subsequent offender pursuant to this section.

For the purposes of this section, an offense is considered a second or subsequent offense or a previous conviction of aggravated sexual assault, sexual assault, aggravated criminal sexual contact or endangering the welfare of a child, as the case may be, if the actor has at any time been convicted pursuant to this section or under any similar statute of the United States, this State or any other state for an offense that is substantially equivalent to this section or substantially equivalent to aggravated sexual assault, sexual assault, aggravated criminal sexual contact or endangering the welfare of a child.

PRACTICAL APPLICATION OF STATUTE

Mercury Anderson is guilty of violating 3-6 for luring Frank Pileggi into his automobile. Per the statute, a person commits this second degree offense if he attempts to lure or entice a child into a motor vehicle or other isolated area with the purpose to commit a criminal offense with or against the child.

Frank Pileggi, age ten, was lured into a motor vehicle via Mercury Anderson's offering a set of baseball cards. Once Pileggi was inside the automobile, Anderson committed the offense of aggravated criminal sexual contact by rubbing Pileggi's buttocks and groin area. Accordingly, in addition to being charged with sexual assault, Anderson should be charged under 3-6 for luring this ten-year-old child into his automobile and sexually violating him therein.

3-7.   **Luring, enticing an adult, certain circumstances, third degree felony**

A person commits a felony of the third degree if he attempts, via electronic or any other means, to lure or entice a person into a motor vehicle, structure or isolated area, or to meet or appear at any place, with the purpose to commit a criminal offense with or against the person lured or enticed or against any other person.

"Electronic means" as used in this section includes, but is not limited to, the Internet. "Internet" means the international computer network of both federal and non-federal interoperable packet switched data networks. "Structure" shall have the meaning set forth in 3-6.

Nothing herein shall be deemed to preclude, if the evidence so warrants, an indictment and conviction for attempted kidnapping under the provisions of 3-1 or for any other felony or offense.

A conviction under this section shall not merge with a conviction of any other criminal offense, nor shall such other conviction merge with a conviction under this section, and the court shall impose separate sentences upon each violation of this section and any other criminal offense. The court may not suspend or make any other non-custodial disposition of any person sentenced pursuant to this section.

PRACTICAL APPLICATION OF STATUTE

If Frank Pileggi were 28 instead of ten, could Mercury Anderson be convicted of luring him into an automobile? The answer is yes—pursuant to elements set forth in 3-7. Section 3-7 was created to supplement its parent statute, 3-6, which only protects minors. This newer statute, as a third degree felony, is a lower-graded offense than luring a child (which is a felony of the second degree).

Mercury Anderson is guilty of violating this statute if he "attempts, via electronic or any other means, to lure or entice *a person*" (emphasis added) into motor vehicles, structures or any place whatsoever. That is, of course, if he does so "with the purpose to commit a criminal offense with or against the person lured or enticed or against any other person."

The significance of 3-7 is that adults are now protected against luring. Joining the tremendous technological advances that society has gained through the Internet have been tremendous advances by predatory criminals.

Let's say Mercury Anderson contacts Frank Pileggi, Sr., 28, in an Internet chat room about rare baseball cards. During their electronic discussion, Anderson offers to give Pileggi a 1951 Ted Williams card for free. He types a final note to Pileggi, advising him to meet up in a mall parking lot—inside Anderson's white Honda Prelude.

Anderson's purpose, though, is not to give a free baseball card to Pileggi. His true purpose is to force sexual intercourse upon the adult man. Pileggi arrives, enters the Honda and is indeed sexually assaulted.

In the above example, Anderson is guilty of luring an adult under 3-7 in addition to aggravated sexual assault. He utilized the Internet chat room to lure *a person*, Frank Pileggi, into a motor vehicle. His purpose was to commit a criminal offense, aggravated sexual assault, against the man. Accordingly, Anderson is guilty of this third degree felony.

It is important to note that neither luring an adult (3-7) or nor luring a child (3-6) requires the use of the Internet, or other electronic means, for a conviction. The defendant is equally culpable if he lures or entices the victim by "any means." Also, the location where the victim is lured to is not dispositive. Although the statutes specifically itemize "motor vehicle," "structure" and "isolated area," the general language of "to meet or appear at *any place*" means an actor will not escape conviction if the victim is lured to a carnival, playground or football game.

3-8.   **Human trafficking**

   a. A person commits the felony of human trafficking if he:

      (1) Knowingly holds, recruits, lures, entices, harbors, transports, provides or obtains, by any means, another, to engage in sexual activity as defined in the offense of prostitution or to provide labor or services:

         (a) By threats of serious bodily harm or physical restraint against the person or any other person;

         (b) By means of any scheme, plan or pattern intended to cause the person to believe that the person or any other person would suffer serious bodily harm or physical restraint;

         (c) By committing a violation of the offense of criminal coercion against the person; or

         (d) By destroying, concealing, removing, confiscating or possessing any passport, immigration-related document or other document issued by a governmental agency to any person which could be used as a means of verifying the person's identity or age or any other personal identifying information; or

         (e) By means of the abuse or threatened abuse of the law or legal process; or

      (2) Receives anything of value from participation as an organizer, supervisor, financier or manager in a scheme or course of conduct which violates paragraph (1) of this subsection.

   b. An offense under this section constitutes a felony of the first degree.

   c. It is an affirmative defense to prosecution for a violation of this section that, during the time of the alleged commission of the offense of human trafficking created by this section, the defendant was a victim of human trafficking.

   d. The term of imprisonment imposed for a felony of the first degree under paragraph (2) of subsection a. shall be either a term of 20 years during which the actor shall not be eligible for parole or a specific term between 20 years and life imprisonment, of which the actor shall serve 20 years before being eligible for parole.

   e. In addition to any other disposition authorized by law, any person who violates the provisions of this section shall be sentenced to make restitution to any victim. The court shall award to the victim restitution which is the gross income or value to the defendant of the victim's labor or services.

PRACTICAL APPLICATION OF STATUTE

Section 3-8 basically proscribes modern-day slavery. Race, ethnicity, religion, gender, age and any class or status whatsoever are irrelevant in this statute. The bondage, or human trafficking, of any person, of any background, is a first degree felony under 3-8.

Per subsection a.(1), two types of compelled activities are specifically prohibited—prostitution and forced labor/services. However, for a person to be convicted of human trafficking, he must force the prostitution or labor by one of the several methods as defined in subsections a.(1)(a) through (e). These methods include threats of serious bodily harm, physical restraint, coercion as defined in 3-5 and destroying or concealing a victim's passport or other immigration-related document. Per subsection a.(2), a defendant is equally culpable as an "organizer, supervisor, financier or manager" if he "receives anything of value" in a scheme or course of human trafficking.

Here's how this statute works. Marty, Fred, Betty, Orange and Blue wanted to instantly become millionaires. Since they were lowlifes and were too lazy to work to obtain monetary success, they decided to open a "business" where they could just kick back and drink beer while others perform the labor.

Marty organized the group, calling the others up and presenting the business plan. Fred and Betty were tapped to run the day-to-day operations. Orange and Blue were just money guys. Each held an equal monetary share in the business. The place of operation was an old warehouse in Cypress City.

Susan, Sally and Samantha were "recruited" to perform massages at the business. Once they arrived, however, Susan, Sally and Samantha were locked in the warehouse's penthouse by Fred and Betty. Although they were provided gourmet meals, nice lingerie and comfortable beds, the women were physically restrained and not allowed to leave, except once a week to visit with family. Even more so, they were ordered to have sexual intercourse with hundreds of men, who paid for the services. They were told that if they didn't engage in the sexual acts, their families would be killed. They were also personally threatened with maiming and death.

Marty, Fred, Betty, Orange and Blue are all guilty of human trafficking. Susan, Sally and Samantha were "recruited" to engage in prostitution. The women were "held" in this service of sexual activities via two methods: actual physical restraint and threats of serious bodily harm to themselves and their families. Fred and Betty are guilty of this offense, as they carried out the actual restraint and threats. Marty is equally guilty as the organizer of the human trafficking, and Orange and Blue as its financiers.

The defendants have violated this statute even though the women, at times, were permitted to leave their roles as forced laborers. Similarly, they are guilty regardless of whether the women were paid for their prostitution services. Simply because the women were compelled to perform the labor "by threats of serious bodily harm," the defendants are guilty of the first degree felony of human trafficking.

Affirmative Defense

A defendant is afforded an affirmative defense under this statute if "during the time of the alleged commission of the offense . . . the defendant was a victim of human trafficking." How does this work? Let's say that during Susan's forced prostitution participation, she was compelled to supervise Samantha and Sally, making sure that they carried out their sexual duties. Since Susan herself was a victim of the human trafficking scheme, she is relieved of culpability and would have an affirmative defense to the felony.

END OF CHAPTER REVIEW

Multiple-Choice Questions

1. Mercury Anderson, 50, enters the automobile of Kung Po, 30. Anderson locks the vehicle's doors and refuses to allow Po to leave the car for approximately 15 minutes. Anderson's actions amount to which offense?
    a. criminal restraint—as long as his restraint did not subject Po to a risk of serious bodily injury
    b. false imprisonment—as long as his restraint did not subject Po to a risk of serious bodily injury
    c. kidnapping—as long as his restraint was not due to a familial relationship
    d. involuntary servitude—as long as his restraint was not consensual
    e. all of the above

2. In order to be convicted of criminal coercion:
    a. the defendant must purposefully and unlawfully act to restrict another's freedom of action to engage or refrain from engaging in conduct
    b. the defendant must recklessly and unlawfully act to restrict another's freedom of action to engage or refrain from engaging in conduct
    c. the defendant must purposefully lure the victim to engage in specific conduct
    d. the defendant must, with knowledge, lure the victim to engage in specific conduct
    e. the defendant must coerce the victim into buying a sport-utility vehicle

3. Kidnapping is:
    a. a felony of the third degree only
    b. a felony of the second degree only
    c. a felony of the first degree only
    d. a felony of the first, second or third degree, depending on the circumstances
    e. a felony of the first or second degree, depending on the circumstances

4. "Involuntary servitude" is part of which offense?
    a. criminal restraint
    b. false imprisonment
    c. kidnapping
    d. luring
    e. aggravated sexual assault

The following fact pattern pertains to questions 5–6.

Bethany Anderson had the sole physical and legal custody of Rainbow Anderson, age ten. Mercury Anderson, Rainbow's father, secretly took his daughter from Bethany. Mercury Anderson kept the minor in his custody for three years, never advising Bethany of her child's whereabouts. Rainbow was never harmed by Anderson. Th police captured Anderson, with Rainbow, in a hideaway house in Sussex County.

5. The best offense to charge Mercury Anderson with is:
    a. interference of custody and not kidnapping, because the abducted child was the daughter of Anderson
    b. interference of custody and not kidnapping, because the abducted child was not harmed by Anderson
    c. kidnapping and not interference of custody, because Anderson's actions amounted to permanently depriving the mother of her lawful custody of the child
    d. neither kidnapping nor interference of custody but criminal restraint, since Anderson did not harm his daughter
    e. neither kidnapping nor interference of custody but false imprisonment, since Anderson did not harm his daughter

6. What would be an affirmative defense for Mercury Anderson, wherein he could avoid any criminal conviction for his taking of Rainbow?
    a. if Anderson had a pending custody action in family court
    b. if Anderson had a psychological report, from a licensed medical doctor, stating that Bethany Anderson was legally insane
    c. if Anderson was advised by a police officer or prosecutor that he could legally take Rainbow
    d. if Rainbow was 15 years old—and not ten—when Mercury Anderson took her and Anderson did not take her with the purpose to commit a felony against or with her
    e. there is no affirmative defense available to him

7. Virginia can't find her 13-year-old son, Marcus, who has wandered off in the Westview Mall. Finally, she locates him, chastises him and takes him to the car. Once in the car, Virginia won't let Marcus leave, although he is demanding to be let out to go back into the mall. After about ten minutes of arguing, Virginia drives off, taking Marcus back home. Which of the following offenses should Virginia be charged with?
    a. kidnapping
    b. criminal restraint
    c. false imprisonment
    d. interference with custody
    e. nothing, because she has an affirmative defense in that her sole purpose was to assume control of her minor child

Essay Questions

1. Mercury Anderson, 50, took Candice Wesley, 29, from her automobile against her will. Anderson brought Wesley to an East Pinedale apartment and demanded a $50,000 ransom. For some reason, he released her at a diner six hours later, unharmed. Anderson was apprehended for the offense five months later but escaped from custody within a week. Explain why Anderson is guilty of kidnapping for his abduction of Candice Wesley; specifically detail the elements of this offense that make him guilty. Is this a first or second degree kidnapping? Explain.

2. Lucy, 51, enticed Alex, 8, into an alley by offering the young girl a popsicle. Alex took the popsicle, and then Lucy committed the offense of sexual assault by rubbing Alex's breasts and groin area. She then released the girl. In addition to sexual assault, what other offense should Lucy be charged with? Why can she be charged with this offense? Is this offense a felony or misdemeanor? What degree is it? If Alex were 65 instead of 8, is there any offense that Lucy could be charged with? If so, name it and its degree.

4

SEXUAL ASSAULT

4-1. **Definitions**

The following definitions apply to this chapter:

a. "Actor" means a person accused of an offense proscribed under this act.

b. "Victim" means a person alleging to have been subjected to offenses proscribed by this act.

c. "Sexual penetration" means vaginal intercourse, cunnilingus, fellatio or anal intercourse between persons or insertion of the hand, finger or object into the anus or vagina either by the actor or upon the actor's instruction. The depth of insertion shall not be relevant as to the question of commission of the felony.

d. "Sexual contact" means an intentional touching by the victim or actor, either directly or through clothing, of the victim's or actor's intimate parts for the purpose of degrading or humiliating the victim or sexually arousing or sexually gratifying the actor. Sexual contact of the actor with himself must be in view of the victim whom the actor knows to be present.

e. "Intimate parts" means the following body parts: sexual organs, genital area, anal area, inner thigh, groin, buttock or breast of a person.

f. "Severe personal injury" means severe bodily injury, disfigurement, disease, incapacitating mental anguish or chronic pain.

g. "Physically helpless" means that condition in which a person is unconscious or is physically unable to flee or is physically unable to communicate unwillingness to act.

h. "Mentally defective" means that condition in which a person suffers from a mental disease or defect which renders that person temporarily or permanently incapable of understanding the nature of his conduct, including, but not limited to, being incapable of providing consent.

i. "Mentally incapacitated" means that condition in which a person is rendered temporarily incapable of understanding or controlling his conduct due to the influence of a narcotic, anesthetic, intoxicant or other substance administered to that person without his prior knowledge or consent, or due to any other act committed upon that person which rendered that person incapable of appraising or controlling his conduct.

j. "Coercion" as used in this chapter shall refer to those acts which are defined as criminal coercion in that statute as found in chapter 3.

4-2. **Sexual assault**

a. An actor is guilty of aggravated sexual assault if he commits an act of sexual penetration with another person under any one of the following circumstances:

(1) The victim is less than 13 years old;

(2) The victim is at least 13 but less than 16 years old; and

(a) The actor is related to the victim by blood or affinity to the third degree, or

(b) The actor has supervisory or disciplinary power over the victim by virtue of the actor's legal, professional or occupational status; or

(c) The actor is a resource family parent, a guardian or stands *in loco parentis* within the household;

(3) The act is committed during the commission, or attempted commission, whether alone or with one or more other persons, of robbery, kidnapping, homicide, aggravated assault on another, burglary, arson or criminal escape;

(4) The actor is armed with a weapon or any object fashioned in such a manner as to lead the victim to reasonably believe it to be a weapon and threatens by word or gesture to use the weapon or object;

(5) The actor is aided or abetted by one or more other persons and the actor uses physical force or coercion;

(6) The actor uses physical force or coercion and severe personal injury is sustained by the victim;

(7) The victim is one whom the actor knew or should have known was physically helpless, mentally defective or mentally incapacitated.

Aggravated sexual assault is a felony of the first degree.

b. An actor is guilty of sexual assault if he commits an act of sexual contact with a victim who is less than 13 years old and the actor is at least four years older than the victim.

c. An actor is guilty of sexual assault if he commits an act of sexual penetration with another person under any one of the following circumstances:

(1) The actor uses physical force or coercion, but the victim does not sustain severe personal injury;

(2) The victim is on probation or parole or is detained in a hospital, prison or other institution and the actor has supervisory or disciplinary power over the victim by virtue of the actor's legal, professional or occupational status;

(3) The victim is at least 16 but less than 18 years old and:

(a) The actor is related to the victim by blood or affinity to the third degree; or

(b) The actor has supervisory or disciplinary power of any nature or in any capacity over the victim; or

(c) The actor is a resource family parent, a guardian or stands *in loco parentis* within the household;

(4) The victim is at least 13 but less than 16 years old and the actor is at least four years older than the victim.

Sexual assault is a felony of the second degree.

PRACTICAL APPLICATION OF STATUTE

Aggravated Sexual Assault—Generally

Aggravated sexual assault is a felony of the first degree. A variety of actions constitute the commission of this offense. Under some circumstances, an actor is guilty only where sexual penetration was not consented to; in other circumstances, however, consent is not a required element of the offense. In all cases, an act of sexual penetration must occur for a conviction under this statute. Sexual penetration, as defined under 4-1, means vaginal intercourse, cunnilingus, fellatio, anal intercourse between persons or the insertion of the hand, finger or object into the anus or vagina of another. The actor need not conduct the insertion himself; his instruction of an insertion will suffice to constitute an act of sexual penetration.

Regardless of age, an individual is guilty of aggravated sexual assault if he commits an act of sexual penetration during the commission of violent felonies such as robbery, kidnapping or murder (see 4-2a.(3)). He is similarly guilty of aggravated sexual assault where he utilizes a weapon to force another into an act of sexual penetration (see 4-2a.(4)). This first degree felony is also committed where the actor uses physical force *and* "severe personal injury" is sustained by the victim (see 4-2a.(6)). Likewise, an actor who uses physical force *and* is "aided or abetted by one or more other persons" is guilty of aggravated sexual assault (see 4-2a.(5)).

Mercury Anderson is guilty of aggravated sexual assault for his nonconsensual sexual penetration of Jerri Sloane. First, he violated 4-2a.(3), as he had sexual intercourse with Sloane during her kidnapping. He is guilty of the offense, per the tenets of 4-2a.(4), because he armed himself with a handgun while he sexually penetrated her. Neither of these two subsections requires that personal injury result from the sexual act. Anderson, however, is also guilty of aggravated sexual assault under 4-2a.(6). Why? Because he used physical force against Sloane *and* personal injury resulted. Anderson beat her violently, breaking her nose with the butt of a handgun.

If Anderson had been aided by an accomplice and used physical force to have sexual intercourse with Sloane, he would have violated 4-2a.(5). This subsection, though, like a.(3) and a.(4), again does not require personal injury to be caused for an aggravated sexual assault conviction.

Aggravated Sexual Assault—Victim Under 13

Mercury Anderson is guilty of aggravated sexual assault for having sexual intercourse with Samantha Cora, even though she consented to the act. Under 4-2a., an actor is guilty of aggravated sexual assault if he commits an act of "sexual penetration" with a victim less than 13 years old. This is a felony of strict liability, here meaning that it is irrelevant if the offender knew the victim was under 13 or if the victim consented to the sexual penetration.

Samantha Cora, 12 years old, consented to having sexual intercourse, an act of sexual penetration, with Mercury Anderson; however, her consent is not a defense to 4-2a.(1). Simply stated, having sexual intercourse with an individual under 13 makes an actor guilty of aggravated sexual assault. Accordingly, Mercury Anderson should be charged with this first degree felony for having sexual intercourse with Samantha Cora.

Aggravated Sexual Assault—Victim at Least 13 But Under 16

If Samantha Cora was 15 rather than 12, Mercury Anderson could still be charged with aggravated sexual assault for his sexual intercourse with the girl. However, in addition to the minor's age being 13, 14 or 15, one of three factors must be present for a conviction. If the actor was related by blood to a victim whose age is 13, 14 or 15, he is guilty. If Anderson had supervisory or disciplinary powers over a victim whose age is 13, 14 or 15, he is guilty. If he was a foster parent or otherwise had guardian control of a victim with an age of 13, 14 or 15, he is guilty.

In sum, if any of the factors mentioned in the above paragraph existed, in addition to Samantha Cora being 15 years old, Mercury Anderson would be guilty of aggravated sexual assault for having sexual intercourse with this girl—even though she consented to the act. If none of the aforesaid additional factors were present, however, an act of sexual penetration with a person 13, 14 or 15 years old is the lesser felony of sexual assault. This felony will be discussed later in this Practical Application section.

Aggravated Sexual Assault—Mentally Defective or Incapacitated Victim

Under 4-2a.(7), a defendant is guilty of aggravated sexual assault if the "victim is one whom the actor knew or should have known was physically helpless, mentally defective or mentally incapacitated." This is a felony of strict liability where consent is not a defense. Many of the terms of this subsection make the conviction of a defendant dependent on expert testimony. Although "mentally defective" and "mentally incapacitated" are defined in 4-1, expert psychological testimony is a must to determine whether or not an individual "knew" or "should have known" the victim's condition. Accordingly, even before charging an individual under this subsection, law enforcement officers should have a viable reason to believe that the victim was "mentally incapacitated," "mentally defective" or "physically helpless."

Sexual Assault—Generally

Like aggravated sexual assault, there are multiple scenarios that amount to the commission of sexual assault. The offenses range from situations involving nonconsensual sexual penetration where an actor uses force to situations of consensual sexual penetration where a victim is 13, 14 or 15. Each type of offense, though, has special circumstances in order for the act to be considered a sexual assault.

As set forth in the previous sections, Mercury Anderson is guilty of aggravated sexual assault for the forced sexual intercourse he had with Jerri Sloane; however, if the facts were modified, he would face the lesser charge of sexual assault instead. For example, Anderson would be guilty of sexual assault, under 4-2c.(1), if he used physical force to have nonconsensual sexual intercourse with Jerri Sloane, an adult, in her own home or another location. For him to be guilty of sexual assault under these circumstances—rather than aggravated sexual assault—Sloane could not have suffered "severe personal injury" due to the forceful attack. Also, for the charge to be the lesser offense of sexual assault, there could be no kidnapping involved—remember, an act of sexual penetration that occurs during the commission of felonies such as kidnapping, murder and robbery automatically becomes an aggravated sexual assault.

Sexual Assault—Sexual Contact with Victim Under 13

Mercury Anderson should be charged with sexual assault, and not the lower felony of criminal sexual contact, for his touching of ten-year-old Frank Pileggi's buttocks and groin area. Sexual contact, as defined in 4-1, means intentional touching by the victim or actor—either directly or through clothing—of the victim's or actor's intimate parts. Intimate parts include genitals, anal area, buttocks, groin, breast and inner thigh.

Also, for the contact to be illegal, it must be perpetrated for the purpose of "degrading or humiliating the victim" or "sexually arousing or gratifying the actor."

Section 4-2b. elevates a "sexual contact," as described above, from a charge of criminal sexual contact to sexual assault where the victim is less than 13 years old. Mercury Anderson lured a ten-year-old boy, Frank Pileggi, into his automobile. There, Anderson touched the boy's groin and buttocks through his clothing. Anderson had no appropriate purpose to conduct these sexual contacts; obviously, the touching was conducted to sexually arouse and gratify Anderson. Accordingly, Anderson would be charged with the second degree felony of sexual assault for this illegal contact with Pileggi. Given Pileggi's youthful age, this charge is appropriate even if the boy consented to the contact.

Sexual Assault—Actor with Supervisory Power over Victim in Institution or on Parole

Under 4-2c.(2), a corrections officer or medical doctor is guilty of sexual assault if he engages in an act of sexual penetration with an inmate or detained hospital patient. This subsection provides that an individual having supervisory/disciplinary power over a person on probation or parole is guilty of sexual assault if he engages in an act of sexual penetration with that supervised person. Similarly, an individual having supervisory/disciplinary power over a detained prison inmate or hospital patient is guilty of sexual assault if he engages in an act of sexual penetration with that confined person.

The subsection does not require force or coercion as an element of the offense. Accordingly, it seems that if a parole officer has sexual intercourse—even if it is consensual—with a parolee, he is guilty of the second degree felony of sexual assault. Similarly, a prison guard who engages in fellatio (an act of sexual penetration) with an inmate is guilty of sexual assault, and a medical doctor who engages in cunnilingus (an act of sexual penetration) with a detained hospital patient is guilty of sexual assault.

4-3.   **Aggravated criminal sexual contact; criminal sexual contact**

a. An actor is guilty of aggravated criminal sexual contact if he commits an act of sexual contact with the victim under any of the circumstances set forth in 4-2a.(2) through (7). Aggravated criminal sexual contact is a felony of the third degree.

b. An actor is guilty of criminal sexual contact if he commits an act of sexual contact with the victim under any of the circumstances set forth in section 4-2c.(1) through (4). Criminal sexual contact is a felony of the fourth degree.

PRACTICAL APPLICATION OF STATUTE

Aggravated Criminal Sexual Contact and Criminal Sexual Contact

Per the definitions set forth under 4-1, sexual contact is an intentional touching by the victim or actor—either directly or through clothing—of the victim's or actor's intimate parts. Intimate parts include genitals, anal area, buttocks, groin, breast and inner thigh. Also, for the contact to be illegal, it must be perpetrated for the purpose of "degrading or humiliating the victim" or "sexually arousing or gratifying the actor."

Section 4-3 has two subsections. Subsection a. sets forth the provisions for the third degree felony of aggravated sexual contact, and subsection b. covers the fourth degree felony of sexual contact. Basically, aggravated sexual contact is a lower form of aggravated sexual assault, and sexual contact is the lesser version of sexual assault. Aggravated criminal sexual contact follows the same circumstances set forth in the aggravated sexual assault statute—4-2a.(2) through (7). Criminal sexual contact follows the same circumstances set forth in the sexual assault statute—4-2c.(1) through (4). The difference is that a sexual contact rather than a sexual penetration must occur.

Following are some examples of aggravated criminal sexual contact: a football coach who touches a 15-year-old boy's groin in an effort to gratify himself; a man who rubs a woman's breasts over her shirt during a kidnapping; a woman who wields a knife while she touches another woman's genitals; a man, accompanied by two other men, who uses physical force to rub a woman's genitals over her pants; a man who uses physical force to rub another man's buttocks and causes severe personal injury to that victim; and a man who fondles the breasts of a woman who he knows is mentally incapacitated.

Examples of criminal sexual contact include the following: A man uses physical force to rub another man's buttocks, but severe personal injury is not suffered by the victim; a prison guard rubs the breasts of an inmate; a high school teacher touches a 17-year-old student's genitals over her pants; and a 25-year-old-man rubs the groin of a 15-year-old girl.

It is important to note that, just like the provisions of the aggravated sexual assault and the sexual assault statutes, in many cases an actor is guilty of aggravated criminal sexual contact and criminal sexual contact even where a victim consents. Many of the above examples fall within this framework (the high school teacher cannot claim a defense of consent where he touches his 17-year-old student's genitals over her pants; the 25-year-old man is still guilty of criminal sexual contact even if the 15-year-old girl consented to his rubbing her groin).

4-4. **Lewdness**

a. A person commits a misdemeanor A if he does any flagrantly lewd and offensive act which he knows or reasonably expects is likely to be observed by other nonconsenting persons who would be affronted or alarmed.

b. A person commits a felony of the fourth degree if:

(1) He exposes his intimate parts for the purpose of arousing or gratifying the sexual desire of the actor or of any other person under circumstances where the actor knows or reasonably expects he is likely to be observed by a child who is less than 13 years of age where the actor is at least four years older than the child.

(2) He exposes his intimate parts for the purpose of arousing or gratifying the sexual desire of the actor or of any other person under circumstances where the actor knows or reasonably expects he is likely to be observed by a person who because of mental disease or defect is unable to understand the sexual nature of the actor's conduct.

c. As used in this section:

"Lewd acts" shall include the exposing of the genitals for the purpose of arousing or gratifying the sexual desire of the actor or of any other person.

PRACTICAL APPLICATION OF STATUTE

Lewdness as a Misdemeanor A

Mercury Anderson is guilty of the misdemeanor A of lewdness for exposing his genitals to 20-year-old Eric Mesos. Lewdness is a misdemeanor A where a person performs any flagrantly lewd and offensive act that he knows or reasonably expects to be observed by other nonconsenting persons who would be alarmed by the act. Lewd acts include exposing the genitals for the purpose of arousing or gratifying the sexual desires of the actor or another.

Anderson twice exposed his genitals to Eric Mesos while the two were seated in an automobile. Mesos did not consent to these acts, as he was only in the automobile under the threat that his mother would be killed if he left. Clearly, Anderson only exposed his genitals for his own sexual gratification, and he had to reasonably expect these lewd acts would alarm Mesos. Accordingly, Mercury Anderson is guilty of the misdemeanor A of lewdness.

Lewdness as a Fourth Degree Felony

Lewdness becomes a fourth degree felony under two circumstances—where an actor exposes his genitals to a child under 13 (and the actor is at least four years older than the child), and where an actor exposes his genitals to a person who is mentally defective (a person who has a mental disease or defect that makes him unable to understand the sexual nature of the actor's conduct). In both cases, the actor must expose his genitals for the purpose of arousing or gratifying his own sexual desires or the sexual desires of another. Mercury Anderson's flashing of his genitals to Eric Mesos would therefore be elevated to a fourth degree lewdness if either Mesos had been under 13 or he was proven to be mentally defective.

4-5.   **Invasion of privacy, degree of felony; defenses, privileges**

a. An actor commits a felony of the fourth degree if, knowing that he is not licensed or privileged to do so, and under circumstances in which a reasonable person would know that another may expose intimate parts or may engage in sexual penetration or sexual contact, he observes another person without that person's consent and under circumstances in which a reasonable person would not expect to be observed.

b. An actor commits a felony of the third degree if, knowing that he is not licensed or privileged to do so, he photographs, films, videotapes, records or otherwise reproduces in any manner the image of another person whose intimate parts are exposed or who is engaged in an act of sexual penetration or sexual contact, without that person's consent and under circumstances in which a reasonable person would not expect to be observed.

c. An actor commits a felony of the third degree if, knowing that he is not licensed or privileged to do so, he discloses any photograph, film, videotape, recording or any other reproduction of the image of another person whose intimate parts are exposed or who is engaged in an act of sexual penetration or sexual contact, unless that person has consented to such disclosure. For purposes of this subsection, "disclose" means sell, manufacture, give, provide, lend, trade, mail, deliver, transfer, publish, distribute, circulate, disseminate, present, exhibit, advertise or offer. A fine not to exceed $30,000 may be imposed for a violation of this subsection.

d. It is an affirmative defense to a felony under this section that:

    (1) The actor posted or otherwise provided prior notice to the person of the actor's intent to engage in the conduct specified in subsection a., b., or c.; and

    (2) The actor acted with a lawful purpose.

e. (1) It shall not be a violation of subsection a. or b. to observe another person in the access way, foyer or entrance to a fitting room or dressing room operated by a retail establishment or to photograph, film, videotape, record or otherwise reproduce the image of such person, if the actor conspicuously posts at the entrance to the fitting room or dressing room prior notice of his intent to make the observations, photographs, films, videotapes, recordings or other reproductions.

    (2) It shall be a violation of subsection c. to disclose in any manner any such photograph, film, videotape or recording of another person using a fitting room or dressing room except under the following circumstances:

        (a) To law enforcement officers in connection with a criminal prosecution;

        (b) Pursuant to subpoena or court order for use in a legal proceeding; or

        (c) To a co-worker, manager or supervisor acting within the scope of his employment.

f. It shall be a violation of subsection a. or b. to observe another person in a private dressing stall of a fitting room or dressing room operated by a retail establishment or to photograph, film, videotape, record or otherwise reproduce the image of another person in a private dressing stall of a fitting room or dressing room.

g. For purposes of this act, a law enforcement officer, or a corrections officer or guard in a correctional facility or jail, who is engaged in the official performance of his duties shall be deemed to be licensed or privileged to make and to disclose observations, photographs, films, videotapes, recordings or any other reproductions.

h. A conviction arising under subsection b. of this section shall not merge with a conviction under subsection c. of this section, nor shall a conviction under subsection c. merge with a conviction under subsection b.

PRACTICAL APPLICATION OF STATUTE

This statute is basically an extension of the "peeking into windows" subsection found in 8-3. It was enacted to criminalize more than just the typical "peeping Tom" activities, as 8-3c. only covers privacy invasions where an actor "peers into a window or other opening of a dwelling or other structure adapted for overnight accommodation."

But what if a person photographs another in a dressing room? Or in a business office? These locations are not a "dwelling" or a "structure adapted for overnight accommodation." This is where section 4-5 comes in.

Observing Another Exposed or Engaging in Sexual Acts

Per subsection a. of 4-5, an actor commits a fourth degree felony if he observes another person (without that other person's consent) exposing "intimate parts" or engaging in "sexual penetration or sexual contact." In order for this to be a felony, however, the actor must commit the offense "knowing that he is not licensed to do so" and "under circumstances in which a reasonable person would not expect to be observed."

Mercury Anderson is guilty of a fourth degree felony under 4-5a. Anderson followed Kami Subron, a 26-year-old attorney, to the office where she worked. Inside her private office, Anderson hid in the closet. There he consumed beer and secretly watched Subron engage in sexual relations with her lover, Suave.

Here, Mercury Anderson watched Subron and Suave "engage in sexual penetration." Anderson knew he was "not licensed or privileged" to be in Subron's office—and he observed them "without consent." Obviously, in her private law office, Subron had a reasonable expectation of privacy; under these circumstances, "a reasonable person would not expect to be observed." Accordingly, Anderson is guilty of a fourth degree felony per subsection a. of 4-5.

Photographing Another Exposed or Engaging in Sexual Acts

Subsection b. of this statute increases the degree of the offense—to a third degree felony—where the actor "photographs, films, videotapes," etc., while engaging in the observational conduct prohibited in subsection a. Mercury Anderson is guilty of violating this subsection as well.

In a department store, Anderson set up a hidden camera in the women's dressing room. There he videotaped Kami Subron, naked, as she changed into various articles of lingerie. In the dressing room, Subron had a reasonable expectation that she would not be observed changing. Anderson's observation of Subron naked was without her consent, and Anderson knew that he was not licensed or privileged to make the observation. Even if Anderson was an owner or employee of the department store, he would have no legal right to observe Subron in these circumstances. Videotaping Subron in this situation renders him guilty of a third degree felony.

Disclosing Photographs or Videos of Another Exposed or Engaged in Sexual Acts

An additional third degree felony is committed where an actor "discloses" photographs, videos, etc., that were obtained in violation of section 4-5. Per subsection c., "disclose" means "sell, manufacture, give, provide, lend, trade, mail, deliver, transfer, publish, distribute, circulate, disseminate, present, exhibit, advertise or offer."

For selling the videotape of Kami Subron, which depicted her naked as she changed in a department store dressing room, Mercury Anderson is guilty of a third degree felony per subsection c. of 4-5. Even if he had "lent" the videotape to a friend, he could be convicted of this additional offense.

It is interesting to note here that under subsection h. of this statute, a conviction of subsection b. (performing the photographing, etc.) may not merge with a conviction of subsection c. (disclosing the photographs, etc.). This means that an actor who "discloses" his photographs, etc., to another will necessarily face two separate convictions under section 4-5.

Defenses

Subsections e. and f. provide certain defenses and circumstances where a felony is not committed under this statute. These include where a person is observed or photographed in the "access way, foyer or entrance" to a "fitting room or dressing room" and where conspicuous notice has been provided—and where such photographs, etc., are disclosed to law enforcement officers in connection with criminal prosecution.

4-6.   **Registration of sex offenders; definition; requirements**

a. (1) A person who has been convicted, adjudicated delinquent or found not guilty by reason of insanity for commission of a sex offense as defined in subsection b. of this section shall register as provided in subsections c. and d. of this section.

(2) A person who in another jurisdiction is required to register as a sex offender and (a) is enrolled on a full-time or part-time basis in any public or private educational institution in this State, including any secondary school, trade or professional institution, institution of higher education or other post-secondary school, or (b) is employed or carries on a vocation in this State, on either a full-time or a part-time basis, with or without compensation, for more than 14 consecutive days or for an aggregate period exceeding 30 days in a calendar year, shall register in this State as provided in subsections c. and d. of this section. A person who fails to register as required under this act shall be guilty of a felony of the fourth degree.

b. For the purposes of this act a sex offense shall include the following:

(1) Aggravated sexual assault, sexual assault, aggravated criminal sexual contact, kidnapping pursuant to paragraph (2) of subsection c. of 3-1 or an attempt to commit any of these felonies if the court found that the offender's conduct was characterized by a pattern of repetitive, compulsive behavior, regardless of the date of the commission of the offense or the date of conviction;

(2) A conviction, adjudication of delinquency or acquittal by reason of insanity for aggravated sexual assault; sexual assault; aggravated criminal sexual contact; kidnapping pursuant to paragraph (2) of subsection c. of 3-1; endangering the welfare of a child by engaging in sexual conduct which would impair or debauch the morals of the child pursuant to subsection a. of 12-2; endangering the welfare of a child pursuant to paragraph (3) or (4) or subparagraph (a) of paragraph (5) of subsection b. of 12-2; luring or enticing pursuant to section 3-6; criminal sexual contact pursuant to 4-3b. if the victim is a minor; kidnapping pursuant to 3-1, criminal restraint pursuant to 3-2 or false imprisonment pursuant to 3-3 if the victim is a minor and the offender is not the parent of the victim; knowingly promoting prostitution of a child pursuant to paragraph (3) or paragraph (4) of subsection b. of 19-1; or an attempt to commit any of these enumerated offenses if the conviction, adjudication of delinquency or acquittal by reason of insanity is entered on or after the effective date of this act or the offender is serving a sentence of incarceration, probation, parole or other form of community supervision as a result of the offense or is confined following acquittal by reason of insanity or as a result of civil commitment on the effective date of this act;

(3) A conviction, adjudication of delinquency or acquittal by reason of insanity for an offense similar to any offense enumerated in paragraph (2) or a sentence on the basis of criteria similar to the criteria set forth in paragraph (1) of this subsection entered or imposed under the laws of the United States, this State or another state.

c. A person required to register under the provisions of this act shall do so on forms to be provided by the designated registering agency as follows:

(1) A person who is required to register and who is under supervision in the community on probation, parole, furlough, work release or a similar program shall register at the time the person is placed under supervision or no later than 120 days after the effective date of this act, whichever is later, in accordance with procedures established by the Department of Corrections, the Department of Human Services, the Juvenile Justice Commission or the Administrative Office of the Courts, whichever is responsible for supervision;

(2) A person confined in a correctional or juvenile facility or involuntarily committed who is required to register shall register prior to release in accordance with procedures established by the Department of Corrections, the Department of Human Services or the Juvenile Justice Commission;

(3) A person moving to or returning to this State from another jurisdiction shall register with the chief law enforcement officer of the municipality in which the person will reside or, if the municipality does not have a local police force, the Superintendent of State Police within 120 days of the effective date of this act or ten days of first residing in or returning to a municipality in this State, whichever is later;

(4) A person required to register on the basis of a conviction prior to the effective date who is not confined or under supervision on the effective date of this act shall register within 120 days of the effective date of this act with the chief law enforcement officer of the municipality in which the person will reside or, if the municipality does not have a local police force, the Superintendent of State Police;

(5) A person who in another jurisdiction is required to register as a sex offender and who is enrolled on a full-time or part-time basis in any public or private educational institution in this State, including any secondary school, trade or professional institution, institution of higher education or other post-secondary school, shall, within ten days of commencing attendance at such educational institution, register with the chief law enforcement officer of the municipality in which the educational institution is located or, if the municipality does not have a local police force, the Superintendent of State Police;

(6) A person who in another jurisdiction is required to register as a sex offender and who is employed or carries on a vocation in this State, on either a full-time or a part-time basis, with or without compensation, for more than 14 consecutive days or for an aggregate period exceeding 30 days in a calendar year, shall, within ten days after commencing such employment or vocation, register with the chief law enforcement officer of the municipality in which the employer is located or where the vocation is carried on, as the case may be, or, if the municipality does not have a local police force, the Superintendent of State Police;

(7) In addition to any other registration requirements set forth in this section, a person required to register under this act who is enrolled at, employed by or carries on a vocation at an institution of higher education or other post-secondary school in this State shall, within ten days after commencing such attendance, employment or vocation, register with the law enforcement unit of the educational institution, if the institution has such a unit.

d. Upon a change of address, a person shall notify the law enforcement agency with which the person is registered and shall re-register with the appropriate law enforcement agency no less than ten days before he intends to first reside at his new address. Upon a change of employment or school enrollment status, a person shall notify the appropriate law enforcement agency no later than five days after any such change. A person who fails to notify the appropriate law enforcement agency of a change of address or status in accordance with this subsection is guilty of a felony of the fourth degree.

e. A person required to register under paragraph (1) of subsection b. of this section or under paragraph (3) of subsection b. due to a sentence imposed on the basis of criteria similar to the criteria set forth in paragraph (1) of subsection b. shall verify his address with the appropriate law enforcement agency every 90 days in a manner prescribed by the Attorney General. A person required to register under paragraph (2) of subsection b. of this section or under paragraph (3) of subsection b. on the basis of a conviction for an offense similar to an offense enumerated in paragraph (2) of subsection b. shall verify his address annually in a manner prescribed by the Attorney General. One year after the effective date of this act, the Attorney General shall review, evaluate and, if warranted, modify, pursuant to the "Administrative Procedure Act," the verification requirement.

f. Except as provided in subsection g. of this section, a person required to register under this act may make application to the Superior Court of this State to terminate the obligation upon proof that the person has not committed an offense within 15 years following conviction or release from a correctional facility for any term of imprisonment imposed, whichever is later, and is not likely to pose a threat to the safety of others.

g. A person required to register under this section who has been convicted of, adjudicated delinquent or acquitted by reason of insanity for more than one sex offense as defined in subsection b. of this section or who has been convicted of, adjudicated delinquent or acquitted by reason of insanity for aggravated sexual assault pursuant to subsection a. of 4-2 or sexual assault pursuant to paragraph (1) of subsection c. of 4-2 is not eligible under subsection f. of this section to make application to the Superior Court of this State to terminate the registration obligation.

h. The effective date of this act is January 1, 1993.

PRACTICAL APPLICATION OF STATUTE

Mercury Anderson should be charged with a fourth degree "Megan's Law" felony for failing to register as a sex offender, in addition to the multiple other serious felonies he committed. Anderson's charge under 4-6 arises out of a 30-year-old conviction of sexual assault and his failure to ever register as a sex offender in the municipality where he resided.

Subsection b. of 4-6 defines what offenses are sex offenses for purposes of this act. Among the felonies included are aggravated criminal sexual contact, kidnapping offenses, multiple offenses related to minors and, of course, sexual assault and aggravated sexual assault. Subsections c. and d. provide for the appropriate locations and timetables that sex offenders must register their status as a sex offender. Particularly, subsection c.(4) provides that a person who was convicted of a sex offense prior to the effective date of the act and who was not confined or under supervision on the effective date of the act "shall register within 120 days of the effective date of this act with the chief law enforcement officer of the municipality in which the person will reside."

Mercury Anderson was convicted of sexual assault 30 years ago. His term of incarceration had expired years before section 4-6's effective date, which was January 1, 1993. Anderson, however, failed to register his status as a convicted sex offender within 120 days of the act's effective date; in fact, he never registered with the chief law enforcement officer of the municipality where he resided. Accordingly, it would be correct for the police to charge him with a fourth degree felony for violating section 4-6's registration requirements.

It is important to note that subsections c. and d. provide for varied registration requirements depending on the sex offender's confinement status and his residential living arrangements. For example, per c.(1), a sex offender under a supervisory program such as probation or parole is required to register "at the time the person is placed under supervision." Under subsection d., a sex offender who changes his address must "re-register with the appropriate law enforcement agency no less than ten days before he intends to first reside at his new address." It is also important to note that under 4-6, an individual cannot avoid sex offender registration if his sex offense conviction occurred as a minor (convictions as a minor are correctly referred to as "adjudicated delinquent"). Similarly, if he was found "not guilty by reason of insanity" for commission of a sex offense, he still must register per the requirements of the statute.

END OF CHAPTER REVIEW

Multiple-Choice Questions

1. What is always an element of aggravated sexual assault?
    a. nonconsensual sexual intercourse
    b. nonconsensual sexual contact
    c. sexual penetration
    d. violence
    e. all of the above

2. In a department store, Mercury Anderson set up a hidden camera in the women's dressing room. There, he videotaped Kami Subron, naked, as she changed into various articles of lingerie. What is the best offense to charge Anderson with?
    a. a misdemeanor A of invasion of privacy
    b. a third degree felony of invasion of privacy
    c. a fourth degree felony of peering
    d. a misdemeanor B of disorderly conduct
    e. unfortunately, Anderson's actions do not amount to an offense because people must expect that they may be videotaped in a dressing room

3. Joan rubs Esmeralda's vagina as she is taking a bath. Esmeralda is 17 and the act was consented to. Joan can be convicted of what offense?
    a. criminal sexual contact if Esmeralda is related to Joan by blood as a first cousin
    b. criminal sexual contact if Joan is Esmeralda's volleyball coach
    c. criminal sexual contact if Joan is Esmeralda's foster parent
    d. nothing, if Joan only knew Esmeralda from the restaurant where she works as a waitress
    e. all of the above

4. Mercury Anderson met Samantha Cora, 12, at a carnival. He bought her cotton candy and ice cream and then asked if she would join him at his apartment. Cora agreed, and at the apartment, she consensually engaged in sexual intercourse with Anderson. Anderson is guilty of which offense?
    a. nothing, the act was consensual
    b. aggravated criminal sexual contact
    c. sexual assault
    d. aggravated sexual assault
    e. kidnapping

5. Janice, using physical force, grabs Melinda's breast through Melinda's clothing. Janice did this for her own sexual gratification. Melinda, an adult, did not consent to this touching. Janice is guilty of what offense?

 a. aggravated sexual assault

 b. sexual assault

 c. aggravated criminal sexual contact

 d. criminal sexual contact

 e. invasion of privacy

6. Same facts as above, but Melinda is 12 and Janice is her math teacher. What offense is Janice guilty of violating?

 a. aggravated sexual assault

 b. sexual assault

 c. aggravated criminal sexual contact

 d. criminal sexual contact

 e. invasion of privacy

7. Corky was "acquitted by reason of insanity" of luring a 12-year-old child into his automobile where he exposed his genitals to the child. Is Corky required to register as a sex offender?

 a. no, because he was acquitted of the offense by reason of insanity

 b. no, because the felony of luring does not give rise to a requirement for someone to register as a sex offender

 c. no, because the child must be ten years old or younger

 d. no, because of the "Affirmative Defense Doctrine"

 e. yes, Corky must register as a sex offender

Essay Questions

1. Martin kidnaps Kerry, 25, taking her to a cave in Sparta. There, against her will, Martin forces Kerry to have sexual intercourse with him. Kerry does not suffer severe personal injury and does not go to the hospital after the attack. What is the most appropriate offense to charge Martin with and why? What degree is this offense? Use the same facts as aforementioned, except Martin does not kidnap Kerry; instead, the nonconsensual intercourse occurs during a "date rape" at Kerry's apartment. What is the most appropriate offense to charge Martin with under these circumstances and why? What is the degree of this offense?

2. Grandpa, 72, rubs the groin of Perry, his 15-year-old grandson, without Perry's consent. Grandpa does this because he's attempting to wipe tomato sauce off Perry's pants. Is Grandpa guilty of sexual assault, aggravated criminal sexual contact, criminal sexual contact or nothing at all? The next week, Grandpa urinates in a city alleyway where he is spotted by a police officer and a bartender. For this act, can Grandpa be convicted of lewdness? Explain your answers, explaining the elements of the offenses.

5

ROBBERY

FACT PATTERN (PERTAINING TO CHAPTERS 5–7)

Investigative reporter Chang Lee contacted Petersville Police Captain Sterling Marley after he uncovered the hideout of Mickey Vice, a deranged parolee who had recently committed a tirade of violent thefts and property damage. Marley headed Petersville's elite robbery squad and had been seeking Vice's capture for several weeks, following a chain of criminal events that were not similar to any other in his 25-year career. Accordingly, Captain Marley immediately met with the reporter to learn Vice's location.

At their meeting Marley recounted Vice's felonies—off the record. Mickey Vice orchestrated and carried out five separate criminal actions over a five-week period. His first victim, Horace Wille, a 50-year-old American Indian, was punched in the face several times as Vice stole $500 from the man's wallet. As Wille was beaten, Vice told him, "This is payback for all the money your Indian casinos steal from us. Indians stink."

Exactly one week later, Vice entered Nelson Simone's BMW, pointed a pistol at him and ordered, "Listen, you homosexual, go into your glove box and hand me the hundred dollar bill I know is in there." After Simone turned over the money, Vice violently beat him with the gun, knocking the man unconscious. Then Vice pushed Simone out of his car and fled. Nelson Simone was hospitalized but survived the incident.

For the third week's felony, Vice appeared at his prior residence on Fifth Street in Petersville. Still living at the home was his estranged wife, Carrie. According to Carrie, Vice initially was calm, even congenial, toward her. Things, however, became "odd" as she described it, when Vice suggested that "they burn down the house to collect insurance money and to avoid Petersville's requirement that they pay to have fire escapes erected and junk removed from the backyard." When Carrie refused, Vice forced her to have sexual intercourse with him and then hit her over the head with a baseball bat, causing her to become unconscious. Immediately thereafter, he poured gasoline in the home's living room and lit a match to it. Vice's house, as well as the two row houses connected to it, burned to the ground. Carrie and the other dwellings' occupants were all rescued by Petersville firefighters.

In the fourth week, Vice's criminal activities began with a simple car theft. His first order of business began with the removal of the automobile's vehicle identification number. After he completed this task, Vice attempted to start the car; however, his skills had apparently deteriorated and he was unable to start the engine. Angry, Vice exited the vehicle, repeatedly kicked its doors and smashed all of its windows. The total losses resulting from this damage were $1,550. His attention then turned to a multi-unit building located across the street. He found the structure particularly interesting because it was owned by Carrie's father. Two hours later, Vice returned to the building with dynamite and exploded the same at the base of the building. Although miraculously no one was killed, 17 people suffered serious bodily injuries such as broken bones and loss of eyesight, and over 30 homes were destroyed.

Vice, excited by this recent widespread damage, concocted a particularly vile plan for his fifth week's felonies. Posing as a government nuclear radiation inspector, he gained entrance into a newly constructed nuclear power plant in the industrial section of Petersville. Once inside, Vice spray painted in a woman's bathroom "I am the king. I hate all people who are not just like me." He then released a container of poisonous gas in the facility's hallway, causing most of the workers to flee to open air. As the employees exited, Vice raced to the plant's protected area—where the machinery generating the nuclear power was located. There, he fired shots at the men and women remaining at their job sites and threw a stick of dynamite into the machinery, hoping to release radiation. Fortunately, the dynamite failed to cause any significant damage, and no one was injured by his gunfire. Vice escaped, however, utilizing the melee to avoid capture.

As Captain Marley concluded his last words about Vice's violent five-week tirade, Chang Lee passed him a napkin with an address. Marley cordially thanked the reporter and then raced to his police cruiser. Within 30 minutes, Vice's hideout—an apartment situated atop a hamburger restaurant—was surrounded by over 50 law enforcement personnel. He surrendered, but not without incident. After two hours of gunfire directed at the police officers, he ran out of ammunition. Suddenly, he appeared on the street with his hands raised above his head. Captain Marley personally subdued Vice and took him into custody.

5-1. **Robbery**

a. Robbery defined. A person is guilty of robbery if, in the course of committing a theft, he:

   (1) Inflicts bodily injury or uses force upon another; or

   (2) Threatens another with or purposely puts him in fear of immediate bodily injury; or

   (3) Commits or threatens immediately to commit any felony of the first or second degree.

      An act shall be deemed to be included in the phrase "in the course of committing a theft" if it occurs in an attempt to commit theft or in immediate flight after the attempt or commission.

b. Grading. Robbery is a felony of the second degree, except that it is a felony of the first degree if in the course of committing the theft the actor attempts to kill anyone, or purposely inflicts or attempts to inflict serious bodily injury, or is armed with, or uses or threatens the immediate use of a deadly weapon.

PRACTICAL APPLICATION OF STATUTE

Robbery can be either a first or second degree offense. The determining factor to make it a felony of the first degree is whether a deadly weapon is utilized during the commission of theft—or if a defendant attempts to kill someone or purposely inflicts or attempts to inflict *serious* bodily injury during a theft. Robbery is a lesser second degree offense where the offender threatens or inflicts bodily injury during a theft or in circumstances where force (without a deadly weapon) is used during the commission of a theft. The statute also provides that an offender is guilty of second degree robbery if, during the commission of a theft, he threatens to commit any first or second degree felony such as kidnapping, arson or sexual assault.

Mickey Vice is guilty of the second degree robbery of Horace Wille. Vice lifted $500 from the man. During this theft, he caused bodily injury to Wille by punching him in the face several times. Serious bodily injury did not result from the beating, nor was Wille's life threatened by Vice; a deadly weapon was not utilized in the felony. Accordingly, this strong-arm robbery is a second degree offense.

Vice's robbery of Nelson Simone, however, is a felony of the first degree. Nelson Simone watched, horrified, as Mickey Vice pointed a gun at him and stole $100. The felony didn't end there, though, as Vice pistol-whipped his victim about the head, causing Simone to be rendered unconscious. This is a first degree robbery for two reasons—a deadly weapon was used during the theft, and serious bodily injury resulted from Vice's purposeful beating.

It is important to note that Vice would be guilty of first degree robbery if he simply threatened to use a deadly weapon during the theft or if he attempted to cause serious bodily injury during the offense. "Threatened" and "attempted' are the key words here. Accordingly, had Vice never brandished a weapon but instead threatened "I will shoot you with a gun," he still would be guilty of first degree robbery. Similarly, had Vice's violent gun whipping merely resulted in a couple of stitches, he still could be charged with this highest-graded felony. Why? Because repeatedly beating someone in the head with a pistol is a purposeful attempt to cause serious bodily injury.

5-2.   **Carjacking**

   a. Carjacking defined. A person is guilty of carjacking if, in the course of committing an unlawful taking of a motor vehicle or in an attempt to commit an unlawful taking of a motor vehicle, he

   (1) Inflicts bodily injury or uses force upon an occupant or person in possession or control of a motor vehicle;

   (2) Threatens an occupant or person in control with, or purposely or knowingly puts an occupant or person in control of the motor vehicle in fear of, immediate bodily injury;

   (3) Commits or threatens immediately to commit any felony of the first or second degree; or

   (4) Operates or causes said vehicle to be operated with the person who was in possession or control or was an occupant of the motor vehicle at the time of the taking remaining in the vehicle.

   An act shall be deemed to be "in the course of committing an unlawful taking of a motor vehicle" if it occurs during an attempt to commit the unlawful taking of a motor vehicle or during an immediate flight after the attempt or commission.

   b. Grading. Carjacking is a felony of the first degree, and upon conviction thereof a person may be sentenced to an ordinary term of imprisonment between ten and 30 years. A person convicted of carjacking shall be sentenced to a term of imprisonment and that term of imprisonment shall include the imposition of a minimum term of at least five years during which the defendant shall be ineligible for parole.

PRACTICAL APPLICATION OF STATUTE

Mickey Vice is guilty of carjacking, a first degree felony, for his unlawful taking of Nelson Simone's BMW. But why isn't Vice guilty of just theft or robbery?

Section 5-2 elevates a theft or robbery of an automobile to carjacking if the unlawful taking of the vehicle involves one of several violent actions against or threats to an occupant or person in control of the vehicle. For instance, under subsection a.(1), if the thief inflicts bodily injury or uses force, the felony is carjacking. Under a.(2), if he threatens the victim with immediate bodily injury, it is a carjacking. Per a.(3), if the actor commits or threatens any first or second degree felony (e.g., aggravated assault, sexual assault, arson), he is guilty of carjacking. Finally, pursuant to a.(4), the actor is guilty of carjacking if he forces the victim to remain in the vehicle—either as driver or passenger—at the time of the unlawful taking.

Per the provisions of subsection a.(1), Mickey Vice should be convicted of carjacking. He entered Nelson Simone's BMW and stole $100 from him. Immediately thereafter, he inflicted bodily injury on the man by beating him in the head with a pistol. Vice then pushed his victim from the BMW and fled in the vehicle. Vice's unlawful taking of Nelson Simone's automobile, coupled with his infliction of bodily injury, makes him guilty of carjacking.

END OF CHAPTER REVIEW

Multiple-Choice Questions

1. Robbery of an automobile is considered carjacking if during the unlawful taking:
   a. the actor inflicts bodily injury on an occupant of the vehicle
   b. the actor threatens an occupant of the vehicle with immediate bodily injury
   c. the actor threatens an occupant of the vehicle with arson
   d. all of the above
   e. none of the above

The following fact pattern pertains to questions 2–3.

Mickey Vice enters Nelson Simone's BMW and violently pistol-whips him, leaving him unconscious in the passenger seat. Vice kisses Simone on the lips and then speeds off in the vehicle, driving from Petersville to New Brunswick. Once in New Brunswick, Vice exits the vehicle and proceeds to a gas station where he breaks the attendant's nose while stealing a gas canister and cigarettes from him.

2. For his actions leveled against Simone, what is the best offense to charge Mickey Vice with?
   a. carjacking
   b. aggravated assault
   c. aggravated sexual assault
   d. all of the above
   e. a and b only

3. What offense is Vice guilty of for his unlawful taking of the gas canister and cigarettes?

    a. second degree robbery because breaking the attendant's nose amounts to only bodily injury and not serious bodily injury

    b. first degree robbery if he was armed with a pistol during the offense

    c. carjacking because the offense occurred at a gas station

    d. a and b only

    e. a and c only

4. While Snake is in the outhouse, Goose jumps into the driver's seat of Snake's pickup truck and begins to drive off. Snake, alerted to Goose's driving by the rumbling of the truck's muffler, hurriedly exits the outhouse and chases Goose down, catching him at a red light. Snake rips Goose from the truck and physically beats him. Snake then drives off, leaving Goose with two less teeth and a concussion. Snake is guilty of what offense?

    a. carjacking because Snake inflicted bodily injury on Goose in taking the truck back

    b. robbery and not carjacking because the vehicle belonged to Goose

    c. neither carjacking nor robbery because there was no unlawful taking by Snake

    d. neither carjacking nor robbery because the truck obviously was of little value

    e. none of the above

Essay Question

1. Tubby grabs Sissy by the arm in a Petersville bar. He threatens to rape her if she does not turn over $1,000 in cash to him. Sissy gives Tubby the money and then leaves. Does this act constitute a robbery of the first degree? A robbery of the second degree? Or is it not a robbery at all? Explain your answer, focusing on the elements of the statute.

6

BIAS FELONIES

6-1. **Bias intimidation**

    a. Bias intimidation. A person is guilty of the felony of bias intimidation if he commits, attempts to commit, conspires with another to commit or threatens the immediate commission of an offense specified in chapters 1 through 8 of this Criminal Code:

        (1) With the purpose to intimidate an individual or group of individuals because of race, color, religion, gender, handicap, sexual orientation or ethnicity; or

        (2) Knowing that the conduct constituting the offense would cause an individual or group of individuals to be intimidated because of race, color, religion, gender, handicap, sexual orientation or ethnicity; or

        (3) Under circumstances that caused any victim of the underlying offense to be intimidated and the victim, considering the manner in which the offense was committed, reasonably believed either that (a) the offense was committed with the purpose to intimidate the victim or any person or entity in whose welfare the victim is interested because of race, color, religion, gender, handicap, sexual orientation or ethnicity, or (b) the victim or the victim's property was selected to be the target of the offense because of the victim's race, color, religion, gender, handicap, sexual orientation or ethnicity.

    b. Permissive inference concerning selection of targeted person or property. Proof that the target of the underlying offense was selected by the defendant, or by another acting in concert with the defendant, because of race, color, religion, gender, handicap, sexual orientation or ethnicity shall give rise to a permissive inference by the trier of fact that the defendant acted with the purpose to intimidate an individual or group of individuals because of race, color, religion, gender, handicap, sexual orientation or ethnicity.

    c. Grading. Bias intimidation is a felony of the fourth degree if the underlying offense referred to in subsection a. is a misdemeanor A or misdemeanor B. Otherwise, bias intimidation is a felony one degree higher than the most serious underlying felony referred to in subsection a., except that where the underlying felony is a felony of the first degree, bias intimidation is a first degree felony and the defendant upon conviction thereof may be sentenced to an ordinary term of imprisonment between 15 years and 30 years, with a presumptive term of 20 years.

    d. Gender exemption in sexual offense prosecutions. It shall not be a violation of subsection a. if the underlying criminal offense is a violation of chapter 4 of this Criminal Code and the circumstance specified in paragraph (1), (2) or (3) of subsection a. of this section is based solely upon the gender of the victim.

    e. Merger. A conviction for bias intimidation shall not merge with a conviction of any of the underlying offenses referred to in subsection a. of this section, nor shall any conviction for such underlying offense merge with a conviction for bias intimidation. The court shall impose separate sentences upon a conviction for bias intimidation and a conviction of any underlying offense.

PRACTICAL APPLICATION OF STATUTE

Mickey Vice should be charged with first degree bias intimidation for his offenses perpetrated against Horace Wille. It is Vice's personal motivation behind his criminal actions that permits a charge under section 6-1, and it is the seriousness of his offenses against Wille that make the bias intimidation charge one of the first degree.

The bias intimidation statute basically creates a separate and distinct felony for committing certain offenses based on a victim's race, color, religion, gender, handicap, sexual orientation or ethnicity. Subsection a. of the statute enumerates the only underlying offenses that can give rise to a bias intimidation charge. These offenses are all those found in chapters 1 through 8 of this Criminal Code (e.g., murder, manslaughter, assault, kidnapping, criminal restraint, sexual assault, robbery, arson, criminal mischief, burglary, etc.).

If, during the commission of one of the above-enumerated offenses, an offender acts with the purpose to intimidate the victim based on his background (race, religion, etc.), the offender is guilty of bias intimidation. Likewise, if during the commission of one of the enumerated offenses, the offender knows his conduct would cause the victim to be intimidated because of his background, he is guilty of bias intimidation. Now what does all this mean? It means that a defendant's personal motivations for committing a felony—in some instances—can give rise to a separate and distinct charge of bias intimidation; in other instances, however, a defendant's personal motivations will not result in an additional charge. For example, if a victim is stabbed because he is a Mormon or a homosexual, then the offender will be charged with aggravated assault and bias intimidation. However, if the victim was stabbed because the offender lost a chess game to him, then the offender will be charged with only one felony—aggravated assault. So what about Mickey Vice? What should he be charged with for his actions against Horace Wille?

Mickey Vice committed a second degree robbery of Horace Wille, an American Indian. Vice stole cash from Wille and punched him in the face several times. He told his victim, "This is payback for all the money your Indian casinos stole from us. Indians stink." Clearly, Vice committed the felony of robbery with the purpose to intimidate Wille because of his background as an American Indian. At minimum, Vice knew his conduct would cause his victim to be intimidated because of his race—Vice told him the robbery was payback for the Indian casinos. Accordingly, Mickey Vice is guilty of first degree bias intimidation as well as the second degree robbery offense. But why is this a first degree felony when the underlying offense is a second degree felony?

Subsection c. of the statute provides the grading of bias intimidation offenses. Bias intimidation is a fourth degree felony if the underlying offense is a misdemeanor A or misdemeanor B. In all other situations, "bias intimidation is a felony one degree higher than the most serious underlying felony" committed against the victim. Since the most serious felony Vice committed against Wille was a second degree robbery, his separate and distinct bias intimidation charge would appropriately be a first degree offense—one degree higher than the underlying second degree robbery.

Gender Exemption

Mickey Vice should not be charged with the separate felony of bias intimidation based on the aggravated sexual assault of his estranged wife, Carrie. Subsection d. of the statute provides a gender exemption that prohibits prosecution for bias intimidation where the underlying offense is of a sexual nature and the defendant's actions are "based solely upon the gender of the victim." Given that no factor listed in section 6-1, other than perhaps gender, was a motivation behind Vice's rape of Carrie, he should not be charged with bias intimidation; however, he should, of course, face a charge of aggravated sexual assault.

END OF CHAPTER REVIEW

Multiple-Choice Questions

1. Allan loses a chess game to Junior, a Catholic man. After the chess game, Allan stabs Junior in the chest. Junior survives the attack. What offense is Allan guilty of violating?
   a. aggravated assault because of the deadly weapon involved
   b. simple assault because Junior survived
   c. bias intimidation if the stabbing was committed with the purpose to intimidate the victim because of his Catholic religion
   d. a and c only
   e. b and c only

The following fact pattern pertains to questions 2–4.

Charlotte is a resident of Maplewood. She has short blond hair and is a Mormon. She was born in Cuba and once broke her nose in a boxing match. Charlotte also previously posed naked in a magazine and is heterosexual. Her hobbies include baking, flying kites and plumbing. Pat sexually assaulted Charlotte with the purpose to intimidate her because of something in her personal background.

2. What part of Charlotte's background could *not* trigger a bias intimidation charge?
   a. that she is of Cuban ethnicity
   b. that she is heterosexual
   c. that she resides in Maplewood
   d. a and b only
   e. b and c only

3. What part of Charlotte's background could trigger a bias intimidation charge against Pat?
   a. her blond hair
   b. her past broken nose
   c. her plumbing hobby
   d. all of the above
   e. none of the above

4. If Pat sexually assaulted Charlotte based solely on the fact that Charlotte is a woman, could he be convicted of bias intimidation?

  a. no, because of the gender exemption in sexual offenses
  b. no, because she also has blond hair
  c. yes, because gender is a protected class
  d. yes, because women have special protections under the statute
  e. yes, because of *res ipsa loquitor*

7

ARSON, CRIMINAL MISCHIEF AND OTHER PROPERTY DESTRUCTION

7-1.   **Arson and related offenses**

a. Aggravated arson. A person is guilty of aggravated arson, a felony of the second degree, if he starts a fire or causes an explosion, whether on his own property or another's:

    (1) Thereby purposely or knowingly placing another person in danger of death or bodily injury; or

    (2) With the purpose of destroying a building or structure of another; or

    (3) With the purpose of collecting insurance for the destruction or damage to such property under circumstances which recklessly place any other person in danger of death or bodily injury; or

    (4) With the purpose of destroying or damaging a structure in order to exempt the structure, completely or partially, from the provisions of any State, county or local zoning, planning or building law, regulation, ordinance or enactment under circumstances which recklessly place any other person in danger of death or bodily injury; or

    (5) With the purpose of destroying or damaging any forest.

b. Arson. A person is guilty of arson, a felony of the third degree, if he purposely starts a fire or causes an explosion, whether on his own property or another's:

    (1) Thereby recklessly placing another person in danger of death or bodily injury; or

    (2) Thereby recklessly placing a building or structure of another in danger of damage or destruction; or

    (3) With the purpose of collecting insurance for the destruction or damage to such property; or

    (4) With the purpose of destroying or damaging a structure in order to exempt the structure, completely or partially, from the provisions of any State, county or local zoning, planning or building law, regulation, ordinance or enactment; or

    (5) Thereby recklessly placing a forest in danger of damage or destruction.

c. Failure to control or report a dangerous fire. A person who knows that a fire is endangering life or a substantial amount of property of another and either fails to take reasonable measures to put out or control the fire, when he can do so without substantial risk to himself, or to give prompt fire alarm, commits a felony of the fourth degree if:

    (1) He knows that he is under an official, contractual or other legal duty to prevent or combat the fire; or

    (2) The fire was started, albeit lawfully, by him or with his assent, or on property in his custody or control.

d. Any person who, directly or indirectly, pays or accepts or offers to pay or accept any form of consideration including, but not limited to, money or any other pecuniary benefit, regardless of whether any consideration is actually exchanged, for the purpose of starting a fire or causing an explosion in violation of this section commits a felony of the first degree.

e. Notwithstanding the provisions of any section of this Criminal Code to the contrary, if a person is convicted of aggravated arson pursuant to the provisions of subsection a. of this section and the structure which was the target of the offense was a health care facility or a physician's office, the sentence imposed shall include a term of imprisonment. The court may not suspend or make any other noncustodial disposition of a person sentenced pursuant to the provisions of this subsection.

f. Definitions. "Structure" is defined in section 8-1. Property is that of another, for the purpose of this section, if any one other than the actor has a possessory, or legal or equitable proprietary interest therein. Property is that of another, for the purpose of this section, if anyone other than the actor has a legal or equitable interest in the property including, but not limited to, a mortgage, pledge, lien or security interest therein. If a building or structure is divided into separately occupied units, any unit not occupied by the actor is an occupied structure of another.

    As used in this section, "forest" means and includes any forest, brush land, grass land, salt marsh, wooded area and any combination thereof, including but not limited to an open space area, public lands, wetlands, park lands, natural habitats, a State conservation area, a wildlife refuge area or any other designated undeveloped open space whether or not it is subject to specific protection under law.

g. Notwithstanding the provisions of any section of this Criminal Code to the contrary, if a person is convicted pursuant to the provisions of subsection a., b. or d. of this section and the structure which was the target of the offense was a church, synagogue, temple or other place of public worship, that person commits a felony of the first degree and the sentence imposed shall include a term of imprisonment. The term of imprisonment shall include a minimum term of 15 years, during which the defendant shall be ineligible for parole. The court may not suspend or make any other noncustodial disposition of a person sentenced pursuant to the provisions of this subsection.

PRACTICAL APPLICATION OF STATUTE

Aggravated Arson and Arson Generally

The primary difference between aggravated arson and arson rests in the mental state of the defendant. For example, if an actor starts a fire "purposely" or "knowingly," placing another person in danger of death or bodily injury, he is guilty of aggravated arson, a second degree felony. However, if he starts the fire "recklessly," placing another person in danger of death or bodily injury, he is guilty of the lesser third degree felony, arson.

    This "purposeful"/"knowing" differentiation from "recklessness" becomes convoluted, however, when the actor's reason for committing the fire involves either collecting insurance or avoiding zoning/building laws. For example, if an actor sets a fire in order to collect insurance on the property *and* thereby "recklessly" places another in danger of death or bodily injury, he is guilty of aggravated arson. If he starts the fire to collect insurance and no one is placed in such danger, however, then he is only guilty of arson.

Please note that aggravated arson and arson are considered to be committed in circumstances where an actor starts a fire or causes an explosion. Also, one can commit either of these offenses whether on his own property or another's property.

Aggravated Arson—Purposely/Knowingly Placing Another in Danger

Under section 7-1a.(1), Mickey Vice is guilty of aggravated arson for the fire he started at his own house. Vice started this fire after he had sexually assaulted his estranged wife, Carrie. He knocked her unconscious and then poured gasoline in the home's living room, striking a match to the scene. Leaving the woman in the house as it burned to the ground, he necessarily "purposely," or at least "knowingly," placed her in danger of death or bodily injury. Accordingly, Mickey Vice is guilty of aggravated arson under subsection a.(1) of the statute.

Aggravated Arson—Purposely Destroying a Building of Another

Subsection a.(2) provides that a person is guilty of aggravated arson if he starts a fire or causes an explosion "with the purpose of destroying a building or structure of another." Mickey Vice is guilty of aggravated arson under this subsection for the explosion he carried out at his father-in-law's multi-unit building.

Vice purposely placed and detonated dynamite at the base of the building. Over 30 homes were destroyed and numerous people suffered serious bodily injuries. Certainly, Vice's purpose in exploding the dynamite was to destroy his father-in-law's building, so he should be charged and convicted of aggravated arson for this brutal act.

Aggravated Arson—Starting a Fire to Collect Insurance or to Avoid Zoning/Building Laws

Mickey Vice is guilty of aggravated arson under both subsections a.(3) and a.(4) for the fire he started at his own house. Section 7-1a.(3) provides that an actor has committed aggravated arson where he starts a fire to collect insurance; section 7-1a.(4) makes the fire-starter guilty of aggravated arson where his purpose was to destroy the structure to have it exempt from a zoning or building law. Under both a.(3) and a.(4), the actor's fire must recklessly place another person in danger of death or bodily injury for the felony to be aggravated arson and not just arson.

When Vice started the fire at his house, his wife was unconscious. Not only did he leave her for dead in the burning structure, the fire spread to two adjoining row houses where people lived. In starting this fire, Vice recklessly placed his neighbors in danger of death or bodily injury as he had to know that the fire could easily spread to the homes connected to his house—certainly any reasonable person would know this. Vice's actions rise above recklessness as he purposely or knowingly placed his wife in danger of death by starting the fire. With this all being the case, the reckless element of a.(3) and a.(4) is met.

But why did Mickey Vice start the fire? Vice told his wife that they should "burn down the house to collect insurance money and to avoid Petersville's requirement that they pay to have fire escapes erected and junk removed from the backyard." Accordingly, he is guilty of a.(3) because part of his purpose in starting the fire was to collect insurance for the destruction of the property; likewise, he is guilty of a.(4) because he also started the fire to avoid building ordinances of erecting a fire escape and removing junk from the yard.

Vice would be guilty of third degree arson, rather than second degree aggravated arson, if he had started the fire for the same reasons as above—to collect insurance or to avoid zoning/building laws—and no persons were recklessly placed in danger. Under b.(3) of the statute, an actor is guilty of arson if he starts a fire to collect insurance, and under b.(4), he is guilty of arson if he starts a fire to avoid a building or zoning law.

Arson—Recklessly Placing Another in Danger

Subsection b.(1) provides that an actor is guilty of arson if he starts a fire that "recklessly" places another in danger of death or bodily injury. The facts can be changed in Mickey Vice's burning of his home to exemplify this type of arson.

Let's say Vice never argued with his wife on the day of the fire—he never even saw her. However, ignorant of her whereabouts, he starts the fire at his house. Under these circumstances—not knowing if she was in the house—he would be recklessly placing his wife in danger of death or bodily injury. Similarly, Vice's actions would recklessly place his neighbors in danger given the design of their homes as row houses that are connected to each other. It is quite possible that the fire would spread, which would put them in danger of death or bodily injury. Accordingly, under these circumstances, Vice would be guilty of arson under 7-1b.(1).

Arson—Recklessly Placing the Building of Another in Danger of Destruction

Vice should be charged with arson under subsection b.(2) for recklessly placing his neighbors' homes in danger of destruction. As stated above, their row houses were connected to Vice's, and given this type of structure, Vice had to reasonably know that the fire he started at his own home would likely spread to his neighbors' homes. Accordingly, he is guilty of arson under this subsection.

Fire Placing a Forest in Danger

An actor who starts a fire to "purposely" destroy a forest is guilty of aggravated arson under subsection a.(5). If he starts a fire that "recklessly" places a forest in danger of destruction, he is guilty of arson under b.(5).

Paying to Start a Fire

If Mickey Vice had paid another person (or been the one who was paid) to start the fire at his home, he would be guilty of a first degree offense. Under subsection d. of the statute, aggravated arson and arson are elevated to a first degree felony where money or pecuniary value is exchanged to start a fire. Both the person who pays the money and the one who accepts it are guilty per this provision. It is important to note that the money does not actually need to be exchanged for conviction—an agreement simply must be in place.

Failure to Control or Report a Dangerous Fire

Subsection c. of the statute is interesting as it is somewhat akin to a "Good Samaritan" law. As examples, the following people would be guilty of a fourth degree offense per the elements of this subsection: a firefighter who does nothing while he watches a house filled with people burn to the ground—even though he could have taken measures to control the fire without putting himself at substantial risk; a police officer who does not notify the fire department of a raging building fire that likely will destroy the property. Another example is if John Smith starts a controlled burn of a leaf pile in the far corner of his yard, and after an unexpected gust of wind, several burning leaves fly off the pile and onto his old tool shed, igniting the roof and quickly engulfing the entire shed. Despite having a cell phone and easy access to a garden hose that could have easily been used to quench the smoldering leaves on the roof, he runs inside his home and watches the flames spread to the neighboring property. As a final example, at a corporate Christmas party, Jim Exec lights a fire in the fireplace of his deluxe office into which he and his guests proceed to throw napkins and other combustibles. One of these napkins falls outside the hearth, starting a small fire on the Persian rug. Despite knowing that he has a fire extinguisher in his office, Jim and his guests run out to the street and watch the building burn to the ground—and don't even bother to report it.

7-2.

Causing or risking widespread injury or damage

    a. (1) A person who, purposely or knowingly, unlawfully causes an explosion, flood, avalanche, collapse of a building, release or abandonment of poison gas, radioactive material or any other harmful or destructive substance commits a felony of the second degree. A person who, purposely or knowingly, unlawfully causes widespread injury or damage in any manner commits a felony of the second degree.

       (2) A person who, purposely or knowingly, unlawfully causes a hazardous discharge required to be reported pursuant to the "Spill Compensation and Control Act" or any rules and regulations adopted pursuant thereto, or who, purposely or knowingly, unlawfully causes a release or abandonment of hazardous waste as defined in the "Spill Compensation and Control Act" commits a felony of the second degree. Any person who recklessly violates the provisions of this paragraph is guilty of a felony of the third degree.

    b. A person who recklessly causes widespread injury or damage is guilty of a felony of the third degree.

    c. A person who recklessly creates a risk of widespread injury or damage commits a felony of the fourth degree, even if no such injury or damage occurs. A violation of this subsection is a felony of the third degree if the risk of widespread injury or damage results from the reckless handling or storage of hazardous materials. A violation of this subsection is a felony of the second degree if the handling or storage of hazardous materials violated any law, rule or regulation intended to protect the public health and safety.

    d. A person who knowingly or recklessly fails to take reasonable measures to prevent or mitigate widespread injury or damage commits a felony of the fourth degree if:

       (1) He knows that he is under an official, contractual or other legal duty to take such measures; or

       (2) He did or assented to the act causing or threatening the injury or damage.

   e. For purposes of this section, widespread injury or damage means serious bodily injury to five or more people or damage to five or more habitations or to a building which would normally have contained 25 or more persons at the time of the offense.

PRACTICAL APPLICATION OF STATUTE

Mickey Vice should be charged with causing widespread injury and damage under 7-2a. for the dynamite blasting of his father-in-law's building. This statute provides that a person who "purposely," "knowingly"—and unlawfully—causes disasters such as an explosion, collapse of a building, avalanche or flood is guilty of a second degree offense. Widespread injury or damage means serious bodily injury to five or more people or damage to five or more habitations.

Vice purposely placed dynamite at the base of his father-in-law's building. After setting it there, he detonated the explosives. Although no one was killed, 17 people suffered serious bodily injuries (broken bones, loss of eyesight) and over 30 homes were destroyed. Given this massive destruction carried out by Vice, he should be charged with a second degree felony under 7-2.

It should be noted that the statute sets forth lower degree felonies where a less culpable mental state is involved and where damage does not actually occur. For example, under subsection b., if the defendant "recklessly" causes widespread injury or damage, he is guilty of a third degree offense. Under subsection c., if he "recklessly" creates a *risk* of widespread injury or damage, he is guilty of a fourth degree felony— even if no such injury or damage occurs.

7-3.   **Criminal mischief**

   a. Offense defined. A person is guilty of criminal mischief if he:

     (1) Purposely or knowingly damages tangible property of another or damages tangible property of another recklessly or negligently in the employment of fire, explosives or other dangerous means listed in subsection a. of 7-2; or

     (2) Purposely, knowingly or recklessly tampers with tangible property of another so as to endanger person or property, including the damaging or destroying of a rental premises by a tenant in retaliation for institution of eviction proceedings.

   b. Grading.

     (1) Criminal mischief is a felony of the third degree if the actor purposely or knowingly causes pecuniary loss of $2,000 or more.

     (2) Criminal mischief is a felony of the fourth degree if the actor causes pecuniary loss in excess of $500 but less than $2,000. It is a misdemeanor A if the actor causes pecuniary loss of $500 or less.

     (3) Criminal mischief is a felony of the third degree if the actor damages, defaces, eradicates, alters, receives, releases or causes the loss of any research property used by the research facility or otherwise causes physical disruption to the functioning of the research facility. The term "physical disruption" does not include any lawful activity that results from public, governmental or research facility employee reaction to the disclosure of information about the research facility.

     (4) Criminal mischief is a felony of the fourth degree if the actor damages, removes or impairs the operation of any device, including, but not limited to, a sign, signal, light or other equipment, which serves to regulate or ensure the safety of air traffic at any airport, landing field, landing strip, heliport, helistop or any other aviation facility;

however, if the damage, removal or impediment of the device recklessly causes bodily injury or damage to property, the actor is guilty of a felony of the third degree, or if it recklessly causes a death, the actor is guilty of a felony of the second degree.

(5) Criminal mischief is a felony of the fourth degree if the actor interferes or tampers with any airport, landing field, landing strip, heliport, helistop or any other aviation facility; however, if the interference or tampering with the airport, landing field, landing strip, heliport, helistop or other aviation facility recklessly causes bodily injury or damage to property, the actor is guilty of a felony of the third degree, or if it recklessly causes a death, the actor is guilty of a felony of the second degree.

(6) Criminal mischief is a felony of the third degree if the actor tampers with a grave, crypt, mausoleum or other site where human remains are stored or interred, with the purpose to desecrate, destroy or steal such human remains or any part thereof.

(7) Criminal mischief is a felony of the third degree if the actor purposely or knowingly causes a substantial interruption or impairment of public communication, transportation, supply of water, oil, gas or power or other public service. Criminal mischief is a felony of the second degree if the substantial interruption or impairment recklessly causes death.

(8) Criminal mischief is a felony of the fourth degree if the actor purposely or knowingly breaks, digs up, obstructs or otherwise tampers with any pipes or mains for conducting gas, oil or water, or any works erected for supplying buildings with gas, oil or water, or any appurtenances or appendages therewith connected, or injures, cuts, breaks down, destroys or otherwise tampers with any electric light wires, poles or appurtenances, or any telephone, telecommunications, cable television or telegraph wires, lines, cable or appurtenances.

c. A person convicted of an offense of criminal mischief that involves an act of graffiti may, in addition to any other penalty imposed by the court, be required to pay to the owner of the damaged property monetary restitution in the amount of the pecuniary damage caused by the act of graffiti and to perform community service, which shall include removing the graffiti from the property, if appropriate. If community service is ordered, it shall be for either not less than 20 days or not less than the number of days necessary to remove the graffiti from the property.

d. As used in this section:

(1) "Act of graffiti" means the drawing, painting or making of any mark or inscription on public or private real or personal property without the permission of the owner.

(2) "Spray paint" means any paint or pigmented substance that is in an aerosol or similar spray container.

e. A person convicted of an offense of criminal mischief that involves the damaging or destroying of a rental premises by a tenant in retaliation for institution of eviction proceedings may, in addition to any other penalty imposed by the court, be required to pay to the owner of the property monetary restitution in the amount of the pecuniary damage caused by the damage or destruction.

PRACTICAL APPLICATION OF STATUTE

Criminal Mischief

Criminal mischief can be a second degree, third degree or fourth degree offense or a misdemeanor A. The seriousness of the charge primarily depends on the monetary loss a defendant causes to property that he damages. Losses of $2,000 or more mean the defendant is guilty of a third degree felony, and losses in excess of $500 but less than $2,000 make the defendant susceptible to a fourth degree felony. If the defendant causes damage that results in a pecuniary loss of $500 or less, he is guilty of only a misdemeanor A.

Mickey Vice is guilty of two counts of criminal mischief. First, after Vice failed to hot-wire an automobile, he repeatedly kicked its doors and smashed in all of its windows. For this damage, he should be charged with fourth degree criminal mischief as the total losses were $1,550—in excess of $500 but less than $2,000. Vice should be convicted of a misdemeanor A of criminal mischief for the spray painting he did in the women's bathroom at the nuclear power plant. The costs to remedy the graffiti would likely be under $500, and therefore the charge would appropriately be a misdemeanor A.

Second, Third or Fourth Degree Criminal Mischief Automatic for Specific Types of Damages and Acts

It is interesting to note that specific types of damages will automatically render a fourth, third or even second degree charge regardless of the monetary loss. These specific damages are itemized in subsections b.(3) through b.(8). For instance, under subsection b.(7), a person is guilty of third degree criminal mischief if he purposely or knowingly causes a substantial interruption of public services such as gas, water or transportation. It becomes a felony of the second degree where such criminal mischief "recklessly causes death." Under b.(6), a third degree offense is committed in circumstances where damage is purposely caused to places where human remains are kept (e.g., a grave, crypt or mausoleum).

Tenant Destroying Rental Premises

A provision in subsection a.(2) specifically protects landlords from vindictive tenants. Even though the statute, by its nature, already comprehensively covers "purposely, knowingly or recklessly" damaging any tangible property of another, it contains the following special clause—"including the damaging or destroying of a rental premises by a tenant in retaliation for the institution of eviction proceedings."

7-3.1.   **Traffic sign, signal damage, removal, violation**

A person who purposely, knowingly, recklessly or negligently defaces, injures or removes an official traffic sign or signal described in the Motor Vehicle Statutes of this State is guilty of a misdemeanor A.

If a juvenile who is adjudicated delinquent for an act which, if committed by an adult, would constitute a violation of this section is assessed a fine and the court determines that the juvenile is unable to pay the fine, the juvenile's parents or legal guardian shall be responsible for the imposed fine.

PRACTICAL APPLICATION OF STATUTE

An example of an offense under 7-3.1 is Mickey Vice "purposely" ripping down a stop sign. Another example is if, "for kicks," he climbed up a traffic light. While swinging on the light, he "recklessly" causes it to snap and crash to the ground. Both of these acts render Vice guilty of a misdemeanor A per 7-3.1.

7-4. **Motor vehicles; removal or alteration of identification number or mark; possession; penalty**

a. A person who removes, defaces, alters, changes, destroys, covers or obliterates any trademark, distinguishing or identification number, serial number or mark on or from any motor vehicle for an unlawful purpose is guilty of a felony of the third degree.

b. A person who, for an unlawful purpose, knowingly possesses any motor vehicle, or any of the parts thereof, from or on which any trademark, distinguishing or identification number, or serial number or mark has been removed, covered, altered, changed, defaced, destroyed or obliterated is guilty of an offense, unless, within ten days after the motor vehicle or any part thereof shall have come into his possession, he files with the Director of the Division of Motor Vehicles of this State a verified statement showing the source of his title, the proper trademark, identification or distinguishing number, or serial number or mark, if known, and if known, the manner of and reason for the mutilation, change, alteration, concealment or defacement, the length of time the motor vehicle or part has been held and the price paid therefore.

  If the value of the motor vehicle or parts possessed exceeds $500, the offense is a felony of the third degree. If the value is at least $200 but does not exceed $500, it is a felony of the fourth degree, but if the value is less than $200, it is a misdemeanor A.

c. As used in this section, "motor vehicle" includes motor bicycles, motorcycles, automobiles, trucks, tractors or other vehicles designed to be self-propelled by mechanical power, and otherwise than by muscular power, except motor vehicles running upon or guided by rails or tracks.

PRACTICAL APPLICATION OF STATUTE

For removing the vehicle identification number of an automobile he attempted to steal, Mickey Vice is guilty of a third degree offense. Simply put, section 7-4a. provides that any person who removes or defaces any trademark or serial number from a motor vehicle—for an unlawful purpose—is guilty of a third degree felony. Vice removed the vehicle identification number for the unlawful purpose of hiding the automobile's identity after he stole it; accordingly, he is guilty of this third degree felony.

7-5. **Tampering, damage involving nuclear electric generating plant; felony of first degree**

The provisions of 7-2 to the contrary notwithstanding, any person who purposely or knowingly damages or tampers with any machinery, device or equipment at a nuclear electric generating plant with the purpose to cause or threaten to cause an unauthorized release of radiation commits a felony of the first degree and may be sentenced to an extended term of imprisonment, provided, however, that if the defendant is not sentenced to an extended term of imprisonment, the defendant shall be sentenced to an ordinary term of imprisonment between 15 and 30 years.

PRACTICAL APPLICATION OF STATUTE

Mickey Vice has violated the provisions of section 7-5 for his attempt to release radiation during his melee at the nuclear power plant. The charge is valid even though no radiation was actually released.

Section 7-5 provides that any person who purposely or knowingly damages machinery at a nuclear electric generating plant, with the intent to release radiation, is guilty of a first degree felony. Vice shot at power plant employees and threw a stick of dynamite into nuclear generating machinery, hoping to release radiation. Accordingly, even though he failed in his attempt, Vice is guilty of a section 7-5 first degree offense.

7-6.   **Nuclear electric generating plant; damaging or tampering with equipment which results in death; felony of first degree**

Any person who purposely or knowingly damages or tampers with any machinery, device or equipment at a nuclear electric generating plant which results in the death of another due to exposure to radiation commits a felony of the first degree and may be sentenced to an extended term of imprisonment, provided, however, that if the defendant is not sentenced to an extended term of imprisonment, the defendant shall be sentenced to an ordinary term of imprisonment between 15 and 30 years.

PRACTICAL APPLICATION OF STATUTE

If Mickey Vice had succeeded in his quest to release radiation and death had resulted from his damage, then he would be guilty of a first degree felony per section 7-6.

7-7.   **Nuclear electric generating plant; damaging or tampering with equipment which results in injury; felony of second degree**

Any person who purposely or knowingly damages or tampers with any machinery, device or equipment at a nuclear electric generating plant which results in the injury of another due to exposure to radiation commits a felony of the second degree and may be sentenced to an extended term of imprisonment, provided, however, that if the defendant is not sentenced to an extended term of imprisonment, the defendant shall be sentenced to an ordinary term of imprisonment between 15 and 30 years.

PRACTICAL APPLICATION OF STATUTE

If Mickey Vice had succeeded in his attempt to release radiation and at least one other person was injured by his damages, then he would be guilty of a second degree felony per section 7-7.

END OF CHAPTER REVIEW

Multiple-Choice Questions

The following fact pattern pertains to questions 1–2.

After munching on a raw potato, Maglio smashed the remainder of it into the car window of Carlos, his nemesis. The window broke, resulting in $205 damage to Carlos' car.

1. The best offense to charge Maglio with for damaging Carlos' car is:
    a. defiant trespass
    b. burglary
    c. criminal mischief
    d. peering into windows
    e. vegetative destruction

2. The degree of Maglio's offense is:
    a. a misdemeanor A because the pecuniary loss was $500 or less
    b. a fourth degree felony because the pecuniary loss was more than $200 but less than $500
    c. a misdemeanor A because the property damaged was a private automobile and not a private plane
    d. a misdemeanor B because of the *rex tex tung* doctrine
    e. a and c only

3. Mickey Vice placed and detonated dynamite at the base of his father-in-law's Petersville building. Over 30 homes were destroyed and numerous people suffered serious bodily injuries. Mickey Vice is guilty of what offense?
    a. arson
    b. aggravated arson
    c. aggravated assault
    d. a and c
    e. b and c

4. Jordi flew in from Canada to visit Veronica at her new three-bedroom ranch in White Meadow. While Veronica was at work, Jordi put a log in the fireplace and ignited it with the aid of a newspaper. The fire accidentally grew out of control, though, catching nearby drapes. Jordi, nervous and embarrassed, ran out of the house, which was now engulfed in flames. She drove to a park nearby to pass some time and then came back to the ranch and watched the volunteer firefighters put out the blaze. Veronica's new ranch was completely destroyed. White Meadow police should charge Jordi with what offense?
    a. nothing, the fire started accidentally
    b. a fourth degree felony for failing to report a dangerous fire
    c. a third degree felony of arson
    d. a misdemeanor A of arson
    e. aggravated arson because the structure was completely destroyed by the fire

5. Use the same facts as above, except Jordi purposely burned down Veronica's house because she was jealous of her. Here, Jordi is guilty of what offense?
    a. aggravated arson
    b. arson
    c. manslaughter
    d. a and c
    e. b and c

6. Stupid Sam purposely defaces a heliport in New Waterford, making the landing area uneven and slippery. When the next helicopter arrived, it tumbled over due to Stupid Sam's mischievous activities. The pilot was killed as a result. In addition to a homicide offense, what else could Stupid Sam be charged with?

   a. aggravated arson
   b. arson
   c. a misdemeanor A of criminal mischief
   d. a second degree felony of criminal mischief
   e. there's nothing in this Criminal Code to additionally charge him with

7. Eli goes to the newly created dam in Palladin and purposely causes an explosion, with the intent to cause a flood. The dam indeed breaks and water floods half the city of Palladin, resulting in millions of dollars in property damage, including the destruction of over 100 families' homes. Eli is guilty of:

   a. a second degree felony for causing widespread damage
   b. a fourth degree felony for causing widespread damage
   c. arson
   d. a and c
   e. b and c

Essay Questions

1. Maria always hated her brother Bobby's baseball card collection. Although now both adults, they both still hung out in their tree house located in their parents' backyard. One day, Maria stopped by Mommy and Daddy's house and went directly to the tree house. There, at the base of the tree, was Bobby's baseball card collection. In a sudden fit of rage, Maria poured gasoline on the cards, lit them on fire and ran away. The result was the burning and complete destruction of the baseball cards and the tree house. Bobby, unbeknownst to Maria, was in the tree house at the time of the fire, but he escaped without injury. Is Maria guilty of arson? Aggravated arson? Is the tree house a "structure"? If not, could Maria be convicted of either arson or aggravated arson? Are there any other offenses in chapter 7 that Maria could be convicted of?

2. What are the only two circumstances that can raise aggravated arson from a second degree felony to a first degree felony? Provide examples for each, and cite the specific subsections in your answer.

8

BURGLARY AND OTHER CRIMINAL INTRUSIONS

FACT PATTERN (PERTAINING TO CHAPTERS 8 AND 9)

As a personal birthday present, Ignacio Marini determined to obtain a wish list of items: $50,000 in cash, a Mercedes, a gold pinky ring, a diamond earring, a moose, two kilograms of cocaine, one pound of marijuana, a gerbil, the mechanical repair of his lawn mower and a box of Devil Dogs. Ignacio determined that two days' worth of activities would net him all his desired presents.

Day One

To carry out his goals, Ignacio procured a stocking from his sister's bedroom and exited his Abner co-op home. His first stop—a supermarket approximately six blocks from his residence. The man was hungry.

Once inside the food chain conglomerate, Ignacio surreptitiously traveled down several of the store's aisles. He stopped when he reached the baked goods; there, he quickly grabbed a box of 16 Devil Dogs and stuffed the pastry items into his coat pocket. He then exited the store with swift calculation.

Outside, Ignacio spotted a brand-new white convertible Mercedes-Benz. He gave a cursory glance at his surroundings, forced a Devil Dog in his mouth, swallowed it with two bites and then hot-wired the vehicle, which was valued at $85,000.

From the supermarket's parking lot, Ignacio traveled one municipality to the town of Falkner. Checking notes to himself, he arrived at a home on Century Road. At this location, he affixed a tie to his shirt, procured a briefcase, approached the door and rang the bell. Moments later, 73-year-old Fanny Moses answered. Ignacio advised her that he was the township's tax collector and that he was present to collect $52,500—the amount she was overdue in her property taxes. Ms. Moses was not in any arrears in her taxes, and Ignacio knew this. Similarly, Ignacio was not the township's tax collector nor a member of any government agency. He was aware, however, that Ms. Moses suffered from Alzheimer's disease. Ms. Moses handed over a check without objection.

Ignacio's next stop was two doors away at the home of Sandy Jerusalem. At Mr. Jerusalem's residence, Ignacio removed his tie and placed a top hat on his head. He then banged furiously on the door until Jerusalem responded. Once the greeting was complete, Ignacio simply told Jerusalem, "Kindly turn over your gold pinky ring to me or I will advise the media that you regularly frequent a nudist camp in Baja." Jerusalem immediately removed his pinky ring, valued at $3,500, and handed it to his blackmailer.

Ignacio then reentered his new Mercedes and traveled north to Larkspur, where he stopped on a quiet residential street just after night fell. Placing the stocking over his head, Ignacio walked briskly to the street's last house. There he utilized a screwdriver to pry open a screen; once through the open window, he went directly to the home's only juvenile room. It was empty except for a caged gerbil that was enjoying a relaxing moment on a pile of wood chips. Ignacio heisted the tiny animal and exited.

Day Two

Bright and early the next morning, Ignacio rose from a pleasant night's sleep and immediately traveled to a Rickert Park mechanical repair shop. Posing as a local councilman, Ignacio asked to have his lawn mower repaired by day's end and to have an invoice sent to his home. The shop owner agreed—Ignacio, of course, never paid the bill, which amounted to $165.

A shipping center in the town of Marlowe was Ignacio's next stop. At this store, Ignacio maintained a box to receive mail. Waiting for him was a single letter addressed to "Ignacio B. Marini." Ignacio, aware that this letter was sent to him by mistake—as his uncle was "Ignacio B. Marini" and he himself was "Ignacio S. Marini"—opened the letter anyway. Inside was an insurance check for $25,000. Ignacio expeditiously deposited the check into his personal bank account and then drove to a friend's house.

Although Ignacio was over 40, his closest friend was Charles Bigby, a 17-year-old high school dropout. Charles was elated with Ignacio's new stolen car; his older pal, noting this, asked Charles to come along for "some more fun."

Simply driving down the block from Charles' house, the two arrived at a horse farm. Even though the property was marked with "No Trespassing" signs, the friends bypassed the same and jumped on two horses. They galloped off, riding the saddled animals on the city streets of Abner for nearly an hour. When they were finished, they tied the horses to a tree and proceeded to a late-model BMW.

Ignacio coaxed Charles to hot-wire the automobile and to thereafter meet him at Mickey's Auto Body Shop in East Radcliffe. Charles agreed, and 30 minutes later they were each paid $10,000 by Mickey Morabito, an unassuming man in his sixties who ran an intricate auto theft ring. Under his control were over 50 men who routinely stole automobiles for payment. Mickey, in turn, would either resell the automobiles for a huge profit or chop them up for parts and then sell them.

Before Ignacio and Charles left Mickey's headquarters, they ducked into the conference room. There, Ignacio enlisted Charles to assist him in carrying two heavy boxes—one box containing nearly a pound of marijuana and the other holding two kilograms of cocaine. They avoided detection by Mickey and his employees, jumped into a pickup truck owned by a regular shop customer and fled. Laughing raucously as they counted their money and drugs, Ignacio ran stoplights and drove at excessive speeds. They sideswiped two parked automobiles and then finally arrived back at the horse farm—about 15 minutes after leaving Mickey's. The pickup truck was abandoned by a stable.

Once again posing as a Rickert Park councilman, Ignacio presented the owner of the horse farm with a handshake and the promise to make four payments of $1,000. The future payments were supposed to be in exchange for a prize moose that the horse farm held on its premises. Per their agreement, Ignacio was required to make four payments of $1,000 on the first of the month for four consecutive months. The moose was then loaded onto a trailer attached to a SUV; Marini and Bigby drove off the farm. Of course, no payments were ever delivered.

Tired by the day's events and late for supper, Charles asked to be brought home. Ignacio complied, driving his young friend to his doorstep. Before Ignacio could depart, however, Charles presented him with his birthday gift—a brand-new 32-inch color television set valued at $1,000. Charles told his mentor, "It's a little hot, but I chiseled off the serial numbers. Enjoy." Ignacio thanked his best friend and then departed.

Driving with the moose and television set, Ignacio decided to make his final stop at BB's Home of Appliances. Upon entering the establishment, he was immediately greeted by Franz Bellenwood. The two sipped espresso as Ignacio explained that he had a $1,000 television set with the serial numbers removed. Franz directed Ignacio to follow normal business procedure and bring the set around back.

Moments later, the two men met at the rear of the building. Ignacio then followed Franz to the basement, where he placed the television set next to hundreds of other appliances and electronic equipment with similarly defaced serial numbers. In exchange for the TV, Franz supplied Ignacio with a one-half-carat diamond earring.

Satisfied that all his birthday gifts had been received, Ignacio asked Franz to join him for a celebratory dinner. Franz consented and prepared to lock up his basement of goods. All of a sudden, however, a battalion of Abner police officers and investigators from the County Prosecutor's Office entered the room armed with arrest warrants. Ignacio shared a glass of tap water and a bologna sandwich with Franz as the birthday celebration was carried out in the Abner County Jail.

8-1. Definition

In this chapter, unless a different meaning plainly is required, "structure" means any building, room, ship, vessel, car, vehicle or airplane and also means any place adapted for overnight accommodation of persons, or for carrying on business therein, whether or not a person is actually present.

8-2. Burglary

a. Burglary defined. A person is guilty of burglary if, with the purpose to commit an offense therein, he:

   (1) Enters a research facility, structure or a separately secured or occupied portion thereof unless the structure was at the time open to the public or the actor is licensed or privileged to enter; or

   (2) Surreptitiously remains in a research facility, structure or a separately secured or occupied portion thereof knowing that he is not licensed or privileged to do so.

b. Grading. Burglary is a felony of the second degree if, in the course of committing the offense, the actor:

   (1) Purposely, knowingly or recklessly inflicts, attempts to inflict or threatens to inflict bodily injury on anyone; or

   (2) Is armed with or displays what appears to be explosives or a deadly weapon.

Otherwise burglary is a felony of the third degree. An act shall be deemed "in the course of committing" an offense if it occurs in an attempt to commit an offense or in immediate flight after the attempt or commission.

PRACTICAL APPLICATION OF STATUTE

Burglary is an offense primarily predicated on two basic elements—entering a structure with the purpose to commit an offense once inside it. The offense inside, however, need not actually be committed; an attempt is sufficient for conviction under this statute. Ignacio Marini is guilty of burglary for his break-in and gerbil theft at the Larkspur home.

Ignacio Marini planned to obtain a gerbil as one of his birthday presents. In order to accomplish this goal, he used a screwdriver to pry open a screen and illegally enter the home in Larkspur. His purpose in entering this home was to commit the offense of theft—the theft of the gerbil. Accordingly, Ignacio is guilty of burglary, which is a third degree offense in this case.

Ignacio's aforementioned burglary is a third degree felony because he neither injured another during the offense nor was armed with a deadly weapon. In burglaries where a defendant inflicts (or threatens to inflict) bodily injury or where a defendant is armed with a deadly weapon, the defendant is guilty of second degree burglary.

8-3.   **Unlicensed entry of structures; defiant trespasser; peering into dwelling places; defenses**

    a. Unlicensed entry of structures. A person commits an offense if, knowing that he is not licensed or privileged to do so, he enters or surreptitiously remains in any research facility, structure or separately secured or occupied portion thereof. An offense under this subsection is a felony of the fourth degree if it is committed in a school or on school property. The offense is a felony of the fourth degree if it is committed in a dwelling. An offense under this section is a felony of the fourth degree if it is committed in a research facility, power generation facility, waste treatment facility, public sewage facility, water treatment facility, public water facility, nuclear electric generating plant or any facility which stores, generates or handles any hazardous chemical or chemical compounds. Otherwise it is a misdemeanor A.

    b. Defiant trespasser. A person commits a misdemeanor B if, knowing that he is not licensed or privileged to do so, he enters or remains in any place as to which notice against trespass is given by:

        (1) Actual communication to the actor; or

        (2) Posting in a manner prescribed by law or reasonably likely to come to the attention of intruders; or

        (3) Fencing or other enclosure manifestly designed to exclude intruders.

    c. Peering into windows or other openings of dwelling places. A person commits a felony of the fourth degree if, knowing that he is not licensed or privileged to do so, he peers into a window or other opening of a dwelling or other structure adapted for overnight accommodation for the purpose of invading the privacy of another person and under circumstances in which a reasonable person in the dwelling or other structure would not expect to be observed.

    d. Defenses. It is an affirmative defense to prosecution under this section that:

        (1) A structure involved in an offense under subsection a. was abandoned;

(2) The structure was at the time open to members of the public and the actor complied with all lawful conditions imposed on access to or remaining in the structure; or

(3) The actor reasonably believed that the owner of the structure, or other person empowered to license access thereto, would have licensed him to enter or remain, or, in the case of subsection c. of this section, to peer.

PRACTICAL APPLICATION OF STATUTE

Unlicensed Entry of Structures

If Ignacio Marini had no intent to steal the gerbil, or commit any other felony in the Larkspur home he entered, then he would be guilty of fourth degree trespassing rather than burglary. Section 8-3a. sets forth the elements that make it illegal to enter a structure without license or privilege to do so. Key to this offense is the mental state of "knowledge"—the actor must know that he has no right to enter the structure. Criminal trespass is a fourth degree felony if the structure entered is a dwelling, school or facility such as a research facility, power generation facility or public water facility. Otherwise, it is a misdemeanor A.

Ignacio Marini entered the house in Larkspur. He did so by prying open a window and climbing through the vacated space, so he obviously knew he was not licensed to enter this dwelling. Accordingly, had he just remained in the house and watched television (and never stolen the gerbil or committed any other felony), then he would be guilty of fourth degree trespassing.

Defiant Trespass

Per the provisions of 8-3b., Ignacio Marini and his friend, Charles Bigby, are guilty of the misdemeanor B of defiant trespass. This is due to their entry onto the horse farm in face of the posted "No Trespassing" signs.

Defiant trespass covers the many different types of property not enumerated in subsection a. of the statute. A person commits this offense if he enters any property where "notice against trespass is given." Notice can be afforded through actual communication or a posting that is clear. Individuals intending to enter property should also regard fencing (or other similar closures) as notice not to trespass.

The horse farm was clearly marked with "No Trespassing" signs. Ignacio and Charles saw the signs, ignored them and entered the property. Accordingly, they are guilty of defiant trespass, one of the lowest-graded offenses under this Criminal Code as it is a misdemeanor B. Their horse thefts, of course, make them guilty of separate, more serious offenses.

Peering into Windows

Simply stated, one who peers into the windows (or other openings) of a dwelling without permission of the occupants is guilty of a fourth degree felony. Two elements, however, must be present for a conviction—the peering is "for the purpose of invading privacy" and a "reasonable person in the dwelling would not expect to be observed."

An example of this felony is the typical "Peeping Tom." Linda is undressing in her bedroom. Tom climbs a ladder and peeks through the curtains. Tom is guilty of a fourth degree offense under 8-3c.

Defenses

It is important to note that the criminal trespass statute provides specific affirmative defenses to the offenses defined therein. If a structure such as a dwelling or research facility was abandoned at the time of entry, the abandonment is an affirmative defense. Likewise, if the structure was open to members of the public at the time of entry and the actor was not required to leave by any law, then he has an affirmative defense to trespass. Finally, if the actor reasonably believed that he was licensed to enter the property, then he cannot be convicted of an offense under this statute.

8-4.   ### Lands defined

As used in this chapter, "lands" means agricultural or horticultural lands devoted to the production for sale of plants and animals useful to man, encompassing plowed or tilled fields, standing crops or their residues, cranberry bogs and appurtenant dams, dikes, canals, ditches and pump houses, including impoundments, man-made reservoirs and the adjacent shorelines thereto, orchards, nurseries and lands with a maintained fence for the purpose of restraining domestic livestock. "Lands" shall also include lands in agricultural use where public notice prohibiting trespass is given by actual communication to the actor, conspicuous posting or fencing or other enclosure manifestly designed to exclude intruders.

8-5.   ### Knowingly or recklessly operating motor vehicle or riding horseback on lands of another without written permission, or damaging or injuring tangible property

It is a misdemeanor A under this act to:

a. Knowingly or recklessly operate a motorized vehicle or to ride horseback upon the lands of another without obtaining and being in possession of the written permission of the owner, occupant or lessee thereof.

b. Knowingly or recklessly damage or injure any tangible property, including, but not limited to, any fence, building, feedstocks, crops, live trees or any domestic animals, located on the lands of another.

PRACTICAL APPLICATION OF STATUTE

Operating Motor Vehicle/Riding Horseback on Another's Property

This statute is rarely invoked; however, if it is violated, a misdemeanor A has been committed. Simply put, the law is broken where an individual "knowingly" or "recklessly" operates a motor vehicle or rides horseback on another's property without proper permission.

Damaging Tangible Property

Under subsection b. of this statute, an individual can be convicted of a third degree felony, fourth degree felony or misdemeanor A for causing damage to tangible property such as buildings, homes, crops, domestic animals and live trees. The difference among the gradation of offenses is defined in the subsequent statute—8-6—and depends on the monetary amount of damage caused by the defendant. If there is a pecuniary loss of $2,000 or more, a third degree felony has been committed. A fourth degree felony has occurred if damages are between $500 and $2,000, and the defendant is guilty of a misdemeanor A if he causes monetary loss of $500 or less.

This statute is remarkably similar to criminal mischief as set forth in 7-3. A minor difference appears to be in the language "knowingly or *recklessly*" damaging the tangible property of another. Criminal mischief has a subsection that allows for a conviction with a "reckless" mental state, but it requires that the actor damage the tangible property "so as to endanger person or property." The statute here has no such requirement—simply damaging tangible property through reckless behavior renders a person guilty.

8-6.   **Offenses; penalties; restitution**

     a. An offense pursuant to this chapter is a felony of the third degree if the actor causes pecuniary loss of $2,000 or more; a felony of the fourth degree if the actor causes pecuniary loss in excess of $500 but less than $2,000; and a misdemeanor A if he causes pecuniary loss of $500 or less.

     b. In addition to any other sentence which the court may impose, a person convicted of an offense under this act shall be sentenced to make restitution and to pay a fine of not less than $500 if the offense is a felony of the third degree; to pay a fine of not less than $200 if the offense is a felony of the fourth degree; and to pay a fine of not less than $100 when the conviction is of a misdemeanor A.

END OF CHAPTER REVIEW

Multiple-Choice Questions

1. Ignacio Marini used a screwdriver to pry open a screen and illegally enter a home in Larkspur. His purpose of entering the house was to steal a gerbil inside it. What is the *best* offense to charge Marini with?
    a. defiant trespass
    b. burglary
    c. peering into windows
    d. robbery
    e. harassment

2. The primary difference between theft and burglary is:
    a. a theft involves the taking of money
    b. burglary involves wearing a mask
    c. burglary involves entering a structure with the intent to commit an offense once inside
    d. burglary requires surreptitiously gaining access to a dwelling with burglary tools
    e. theft is a felony of the second degree

3. A horse farm is clearly marked with "No Trespassing" signs. Bigby sees the signs, ignores them and enters the farm. Once there, he consumes two cans of cola and a beer. Bigby is guilty of:
    a. defiant trespass
    b. burglary
    c. drinking in public
    d. cola-ascoptemy
    e. partying

4. Alex converses with Ellen on the phone. During their conversation, Ellen tells Alex to come by her house and look into her kitchen window, as she "has a surprise for him." Alex follows her instructions, stops by, looks in her window and sees Ellen, completely naked, baking cookies. Alex is guilty of what offense?
    a. burglary
    b. defiant trespass
    c. fourth degree peering into windows
    d. misdemeanor A of peering into windows
    e. no offense at all

Essay Question

1. Fidel cuts a hole through the roof of Sharon's house in order to sexually assault her. Fidel carries out his plan and rapes Sharon in her bedroom. Has a burglary been committed even though Fidel didn't steal anything from Sharon or her house? Why or why not? Also, identify what elements elevate burglary from a third degree felony to a second degree felony. Cite the specific subsection of the statute that applies.

9

THEFT AND RELATED OFFENSES

9-1.   **Definitions**

In chapters 9 and 10, unless a different meaning plainly is required:

a. "Deprive" means:
    (1) To withhold or cause to be withheld property of another permanently or for so extended a period as to appropriate a substantial portion of its economic value, or with the purpose to restore only upon payment of reward or other compensation; or
    (2) To dispose or cause disposal of the property so as to make it unlikely that the owner will recover it.

b. "Fiduciary" means an executor, general administrator of an intestate, administrator with the will annexed, substituted administrator, guardian, substituted guardian, trustee under any trust, express, implied, resulting or constructive, substituted trustee, executor, conservator, curator, receiver, trustee in bankruptcy, assignee for the benefit of creditors, partner, agent or officer of a corporation, public or private, temporary administrator, administrator, administrator *pendente lite,* administrator *ad prosequendum,* administrator *ad litem* or other person acting in a similar capacity.

c. "Financial institution" means a bank, insurance company, credit union, savings and loan association, investment trust or other organization held out to the public as a place of deposit of funds or medium of savings or collective investment.

d. "Government" means the United States, any state, county, municipality or other political unit, or any department, agency or subdivision of any of the foregoing, or any corporation or other association carrying out the functions of government.

e. "Movable property" means property the location of which can be changed, including things growing on, affixed to or found in land, and documents, although the rights represented thereby have no physical location. "Immovable property" is all other property.

f. "Obtain" means (1) in relation to property, to bring about a transfer or purported transfer of a legal interest in the property, whether to the obtainer or another; or (2) in relation to labor or service, to secure performance thereof.

g. "Property" means anything of value, including real estate, tangible and intangible personal property, trade secrets, contract rights, choses in action and other interests in or claims to wealth, admission or transportation tickets, captured or domestic animals, food and drink, electric, gas, steam or other power, financial instruments, information, data and computer software, in either human readable or computer readable form, copies or originals.

h. "Property of another" includes property in which any person other than the actor has an interest which the actor is not privileged to infringe, regardless of the fact that the actor also has an interest in the property and regardless of the fact that the other person might be precluded from civil recovery because the property was used in an unlawful transaction or was subject to forfeiture as contraband. Property in possession of the actor shall not be deemed property of another who has only a security interest therein, even if legal title is in the creditor pursuant to a conditional sales contract or other security agreement.

i. "Trade secret" means the whole or any portion or phase of any scientific or technical information, design, process, procedure, formula or improvement which is secret and of value. A trade secret shall be presumed to be secret when the owner thereof takes measures to prevent it from becoming available to persons other than those selected by the owner to have access thereto for limited purposes.

j. "Dealer in property" means a person who buys and sells property as a business.

k. "Traffic" means:

   (1) To sell, transfer, distribute, dispense or otherwise dispose of property to another person; or

   (2) To buy, receive, possess or obtain control of or use property, with intent to sell, transfer, distribute, dispense or otherwise dispose of such property to another person.

l. "Broken succession of title" means lack of regular documents of purchase and transfer by any seller except the manufacturer of the subject property, or possession of documents of purchase and transfer by any buyer without corresponding documents of sale and transfer in possession of seller, or possession of documents of sale and transfer by seller without corresponding documents of purchase and transfer in possession of any buyer.

m. "Person" includes any individual or entity or enterprise, as defined herein, holding or capable of holding a legal or beneficial interest in property.

n. "Anything of value" means any direct or indirect gain or advantage to any person.

o. "Interest in property which has been stolen" means title or right of possession to such property.

p. "Stolen property" means property that has been the subject of any unlawful taking.

q. "Enterprise" includes any individual, sole proprietorship, partnership, corporation, business trust, association or other legal entity and any union or group of individuals associated in fact, although not a legal entity, and it includes illicit as well as licit enterprises and governmental as well as other entities.

r. "Attorney General" includes the State Attorney General, his assistants and deputies. The term shall also include a county prosecutor or his designated assistant prosecutor, if a county prosecutor is expressly authorized in writing by the Attorney General to carry out the powers conferred on the Attorney General by this chapter.

s. "Access device" means property consisting of any telephone calling card number, credit card number, account number, mobile identification number, electronic serial number, personal identification number or any other data intended to control or limit access to telecommunications or other computer networks in either human readable or computer readable form, either copy or original, that can be used to obtain telephone service. Access device also means property consisting of a card, code or other means of access to an account held by a financial institution, or any combination thereof, that may be used by the account holder for the purpose of initiating electronic fund transfers.

t. "Defaced access device" means any access device, in either human readable or computer readable form, either copy or original, which has been removed, erased, defaced, altered, destroyed, covered or otherwise changed in any manner from its original configuration.

u. "Domestic companion animal" means any animal commonly referred to as a pet or one that has been bought, bred, raised or otherwise acquired, in accordance with local ordinances and State and federal law, for the primary purpose of providing companionship to the owner, rather than for business or agricultural purposes.

v. "Personal identifying information" means any name, number or other information that may be used, alone or in conjunction with any other information, to identify a specific individual and includes, but is not limited to, the name, address, telephone number, date of birth, social security number, official State issued identification number, employer or taxpayer number, place of employment, employee identification number, demand deposit account number, savings account number, credit card number, mother's maiden name, unique biometric data, such as fingerprint, voice print, retina or iris image or other unique physical representation, or unique electronic identification number, address or routing code of the individual.

9-1.1. Offense involving access device; presumption of unlawful purpose

In any prosecution for an offense enumerated in chapter 9 of the Criminal Code involving a defaced access device, any removal, erasure, defacement, alteration, destruction, covering or other change in such access device from its original configuration performed by any person other than an authorized manufacturer of, or service provider to, access devices shall be presumed to be for an unlawful purpose.

9-2. Consolidation of theft offenses; grading; provisions applicable to theft generally

a. Consolidation of theft and computer criminal activity offenses. Conduct denominated theft or computer criminal activity in this chapter constitutes a single offense, but each episode or transaction may be the subject of a separate prosecution and conviction. A charge of theft or computer criminal activity may be supported by evidence that it was committed in any manner that would be theft or computer criminal activity under this chapter, notwithstanding the specification of a different manner in the indictment or accusation, subject only to the power of the court to ensure fair trial by granting a bill of particulars, discovery, a continuance or other appropriate relief where the conduct of the defense would be prejudiced by lack of fair notice or by surprise.

b. Grading of theft offenses.

(1) Theft constitutes a felony of the second degree if:

(a) The amount involved is $75,000 or more;

(b) The property is taken by extortion;

(c) The property stolen is a controlled dangerous substance or controlled substance analog and the quantity is in excess of one kilogram;

(d) The property stolen is a person's benefits under federal or state law, or from any other source, which the Department of Human Services or an agency acting on its behalf has budgeted for the person's health care and the amount involved is $75,000 or more; or

(e) The property stolen is human remains or any part thereof.

(2) Theft constitutes a felony of the third degree if:

(a) The amount involved exceeds $500 but is less than $75,000;

(b) The property stolen is a firearm, motor vehicle, vessel, boat, horse, domestic companion animal or airplane;

(c) The property stolen is a controlled dangerous substance or controlled substance analog and the amount involved is less than $75,000 or is undetermined and the quantity is one kilogram or less;

     (d) It is from the person of the victim;

     (e) It is in breach of an obligation by a person in his capacity as a fiduciary;

     (f) It is by threat not amounting to extortion;

     (g) It is of a public record, writing or instrument kept, filed or deposited according to law with or in the keeping of any public office or public servant;

     (h) The property stolen is a person's benefits under federal or state law, or from any other source, which the Department of Human Services or an agency acting on its behalf has budgeted for the person's health care and the amount involved is less than $75,000;

     (i) The property stolen is any real or personal property related to, necessary for or derived from research, regardless of value, including, but not limited to, any sample, specimens and components thereof, research subject, including any warm-blooded or cold-blooded animals being used for research or intended for use in research, supplies, records, data or test results, prototypes or equipment, as well as any proprietary information or other type of information related to research;

     (j) The property stolen is a State prescription blank;

     (k) The property stolen consists of an access device or a defaced access device; or

     (l) The property stolen consists of anhydrous ammonia and the actor intends it to be used to manufacture methamphetamine.

  (3) Theft constitutes a felony of the fourth degree if the amount involved is at least $200 but does not exceed $500. If the amount involved was less than $200, the offense constitutes a misdemeanor A.

  (4) The amount involved in a theft or computer criminal activity shall be determined by the trier of fact. The amount shall include, but shall not be limited to, the amount of any State tax avoided, evaded or otherwise unpaid, improperly retained or disposed of. Amounts involved in thefts or computer criminal activities committed pursuant to one scheme or course of conduct, whether from the same person or several persons, may be aggregated in determining the grade of the offense.

c. Claim of right. It is an affirmative defense to prosecution for theft that the actor:

  (1) Was unaware that the property or service was that of another;

  (2) Acted under an honest claim of right to the property or service involved or that he had a right to acquire or dispose of it as he did; or

  (3) Took property exposed for sale, intending to purchase and pay for it promptly, or reasonably believing that the owner, if present, would have consented.

d. Theft from spouse. It is no defense that theft or computer criminal activity was from or committed against the actor's spouse, except that misappropriation of household and personal effects, or other property normally accessible to both spouses, is theft or computer criminal activity only if it occurs after the parties have ceased living together.

PRACTICAL APPLICATION OF STATUTE

Grading of Theft Offenses

Theft can be a second, third or fourth degree felony, as well as a misdemeanor A. The grading differences are primarily determined by the pecuniary loss suffered but also may be the consequence of other substantive matters.

An individual who commits a theft involving a pecuniary loss of $75,000 or more is guilty of second degree theft. Similarly, if the property is taken by extortion or if a person steals over one kilogram of a controlled dangerous substance (CDS), he is guilty of a second degree felony. The theft of human remains is also a felony of the second degree.

Third degree thefts include the theft of firearms, motor vehicles, boats, airplanes, dogs, cats and other domestic companion animals. Also, thefts from the person (purse snatching), CDS under a kilogram in weight and blank prescription pads are third degree felonies. If the amount involved in any theft exceeds $500 but is less than $75,000, a felony of the third degree has been committed.

A fourth degree theft has occurred when the amount involved is between $200 and $500. It is a misdemeanor A when an actor has stolen matter with a value less than $200. Particular types of theft offenses will be discussed in detail in the Practical Application sections following each category in this chapter (e.g., theft of services, theft by deception).

9-3.

Theft by unlawful taking or disposition

a. Movable property. A person is guilty of theft if he unlawfully takes, or exercises unlawful control over, movable property of another with the purpose to deprive him thereof.

b. Immovable property. A person is guilty of theft if he unlawfully transfers any interest in immovable property of another with the purpose to benefit himself or another not entitled thereto.

PRACTICAL APPLICATION OF STATUTE

Movable Property

Ignacio Marini's theft of the convertible Mercedes is a theft of movable property by unlawful taking. This theft would normally be a third degree felony, as thefts of motor vehicles automatically are graded as third degree offenses. However, it is a second degree offense here because the value of the automobile exceeds $75,000—the Mercedes was worth $85,000 at the time it was unlawfully taken.

Other movable property stolen by Ignacio included two kilograms of cocaine, a pound of marijuana and the gerbil. The theft of the cocaine is a second degree offense because it is a CDS that exceeds one kilogram in weight; the marijuana heist is a felony of the third degree because its weight is less than one kilogram. The gerbil theft is also a third degree theft, as a gerbil is a domestic companion animal.

Under all of the above circumstances, Ignacio is guilty of theft by unlawful taking under section 9-3a. This is because he unlawfully heisted the movable property with the purpose to deprive the owner of it.

Immovable Property

Thefts of immovable property include the transfer of health benefits and titles in real estate property. The seriousness of the offense depends on the amount of pecuniary loss involved in the theft.

9-4.   **Theft by deception**

A person is guilty of theft if he purposely obtains property of another by deception. A person deceives if he purposely:

a. Creates or reinforces a false impression, including false impressions as to law, value, intention or other state of mind, and including, but not limited to, a false impression that the person is soliciting or collecting funds for a charitable purpose; but deception as to a person's intention to perform a promise shall not be inferred from the fact alone that he did not subsequently perform the promise;

b. Prevents another from acquiring information which would affect his judgment of a transaction; or

c. Fails to correct a false impression which the deceiver previously created or reinforced, or which the deceiver knows to be influencing another to whom he stands in a fiduciary or confidential relationship.

The term "deceive" does not, however, include falsity as to matters having no pecuniary significance or puffing or exaggeration by statements unlikely to deceive ordinary persons in the group addressed.

PRACTICAL APPLICATION OF STATUTE

For his theft of a $52,500 check from Alzheimer's sufferer Fanny Moses, Ignacio Marini should be charged with theft by deception. This is a felony of the third degree because the pecuniary loss involved exceeds $500 but is less than $75,000.

Theft by deception in its simplest sense involves deceiving another in order to obtain items of value. Under subsection a., an actor deceives if he "creates or reinforces a false impression." Under subsection b., he deceives if he "prevents another from acquiring information which would affect his judgment of a transaction." Finally, per subsection c., a deception has occurred if the con man "fails to correct a false impression" that he previously created or if he knows that the false impression is "influencing another to whom he stands in a fiduciary or confidential duty."

Ignacio Marini's guilt lies in deceptive behavior best defined in subsection a. of the statute. Posing as the Falkner tax collector, Ignacio advised 73-year-old Fanny Moses that she was $52,500 in arrears in her property taxes. Ignacio created a false impression as to his identity—he was actually not the town's tax collector—and he created a false impression as to Ms. Moses' property taxes—she was not in any arrears. Ignacio's ultimate receipt of Moses' $52,500 check, therefore, constitutes a theft by deception.

The fact that Ms. Moses suffered from Alzheimer's disease only makes his felony that much more egregious. That negates any defense that his statements would be unlikely to deceive an ordinary person in her situation.

9-5.   **Theft by extortion**

A person is guilty of theft by extortion if he purposely and unlawfully obtains property of another by extortion. A person extorts if he purposely threatens to:

a. Inflict bodily injury on or physically confine or restrain anyone or commit any other criminal offense;

b. Accuse anyone of an offense or cause charges of an offense to be instituted against any person;

   c. Expose or publicize any secret or any asserted fact, whether true or false, tending to subject any person to hatred, contempt or ridicule or to impair his credit or business repute;

   d. Take or withhold action as an official, or cause an official to take or withhold action;

   e. Bring about or continue a strike, boycott or other collective action, if the property is not demanded or received for the benefit of the group in whose interest the actor purports to act;

   f. Testify or provide information or withhold testimony or information with respect to another's legal claim or defense; or

   g. Inflict any other harm which would not substantially benefit the actor but which is calculated to materially harm another person.

It is an affirmative defense to prosecution based on paragraphs b, c, d or f that the property obtained was honestly claimed as restitution or indemnification for harm done in the circumstances or as lawful compensation for property or services.

PRACTICAL APPLICATION OF STATUTE

Sandy Jerusalem is the victim of theft by extortion arising out of Ignacio Marini's taking of his gold pinky ring. This theft is automatically a second degree felony, regardless of the pecuniary value of the ring, because it was stolen through extortion measures.

In order to be guilty of theft by extortion, the defendant's actions must be "purposeful." A defendant extorts if he purposely threatens matters such as inflicting bodily injury, accusing another of a criminal offense or exposing a secret that would subject another to hatred, contempt or ridicule.

Ignacio appeared at Sandy Jerusalem's home with the intent to steal his gold pinky ring—one of the items Ignacio determined to obtain as a birthday present for himself. Ignacio told Jerusalem, "Kindly turn over your gold pinky ring to me or I will advise the media that you regularly frequent a nudist camp in Baja." Jerusalem, in turn, handed over the ring. Ignacio's purposeful threat certainly would expose a secret that would subject Jerusalem to public contempt and ridicule. Accordingly, this is theft by extortion, and even though the value of the ring was only $3,500, it is a second degree offense.

9-6.   **Theft of property lost, mislaid, or delivered by mistake**

A person who comes into control of property of another that he knows to have been lost, mislaid or delivered under a mistake as to the nature or amount of the property or the identity of the recipient is guilty of theft if, knowing the identity of the owner and with the purpose to deprive said owner thereof, he converts the property to his own use.

PRACTICAL APPLICATION OF STATUTE

The correct charge for Ignacio Marini's depositing of his uncle's insurance check is under section 9-6, as he took control of a check that was delivered to him by mistake. This is a third degree felony because the amount of the check was $25,000—in excess of $500 but less than $75,000.

This statute makes the taking of property illegal where the actor knows that the property was lost, mislaid or delivered by mistake *and* where he knows the identity of the owner. Also, the actor must convert the property to his own use with the "purpose" to deprive the owner of it.

A $25,000 insurance check was delivered to Ignacio by mistake. The true recipient of the check was supposed to be Ignacio's uncle and Ignacio knew this. With the purpose to deprive his uncle of the proceeds of the check, Ignacio deposited the funds into his personal bank account. Accordingly, he is guilty of theft under 9-6.

9-7.   **Receiving stolen property**

    a. Receiving. A person is guilty of theft if he knowingly receives or brings into this State movable property of another knowing that it has been stolen or believing that it is probably stolen. It is an affirmative defense that the property was received with the purpose to restore it to the owner. "Receiving" means acquiring possession, control or title or lending on the security of the property.

    b. Presumption of knowledge. The requisite knowledge or belief is presumed in the case of a person who:

        (1) Is found in possession or control of two or more items of property stolen on two or more separate occasions; or

        (2) Has received stolen property in another transaction within the year preceding the transaction charged; or

        (3) Being a person in the business of buying or selling property of the sort received, acquires the property without having ascertained by reasonable inquiry that the person from whom he obtained it had a legal right to possess and dispose of it; or

        (4) Is found in possession of two or more defaced access devices.

PRACTICAL APPLICATION OF STATUTE

Generally

Ignacio Marini should be convicted of theft under section 9-7 for his receipt of a television set he knew to be stolen. Since the television set's value was more than $500 but less than $75,000, this is a third degree felony.

A person is guilty of receiving stolen property if "he knowingly receives or brings into this State movable property of another knowing that it has been stolen or believing that it is probably stolen." Ignacio's best friend, Charles Bigby, gave him a brand-new 32-inch color television set, valued at $1,000, as a birthday present. Charles told Ignacio, "It's a little hot, but I chiseled off the serial numbers. Enjoy." Ignacio knowingly received the television set, which he knew was stolen. With this being the case, Ignacio is guilty of receiving stolen property, a third degree theft offense given the TV's $1,000 value.

Presumption of Knowledge

It is important to note that the receiving stolen property statute provides that there is a "presumption of knowledge" (that the property is stolen) under certain circumstances. Per subsection b. of the statute, a person is "presumed" to know—or believe—that an item is probably stolen in four scenarios.

An example where knowledge of stolen property is presumed is as follows. Mark the Manipulator is in the pawnbroker business. He regularly buys items of jewelry, television sets, stereo systems and home appliances. Jerry, a man who Mark knows to be a drug addict, stops by his store with a diamond ring. Mark asks Jerry neither for proof of ownership of the ring (e.g., a receipt or warranty) nor the location where he obtained the ring. Mark simply buys the ring from Jerry. The ring turns out to be stolen.

Section 9-7b.(3) provides that knowledge or belief is presumed in the case of a person who, "being a person in the business of buying or selling property of the sort received, acquires the property without having ascertained by reasonable inquiry that the person from whom he obtained it had a legal right to possess or dispose of it." Mark was in the business of buying diamond rings. When Jerry attempted to sell the diamond ring to him, Mark did not make any reasonable inquiry into whether Jerry had a legal right to possess or dispose of the ring. Accordingly, per subsection b.(3), Mark may be "presumed" to have knowledge that the diamond ring was stolen.

9-7.1.   Fencing

    a. Possession of altered property. Any dealer in property who knew or should have known that the identifying features such as serial numbers and permanently affixed labels of property in his possession have been removed or altered without the consent of the manufacturer is guilty of possession of altered property. It is a defense to a prosecution under this subsection that a person lawfully possesses the usual indicia of ownership in addition to mere possession.

    b. Dealing in stolen property. A person is guilty of dealing in stolen property if he traffics in or initiates, organizes, plans, finances, directs, manages or supervises trafficking in stolen property.

    c. The value of the property involved in the violation of this section shall be determined by the trier of fact. The value of the property involved in the violation of this section may be aggregated in determining the grade of the offense where the acts or conduct constituting a violation was committed pursuant to one scheme or course of conduct, whether from the same person or several persons.

    d. It is an affirmative defense to a prosecution under this section that the actor:

        (1) Was unaware that the property or service was that of another;

        (2) Acted under an honest claim of right to the property or service involved or that he had a right to acquire or dispose of it as he did.

    e. In addition to the presumptions contained in 9-7b., the following presumptions are available in the prosecution for a fencing offense:

        (1) Proof of the purchase or sale of property at a price substantially below its fair market value, unless satisfactorily explained, gives rise to an inference that the person buying or selling the property knew that it had been stolen;

        (2) Proof of the purchase or sale of property by a dealer in that property, out of the regular course of business, or without the usual indicia of ownership other than mere possession, or the property or the job lot of which it is a part was bought, received, possessed or controlled in broken succession of title so that it cannot be traced, by appropriate documents, in unbroken succession to the manufacturer, in all cases where the regular course of business reasonably indicates records of purchase, transfer or sale, unless satisfactorily explained, gives rise to an inference that the person buying or selling the property knew that it had been stolen; and

        (3) Proof that a person buying or selling property of the sort received obtained such property without having ascertained by reasonable inquiry that the person from whom he obtained it had a legal right to possess or control it gives rise to an inference that such person knew that it had been stolen.

PRACTICAL APPLICATION OF STATUTE

Franz Bellenwood, Ignacio's intended fence for his stolen television set, is guilty of a third degree felony as the value of the TV was $1,000. Bellenwood's guilt is predicated on his personal knowledge that the television was stolen; however, knowledge could be imputed to him, under 9-7.1, for a variety of reasons.

The fencing statute differs from receiving stolen property in that it specifically prohibits criminal behavior involving "dealers"—individuals who sell property for a living. Subsection a. of the statute makes it illegal for a dealer to possess property that he "knows or should have known" has identifying features (such as serial numbers) that have been altered. Subsection b., the more serious component of the statute, sets forth the elements that make a dealer guilty of "dealing" in stolen property. If he "traffics in or initiates, organizes, plans, finances, directs, manages or supervises trafficking in stolen property," he has violated subsection b. of the fencing statute.

Franz Bellenwood is guilty of fencing under subsection b. of the statute. Ignacio met Bellenwood at his place of business. He explained to Bellenwood that the TV had defaced serial numbers and that he wished to sell it to him. Bellenwood responded by bringing Ignacio to the basement of the business where numerous stolen appliances, with defaced serial numbers, were maintained. There, the television set was exchanged for a one-half-carat diamond earring. Given that Bellenwood obviously engaged in a business of dealing in stolen property, he is guilty of a third degree felony under 9-7.1b.

Law enforcement officers charging under 9-7.1 should take note that subsection e. of the statute provides the prosecution with several "presumptions of knowledge" that the items in question were stolen. For example, e.(1) provides that if property is either purchased or sold at a price "substantially below its fair market value," there is a presumption that the dealer knew the property was stolen. This presumption of knowledge exists unless the dealer can "satisfactorily explain" the low purchase cost or sale price. While these presumptions should certainly be taken into consideration by law enforcement personnel investigating individuals and charging pursuant to the statute, the ultimate determination of "knowledge" is a legal question and will be determined by the trier of fact—a jury or judge.

9-8.

Theft of services

a. A person is guilty of theft if he purposely obtains services which he knows are available only for compensation, by deception or threat, or by false token, slug or other means, including but not limited to mechanical or electronic devices or through fraudulent statements, to avoid payment for the service. "Services" includes labor or professional service; transportation, telephone, telecommunications, electric, water, gas, cable television or other public service; accommodation in hotels, restaurants or elsewhere; entertainment; admission to exhibitions; use of vehicles or other movable property. Where compensation for service is ordinarily paid immediately upon the rendering of such service, as in the case of hotels and restaurants, absconding without payment or offer to pay gives rise to a presumption that the service was obtained by deception as to intention to pay.

b. A person commits theft if, having control over the disposition of services of another, to which he is not entitled, he knowingly diverts such services to his own benefit or to the benefit of another not entitled thereto.

c. Any person who, without permission and for the purpose of obtaining electric current, gas or water with intent to defraud any vendor of electricity, gas or water or a person who is furnished by a vendor with electric current, gas or water:

   (1) Connects or causes to be connected by wire or any other device with the wires, cables or conductors of any such vendor or any other person; or

   (2) Connects or disconnects the meters, pipes or conduits of such vendor or any other person or in any other manner tampers or interferes with such meters, pipes or conduits or connects with such meters, pipes or conduits by pipes, conduits or other instruments—is guilty of a misdemeanor A.

      The existence of any of the conditions with reference to meters, pipes, conduits or attachments, described in this subsection, is presumptive evidence that the person to whom gas, electricity or water is at the time being furnished by or through such meters, pipes, conduits or attachments has, with intent to defraud, created or caused to be created with reference to such meters, pipes, conduits or attachments the condition so existing; provided, however, that the presumption shall not apply to any person so furnished with gas, electricity or water for less than 31 days or until there has been at least one meter reading.

      A violation of this subsection shall be deemed to be a continuing offense as long as the conditions described in this subsection exist.

d. Any person who, without permission or authority, connects or causes to be connected by wires or other devices any meter erected or set up for the purpose of registering or recording the amount of electric current supplied to any customer by any vendor of electricity within this State, or changes or shunts the wiring leading to or from any such meter, or by any device, appliance or means whatsoever tampers with any such meter so that the meter will not measure or record the full amount of electric current supplied to such customer is guilty of a misdemeanor A.

      The existence of any of the conditions with reference to meters or attachments described in this subsection is presumptive evidence that the person to whom electricity is at the time being furnished by or through such meters or attachments has, with intent to defraud, created or caused to be created, with reference to such meters or attachments, the condition so existing; provided, however, that the presumption shall not apply to any person so furnished with electricity for less than 31 days or until there has been at least one meter reading.

      A violation of this subsection shall be deemed to be a continuing offense as long as the conditions described in this subsection exist.

e. Any person who, with intent to obtain cable television service without payment, in whole or in part, of the lawful charges therefor, or with intent to deprive another of the lawful receipt of such service, damages, cuts, tampers with, installs, taps or makes any connection with, or who displaces, removes, injures or destroys any wire, cable, conduit, apparatus or equipment of a cable television company operating a CATV system; or who, without authority of a cable television company, intentionally prevents, obstructs or delays, by any means or contrivance, the sending, transmission, conveyance, distribution or receipt of programming material carried by equipment of the cable television company operating a CATV system is guilty of a misdemeanor A.

      The existence of any of the conditions with reference to wires, cables, conduits, apparatus or equipment described in this subsection is presumptive evidence that the person to whom cable television service is at the time being furnished has, with intent to obtain cable television service without authorization or compensation or to otherwise defraud, created or caused to be created the condition so existing.

f. Any person who purposely or knowingly manufactures, constructs, sells, offers for sale, distributes or installs any equipment, device or instrument designed or intended to facilitate the interception, decoding or receipt of any cable television service with intent to obtain such service and avoid the lawful payment of the charges therefor to the provider, in whole or in part, is guilty of a misdemeanor A.

Any communications paraphernalia prohibited under this subsection shall be subject to forfeiture and may be seized by the State or any law enforcement officer.

g. Any person who purposely or knowingly maintains or possesses any equipment, device or instrument of the type described in subsection f. of this section or maintains or possesses any equipment, device or instrument actually used to facilitate the interception, decoding or receipt of any cable television service with intent to obtain such service and avoid the lawful payment, in whole or in part, of the charges therefor to the provider, is guilty of a misdemeanor A.

Any communications paraphernalia prohibited under this subsection shall be subject to forfeiture and may be seized by the State or any law enforcement officer.

h. Any person who, with the intent of depriving a telephone company of its lawful charges therefor, purposely or knowingly makes use of any telecommunications service by means of the unauthorized use of any electronic or mechanical device or connection, or by the unauthorized use of billing information, or by the use of a computer, computer equipment or computer software, or by the use of misidentifying or misleading information given to a representative of the telephone company is guilty of a felony of the third degree.

The existence of any of the conditions with reference to electronic or mechanical devices, computers, computer equipment or computer software described in this subsection is presumptive evidence that the person to whom telecommunications service is at the time being furnished has, with intent to obtain telecommunications service without authorization or compensation or to otherwise defraud, created or caused to be created the condition so existing.

i. Any person who purposely or knowingly manufactures, constructs, sells, offers for sale, distributes, installs or otherwise provides any service, equipment, device, computer, computer equipment, computer software or instrument designed or intended to facilitate the receipt of any telecommunications service and avoid the lawful payment of the charges therefor to the provider, in whole or in part, is guilty of a felony of the third degree.

Any communications paraphernalia, computer, computer equipment or computer software prohibited under this subsection shall be subject to forfeiture and may be seized by the State or any law enforcement officer.

j. Any person who purposely or knowingly maintains or possesses any equipment, device, computer, computer equipment, computer software or instrument of the type described in subsection i. of this section, or maintains or possesses any equipment, device, computer, computer equipment, computer software or instrument actually used to facilitate the receipt of any telecommunications service with intent to obtain such service and avoid the lawful payment, in whole or in part, of the charges therefor to the provider, is guilty of a felony of the third degree.

Any communications paraphernalia, computer, computer equipment or computer software prohibited under this subsection shall be subject to forfeiture and may be seized by the State or any law enforcement officer.

k. In addition to any other disposition authorized by law, every person who violates this section shall be sentenced to make restitution to the vendor and to pay a minimum fine of $500 for each offense. In determining the amount of restitution, the court shall consider the costs expended by the vendor, including but not limited to the repair and replacement of damaged equipment, the cost of the services unlawfully obtained, investigation expenses and attorney fees.

l. The presumptions of evidence applicable to offenses defined in subsections c., d., e. and h. of this section shall also apply in any prosecution for theft of services brought pursuant to the provisions of subsection a. or b. of this section.

PRACTICAL APPLICATION OF STATUTE

The appropriate charge for Ignacio Marini's trickery with the lawn mower repair shop owner is theft of services. Given that the total owed, but never recovered, was $165, this theft constitutes a misdemeanor A.

Although 9-8 is a statute containing considerable language, it primarily provides that a person is guilty of theft of services if he fraudulently dupes another to provide labor or services—with no intention to pay for said services. Basically, any services stolen through deception will result in a conviction under this statute; however, many items are specifically enumerated, including professional services (e.g., lawyers, doctors), transportation, telecommunications, restaurants, hotels and entertainment. Subsections c., d., e., f., g., h., i. and j. set forth special provisions for thefts involving gas, electric, cable television and telecommunications services.

Ignacio Marini didn't rip off any large private corporation or government agency in order to obtain repairs to his lawn mower. He did, however, defraud a small business owner. Posing as a Rickert Park councilman, Ignacio asked to have his lawn mower repaired—and to thereafter have an invoice sent to his home. Ignacio, of course, was not a Rickert Park councilman, nor did he ever intend to pay the bill. Accordingly, since he deceived the business owner, causing him to provide services that were never paid for, Ignacio Marini is guilty of theft of services.

9-9.   **Theft by failure to make required disposition of property received**

A person who purposely obtains or retains property upon agreement or subject to a known legal obligation to make specified payment or other disposition, whether from such property or its proceeds or from his own property to be reserved in equivalent amount, is guilty of theft if he deals with the property obtained as his own and fails to make the required payment or disposition. The foregoing applies notwithstanding that it may be impossible to identify particular property as belonging to the victim at the time of the actor's failure to make the required payment or disposition. An officer or employee of the government or of a financial institution is presumed (a) to know any legal obligation relevant to his criminal liability under this section and (b) to have dealt with the property as his own if he fails to pay or account upon lawful demand or if an audit reveals a shortage or falsification of accounts. The fact that any payment or other disposition was made with a subsequently dishonored negotiable instrument shall constitute *prima facie* evidence of the actor's failure to make the required payment or disposition, and the trier of fact may draw a permissive inference therefrom that the actor did not intend to make the required payment or other disposition.

PRACTICAL APPLICATION OF STATUTE

Theft by failure to make required disposition is predicated on the mental state of "purpose." One who "purposely" obtains or retains property by a known agreement to make payment (a disposition) is guilty of theft under this statute if he maintains the property as his own and fails to make the disposition. Ignacio Marini is guilty of theft per the elements of 9-9 for his taking of the prize moose from the farm owner.

Ignacio and the owner of the horse farm shook hands on a deal that required Ignacio to make four payments of $1,000 in exchange for the prize moose. The farm owner delivered on his promise and provided Ignacio with the moose; Ignacio took the moose, never intending to make the required payments for the animal. Given that he "purposely" obtained this property—the prize moose—by a known agreement to make a disposition (four payments of $1,000) and thereafter retained the moose without ever making the payments, he is guilty of theft under 9-9. This is a third degree felony, as the amount of money involved exceeds $500 but is less than $75,000.

9-10.   **Unlawful taking of means of conveyance**

   a. A person commits a misdemeanor A if, with the purpose to withhold temporarily from the owner, he takes, operates or exercises control over any means of conveyance, other than a motor vehicle, without consent of the owner or other person authorized to give consent. "Means of conveyance" includes but is not limited to motor vehicles, bicycles, motorized bicycles, boats, horses, vessels, surfboards, rafts, skimobiles, airplanes, trains, trams and trailers. It is an affirmative defense to prosecution under subsections a., b. and c. of this section that the actor reasonably believed that the owner or any other person authorized to give consent would have consented to the operation had he known of it.

   b. A person commits a felony of the fourth degree if, with the purpose to withhold temporarily from the owner, he takes, operates or exercises control over a motor vehicle without the consent of the owner or other person authorized to give consent.

   c. A person commits a felony of the third degree if, with the purpose to withhold temporarily from the owner, he takes, operates or exercises control over a motor vehicle without the consent of the owner or other person authorized to give consent and operates the motor vehicle in a manner that creates a risk of injury to any person or a risk of damage to property.

   d. A person commits a felony of the fourth degree if he enters and rides in a motor vehicle knowing that the motor vehicle has been taken or is being operated without the consent of the owner or other person authorized to consent.

PRACTICAL APPLICATION OF STATUTE

Theft of Means of Conveyance

Ignacio Marini is guilty of the third degree felony of unlawful taking of a means of conveyance for his taking of the pickup truck from Mickey's Auto Body Shop. This is not considered a normal auto theft given the "temporary" taking of the motor vehicle. In Ignacio's case, the felony reaches the third degree level only because he drove the automobile in a manner that created a "risk of injury" to others.

Pursuant to subsection c. of 9-10, a person who purposely "temporarily" withholds or operates another's motor vehicle without consent is guilty of a third degree felony if he operates the vehicle "in a manner that creates a risk of injury to any person or a risk of damage to property." After stealing cocaine and marijuana from Mickey, Ignacio and Charles drove away in a pickup truck owned by one of Mickey's customers. They did not have the owner's consent to drive the vehicle. Laughing raucously as they counted their heisted money and drugs, Ignacio ran stop signs and drove at excessive speeds. During this rampage, he even sideswiped two parked cars. The siege of the truck, though, lasted merely 15 minutes.

Here, all elements of the offense have been met. The pickup truck was only heisted "temporarily" (15 minutes)—but it was taken without the owner's consent. In addition, Ignacio's driving clearly put other people at risk of injury, and he actually caused property damage. Accordingly, he is guilty of a third degree felony under 9-10c.

It is interesting to note that under subsection b. of the statute, if Ignacio had not driven in this "risky" manner, he would only be guilty of a fourth degree felony. Also, per subsection a., if he had taken a means of conveyance other than a motor vehicle (e.g., a bike or horse), he would be guilty of only a misdemeanor A.

Knowingly Riding in Motor Vehicle That Is Being Operated Without Owner's Consent

Per subsection d. of 9-10, an individual is guilty of a fourth degree felony if he "knowingly" rides in a motor vehicle that is being operated without the owner's consent. Given that Charles "knew" that he and Ignacio were driving in the pickup truck without the owner's consent, he is guilty of this fourth degree offense.

9-11.   **Shoplifting**

a. Definitions. The following definitions apply to this section:

(1) "Shopping cart" means those push carts of the type or types which are commonly provided by grocery stores, drug stores or other retail mercantile establishments for the use of the public in transporting commodities in stores and markets and, incidentally, from the stores to a place outside the store;

(2) Store or other retail mercantile establishment" means a place where merchandise is displayed, held, stored or sold or offered to the public for sale;

(3) "Merchandise" means any goods, chattels, foodstuffs or wares of any type and description, regardless of the value thereof;

(4) "Merchant" means any owner or operator of any store or other retail mercantile establishment or any agent, servant, employee, lessee, consignee, officer, director, franchisee or independent contractor of such owner or proprietor;

(5) "Person" means any individual or individuals, including an agent, servant or employee of a merchant where the facts of the situation so require;

(6) "Conceal" means to conceal merchandise so that, although there may be some notice of its presence, it is not visible through ordinary observation;

(7) "Full retail value" means the merchant's stated or advertised price of the merchandise;

(8) "Premises of a store or retail mercantile establishment" means and includes but is not limited to, the retail mercantile establishment; any common use areas in shopping centers and all parking areas set aside by a merchant or on behalf of a merchant for the parking of vehicles for the convenience of the patrons of such retail mercantile establishment;

(9) "Under-ring" means to cause the cash register or other sale recording device to reflect less than the full retail value of the merchandise;

(10) "Antishoplifting or inventory control device countermeasure" means any item or device which is designed, manufactured, modified or altered to defeat any antishoplifting or inventory control device.

b. Shoplifting. Shoplifting shall consist of any one or more of the following acts:

(1) For any person purposely to take possession of, carry away, transfer or cause to be carried away or transferred any merchandise displayed, held, stored or offered for

sale by any store or other retail mercantile establishment with the intention of depriving the merchant of the possession, use or benefit of such merchandise or converting the same to the use of such person without paying to the merchant the full retail value thereof.

(2) For any person purposely to conceal upon his person or otherwise any merchandise offered for sale by any store or other retail mercantile establishment with the intention of depriving the merchant of the processes, use or benefit of such merchandise or converting the same to the use of such person without paying to the merchant the value thereof.

(3) For any person purposely to alter, transfer or remove any label, price tag or marking indicia of value or any other markings which aid in determining value affixed to any merchandise displayed, held, stored or offered for sale by any store or other retail mercantile establishment and to attempt to purchase such merchandise personally or in consort with another at less than the full retail value with the intention of depriving the merchant of all or some part of the value thereof.

(4) For any person purposely to transfer any merchandise displayed, held, stored or offered for sale by any store or other retail merchandise establishment from the container in or on which the same shall be displayed to any other container with intent to deprive the merchant of all or some part of the retail value thereof.

(5) For any person purposely to under-ring with the intention of depriving the merchant of the full retail value thereof.

(6) For any person purposely to remove a shopping cart from the premises of a store or other retail mercantile establishment without the consent of the merchant given at the time of such removal with the intention of permanently depriving the merchant of the possession, use or benefit of such cart.

c. Gradation.

(1) Shoplifting constitutes a felony of the second degree under subsection b. of this section if the full retail value of the merchandise is $75,000 or more.

(2) Shoplifting constitutes a felony of the third degree under subsection b. of this section if the full retail value of the merchandise exceeds $500 but is less than $75,000.

(3) Shoplifting constitutes a felony of the fourth degree under subsection b. of this section if the full retail value of the merchandise is at least $200 but does not exceed $500.

(4) Shoplifting is a misdemeanor A under subsection b. of this section if the full retail value of the merchandise is less than $200. Additionally, any person convicted of a shoplifting offense shall be sentenced to perform community service as follows: for a first offense, at least ten days of community service; for a second offense, at least 15 days of community service; and for a third or subsequent offense, a maximum of 25 days of community service and any person convicted of a third or subsequent shoplifting offense shall serve a minimum term of imprisonment of not less than 90 days.

d. Presumptions. Any person purposely concealing unpurchased merchandise of any store or other retail mercantile establishment, either on the premises or outside the premises of such store or other retail mercantile establishment, shall be *prima facie* presumed to have so concealed such merchandise with the intention of depriving the merchant of the possession, use or benefit of such merchandise without paying the full retail value thereof, and the finding of such merchandise concealed upon the person or among the belongings of such person shall be *prima facie* evidence of purposeful concealment; and if such person conceals, or causes to be concealed, such merchandise upon the person or among the belongings of another, the finding of the same shall also be *prima facie* evidence of willful concealment on the part of the person so concealing such merchandise.

e. A law enforcement officer, a special officer or a merchant, who has probable cause for believing that a person has willfully concealed unpurchased merchandise and that he can recover the merchandise by taking the person into custody, may, for the purpose of attempting to effect recovery thereof, take the person into custody and detain him in a reasonable manner for not more than a reasonable time, and the taking into custody by a law enforcement officer or special officer or merchant shall not render such person criminally or civilly liable in any manner or to any extent whatsoever.

Any law enforcement officer may arrest without warrant any person he has probable cause for believing has committed the offense of shoplifting as defined in this section.

A merchant who causes the arrest of a person for shoplifting, as provided for in this section, shall not be criminally or civilly liable in any manner or to any extent whatsoever where the merchant has probable cause for believing that the person arrested committed the offense of shoplifting.

f. Any person who possesses or uses any antishoplifting or inventory control device countermeasure within any store or other retail mercantile establishment is guilty of a misdemeanor A.

PRACTICAL APPLICATION OF STATUTE

Shoplifting

Shoplifting isn't just stealing candy, batteries and T-shirts. The offense actually ranges from a misdemeanor A all the way to a second degree felony—this range depends on the amount of monetary loss involved in the theft. In the case of Ignacio Marini, however, he is only guilty of the lowest level shoplifting offense as he merely took a box of Devil Dogs from his local supermarket.

Subsection b. of the statute enumerates the different types of acts that constitute shoplifting. They include the following: taking/carrying away merchandise offered for sale (b.(1)); concealing merchandise (b.(2)); altering price tags (b.(3)); transferring merchandise from one container to another (b.(4)); under-ringing at the register (b.(5)); and removing a shopping cart from a store (b.(6)). All forms of shoplifting require that the thief act "purposely."

Ignacio Marini could appropriately be charged with shoplifting under b.(1) or b.(2) for his theft of the Devil Dogs. After entering his local supermarket, Ignacio proceeded to the store's aisle that contained baked goods; there, he grabbed a box of Devil Dogs and stuffed them in his coat pocket. He then exited the store without paying for the items.

Ignacio "purposely" took possession of the Devil Dogs and carried them away from the store. His intent was obviously to deprive the merchant of possession of these items without paying for the same. Accordingly, he could be charged with shoplifting under b.(1) of the statute. Likewise, Ignacio could be charged under b.(2) as he "purposely" concealed the merchandise on his person. Since he did this in an effort to deprive the supermarket of the benefit of the items and did not pay for them, he could be convicted per this subsection. So which subsection should Ignacio be charged under?

Really, either fits, but b.(1) is probably the better choice as b.(2) is more geared toward situations where a thief gets caught (e.g., he concealed the items in his clothes but never actually made it out of the store).

Grading

Subsection c. of the statute sets forth the requirements for grading shoplifting offenses. Basically, they fall under the same parameters as other theft offenses. If the full retail value of the item(s) stolen is $75,000 or more, a second degree felony has been committed. Shoplifting constitutes a third degree felony if the value exceeds $500 but is less than $75,000, and it is a fourth degree felony where the value of the merchandise is between $200 and $500; a misdemeanor A is committed if the merchandise is worth less than $200. Ignacio Marini's shoplifting offense is just this, as the Devil Dogs' full retail value was well under $200.

Detaining Shoplifting Suspects

Pursuant to the provisions of subsection e., a law enforcement officer, a special officer or a merchant may detain a shoplifting suspect—when having probable cause to believe that the suspect has "willfully concealed unpurchased merchandise." Also, the detainer must believe that "he can recover the merchandise by taking the person into custody."

It is crucial to note that the above-referenced custody must be performed in a "reasonable manner" and can occur for "not more than a reasonable time." If the tenets of this subsection are handled "reasonably" and with probable cause, then any officer or merchant effecting such a detention cannot be held criminally or civilly liable for his conduct. But one should be careful because what is considered a "reasonable manner of detention" and a "reasonable time of detention" are matters to be interpreted by the courts.

Possessing/Using Antishoplifting Countermeasure— Misdemeanor A

As provided in subsection f., one who possesses or uses any "antishoplifting or inventory control device countermeasure" within any store is guilty of a misdemeanor A. What is such an item? Subsection a. of the statute, which provides definitions pertaining to special terms contained in it, doesn't do much to define this phrase; however, examples of "antishoplifting or inventory control device countermeasures" are devices that change bar codes and devices that de-magnetize magnetic antishoplifting strips. Given that their purpose is to defeat antishoplifting devices, their possession and/or use (within a store) is a misdemeanor A.

9-12.　　**Operation of facility for sale of stolen automobile parts, penalties**

    a. A person who knowingly maintains or operates any premises, place or facility used for the remodeling, repainting or separating of automobile parts for resale of any stolen automobile is guilty of a felony of the second degree.

    b. Notwithstanding any provision of law to the contrary, any person convicted of a violation of this section shall forthwith forfeit his right to operate a motor vehicle in this State for a period to be fixed by the court at not less than three nor more than five years. The court shall cause a report of the conviction to be filed with the Director of the Division of Motor Vehicles.

PRACTICAL APPLICATION OF STATUTE

Mickey Morabito is guilty of maintaining a facility for selling stolen automobiles and their parts. This is a felony of the second degree.

Simply stated, one who "knowingly" maintains or operates a facility used for reselling stolen automobiles or for chopping up stolen automobiles and reselling the parts is guilty of violating this statute. In East Radcliffe, Mickey maintained such a facility. Posing as a legitimate auto body shop owner, Mickey routinely brought in stolen cars, which he either immediately resold for a huge profit or chopped up into parts and then resold the individual items. The Mercedes and BMW sold to him by Ignacio and Charles were just examples of his huge enterprise. Accordingly, since Mickey actively engaged in this business, he is guilty of a second degree felony under 9-12.

9-13. **Use of juvenile in theft of automobiles, penalty**

a. A person who is at least 18 years of age who knowingly uses, solicits, directs, hires or employs a person who is in fact 17 years of age or younger to commit theft of an automobile is guilty of a felony of the second degree. A conviction under this section shall not merge with a conviction for theft of an automobile. Nothing contained in this act shall prohibit the court from imposing an extended term; nor shall this act be construed in any way to preclude or limit the prosecution or conviction of any person for conspiracy, or any prosecution or conviction for any other offense.

b. It shall be no defense to a prosecution under this section that the actor mistakenly believed that the person which the actor used, solicited, directed, hired or employed was older than 17 years of age, even if such mistaken belief was reasonable.

PRACTICAL APPLICATION OF STATUTE

Ignacio Marini's use of his 17-year-old friend, Charles, to steal a BMW renders Ignacio guilty of a second degree felony per the elements of 9-13. It is not a defense if Ignacio wasn't aware of Charles' age or if Charles willingly engaged in the theft.

Section 9-13, in a nutshell, provides that any person who is at least 18 who knowingly uses, solicits or employs someone 17 or younger to steal an automobile is guilty of a second degree felony. Ignacio asked Charles to hot-wire and drive away a late-model BMW. Charles agreed and thereafter took the stolen car to Mickey's Auto Body Shop where they received a $10,000 payment for it. Given that Ignacio is well over 18 and that he solicited 17-year-old Charles to steal the BMW, Ignacio is guilty of violating this statute.

9-14. **Leader of auto theft trafficking network, penalty**

A person is a leader of an auto theft trafficking network if he conspires with others as an organizer, supervisor, financier or manager to engage for profit in a scheme or course of conduct to unlawfully take, dispose of, distribute, bring into or transport in this State automobiles as stolen property. Leader of auto theft trafficking network is a felony of the second degree. The court may impose a fine not to exceed $250,000 or five times the retail value of the automobiles seized at the time of the arrest, whichever is greater.

A conviction of leader of auto theft trafficking network shall not merge with the conviction for any offense which is the object of the conspiracy. Nothing contained in this act shall prohibit the court from imposing an extended term; nor shall this act be construed in any way to preclude or limit the prosecution or conviction of any person for conspiracy or any prosecution or conviction for any other offense.

It shall not be necessary in any prosecution under this act for the State to prove that any intended profit was actually realized. The trier of fact may infer that a particular scheme or course of conduct was undertaken for profit from all of the attending circumstances, including but not limited to the number of persons involved in the scheme or course of conduct, the actor's net worth and his expenditures in relation to his legitimate sources of income, the number of automobiles involved or the amount of cash or currency involved.

It shall not be a defense to a prosecution under this act that the automobile was brought into or transported in this State solely for ultimate distribution in another jurisdiction; nor shall it be a defense that any profit was intended to be made in another jurisdiction.

PRACTICAL APPLICATION OF STATUTE

To be convicted of being a leader of an auto theft trafficking network, the defendant must "conspire" with others as an "organizer, supervisor, financier or manager" to make a profit from the theft of automobiles. Mickey Morabito could be convicted of this second degree felony.

Mickey maintained and operated a chop shop in East Radcliffe, where he routinely bought stolen automobiles. He either immediately resold the vehicles for a huge profit or chopped them up and then sold the stolen parts. The fact that he maintained such a facility and made a profit from the stolen vehicles alone does not make him guilty of violating 9-14, though. The evidence must show that Mickey "conspired" with others and that he somehow headed the theft ring.

Since his business necessarily involved paying thieves, such as Ignacio and Charles, for stolen automobiles, it is clear that Mickey conspired with others. Similarly, it would probably be easy to show that he organized and/or supervised the network, as he was the individual responsible for paying for the vehicles and reselling them. The sum total of his actions, therefore, makes it likely that he would be convicted of being a leader of an auto theft trafficking network if he was indeed charged with this offense.

9-15.   **Definitions**

As used in this act:

a. "Access" means to instruct, communicate with, store data in, retrieve data from or otherwise make use of any resources of a computer, computer storage medium, computer system or computer network.

b. "Computer" means an electronic, magnetic, optical, electrochemical or other high-speed data processing device or another similar device capable of executing a computer program, including arithmetic, logic, memory, data storage or input-output operations, and includes all computer equipment connected to such a device, computer system or computer network but shall not include an automated typewriter or typesetter or a portable, hand-held calculator.

c. "Computer equipment" means any equipment or devices, including all input, output, processing, storage, software or communications facilities, intended to interface with the computer.

d. "Computer network" means the interconnection of communication lines, including microwave or other means of electronic communications, with a computer through remote terminals, or a complex consisting of two or more interconnected computers, and shall include the Internet.

e. "Computer program" means a series of instructions or statements executable on a computer, which directs the computer system in a manner to produce a desired result.

f. "Computer software" means a set of computer programs, data, procedures and associated documentation concerned with the operation of a computer system.

g. "Computer system" means a set of interconnected computer equipment intended to operate as a cohesive system.

h. "Data" means information, facts, concepts or instructions contained in a computer, computer storage medium, computer system or computer network. It shall also include, but not be limited to, any alphanumeric, hexadecimal, octal or binary code.

i. "Database" means a collection of data.

j. "Financial instrument" includes but is not limited to a check, draft, warrant, money order, note, certificate of deposit, letter of credit, bill of exchange, credit or debit card, transaction authorization mechanism, marketable security and any computer representation of these items.

k. "Services" includes but is not limited to the use of a computer system, computer network, computer programs, data prepared for computer use and data contained within a computer system or computer network.

l. "Personal identifying information" shall have the meaning set forth in subsection a. of 10-17 and shall also include passwords and other codes that permit access to any data, database, computer, computer storage medium, computer program, computer software, computer equipment, computer system or computer network where access is intended to be secure, restricted or limited.

m. "Internet" means the international computer network of both federal and non-federal interoperable packet switched data networks.

n. "Alter," "damage" or "destroy" shall include, but not be limited to, any change or impairment to the integrity or availability of any data or other information, database, computer program, computer software, computer equipment, computer, computer storage medium, computer system or computer network by any means including introduction of a computer contaminant.

o. "User of computer services" shall include, but not be limited to, any person, business, computer, computer network, computer system, computer equipment or any other device which makes use of any resources of a computer, computer network, computer system, computer storage medium, computer equipment, data or database.

p. "Computer contaminant" means any set of computer instructions that is designed to alter, damage, destroy, record or transmit information within a computer, computer system or computer network without the authorization of the owner of the information. They include, but are not limited to, a group of computer instructions commonly called viruses or worms that are self-replicating or self-propagating and are designed to contaminate other computer programs or computer data, consume computer resources, alter, damage, destroy, record or transmit data or in some other fashion usurp the normal operation of the computer, computer program, computer operations, computer services or computer network.

q. "Authorization" means permission, authority or consent given by a person who possesses lawful authority to grant such permission, authority or consent to another person to access, operate, use, obtain, take, copy, alter, damage or destroy a computer, computer network, computer system, computer equipment, computer software, computer program, computer storage medium or data. An actor has authorization if a reasonable person would believe that the act was authorized.

9-16.   Value of property of services; additional measures

For the purposes of this act, the value of any property or services, including the use of computer time, shall be their fair market value, if it is determined that a willing buyer and willing seller exist. Value shall include the cost of repair or remediation of any damage caused by an unlawful act and the gross revenue from any lost business opportunity caused by the unlawful act. The value of any lost business opportunity may be determined by comparison to gross revenue generated before the unlawful act that resulted in the lost business opportunity. Value shall include, but not be limited to, the cost of generating or obtaining data and storing it within a computer or computer system.

9-17.   Computer criminal activity; degree of felony; sentencing

A person is guilty of computer criminal activity if the person purposely or knowingly and without authorization, or in excess of authorization:

a. Accesses any data, database, computer storage medium, computer program, computer software, computer equipment, computer, computer system or computer network;

b. Alters, damages or destroys any data, database, computer, computer storage medium, computer program, computer software, computer system or computer network or denies, disrupts or impairs computer services, including access to any part of the Internet, that are available to any other user of the computer services;

c. Accesses or attempts to access any data, database, computer, computer storage medium, computer program, computer software, computer equipment, computer system or computer network for the purpose of executing a scheme to defraud or to obtain services, property, personal identifying information or money from the owner of a computer or any third party;

d. Obtains, takes, copies or uses any data, database, computer program, computer software, personal identifying information or other information stored in a computer, computer network, computer system, computer equipment or computer storage medium; or

e. Accesses and recklessly alters, damages or destroys any data, data base, computer, computer storage medium, computer program, computer software, computer equipment, computer system or computer network.

f. A violation of subsection a. of this section is a felony of the third degree. A violation of subsection b. is a felony of the second degree. A violation of subsection c. is a felony of the third degree, except that it is a felony of the second degree if the value of the services, property, personal identifying information or money obtained or sought to be obtained exceeds $5,000. A violation of subsection e. is a felony of the third degree, except that it is a felony of the second degree if the data, database, computer program, computer software or information:

(1) Is or contains personal identifying information, medical diagnoses, treatments or other medical information concerning an identifiable person;

(2) Is or contains governmental records or other information that is protected from disclosure by law, court order or rule of court; or

(3) Has a value exceeding $5,000.

A violation of subsection f. is a felony of the fourth degree, except that it is a felony of the third degree if the value of the damage exceeds $5,000.

A violation of any subsection of this section is a felony of the first degree if the offense results in:

(1) A substantial interruption or impairment of public communication, transportation, supply of water, gas or power or other public service. The term "substantial interruption or impairment" shall mean such interruption or impairment that:

    (a) Affects ten or more structures or habitations;

    (b) Lasts for two or more hours; or

    (c) Creates a risk of death or significant bodily injury to any person

(2) Damages or loss in excess of $250,000; or

(3) Significant bodily injury to any person.

Every sentence of imprisonment for a felony of the first degree committed in violation of this section shall include a minimum term of one-third to one-half of the sentence imposed, during which term the defendant shall not be eligible for parole.

g. Every sentence imposed upon a conviction pursuant to this section shall, if the victim is a government agency, include a period of imprisonment. The period of imprisonment shall include a minimum term of one-third to one-half of the sentence imposed, during which term the defendant shall not be eligible for parole. The victim shall be deemed to be a government agency if a computer, computer network, computer storage medium, computer system, computer equipment, computer program, computer software, computer data or database that is a subject of the felony is owned, operated or maintained by or on behalf of a governmental agency or unit of State or local government or a public authority. The defendant shall be strictly liable under this subsection and it shall not be a defense that the defendant did not know or intend that the victim was a government agency or that the defendant intended that there be other victims of the felony.

A violation of any subsection of this section shall be a distinct offense from a violation of any other subsection of this section, and a conviction for a violation of any subsection of this section shall not merge with a conviction for a violation of any other subsection of this section or section 9-18, or for conspiring or attempting to violate any subsection of this section or section 9-18, and a separate sentence shall be imposed for each such conviction.

When a violation of any subsection of this section involves an offense committed against a person under 18 years of age, the violation shall constitute an aggravating circumstance to be considered by the court when determining the appropriate sentence to be imposed.

PRACTICAL APPLICATION OF STATUTE

Allen, Bob, and Charles are three disgruntled employees of Arnoldi Asset Management, Inc. After recent cuts in pay and the looming threat of job loss due to a sagging economy, the three employees decide to sabotage the company before all mutually quitting their jobs within the next month. Using Allen's building key, the three individuals enter Arnoldi's offices late one evening without authorization. The lone security guard is accustomed to employees coming in at random hours and doesn't give it a second thought. Bob, one of the tech administrators, leads the group to the computer area where the group splits up to execute their plan.

Allen, a member of the marketing department, logs on to marketing's database of current and potential high-net-worth investors and saves the list to a zip disk so that he may later solicit these individuals to invest in a scam he intends to set up. Bob, the tech administrator, logs on to the network and plants a malicious virus, which is designed to completely erase the hard drive of the network and cripple the company's email capabilities. Finally, Charles, one of the traders, transfers the profiles of the department's Lexis-Nexis users from the local computer in the trading room to his personal laptop so that he may access the service at home for his own purposes without paying the normal fee.

Despite each individual's computer prowess, they were all easily caught soon after things started going wrong. Each individual was charged with computer-related theft—each under a different subsection of 9-17.

While all the actions of the three employees meet the criteria of "purposely or knowingly and without authorization," their specific actions lie within the four separate subsections. Allen should be charged under 9-17a. for taking the investor database for his own use, and Bob should be charged under subsection b. for damaging or destroying the actual computer system or computer network when he planted the malicious virus. Charles should be charged under subsection c., since he accessed a computer for the purpose of executing a scheme to wrongfully obtain services—the Lexis-Nexis application—from the company's computer.

9-18.   **Wrongful access, disclosure of information; degree of felony; sentencing**

a. A person is guilty of a felony of the third degree if the person purposely or knowingly and without authorization, or in excess of authorization, accesses any data, database, computer, computer storage medium, computer software, computer equipment or computer system and knowingly or recklessly discloses or causes to be disclosed any data, database, computer software, computer programs or personal identifying information.

b. A person is guilty of a felony of the second degree if the person purposely or knowingly and without authorization, or in excess of authorization, accesses any data, database, computer, computer storage medium, computer software, computer equipment, computer system or computer network and purposely or knowingly discloses or causes to be disclosed any data, database, computer software, computer program or other information that is protected from disclosure by any law, court order or rule of court. Every sentence imposed upon a conviction pursuant to this subsection shall include a period of imprisonment. The period of imprisonment shall include a minimum term of one-third to one-half of the sentence imposed, during which term the defendant shall not be eligible for parole.

PRACTICAL APPLICATION OF STATUTE

Michele, while temping at Big Dude's Auto, is exposed to a computer program that can simulate riding in the new Turbo-Pro model cars planned to go into production in the coming months. Without authorization, Michele decides to play around with the program a little and in the process inadvertently accesses the design plans for a top-secret stealth car that is being researched for the military. In an effort to impress several friends, she saves the program to a disk and, over the next week, shows the program to a few acquaintances. Daniel, whose computer Michele had accessed, notices the unauthorized use and realizes that the top-secret file has been accessed and saved. He reports the incident to his superiors, who eventually trace the breach to Michele.

Here, Michele could be charged under section 9-18 for disclosure of data from wrongful access, a felony of the third degree. A conviction of this offense can occur despite the fact that damages could not be assessed.

9-19.

Obtaining, copying, accessing program, software valued at $1,000 or less

It is an affirmative defense to a prosecution pursuant to subsection e. of 9-17, which shall be proved by clear and convincing evidence, that the actor obtained, copied or accessed a computer program or computer software that had a retail value of less than $1,000 and the actor did not disseminate or disclose the program or software to any other person.

PRACTICAL APPLICATION OF STATUTE

Tom and his buddies are typical teenagers with too much time on their hands. Through instructions easily found online, they have figured out how to use their CD burner to make copies of their favorite games and DVDs on disks. Here, their conduct does not constitute theft per the language of 9-19. Why? Because the teenagers are not mass-producing these copies for resale, and the retail value of their copied material is under $1,000.

9-20.

Situs of offense; determination

For the purpose of prosecution under this act, and in addition to determining the situs of the offense, the situs of an offense of computer criminal activity shall also be the location of the computer, computer storage medium, computer program, computer software, computer equipment, computer system or computer network which is accessed, or where the computer, computer storage medium, computer program, computer software, computer equipment, computer system, computer network or other device used in the offense is situated or where the actual damage occurs.

9-21.

Definitions

As used in this act:

"ATP card" means a document issued by a State or federal agency, to a certified household, to show the food stamp allotment a household is authorized to receive on presentation.

"Benefit card" means a card used or intended for use to access the State Work First Program, food stamp or other benefits as determined by the Commissioner of Human Services under the electronic benefit distribution system established pursuant to the "Public Assistance Electronic Benefit Distribution System Act."

"Department" means the Department of Human Services.

"Food stamp coupon" means any coupon or stamp used or intended for use in the purchase of food pursuant to the federal food stamp program authorized by Title XIII of the "Food and Agriculture Act of 1977" or the State Supplementary Food Stamp Program.

9-22.   **Misuse of food stamp coupons, ATP card, benefit card, value equal or greater than $150**

If the face value of food stamp coupons or an ATP card or benefit card is equal to or greater than $150, an individual shall be guilty of a felony of the fourth degree if he purposely or knowingly and without authorization:

a.   Receives or uses the proceeds of food stamp coupons or an ATP card or benefit card for which he has not applied or has not been approved by the department to use;

b.   Engages in any transaction to convert food stamp coupons or an ATP card or benefit card to other property contrary to federal and State government rules and regulations governing the State Work First Program, the federal food stamp program, the State Supplementary Food Stamp Program or any other program included in the electronic benefit distribution system; or

c.   Transfers food stamp coupons or an ATP card or benefit card to another person who is not lawfully entitled or approved by the department to use the coupons or ATP card or benefit card.

PRACTICAL APPLICATION OF STATUTE

Daniel Deadbeat has been collecting food stamp coupons since he lost his job nearly a year ago. Instead of using the coupons for food, however, Daniel regularly "sells" his $250 stamps on the black market for slightly less than their face value in order to buy alcohol and cigarettes. Through a sting operation set up to catch this sort of behavior, Daniel ends up "selling" his stamps to an undercover officer.

Daniel should be charged under 9-22. with a felony of the fourth degree for engaging "in any transaction to convert food stamp coupons or an ATP card or benefit card to other property contrary to federal and State government rules and regulations governing the State Work First Program, the federal food stamp program, the State Supplementary Food Stamp Program or any other program included in the electronic benefit distribution system"—where the face value of the food stamp coupon is "equal to or greater than $150."

If Daniel had been selling his $250 coupons to an individual (rather than an undercover officer) and that individual used the coupons for his own unauthorized use, he would be guilty of a fourth degree felony under subsection a. of this same statute. Why? Because this individual received "the proceeds of food stamp coupons or an ATP card or benefit card for which he has not applied or has not been approved by the department to use"—where the food stamps have a face value equal to or greater than $150.

9-23.   **Misuse of food stamp coupons, ATP card, benefit card, value less than $150**

If the face value of food stamp coupons or an ATP card or benefit card is less than $150, an individual shall be guilty of a misdemeanor A if he purposely or knowingly and without authorization:

a.   Receives or uses the proceeds of food stamp coupons or an ATP card or benefit card for which he has not applied or has not been approved, by the department, to use;

b.   Engages in any transaction to convert food stamp coupons or an ATP card or benefit card to other property contrary to federal and State government rules and regulations governing the State Work First Program, the federal food stamp program, the State Supplementary Food Stamp Program or any other program included in the electronic benefit distribution system; or

c. Transfers food stamp coupons or an ATP card or benefit card to another person who is not lawfully entitled or approved, by the department, to use the coupons or ATP card or benefit card.

PRACTICAL APPLICATION OF STATUTE

Daniel's offense (as described in 9-22's Practical Application section) would be considered a misdemeanor A if, under the same circumstances, the face value of the food stamp coupons was less than $150.

END OF CHAPTER REVIEW

Multiple-Choice Questions

1. Chacon and Maple are adult brothers who live in the same house. Chacon steals $1,000 cash off Maple's dresser. Chacon is guilty of:
   a. second degree theft
   b. third degree theft
   c. second degree burglary
   d. a and c
   e. b and c

2. The following is an example of a second degree theft:
   a. Gary steals two kilograms of cocaine from Jason.
   b. Maude heists the human remains of her former boss from a funeral parlor.
   c. Penelope, knowing she has only $200 to her name, has Robert build a shore house for her at a cost of $450,000. Penelope never pays Bob.
   d. all of the above
   e. none of the above

3. Mickey Morabito maintained and operated a shop in East Radcliffe where he routinely bought stolen automobiles from various thieves. He either immediately resold the vehicles for a huge profit or chopped them up and then sold the stolen parts. Morabito could be convicted of which offense?
   a. theft by extortion
   b. fencing
   c. leader of auto trafficking network
   d. all of the above
   e. b and c only

The following fact pattern pertains to questions 4–5.

Mark is in the pawnbroker business. He regularly buys items of jewelry, television sets, stereos and home appliances. Jerry, a man who Mark knows to be a drug addict, stops by his store with a diamond ring. Mark asks Jerry neither for proof of ownership of the ring (e.g., a receipt or warranty) nor where he obtained the ring. The ring, valued at $110,000, turns out to have been stolen by Jerry.

4. Mark could be convicted of what offense?
   a. theft by extortion because he could have exposed Jerry as a drug addict
   b. theft by deception because he reinforced a false impression that the ring was lawfully obtained
   c. shoplifting because the ring is a stolen good now for sale in a lawful business
   d. receiving stolen property because, under the circumstances, he is presumed to have knowledge that the ring was stolen
   e. theft of services because he knowingly converted the ring to his benefit

5. For stealing the ring, Jerry is guilty of:
   a. first degree theft
   b. second degree theft
   c. third degree theft
   d. an additional count of grand larceny
   e. *modus operandi*

6. A person who knowingly rides as a passenger in a motor vehicle that is being operated without the owner's consent is guilty of:
   a. a first degree felony
   b. a fourth degree felony
   c. a misdemeanor B
   d. a motor vehicle offense for driving on the revoked list
   e. no offense at all because he was just a passenger and isn't culpable for the driver's heist of the vehicle

7. Ignacio Marini and an owner of a horse farm shook hands on a deal that required Marini to make four payments of $1,000 in exchange for a prize moose. Marini took the moose but never made the payments. Which of the following statements is true?
   a. Marini could be convicted of an offense under section 10-9 for theft by failure to make required disposition if he purposely obtained the moose with no intention of ever making the payments.
   b. If Marini is guilty of a theft under section 10-9, it would be a third degree felony because the value involved exceeds $500 but is less than $75,000.
   c. Marini could not be convicted of any offense in the criminal code because this is purely a contract dispute.
   d. a and b only
   e. none of the above

Essay Questions

1. Sol threatens to inflict bodily injury on Julie if Julie doesn't sign over the title of her car to him. Is this an act of theft? If so, what type of theft is it, what is the statute number and what is the degree of the offense? Jim is a defendant in a civil suit. Sol threatens to testify against Jim if Jim does not give Sol the motorcycle in his garage. Is this an act of theft? If so, what type of theft is it, what is the statute number and what is the degree of the offense? Be sure to explain your answers, focusing on the elements of the offenses.

2. Marlo delivered a $100,000 money order to Paul Canapa, a bubble gum manufacturer. The problem is, Marlo was supposed to deliver the money order to Francisco Maxgoose, a tractor trailer company owner. Canapa knew that he was not supposed to receive this money order and that it actually was supposed to have been delivered to Maxgoose. With the purpose to deprive Maxgoose of the proceeds of the money order, Canapa deposited the $100,000 in his personal bank account. What is the most appropriate theft offense to charge Canapa with and why? Cite the statute number. Also, is this a second, third or fourth degree offense and why?

10

FORGERY AND FRAUDULENT PRACTICES

At the urging of the mayor of Capwell and the Upton County Prosecutor, Christian Star was appointed to be the new director of the Upton County Police Academy. Star's appointment was quite a feat given that he was only 33 years old at the time of the announcement. Accomplishing great things at a young age, though, was nothing new to Christian Star. Already, he had moved from patrolman to sergeant to lieutenant to captain in the Capwell Police Department, and he had personally cracked the largest forgery and fraudulent business scam in the state. This is what led to his Police Academy Director post—who better to train the county's recruits? The first class under his leadership listened closely as one of the academy's instructors explained the story of Director Star's monumental bust.

Maxwell Borscht, a former Ivy League valedictorian, resigned from an executive position with a top corporate firm on the West Coast after a power struggle with other bosses. Borscht told family, friends and business colleagues that he intended to pursue a career in acting as he was "finished with corporate America." He said he was moving to the East Coast. Borscht, though, was lying.

Trading in his West Coast penthouse for a spacious Victorian home in Capwell, Borscht assumed the name "Kalman Greenwald" and began operating "Jackpot Entertainment Insurance," which he held out to be a specialized subsidiary company of one of the nation's largest insurance companies, The Pellman Group. The problem was, Jackpot Entertainment Insurance was as fake as his new name.

Borscht had acquired his alias, Kalman Greenwald, through an arranged meeting with Ellsworth businessman Michael "The Hunk" Pardemena. The Hunk made a career of manufacturing various phony forms of identification as well as obtaining some genuine items. For example, he recently purchased an Ellsworth police badge from his friend, Manny Rando. In the same day, The Hunk "restructured" Manny's father's will to make Manny the sole beneficiary of his dad's estate. The Hunk did this by dissolving the printed ink and replacing it with language favorable to Manny.

The Hunk also visited the home of Manny's father-in-law; there, he destroyed the man's will—which left all his assets to a charity. The purpose of this destruction was so that the man would die "intestate," thereby requiring that his assets would go to his closest living immediate family member, which was Manny's wife.

Now, back to The Hunk's dealings with Borscht. The Hunk, on the spot, made a state driver's license for Borscht that falsely purported Borscht to be Kalman Greenwald. The Hunk sold the license to Borscht for $500, and in the same transaction, The Hunk sold Borscht a fake motor vehicle insurance card.

Ironically, Christian Star's first interaction with Borscht was on the evening Borscht purchased his illicit identification cards from The Hunk. Star, in his supervisor cruiser, pulled over Borscht, who presented the newly purchased driver's license and insurance card. The cards, even to an expert eye, appeared authentic; Borscht went on his way with a warning for speeding.

The following days were dedicated to setting up and financing Borscht's fictitious business, Jackpot Entertainment Insurance. In an unusual move to obtain start-up capital, Borscht created a manuscript that he claimed to be an authentic writing of Ernest Hemingway. It was handwritten—and the writing so closely resembled Hemingway's that knowledgeable collectors were fooled by it. The highest bidder took it home for $50,000. Borscht's next order of business was to alter actual records pertaining to Kalman Greenwald—Greenwald was indeed a real person.

Borscht changed an important diagnosis made by Greenwald's cardiologist. The document was altered to read that Greenwald had "chronic heart disease . . . which necessitated a heart transplant," whereas the real diagnosis was a "heart murmur." Borscht took this diagnostic record to sympathetic wealthy members of Upton County's Chamber of Commerce and solicited over $25,000 in funds to pay costs that insurance would not cover in the "heart transplant." Borscht then went to a doctor friend, Elias Williamson, M.D., who agreed to act as if he had performed the surgery. Williamson submitted claims to Greenwald's insurance company and then split the proceeds of the insurance payments with Borscht.

Borscht continued his fund-raising campaign by the use of credit cards. His first act was to simply pluck two credit cards from the home of Kalman Greenwald. Greenwald, a former business associate of Borscht, was moving to Portugal, and Borscht attended his "going away" party. Borscht then "maxed out" the cards via cash advances. He later used them, along with his phony driver's license, as part of the application process to obtain additional credit cards. In those applications, he falsely purported to be Kalman Greenwald, signing Greenwald's name to the paperwork and listing phony business references.

Utilizing Greenwald's identity, Borscht visited several businesses in the northern part of the state that were familiar with Greenwald's reputation but not his physical appearance. Borscht's false pretense allowed him to obtain on invoice several items of value, including office furniture, equipment and handmade suits. Borscht, as Greenwald, agreed to pay the vendors within 30 days; payment, of course, was never remitted. During these visits, Borscht actually paid for an item—a large jar of "anti-aging" pills. The merchant claimed on the jar's label that the pills were made from a coral found only off the coast of Australia, when in fact he produced them in his basement, utilizing various ingredients from his own kitchen. When Borscht found out he was misled, he returned to the store and issued a check for $3,500 in exchange for various livestock that the merchant retained at a farm in Sussex County. The merchant wasn't pleased, though, when he learned the check was from a bank account that had been closed for nearly a year. Borscht laughed heartily, knowing the account no longer existed.

Fully funded and equipped, Borscht was now ready to begin work. At the headquarters of the insurance conglomerate, The Pellman Group, Borscht met with Sandy Ireland, one of the company's board of directors. Ireland had previously worked hand-in-hand with none other than Kalman Greenwald, Pellman's recently retired chief financial officer.

Borscht paid Ireland $50,000 to form a subsidiary company named Jackpot Entertainment Insurance, which actually wouldn't be started for 24 months, as it would take that period of time to clear the internal bureaucratic red tape and administrative matters. The name, though, would be in place and tied to The Pellman Group, and anyone checking into Jackpot could confirm this. Borscht convinced Ireland that she was at no risk because if things went afoul, Ireland could easily claim that Borscht simply stole the name. Ireland took the money and had the subsidiary company formed, even though she knew it could be to the detriment of Pellman and its shareholders. At the same board of directors meeting where she proposed the formation of Jackpot, Ireland agreed with other board members to issue each board member a $150,000 dividend, holding it out to be a "Presidents' Day bonus," although they knew the corporation didn't allow for such a dividend distribution.

Borscht then began soliciting high-level film production companies, purporting to sell them liability and other entertainment insurance policies for their film productions. Posing as Kalman Greenwald, former CFO of The Pellman Group and now CEO of Jackpot, Borscht met with the top executives of numerous production companies. Because The Pellman Group had never sold such insurance, the executives were interested in meeting with Borscht/Greenwald. They immediately purchased the insurance because the rates were so much lower than competitors'.

To avoid any detection of fraud, Borscht created policy documents that replicated in letterhead, typeset and stock language other documents delivered by The Pellman Group. He issued the policies under the name "Jackpot Entertainment Insurance Company—A Subsidiary of The Pellman Group," and he signed Kalman Greenwald's name to each policy—all this, even though he had no consent whatsoever from Greenwald or The Pellman Group to issue such policies. As a special touch, Borscht applied The Pellman Group's signatory wax seal; he had created equipment that could perfectly match the seal.

Within six months of opening shop, Borscht had sold such a large number of fictitious insurance policies to production companies throughout the state that he had netted himself over $3 million. At this point, he was committed to wind up the business as claims were beginning to come in; heat was sure to be coming, as he had absolutely no plans to pay any of the claims. He had one problem, however—Capwell Police Officer Christian Star.

The young captain responded to a call from a local restaurateur that a "new guy in town" was dancing on one of his tables, screaming "I'm 53, but only look 35 . . . Don't you all love me?" When Star arrived, Borscht was off the table but rolling on the floor instead, yelling, "I'm in the movie business . . . rich and handsome . . . rich and handsome." Star immediately recognized him as a man he had previously pulled over. Having an incredible memory, he tapped Borscht on the shoulder and said, "Mr. Greenwald, could you stand up?"

Borscht didn't stand but lifted his head and said, "I'm Borscht . . . Would you like an apple martini?" Captain Star noted the name change but also noted Borscht's drunkenness. He lifted the man up from the floor, threw him over his shoulder and carried him to his police vehicle. Then he gave him a courtesy ride home.

On instinct, Star ran a check on the "new guy in town." He quickly learned that a Kalman Greenwald had recently sold his home in Cape Marna and also found out that Greenwald was previously the CFO of The Pellman Group. Human resources advised that he had just retired and thought that he had moved out of the country. They mentioned, though, that Greenwald was a private man and perhaps wanted to remain anonymous in the United States for a while. This seemed to conflict with the behavior Star had just witnessed at the restaurant, but he had no real reason to suspect Greenwald of a felony, so he thought he would just monitor the man—until he got a call from Sandy Ireland.

The Pellman Group director freaked when she heard that law enforcement was inquiring about Kalman Greenwald. Did they know about Borscht's subsidiary company? Were they on to the bribe? Is it possible that Borscht killed Kalman Greenwald? Ireland didn't want to face culpability for any of this—so she made an appointment with Captain Star and spilled everything.

An arrest of Borscht was not easy, however. By the time Star arrived with an arrest warrant, Borscht was gone. The home, though, did provide clues as to his whereabouts. Above a ceiling panel, Star found several thousand dollars in cash, which Borscht had forgotten in his rush to leave. Underneath a floor tile, Star discovered where the money was derived from—three pizza parlors in Hamilton County.

Borscht had bought the establishments in his real name before creating the Jackpot Entertainment Insurance scam. What Star ultimately learned was that Borscht was selling heroin when he first came to the state, utilizing the pizza places to disguise the real manner in which he earned funds. His goal was to act like the money was made legitimately via the restaurants, sending it through those businesses' records as if an enormous number of pizzas and calzones had been sold.

Star then hooked up with investigators from the Hamilton County Prosecutor's Office to have surveillance set up at the various pizza parlors. Borscht, however, never appeared. At this point, Star thought that perhaps Borscht had simply fled the county with the millions he had deceptively earned, but then he thought about something Sandy Ireland had said in her babbling confession—a great-uncle of Borscht's was buried in an unmarked grave in Orange Hill. The significance was that there was a family myth that buried along with the uncle was $5 million in gold bullion.

Star, discouraged with the Hamilton County stakeouts, drove across the state to Orange Hill, figuring he'd stop by the local racetrack if nothing turned up at the cemeteries. But something did—as he approached his third graveyard, he found Borscht, shovel in hand, breaking open a pine box casket in an unmarked grave. Borscht pulled the human remains from the box, tossed them aside and threw up his hands. He then kicked the unfortunate unmarked man's skeleton and cried, "Where's the bullion, you bony fool?" At this point, Christian Star pointed his pistol at Borscht, dangling handcuffs from his free hand. The young officer had captured his man—the police academy promotion came just one month later.

10-1.   **Forgery and related offenses**

a. Forgery. A person is guilty of forgery if, with the purpose to defraud or injure anyone, or with knowledge that he is facilitating a fraud or injury to be perpetrated by anyone, the actor:

(1) Alters or changes any writing of another without his authorization;

(2) Makes, completes, executes, authenticates, issues or transfers any writing so that it purports to be the act of another who did not authorize that act or of a fictitious person, or to have been executed at a time or place or in a numbered sequence other than was in fact the case, or to be a copy of an original when no such original existed; or

(3) Utters any writing which he knows to be forged in a manner specified in paragraph (1) or (2).

"Writing" includes printing or any other method of recording information, money, coins, tokens, stamps, seals, credit cards, badges, trademarks, access devices and other symbols of value, right, privilege or identification, including retail sales receipts, universal product code (UPC) labels and checks. This section shall apply without limitation to forged, copied or imitated checks.

As used in this section, "information" includes, but is not limited to, personal identifying information as defined in subsection v. of 9-1.

b. Grading of forgery. Forgery is a felony of the third degree if the writing is or purports to be part of an issue of money, securities, postage or revenue stamps or other instruments, certificates or licenses issued by the government, State prescription blanks or part of an issue of stock, bonds or other instruments representing interest in or claims against any property or enterprise, personal identifying information or an access device. Forgery is a felony of the third degree if the writing is or purports to be a check. Forgery is a felony of the third degree if the writing is or purports to be 15 or more forged or altered retail sales receipts or universal product code labels.

Otherwise forgery is a felony of the fourth degree.

c. Possession of forgery devices. A person is guilty of possession of forgery devices, a felony of the third degree, when with the purpose to use, or to aid or permit another to use, the same for purposes of forging written instruments, including access devices and personal identifying information, he makes or possesses any device, apparatus, equipment, computer, computer equipment, computer software or article specially designed or adapted to such use.

PRACTICAL APPLICATION OF STATUTE

Michael "The Hunk" Pardemena could appropriately be found guilty of forgery under subsection a.(1) of the above statute due to his "restructuring" of Manny's father's will. In The Hunk's case, this would be a felony of the third degree.

Subsection b. of this statute makes the offense of forgery a felony of the third degree under certain listed circumstances and a felony of the fourth degree in all remaining instances. Circumstances in which forgery is a felony of the third degree include matters such as where the forged documents are government-issued certificates or licenses (e.g., money, securities or postage stamps); stocks or bonds; State prescription blanks; and "instruments representing interest in or claims against any property or enterprise."

Although the statute does not specifically mention wills, it could certainly be argued that a will would fall into the category of an "instrument representing an interest in property," therefore making The Hunk's actions a felony of the third degree.

At its core, the felony of forgery consists of two elements: 1) the intent to defraud and 2) the false making or materially altering of any writing, which, if genuine, would have some legal effect on the rights of others. Although intent can occasionally be a tricky element, the very act of forgery itself is probably sufficient to imply an intent to defraud. In The Hunk's case, both elements are met. First, he clearly intended to defraud the two beneficiaries of Manny's father—he dissolved the printed ink of the will and replaced it with language favorable to Manny. Second, the material altering of the will would certainly have a legal effect on others, as it would deprive the true beneficiaries of the will's grants and proceeds. Accordingly, The Hunk is guilty of third degree forgery per subsection a.(1) of the statute.

Possession of Forgery Devices

Maxwell Borscht is guilty of possessing forgery devices as part of his phony insurance company, Jackpot Entertainment Insurance. This is a felony of the third degree.

Per subsection c. of 10-1, a person who possesses any device, apparatus or equipment with a purpose to use the same to aid in forging a written instrument is guilty of a third degree felony. Borscht had created equipment that could perfectly match the signature wax seal of one of the nation's largest insurance companies, The Pellman Group. Borscht used this equipment in an effort to make his own phony insurance documents look authentic. Since he used this seal device for the purpose of aiding in forging written instruments, Borscht is guilty of violating subsection c. of 10-1.

10-2. ### Criminal simulation

A person commits a felony of the fourth degree if, with the purpose to defraud anyone or with knowledge that he is facilitating a fraud to be perpetrated by anyone, he makes, alters or utters any object so that it appears to have value because of antiquity, rarity, source or authorship which it does not possess.

PRACTICAL APPLICATION OF STATUTE

When Maxwell Borscht created his sham Ernest Hemingway manuscript, he committed the fourth degree felony of criminal simulation. This statute simply requires that a person (with the purpose to defraud) make or alter any object so that it appears to have value because of "antiquity, rarity, source or authorship which it does not possess." By forging an Ernest Hemingway manuscript for the sole purpose of pawning it off as an original and subsequently reaping the ill-received gains from an unknowing bidder, Borsht falls squarely within the statute. Accordingly, he is guilty of a fourth degree felony as defined in 10-2.

10-2.1. ### Offenses involving false government documents, degree of felony

a. A person who knowingly sells, offers or exposes for sale or otherwise transfers, or possesses with the intent to sell, offer or expose for sale or otherwise transfer, a document, printed form or other writing which falsely purports to be a driver's license, birth certificate or other document issued by a governmental agency and which could be used as a means of verifying a person's identity or age or any other personal identifying information is guilty of a felony of the second degree.

b. A person who knowingly makes, or possesses devices or materials to make, a document or other writing which falsely purports to be a driver's license, birth certificate or other document issued by a governmental agency and which could be used as a means of verifying a person's identity or age or any other personal identifying information is guilty of a felony of the second degree.

c. A person who knowingly exhibits, displays or utters a document or other writing which falsely purports to be a driver's license, birth certificate or other document issued by a governmental agency and which could be used as a means of verifying a person's identity or age or any other personal identifying information is guilty of a felony of the third degree. A violation of tampering with public records, constituting a misdemeanor A, in a case where the person uses the personal identifying information of another to illegally purchase an alcoholic beverage or for using the personal identifying information of another to misrepresent his age for the purpose of obtaining tobacco or other consumer product denied to persons under 18 years of age shall not constitute an offense under this subsection if the actor received only that benefit or service and did not perpetrate or attempt to perpetrate any additional injury or fraud on another.

d. A person who knowingly possesses a document or other writing which falsely purports to be a driver's license, birth certificate or other document issued by a governmental agency and which could be used as a means of verifying a person's identity or age or any other personal identifying information is guilty of a felony of the fourth degree. A violation of tampering with public records, constituting a misdemeanor A, in a case where the person uses the personal identifying information of another to illegally purchase an alcoholic beverage or for using the personal identifying information of another to misrepresent his age for the purpose of obtaining tobacco or other consumer product denied to persons under 18 years of age shall not constitute an offense under this subsection if the actor received only that benefit or service and did not perpetrate or attempt to perpetrate any additional injury or fraud on another.

Practical Application of Statute

Section 10-2.1 generally makes it a felony to sell, make, exhibit or possess any document that falsely purports to be a driver's license or other document issued by the government that could be used as a means of verifying a person's identity or age. Subsections a. and b. specify that it is a felony of the second degree to "sell" or "make" such IDs.

Subsection c. makes it a felony of the third degree to "display" or "exhibit" the IDs. Finally, per subsection d., it is felony of the fourth degree for a person to knowingly "possess" a fake ID. However, there shall be no violation of this statute if the actor simply uses the personal identifying information of another to only illegally purchase alcohol or tobacco (or other consumer product denied to persons under age 18)—and the actor "did not perpetrate or attempt to perpetrate any additional injury or fraud on another." This is because the actor would already be guilty of committing a misdemeanor A under the statutes for tampering with public records or possessing or consuming alcohol while under age.

The Hunk and Maxwell Borscht are both guilty of felonies under this statute. The Hunk should be found guilty of the more severe second degree offenses found under subsections a. and b. of 10-2.1. Why? Because he both made and sold Borscht a fake driver's license that falsely purported Borscht to be Kalman Greenwald.

Borscht's possession of this ID makes him guilty of a fourth degree felony under subsection d. Later, when he presented it to Police Lieutenant Christian Star at a motor vehicle stop, Borscht's offense rose to a felony of the third degree as provided for in subsection c. of the statute.

10-2.2.   Ban on police badge transfers

It shall be a misdemeanor A to:

a. Sell a law enforcement agency badge, the prescribed form of which is presently in use or has been in use in the state during any of the five years preceding the sale, to a person other than a member of a law enforcement agency who presents a letter authorizing the purchase, signed by the commanding officer of that law enforcement agency;

b. Purchase a law enforcement agency badge, described in subsection a. of this section, unless the purchaser is a member of a law enforcement agency who presents a letter authorizing the purchase, signed by the commanding officer of that law enforcement agency; or

c. Give or lend a law enforcement agency badge described in subsection a. of this section, unless the person to whom a badge was given or loaned is a member of a law enforcement agency who presents a letter authorizing the transfer, signed by the commanding officer of that law enforcement agency.

PRACTICAL APPLICATION OF STATUTE

The Hunk continues his stroll down fraudulent lane by violating subsection 10-2.2.b., which makes it a misdemeanor A for non–law enforcement personnel to buy a law enforcement agency badge. This act is an offense where the badge is either presently in use or has been in use in the state during any of the five years prior to the sale.

Manny, the seller of the badge, is also in violation of the statute because subsection a. forbids the sale of any such badge to anyone but authorized law enforcement personnel who present a letter authorizing the purchase, signed by the commanding officer of that law enforcement agency. Manny is not a law enforcement officer, and even if he was, he did not have the appropriate authorization to sell an Ellsworth police badge to The Hunk. Accordingly, he is guilty of a misdemeanor A under 10-2.2.

The only issue that might get these two off the hook is if it turned out that the Ellsworth police badge that Manny sold to The Hunk had not been in use for over five years prior to the sale. If this were the case, it appears the statute provides that there would be no offense.

Christian Star and the other law enforcement officers should take note of subsection c. of this statute, which proscribes giving or loaning their badges to anyone except a fellow member of a law enforcement agency. Even in that case, the law enforcement officer must present a letter authorizing the transfer, signed by the commanding officer of that law enforcement agency. Anyone, officer or civilian, can be found guilty of a misdemeanor A if the person is in violation of this subsection.

10-2.3.   Producing, selling, offering, displaying, possessing fraudulent motor vehicle insurance ID cards; penalties

a. A person who knowingly produces, sells, offers or exposes for sale a document, printed form or other writing which simulates a motor vehicle insurance identification card is guilty of a felony of the third degree. In addition to any other penalty imposed, a person convicted under this section shall be ordered by the court to perform community service for a period of 30 days.

b. A person who exhibits or displays to a law enforcement officer, or a person conducting a motor vehicle inspection, a falsely made, forged, altered, counterfeited or simulated motor vehicle insurance identification card, knowing that the insurance identification card was falsely made, forged, altered, counterfeited or simulated, commits a felony of the fourth degree.

c. A person who possesses a falsely made, forged, altered, counterfeited or simulated motor vehicle insurance identification card, knowing that the insurance identification card was falsely made, forged, altered, counterfeited or simulated, commits a misdemeanor A.

PRACTICAL APPLICATION OF STATUTE

The Hunk and Maxwell Borscht violated 10-2.3 during their illicit transactions where The Hunk also produced and sold a fake motor vehicle insurance card to Borscht. Subsection a. makes it a third degree felony for a person to knowingly produce, sell, offer or expose for sale a fake motor vehicle insurance identification card. The Hunk actually is guilty of two counts under this statute since he both produced and sold the bogus ID.

Subsections b. and c. distinguish between the act of knowingly displaying a fake insurance ID card to a law enforcement officer (or motor vehicle inspector) and merely possessing such ID with the knowledge that it was falsely made. In the former subsection, the felony is of the fourth degree, whereas mere possession is considered a misdemeanor A. Obviously, Borscht could be found guilty of both because he bought and subsequently displayed to Christian Star this fake insurance card while knowing full well it was bogus.

10-2.4.   **Possession of certain fraudulent receipts, universal product code (UPC) labels and checks**

a. Except as provided in subsection b. of this section, any person who knowingly possesses a forged or altered retail sales receipt, universal product code (UPC) label or check for the purpose of defrauding a retail merchant shall be guilty of a misdemeanor A.

b. Any person who knowingly possesses 15 or more forged or altered retail sales receipts, universal product code labels or checks for the purpose of defrauding a retail merchant shall be guilty of a felony of the fourth degree.

PRACTICAL APPLICATION OF STATUTE

Let's say the facts in Maxwell Borscht's case were a bit different. Instead of creating the bogus Hemingway manuscript to obtain start-up capital, Borscht obtained hundreds of fake universal product code (UPC) labels and sales receipts for MacroHard computer software that just so happened to be offering a $300 rebate to everyone sending in their UPC codes and sales receipts. His intent was to send in the items in order to reap the monetary benefits of the rebate.

If the above were the case, Borscht would be guilty of an offense under 10-2.4 for possession of forged or altered receipts and UPC labels. The grifter would be guilty of the fourth degree version of this felony under subsection b., since he knowingly possessed 15 or more such items with the purpose of defrauding a retail merchant.

If, under the same circumstances, Borscht had possessed fewer than 15 of the forged items, he would be guilty of a misdemeanor A as per subsection a. of the statute.

10-3. Frauds relating to public records and recordable instruments

a. Fraudulent destruction, removal or concealment of recordable instruments. A person commits a felony of the third degree if, with the purpose to deceive or injure anyone, he destroys, removes or conceals any will, deed, mortgage, security instrument or other writing for which the law provides public recording.

b. Offering a false instrument for filing. A person is guilty of a misdemeanor A when, knowing that a written instrument contains a false statement or false information, he offers or presents it to a public office or public servant with knowledge or belief that it will be filed with, registered or recorded in or otherwise become a part of the records of such public office or public servant.

PRACTICAL APPLICATION OF STATUTE

The Hunk tops off his devious activities with a visit to the home of Manny's father-in-law, where he destroyed the man's will with the purpose of leaving him "intestate." This would require that the man's assets go to his closest living immediate family member, Manny's wife. This action plainly violates subsection a. of 10-3, which makes it a third degree felony if, with the purpose to deceive or injure anyone, a person destroys, removes or conceals any will, deed, mortgage, security investment or other writing for which the law provides public recording.

Manny's father-in-law had determined that all his assets would be transferred to charitable organizations upon his death. In destroying the man's will, The Hunk certainly had a purpose to deceive and injure the charities, which would have otherwise received the man's wealth. Accordingly, The Hunk is guilty of a third degree felony as set forth in subsection a. of 10-3. This subsection makes it a third degree felony if, with the purpose to deceive or injure anyone, he destroys, removes or conceals any will, deed, mortgage, security instrument or other writing for which the law provides public recording. The Hunk certainly had a purpose to injure the charities, which would have otherwise received the proceeds of the will, by destroying the will.

Subsection b. of this statute does not apply in this case; however, it should be noted that any individual who offers a document he knows contains false information for filing with any public office is guilty of a misdemeanor A. This subsection, though, applies only where the individual did not actually and intentionally make the false statement or record but only has the knowledge that the information contained in the document is false. An example would be where someone noticed a typo in a boundary line agreement yet proceeded to file the agreement with the state in hopes that he might receive the benefit of the error. Remember that the actual making of such false statements or documents is a third degree offense of forgery under 10-1.

10-4. Falsifying or tampering with records

a. Except as provided in subsection b. of this section, a person commits a felony of the fourth degree if he falsifies, destroys, removes or conceals any writing or record, or utters any writing or record, knowing that it contains a false statement or information, with the purpose to deceive or injure anyone or to conceal any wrongdoing.

b. Issuing a false financial statement. A person is guilty of issuing a false financial statement, a felony of the third degree, when, with the purpose to deceive or injure anyone or to conceal any wrongdoing, he by oath or affirmation:

(1) Knowingly makes or utters a written instrument which purports to describe the financial condition or ability to pay of some person and which is inaccurate in some substantial respect; or

(2) Represents in writing that a written instrument purporting to describe a person's financial condition or ability to pay as of a prior date is accurate with respect to such person's current financial condition or ability to pay, whereas he knows it is substantially inaccurate in that respect.

PRACTICAL APPLICATION OF STATUTE

Essentially, section 10-4 deals with the falsification, destruction, removal or concealing of any writing or record with the purpose to deceive anyone or to conceal wrongdoing. Subsection b. of the statute deals specifically with issuing false financial statements.

Here's an example of an offense under this statute. Let's say Maxwell Borscht had actually stayed in business for a while, somehow eluding the authorities and The Pellman Group as to the true nature of his business. During this time, he submits false reports as to the fiscal condition of the company to banks or other corporate insurance agencies in order to obtain loans or insurance coverage. Here, Borscht would be guilty of a third degree felony under subsection b.(1) of this statute. Why? Because b.(1) makes it an offense when, "with the purpose to deceive, " a person knowingly submits an instrument purporting to describe the financial condition of a person or entity and the instrument is inaccurate in some substantial respect.

10-4.1.   **Destruction, alteration, falsification of records, felony of fourth degree**

A person is guilty of a felony of the fourth degree if he purposefully destroys, alters or falsifies any record relating to the care of a medical or surgical or podiatric patient in order to deceive or mislead any person as to information, including, but not limited to, a diagnosis, test, medication, treatment or medical or psychological history, concerning the patient.

PRACTICAL APPLICATION OF STATUTE

Per 10-4.1, a defendant is guilty of a felony of the fourth degree if he purposefully destroys, alters or falsifies any record relating to care of a medical patient for the purpose of deceiving a person as to such information. Maxwell Borscht is guilty of a felony under this statute. Borscht assumed the identity of corporate executive Kalman Greenwald. After doing so, he obtained Greenwald's medical records and began to alter them. Specifically, Borscht changed a diagnosis made by Kalman Greenwald's cardiologist from "heart murmur" to "chronic heart disease necessitating a heart transplant" for the purpose of soliciting funds to pay for bogus costs associated with the "heart transplant." Here, Borscht held the necessary *mens rea* of intent to deceive and certainly committed the *actus reus* by purposefully altering the medical record. Accordingly, he is guilty of the fourth degree felony set forth in 10-4.1.

10-4.2.   **Definitions relative to health care claims fraud**

As used in this act:

a. "Health care claims fraud" means making, or causing to be made, a false, fictitious, fraudulent or misleading statement of material fact in, omitting a material fact from or causing a material fact to be omitted from any record, bill, claim or other document, in writing, electronically or in any other form, that a person attempts to submit, submits, causes to be submitted or attempts to cause to be submitted for payment or reimbursement for health care services.

b. "Practitioner" means a person licensed in this State to practice medicine and surgery, chiropractic, podiatric medicine, dentistry, optometry, psychology, pharmacy, nursing, physical therapy or law, any other person licensed, registered or certified by any state agency to practice a profession or occupation in this State or any person similarly licensed, registered or certified in another jurisdiction.

10-4.3.   **Health care claims fraud, degree of felony; prosecution guidelines**

a. A practitioner is guilty of a felony of the second degree if that person knowingly commits health care claims fraud in the course of providing professional services. In addition to all other criminal penalties allowed by law, a person convicted under this subsection may be subject to a fine of up to five times the pecuniary benefit obtained or sought to be obtained.

b. A practitioner is guilty of a felony of the third degree if that person recklessly commits health care claims fraud in the course of providing professional services. In addition to all other criminal penalties allowed by law, a person convicted under this subsection may be subject to a fine of up to five times the pecuniary benefit obtained or sought to be obtained.

c. A person, who is not a practitioner subject to the provisions of subsection a. or b. of this section, is guilty of a felony of the third degree if that person knowingly commits health care claims fraud. A person, who is not a practitioner subject to the provisions of subsection a. or b. of this section, is guilty of a felony of the second degree if that person knowingly commits five or more acts of health care claims fraud and the aggregate pecuniary benefit obtained or sought to be obtained is at least $1,000. In addition to all other criminal penalties allowed by law, a person convicted under this subsection may be subject to a fine of up to five times the pecuniary benefit obtained or sought to be obtained.

d. A person, who is not a practitioner subject to the provisions of subsection a. or b. of this section, is guilty of a felony of the fourth degree if that person recklessly commits health care claims fraud. In addition to all other criminal penalties allowed by law, a person convicted under this subsection may be subject to a fine of up to five times the pecuniary benefit obtained or sought to be obtained.

e. Each act of health care claims fraud shall constitute an additional, separate and distinct offense, except that five or more separate acts may be aggregated for the purpose of establishing liability pursuant to subsection c. of this section. Multiple acts of health care claims fraud which are contained in a single record, bill, claim, application, payment, affidavit, certification or other document shall each constitute an additional, separate and distinct offense for purposes of this section.

f. (1) The falsity, fictitiousness, fraudulence or misleading nature of a statement may be inferred by the trier of fact in the case of a practitioner who attempts to submit, submits, causes to be submitted or attempts to cause to be submitted any record, bill, claim or other document for treatment or procedure without the practitioner, or an associate of the practitioner, having performed an assessment of the physical or mental condition of the patient or client necessary to determine the appropriate course of treatment.

(2) The falsity, fictitiousness, fraudulence or misleading nature of a statement may be inferred by the trier of fact in the case of a person who attempts to submit, submits, causes to be submitted or attempts to cause to be submitted any record, bill, claim or other document for more treatments or procedures than can be performed during the time in which the treatments or procedures were represented to have been performed.

(3) Proof that a practitioner has signed or initialed a record, bill, claim or other document gives rise to an inference that the practitioner has read and reviewed that record, bill, claim or other document.

g. In order to promote the uniform enforcement of this act, the Attorney General shall develop health care claims fraud prosecution guidelines and disseminate them to the county prosecutors within 120 days of the effective date of this act.

h. For the purposes of this section, a person acts recklessly with respect to a material element of an offense when he consciously disregards a substantial and unjustifiable risk that the material element exists or will result from his conduct. The risk must be of such a nature and degree that, considering the nature and purpose of the actor's conduct and the circumstances known to him, its disregard involves a gross deviation from the standard of conduct that a reasonable person would observe in the actor's situation.

i. (1) Nothing in this act shall preclude an indictment and conviction for any other offense defined by the laws of this State.

(2) Nothing in this act shall preclude an assignment judge from dismissing a prosecution of health care claims fraud if the assignment judge determines the conduct charged to be a *de minimis* infraction.

PRACTICAL APPLICATION OF STATUTE

Both Maxwell Borscht and Dr. Elias Williamson would be guilty of felonies under 10-4.3. This statute generally makes it a felony of varying degrees to either "knowingly" or "recklessly" commit health care claims fraud as defined by 10-4.2. In a nutshell, health care claims fraud means the making of any false or misleading statement for the purpose of obtaining some fiduciary benefit as a result of such statement. Section 10-4.3 breaks down this sort of fraud into different degrees, depending on whether the defendant is a "practitioner" and whether the *mens rea* was "knowing" or "reckless."

Maxwell Borscht went to his friend Dr. Williamson and asked him to act as if he performed heart transplant surgery for Borscht—of course, no such surgery was ever performed. Thereafter, Williamson submitted claims to the appropriate insurance company to cover the "surgery" costs; the proceeds of the insurance payments were split between the doctor and Borscht.

Our good doctor would be guilty of the most severe second degree felony of health care claims fraud because he qualifies as a "practitioner" (defined in 10-4.2 generally as any person licensed in the state to practice medicine or other qualified medical practice) and because he "knowingly" submitted the bogus claims to the insurance company. Had Dr. Williamson submitted the claim without making reasonable efforts to confirm its authenticity but without actually knowing the claim was false, he would have likely been found to be "reckless" under subsection b. of the statute and therefore guilty of the lesser third degree offense.

Since Borscht does not qualify as a "practitioner," his offense would fall under either subsection c. or d. of the statute. Given that he "knowingly" committed health care claims fraud, Borscht would be guilty of the third degree felony under subsection c. It is important to note that under this subsection, there is a provision that would increase this felony to the second degree if the "nonpractitioner" was found to have "knowingly" committed five or more acts of health care claims fraud with an aggregate pecuniary benefit of $1,000 or more. Subsection d. makes the offense one of the fourth degree when the intent is merely "reckless" as opposed to "knowing."

It is interesting to note that the legislature has included several "presumptions" favorable to the prosecution of health care claims fraud; these are found within subsection f. of the statute. The presumptions essentially list certain behaviors or acts that, if shown at trial, automatically create an inference of fraudulent intent by the defendant. In general, these activities include submission of claims without performing an assessment of the patient and submission of claims for more treatments or procedures than could be performed during the time in which they were represented to have been performed. It may also be inferred by the trier of fact that any document signed or initialed by the practitioner has been read and reviewed by the practitioner.

10-4.4.   **Definitions relative to insurance fraud**

As used in 10-4.5 and 10-4.5, unless the context otherwise requires, the following words and terms shall have the following meanings:

a. "Insurance company" means any person, company, corporation, unincorporated association, partnership, professional corporation, agency of government and any other entity authorized or permitted to do business in the State, subject to regulation by the State or incorporated or organized under the laws of any other state of the United States or of any foreign nation or of any province or territory thereof, to indemnify another against loss, damage, risk or liability arising from a contingent or unknown event.

b. "Insurance company" includes, but is not limited to, an insurance company as that term is defined in the Insurance Regulatory Act of this State, self-insurer, re-insurer, reciprocal exchange, inter-insurer, hospital, medical or health service corporation, health maintenance organization, surety, assigned risk plan, joint insurance fund and any other entity legally engaged in the business of insurance as authorized or permitted by this State, including but not limited to any such entity incorporated or organized under the laws of any other state of the United States or of any foreign nation or of any province or territory thereof.

c. "Insurance policy" means the instrument, in writing, electronically or in any other form, in which are set forth the terms of any certificate of insurance, binder of coverage, contract of insurance or contract of re-insurance, issued by an insurance company, including, but not limited to, a state-assigned risk plan, plan of indemnity protection provided by or on behalf of a joint insurance fund or benefit plan, motor club service plan or guaranty bond, surety bond, cash bond or any other alternative to insurance authorized or permitted by this state.

d. "Insurance transaction" means a transaction by, between or among (1) an insurance company and (2) an insured, claimant, applicant for insurance, public adjuster, insurance professional, practitioner as defined by section 2 of 10-4.2, attorney or any person who acts on behalf of any of the foregoing for the purpose of obtaining insurance or re-insurance, calculating insurance premiums, submitting a claim, negotiating or adjusting a claim or otherwise obtaining insurance, self-insurance or re-insurance or obtaining the benefits or annuities thereof or therefrom.

e. "Premium finance transaction" means a transaction involving or related to insurance premium financing which is subject to the Insurance Premium Finance Company Act.

10-4.5.   **Felony of insurance fraud**

a. A person is guilty of the felony of insurance fraud if that person knowingly makes, or causes to be made, a false, fictitious, fraudulent or misleading statement of material fact in, omits a material fact from or causes a material fact to be omitted from any record, bill, claim or other document, in writing, electronically, orally or in any other form, that a person attempts to submit, submits, causes to be submitted or attempts to cause to be submitted as part of, in support of or opposition to or in connection with: (1) a claim for payment, reimbursement or other benefit pursuant to an insurance policy or from an insurance company; (2) an application to obtain or renew an insurance policy; (3) any payment made or to be made in accordance with the terms of an insurance policy or premium finance transaction; or (4) an affidavit, certification, record or other document used in any insurance or premium finance transaction.

b. Insurance fraud constitutes a felony of the second degree if the person knowingly commits five or more acts of insurance fraud, including acts of health care claims fraud pursuant to section 2 of 10-4 and if the aggregate value of property, services or other benefit wrongfully obtained or sought to be obtained is at least $1,000. Otherwise, insurance fraud is a felony of the third degree. Each act of insurance fraud shall constitute an additional, separate and distinct offense, except that five or more separate acts may be aggregated for the purpose of establishing liability pursuant to this subsection. Multiple acts of insurance fraud which are contained in a single record, bill, claim, application, payment, affidavit, certification or other document shall each constitute an additional, separate and distinct offense for purposes of this subsection.

c. Proof that a person has signed or initialed an application, bill, claim, affidavit, certification, record or other document may give rise to an inference that the person has read and reviewed the application, bill, claim, affidavit, certification, record or other document.

d. In order to promote the uniform enforcement of this act, the Attorney General shall develop insurance fraud prosecution guidelines and disseminate them to county prosecutors within 180 days of the effective date of this act.

e. Nothing in this act shall preclude an indictment and conviction for any other offense defined by the laws of this State.

PRACTICAL APPLICATION OF STATUTE

Acts Constituting Second Degree Insurance Fraud

Last year, Dr. Charlotte P. Bimmany, a chiropractic physician, sent over a thousand "Claims for Payment" to various insurance companies; Anil Kamal, a deputy attorney general, however, learned that 30 of the claims were false. Specifically, Kamal obtained statements from 30 patients that their herniated disks, as reported by Dr. Bimmany, were false. In the aggregate, Dr. Bimmany received over $100,000 from these claims.

Several of the patients admitted that they knew that Dr. Bimmany was submitting fictitious claims. They advised Kamal that they agreed to have the false claims submitted so that they could obtain lucrative settlements for car accidents in which they were involved. Even more so, they admitted that almost all monies sought by Dr. Bimmany were for medical visits that never actually occurred.

Dr. Bimmany is guilty of a second degree felony of insurance fraud. Per subsection a. of 10-4.5, a person has committed insurance fraud where he "knowingly" makes a "false, fictitious, fraudulent or misleading statement of material fact" in connection with a submission for "payment" or other "benefit" from an "insurance company" or the "Unsatisfied Claim and Judgment Fund Law." Subsection b. of the statute sets forth the grading of the offense.

A second degree felony has been committed if the person knowingly commits "five or more acts of insurance fraud" *and* if the aggregate value involved is "at least $1,000." Otherwise, insurance fraud is a third degree felony.

Dr. Bimmany, as a practice, submitted fictitious claims of herniated disk injuries to insurance companies in order to bolster her patients' monetary recovery in automobile accident cases; moreover, she submitted claims for payment for numerous medical visits that never occurred. She clearly "knew" her claims for payment were false. The aggregate value involved in her fraudulent claims was over $100,000, far exceeding the $1,000 figure itemized in subsection b. Also, significantly more than five acts of insurance fraud were committed by Dr. Bimmany, as her false submissions involved 30 patients. Accordingly, she is guilty of a second degree felony.

Acts Constituting Third Degree Insurance Fraud

Annie Avalanche contacts the insurance company for Cool Mint Supermarket, seeking payment because she "slipped on a banana peel" in the store and broke her ankle. The truth is that she broke her ankle in a bizarre piano accident. Honest Eddie Bonino seeks a new automobile insurance policy. To avoid the company's detection of the seven car accidents he had in the last five years, Eddie lists his last name as "Smith" on the application.

Both Annie Avalanche and Honest Eddie are guilty of third degree felonies under 10-4.5. In each case, the actor only committed one act of insurance fraud and therefore faces the lower degree charge.

It is important to note here, though, that an actor can always be charged with other felonies (e.g., theft offenses), in addition to insurance fraud, where such is warranted. Subsection e. of 10-4.5 provides that "nothing in this act shall preclude an indictment and conviction for any other offense defined by the laws of this State." Accordingly, if Annie Avalanche collected $200,000 pursuant to her fictitious claim, she could be convicted of a second degree theft offense (the dollar value exceeds $75,000) in addition to a third degree offense of insurance fraud.

10-5.   **Bad checks**

A person who issues or passes a check or similar sight order for the payment of money, knowing that it will not be honored by the drawee, commits an offense as provided for in subsection c. of this section. For the purposes of this section as well as in any prosecution for theft committed by means of a bad check, an issuer is presumed to know that the check or money order (other than a post-dated check or order) would not be paid, if:

a. The issuer had no account with the drawee at the time the check or order was issued; or

b. Payment was refused by the drawee for lack of funds, or due to a closed account, after a deposit by the payee into a bank for collection or after presentation to the drawee within 46 days after issue, and the issuer failed to make good within ten days after receiving notice of that refusal or after notice has been sent to the issuer's last known address. Notice of refusal may be given to the issuer orally or in writing in any reasonable manner by any person.

    c. An offense under this section is:
- (1) A felony of the second degree if the check or money order is $75,000 or more;
- (2) A felony of the third degree if the check or money order is $1,000 or more but is less than $75,000;
- (3) A felony of the fourth degree if the check or money order is $200 or more but is less than $1,000;
- (4) A misdemeanor A if the check or money order is less than $200.

PRACTICAL APPLICATION OF STATUTE

Section 10-5 makes it an offense to write a check "knowing" that it will not be honored by the drawee (generally a bank) under one of two circumstances. Subsection a. applies to those issuing a check where the issuer has no account with the drawee at the time the check was issued. Subsection b. applies when after the check has been refused by the drawee for lack of funds, notice is given to the issuer, and he fails to make good on the amount due within ten days after receiving notice of the refusal.

Maxwell Borscht issued a check for $3,500 in exchange for various livestock that a farmer owned in Sussex County, but Borscht "knew" his check was bad—at the time he issued the check, he was aware that no bank account existed to cover it. Accordingly, he is guilty of an offense under 10-5a.

If there had been an active account but it did not hold sufficient funds to cover the check, Borscht probably would have been guilty under subsection b., since it is unlikely he would have responded to notice of the bank's refusal to pay. It is important to note that this statute only applies to those who know that the check will not clear for any of the above reasons; therefore, individuals who accidentally overdraft their account would not be guilty of an offense under this statute.

Subsection c. of the statute lays out the degrees of offense determined by the amount of the check or money order. The degrees/amounts are set forth as follows: second degree felony for amounts of $75,000 or more; third degree felony for amounts of $1,000 or more but less than $75,000; fourth degree felony for amounts of $200 or more but less than $1,000; and misdemeanor A if the check or money order is less than $200. Given that Borscht's bad check to the farmer was for $3,500, he is guilty of a third degree felony.

10-6.   **Credit cards**

    a. Definitions. As used in this section:
- (1) "Cardholder" means the person or organization named on the face of a credit card to whom or for whose benefit the credit card is issued by an issuer.
- (2) "Credit card" means any tangible or intangible instrument or device issued with or without fee by an issuer that can be used, alone or in connection with another means of account access, in obtaining money, goods, services or anything else of value on credit, including credit cards, credit plates, account numbers or any other means of account access.
- (3) "Expired credit card" means a credit card which is no longer valid because the term shown either on it or on documentation provided to the cardholder by the issuer has elapsed.

(4) "Issuer" means the business organization or financial institution which issues a credit card or its duly authorized agent.

(5) "Receives" or "receiving" means acquiring possession or control or accepting a credit card as security for a loan.

(6) "Revoked credit card" means a credit card which is no longer valid because permission to use it has been suspended or terminated by the issuer.

b. False statements made in procuring issuance of credit card. A person who makes or causes to be made, either directly or indirectly, any false statement in writing, knowing it to be false and with intent that it be relied on, respecting his identity or that of any other person, firm or corporation, or his financial condition or that of any other person, firm or corporation, for the purpose of procuring the issuance of a credit card is guilty of a felony of the fourth degree.

c. Credit card theft.

(1) A person who takes or obtains a credit card from the person, possession, custody or control of another without the cardholder's consent or who, with knowledge that it has been so taken, receives the credit card with intent to use it or to sell it, or to transfer it to a person other than the issuer or the cardholder is guilty of a felony of the fourth degree. Taking a credit card without consent includes obtaining it by any conduct defined and prescribed in Chapter 9 of this title, Theft and Related Offenses.

A person who has in his possession or under his control (a) credit cards issued in the names of two or more other persons or (b) two or more stolen credit cards is presumed to have violated this paragraph.

(2) A person who receives a credit card that he knows to have been lost, mislaid or delivered under a mistake as to the identity or address of the cardholder and who retains possession with intent to use it or to sell it or to transfer it to a person other than the issuer or the cardholder is guilty of a felony of the fourth degree.

(3) A person other than the issuer who sells a credit card or a person who buys a credit card from a person other than the issuer is guilty of a felony of the fourth degree.

(4) A person who, with intent to defraud the issuer, a person or organization providing money, goods, services or anything else of value or any other person, obtains control over a credit card as security for debt is guilty of a felony of the fourth degree.

(5) A person who, with intent to defraud a purported issuer, a person or organization providing money, goods, services or anything else of value or any other person, falsely makes or falsely embosses a purported credit card or utters such a credit card is guilty of a third degree offense. A person other than the purported issuer who possesses two or more credit cards which are falsely made or falsely embossed is presumed to have violated this paragraph. A person "falsely makes" a credit card when he makes or draws, in whole or in part, a device or instrument which purports to be the credit card of a named issuer, but which is not such a credit card because the issuer did not authorize the making or drawing, or alters a credit card which was validly issued. A person "falsely embosses" a credit card when, without the authorization of the named issuer, he completes a credit card by adding any of the matter, other than the signature of the cardholder, which an issuer requires to appear on the credit card before it can be used by a cardholder.

(6) A person other than the cardholder or a person authorized by him who, with intent to defraud the issuer or a person or organization providing money, goods, services or anything else of value or any other person, signs a credit card is guilty of a felony of the fourth degree. A person who possesses two or more credit cards which are so signed is presumed to have violated this paragraph.

d. Intent of cardholder to defraud; penalties; knowledge of revocation. A person who, with intent to defraud the issuer, a person or organization providing money, goods, services or anything else of value or any other person, (1) uses for the purpose of obtaining money, goods, services or anything else of value a credit card obtained or retained in violation of subsection c. of this section or a credit card which he knows is forged, expired or revoked, or (2) obtains money, goods, services or anything else of value by representing without the consent of the cardholder that he is the holder of a specified card or by representing that he is the holder of a card and such card has not in fact been issued is guilty of a felony of the third degree. Knowledge of revocation shall be presumed to have been received by a cardholder four days after it has been mailed to him at the address set forth on the credit card or at his last known address by registered or certified mail, return receipt requested, or, if the address is more than 500 miles from the place of mailing, by air mail. If the address is located outside the United States, Puerto Rico, the Virgin Islands, the Canal Zone and Canada, notice shall be presumed to have been received ten days after mailing by registered or certified mail.

e. Intent to defraud by person authorized to furnish money, goods or services; penalties.

(1) A person who is authorized by an issuer to furnish money, goods, services or anything else of value upon presentation of a credit card by the cardholder, or any agent or employees of such person, who, with intent to defraud the issuer or the cardholder, furnishes money, goods, services or anything else of value upon presentation of a credit card obtained or retained in violation of subsection c. of this section or a credit card which he knows is forged, expired or revoked violates this paragraph and is guilty of a felony of the third degree.

(2) A person who is authorized by an issuer to furnish money, goods, services or anything else of value upon presentation of a credit card by the cardholder fails to furnish money, goods, services or anything else of value which he represents in writing to the issuer that he has furnished is guilty of a felony of the fourth degree.

f. Incomplete credit cards; intent to complete without consent. A person other than the cardholder possessing two or more incomplete credit cards, with intent to complete them without the consent of the issuer or a person possessing, with knowledge of its character, machinery, plates or any other contrivance designed to reproduce instruments purporting to be the credit cards of an issuer who has not consented to the preparation of such credit cards, is guilty of a felony of the third degree. A credit card is "incomplete" if part of the matter other than the signature of the cardholder, which an issuer requires to appear on the credit card before it can be used by a cardholder, has not yet been stamped, embossed, imprinted or written on it.

g. Receiving anything of value knowing or believing that it was obtained in violation of subsection d. of 10-6. A person who receives money, goods, services or anything else of value obtained in violation of subsection d. of this section, knowing or believing that it was so obtained, is guilty of a felony of the fourth degree. A person who obtains, at a discount price, a ticket issued by an airline, railroad, steamship or other transportation company which was acquired in violation of subsection d. of this section without reasonable inquiry to ascertain that the person from whom it was obtained had a legal right to possess it shall be presumed to know that such ticket was acquired under circumstances constituting a violation of subsection d. of this section.

h. Fraudulent use of credit cards. A person who knowingly uses any counterfeit, fictitious, altered, forged, lost, stolen or fraudulently obtained credit card to obtain money, goods, services or anything else of value or who, with unlawful or fraudulent intent, furnishes, acquires or uses any actual or fictitious credit card, whether alone or together with names of cardholders, or other information pertaining to a credit card account in any form is guilty of a felony of the third degree.

PRACTICAL APPLICATION OF STATUTE

Section 10-6 is a long and complex statute dealing with credit card theft and fraudulent use of either unlawfully acquired credit cards or falsely made cards. In Maxwell Borscht's case, he could rightfully be found guilty of offenses under subsections b., c. and d. of this statute.

Subsection c. makes it a felony of the fourth degree to obtain a credit card from a person without the cardholder's consent—and with intent to use it. Obviously, when Borscht stole the two cards from the Cape Marna home of Kalman Greenwald, he did so "without the cardholder's consent." His intent to use them was clearly manifested when he later presented the cards to obtain cash advances. With these two elements met, Maxwell Borscht could be convicted of a fourth degree felony as provided for in 10-6c.; however, his felony should probably be elevated to one of the third degree.

Subsection c., as discussed above, deals with the possession of credit cards "with intent to defraud." Once the defendant actually uses the cards for the purpose of obtaining money, goods, services or anything else of value, he falls into subsection d. of the statute, which automatically makes such behavior a felony of the third degree. In our case, once Borscht "maxed out" the cards via cash advances, he moved from the fourth degree felony of mere possession with intent to defraud to the third degree offense of actually using them to defraud the issuer.

In addition to this offense, Borscht violated subsection b. when he used the stolen cards, along with his phony driver's license, to apply for additional credit cards in Kalman Greenwald's name. Under subsection b. of the statute, it is a felony of the fourth degree to make false statements for the purpose of procuring the issuance of a credit card.

10-6.1.   **Definitions relative to scanning devices, reencoders; criminal use, degree of felony**

a. Definitions. As used in this section:

   (1) "Merchant" means any owner or operator of any store or other retail mercantile establishment or any agent, servant, employee, lessee, consignee, officer, director, franchisee or independent contractor of such owner or proprietor.

   (2) "Payment card" means a credit card, charge card, debit card or any other card that is issued to an authorized card user and that allows the user to obtain, purchase or receive goods, services, money or anything of value from a merchant.

   (3) "Reencoder" means an electronic device that places encoded information from the magnetic strip or stripe of a payment card onto the magnetic strip or stripe of a different payment card or any electronic medium that allows a transaction to occur.

   (4) "Scanning device" means a scanner, skimmer, reader or any other electronic device that is used to access, read, scan, obtain, memorize or store, temporarily or permanently, information encoded on the magnetic strip or stripe of a payment card.

b. It shall be a felony of the third degree for a person, with the intent to defraud an authorized user of a payment card, the issuer of the authorized user's payment card or a merchant, to use:

   (1) A scanning device to access, read, obtain, memorize or store, temporarily or permanently, information encoded on the magnetic strip or stripe of a payment card, without the permission of the authorized user of the payment card; or

(2) A reencoder to place information encoded on the magnetic strip or stripe of a payment card onto the magnetic strip or stripe of a different card or any electronic medium that allows a transaction to occur without the permission of the authorized user of the card from which the information is being reencoded.

c. It shall be a felony of the fourth degree for a person to knowingly possess with intent to commit a violation of paragraph (1) or (2) of subsection b. of this section any device, apparatus, equipment, software, article, material, good, property or supply that is specifically designed or adapted for use as or in a scanning device or reencoder.

Practical Application of Statute

This statute was created to meet the technological advances of criminals who seek to steal information from "payment cards" (e.g., credit cards, debit cards). New phrases such as "reencoder" and "scanning device" are introduced and defined in subsection a. of 10-6.1.

A "reencoder" is a device that electronically takes information from one payment card and transfers it to another payment card. A "scanning device" is utilized to access and/or store information encoded on a payment card.

Per subsection b. of the statute, an individual who uses a scanning device or reencoder to take information from another's payment card (or to engage in a transaction using another's payment card) is guilty of a third degree felony. However, the actor is only guilty if he does so "without the permission of the authorized user" of the payment card and where he acts "with the intent to defraud" the authorized user.

Under subsection c., it can be a fourth degree felony to simply possess a reencoder or scanning device—or any paraphernalia related to these potentially illicit items. However, the possession only actually becomes a felony if the defendant knowingly possesses them "with intent to commit" the illegal transactions and acts defined in subsection b. of this statute.

10-7.   **Deceptive business practices**

A person commits an offense if in the course of business he:

a. Uses or possesses for use a false weight or measure, or any other device for falsely determining or recording any quality or quantity;

b. Sells, offers or exposes for sale, or delivers less than the represented quantity of any commodity or service;

c. Takes or attempts to take more than the represented quantity of any commodity or service when as buyer he furnishes the weight or measure;

d. Sells, offers or exposes for sale adulterated or mislabeled commodities;

e. Makes a false or misleading statement in any advertisement addressed to the public or to a substantial segment thereof for the purpose of promoting the purchase or sale of property or services;

f. Makes a false or misleading written statement for the purpose of obtaining property or credit; or

g. Makes a false or misleading written statement for the purpose of promoting the sale of securities, or omits information required by law to be disclosed in written documents relating to securities.

The offense is a felony of the fourth degree if subsection f. or g. is violated. Otherwise it is a misdemeanor A.

It is an affirmative defense to prosecution under this section if the defendant proves by a preponderance of the evidence that his conduct was not knowingly or recklessly deceptive.

"Adulterated" means varying from the standard of composition or quality prescribed by or pursuant to any statute providing criminal penalties for such variance or set by established commercial usage. "Mislabeled" means varying from the standard of truth or disclosure in labeling prescribed by or pursuant to any statute providing criminal penalties for such variance or set by established commercial usage.

PRACTICAL APPLICATION OF STATUTE

Perhaps it is only fitting that Maxwell Borscht became a victim of fraud at some point during his own series of deception. When Borscht actually paid for a large jar of "anti-aging" pills that were labeled as being made from rare coral found only off the coast of Australia, the merchant was in violation of 10-7d. Why? Because it turned out that the merchant had actually produced the pills in his own basement from common household ingredients.

Section 10-7d. makes it a misdemeanor A to sell, offer or expose for sale mislabeled commodities. The statute, in total, deals with various deceptive means of selling a falsely determined quality or quantity of any sort of commodity or service. While subsection d. qualifies as misdemeanor A, there are two subsections of 10-7 that deal with offenses considered fourth degree felonies. These subsections, f. and g., make it a fourth degree felony to either make false or misleading written statements for the purpose of obtaining property or credit or make false or misleading written statements (or to omit information required by law to be disclosed), for the purpose of promoting the sale of securities.

In the case of the "anti-aging" pill merchant, he is guilty of 10-7's lesser offense. He misrepresented where the pills' ingredients were derived in order to facilitate sales; accordingly, he violated subsection d. of the statute and is guilty of a misdemeanor A.

10-7.1.   **Definitions**

As used in this act:

a. "Advertise" means engaging in promotional activities including, but not limited to, newspaper, radio and television advertising; the distribution of fliers and circulars; and the display of window and interior signs.

b. "Food," "food product" or "food commodity" means any food, food product or food preparation, whether raw or prepared for human consumption, and whether in a solid or liquid state, including, but not limited to, any meat, meat product or meat preparation; any milk, milk product or milk preparation; and any alcoholic or non-alcoholic beverage.

c. "Food commodity in package form" means a food commodity put up or packaged in any manner in advance of sale in units suitable for retail sale and which is not intended for consumption at the point of manufacture.

d. "Kosher" means prepared under and maintained in strict compliance with the laws and customs of the Orthodox Jewish religion and includes foods prepared for the festival of Passover and represented to be "kosher for Passover."

10-7.2.   **False representations**

    a. A false representation prohibited by this act shall include any oral or written statement that directly or indirectly tends to deceive or otherwise lead a reasonable individual to believe that a non-kosher food or food product is kosher.

    b. The presence of any non-kosher food or food product in any place of business that advertises or represents itself in any manner as selling, offering for sale, preparing or serving kosher food or food products only is presumptive evidence that the person in possession offers the same for sale in violation of this act.

    c. It shall be a complete defense to a prosecution under this act that the defendant relied in good faith upon the representations of a slaughterhouse, manufacturer, processor, packer or distributor or any person or organization which certifies or represents any food or food product at issue to be kosher, kosher for Passover or as having been prepared under or sanctioned by Orthodox Jewish religious requirements.

10-7.3.   **Misdemeanor A**

A person commits a misdemeanor A if, in the course of business, he:

    a. (1) Falsely represents any food sold, prepared, served or offered for sale to be kosher or kosher for Passover;

        (2) Removes or destroys, or causes to be removed or destroyed, the original means of identification affixed to food commodities to indicate that same are kosher or kosher for Passover, except that this paragraph shall not be construed to prevent the removal of the identification if the commodity is offered for sale as non-kosher; or

        (3) Sells, disposes of or has in his possession for the purpose of resale as kosher any food commodity to which a slaughterhouse plumba, mark, stamp, tag, brand, label or other means of identification has been fraudulently attached.

    b. (1) Labels or identifies a food commodity in package form to be kosher or kosher for Passover or possesses such labels or means of identification, unless he is the manufacturer or packer of the food commodity in package form;

        (2) Labels or identifies an article of food not in package form to be kosher or kosher for Passover or possesses such labels or other means of identification, unless he is the manufacturer of the article of food;

        (3) Falsely labels any food commodity in package form as kosher or kosher for Passover by having or permitting to be inscribed on it, in any language, the words "kosher" or "kosher for Passover," "parve," "glatt" or any other words or symbols which would tend to deceive or otherwise lead a reasonable individual to believe that the commodity is kosher or kosher for Passover; or

        (4) Labels any food commodity in package form by having or permitting to be inscribed on it the words "kosher-style," "kosher-type," "Jewish" or "Jewish-style," unless the product label also displays the word "non-kosher" in letters at least as large and in close proximity.

    c. (1) Sells, offers for sale, prepares or serves in or from the same place of business both unpackaged non-kosher food and unpackaged food he represents to be kosher unless he posts a window sign at the entrance of his establishment which states in block letters at least four inches in height: "Kosher and Non-Kosher Foods Sold Here," or "Kosher and Non-Kosher Foods Served Here" or a statement of similar import; or

        (2) Employs any Hebrew word or symbol in any advertising of any food offered for sale or place of business in which food is prepared, whether for on-premises or

off-premises consumption, unless the advertisement also sets forth in conjunction therewith and in English, the words "We Sell Kosher Food Only," "We Sell Both Kosher and Non-Kosher Foods" or words of similar import, in letters of at least the same size as the characters used in Hebrew. For the purpose of this paragraph, "Hebrew symbol" means any Hebrew word or letter or any symbol, emblem, sign, insignia or other mark that simulates a Hebrew word or letter.

d. (1) Displays for sale in the same show window or other location on or in his place of business, both unpackaged food represented to be kosher and unpackaged non-kosher food, unless he:

    (a) Displays over the kosher and non-kosher food signs that read, in clearly visible block letters, "kosher food" and "non-kosher food," respectively, or, as to the display of meat alone, "kosher meat" and "non-kosher meat," respectively;

    (b) Separates the kosher food products from the non-kosher food products by keeping the products in separate display cabinets or by segregating kosher items from non-kosher items by use of clearly visible dividers; and

    (c) Slices or otherwise prepares the kosher food products for sale with utensils used solely for kosher food items;

(2) Prepares or serves any food as kosher whether for consumption in his place of business or elsewhere if in the same place of business he also prepares or serves non-kosher food, unless he:

    (a) Uses and maintains separate and distinctly labeled or marked dishes and utensils for each type of food; and

    (b) Includes in clearly visible block letters the statement "Kosher and Non-Kosher Foods Prepared and Sold Here" in each menu or sign used or posted on the premises or distributed or advertised off the premises;

(3) Sells or has in his possession for the purpose of resale as kosher any food commodity not having affixed thereto the original slaughterhouse plumba, mark, stamp, tag, brand, label or other means of identification employed to indicate that the food commodity is kosher or kosher for Passover; or

(4) Sells or offers for sale, as kosher, any fresh meat or poultry that is identified as "soaked and salted," unless (a) the product has in fact been soaked and salted in a manner which makes it kosher, and (b) the product is marked "soaked and salted" on the package label or, if the product is not packaged, on a sign prominently displayed in conjunction with the product. For the purpose of this paragraph, "fresh meat or poultry" shall mean meat or poultry that has not been processed except for salting and soaking.

PRACTICAL APPLICATION OF STATUTE

Sections 10-7.1, 10-7.2 and 10-7.3 work together to make it a misdemeanor A to "knowingly" misrepresent non-kosher foods as being kosher or kosher for Passover. Section 10-7.1 contains the general definitions to be used in these related statutes—they are basically self-explanatory. Section 10-7.2 contains some further definitional subsections, explaining that a "false representation" prohibited by the act constitutes any oral or written statement that either directly or indirectly leads a person believe that non-kosher food or food products are kosher.

It is important to note, however, that subsection c. of 10-7.2 provides a complete defense to any prosecution under the three statutes. If the defendant relied in good faith on the representations of an organization such as a slaughterhouse, which certified any food at issue to be kosher (or having been prepared under Orthodox Jewish religious requirements), then he has an affirmative defense.

The heart of these three statutes lies in 10-7.3, which provides an extensive list of offenses, all considered misdemeanor As, dealing with the knowing misrepresentation of non-kosher foods as being kosher. Although the entire list boils down to the aforementioned knowing misrepresentation, the specifics include activities such as mislabeling or falsely labeling any food commodity as kosher and removing the original means of identification indicating that foods are kosher. There are additional requirements mentioned, such as the use of separate utensils for serving or preparing kosher and non-kosher foods, but the bottom line is that one cannot falsely serve, label, prepare, display or otherwise promote packaged or nonpackaged food as kosher unless he has followed the strict Orthodox Jewish religious requirements. Knowing failure to do so may result in a conviction of a misdemeanor A.

10-8.   **Misrepresentation of mileage of motor vehicle**

A person commits a misdemeanor A when he sells, exchanges, offers for sale or exchange or exposes for sale or exchange a used motor vehicle on which he has changed or disconnected the mileage registering instrument on the vehicle to show a lesser mileage reading than that actually recorded on the vehicle or on the instrument with the purpose to misrepresent the mileage of the vehicle. This provision shall not prevent the servicing, repair or replacement of a mileage registering instrument which by reason of normal wear or through damage requires service, repair or replacement if the instrument is then set at zero or at the actual previously recorded mileage.

In addition to the penalty authorized for violation of this section, the Director of the Division of Motor Vehicles may, after notice and hearing, revoke the license of any motor vehicle dealer so convicted.

PRACTICAL APPLICATION OF STATUTE

Let us assume that Maxwell Borscht had come up with yet another scheme for raising start-up capital for his fraudulent business, Jackpot Entertainment Insurance. This time, he happens to find several cars in Kalman Greenwald's garage and decides to modify the odometer on a few of them. He then sells them for more money than their fair market value would have yielded if the true mileage were presented. Here, Borscht would have committed a misdemeanor A under section 10-8. This statute proscribes the sale or exchange, or offer for sale or exchange, of any used motor vehicle on which a person has changed the mileage on the vehicle to show a lesser mileage than actually recorded on the vehicle. In order to be convicted under 10-8, the defendant must act "with the purpose to misrepresent the mileage of the vehicle." But why else would someone set back the mileage of a vehicle? Perhaps accidentally?

10-8.1.   **Definition; determination of degree of offense**

a. As used in chapter 10, unless a different meaning plainly is required:

"Benefit derived" means the loss resulting from the offense or any gain or advantage to the actor, or coconspirators or any person in whom the actor is interested, whichever is greater, whether loss, gain or advantage takes the form of money, property, commercial interests or anything else, the primary significance of which is economic gain.

b. The benefit derived or resulting harm in violation of chapter 10 shall be determined by the trier of fact. The benefit derived or resulting harm pursuant to one scheme or course of conduct, whether in relation to the same person or several persons, may be aggregated in determining the degree of the offense.

10-9. **Misconduct by corporate official**

A person is guilty of a felony when:

a. Being a director of a corporation, he knowingly, with the purpose to defraud, concurs in any vote or act of the directors of such corporation, or any of them, which has the purpose of:

  (1) Making a dividend except in the manner provided by law;

  (2) Dividing, withdrawing or in any manner paying to any stockholder any part of the capital stock of the corporation except in the manner provided by law;

  (3) Discounting or receiving any note or other evidence of debt in payment of an installment of capital stock actually called in and required to be paid, or with the purpose of providing the means of making such payment;

  (4) Receiving or discounting any note or other evidence of debt with the purpose of enabling any stockholder to withdraw any part of the money paid in by him on his stock; or

  (5) Applying any portion of the funds of such corporation, directly or indirectly, to the purchase of shares of its own stock, except in the manner provided by law.

b. Being a director or officer of a corporation, he, with the purpose to defraud:

  (1) Issues, participates in issuing or concurs in a vote to issue any increase of its capital stock beyond the amount of the capital stock thereof, duly authorized by or in pursuance of law; or

  (2) Sells, agrees to sell or is directly interested in the sale of any share of stock of such corporation, or in any agreement to sell the same, unless at the time of such sale or agreement he is an actual owner of such share, provided that the foregoing shall not apply to a sale by or on behalf of an underwriter or dealer in connection with a *bona fide* public offering of shares of stock of such corporation.

c. He purposely or knowingly uses, controls or operates a corporation for the furtherance or promotion of any criminal object.

If the benefit derived from a violation of this section is $75,000, or more, the offender is guilty of a felony of the second degree. If the benefit derived exceeds $1,000, but is less than $75,000, the offender is guilty of a felony of the third degree. If the benefit derived is $1,000, or less, the offender is guilty of a felony of the fourth degree.

PRACTICAL APPLICATION OF STATUTE

Aside from the problems that Maxwell Borscht likely caused The Pellman Group, Sandy Ireland and the other board members of that company could be facing serious second degree criminal charges themselves for their arbitrary decision to issue a $150,000 "Presidents' Day bonus" dividend to each other while knowing this was in violation of the corporation's bylaws.

Section 10-9a.(1) specifically proscribes the board members' actions by making it a felony for a director of a corporation to "knowingly," with the purpose to defraud, vote in his capacity as a director to issue a dividend. Only dividends issued in "the manner provided by law" are permissible per this statute. Since the board members were aware that this "Presidents' Day bonus" was not allowed, they certainly had the requisite *mens rea*—"knowingly with the purpose to defraud"—necessary for conviction under this statute.

Section 10-9 breaks down these offenses into degree based on the monetary benefit derived from the violation. Given that each board member voted for a bonus of $150,000 for each individual, they would fall into the most severe category, which makes it a second degree felony when the benefit derived is $75,000 or more. Amounts over $1,000 but less than $75,000 fall into the third degree category, and amounts of $1,000 or less are fourth degree felonies.

10-10.   **Commercial bribery and breach of duty to act disinterestedly**

  a. A person commits a felony if he solicits, accepts or agrees to accept any benefit as consideration for knowingly violating or agreeing to violate a duty of fidelity to which he is subject as:

  (1) An agent, partner or employee of another;

  (2) A trustee, guardian, or other fiduciary;

  (3) A lawyer, physician, accountant, appraiser or other professional adviser or informant;

  (4) An officer, director, manager or other participant in the direction of the affairs of an incorporated or unincorporated association;

  (5) A labor official, including any duly appointed representative of a labor organization or any duly appointed trustee or representative of an employee welfare trust fund; or

  (6) An arbitrator or other purportedly disinterested adjudicator or referee.

  b. A person who holds himself out to the public as being engaged in the business of making disinterested selection, appraisal or criticism of commodities, real properties or services commits a felony if he solicits, accepts or agrees to accept any benefit to influence his selection, appraisal or criticism.

  c. A person commits a felony if he confers, or offers or agrees to confer, any benefit the acceptance of which would be criminal under this section.

  d. If the benefit offered, conferred, agreed to be conferred, solicited, accepted or agreed to be accepted in violation of this section is $75,000 or more, the offender is guilty of a felony of the second degree. If the benefit exceeds $1,000 but is less than $75,000, the offender is guilty of a felony of the third degree. If the benefit is $1,000 or less, the offender is guilty of a felony of the fourth degree.

PRACTICAL APPLICATION OF STATUTE

Sandy Ireland, one of The Pellman Group's Board of Directors, accepted $50,000 from Maxwell Borscht in return for granting the formation of a subsidiary company named Jackpot Entertainment Insurance. She knew that the creation of this subsidiary company could be detrimental to The Pellman Group and its shareholders. This act renders her guilty of a third degree felony.

Section 10-10 makes it a felony for a director, such as Ireland, to accept any benefit as consideration for "knowingly" violating a duty of fidelity to the company that she serves. Subsection a. lists various positions from which a duty of fidelity to another person or entity is implied. In Ireland's case, she falls within subsection a.(4) as a director of "an incorporated or unincorporated association," violating her fiduciary duty not only to The

Pellman Group but to its shareholders as well. Her acceptance of $50,000 in return for the formation of the subsidiary without any sort of research into the proposed subsidiary or Borscht himself would probably constitute a breach of fiduciary duty. Given that Ireland "knew" what Borscht was up to—in creating a sham subsidiary—she certainly breached this fiduciary duty and committed a felony under 10-10.

Similar to the previous statute, the degree of felony associated with a violation of 10-10 is broken down by the dollar amount of the benefit offered, conferred, accepted or agreed to. The most severe second degree felony is reserved for benefits of $75,000 or more. Amounts less than $75,000 but more than $1,000 are third degree felonies, and benefits of $1,000 or less are considered felonies of the fourth degree. Ireland's acceptance of $50,000 would place her within the third degree version of this felony.

10-11.   **Rigging publicly exhibited contest**

    a. A person commits a felony if, with the purpose to prevent a publicly exhibited contest from being conducted in accordance with the rules and usages which govern it, he:

        (1) Confers or offers or agrees to confer any benefit upon or threatens any injury to a participant, official or other person associated with the contest or exhibition; or

        (2) Tampers with any person, animal or thing.

    b. Soliciting or accepting benefit for rigging. A person commits a felony if he knowingly solicits, accepts or agrees to accept any benefit the giving of which would be criminal under subsection a.

    c. If the benefit offered, conferred, agreed to be conferred, solicited, accepted or agreed to be accepted in violation of subsections a. and b. of this section is $75,000 or more, the offender is guilty of a felony of the second degree. If the benefit exceeds $1,000 but is less than $75,000, the offender is guilty of a felony of the third degree. If the benefit is $1,000 or less, the offender is guilty of a felony of the fourth degree.

    d. Failure to report solicitation for rigging. A person commits a misdemeanor A if he fails to report, with reasonable promptness, a solicitation to accept any benefit or to do any tampering, the giving or doing of which would be criminal under subsection a.

    e. Participation in rigged contest. A person commits a felony of the fourth degree if he knowingly engages in, sponsors, produces, judges or otherwise participates in a publicly exhibited contest knowing that the contest is being conducted in violation of subsection a. of this section.

PRACTICAL APPLICATION OF STATUTE

Section 10-11 makes it criminal, in varying degrees, to engage in activities involving the rigging of contests. Very simply, a person commits a felony if he attempts to either confer any benefit on or threaten injury to a participant, official or other person associated with the contest "with the purpose" to prevent the contest from being conducted in accordance with its rules. This applies to a number of situations, including anyone who would tamper with a person, animal or thing in an attempt to alter the outcome. For instance, if a jockey were found to have used some sort of electrical shock system, forbidden by the horse racing rules, in order to get his horse to outperform the rest of the horses, he could be convicted of an offense under this statute. Depending on the amount of benefit offered, conferred or agreed to, the offense would vary in degree from a second degree felony to a felony of the fourth degree. Amounts of $75,000 or more are second degree offenses, amounts less than $75,000 but more than $1,000 are third degree felonies and amounts of $1,000 or less are fourth degree felonies.

The statute also makes it a misdemeanor A to fail to report solicitation for such rigging. If a person is solicited to accept any benefit or do any tampering that would constitute illegal tampering, he is required to report such solicitation with "reasonable promptness." Although the statute does not give a specific timeline of what "reasonable promptness" is, it would be safe to assume that the solicitee would be required to report the solicitation at the earliest opportune moment under the facts and circumstances of the matter.

10-12.   Defrauding secured creditors

A person is guilty of a felony of the fourth degree when he destroys, removes, conceals, encumbers, transfers or otherwise deals with property subject to a security interest with the purpose to hinder enforcement of that interest.

PRACTICAL APPLICATION OF STATUTE

Let's say Maxwell Borscht had rightful possession of a mortgaged truck that he used in his pizza business. If he, with the intent to defraud the mortgagee, removed the truck from the state when he fell behind in payments and received notice of repossession, he would be guilty of the fourth degree felony of defrauding secured creditors. Section 10-12 makes it a felony to remove property subject to a security interest with the purpose of hindering enforcement of that interest. It is important to note that there must be an intent to defraud in order to be convicted under this statute; therefore, if Borscht had simply been operating his truck in the tri-state area as part of his normal course of business (and not to hinder the lawful repossession of it), his removal of the property from the state would not constitute a violation of this statute.

10-13.   Fraud in insolvency

A person commits a felony if, knowing that proceedings have been or are about to be instituted for the appointment of a receiver or other person entitled to administer property for the benefit of creditors or that any other composition or liquidation for the benefit of creditors has been or is about to be made, he:

a. Destroys, removes, conceals, encumbers, transfers or otherwise deals with any property or obtains any substantial part of or interest in the debtor's estate with the purpose to defeat or obstruct the claim of any creditor or otherwise to obstruct the operation of any law relating to administration of property for the benefit of creditors;

b. Knowingly falsifies any writing or record relating to the property; or

c. Knowingly misrepresents or refuses to disclose to a receiver or other person entitled to administer property for the benefit of creditors the existence, amount or location of the property or any other information which the actor could be legally required to furnish in relation to such administration.

If the benefit derived from a violation of this section is $75,000 or more, the offender is guilty of a felony of the second degree. If the benefit derived exceeds $1,000 but is less than $75,000, the offender is guilty of a felony of the third degree. If the benefit derived is $1,000 or less, the offender is guilty of a felony of the fourth degree.

PRACTICAL APPLICATION OF STATUTE

Returning to the pizza parlor example, let's say Maxwell Borscht had become insolvent and received notice that proceedings had been started for the repossession of the parlors and all his materials used in the business. The proceedings were initiated to repay creditors to which he owed money. Borscht, though, decides that he is not going to allow authorities to take his things; instead, he destroys everything that he can't remove from the parlors and hides everything else in a warehouse that he secretly rented under another name. Here, he would have committed the felony of fraud in insolvency as defined in 10-13.

Subsection a. of this statute makes it a felony when a person, "knowing" that proceedings have been instituted for repossession of property for the benefit of creditors, destroys, removes, conceals, encumbers or transfers any property "with the purpose to defeat or obstruct the claim of any creditor." Since this is exactly what Borscht did in the above example, he is guilty of violating subsection a. of 10-13.

If the repossession team knew Borscht had hidden certain materials and he refused to disclose the location of such materials upon request, Borscht's behavior would fall within subsection c. of the statute. This subsection makes it a felony to knowingly misrepresent the existence, amount or location of such property.

Given that the value of Borscht's materials that were either demolished or hidden would likely exceed $75,000, Borscht would be convicted of the second degree version of this felony. This statute follows many of the preceding statutes in determining the degree of the felony in association with the dollar amount of benefit derived: second degree for amounts over $75,000, third degree for amounts above $1,000 but less than $75,000 and fourth degree for amounts of $1,000 or less.

10-14.   Receiving deposits in a failing financial institution

An officer, manager or other person directing or participating in the direction of a financial institution commits a felony of the fourth degree if he receives or permits the receipt of a deposit, premium payment or other investment in the institution knowing that:

a. Due to financial difficulties the institution is about to suspend operations or go into receivership or reorganization; and

b. The person making the deposit or other payment is unaware of the precarious situation of the institution.

PRACTICAL APPLICATION OF STATUTE

This fairly straightforward statute makes it a felony of the fourth degree for a financial institution or authorized person thereof to accept deposits, premium payments or other investments in the institution knowing that the institution is about to stop operations due to financial difficulties and knowing that the person making the deposit or other payment is unaware of the precarious situation of the institution. It is important to note that this felony requires the knowledge of both prongs of the offense. Therefore, regardless of the institution's financial problems, if the person making the deposit is aware of this "precarious situation" and still makes the deposit, the institution or its managers have not committed an offense under this statute. Obviously, a teller or other employee of the institution accepting deposits without the requisite knowledge of the institution's financial condition should not be found guilty of this felony.

10-15.   **Misapplication of entrusted property and property of government or financial institution**

A person commits a felony if he applies or disposes of property that has been entrusted to him as a fiduciary or property belonging to or required to be withheld for the benefit of the government or of a financial institution in a manner which he knows is unlawful and involves substantial risk of loss or detriment to the owner of the property or to a person for whose benefit the property was entrusted whether or not the actor has derived a pecuniary benefit. "Fiduciary" includes trustee, guardian, executor, administrator, receiver and any person carrying on fiduciary functions on behalf of a corporation or other organization which is a fiduciary.

If the benefit derived from a violation of this section is $75,000 or more, the offender is guilty of a felony of the second degree. If the benefit derived exceeds $1,000 but is less than $75,000, the offender is guilty of a felony of the third degree. If the benefit derived is $1,000 or less, the offender is guilty of a felony of the fourth degree.

For the purposes of this section, the term "benefit derived" shall include but shall not be limited to the amount of any tax avoided, evaded or otherwise unpaid or improperly retained or disposed of.

PRACTICAL APPLICATION OF STATUTE

Extending the facts of Maxwell Borscht's case can help explain this statute. Borscht hires a few employees for his bogus company Jackpot Entertainment Insurance. In an attempt to make the company appear as legitimate as possible, he institutes 401k plans for these employees. Instead of using the money contributed by the employees for the plan, though, he uses this money to cover his company's expenses. Here, Borscht could rightfully be found guilty of a felony under 10-15.

This statute makes it criminal to apply or dispose of property that has been entrusted to a person as a fiduciary "in a manner which he knows is unlawful and involves substantial risk of loss or detriment to the owner of the property or to a person for whose benefit the property was entrusted." Clearly, Borscht, posing as the head of Jackpot Entertainment Insurance, would be considered a fiduciary in respect to the money given to him by the employees for the 401k plan. Obviously, Borscht knew that using this money for company expenses was unlawful and involved a substantial risk of loss and detriment to the employees. Accordingly, he is guilty of violating 10-15; in this case, the felony would probably be one of the second degree, as the amount involved likely would exceed $75,000.

Like many of the other statutes in Chapter 10, the offense is broken into degrees based on the dollar amount of the benefit. Amounts of $75,000 or more are second degree offenses, amounts less than $75,000 but more than $1,000 are third degree offenses and amounts of $1,000 or less are fourth degree offenses. As mentioned earlier, the failure to report solicitation for rigging is a misdemeanor A.

10-16.   **Securing execution of documents by deception**

A person commits a felony of the fourth degree if, by deception as to the contents of the instrument, he causes or induces another to execute any instrument affecting, purporting to affect or likely to affect the pecuniary interest of any person.

PRACTICAL APPLICATION OF STATUTE

This short statute makes it a fourth degree felony to cause another to execute any instrument affecting the pecuniary interest of any person by means of deception as to the contents of the instrument. If we return to The Hunk's "restructuring" of Manny's father's will (making Manny the sole beneficiary of his dad's estate), we can apply this statute by modifying the facts a bit.

Instead of dissolving the will's ink and replacing it, The Hunk creates a new will containing language favorable to Manny. The Hunk then proceeds to Manny's father and convinces him that the document is merely a receipt, acknowledging the delivery of a package which requires his signature. If the man signed the will, thinking it was merely a receipt, The Hunk would have violated this statute and could rightfully be charged with a fourth degree felony.

10-17.   **Impersonation; theft of identity; felony**

    a. A person is guilty of an offense if the person:

        (1) Impersonates another or assumes a false identity and does an act in such assumed character or false identity for the purpose of obtaining a benefit for himself or another or to injure or defraud another;

        (2) Pretends to be a representative of some person or organization and does an act in such pretended capacity for the purpose of obtaining a benefit for himself or another or to injure or defraud another;

        (3) Impersonates another, assumes a false identity or makes a false or misleading statement regarding the identity of any person, in an oral or written application for services, for the purpose of obtaining services; or

        (4) Obtains any personal identifying information pertaining to another person and uses that information, or assists another person in using the information, in order to assume the identity of or represent themselves as another person, without that person's authorization and with the purpose to fraudulently obtain or attempt to obtain a benefit or services or avoid the payment of debt or other legal obligation or avoid prosecution for a felony by using the name of the other person.

           As used in this section:

           "Benefit" means, but is not limited to, any property, any pecuniary amount, any services, any pecuniary amount sought to be avoided or any injury or harm perpetrated on another where there is no pecuniary value.

    b. A person is guilty of an offense if, in the course of making an oral or written application for services, the person impersonates another, assumes a false identity or makes a false or misleading statement with the purpose of avoiding payment for prior services. Purpose to avoid payment for prior services may be presumed upon proof that the person has not made full payment for prior services and has impersonated another, assumed a false identity or made a false or misleading statement regarding the identity of any person in the course of making oral or written application for services.

    c. (1) If the actor obtains a benefit or deprives another of a benefit in an amount less than $500 and the offense involves the identity of one victim, the actor shall be guilty of a felony of the fourth degree.

        (2) For a second or subsequent offense, or if the actor obtains a benefit or deprives another of a benefit in an amount of at least $500 but less than $75,000, or the

offense involves the identity of at least two but less than five victims, the actor shall be guilty of a felony of the third degree.

(3) If the actor obtains a benefit or deprives another of a benefit in the amount of $75,000 or more, or the offense involves the identity of more than five victims, the actor shall be guilty of a felony of the second degree.

d. A violation of using the personal identifying information of another to illegally purchase an alcoholic beverage or for using the personal identifying information of another to misrepresent his age for the purpose of obtaining tobacco or other consumer product denied to persons under 18 years of age shall not constitute an offense under this section if the actor received only that benefit or service and did not perpetrate or attempt to perpetrate any additional injury or fraud on another.

PRACTICAL APPLICATION OF STATUTE

After Maxwell Borscht stole Kalman Greenwald's credit cards and created a phony driver's license in Greenwald's name, he set out to visit several businesses throughout the state. Pursuant to these visits, he obtained, through impersonation of Greenwald, several items on credit from merchants. The merchants were familiar with Greenwald's reputation but not his physical appearance. By carrying through these acts, Borscht could add to his list of offenses an offense under 10-17, subsection a.(1).

This statute makes it a felony to impersonate another, or assume a false identity, and perform an act under such assumed character. The illicit act must be done for the "purpose of obtaining a benefit for himself or another or to injure or defraud another."

Borscht used Greenwald's identity to defraud merchants and obtain benefit. Specifically, the false pretense allowed him to obtain on invoice several items of value, including office furniture, equipment and handmade suits. Borscht, as Greenwald, agreed to pay the vendors within 30 days; payment, of course, was never remitted. With this being the case, Borscht is guilty of a felony under 10-17a.(1).

The offenses defined in this statute are broken down by degree in accordance with the pecuniary amount involved or the number of false identities assumed. Amounts of $75,000 or more or more than five false identities are considered felonies in the second degree; amounts less than $75,000 but more than $500 or at least two but less than five false identities are felonies of the third degree; for amounts less than $500 or one false identity, the offender is guilty of a felony of the fourth degree.

It appears from the facts in Borscht's case that he would be guilty of at least the third degree version of this felony. Possibly, he could be guilty of a felony of the second degree, since it is feasible that the office equipment, furniture and handmade suits could come to an amount over $75,000.

It should be noted that if the impersonation was merely for the purpose of obtaining a driver's license or motor vehicle registration or purchasing alcohol while a person is under age, it will not be considered an offense under this section if the actor received only that benefit or service and did not perpetrate or attempt to perpetrate any additional injury or fraud on another. This type of behavior is addressed and proscribed in other statutes found in the Code.

10-17.1.   **Use of personal identifying information of another, certain; second degree felony**

    a. A person is guilty of a felony of the second degree if, in obtaining or attempting to obtain a driver's license, birth certificate or other document issued by a governmental agency which could be used as a means of verifying a person's identity, age or any other personal identifying information, that person knowingly exhibits, displays or utters a document or other writing which falsely purports to be a driver's license, birth certificate or other document issued by a governmental agency or which belongs or pertains to a person other than the person who possesses the document.

    b. A conviction under this section shall not merge with a conviction of any other criminal offense, nor shall such other conviction merge with a conviction under this section, and the court shall impose separate sentences upon each violation of this section and any other criminal offense.

    c. A violation of tampering with public records, constituting a misdemeanor A, in a case where the person uses the personal identifying information of another to illegally purchase an alcoholic beverage or for using the personal identifying information of another to misrepresent his age for the purpose of obtaining tobacco or other consumer product denied to persons under 18 years of age shall not constitute an offense under this section if the actor received only that benefit or service and did not perpetrate or attempt to perpetrate any additional injury or fraud on another.

PRACTICAL APPLICATION OF STATUTE

This statute apparently makes it a second degree felony to obtain or attempt to obtain a driver's license (or other government document that can be used as personal identification) by "knowingly" exhibiting a document "which falsely purports to be a driver's license or other document issued by a governmental agency or which belongs or pertains to a person other than the person who possesses the document." The case of Maxwell Borscht can help explain this statute.

    Let's say Borscht appears at the Division of Motor Vehicles and presents a fictitious out-of-state driver's license in the name of Frank Malpone. Borscht claims to be Malpone and is now seeking a state driver's license in that name. Here, Borscht "knowingly" exhibited a government document that "falsely purported" to be a "driver's license" of another and did this in an effort to fraudulently obtain a state driver's license. Accordingly, he is guilty of violating 10-17.1.

Exception for Alcohol and Tobacco Purchases

Subsection c. of 10-17.1 carves out an exception wherein the statute shall not apply. A person may avoid conviction under 10-17.1 if he:

1. Uses the personal identifying information of another for the purpose of illegally purchasing alcohol; or

2. Uses the personal identifying information of another "to misrepresent his age for the purpose of obtaining tobacco or other consumer product denied to persons under 18 years of age."

The aforementioned acts shall not constitute an offense under 10-17.1 if the actor received *only* the above benefits or services and if the actor "did not perpetrate or attempt to perpetrate any additional injury or fraud on another."

10-17.2.   **Trafficking in personal identifying information pertaining to another person, certain; felony degrees; terms defined**

a. A person who knowingly distributes, manufactures or possesses any item containing personal identifying information pertaining to another person, without that person's authorization, and with knowledge that the actor is facilitating a fraud or injury to be perpetrated by anyone is guilty of a felony of the fourth degree.

b. (1) If the person distributes, manufactures or possesses 20 or more items containing personal identifying information pertaining to another person, or five or more items containing personal information pertaining to five or more separate persons, without authorization, and with knowledge that the actor is facilitating a fraud or injury to be perpetrated by anyone, the person is guilty of a felony of the third degree.

(2) If the person distributes, manufactures or possesses 50 or more items containing personal identifying information pertaining to another person, or ten or more items containing personal identifying information pertaining to five or more separate persons, without authorization, and with knowledge that the actor is facilitating a fraud or injury to be perpetrated by anyone, the person is guilty of a felony of the second degree.

c. Distribution, manufacture or possession of 20 or more items containing personal identifying information pertaining to another person or of items containing personal identifying information pertaining to five or more separate persons without authorization shall create an inference that the items were distributed, manufactured or possessed with knowledge that the actor is facilitating a fraud or injury to be perpetrated by anyone.

d. As used in this section:

"Distribute" means, but is not limited to, any sale, purchase, transfer, gift, delivery or provision to another, regardless of whether the distribution was for compensation.

"Item" means a writing or document, whether issued by a governmental agency or made by any business or person, recorded by any method that contains personal identifying information. Item includes, but is not limited to, an access device, book, check, paper, card, instrument or information stored in electronic form by way of email or otherwise, on any computer, computer storage medium, computer program, computer software, computer equipment, computer system or computer network or any part thereof or by other mechanical or electronic device such as cellular telephone, pager or other electronic device capable of storing information.

PRACTICAL APPLICATION OF STATUTE

Section 10-17.2 was enacted to combat the trafficking of individuals' personal identifying information. It prohibits the distribution, manufacture or possession of "any item containing personal identifying information" of another person. To be convicted under this statute, the actor must commit the proscribed acts without the other person's authorization and "with knowledge" that the actor "is facilitating a fraud or injury to be perpetrated by anyone." An example where 10-17.2 can be implemented is set forth below.

The Hunk, with knowledge that he is facilitating fraud, manufactures a birth certificate in the name of Selma Gonzalez. He does this without Gonzalez's authorization and sells the identifying documents to Carmella Swiss. Here, The Hunk has committed a fourth degree felony per subsection a. of 10-17.2.

The severity of this offense increases where the actor unlawfully distributes, manufactures or possesses multiple items containing personal identifying information.

Subsections b.(1) and b.(2) define where the offense increases to a third degree felony and a second degree felony, respectively.

10-18.

Slugs

A person is guilty of a misdemeanor A when other than under such circumstances as would constitute a violation of any of the provisions of the "Casino Control Act":

(1) He inserts or deposits a slug, key, tool, instrument, explosive or device in a coin, currency or credit card activated machine with the purpose to defraud; or

(2) He makes, possesses or disposes of a slug, key, tool, instrument, explosive or device or a drawing, print or mold of a key, tool, instrument, explosive or device with the purpose to enable a person to insert or deposit it in a coin, currency or credit card activated machine.

"Slug" means an object or article which, by virtue of its size, shape or any other quality, is capable of being inserted or deposited in a coin, currency or credit card activated machine as an improper substitute for money.

PRACTICAL APPLICATION OF STATUTE

Simply put, it is a misdemeanor A for a person to use any sort of slug (defined as any object that is capable of being inserted "in a coin, currency or credit card activated machine as an improper substitute for money") in any machine meant to accept legal currency or credit cards. An example of this offense is a person inserting a round metal object that substitutes as a quarter into a vending machine. Please note that it is also a misdemeanor A to possess any tool, instrument or other paraphernalia that would enable a person to create or use a slug.

10-19.

Wrongful credit practices and related offenses

a. Criminal usury. A person is guilty of criminal usury when not being authorized or permitted by law to do so, he:

(1) Loans or agrees to loan, directly or indirectly, any money or other property at a rate exceeding the maximum rate permitted by law; or

(2) Takes, agrees to take or receives any money or other property as interest on the loan or on the forbearance of any money or other interest in excess of the maximum rate permitted by law.

For the purposes of this section and notwithstanding any law of this State which permits as a maximum interest rate a rate or rates agreed to by the parties of the transaction, any loan or forbearance with an interest rate which exceeds 30% per annum shall not be a rate authorized or permitted by law, except if the loan or forbearance is made to a corporation, limited liability company or limited liability partnership, in which case any rate not in excess of 50% per annum shall be a rate authorized or permitted by law.

Criminal usury is a felony of the second degree if the rate of interest on any loan made to any person exceeds 50% per annum or the equivalent rate for a longer or shorter period. It is a felony of the third degree if the interest rate on any loan made to any person except a corporation, limited liability company or limited liability partnership does not exceed 50% per annum but the amount of the loan or forbearance exceeds $1,000. Otherwise, making a loan to any person in violation of subsections a.(1) and a.(2) of this section is a misdemeanor A.

b. Business of criminal usury. Any person who knowingly engages in the business of making loans or forbearances in violation of subsection a. of this section is guilty of a felony of the second degree and shall be subject to a fine of not more than $250,000 and any other appropriate disposition.

c. Possession of usurious loan records. A person is guilty of a felony of the third degree when, with knowledge of the nature thereof, he possesses any writing, paper instrument or article used to record criminally usurious transactions prohibited by subsection a. of this section.

d. Unlawful collection practices. A person is guilty of a misdemeanor A when, with the purpose to enforce a claim or judgment for money or property, he sends, mails or delivers to another person a notice, document or other instrument which has no judicial or official sanction and which in its format or appearance simulates a summons, complaint, court order or process or an insignia, seal or printed form of a federal, state or local government or an instrumentality thereof or is otherwise calculated to induce a belief that such notice, document or instrument has a judicial or official sanction.

e. Making a false statement of credit terms. A person is guilty of a misdemeanor A when he understates or fails to state the interest rate or makes a false or inaccurate or incomplete statement of any other credit terms.

f. Debt adjusters. Any person who shall act or offer to act as a debt adjuster shall be guilty of a felony of the fourth degree.

"Debt adjuster" means a person (1) who either acts or offers to act for a consideration as an intermediary between a debtor and his creditors for the purpose of settling, compounding or otherwise altering the terms of payment of any debts of the debtor or (2) who, to that end, receives money or other property from the debtor, or on behalf of the debtor, for payment to, or distribution among, the creditors of the debtor. "Debtor" means an individual or two or more individuals who are jointly and severally, or jointly or severally indebted.

The following persons shall not be deemed debt adjusters for the purposes of this section: an attorney at law of this State who is not principally engaged as a debt adjuster; a nonprofit social service or consumer credit counseling agency; a person who is a regular, full-time employee of a debtor, and who acts as an adjuster of his employer's debts; a person acting pursuant to any order or judgment of court, or pursuant to authority conferred by any law of this State or of the United States; a person who is a creditor of the debtor, or an agent of one or more creditors of the debtor, and whose services in adjusting the debtor's debts are rendered without cost to the debtor; or a person who, at the request of the debtor, arranges for or makes a loan to the debtor, and who, at the authorization of the debtor, acts as an adjuster of the debtor's debts in the disbursement of the proceeds of the loan, without compensation for the services rendered in adjusting such debts.

PRACTICAL APPLICATION OF STATUTE

Section 10-19 proscribes all forms of criminal usury, more commonly know as "loan-sharking." A person is guilty of criminal usury when, not being authorized by the law to do so, he loans or otherwise engages in the exchange of money or property as interest on a loan in excess of the maximum rates permitted by law. Anyone who makes loan-sharking his business, or is even found to be in knowing possession of usurious loan records, is also guilty of a felony. For the purposes of this statute, any loan with an interest rate over 30% per annum is in excess of the maximum rates permitted by law—except if the loan is made to a corporation or other business entity, in which case any rate over 50% per annum is in excess of the maximum permitted by law.

The degree of offense varies from a felony of the second degree down to a misdemeanor A, depending on the nature of the activity. Pursuant to subsection a. of the statute, the highest second degree version applies to any person found guilty of making any loan to another person with an interest rate over 50% per year. Per subsection b., any person who "knowingly engages in the business of making loans or forbearances" is similarly guilty of a second degree felony.

Returning to subsection a., the third degree type applies when the loans are less than 50% but over 30% and the amount of the loan is more than $1,000. This provision, however, is not applicable if such a loan is made to a corporation, limited liability company or limited liability partnership.

As subsection c. provides, it is a third degree felony to possess usurious loan records, provided that the defendant held the requisite knowledge of the nature of such records. All other loans in violation of this section are misdemeanor As; unlawful collection practices constitute a misdemeanor A as well. Unlawful collection practices are basically the issuance of any sort of notice or document that has no actual judicial or official effect. Such a notice or document simulates a summons, court order or other official instrument for the purpose of collecting a debt, and as such, it makes the debtor believe that the notice has a valid judicial or official sanction.

10-20.   ## Unlicensed practice of medicine, surgery, podiatric medicine, felony of third degree

A person is guilty of a felony of the third degree if he knowingly does not possess a license or permit to practice medicine and surgery or podiatric medicine, or knowingly has had the license or permit suspended, revoked or otherwise limited by an order entered by the state Board of Medical Examiners, and he:

a. Engages in that practice;

b. Exceeds the scope of practice permitted by the board order;

c. Holds himself out to the public or any person as being eligible to engage in that practice;

d. Engages in any activity for which such license or permit is a necessary prerequisite, including, but not limited to, the ordering of controlled dangerous substances or prescription legend drugs from a distributor or manufacturer; or

e. Practices medicine or surgery or podiatric medicine under a false or assumed name or falsely impersonates another person licensed by the board.

PRACTICAL APPLICATION OF STATUTE

What if our buddy Maxwell Borscht had decided to get especially gutsy and had The Hulk forge a medical license and other documentation that allowed him to set up a bogus liposuction clinic in Jasper City? In that case, he could be convicted of a third degree felony per 10-20.

Figuring he could score some quick and easy income by reading a few books on the subject and then sucking the cellulite and the cash out of some of the area's more wealthy and vain residents, Borscht sets up shop. However, he is busted when his first client gets suspicious of his "get tough" no-anesthesia approach and hastily reports him to the authorities.

Borscht would likely be able to add section 10-20 to his list of offenses if the above were true. Why? Because this statute makes it a third degree felony for a person, knowing he does not possess a license to practice medicine, surgery or podiatry or knowing that the license has been suspended or otherwise limited, to engage in any activity for which such a license is required. Performing liposuction surgery without a valid license certainly violates this statute.

10-21.   **Short title; definitions; offenses; penalties**

a. This act shall be known and may be cited as the "Anti-Piracy Act."

b. As used in this act:

    (1) "Sound recording" means any phonograph record, disc, tape, film, wire, cartridge, cassette, player piano roll or similar material object from which sounds can be reproduced either directly or with the aid of a machine.

    (2) "Owner" means (a) the person who owns the sounds fixed in any master sound recording on which the original sounds were fixed and from which transferred recorded sounds are directly or indirectly derived; or (b) the person who owns the rights to record or authorize the recording of a live performance.

    (3) "Audiovisual work" means any work that consists of a series of related images which are intrinsically intended to be shown by the use of machines or devices such as projectors, viewers or electronic equipment, together with accompanying sounds, if any, regardless of the nature of the material object, such as film or tape, in which the work is embodied. "Audiovisual work" includes but is not limited to a motion picture.

    (4) "Audiovisual recording function" means the capability of a device to record or transmit a motion picture or any part thereof by means of any technology.

    (5) "Facility" means any theater, screening room, indoor or outdoor screening venue, auditorium, ballroom or other premises where motion pictures are publicly exhibited but does not include a library or retail establishment.

c. A person commits an offense who:

    (1) Knowingly transfers, without the consent of the owner, any sounds recorded on a sound recording with intent to sell the sound recording onto which the sounds are transferred or to use the sound recording to promote the sale of any product, provided, however, that this paragraph shall only apply to sound recordings initially fixed prior to February 15, 1972.

    (2) Knowingly transports, advertises, sells, resells, rents or offers for rental, sale or resale any sound recording or audiovisual work that the person knows has been produced in violation of this act.

    (3) Knowingly manufactures or transfers, directly or indirectly by any means, or records or fixes a sound recording or audiovisual work, with the intent to sell or distribute for commercial advantage or private financial gain, a live performance with the knowledge that the live performance has been recorded or fixed without the consent of the owner of the live performance.

    (4) For commercial advantage or private financial gain, knowingly advertises or offers for sale, resale or rental or sells, resells, rents or transports a sound recording or audiovisual work or possesses with intent to advertise, sell, resell, rent or transport any sound recording or audiovisual work, the label, cover, box or jacket of which does not clearly and conspicuously disclose the true name and address of the manufacturer and, in the case of a sound recording, the name of the actual performer or group.

     (5) Knowingly operates an audiovisual recording function of a device in a facility while a motion picture is being exhibited, for the purpose of recording the motion picture, without the consent of both the licensor of the motion picture and the owner or lessee of the facility.

d. Grading; fine:

     (1) Any offense set forth in this act which involves at least 1,000 unlawful sound recordings or at least 65 audiovisual works within any 180-day period shall be punishable as a felony of the third degree and a fine of up to $250,000 may be imposed.

     (2) Any offense which involves more than 100 but less than 1,000 unlawful sound recordings or more than 7 but less than 65 unlawful audiovisual works within any 180-day period shall be punishable as a felony of the third degree and a fine of up to $150,000 may be imposed.

     (3) Any offense punishable under the provisions of this act not described in paragraph (1) or (2) of this subsection shall be punishable for the first offense as a felony of the fourth degree and a fine of up to $25,000 may be imposed. For a second and subsequent offense pursuant to this paragraph, a person shall be guilty of a felony of the third degree. A fine of up to $50,000 may be imposed for a second offense pursuant to this paragraph and a fine of up to $100,000 for a third and subsequent offense may be imposed.

e. All unlawful sound recordings and audiovisual works and any equipment or components used in violation of the provisions of this act shall be subject to forfeiture.

f. The provisions of this act shall not apply to:

     (1) Any broadcaster who, in connection with or as part of a radio or television broadcast transmission, or for the purposes of archival preservation, transfers any sounds or images recorded on a sound recording or audiovisual work.

     (2) Any person who, in his own home, for his own personal use, and without deriving any profit, transfers any sounds or images recorded on a sound recording or audiovisual work.

     (3) Any law enforcement officer who, while engaged in the official performance of his duties, transfers any sounds or images recorded on a sound recording or audiovisual work.

g. A law enforcement officer, an owner or lessee of a facility where a motion picture or a live performance is being exhibited, the authorized agent or employee of the owner or lessee, the licensor of the motion picture or the live performance or the authorized agent or employee of the licensor, who has probable cause for believing that a person has operated an audiovisual recording function of a device in violation of this section and that he can recover the recording by taking the person into custody, may, for the purpose of attempting to effect recovery thereof, take the person into custody and detain him in a reasonable manner for not more than a reasonable time, and the taking into custody by a law enforcement officer, owner, lessee, licensor, authorized agent or employee shall not render such person criminally or civilly liable in any manner or to any extent whatsoever.

     Any law enforcement officer may arrest without warrant any person he has probable cause for believing has operated an audiovisual recording function of a device in violation of this section.

     An owner or lessee of a facility, the authorized agent or employee of the owner or lessee, the licensor of the motion picture or the live performance or the authorized agent or employee of the licensor who causes the arrest of a person for operating an audiovisual recording function of a device in violation of this section shall not be criminally or civilly liable in any manner or to any extent whatsoever where the owner, lessee, licensor, authorized agent or employee has probable cause for believing that the person arrested committed the offense.

PRACTICAL APPLICATION OF STATUTE

This statute was enacted and has been amended in an attempt to keep up with the growing industry and technological advances associated with the unlawful taking and distribution of audiovisual recordings without the consent of the owners of such media. Aside from any separate federal copyright or trademark issues that could come into play with such an offense, section 10-21 makes it a felony of various degrees to knowingly, and with the intent to gain commercial advantage or private financial gain, transfer, record, transport, advertise, sell, rent or offer for sale or rental any sound recording or audiovisual work without the consent of the rightful owner.

This statute also includes a "truth in labeling" provision, which makes it a felony to sell, rent, possess, transport or otherwise unlawfully deal in any sound recording or audiovisual work that does not clearly and conspicuously disclose the true name and address of the manufacturer and, in the case of a sound recording, the name of the actual performer or group. It should be noted that there are exceptions to this statute that generally allow for any "fair use" of such materials. Therefore, the provisions of this statute do not apply to any persons who record or transfer such materials for their own personal nonprofit use or to any broadcaster who, in connection with a radio or television broadcast or for archival preservation, transfers such sound or audiovisual works.

An example of an offense under this statute is as follows. Slick Timmy knows that Bobberino wants 100 different movies to start a video collection. Slick Timmy then hooks up two separate VCRs to his television set and records 100 different movies onto blank VHS tapes. He then sells the VHS copies he made to Bobberino for $500. The entirety of his work, from copying to sale, took two weeks. Slick Timmy did not have the consent of any of the movies' owners to perform such transfers or sales.

The number and type of offenses under this statute determine the degree of the felony. For instance, any offense under this statute that involves 1,000 or more unlawful sound recordings or at least 65 audiovisual works within any 180-day period will constitute a felony of the third degree. Slick Timmy, without the owners' consent, transferred and sold 100 audiovisual works (the movies) in a two-week period. Therefore, he is guilty of a third degree felony under 10-21.

10-22.   **Unauthorized practice of law, penalties**

    a. A person is guilty of a misdemeanor A if the person knowingly engages in the unauthorized practice of law.

    b. A person is guilty of a felony of the fourth degree if the person knowingly engages in the unauthorized practice of law and:

        (1) Creates or reinforces a false impression that the person is licensed to engage in the practice of law; or

        (2) Derives a benefit; or

        (3) In fact causes injury to another.

    c. For the purposes of this section, the phrase "in fact" indicates strict liability.

PRACTICAL APPLICATION OF STATUTE

Section 10-22 makes it a misdemeanor A for a person to knowingly engage in the unauthorized practice of law. The degree of the felony is increased to the fourth degree if, while engaging in this unauthorized practice, he derives a benefit, actually causes injury to another or "creates or reinforces a false impression" that he is licensed to engage in the practice of law. But what is the difference between the misdemeanor A of "unauthorized practice of law" and the fourth degree felony of the unauthorized practice of law where the person "creates or reinforces a false impression" that he is licensed to engage in the practice of law?

Here's an example. Bart, an aspiring law student, witnesses a car accident and approaches the driver of the vehicle who he feels is at fault. Bart tells the driver, Eddie, that although he is not a lawyer, he is an expert in law and advises Eddie that in order to escape liability for the accident, he should issue a ticket for speeding against the other driver. Bart then meets with Eddie the next day and drafts a civil complaint naming Eddie as the plaintiff and the other driver as the defendant. Eddie likes the complaint, so Bart sends it to the court for filing and mails a copy to the "defendant."

Bart obviously engaged in the "unauthorized practice of law." However, he didn't "create or reinforce a false impression" that he was *licensed* to engage in the practice of law; in fact, he advised that he was not a lawyer. Accordingly, as long as Bart didn't charge Eddie any money or derive any other benefit—and as long as no one was ultimately injured, financially or otherwise, by his actions—Bart would be guilty of the misdemeanor A of engaging in the "unauthorized practice of law." His offense would be elevated to a felony of the fourth degree, though, if he had told Eddie that he was a lawyer or had otherwise created such a false impression.

10-22.1.   **Definitions relative to use of runners; felony; sentencing**

a. As used in this section:

"Provider" means an attorney, a health care professional, an owner or operator of a health care practice or facility, any person who creates the impression that he or his practice or facility can provide legal or health care services or any person employed or acting on behalf of any of the aforementioned persons.

"Public media" means telephone directories, professional directories, newspapers and other periodicals, radio and television, billboards and mailed or electronically transmitted written communications that do not involve in-person contact with a specific prospective client, patient or customer.

"Runner" means a person who, for a pecuniary benefit, procures or attempts to procure a client, patient or customer at the direction of, request of or in cooperation with a provider whose purpose is to seek to obtain benefits under a contract of insurance or assert a claim against an insured or an insurance carrier for providing services to the client, patient or customer. "Runner" shall not include a person who procures or attempts to procure clients, patients or customers for a provider through public media or a person who refers clients, patients or customers to a provider as otherwise authorized by law.

b. A person is guilty of a felony of the third degree if that person knowingly acts as a runner or uses, solicits, directs, hires or employs another to act as a runner.

c. The court shall deal with a person who has been convicted of a violation of this section by imposing a sentence of imprisonment unless, having regard to the character and condition of the person, the court is of the opinion that imprisonment would be a serious injustice which overrides the need to deter such conduct by others. If the court imposes a noncustodial or probationary sentence, such sentence shall not become final for ten days in order to permit the appeal of such sentence by the prosecution. Nothing in this section shall preclude an indictment and conviction for any other offense defined by the laws of this State.

PRACTICAL APPLICATION OF STATUTE

Although this statute is primarily a definitional section, it is notable in its definition and prohibition of being a "runner." A person commits the third degree felony of being a "runner" if, for pecuniary benefit, he procures or attempts to procure a client, patient or customer at the direction of any type of "provider," whose purpose is to obtain benefits under any type of insurance contract. A "provider" is basically defined in this section as any attorney or health care provider or owner/operator of such a facility. The "provider" also may be convicted of a third degree felony under this statute—that is, if the "provider . . . uses, solicits, directs, hires or employs to act as a runner."

It is important to note that the term "runner" does not include a person "who procures or attempts to procure clients, patients or customers for a provider through public media or a person who refers clients, patients or customers to a provider as otherwise authorized by law." Accordingly, persons who act in the aforementioned capacities are not violating the provisions of 10-22.1.

10-23.   **Definitions**

As used in this act:

> "Attorney General" includes the Attorney General of this State and the Attorney General's assistants and deputies. The term also shall include a county prosecutor or the county prosecutor's designated assistant prosecutor if a county prosecutor is expressly authorized in writing by the Attorney General pursuant to this act.
>
> "Derived from" means obtained directly or indirectly from, maintained by or realized through.
>
> "Person" means any corporation, unincorporated association or any other entity or enterprise, as defined in subsection q. of 9-1, which is capable of holding a legal or beneficial interest in property.
>
> "Property" means anything of value, as defined in subsection g. of 9-1, and includes any benefit or interest without reduction for expenses incurred for acquisition, maintenance or any other purpose.

10-24.   **Money laundering, illegal investment, felony**

A person is guilty of a felony if the person:

a. Transports or possesses property known or which a reasonable person would believe to be derived from criminal activity; or

b. Engages in a transaction involving property known or which a reasonable person would believe to be derived from criminal activity:

(1) With the intent to facilitate or promote the criminal activity; or

(2) Knowing that the transaction is designed in whole or in part:

(a) To conceal or disguise the nature, location, source, ownership or control of the property derived from criminal activity; or

(b) To avoid a transaction reporting requirement under the laws of this State or any other state or of the United States; or

c. Directs, organizes, finances, plans, manages, supervises or controls the transportation of or transactions in property known or which a reasonable person would believe to be derived from criminal activity.

d. For the purposes of this act, property is known to be derived from criminal activity if the person knows that the property involved represents proceeds from some form, though not necessarily which form, of criminal activity. Among the factors that the finder of fact may consider in determining that a transaction has been designed to avoid a transaction reporting requirement shall be whether the person, acting alone or with others, conducted one or more transactions in currency, in any amount, at one or more financial institutions, on one or more days, in any manner. The phrase "in any manner" includes the breaking down of a single sum of currency exceeding the transaction reporting requirement into smaller sums, including sums at or below the transaction reporting requirement, or the conduct of a transaction, or series of currency transactions, including transactions at or below the transaction reporting requirement. The transaction or transactions need not exceed the transaction reporting threshold at any single financial institution on any single day in order to demonstrate a violation of subparagraph (b) of paragraph (2) of subsection b. of this section.

e. A person is guilty of a felony if, with the purpose to evade a transaction reporting requirement of this State, he:

(1) Causes or attempts to cause a financial institution, including a foreign or domestic money transmitter or an authorized delegate thereof, casino, check casher, person engaged in a trade or business or any other individual or entity required by State or federal law to file a report regarding currency transactions or suspicious transactions to fail to file a report; or

(2) Causes or attempts to cause a financial institution, including a foreign or domestic money transmitter or an authorized delegate thereof, casino, check casher, person engaged in a trade or business or any other individual or entity required by State or federal law to file a report regarding currency transactions or suspicious transactions to file a report that contains a material omission or misstatement of fact; or

(3) Structures or assists in structuring, or attempts to structure or assist in structuring, any transaction with one or more financial institutions, including foreign or domestic money transmitters or an authorized delegate thereof, casinos, check cashers, persons engaged in a trade or business or any other individuals or entities required by State or federal law to file a report regarding currency transactions or suspicious transactions. "Structure" or "structuring" means that a person, acting alone or in conjunction with, or on behalf of, other persons, conducts or attempts to conduct one or more transactions in currency, in any amount, at one or more financial institutions, on one or more days, in any manner, for the purpose of evading currency transaction reporting requirements provided by State or federal law. "In any manner" includes, but is not limited to, the breaking down into smaller sums of a single sum of currency meeting or exceeding that which is necessary to trigger a currency reporting requirement or the conduct of a transaction, or series of currency transactions, at or below the reporting requirement. The transaction or transactions need not exceed the reporting threshold at any single financial institution on any single day in order to meet the definition of "structure" or "structuring" provided in this paragraph.

PRACTICAL APPLICATION OF STATUTE

Topping off Maxwell Borscht's impressive résumé of violations under this statute was his act of money laundering. Sections 10-24 through 10-26 all deal with the felony and punishment of money laundering and any activities facilitating the act of this offense.

Prior to Borscht's Jackpot Entertainment Insurance scam, he sold heroin. When he first arrived in the state, he utilized pizza places to disguise the real manner in which he earned his funds. His goal was to act like the money was made legitimately via the restaurants, sending it through these businesses' records as if an enormous number of pizzas and calzones were sold, but in reality, the money was being made from his illicit drug distribution.

Maxwell Borscht's above-referenced activity falls squarely within the prohibitions of 10-24b.(2)(a). This subsection makes it a felony to engage in any transactions involving property derived from criminal activity while knowing that the transaction is designed to conceal the nature of the property derived from criminal activity.

Although the term "property" conjures up an image of some tangible object, the cash Borscht had made through his illegal heroin sales is considered property for the purposes of this statute. Making the money/property look as though it was made through the restaurants by sending it through their business records, Borscht knowingly conducted these transactions with the purpose to conceal the nature of where the money actually came from. Therefore, he is guilty of money laundering.

The gradations of money laundering offenses are found in section 10-26. Depending on how lucrative Borscht's heroin racket was, he could face up to a first degree criminal charge. For the offenses defined in subsections a., b. and c. of 10-24 (Borscht's offense falls under subsection b.), it is a felony of the first degree if the amount involved is $500,000 or more. If the amount is at least $75,000 but less than $500,000, the offense constitutes a felony of the second degree; for all other amounts, it is a felony of the third degree.

10-25.   Knowledge inferred

For the purposes of this act, the requisite knowledge may be inferred where the property is transported or possessed in a fashion inconsistent with the ordinary or usual means of transportation or possession of such property and where the property is discovered in the absence of any documentation or other indicia of legitimate origin or right to such property.

10-26.   Degrees of offense; penalties; nonmerger

The offense defined in subsections a., b. and c. of 10-24 constitutes a felony of the first degree if the amount involved is $500,000 or more. If the amount involved is at least $75,000 but less than $500,000, the offense constitutes a felony of the second degree; otherwise, the offense constitutes a felony of the third degree. The offense defined in subsection e. of 10-24 constitutes a felony of the third degree. The court may also impose a fine up to $500,000. The amount involved in a prosecution for violation of this section shall be determined by the trier of fact. Amounts involved in transactions conducted pursuant to one scheme or course of conduct may be aggregated in determining the degree of the offense. A person convicted of a felony of the first degree pursuant to the provisions of this subsection shall be sentenced to a term of imprisonment that shall include the imposition of a minimum term which shall be fixed at, or between, one-third and one-half of the sentence imposed, during which time the defendant shall not be eligible for parole.

10-27.   **Unlawful practice of dentistry; third degree felony**

A person is guilty of a felony of the third degree if he knowingly does not possess a license to practice dentistry ,or knowingly has had the license suspended, revoked or otherwise limited by an order entered by the State Board of Dentistry, and he:

    a. Engages in that practice;

    b. Exceeds the scope of practice permitted by a board order;

    c. Holds himself out to the public or any person as being eligible to engage in that practice;

    d. Engages in any activity for which such license is a necessary prerequisite, including, but not limited to, the ordering of controlled dangerous substances or prescription legend drugs from a distributor or manufacturer; or

    e. Practices dentistry under a false or assumed name or falsely impersonates another person licensed by the board.

PRACTICAL APPLICATION OF STATUTE

Section 10-27 simply proscribes the unlawful practice of dentistry. A violation under this statute is a third degree felony. Please note that 10-27 requires that the defendant "knowingly" engage in the prohibited activities. This intent requirement would presumably prevent any sort of prosecution under circumstances where the individual had inadvertently been working under an expired license or otherwise believed in good faith that he was properly authorized.

10-28.   **Short title; definitions relative to counterfeit marks; offenses**

    a. This act shall be known and may be cited as the "Trademark Counterfeiting Act."

    b. As used in this act:

        (1) "Counterfeit mark" means a spurious mark that is identical with or substantially indistinguishable from a genuine mark that is registered on the principal register in the United States Patent and Trademark Office or registered in this State's Secretary of State's office or a spurious mark that is identical with or substantially indistinguishable from the words, names, symbols, emblems, signs, insignias or any combination thereof of the United States Olympic Committee or the International Olympic Committee and that is used or is intended to be used on, or in conjunction with, goods or services for which the genuine mark is registered and in use.

        (2) "Retail value" means the counterfeiter's regular selling price for the item or service bearing or identified by the counterfeit mark. In the case of items bearing a counterfeit mark which are components of a finished product, the retail value shall be the counterfeiter's regular selling price of the finished product on or in which the component would be utilized.

    c. A person commits the offense of counterfeiting who, with the intent to deceive or defraud some other person, knowingly manufactures, uses, displays, advertises, distributes, offers for sale, sells or possesses with intent to sell or distribute within or in conjunction with commercial activities within this State any item or services bearing, or identified by, a counterfeit mark.

        A person who has in his possession or under his control more than 25 items bearing a counterfeit mark shall be presumed to have violated this section.

d. (1) An offense set forth in this act shall be punishable as a felony of the fourth degree if the offense involves fewer than 100 items bearing a counterfeit mark, the offense involves a total retail value of less than $1,000 for all items bearing, or services identified by, a counterfeit mark or the offense involves a first conviction under this act.

(2) An offense set forth in this act shall be punishable as a felony of the third degree if the offense involves 100 or more but fewer than 1,000 items bearing a counterfeit mark, the offense involves a total retail value of $1,000 or more but less than $15,000 of all items bearing, or services identified by, a counterfeit mark or the offense involves a second conviction under this act.

(3) An offense set forth in this act shall be punishable as a felony of the second degree if the offense involves 1,000 or more items bearing a counterfeit mark, the offense involves a total retail value of $15,000 or more of all items bearing, or services identified by, a counterfeit mark or the offense involves a third or subsequent conviction under this act.

e. For purposes of this act:

(1) The quantity or retail value of items or services shall include the aggregate quantity or retail value of all items bearing, or services identified by, every counterfeit mark the defendant manufactures, uses, displays, advertises, distributes, offers for sale, sells or possesses; and

(2) Any State or federal certificate of registration of any intellectual property shall be *prima facie* evidence of the facts stated therein.

PRACTICAL APPLICATION OF STATUTE

If Maxwell Borscht had decided to raise a little more capital by operating a small stand selling women's purses with the name and logo of a famous clothing designer while "knowing" that the purses were not actually produced with the authorization of this designer, Borscht would be in violation of 10-28. This statute is more commonly known as the Trademark Counterfeiting Act.

Section 10-28 makes it a felony to knowingly manufacture, use, display, advertise, distribute or sell (or possess with intent to sell) any item or service identified by a counterfeit mark. In order to be guilty of an offense under this statute, the defendant must intend to "deceive or defraud" another.

Although 10-28 does not necessarily make it a felony to possess one of these counterfeit items, any person who has possession of more than 25 items bearing a counterfeit mark is presumed to be in violation of this statute. The offenses range from the fourth degree to second degree depending on the number and retail value of the prohibited items. See subsections d.(1), d.(2) and d.(3) for specifics in this respect.

10-29.   **Electrical contracting without business permit, fourth degree felony**

a. A person is guilty of a felony of the fourth degree if that person knowingly engages in the business of electrical contracting without having a business permit issued by the Board of Examiners of Electrical Contractors and:

(1) Creates or reinforces a false impression that the person is licensed as an electrical contractor or possesses a business permit; or

    (2) Derives a benefit, the value of which is more than incidental; or

    (3) In fact causes injury to another.

  b. For the purposes of this section, the phrase "in fact" indicates strict liability.

PRACTICAL APPLICATION OF STATUTE

Those engaging in the "business of electrical contracting" without having a business permit issued by the Board of Examiners of Electrical Contractors may be guilty of a fourth degree felony. This is the case if they do the aforementioned *and* cause injury to another or derive a significant benefit (i.e., monetary) from the work or create a "false impression" that they possess the appropriate license or permit.

10-30.   **Penalty for false contract payment claims, representation, for a government contract; prevailing wage violations; grading**

  a. A person commits a felony if the person knowingly submits to the government any claim for payment for performance of a government contract knowing such claim to be false, fictitious or fraudulent. If the claim submitted is for $25,000 or above, the offender is guilty of a felony of the second degree. If the claim exceeds $2,500 but is less than $25,000, the offender is guilty of a felony of the third degree. If the claim is for $2,500 or less, the offender is guilty of a felony of the fourth degree.

  b. A person commits a felony if the person knowingly makes a material representation that is false in connection with the negotiation, award or performance of a government contract. If the contract amount is for $25,000 or above, the offender is guilty of a felony of the second degree. If the contract amount exceeds $2,500 but is less than $25,000, the offender is guilty of a felony of the third degree. If the contract amount is for $2,500 or less, the offender is guilty of a felony of the fourth degree.

  c. An employer commits a felony if the employer knowingly pays one or more employees employed in public work at a rate less than the rate required. If the contract amount is for $75,000 or above, the employer is guilty of a felony of the second degree; if the contract amount exceeds $2,500 but is less than $75,000, the employer is guilty of a felony of the third degree; and if the contract amount is for $2,500 or less, the employer is guilty of a felony of the fourth degree. In addition, the employer shall be deemed to have caused loss to the employees in the amount by which the employees were underpaid and shall be subject to the provisions regarding fines and restitution to victims and be subject to other pertinent provisions regarding sentencing.

PRACTICAL APPLICATION OF STATUTE

Under section 10-30, a person commits a felony by either knowingly submitting a false claim for payment on a government contract or knowingly making a materially false representation in connection with the negotiation or award of a government contract. For example, this statute could apply to a construction company contracted by the government to build a new firehouse. If the company president submitted claims to the government containing charges for items that were never used or charges in excess of the actual cost of materials, then the company president is ripe for a charge under 10-30. The felony is of the second degree for amounts of $25,000 or more. It is a third degree felony for amounts over $2,500 but less than $25,000 and a felony of the fourth degree for amounts of $2,500 or less.

END OF CHAPTER REVIEW

Multiple-Choice Questions

1. Maxwell Borscht created a sham Ernest Hemingway manuscript with the purpose to defraud Holly. Borscht traded the fake manuscript to Holly for a washer/dryer set. Which of the following is the *best* offense to charge Borscht with?

    a. offering a false instrument for filing under 10-3

    b. criminal simulation under 10-2

    c. criminal solicitation under 10-15.1

    d. piracy under common law

    e. all of the above

2. Which of the following acts violates the Trademark Counterfeiting Act under 10-28?

    a. Artie manufactures 1,000 chimney sweepers, branding each sweeper with the label "Fresco Chimney Sweepers," knowing that the famous sweeper company was not involved with Artie's sweepers.

    b. Mitchell advertises the sale of "Gucci wallets," knowing that the wallets were rip-offs of Gucci.

    c. GeorgeAnne possesses five fake Tag Heuer watches. She wears them frequently, showing them off.

    d. all of the above

    e. a and b only

The following fact pattern pertains to questions 3–4.

Michael "The Hunk" Pardemena "restructured" the will of Salvatore Rando, making Salvatore's son, Manny, the sole beneficiary. The Hunk did this by dissolving the printed ink and replacing it with language favorable to Manny.

3. The *best* offense to charge The Hunk with is:

    a. criminal simulation

    b. forgery

    c. fraud related to public records

    d. falsifying financial statements

    e. a misdemeanor A

4. The degree of The Hunk's offense is:

    a. a first degree felony

    b. a third degree felony

    c. a misdemeanor A

    d. a misdemeanor

    e. none of the above

5. Maxwell Borscht, owner of a pizza parlor, had become insolvent and received the appropriate government notice that proceedings had been started for the repossession of the pizza parlor and all the materials he used in the business. The proceedings were initiated to repay creditors to which he owed money. Borscht

decides he is not going to allow authorities to take his things and hides the various items in a warehouse that he secretly rented under another name. Here, Borscht is guilty of:

   a. a second degree felony of fraud in insolvency if the value of the items exceeded $75,000

   b. a third degree felony of fraud in insolvency if the value of the items exceeded $1,000 but was less than $75,000

   c. a fourth degree felony of fraud in insolvency if the value of the items was $1,000 or less

   d. all of the above

   e. no felony of fraud in insolvency; this is a civil action only

6. Bart, a fireman, overhears Karla, a go-go dancer, explaining that she was arrested in Marlboro for a DWI. In an effort to impress Karla, Bert tells her that he is a lawyer and offers to represent her on the DWI in exchange for a few lap dances. Ultimately, Bart represents her in court, and Karla is convicted of the offense. What is Bart guilty of?

   a. a misdemeanor B for the unauthorized practice of law

   b. a fourth degree felony for the unauthorized practice of law

   c. a first degree felony for the unauthorized practice of law

   d. a *mandamus* writ

   e. a bad rap

7. A person who knowingly engages in the business of criminal usury is guilty of:

   a. a second degree felony

   b. a fourth degree felony

   c. a misdemeanor B

   d. a bad business decision

   e. none of the above

Essay Questions

1. Jameson issues a check in the amount of $15,000 to Schmidt in exchange for a pile of rare Idaho potatoes. The check bounces. Jameson eats the potatoes and never makes good on the check. Under what circumstances is Jameson guilty of issuing a bad check per the provisions of 10-5? Make sure to use the elements of this offense to explain your answer. Would Jameson's bad check charge be a felony or misdemeanor? What degree?

2. For each of the following circumstances, explain if the actor has committed the felony of usury: (a) Premium Loan lends $5,000 to Bob, an individual, at an interest rate of 75% per annum; (b) Premium Loan lends $500,000 to Smack Hack's Bar and Restaurant, a limited liability company, at an interest rate of 75% per annum; and (c) Marty lends $10,000 to his friend's company, Jose Shoes, Inc., at an interest rate of 45% per annum.

11

DISTURBING HUMAN REMAINS

11-1. **Disturbing, desecrating human remains; offenses**

    a. A person commits a felony of the second degree if he:

        (1) Unlawfully disturbs, moves or conceals human remains;

        (2) Unlawfully desecrates, damages or destroys human remains; or

        (3) Commits an act of sexual penetration or sexual contact, as defined in 4-1, upon human remains.

    b. A person commits a felony of the third degree if he purposely or knowingly fails to dispose of human remains in a manner required by law.

    c. As used in this act, "human remains" means the body of a deceased person or the dismembered part of a body of a living person but does not include cremated remains.

    d. Nothing in this section shall be construed to apply to any act performed in accordance with law, including but not limited to the "State Medical Examiner Act," the "Mortuary Science Act," the provisions concerning disposal of dead bodies and cremation; the "State Cemetery Act"; a criminal investigation conducted by a law enforcement authority; or an order of a court of competent jurisdiction or other appropriate legal authority. Nothing in this section shall be construed to criminalize any good-faith action involving interment or disinterment which disturbs, moves, conceals, desecrates, damages or destroys human remains.

PRACTICAL APPLICATION OF STATUTE

Maxwell Borscht violated section 11-1 by disturbing the remains of an unnamed man buried in an Orange Hill cemetery. This is a felony of the second degree.

Pursuant to subsection a. of 11-1, a person commits a second degree felony if he unlawfully disturbs, moves, conceals, desecrates, damages or destroys human remains. Similarly, he is guilty of a second degree felony if he commits an act of sexual penetration or sexual contact upon human remains. Per subsection b., a third degree felony has been committed where a person purposely or knowingly fails to dispose of human remains in a manner required by law.

Borscht is guilty of a second degree felony as provided for in subsection a. He believed a family myth that his great-uncle was buried in an unmarked grave in Orange Hill. The significance of the myth was that $5 million in gold bullion was also said to be buried there.

Capwell Police Lieutenant Christian Star had been searching for Borscht pursuant to a massive insurance scam that he had perpetrated. Relying on a tip from a witness, Star traveled to Orange Hill and began visiting the town's cemeteries. As he approached his third graveyard, he did indeed find Borscht, shovel in hand, breaking open a pine box casket in an unmarked grave.

Borscht pulled the human remains from the box, tossed them aside and threw up his hands. He then kicked the unfortunate unnamed man's skeleton and cried, "Where's the bullion, you bony fool?" At this point, Star pointed his pistol at Borscht, dangling handcuffs from his free hand. Borscht was then appropriately arrested.

Given that Maxwell Borscht had no lawful reason to disturb and damage the human remains of the unnamed man, he is guilty of a second degree felony under section 11-1.

END OF CHAPTER REVIEW

Multiple-Choice Question

1. A person commits a second degree felony if he:
   a. unearths a grave in a cemetery, pulling human remains from a casket and taking the clothes from the remains
   b. fails to dispose of human remains as required by law
   c. has sexual intercourse with human remains
   d. a and b
   e. a and c

12

OFFENSES AGAINST THE FAMILY, CHILDREN AND INCOMPETENTS

FACT PATTERN (PERTAINING TO CHAPTERS 12 AND 13)

Blakeville Police Patrolman Ra Davis reported to an alleged domestic violence dispute at the home of Barbie Penn, a 38-year-old woman who lived with her ten-year-old daughter. Also living in the house were Barbie's 40-year-old mentally incompetent cousin and her 75-year-old mother. Barbie was paid by her late father's estate to care for her mother and cousin on a daily basis.

Once at the Penn residence, Patrolman Davis heard yelling through the front door. Although he could decipher a few words coming from a man's mouth, he was unable to understand the content of the loud talk. The officer rang the doorbell, hoping to interrupt; Barbie Penn answered within seconds.

Standing beside Barbie was Jerry Penn, her husband. Officer Davis immediately observed that Jerry was bleeding from the nose, and upon closer inspection of Barbie, he noted that a small bruise was beginning to form under her eye. Accordingly, he asked what had occurred. Jerry advised that he and Barbie had been separated for about ten months. Per court order, he was permitted to have visitation with their daughter, Suzie, twice a week; however, the daughter was to be picked up and dropped off by Jerry's mother because the court had also issued a restraining order against Jerry where he was not to have any contact with Barbie. When Officer Davis inquired why Jerry was at the house in obvious violation of the restraining order, he only replied with, "Because I heard this lunatic was doing some very bad things in front of my daughter." Barbie then lunged at Jerry, punching him in the chin. As Officer Davis restrained her, she screamed, "And I'm not sorry I broke your nose. You deserved it, because you're ugly." At that, Davis arrested both Jerry and Barbie. He thereafter called the appropriate state agencies to ensure proper care for Suzie and the other women living in the home.

Jerry Penn's statement irked the Blakeville patrolman enough so that he contacted the department's deputy chief, who headed their detective unit. What unfolded pursuant to a one-month follow-up investigation didn't just provide validity to Jerry Penn's words—it shocked the entire town of Blakeville. The following offenses involving Barbie Penn were uncovered:

1. On three separate occasions, Barbie Penn engaged in numerous sexual acts with two men at the same time. These acts, which included sexual intercourse, were performed in the presence of her ten-year-old daughter, Suzie. The men, Frank Roberts and Fred Rodriguez, were not boyfriends—they were both legally married to Barbie. This brought her total number of current marriages to three. Both Roberts and Rodriguez knew that Barbie was married to Jerry Penn when they took their vows to marry her.

2. Frank Roberts brought a video cameraman to Barbie's house for the purpose of shooting footage of ten-year-old Suzie—the video footage was of Suzie having sex with a 13-year-old boy. Barbie permitted the video photography, watching over the entire session. The cameraman, Willie Maxso, turned over the tapes to Roberts, who then sold copies of the same to several residents throughout the state, including a prominent state senator. In addition, Roberts posted the video on the Internet, charging any persons who logged on to his website. Roberts also paid the 13-year-old boy to steal Maxso's camera from him after the shooting was completed. The camera was valued at $1,000.

3. Barbie routinely maltreated and endangered her 75-year-old mother and mentally incompetent adult cousin. On one occasion, "for laughs" as Barbie later described it, she baked brownies laced with marijuana and fed them to her cousin. The Blakeville police also learned that Barbie once locked her elderly mother in her bedroom for 72 hours. The woman's only recourse for nutrition was tap water from the room's adjoining bathroom and two candy bars that she had stashed in her bureau; the mother's food deprivation caused her to be hospitalized.

At the conclusion of the deputy chief's investigation, Barbie Penn was arrested at her home. On the same day, Frank Roberts and Willie Maxso were picked up while they were mingling at a local bar. Frank Rodriguez was nabbed at his place of employment. The state senator turned himself in to police headquarters when he learned that a warrant had been issued for his arrest. All of these adults were charged accordingly, and bail was set.

12-1.   **Bigamy**

a. Bigamy. A married person is guilty of bigamy, a misdemeanor A, if he contracts or purports to contract another marriage, unless at the time of the subsequent marriage:

   (1) The actor believes that the prior spouse is dead;

   (2) The actor and the prior spouse have been living apart for 5 consecutive years throughout which the prior spouse was not known by the actor to be alive;

   (3) A court has entered a judgment purporting to terminate or annul any prior disqualifying marriage, and the actor does not know that judgment to be invalid; or

   (4) The actor reasonably believes that he is legally eligible to remarry.

b. Other party to bigamous marriage. A person is guilty of bigamy if he contracts or purports to contract marriage with another knowing that the other is thereby committing bigamy.

PRACTICAL APPLICATION OF STATUTE

Bigamy

Pursuant to 12-1, Barbie Penn was charged with two counts of bigamy for her marriages to Frank Roberts and Fred Rodriguez. Bigamy is a misdemeanor A.

The statute basically provides that a married person who engages in another marriage is guilty of bigamy—you can't be married to two or three people at once. Since Barbie was only separated from her husband Jerry, and not legally divorced, her subsequent marriages to Frank and Fred make her guilty of bigamy.

It should be noted that under subsections a.(1) through a.(4), certain circumstances vitiate a bigamy offense. These exceptions are varied and include situations such as an actor's belief that the prior spouse is dead and that an erroneous court order had terminated the prior marriage. Barbie, however, does not have these defenses.

Other Party to Bigamous Marriage

Frank Roberts and Fred Rodriguez should also be charged with bigamy as they knew they were marrying a married woman. At the time each man took his wedding vows, he was aware of Barbie's prior existing marriage to Jerry Penn. Accordingly, they are both guilty of this misdemeanor A.

12-2.   **Endangering welfare of children**

a. Any person having a legal duty for the care of a child or who has assumed responsibility for the care of a child who engages in sexual conduct which would impair or debauch the morals of the child, or who causes the child harm that would make the child an abused or neglected child, is guilty of a felony of the second degree. Any other person who engages in conduct or who causes harm as described in this subsection to a child under the age of 16 is guilty of a felony of the third degree.

b. (1) As used in this subsection:

"Child" means any person under 16 years of age.

"Internet" means the international computer network of both federal and non-federal interoperable packet switched data networks.

"Prohibited sexual act" means

(a) Sexual intercourse; or

(b) Anal intercourse; or

(c) Masturbation; or

(d) Bestiality; or

(e) Sadism; or

(f) Masochism; or

(g) Fellatio; or

(h) Cunnilingus; or

(i) Nudity, if depicted for the purpose of sexual stimulation or gratification of any person who may view such depiction; or

(j) Any act of sexual penetration or sexual contact as defined in 4-1. "Reproduction" means, but is not limited to, computer generated images.

(2) A person commits a felony of the second degree if he causes or permits a child to engage in a prohibited sexual act or in the simulation of such an act if the person knows, has reason to know or intends that the prohibited act may be photographed, filmed, reproduced or reconstructed in any manner, including on the Internet, or may be part of an exhibition or performance. If the person is a parent, guardian or other person legally charged with the care or custody of the child, the person shall be guilty of a felony of the first degree.

(3) Any person who photographs or films a child in a prohibited sexual act or in the simulation of such an act or who uses any device, including a computer, to reproduce or reconstruct the image of a child in a prohibited sexual act or in the simulation of such an act is guilty of a felony of the second degree.

(4) (a) Any person who knowingly receives for the purpose of selling or who knowingly sells, procures, manufactures, gives, provides, lends, trades, mails, delivers, transfers, publishes, distributes, circulates, disseminates, presents, exhibits, advertises, offers or agrees to offer, through any means, including the Internet, any photograph, film, videotape, computer program or file, video game or any other reproduction or reconstruction which depicts a child engaging in a prohibited sexual act or in the simulation of such an act is guilty of a felony of the second degree.

(b) Any person who knowingly possesses or knowingly views any photograph, film, videotape, computer program or file, video game or any other reproduction or reconstruction which depicts a child engaging in a prohibited sexual act or in the simulation of such an act, including on the Internet, is guilty of a felony of the fourth degree.

(5) For purposes of this subsection, a person who is depicted as or presents the appearance of being under the age of 16 in any photograph, film, videotape, computer program or file, video game or any other reproduction or reconstruction shall be rebuttably presumed to be under the age of 16. If the child who is depicted as engaging in, or who is caused to engage in, a prohibited sexual act or simulation of a prohibited sexual act is under the age of 16, the actor shall be strictly liable and it shall not be a defense that the actor did not know that the child was under the age of 16, nor shall it be a defense that the actor believed that the child was 16 years of age or older, even if such a mistaken belief was reasonable.

PRACTICAL APPLICATION OF STATUTE

Endangering the Welfare of a Child—Debauching Morals

For engaging in sexual activity with two men in front of her ten-year-old daughter, Barbie Penn was appropriately charged with endangering the welfare of a child. Her legal duty to care for her daughter—as her mother—is the linchpin that makes this a second degree felony.

Per subsection a. of 12-2, a person who has a "legal duty for the care of a child" (or who has assumed responsibility to care for the child) is guilty of a second degree felony if he engages in sexual conduct that would "impair" or "debauch" the child's morals. On three separate occasions, Barbie Penn engaged in numerous sexual acts, including sexual intercourse with two men, in front of her ten-year-old daughter, Suzie. This kind of conduct performed in the presence of such a young child reasonably would "impair" and/or "debauch" the juvenile's morals. Given that Barbie Penn had custody of Suzie and is the child's mother, she had a legal duty to care for her. With these two elements met, Penn is guilty of a second degree felony for endangering her daughter's welfare.

Frank Roberts and Fred Rodriguez should also be charged under subsection a. of the statute, as their sexual conduct similarly would be found to endanger Suzie's welfare. However, their actions, in being the two men having sex with Barbie Penn, only amount to a third degree felony because they did not have a legal duty to care for the ten-year-old girl.

Child Pornography—Permitting Act

Barbie Penn is guilty of a first degree felony for permitting her daughter, Suzie, to be filmed while having sex with a 13-year-old boy. This serious offense is grounded in subsection b. of the endangering welfare of children statute.

Under 12-2b.(3), any person who "causes or permits" a child to engage in a "prohibited sexual act" while such act is photographed or filmed is guilty of a second degree felony. If the person is the child's parent or guardian, the felony is elevated to a first degree offense.

One of Penn's husbands, Frank Roberts, brought a cameraman to her home. Once there, he shot video footage of ten-year-old Suzie having sex with another minor. Not only did Penn allow this deviant act to occur, she actually stood by and watched. Accordingly, this mother is guilty of first degree endangering the welfare of a child.

It should be noted that a "simulated" sexual act—one that appears to be occurring—is prohibited under this statute as well. Also, still photography (or any kind of reproduction of a prohibited act) is illegal. In other words, if Penn had permitted still pictures of Suzie in a simulated sexual act to appear on the Internet, she would still be guilty of this first degree felony.

These additional matters apply not only for subsection b.(2) but also for subsections b.(3) and b.(4).

Child Pornography—Photographing Act

Cameraman Willie Maxso is guilty of a second degree felony for videotaping ten-year-old Suzie having sex with a 13-year-old boy. Simply stated, subsection b.(3) makes it unlawful for anyone to photograph or film a child engaging in any prohibited sexual act.

Child Pornography—The Seller

In selling the videotapes of the sexual acts of the ten-year-old and the 13-year-old, Frank Roberts has endangered the welfare of these children. Under 12-2b.(4)(a), Roberts is guilty of a second degree felony.

This subsection carefully enumerates the multiple manners of distribution of child pornography that will render an individual guilty of this offense. Unlawful distribution-type activities include selling, publishing, circulating and advertising. A person can be convicted under b.(4)(a) even where he has just "received" child pornography material—but only if the prosecution proves that he received it "for the purpose of selling" it.

Child Pornography—The Buyer

One who "knowingly" possesses (or views) child pornography but who is not in the business of selling it is guilty of a fourth degree felony. Accordingly, since the state senator purposely bought the illicit videotape of ten-year-old Suzie, he is guilty of this felony, which is set forth in subsection b.(4)(b) of the endangering welfare of children statute.

The "knowingly" mental state component of this subsection is particularly important. For example, had the state senator unwittingly entered a child porn website while surfing the Internet, he should not be charged with this felony. Likewise, if he attended a party where, all of a sudden, a guest popped a child porn tape into the VCR, he should not be convicted under this statute—unless, of course, he stayed and watched.

12-3. **Endangering the welfare of an incompetent person**

A person is guilty of a misdemeanor A when he knowingly acts in a manner likely to be injurious to the physical, mental or moral welfare of a person who is unable to care for himself because of mental disease or defect.

PRACTICAL APPLICATION OF STATUTE

Barbie Penn should be charged with violating section 12-3 for feeding her adult cousin brownies laced with marijuana. Her action constitutes endangering the welfare of an incompetent person, which is a misdemeanor A.

An individual who knowingly performs an act that likely will be injurious to the "physical, moral or mental welfare" of an incompetent person has violated 12-3. Penn fed her cousin, a mentally incompetent woman, brownies with the illegal controlled dangerous substance marijuana. This act, which she stated she did "for laughs," certainly was likely to be injurious to the woman's "physical" and "mental" welfare. With this being the case, Penn is guilty of violating this statute.

12-4. **Abandonment, neglect of elderly person, disabled adult; third degree felony**

a. A person having a legal duty to care for or who has assumed continuing responsibility for the care of a person 60 years of age or older or a disabled adult who abandons the elderly person or disabled adult or unreasonably neglects to do or fails to permit to be done any act necessary for the physical or mental health of the elderly person or disabled adult is guilty of a felony of the third degree. For purposes of this section "abandon" means the willful desertion or forsaking of an elderly person or disabled adult.

b. A person shall not be considered to commit an offense under this section for the sole reason that he provides or permits to be provided nonmedical remedial treatment by spiritual means through prayer alone in lieu of medical care, in accordance with the tenets and practices of the elderly person's or disabled adult's established religious tradition, to an elderly person or disabled adult whom he has a legal duty to care for or has assumed responsibility to care for.

c. Nothing in this section shall be construed to preclude or limit the prosecution or conviction for any other offense defined in this Code or in any other law of this State.

PRACTICAL APPLICATION OF STATUTE

Endangering the welfare of an elderly or disabled person is a felony of the third degree. Barbie Penn is guilty of this offense for locking her elderly mother in the bedroom for 72 hours straight.

In order to be convicted under this statute, the defendant must have a "legal duty" to care for an elderly (60 years or older) or disabled person—at minimum, the defendant must have assumed a continuing responsibility to provide such care. A violation has occurred where the care provider has abandoned or unreasonably neglected the above-described person.

Barbie Penn was under a legal duty to care for her 75-year-old mother. She was paid by her late father's estate to handle the same on a daily basis. For some reason, Penn locked the elderly lady in her bedroom for 72 consecutive hours. The woman's only recourse for nutrition was tap water from the room's adjoining bathroom and two candy bars that she had stashed in her bureau; the traumatic event caused Penn's mother to be hospitalized for food deprivation.

Barbie Penn's neglect of her mother was clearly unreasonable. Not only did she fail to provide food for the woman, but she precluded her from all the normal activities of daily life—locking a 75-year-old woman in her bedroom is tantamount to imprisonment—not to mention that Penn placed her mother in other considerable danger. If a medical emergency arose, who would know? Under these circumstances, Penn, an individual who had a legal duty to care for her elderly mother, is guilty of violating section 12-4 for endangering her mother's welfare.

Penn probably also should be charged with false imprisonment or perhaps criminal restraint. After all, she did place her mother at risk of serious bodily injury by depriving her of food and general care. Subsection c. of 12-4 provides a special provision advising that a charge under this statute does not preclude prosecution under any other offense defined in the Code. This should be no surprise, though, as any one incident may result in violations of a number of different offenses.

12-5.   **Use of 17-year-old or younger to commit criminal offense; felony**

a. Except as provided in 10-17 and 20-5, any person who is at least 18 years of age who knowingly uses, solicits, directs, hires, employs or conspires with a person who is in fact 17 years of age or younger to commit a criminal offense is guilty of a felony.

b. An offense under this section constitutes a felony of the fourth degree if the underlying offense is a misdemeanor A. Otherwise, an offense under this section shall be classified one degree higher than the underlying offense.

c. A conviction under this section shall not merge with a conviction for the underlying offense, nor shall a conviction for the underlying offense merge with a conviction under this section. Nothing contained in this act shall prohibit the court from imposing an extended term of imprisonment; nor shall this be construed to preclude or limit a prosecution or conviction of any person for conspiracy, or any prosecution or conviction for any offense.

d. It shall be no defense to a prosecution under this act that the actor mistakenly believed that the person which the actor used, solicited, directed, hired or employed was 18 years of age or older, even if such mistaken belief was reasonable.

Practical Application of Statute

Frank Roberts is ripe for a charge under section 12-5 for paying a 13-year-old boy to steal Willie Maxso's camera. Given that the underlying theft offense is a third degree felony, Roberts' charge for criminally employing this juvenile is one of the second degree.

A person is guilty of an offense under 12-5 where he "knowingly" solicits or employs or conspires with a juvenile (17 or younger) to commit a criminal offense. This type of activity is a fourth degree felony where the underlying offense is a misdemeanor A; otherwise, it is a felony one degree higher than the underlying offense.

Frank Roberts actively paid a 13-year-old boy to steal a camera. Accordingly, he should be charged with violating 12-5 as he "knowingly" employed a juvenile to commit a criminal offense. The value of the camera was $1,000, which means the underlying theft offense is a third degree felony (thefts where the amount involved exceeds $500 but is less than $75,000 are third degree felonies). Therefore, since an offense under 12-5 is one degree higher than the underlying offense, Roberts should here be charged with a second degree felony.

No Defense Where Reasonable Belief Actor Is 18 or Older

Pursuant to subsection d., there is no defense available where the actor reasonably believed the juvenile employed was 18 years of age or older. If the juvenile used in the felony was in fact 17 or younger, the actor is automatically guilty of violating this statute.

End of Chapter Review

Multiple-Choice Questions

1. Which of the following constitutes the third degree felony of abandoning/neglecting an elderly person or disabled adult?
    a. Barbie Penn is paid by her late father's estate to care for her 75-year-old mother on a daily basis. She locks her mother in her bedroom for 72 consecutive hours. The woman's only recourse for nutrition was tap water from the room's adjoining bathroom and two candy bars she had stashed in her bureau.
    b. Storm, 33, has a 54-year-old friend, Garth, who is paralyzed from the waist down. Storm frequently visits Garth, often bringing Garth to the supermarket to buy groceries. Storm, however, becomes angry at Garth when he caught his friend using his toothbrush. Storm decides not to visit Garth anymore. Ten weeks later, Garth is rushed to the hospital for lack of nutrition. His cupboards and refrigerator were barren.
    c. Sally Mae, 80, showed her daughter, Ariel, her will, which left everything to her. Ariel, a crack addict, nonetheless rarely visited Sally Mae, who was suffering from several ailments. Sally Mae, upset, told Ariel that she felt "abandoned" and threatened to remove her from the will. The next day, Sally Mae died of a heart attack.
    d. all of the above
    e. none of the above

The following fact pattern pertains to questions 2–4.

Cameraman Willie Maxso videotaped ten-year-old Suzie having sex with a 13-year-old boy. Suzie's mother, Barbie Penn, brought Suzie to Frank Roberts' house in order for the videotaping to occur. She watched the entire shoot. Roberts set up the shoot and thereafter made multiple copies of the videotape and sold them through the Internet.

2. For acting as the cameraman, Maxso is guilty of:
    a. a first degree felony if he knew the children's age
    b. a second degree felony as long as he wasn't the parent or guardian of one of the children
    c. a fourth degree felony if his only role was to film the children
    d. all of the above
    e. a and b only

3. If the children weren't actually having sexual intercourse but were "simulating" sex, Maxso would be guilty of:
    a. no offense at all because the act was not real
    b. a misdemeanor A because the "simulation" lowers the degree
    c. a fourth degree felony if his only role was to film the children
    d. a second degree felony as long as he wasn't the parent or guardian of one of the children
    e. a capital offense

4. Barbie Penn, Suzie's mother, is guilty of:
    a. a first degree felony
    b. a second degree felony
    c. a fourth degree felony
    d. a misdemeanor B
    e. *res ipsa loquitor*

Essay Question

1. State Senator Wilfredo Chavez attended a party where, all of a sudden, a guest popped a child pornography tape into the VCR. If Senator Chavez simply stayed at the party and watched the tape, would he be guilty of any offense? If so, what offense is it, and what would the degree be? What if he took the child porn tape and sold it to a friend? Specifically cite the statute(s) and subsection(s).

13
DOMESTIC VIOLENCE

13-1.   **Definitions**

This act shall be known and may be cited as the "Prevention of Domestic Violence Act."
As used in this act:

a. "Domestic violence" means the occurrence of one or more of the following acts inflicted upon a person protected under this act by an adult or an emancipated minor:
   (1) Homicide
   (2) Assault
   (3) Terroristic threats
   (4) Kidnapping
   (5) Criminal restraint
   (6) False imprisonment
   (7) Sexual assault
   (8) Criminal sexual contact
   (9) Lewdness
   (10) Criminal mischief
   (11) Burglary
   (12) Criminal trespass
   (13) Harassment
   (14) Stalking

   When one or more of these acts are inflicted by an unemancipated minor upon a person protected under this act, the occurrence shall not constitute "domestic violence" but may be the basis for the filing of a petition or complaint.

b. "Law enforcement agency" means a department, division, bureau, commission, board or other authority of the State or of any political subdivision thereof which employs law enforcement officers.

c. "Law enforcement officer" means a person whose public duties include the power to act as an officer for the detection, apprehension, arrest and conviction of offenders against the laws of this State.

d. "Victim of domestic violence" means a person protected under this act and shall include any person who is 18 years of age or older or who is an emancipated minor and who has been subjected to domestic violence by a spouse, former spouse or any other person who is a present or former household member. "Victim of domestic violence" also includes any person, regardless of age, who has been subjected to domestic violence by a person with whom the victim has a child in common, or with whom the victim anticipates having a child in common, if one of the parties is pregnant. "Victim of domestic violence" also includes any person who has been subjected to domestic violence by a person with whom the victim has had a dating relationship.

e. "Emancipated minor" means a person who is under 18 years of age but who has been married, has entered military service, has a child or is pregnant or has been previously declared by a court or an administrative agency to be emancipated.

PRACTICAL APPLICATION OF STATUTE

Domestic Violence—Types of Offenses, Who Is a Victim, Probable Cause and Required Arrests Generally

"Domestic violence" includes offenses ranging from homicide to assault to stalking to harassment (see section 13-1 for a complete list). A "victim of domestic violence" is defined as any person who is 18 years or older—or who is an emancipated minor—who has some type of close relationship with the perpetrator. Per 13-1, relationships that qualify an individual to be protected under the Domestic Violence Act include where the perpetrator is a spouse, former spouse, any person who is a present or former household member or any person who has ever dated the victim. Also, a person can be a "victim of domestic violence," regardless of his age, where the perpetrator is a person who has a child with the victim or who anticipates having a child with the victim, meaning that one of the parties is pregnant.

Where a law enforcement officer finds "probable cause" to believe that an act of domestic violence has occurred, he "can" arrest the person he believes committed the act. The officer "shall"—or "must"—arrest the suspect if one of the following circumstances exists in addition to his finding of probable cause: the victim has a visible sign of injury, a warrant is in effect, the suspect is in contempt of a court order or a weapon was involved in the act of domestic violence. Probable cause—and nothing more—that the suspect utilized a weapon or is in contempt of a court order necessitates that the officer must arrest him. It should be noted that even where none of the aforementioned additional circumstances exist, an officer may still arrest an individual where he simply has probable cause to believe a domestic violence act has been committed.

Arrest Required Due to Probable Cause, Visible Signs of Injuries and Contempt of Court

Blakeville Police Patrolman Ra Davis was in a situation where he "must" have arrested both Barbie Penn and Jerry Penn for committing acts of domestic violence. Officer Davis responded to a report of violence at the home of Barbie Penn. Upon his arrival at her house, he found Barbie with her husband, Jerry Penn. Davis immediately observed that Jerry was bleeding from his nose, and upon closer inspection of Barbie, he noted that a small bruise was beginning to form under her eye. Both parties admitted to physically fighting with each other. Barbie even stated, "And I'm not sorry I broke your nose. You deserved it, because you're ugly." Jerry Penn advised that he was at the house even though there was a court order that forbade him from having contact with Barbie.

He claimed, however, that he was there in an effort to protect his daughter from "bad things" being performed in front of her by Barbie.

Under the totality of the circumstances, Patrolman Davis was required to arrest both Jerry and Barbie Penn for committing acts of domestic violence. First, both parties qualify as "victims" as defined in 13-1. Although separated, they are spouses—even if divorced, however, they would qualify as former spouses or people who previously lived in the same household. Second, Officer Davis had probable cause to believe that both Jerry and Barbie had committed prohibited acts of domestic violence—simple assaults:

1. Both parties admitted to fighting with each other;
2. Barbie even admitted to breaking Jerry's nose;
3. Jerry was obviously upset that Barbie was doing something improper, or perhaps illegal, in front of their daughter, thus giving him a motive to act out violently;
4. Both individuals exhibited signs of injuries.

The visible signs of injuries are important. This factor, in addition to Davis' finding of probable cause that an act of domestic violence occurred, meant that he had to arrest both Barbie and Jerry. It is important to note here, however, that had Davis found that either party had caused injuries to the other by using "reasonable force" to protect himself or herself, then Davis should *not* arrest that person. Section 13-2 sets forth an exception to a "must" arrest where a person has used reasonable force in self-defense from an attack. For example, if Jerry had fought off Barbie—the aggressor who broke his nose because he was "ugly"—then Davis should not arrest Jerry because of visible injuries he noted on Barbie.

Officer Davis, though, had to arrest Jerry in any case—he was in contempt of a court order. Jerry Penn admitted to Officer Davis that he was present at Barbie's home in face of a court order prohibiting his contact with her. This contempt violation, in addition to Davis' finding of probable cause that an act of domestic violence had been committed by Jerry, required Officer Davis to arrest him. The fact that Jerry claimed he was there in an effort to stop his estranged wife from doing "very bad things" in front of their child should not preclude Officer Davis from effectuating the arrest. Based on all of the above, Jerry Penn should be arrested as a domestic violence offender and charged with simple assault; he should further be charged for contempt of court as he violated the court's order to have no contact with his estranged wife. Barbie, too, should be arrested for committing an act of domestic violence, with a charge of simple assault filed against her. Thereafter, the courts will resolve the outcome of the charges.

13-2.

Arrest of alleged attacker; seizure of weapons, etc.

a. When a person claims to be a victim of domestic violence, and where a law enforcement officer responding to the incident finds probable cause to believe that domestic violence has occurred, the law enforcement officer shall arrest the person who is alleged to be the person who subjected the victim to domestic violence and shall sign a criminal complaint if:

(1) The victim exhibits signs of injury caused by an act of domestic violence;

(2) A warrant is in effect;

(3) There is probable cause to believe that the person has violated the contempt statute, and there is probable cause to believe that the person has been served with the order alleged to have been violated. If the victim does not have a copy of a purported order, the officer may verify the existence of an order with the appropriate law enforcement agency; or

(4) There is probable cause to believe that a weapon has been involved in the commission of an act of domestic violence.

b. A law enforcement officer may arrest a person, or may sign a criminal complaint against that person, or may do both, where there is probable cause to believe that an act of domestic violence has been committed, but where none of the conditions in subsection a. of this section applies.

c. (1) As used in this section, the word "exhibits" is to be liberally construed to mean any indication that a victim has suffered bodily injury, which shall include physical pain or any impairment of physical condition. Where the victim exhibits no visible sign of injury but states that an injury has occurred, the officer should consider other relevant factors in determining whether there is probable cause to make an arrest.

(2) In determining which party in a domestic violence incident is the victim where both parties exhibit signs of injury, the officer should consider the comparative extent of the injuries, the history of domestic violence between the parties, if any, and any other relevant factors.

(3) No victim shall be denied relief or arrested or charged under this act with an offense because the victim used reasonable force in self-defense against domestic violence by an attacker.

d. (1) In addition to a law enforcement officer's authority to seize any weapon that is contraband, evidence or an instrumentality of felony, a law enforcement officer who has probable cause to believe that an act of domestic violence has been committed shall:

(a) Question persons present to determine whether there are weapons on the premises; and

(b) Upon observing or learning that a weapon is present on the premises, seize any weapon that the officer reasonably believes would expose the victim to a risk of serious bodily injury. If a law enforcement officer seizes any firearm pursuant to this paragraph, the officer shall also seize any firearm purchaser identification card or permit to purchase a handgun issued to the person accused of the act of domestic violence.

(2) A law enforcement officer shall deliver all weapons, firearms purchaser identification cards and permits to purchase a handgun seized pursuant to this section to the county prosecutor and shall append an inventory of all seized items to the domestic violence report.

(3) Weapons seized in accordance with the "Prevention of Domestic Violence Act" shall be returned to the owner except upon order of the Superior Court. The prosecutor who has possession of the seized weapons may, upon notice to the owner, petition a judge of the Family Part of the Superior Court, Chancery Division, within 45 days of seizure, to obtain title to the seized weapons or to revoke any and all permits, licenses and other authorizations for the use, possession, or ownership of such weapons pursuant to the law governing such use, possession or ownership or may object to the return of the weapons on such grounds as are provided for the initial rejection or later revocation of the authorizations, or on the grounds that the owner is unfit or that the owner poses a threat to the public in general or a person or persons in particular.

A hearing shall be held and a record made thereof within 45 days of the notice provided above. No formal pleading and no filing fee shall be required as a preliminary to such hearing. The hearing shall be summary in nature. Appeals from the results of the hearing shall be to the Superior Court, Appellate Division, in accordance with the law.

If the prosecutor does not institute an action within 45 days of seizure, the seized weapons shall be returned to the owner.

After the hearing the court shall order the return of the firearms, weapons and any authorization papers relating to the seized weapons to the owner if the court determines the owner is not subject to any of the disabilities set forth in chapter 24 of this Criminal Code or the "State Firearms Purchase Act" and finds that the complaint has been dismissed at the request of the complainant and the prosecutor determines that there is insufficient probable cause to indict; or if the defendant is found not guilty of the charges; or if the court determines that the domestic violence situation no longer exists. Nothing in this act shall impair the right of the State to retain evidence pending a criminal prosecution, nor shall any provision of this act be construed to limit the authority of the State or a law enforcement officer to seize, retain or forfeit property.

If, after the hearing, the court determines that the weapons are not to be returned to the owner, the court may:

(a) With respect to weapons other than firearms, order the prosecutor to dispose of the weapons if the owner does not arrange for the transfer or sale of the weapons to an appropriate person within 60 days; or

(b) Order the revocation of the owner's firearms purchaser identification card or any permit, license or authorization, in which case the court shall order the owner to surrender any firearm seized and all other firearms possessed to the prosecutor and shall order the prosecutor to dispose of the firearms if the owner does not arrange for the sale of the firearms to a registered dealer of the firearms within 60 days; or

(c) Order such other relief as it may deem appropriate. When the court orders the weapons forfeited to the State or the prosecutor is required to dispose of the weapons, the prosecutor shall dispose of the property.

(4) A civil suit may be brought to enjoin a wrongful failure to return a seized firearm where the prosecutor refuses to return the weapon after receiving a written request to do so and notice of the owner's intent to bring a civil action pursuant to this section. Failure of the prosecutor to comply with the provisions of this act shall entitle the prevailing party in the civil suit to reasonable costs, including attorney's fees, provided that the court finds that the prosecutor failed to act in good faith in retaining the seized weapon.

(5) No law enforcement officer or agency shall be held liable in any civil action brought by any person for failing to learn of, locate or seize a weapon pursuant to this act or for returning a seized weapon to its owner.

PRACTICAL APPLICATION OF STATUTE

Seizure of Weapons

Where a law enforcement officer has probable cause to believe an act of domestic violence has occurred, he *shall* "seize any weapons that he reasonably believes would expose the victim to a risk of serious bodily injury." This subsection also provides that the officer *shall* "question persons present to determine whether there are weapons on the premises" and "upon observing or learning that a weapon is present on the premises, seize any weapon that the officer reasonably believes would expose the victim to a risk of serious bodily injury." Upon seizure, "a law enforcement officer shall deliver all weapons, firearms purchaser identification cards and permits to purchase a handgun seized pursuant to this section to the county prosecutor."

In updating domestic violence statutes, the legislatures of various states have changed the word "may" to "shall" with reference to provisions like those found in subsection d. herein. The result in this case is that police officers now *must* make the inquiries and seizures as described above.

END OF CHAPTER REVIEW

Multiple-Choice Questions

1. Which of the following offenses is *not* considered an act of "domestic violence" under the Domestic Violence Act?
   a. lewdness
   b. harassment
   c. disorderly conduct
   d. all of the above
   e. b and c only

2. Barbie Penn is visiting her cousin Shauna Penn at a park in Clauseville. There, Barbie gets mad at Shauna and bites her in the arm, leaving teeth indentations and a red mark. Clauseville Police Sergeant Mark Combs responds to the scene and witnesses the teeth indentations and red marks on Shauna's arm. Both women deny anything occurred. Which of the following statements is true?
   a. Without any other facts presented, Officer Combs cannot charge Barbie Penn with simple assault because he did not witness the assault.
   b. Pursuant to the Domestic Violence Act, Officer Combs could arrest Barbie Penn upon a finding of probable cause that a simple assault occurred.
   c. Under the Domestic Violence Act, Officer Combs must arrest Barbie Penn because he witnessed visible signs of injury to Shauna Penn.
   d. Officer Combs should charge Barbie Penn with aggravated assault because biting Shauna exceeds a simple assault.
   e. None of the above are true.

3. During a craps game in Clemente City, Jessica becomes enraged at her roommate Candy and burns her with her cigarette as she is yelling at her. It was obvious, though, that the burning was accidental. Clemente City officers, who witnessed the incident, should:
   a. arrest Jessica because Candy is her roommate and there were visible signs of injuries to her
   b. arrest Jessica because they witnessed the injuries

    c. not arrest Jessica because there was not probable cause to believe a simple assault occurred as the burning was accidental

    d. all of the above

    e. a and b only

4. Shrewsberry Patrolman Elliot Sarmucci arrives at a park, responding to an anonymous call about a verbal dispute. When he arrived, he found Bob and Mike yelling and cursing at each other. Mike had a scratch across the bridge of his nose and was bleeding slightly. After a brief discussion, Patrolman Sarmucci learned that Mike and Bob were lovers who lived together in Stargell County. Which of the following is correct?

    a. Patrolman Sarmucci should advise Mike that he can file a complaint against Bob for simple assault, but the officer cannot arrest Bob because he did not witness the act.

    b. Patrolman Sarmucci could normally arrest Bob under the Domestic Violence Act but can't because Bob lives out of the county.

    c. Patrolman Sarmucci cannot arrest Bob under the Domestic Violence Act because the act only applies to heterosexuals in a dating relationship.

    d. Patrolman Sarmucci must arrest Bob under the Domestic Violence Act.

    e. All of the above are true.

Essay Question

1. Patrolman Terry Simon of the Kenilworth Police Department responds to a call of an argument at the McMoose home. Upon arriving, Officer Simon finds Mr. McMoose and Mrs. McMoose yelling at each other on the front porch of the home. Mr. McMoose, a champion powerlifter and nearly 300 pounds in weight, is bleeding from the nose. Mrs. McMoose, a slight 100 pounds, has no visible signs of injuries. Both Mr. and Mrs. McMoose refuse to provide any statements to Officer Simon, and both advise that they don't want to file any charges. A neighbor, however, told Officer Simon that she saw Mrs. McMoose hurling her arms near Mr. McMoose's face. Are Mr. and/or Mrs. McMoose potential victims under the Prevention of Domestic Violence Act? What is it about their relationship that either allows or disallows them to be protected under the act? What should Officer Simon do in this matter? Can he arrest either person? Must he arrest either person? Would anything change if Officer Simon found that Mrs. McMoose scratched her husband by using reasonable force to protect herself? Explain your answers, citing specific statute subsections.

14

BRIBERY AND CORRUPT INFLUENCE

FACT PATTERN (PERTAINING TO CHAPTERS 14 AND 15)

Meade County Prosecutor Hoyt Wilder called a special press conference outside the gates of his office building. Flanked by his chief of investigators and his first assistant prosecutor, Wilder announced that his office had just completed an investigation that resulted in the arrests and indictments of more than ten individuals, including a number of elected officials and public servants. Unrolling a papyrus-type scroll, he tapped the microphone in front of him and read aloud the names and facts pertaining to a number of the indictments.

So You Want to Be the Police Director?

In Eastlake Township, the mayor and certain members of the town's council sought to pass legislation creating a police director position. Four affirmative votes of the council were necessary in order for the ordinance to pass; however, only three of the local legislators were publicly in favor of the new top cop job. In an attempt to swing the likely dissenting voters to his side, Mayor Packer Winstrol met individually with each councilperson. He was confident that at least one, Caroline Timborelli, would join his cause.

Mayor Winstrol met with Councilwoman Timborelli at her four-bedroom colonial home. After a light dinner, Francis Pinkerton joined them for tea cakes and various herbal teas. Pinkerton, owner of a local hotel and a number of township shops, was the leading candidate for the police director position. After he explained a detailed plan for the success of the Eastlake police force under his leadership, Pinkerton passed the councilwoman an envelope and said, "I hope all of my offerings will secure your vote on the ordinance." Timborelli casually thumbed through the envelope's contents—$5,000 in $20 bills—and replied, "I'm certain they have. You're a good man, Francis Pinkerton."

The ordinance passed the following Thursday, with Councilwoman Timborelli casting the deciding vote. A week later, Mayor Winstrol appointed Pinkerton to the police director post. One month after that, Prosecutor Wilder recorded Mayor Winstrol and Pinkerton in a conversation at one of his shops. During their discussion, the mayor stated to Pinkerton, "I assume you appreciate my appointment. Now, how about helping your old friend out? I don't need any cash. Just put my kid up in your hotel for free—I want him out of the house. You promised you would do this if I ensured your appointment."

Prosecutor Wilder convened a grand jury to seek indictments against Mayor Winstrol, Councilwoman Timborelli and Police Director Pinkerton. Somehow, Pinkerton learned that Timborelli was cooperating with Wilder's office and that she was going to provide testimony against him and Winstrol. The day before she was to appear at the grand jury, Pinkerton tracked down Timborelli in the driveway of her home. With an unidentified man, he wielded a baseball bat in front of her face and told her, "Testify tomorrow and I will break your legs." Timborelli, frightened, simply nodded. Pinkerton, then satisfied, fled with his friend.

The following day, not only did Timborelli unleash all of the payoff information to the grand jury, she also testified about Pinkerton's threats. Mayor Winstrol appeared next. He, however, gave testimony in direct contradiction to Timborelli's. After taking the appropriate oath and swearing to tell the truth, Winstrol told the grand jurors that he was not present at Timborelli's home when she was allegedly paid $5,000 by Pinkerton. He then categorically denied every charge levied against him.

A week later, the grand jury handed down indictments against Mayor Winstrol, Councilwoman Timborelli and Police Director Pinkerton. They were all arrested at the Eastlake Township municipal complex during a council meeting.

Does My Councilman Grow Marijuana?

In Templeton, three local officials and an 18-year-old high school cheerleader were indicted together in an unusual corruption conspiracy. Templeton High School senior Lacey Campbell appeared at a police precinct in the Chambersberg section of the city. She complained to the desk sergeant that one of the city's new council members, Mario Conti, was growing marijuana in his backyard. Upon some questioning, Campbell agreed to provide a written statement. Her statement was then turned over to the department's detective bureau, and an investigation was initiated.

Arriving in a marked Templeton police cruiser, two detectives met Councilman Conti on the street in front of his home. They asked the councilman for permission to check his backyard for marijuana plants. Conti, almost laughing, granted their request and led the detectives through the yard's gate. Next door, hidden in the brush, a tabloid photographer looked on with interest. He watched as the plainclothes officers went from plant to plant. They pulled up tomato vines, smelled basil leaves, closely inspected an oregano plant and eyeballed several other forms of greenery. They finally came to a halt, though, at one particular large growth. Uprooting it from the ground, the detectives conducted a quick field test—it proved positive for marijuana. The photographer shot two rolls of film as the officers bagged the illegal drug and handcuffed the shocked councilman.

The pictures and story of Conti's arrest became headlines in the morning edition of every local newspaper in the Templeton area. Conti's attorney, however, vehemently proclaimed his client's innocence and vowed that they would show that the newly elected public servant had been framed—and indeed they did.

This is what happened. An elderly woman who resided in the house behind Conti's came forward after she read of her neighbor's arrest. She told authorities that a young woman—fitting Lacey Campbell's description—had visited Conti's backyard a week earlier. The senior citizen advised that she saw the girl "planting something" but had dismissed the matter as an innocent botanical act.

The same detectives who arrested Conti questioned Campbell. She immediately folded and explained that she was dating a man much older than herself. Her boyfriend was Michael Stanowitz, chief of the Templeton Fire Department. Stanowitz and Conti were longtime adversaries, who most recently had butted heads over Conti's refusal to vote for an ordinance that would have appropriated over $100,000 toward two new fire engines. Stanowitz, in fact, was already under investigation for allegedly threatening to "ignite into flames" Conti's automobile if he failed to vote for the ordinance. When that didn't persuade the councilman to change his mind, he enlisted Campbell's aid to frame the man. Accordingly, two weeks after Conti and the council rejected the ordinance, Campbell appeared at the Chambersberg precinct and falsely incriminated the councilman of growing marijuana in his backyard.

With Stanowitz's illicit plot uncovered, he was expeditiously arrested and appropriately charged, along with his 18-year-old girlfriend. The charge against Councilman Conti was, of course, dismissed.

14-1.   Definitions

In chapters 14 through 17, unless a different meaning plainly is required:

a. "Benefit" means gain or advantage, or anything regarded by the beneficiary as gain or advantage, including a pecuniary benefit or a benefit to any other person or entity in whose welfare he is interested;

b. "Government" includes any branch, subdivision or agency of the government of the State or any locality within it;

c. "Harm" means loss, disadvantage or injury, or anything so regarded by the person affected, including loss, disadvantage or injury to any other person or entity in whose welfare he is interested;

d. "Official proceeding" means a proceeding heard or which may be heard before any legislative, judicial, administrative or other governmental agency, arbitration proceeding, or official authorized to take evidence under oath, including any arbitrator, referee, hearing examiner, commissioner, notary or other person taking testimony or deposition in connection with any such proceeding;

e. "Party official" means a person who holds an elective or appointive post in a political party in the United States by virtue of which he directs or conducts, or participates in directing or conducting, party affairs at any level of responsibility;

f. "Pecuniary benefit" is benefit in the form of money, property, commercial interests or anything else the primary significance of which is economic gain;

g. "Public servant" means any officer or employee of government, including legislators and judges, and any person participating as juror, advisor, consultant or otherwise, in performing a governmental function, but the term does not include witnesses;

h. "Administrative proceeding" means any proceeding, other than a judicial proceeding, the outcome of which is required to be based on a record or documentation prescribed by law or in which law or regulation is particularized in application to individuals; and

i. "Statement" means any representation but includes a representation of opinion, belief or other state of mind only if the representation clearly relates to state of mind apart from or in addition to any facts which are the subject of the representation.

14-2.   **Bribery in official and political matters**

A person is guilty of bribery if he directly or indirectly offers, confers or agrees to confer upon another or solicits, accepts or agrees to accept from another:

a. Any benefit as consideration for a decision, opinion, recommendation, vote or exercise of discretion of a public servant, party official or voter on any public issue or in any public election; or

b. Any benefit as consideration for a decision, vote, recommendation or exercise of official discretion in a judicial or administrative proceeding; or

c. Any benefit as consideration for a violation of an official duty of a public servant or party official; or

d. Any benefit as consideration for the performance of official duties.

For the purposes of this section, "benefit as consideration" shall be deemed to mean any benefit not authorized by law.

It is no defense to prosecution under this section that a person whom the actor sought to influence was not qualified to act in the desired way whether because he had not yet assumed office or lacked jurisdiction or for any other reason.

In any prosecution under this section of an actor who offered, conferred or agreed to confer or who solicited, accepted or agreed to accept a benefit, it is no defense that he did so as a result of conduct by another constituting theft by extortion or coercion or an attempt to commit either of those felonies.

Any offense proscribed by this section is a felony of the second degree. If the benefit offered, conferred, agreed to be conferred, solicited, accepted or agreed to be accepted is of the value of $200 or less, any offense proscribed by this section is a felony of the third degree.

PRACTICAL APPLICATION OF STATUTE

Both Francis Pinkerton and Councilwoman Caroline Timborelli are guilty of bribery. Section 14-2 makes it illegal for an individual to offer a bribe—and for an individual to accept a bribe. The Pinkerton-Timborelli bribe falls under subsection a. of the statute, and it is a second degree offense.

Section 14-2a. provides that the felony of bribery has occurred where a person has either offered or accepted "a benefit as consideration" for matters such as a "decision" or a "vote" of a "public servant" on any "public issue." It is not necessary that the bribe transaction actually be completed; "agreeing to confer" or "agreeing to accept" the benefit is sufficient for conviction.

Francis Pinkerton wanted an Eastlake Township ordinance creating a police director position to be passed. In an effort to accomplish this goal, he ate tea cakes and drank herbal tea with Councilwoman Timborelli—and he also gave her an envelope with $5,000 cash. Pinkerton, in fact, stated to her, "I hope all of my offerings will secure your vote on the ordinance." The councilwoman replied, "I'm certain they have."

Here, an offer of money—which is the "benefit"—was "accepted" by Councilwoman Timborelli, a "public servant." The money was provided as "consideration" for her "vote" on a "public issue"—the creation of a police director position in Eastlake Township. Accordingly, both Francis Pinkerton and councilwoman Caroline Timborelli are guilty of second degree bribery.

It should be noted that 14-2 makes it illegal to bribe any public servant for basically any violation of an official duty (see subsection c.) or for any "performance" of an official duty (see subsection d.). "Public servants" include elected officials such as mayors, councilmen, state assemblymen, state senators and the governor; it also includes individuals such as board of education members, planning board members and any other employees of the government. Bribery involving party officials (e.g., county chairmen) similarly falls under the prohibitions of the statute.

The offer or acceptance of a bribe by a judge likewise comes under the domain of 14-2. Subsection b. specifically makes it illegal for a person to offer or accept a benefit in exchange for a decision in a judicial or administrative proceeding.

Bribery is a second degree felony unless the value of the benefit involved is $200 or less. In that case, it is a felony of the third degree.

14-3.   **Threats and other improper influence in official and political matters**

   a. Offenses defined. A person commits an offense if he directly or indirectly:

   (1) Threatens unlawful harm to any person with the purpose to influence a decision, opinion, recommendation, vote or exercise of discretion of a public servant, party official or voter on any public issue or in any public election; or

   (2) Threatens harm to any public servant with the purpose to influence a decision, opinion, recommendation, vote or exercise of discretion in a judicial or administrative proceeding; or

   (3) Threatens harm to any public servant or party official with the purpose to influence him to violate his official duty.

   It is no defense to prosecution under this section that a person whom the actor sought to influence was not qualified to act in the desired way, whether because he had not yet assumed office or he lacked jurisdiction, or for any other reason.

   b. Grading. An offense under this section is a felony of the third degree.

PRACTICAL APPLICATION OF STATUTE

Templeton Fire Chief Michael Stanowitz is guilty of violating 14-3 for threatening Councilman Mario Conti. The felony is one of the third degree if the offense is directly related to Conti's position as a public servant.

Section 14-3a.(1) provides that an offense has been committed where a person threatens a public servant with unlawful harm in order to influence matters such as a decision or vote. Chief Stanowitz, a longtime adversary of Councilman Conti, threatened to "ignite into flames" the councilman's automobile if he failed to vote for an ordinance that was designed to appropriate over $100,000 toward two new fire engines. Given that there was a threat of harm (arson) toward a public servant (a councilman) in an attempt to influence a vote (on an ordinance), Chief Stanowitz is guilty of this third degree felony.

14-4.   **Unlawful benefits for official behavior; grading**

   a. A person commits a felony if the person, as a public servant:

   (1) Directly or indirectly, knowingly solicits, accepts or agrees to accept any benefit from another for or because of any official act performed or to be performed by the person or for or because of a violation of official duty;

(2) Directly or indirectly, knowingly receives any benefit from another who is or was in a position, different from that of a member of the general public, to benefit, directly or indirectly, from a violation of official duty or the performance of official duties; or

(3) Directly or indirectly, knowingly receives any benefit from or by reason of a contract or agreement for goods, property or services if the contract or agreement is awarded, made or paid by the agency that employs the person or if the goods, property or services are provided to the government agency that employs the public servant.

b. A person commits a felony if the person offers, confers or agrees to confer a benefit, acceptance of which is prohibited by this section.

c. Any offense proscribed by this section is a felony of the second degree. If the benefit solicited, accepted, agreed to be accepted, offered, conferred or agreed to be conferred is of a value of $200 or less, any offense proscribed by this section is a felony of the third degree.

Practical Application of Statute

This statute is quite similar to bribery as defined in section 14-2; however, this one only appears to apply to "public servants," and each subsection has a particular type of act that it prohibits. Subsection a.(1), for instance, has language that specifically prohibits receipt of any benefit for *past* official behavior. This is the statute that best suits Prosecutor Wilder's needs in a case against Mayor Winstrol for his son's yearlong housing in Francis Pinkerton's hotel.

Section 14-4a.(1) makes it illegal for a public servant to solicit or receive a benefit for any official act previously performed by him or to be performed in the future. Mayor Winstrol appointed Francis Pinkerton to be the police director. One month later, Prosecutor Wilder recorded a conversation between the two men. During this discussion, the mayor stated to Pinkerton, "I assume you appreciate my appointment. Now, how about helping your old friend out? I don't need any cash. Just put my kid up in your hotel for free—I want him out of the house. You promised you would do this if I ensured your appointment." In this circumstance, Mayor Winstrol solicited a benefit—free housing for his son—in exchange for his previously performed official act of appointing Pinkerton to the post of police director. Accordingly, the mayor should be charged under 14-4a.(1), which is a second degree offense.

Benefit for Contracts/Benefit from People in Special Positions

Subsections a.(2) and a.(3) provide interesting specific language. The latter sets forth that a public servant has committed a felony where he receives a benefit for doling out a *contract* (e.g., a mayor gives the city's sewer contract to a specific company in exchange for a Mercedes).

Per subsection a.(2), a public servant is guilty of a felony where he receives a benefit "from another who is or was in a position different from that of a member of the general public." What does this mean? The wife of the mayor of Jackson City receives a speeding ticket in Hackathorn. He approaches Hackathorn's municipal court judge and says, "Do me a favor. Dismiss my wife's ticket. I have a spot for you in Jackson City next year." The Hackathorn judge then dismisses Jackson City's First Lady's speeding ticket. Here, the Jackson City mayor has received a "benefit"—the dismissal of his wife's ticket; the benefit came from a judge—someone who is in a position "different from that of the general public." Therefore, the Jackson City mayor is ripe for a charge under 14-4a.(2).

The grading of the mayor's offense is particularly challenging. It should probably be a third degree felony because the fine for a speeding ticket is generally under $200. But is that really the value of the benefit received by the mayor? He and his wife most likely saved themselves at least a grand in insurance surcharges by the ticket's dismissal. Given that any offense under 14-4, where the benefit solicited or received is over $200, is a second degree felony, perhaps that should be the degree of the mayor's charge.

14-5.   **Retaliation for past official action**

A person commits a felony of the fourth degree if he harms another by any unlawful act with the purpose to retaliate for or on account of the service of another as a public servant.

PRACTICAL APPLICATION OF STATUTE

Prosecutor Wilder appropriately had Templeton Fire Chief Michael Stanowitz charged with violating 14-5 for his retaliatory acts against Councilman Mario Conti. This is a fourth degree felony.

Section 14-5 makes it illegal for a person to retaliate against a public servant for a past official act performed by the official. In order for the retaliation to be a felony, it must be an "unlawful act." In Stanowitz's case, he did just that.

Chief Stanowitz was angry at Councilman Conti, a public servant, for voting against an ordinance that would have appropriated over $100,000 toward two new fire engines. In an effort to retaliate against Conti, Stanowitz conspired with his girlfriend to harm the councilman by engaging in the unlawful act of falsely incriminating him to the police—they attempted to frame Conti for growing marijuana in his backyard. Accordingly, Stanowitz should be charged with violating 14-5 for retaliating unlawfully against the councilman.

14-6.   **Unlawful official business transaction where interest is involved; grading; conditions**

A public servant commits a felony of the fourth degree if, while performing his official functions on behalf of a governmental entity, the public servant knowingly transacts any business with himself, a member of his immediate family or a business organization in which the public servant or an immediate family member has an interest. For purposes of this section, an interest in a business organization shall not include aggregate familial ownership or control of 1% or less of an interest in the capital or equity of the business organization. A public servant shall not be guilty of an offense under this section if the public servant's performance of official functions would not affect the public servant, family member or business organization differently than such performance would affect the public generally or would not affect the public servant, family member or business organization, as a member of a business, profession, occupation or group, differently than such performance would affect any other member of such business, profession, occupation or group.

PRACTICAL APPLICATION OF STATUTE

This is yet another bribery-type statute. Section 14-6, though, sets forth specific language to prohibit circumstances where a public servant "transacts" with himself or members of his immediate family. This means that a mayor or board of education member or state assemblyman (or any other public servant) cannot provide public contracts to his own company or a company owned by people such as his wife, sister or mother.

14-7.   **Acceptance or receipt of unlawful benefit by public servant for official behavior**

a. A public servant commits a felony if, under color of office and in connection with any official act performed or to be performed by the public servant, the public servant, directly or indirectly, knowingly solicits, accepts or agrees to accept any benefit, whether the benefit inures to the public servant or another person, to influence the performance of an official duty or to commit a violation of an official duty.

b. A public servant commits a felony if, under color of office and in connection with any official act performed or to be performed by the public servant, the public servant, directly or indirectly, knowingly receives any benefit, whether the benefit inures to the public servant or another person, to influence the performance of an official duty or to commit a violation of an official duty.

c. In addition to the definition set forth in 14-1, "benefit" as used in this act includes any benefit from or by reason of a contract or agreement for goods, property or services if the contract or agreement is awarded, made or paid by the branch, subdivision or agency of the government that employs the public servant.

d. The provisions of this section shall not apply to:

(1) Fees prescribed by law to be received by a public servant or any other benefit to which the public servant is otherwise legally entitled if these fees or benefits are received in the manner legally prescribed and not bartered for another benefit to influence the performance of an official duty or to commit a violation of an official duty;

(2) Gifts or other benefits conferred on account of kinship or other personal, professional or business relationship independent of the official status of the recipient if these gifts or benefits are within otherwise legally permissible limits and are not bartered for another benefit to influence the performance of an official duty or to commit a violation of an official duty; or

(3) Trivial benefits the receipt of which involves no risk that the public servant would perform official duties in a biased or partial manner.

e. An offense proscribed by this section is a felony of the second degree. If the benefit solicited, accepted, agreed to be accepted or received is of a value of $200 or less, any offense proscribed by this section is a felony of the third degree.

PRACTICAL APPLICATION OF STATUTE

Sections 14-7 and 14-8, the "gifts to public servants" statutes, are basically additional bribery statutes. A public servant who solicits or receives a benefit—"whether the benefit inures to the public servant or another person"—can be convicted of this offense. Per subsection e., this is a felony of the second degree unless the benefit is of a value of $200 or less; in that case, it is a third degree felony.

Illicit gifts can range from vacation packages to a new house roof to sterling silver forks. If they are provided in an effort to influence the public servant in his duties, then the gifts are illegal. Where the gift is considered "trivial," no offense is deemed to be committed at all because such gifts "involve no risk that the public servant would perform official duties in a biased or partial manner." Trivial gifts include items such as a cup of coffee or a pen.

14-8.   **Offer of unlawful benefit to public servant for official behavior**

a. A person commits a felony if the person offers, confers or agrees to confer any benefit, whether the benefit inures to the public servant or another person, to influence a public servant in the performance of an official duty or to commit a violation of an official duty.

b. A person commits a felony if the person, directly or indirectly, confers or agrees to confer any benefit not allowed by law to a public servant.

c. In addition to the definition set forth in 14-1, "benefit" as used in this act includes any benefit from or by reason of a contract or agreement for goods, property or services if the contract or agreement is awarded, made or paid by the branch, subdivision or agency of the government that employs the public servant.

d. The provisions of this section shall not apply to:

   (1) Fees prescribed by law to be received by a public servant or any other benefit to which the public servant is otherwise legally entitled if these fees or benefits are received in the manner legally prescribed and not bartered for another benefit to influence the performance of an official duty or to commit a violation of an official duty;

   (2) Gifts or other benefits conferred on account of kinship or other personal, professional or business relationship independent of the official status of the recipient if these gifts or benefits are within otherwise legally permissible limits and are not bartered for another benefit to influence the performance of an official duty or to commit a violation of an official duty; or

   (3) Trivial benefits the receipt of which involves no risk that the public servant would perform official duties in a biased or partial manner.

e. (1) An offense proscribed by subsection a. of this section is a felony of the second degree. If the benefit solicited, accepted or agreed to be accepted is of a value of $200 or less, any offense proscribed by subsection a. of this section is a felony of the third degree.

   (2) An offense proscribed by subsection b. of this section is a felony of the third degree. If the gift or other benefit is of a value of $200 or less, an offense proscribed by subsection b. of this section is a felony of the fourth degree.

PRACTICAL APPLICATION OF STATUTE

The counterpart to section 14-7, this statute prohibits the offering or conferring of a benefit to a public servant. The grading of the offenses is the same for the one who offers the illicit gift as for the public servant who accepts it. This is true as long as the benefit is offered/conferred "to influence a public servant in the performance of an official duty or to commit a violation of an official duty." Subsection e.(2), however, allows for a lower degree charge (third degree generally and fourth degree where the value of the benefit is $200 or less) where a person offers/confers a benefit to a public servant for some other reason.

END OF CHAPTER REVIEW

Multiple-Choice Questions

1. Renard Bendini, a state assemblyman with an eleventh-grade education, receives a free trip to Europe from Mr. Mogul, an insurance company owner. A year later, Assemblyman Bendini votes to give Mr. Mogul's company a state contract. Should Assemblyman Bendini be charged with an offense?

    a. no, because under the "Deprived Educational Resources Act of 1977," Assemblyman Renard Bendini is exempt from criminal prosecution

    b. yes, if Assemblyman Renard Bendini knowingly accepted the vacation in exchange for his vote

    c. yes, if Assemblyman Renard Bendini at least recklessly accepted the vacation while aware that legislation was pending that could benefit Mr. Mogul's insurance company

    d. yes, if Assemblyman Renard Bendini was an immediate family member of Mr. Mogul

    e. c and d

2. Weinstein, an immigrant from Wales, sweeps the floor of the municipal building in Woodbridge. Newly elected Councilman McAllister tells Weinstein that if he polishes McAllister's toenails for seven consecutive weeks, then McAllister will vote for an ordinance giving him an extra week of vacation. Weinstein agrees. Is McAllister guilty of an offense?

    a. yes, McAllister is guilty of bribery because McAllister, a councilperson, solicited a benefit from Weinstein in exchange for McAllister's exercise of a vote

    b. yes, McAllister is guilty of forgery because his vote would amount to a false writing

    c. no, because there was no exchange of money

    d. no, because Weinstein, although a government custodian, is not an elected official

    e. a and b

3. Which of the following acts is illegal?

    a. Fisk, the Madora City building inspector, issues a permit to Knowles in exchange for a Cross pen set and a cup of chocolate mousse. Knowles never should have received the permit.

    b. Yastremski, the Keansburg property maintenance director, ignores a yard cluttered with an amount of debris that violates town ordinances because the property owner gives him tickets to a minor league baseball game.

    c. Scott, a Casabonne Township fire official, issues a summons to Bernard for a burned-out shed. Scott does this in spite of the fact that Bernard does not own the shed, does not have control over it and is not otherwise responsible for it in any way. Scott issues the summons because Sharanda, a hooker who hates Bernard, offers Scott sex in exchange for issuing the summons to Bernard.

   d. All of the above are illegal.

   e. None of the above are illegal.

4. Under the bribery statute, which of the following is true?

   a. A benefit offered, conferred or solicited that is of the value of $10,000 or less is a third degree felony.

   b. A benefit offered, conferred or solicited that is of the value of $75,000 or more is a first degree felony.

   c. A benefit offered, conferred or solicited that is of the value of $200 or less is a third degree felony.

   d. Only a and b are true.

   e. Only b and c are true.

Essay Question

1. Kingman, an electrician, pays Seaver, an employee of a supermarket chain, $5,000 to lobby the supermarket's president to give the chain's electrical contract to Kingman. Kingman also pays Koosman, the mayor of Bridgewater, $7,500 to ensure the passage of a town ordinance that will help Kingman's company grow. In accepting the $5,000 payment, what offense in Chapter 14, if any, has Seaver committed? Kingman's payment of $7,500 to Mayor Koosman makes him guilty of what offense, if any, in Chapter 14? How about Mayor Koosman? Be sure to cite the statute number(s) and degree of offense(s) in your answer.

15

PERJURY AND OTHER FALSIFICATION IN OFFICIAL MATTERS

15-1.   **Perjury**

    a. Offense defined. A person is guilty of perjury, a felony of the third degree, if in any official proceeding he makes a false statement under oath or equivalent affirmation, or swears or affirms the truth of a statement previously made, when the statement is material and he does not believe it to be true.

    b. Materiality. Falsification is material, regardless of the admissibility of the statement under rules of evidence, if it could have affected the course or outcome of the proceeding or the disposition of the matter. It is no defense that the declarant mistakenly believed the falsification to be immaterial. Whether a falsification is material is a question of law.

    c. Irregularities no defense. It is not a defense to prosecution under this section that the oath or affirmation was administered or taken in an irregular manner. A document purporting to be made upon oath or affirmation at any time when the actor presents it as being so verified shall be deemed to have been duly sworn or affirmed.

    d. Retraction. It is an affirmative defense under this section that the actor retracted the falsification in the course of the proceeding or matter in which it was made prior to the termination of the proceeding or matter without having caused irreparable harm to any party.

    e. Corroboration. No person shall be convicted of an offense under this section where proof of falsity rests solely upon contradiction by testimony of a single person other than the defendant.

PRACTICAL APPLICATION OF STATUTE

Perjury

Mayor Packer Winstrol is guilty of perjury, which is a third degree offense. The mayor's felony results from his willfully false testimony provided before the grand jury.

A person is guilty of perjury where he makes a false statement under oath—and knows it not to be true. Also key to this offense is that the statement is "material," meaning that it is relevant, perhaps crucial, to the proceeding where the testimony is provided. Basically, if the false statement can affect the outcome of the proceeding, it is "material." However, "materiality" is a question to be decided by the courts.

Mayor Winstrol was present at Councilwoman Timborelli's house when she received a $5,000 bribe from Francis Pinkerton; in fact, he set up the meeting. Winstrol also solicited a benefit from Pinkerton—to put up his son, for free, in Pinkerton's hotel. This benefit was requested in exchange for the mayor's past appointment of Pinkerton as the township police director. Mayor Winstrol then willfully lied at grand jury proceedings about these matters—grand jury proceedings which were specifically convened to ascertain the truth about the alleged aforementioned corrupt activities of the mayor, Councilwoman Timborelli and Police Director Pinkerton. Accordingly, the mayor's false statements were obviously "material" because if they were believed, they could have affected the outcome of the proceedings and vindicated the mayor and the others. With this being the case, Mayor Packer Winstrol is guilty of perjury.

Retraction—Affirmative Defense

If a person retracts his false testimony during the course of the proceeding where it was made—and it hasn't caused "irreparable harm" to any party, he has an affirmative defense to perjury. This provision can be found under subsection d. of the statute.

Mayor Winstrol committed perjury when he testified in front of the grand jury, but if he had retracted his false testimony before the end of the grand jury proceedings, he would have had an affirmative defense to a perjury charge and could not be convicted of this offense. The only thing that would vitiate the affirmative defense, though, is if the false testimony had caused irreparable harm to the prosecution (e.g., the false testimony caused another key witness to jump bail and refuse to testify).

No Conviction Where Testimony Contradicted by Just One Party

The prosecution would not be able to convict Mayor Winstrol of perjury if they only had one person to contradict his testimony. Subsection e. of the statute provides that a person cannot be convicted of perjury "where proof of falsity rests solely" on one person's contradictory testimony. Accordingly, if the state could only produce Councilwoman Timborelli to contradict the mayor's false testimony, he could not be convicted of perjury; however, since Prosecutor Wilder possessed tape-recorded conversations of Mayor Winstrol, it is unlikely that the politician could avoid a perjury conviction.

15-2.   **False swearing**

    a. False swearing. A person who makes a false statement under oath or equivalent affirmation, or swears or affirms the truth of such a statement previously made, when he does not believe the statement to be true is guilty of a felony of the fourth degree.

    b. Perjury provisions applicable. Subsections c. and d. of section 15-1 apply to the present section.

    c. Inconsistent statements. Where the defendant made inconsistent statements under oath or equivalent affirmation, both having been made within the period of the statute of limitations, the prosecution may proceed by setting forth the inconsistent statements in a single count alleging in the alternative that one or the other was false and not believed by the defendant. In such case it shall not be necessary for the prosecution to prove which statement was false but only that one or the other was false and not believed by the defendant to be true.

PRACTICAL APPLICATION OF STATUTE

While perjury is a third degree felony, false swearing is a fourth degree felony. The offenses are quite similar, with false swearing having the same retraction defense as found in the perjury statute. The difference lies in the lack of a requirement of materiality.

Basically, where a person takes a statement *under oath* and willfully gives false testimony, he can be convicted under section 15-2 instead of 15-1 as long as the false statement was not material. Of course, in order for a conviction to result, the person must believe the statement is not true when he makes it.

15-3.   **Unsworn falsification to authorities**

a. Statements "under penalty." A person commits a felony of the fourth degree if he makes a written false statement which he does not believe to be true on or pursuant to a form bearing notice, authorized by law, to the effect that false statements made therein are punishable.

b. In general. A person commits a misdemeanor A if, with the purpose to mislead a public servant in performing his function, he:

(1) Makes any written false statement which he does not believe to be true;

(2) Purposely creates a false impression in a written application for any pecuniary or other benefit by omitting information necessary to prevent statements therein from being misleading;

(3) Submits or invites reliance on any writing which he knows to be forged, altered or otherwise lacking in authenticity; or

(4) Submits or invites reliance on any sample, specimen, map, boundary mark or other object which he knows to be false.

c. Perjury provisions applicable. Subsections c. and d. of section 15-1 and subsection c. of 15-2 apply to the present section.

PRACTICAL APPLICATION OF STATUTE

Unsworn Falsification—Generally

This is another perjury-type statute, though the false statement does not need to be made "under oath" in order for a conviction to occur. Per subsection a. of 15-3, a person commits a fourth degree felony if he makes a false statement—which he knows is not true—on a form bearing notice, "authorized by law," that false statements made therein are punishable. What does this mean?

Lacey Campbell, the high school cheerleader and girlfriend of Fire Chief Stanowitz, appeared at the Templeton Police Department. There she spoke to officers, telling them that Councilman Conti was growing marijuana in his backyard. Immediately after her oral recitation, Campbell provided a written statement to the officers, again stating that the councilman was growing marijuana in his backyard. Although Campbell knew her written statement was false, she signed the statement. If this statement provided notice that false statements made within it were punishable under the authorization of state law, then Campbell could be convicted of a fourth degree unsworn falsification charge.

No Notice That False Statements Are Punishable as Authorized by Law

If Campbell's statement did *not* contain any language that false statements are "punishable" as "authorized by law," then she should be charged with a misdemeanor A. This is per subsection b. of the statute.

Per 15-3b.(1), a person commits a misdemeanor A where he makes a written false statement "with the purpose to mislead a public servant." Campbell obviously purposely intended to mislead the Templeton police when she provided her written statement to them—she lied, stating that Councilman Conti was growing marijuana when she in fact planted the illegal vegetation in his backyard. Accordingly, if her written statement did not contain a notice advising that false statements are "punishable" as "authorized by law," then she should be charged with a misdemeanor A under subsection b. of the statute.

15-4.   **False reports to law enforcement authorities**

    a. Falsely incriminating another. A person who knowingly gives or causes to be given false information to any law enforcement officer with the purpose to implicate another commits a felony of the fourth degree.

    b. Fictitious reports. A person commits a misdemeanor A if he:

        (1) Reports or causes to be reported to law enforcement authorities an offense or other incident within their concern knowing that it did not occur; or

        (2) Pretends to furnish or causes to be furnished such authorities with information relating to an offense or incident when he knows he has no information relating to such offense or incident.

PRACTICAL APPLICATION OF STATUTE

Falsely Incriminating Another

Lacey Campbell is guilty of violating section 15-4 for providing false information to the Templeton police that implicated Councilman Conti of illegally growing marijuana. This is a felony of the fourth degree.

A person is guilty of violating this statute where he "knowingly" gives (or causes to be given) false information to any law enforcement officer "with the purpose to implicate another." For a conviction to occur under this statute, the information does not need to be provided under oath or in a written statement.

Campbell appeared at the Templeton Police Department and told officers that Councilman Mario Conti was growing marijuana in his backyard. She knew her statement was false, as she had planted the marijuana in his backyard without the man's permission. Since Campbell "knowingly" gave "false information" to police officers—with the purpose to implicate Councilman Conti of committing a felony—she is guilty of a fourth degree felony under 15-4.

It is interesting to note that Campbell's older boyfriend, Templeton Fire Chief Michael Stanowitz, also would probably be convicted under section 15-4 for Campbell's false incrimination of Councilman Conti. How? He was an accomplice in the commission of the offense. If the state can prove that Stanowitz solicited Campbell or aided her in some way in the commission of the false incrimination, then he also can be convicted of the felony.

Fictitious Reports

A person can be convicted under section 15-4 for reporting fictitious information to law enforcement officers even where the false information does not incriminate another. These types of matters are a misdemeanor A.

Under subsection b.(1) of the statute, if a person reports an offense that he knows did not occur, he is guilty of a misdemeanor A (e.g., Bob tells police that someone broke into his house when no such offense occurred). Per b.(2), a person is guilty of a misdemeanor A if he furnishes authorities with information relating to an offense when "he knows he has no information relating to such offense." An example of this follows. Karla's house falls victim to a burglar who enters the home by kicking down the front door. Frank tells police that he saw a woman in a yellow hat kick down the door. Frank's statement, though, is a lie, as he was in Montana when the burglary occurred. Accordingly, since Frank never saw a woman in a yellow hat and has no true information about the burglary of Karla's house, he is guilty of violating 15-4b.(2) for providing a fictitious report.

15-5.   **Tampering with witnesses and informants; retaliation against them**

a. Tampering. A person commits an offense if, believing that an official proceeding or investigation is pending or about to be instituted, he knowingly attempts to induce or otherwise cause a witness or informant to:

(1) Testify or inform falsely;

(2) Withhold any testimony, information, document or thing;

(3) Elude legal process summoning him to testify or supply evidence; or

(4) Absent himself from any proceeding or investigation to which he has been legally summoned.

The offense is a felony of the second degree if the actor employs force or threat of force. Otherwise it is a felony of the third degree. Privileged communications may not be used as evidence in any prosecution for violations of paragraph (2), (3) or (4).

b. Retaliation against witness or informant. A person commits a felony of the fourth degree if he harms another by an unlawful act with the purpose to retaliate for or on account of the service of another as a witness or informant.

c. Witness or informant taking bribe. A person commits a felony of the third degree if he solicits, accepts or agrees to accept any benefit in consideration of his doing any of the things specified in subsections a.(1) through a.(4) of this section.

PRACTICAL APPLICATION OF STATUTE

Witness Tampering—Generally Third Degree Offense, Second Degree When Force Threatened

Eastlake Township Police Director Francis Pinkerton is guilty of a second degree felony for threatening to break Councilwoman Timborelli's legs if she testified in front of the grand jury. Pinkerton's felony is one of the second degree because of his threat of force; otherwise, he would be guilty of a third degree offense.

Pursuant to 15-5a., a person commits witness tampering if, believing that an official proceeding or investigation is pending, he knowingly attempts to induce a witness to withhold testimony or to testify falsely. Also, this subsection makes it illegal either to attempt to induce a witness to evade a legal process that is summoning him to testify or to withhold any type of evidence.

Francis Pinkerton knew that Councilwoman Timborelli was scheduled to testify before a grand jury; even more so, he knew that she was going to provide testimony that would incriminate him. In an effort to persuade her to not testify, Pinkerton ambushed the councilwoman at her home. Standing in the doorway with an unidentified man, Pinkerton wielded a baseball bat in front of her face and told her, "Testify tomorrow and I will break your legs." The councilwoman, frightened, simply nodded. Pinkerton, then satisfied, fled with his friend.

Police Director Pinkerton's actions constitute witness tampering. Believing the grand jury—an official proceeding—was meeting the next day, Pinkerton knowingly attempted to induce Councilwoman Timborelli to not testify. His attempt to induce her was through wielding a baseball bat and threatening to break her legs. Normally, the police director would be guilty of a third degree felony for engaging in witness tampering; however, since he threatened Councilwoman Timborelli with force during his unlawful activities, his offense is elevated to a felony of the second degree. It should be noted that this subsection, as well as the other subsections in 15-5, apply to informants as well as witnesses.

Retaliation Against Witness—Fourth Degree Offense

If Police Director Pinkerton had hit Councilwoman Timborelli with a baseball bat after she testified, he could be charged with a fourth degree felony under 15-5b. This subsection makes it illegal for a person to harm another "by an unlawful act" in retaliation for the individual's service as a witness. Accordingly, had Pinkerton struck the councilwoman with a baseball bat because he was angry that she testified against him, he would be appropriately charged under this subsection. This charge obviously would be in addition to an aggravated assault charge under section 2-1b.

Witness Taking a Bribe or Some Other Benefit— Third Degree Offense

If Police Director Pinkerton had persuaded Councilwoman Timborelli to not testify by providing her a monetary bribe, then she would be guilty of a third degree felony under 15-5c. Simply put, subsection c. of the statute makes it illegal for a person to solicit or accept a bribe in exchange for withholding testimony or testifying falsely at an official proceeding. Accordingly, had the councilwoman accepted money or some other benefit (or even solicited it) in consideration for withholding her testimony at the grand jury, then she would be guilty of a third degree offense per this subsection.

15-6.   **Tampering with or fabricating physical evidence**

A person commits a felony of the fourth degree if, believing that an official proceeding or investigation is pending or about to be instituted, he:

   a. Alters, destroys, conceals or removes any article, object, record, document or other thing of physical substance with the purpose to impair its verity or availability in such proceeding or investigation; or

b. Makes, devises, prepares, presents, offers or uses any article, object, record, document or other thing of physical substance knowing it to be false and with the purpose to mislead a public servant who is engaged in such proceeding or investigation.

PRACTICAL APPLICATION OF STATUTE

One who destroys, alters or removes any type of evidence in an effort to impair its accuracy or availability in an official proceeding is guilty of a fourth degree felony under subsection (1) of 15-6. Examples of this include destroying a knife that was used in a stabbing, burning a diary where a person admitted to committing a string of burglaries and altering a photograph to make it appear that an individual was not in the picture when he really was in it.

15-7.   **Tampering with public records or information**

a. Offense defined. A person commits an offense if he:
   (1) Knowingly makes a false entry in, or false alteration of, any record, document or thing belonging to, or received or kept by, the government for information or record or required by law to be kept by others for information of the government;
   (2) Makes, presents, offers for filing or uses any record, document or thing knowing it to be false and with the purpose that it be taken as a genuine part of information or records referred to in paragraph (1); or
   (3) Purposely and unlawfully destroys, conceals, removes, mutilates or otherwise impairs the verity or availability of any such record, document or thing.

b. Grading. An offense under subsection a. is a misdemeanor A unless the actor's purpose is to defraud or injure anyone, in which case the offense is a felony of the third degree.

c. A person commits a felony of the fourth degree if he purposely and unlawfully alters, destroys, conceals, removes or disables any camera or other monitoring device including any videotape, film or other medium used to record sound or images that is installed in a patrol vehicle.

PRACTICAL APPLICATION OF STATUTE

Alfredo "The King" Minoso sneaks into Wildwood Police Department. Once inside, he finds a speeding ticket issued against him by one of the town's officers. He then proceeds to change the ticket to read "40 in 35" instead of "70 in 35." The King's alteration of his speeding ticket constitutes an offense as provided for in section 15-7. Generally, such an offense would be graded as a misdemeanor A; this is unless the act is found to "defraud or injure anyone," wherein it would be elevated to a felony of the third degree.

15-8.   **Impersonating a public servant or law enforcement officer**

a. Except as provided in subsection b. of this section, a person commits a misdemeanor A if he falsely pretends to hold a position in the public service with the purpose to induce another to submit to such pretended official authority or otherwise to act in reliance upon that pretense.

b. A person commits a felony of the fourth degree if he falsely pretends to hold a position as an officer or member or employee or agent of any organization or association of law enforcement officers with the purpose to induce another to submit to such pretended official authority or otherwise to act in reliance upon that pretense.

PRACTICAL APPLICATION OF STATUTE

Under subsection a. of this statute, an individual is guilty of a misdemeanor A if he impersonates a public servant such as a mayor, state assemblyman or board of education member. However, to be convicted of this offense, the defendant must do more than just pretend to be a public official. His false pretense must be "with the purpose" to induce another to "submit to such pretended authority." For instance, if Jerry Jamone impersonates the mayor of Newberry in an effort to get city sanitation workers to pick up rubbish from an unsightly construction site located on the street where he resides, then he is guilty of a misdemeanor A; however, if Jamone pretends to be the mayor of Newberry at a party but does nothing in furtherance of his false representation, then he is not ripe for a conviction under this statute.

Please note that per subsection b., the offense is upgraded to a fourth degree felony where a person impersonates a law enforcement officer. Accordingly, if Jamone, pretending to be a police officer, pulled over an operator of a motor vehicle for speeding, then he would be guilty of a fourth degree felony.

END OF CHAPTER REVIEW

Multiple-Choice Questions

1. The difference between perjury and false swearing is:
   a. perjury is a felony of the third degree, while false swearing is a felony of the fourth degree
   b. perjury requires that the false statement must be "material" to the proceedings, while false swearing does not
   c. perjury requires that the defendant does not believe that his statement is true, while false swearing does not
   d. a and b
   e. a and c

2. Karla's house falls victim to a burglar who enters the home by kicking down the front door. Frank orally tells police that he saw a woman in a yellow hat kick down the door. Frank's statement is a lie, as he was in Montana at the time of the alleged event. Frank is guilty of what offense?
   a. perjury, a felony of the third degree
   b. false swearing, a felony of the fourth degree
   c. unsworn falsification, a felony of the fourth degree
   d. making a fictitious police report, a misdemeanor A
   e. no offense at all because people, unfortunately, can lie

3. Knockwurst applies for the job of Pleasantvale Business Administrator, providing his application to the mayor. On Knockwurst's written application, he states that he

previously served as business administrator in three towns in Ohio, but Knockwurst never served as a business administrator in any town, Ohio or otherwise. Knockwurst is guilty of what offense?

    a. no offense at all because he did not make his statements under oath

    b. false swearing, a fourth degree felony, if the mayor adopted Knockwurst's application at a joint unified meeting of the town's electorate

    c. perjury, a third degree felony, if the mayor relied on Knockwurst's application in an authorized town council meeting

    d. unsworn falsification, a fourth degree felony, if his application had a notice on it, authorized by law, stating that false statements made on it are punishable

    e. b, c and d

4. Marcy testifies under oath, at a grand jury proceeding, that she saw the defendant, Sampson, break the window of Kackie's house and enter her home. The grand jury's role is to decide whether or not to indict Sampson for burglary and aggravated sexual assault. It turns out that Marcy lied; she never saw Sampson do anything. Which of the following statements is true?

    a. Marcy cannot be charged with perjury because a perjury charge is not permitted where false statements are made at grand jury proceedings.

    b. Marcy can only be charged with false swearing.

    c. Marcy has an affirmative defense to a perjury charge if she retracted her false statement during the same grand jury proceedings and her false statement did not cause irreparable harm to Sampson.

    d. All of the above are true.

    e. Only a and b are true.

5. A conviction of false swearing requires which of the following elements to be present in the defendant's actions?

    a. making a false statement under oath

    b. knowing that the statement is false

    c. having the false statement be "material" to the proceedings

    d. all of the above

    e. a and b only

6. Which of the following actors has committed a misdemeanor A for impersonating a public servant?

    a. Maxwell, at a masquerade party, pretends to be George Bush, President of the United States.

    b. Gloria tells the members of the Argyle Club that she is the CEO of Chrysler and advises that if any member gives her $1,000, she will lease them any Chrysler they want for $50 per month.

    c. Sergio impersonates the mayor of Newarkville in an effort to get sanitation workers to pick up rubbish from an unsightly construction site on the street where he resides.

    d. Only a and b describe a misdemeanor A.

    e. Only a and c describe a misdemeanor A.

7. Lacey Campbell told Templeton police that City Councilman Mario Conti was growing marijuana in his backyard. She told police this although she knew her statement was false. What is the *best* offense to charge Campbell with?

    a. She should be charged with a fourth degree felony for falsely incriminating another.

    b. She should be charged with a first degree felony for falsely incriminating another.

    c. She should be charged with a fourth degree felony of obstruction of justice.

    d. She should be charged with a misdemeanor A for filing a false police report.

    e. This Criminal Code completely stinks because there is no offense that covers Lacey's despicable act.

Essay Questions

1. Simeone is on trial for murder. Horowitz testifies that Simeone was with him at the Super Bowl at the time of the murder, thus giving Simeone an alibi. The prosecution later produces a witness who testifies that Horowitz was indeed lying because Horowitz was in the hospital at the time of the murder. This is the only evidence the prosecution has to show that Horowitz lied on the witness stand. Is Horowitz's statement "material"? Why or why not? Under which statute in Chapter 15 is "materiality" an element? If Horowitz's statement is "material," what offense (if any) in Chapter 15 is he guilty of committing?

2. Skip manufactured fake mayonnaise and sold it to several delicatessens in South Jersey. He eventually was caught and charged appropriately. Just before his trial, he threatened to bust a five-pound jar of nutmeg over Oscar's head if Oscar testified against him. What offense in Chapter 15 should Skip could be charged with and why? Is this a first, second, third or fourth degree felony and why?

16

OBSTRUCTING GOVERNMENTAL OPERATIONS: ESCAPES

FACT PATTERN (PERTAINING TO CHAPTERS 16 AND 17)

While awaiting sentencing in the Ocean County Jail, two men formed an unlikely friendship and bond. Each man was a resident of Seaside Grove, and each previously held positions as public servants in the sandy shoreside town. The men, however, came from different sides of the political fence and actually had once run against each other for an open board of education seat.

Herman Diaz was a staunch conservative who advocated family values and decreased spending on the public schools. He wanted to see less tax dollars paid by his town's residents into what he called a "luxury vacation center for the town's children and educators." Mark Garner, on the other hand, called for increased budgetary outputs for the school system. He argued that with a better-funded, higher-rated school system, the residents' property value would actually increase. He also proclaimed that it was morally appropriate, and socially necessary, to provide the best education for Seaside Grove children.

Herman Diaz won the political race and later became the president of the Seaside Grove Board of Education and then superintendent of the school system. Mark Garner moved on to become a patrolman in the town's police department and then a sergeant who was cited by the department's chief for his strong leadership capabilities. Through their official capacities, though, both Garner and Diaz independently ultimately found their way into the county's jail population. There, they discussed their woes and collaborated on their plans for the future.

A Swan, a Pumpkin, a Clementine . . . and Diaz

After two years as Seaside Grove's superintendent of schools, Herman Diaz suddenly changed his stance on spending. He began advocating the hiring of several new teachers, ranging from elementary school positions to high school educators to specialized instructors. He also sought the purchase of high-tech computer hardware and upgraded equipment for all of the high school's athletic teams. In fact, he ordered monetary disbursements that he knew exceeded the board's budget and duped the district's business administrator into cutting checks to pay for the new items and services.

A group of local residents, who had formerly supported Diaz, became outraged at his spending spree. Their anger grew when they learned that three of the newly hired teachers were family members of Diaz. The group also suspected impropriety in Diaz's unusual push for Seaside Grove's purchase of a stretch of land that was to be dedicated to the high school as a new sports stadium. Diaz had strongly privately advocated for this purchase when he was president of the board of education; in fact, he initiated a purchase price of $1,000,000 for the land, which was later approved by the town's residents via a referendum vote. What appeared questionable to the group, though, was that prior to the referendum being put on the ballot, a corporation had purchased the land for $500,000; now, pursuant to the referendum victory, Seaside Grove was buying that same land for $1,000,000 from the corporation.

On the day the deal was closed, the group learned that the corporation had only two shareholders: Cecilia Swan and Carmine Mahob. Swan was one of the newly hired teachers and Diaz's sister-in-law. Ms. Swan later advised authorities that Carmine Mahob was the name of a deceased man and that 90% of the proceeds were actually going to Diaz, who orchestrated the deal. Swan said that she agreed to be part of the scam in exchange for her 10% share and the teacher position.

To strengthen their case against Superintendent Diaz, Ocean County Assistant Prosecutor Marjorie Callahan negotiated a plea arrangement with Swan where she would receive a lighter sentence if she agreed to wear a wire and speak to Diaz about their deal. Swan, who was on parole for a prior drug distribution charge, however, fled Seaside Grove before her scheduled meeting with Diaz. Not knowing when (or if) authorities would find Swan, Assistant Prosecutor Callahan ordered the arrest of Diaz, and the superintendent was immediately arrested without incident.

Through a bizarre chain of events, Cecilia Swan was arrested the same day. Her capture was about 85 miles north in the small Balsam County town of Hillsdale, resulting from a 911 call by an elderly woman that her son was just paid $1,000 to not report a burglary of their neighbor's home. When police responded, the woman's son, Strom Milton, admitted that he accepted the payment from a woman whose name he did not know. As Milton was providing the woman's description, he suddenly pointed across the street and said, "That's her!" The woman was Cecilia Swan.

Swan, noting the police presence, fled in her SUV. Two police cruisers, with activated overhead lights and sirens, trailed her at a safe distance as she raced through the town's narrow streets, running stop signs and red lights. They thought the pursuit was finished when Swan crashed into another moving vehicle; Swan, however, had other plans, jumping a fence and running through backyards. One officer followed her as the other tended to possible injured victims in the hit automobile. The chasing officer was unable to catch her.

Hillsdale immediately contacted Ocean County police, and a search for Swan was initiated. Canine units were employed in the manhunt, which proved to be a good choice. One particular dog, Clementine, ranted and barked wildly at the foot of the town's only trailer home. Clementine's partner, Officer Wil Frietag, in full police uniform, knocked on the trailer's door, knowing he did not have a warrant. A man—Peter Pumpcano—answered. Clementine continued to bark wildly as Officer Frietag inquired into whether Pumpcano knew of Cecilia Swan or her whereabouts. When Pumpcano denied knowing Swan, Officer Frietag politely thanked him and determined to leave to procure a warrant and call for backup. As Pumpcano went to shut the door, however, Clementine broke loose from his officer partner and shot through the door.

Officer Frietag chased after the canine but heard a loud yelp before he could visually locate him. As he passed by Pumpcano, Frietag found Cecilia Swan viciously biting Clementine's neck. When she spotted the officer, Swan released the dog from her oral grasp, kicked the patrolman and struggled with him, trying to avoid an arrest. Frietag continually advised her to submit as she was "under arrest." The officer was finally able to restrain Swan after about a 90-second struggle and then handcuffed her.

Pumpcano was arrested by a backup unit that arrived shortly thereafter. Upon questioning, Pumpcano again reiterated that his name was indeed "Peter Pumpcano," and he provided a state driver's license to that effect; however, a quick search of his trailer revealed a birth certificate and another state driver's license that named him as "Peter Jasowitz." Police also found a blond wig, black lipstick, a handgun and $5,000 in cash in a bag that was marked with a note that read "For my love, Cecilia." Pumpcano/Jasowitz was charged accordingly.

Better Ways to Deal with a Toothache

The case against Sergeant Mark Garner began with an innocent toothache, although it was a painful oral matter. Aspirin had failed him, soothing medicated liquid hadn't helped him and he couldn't sleep it off, so the man began to drink—but not tea or coffee. Instead, he tried to comfort himself with bourbon, whiskey and beer. When they didn't remedy the pain, Garner decided to visit a dentist, a wise decision it would seem. The problem, though, is that the dentist was his ex-wife, Cybil Carrington, who had a restraining order against him. The order forbade the officer from having contact with Carrington. The issuing of this court order had almost cost Garner his job with the Seaside Grove Police Department, but his promises that he would stay away from Cybil assuaged their concerns. The liquor and the toothache, however, quickly rekindled the matter.

Garner drove to his ex-wife's house in neighboring Langsdon, waking the woman instantly as he crashed his private sedan into her garage door. When she arrived at the garage and saw the destruction he had caused, she ordered Garner to leave; instead, he said to her, "Honey, I know we're not married anymore, but could you still be my dentist?" Cybil ignored him and began to walk away. As she did, she yelled back, "I'm calling the police." Realizing that he would lose his job, Garner suddenly became enraged, ran up to Cybil and slapped her twice across the face. Cybil then ran in the house, locked the door and phoned the Langsdon Police Department.

Garner made a tactical decision to leave. Still suffering from his toothache and yet to find a remedy, the sergeant drove his dented vehicle to a local drug dealer. There, he inquired about a cocaine purchase. The dealer, having sold to Garner before, advised his client that he did indeed have the substance available, but it would come for a price that was not monetary. He told Garner that he would provide the aching officer with $1,000 worth of coke and $10,000 in cash if he did the following: utilize his position as a Seaside Grove police officer to enter the department's evidence locker and heist 50 pounds of marijuana that had just been confiscated from a rival dealer. Garner, desperate for his drug of choice and believing that he was going to lose his job anyway, agreed to the task. Although the sergeant was successful in the theft, he was arrested a day later when the felony was detected and expeditiously solved.

Bail was set at $100,000 without a 10% option. Ironically, even though Cybil had notified the Langsdon Police Department of Garner's first unlawful act, she felt guilty and posted the bail. He returned her generosity by immediately fleeing the jurisdiction and failing to appear for his first court appearance. The bail was revoked and a manhunt commenced. Garner, however, apparently hadn't learned much from the crafty criminals he often dealt with as a police officer and was spotted at a dentist's office in Cassy Bluffs.

The individual who picked Garner out was a rookie Cassy Bluffs police officer, present for his six-month checkup. What he didn't know, though, was that his dentist, Dr. Sharise Witherspoon, was Garner's most recent lover. When he identified himself as a police officer and attempted to effectuate the man's arrest, Witherspoon jumped in front of him, blocking his path to Garner. Her human barricade lasted just long enough for Garner to slip out of the office's back door. The rookie, a former high school football star, raced after Garner and caught him only two blocks away. The suspended sergeant was arrested along with his lover, Dr. Witherspoon.

The Trials—A Little Help from Lovers Didn't Go a Long Way

Both Mark Garner and Herman Diaz were convicted at their respective trials. Each case was marked with sensation and intrigue. In Garner's case, Dr. Witherspoon attempted to influence a juror to acquit her boyfriend by providing the juror with $20,000 in cash. Another juror attempted to contract with a film production company to sell her knowledge of Garner's case—before the trial was completed.

During Diaz's trial, his wife baked a cake and had it delivered to the former superintendent in his courtroom holding cell. The sheriff's officers, not suspecting the oldest trick in the book, gave the cake to Diaz. Inside the tasty dessert, wrapped in a plastic bag, was a powerful knockout chemical that Diaz was able to slip into the blue raspberry fruit punch being enjoyed by his jailers. As they passed out, he was able to snatch the keys to his cell, unlock it and escape into the courtroom. There, however, he was recaptured by the court stenographer, who tripped him with an umbrella as he attempted to make his way to freedom. She then dove atop Diaz and twisted him in a contorted grappling hold until law enforcement officers rallied to the scene and handcuffed the convict.

The two former public servants, Herman Diaz and Mark Garner, now sulked together in the Ocean County Jail. They awaited their lengthy prison sentences, being tape-recorded by jail officials as they plotted dream plans of escape.

16-1.   **Obstructing administration of law or other governmental function**

    a. A person commits an offense if he purposely obstructs, impairs or perverts the administration of law or other governmental function or prevents or attempts to prevent a public servant from lawfully performing an official function by means of flight, intimidation, force, violence or physical interference or obstacle or by means of any independently unlawful act. This section does not apply to failure to perform a legal duty other than an official duty or any other means of avoiding compliance with law without affirmative interference with governmental functions.

    b. An offense under this section is a felony of the fourth degree if the actor obstructs the detection or investigation of a felony or the prosecution of a person for a felony; otherwise it is a misdemeanor A.

PRACTICAL APPLICATION OF STATUTE

Dr. Sharise Witherspoon is guilty of obstructing the administration of law for jumping in front of a Cassy Bluffs police officer who was attempting to arrest former Seaside Grove Police Sergeant Mark Garner. In Witherspoon's case, this is a felony of the fourth degree.

Pursuant to 16-1a., a person is guilty of obstructing the administration of law where he purposely prevents (or attempts to prevent) a public servant from lawfully performing an official function by actions such as intimidation, force and physical interference. The Cassy Bluffs police officer attempted to arrest Mark Garner in Dr. Witherspoon's dentist office. As he attempted to effectuate the arrest, Witherspoon intentionally jumped in front of the officer, blocking his path to Garner. Here the doctor "purposely" prevented a "public servant"—the police officer—from performing the "official function" of an arrest; she prevented the officer from making the arrest by the "physical interference" of blocking his path. Accordingly, Dr. Witherspoon is guilty of obstructing the administration of law.

Subsection b. of the statute provides the grading of this offense. If the actor obstructs an official function pertaining to a felony, then the actor is guilty of a fourth degree offense; otherwise, the actor is guilty of a misdemeanor A. Since Dr. Witherspoon obstructed the arrest of Mark Garner—a person who was being sought for the felonies of contempt, official misconduct and bail jumping—she is guilty of a fourth degree obstructing the administration of law.

16-2.   **Resisting arrest, eluding officer**

    a.   (1) Except as provided in paragraph (3), a person is guilty of a misdemeanor A if he purposely prevents or attempts to prevent a law enforcement officer from effecting an arrest.

        (2) Except as provided in paragraph (3), a person is guilty of a felony of the fourth degree if he, by flight, purposely prevents or attempts to prevent a law enforcement officer from effecting an arrest.

        (3) An offense under paragraph (1) or (2) of subsection a. is a felony of the third degree if the person:

            (a) Uses or threatens to use physical force or violence against the law enforcement officer or another; or

            (b) Uses any other means to create a substantial risk of causing physical injury to the public servant or another.

            It is not a defense to a prosecution under this subsection that the law enforcement officer was acting unlawfully in making the arrest, provided he was acting under color of his official authority and provided the law enforcement officer announces his intention to arrest prior to the resistance.

    b. Any person, while operating a motor vehicle on any street or highway in this State or any vessel on the waters of this State who knowingly flees or attempts to elude any police or law enforcement officer after having received any signal from such officer to bring the vehicle or vessel to a full stop commits a felony of the third degree; except that a person is guilty of a felony of the second degree if the flight or attempt to elude creates a risk of death or injury to any person. For purposes of this subsection, there shall be a permissive inference that the flight or attempt to elude creates a risk of death or injury to any person if the person's conduct involves a violation of the State motor vehicle statutes. In addition to the penalty prescribed under this subsection or any other section of law, the court shall order the suspension of that person's driver's license or privilege to operate a vessel, whichever is appropriate, for a period of not less than six months or more than two years.

In the case of a person who is at the time of the imposition of sentence less than 17 years of age, the period of the suspension of driving privileges authorized herein, including a suspension of the privilege of operating a motorized bicycle, shall commence on the day the sentence is imposed and shall run for a period as fixed by the court. If the driving or vessel operating privilege of any person is under revocation, suspension or postponement for a violation of any provision of this Title or the State motor vehicle statutes at the time of any conviction or adjudication of delinquency for a violation of any offense defined in this chapter or for drug-related offenses, the revocation, suspension or postponement period imposed herein shall commence as of the date of termination of the existing revocation, suspension or postponement.

Upon conviction the court shall collect forthwith the State driver's license or licenses of the person and forward such license or licenses to the Director of the Division of Motor Vehicles along with a report indicating the first and last day of the suspension or postponement period imposed by the court pursuant to this section. If the court is for any reason unable to collect the license or licenses of the person, the court shall cause a report of the conviction or adjudication of delinquency to be filed with the director. That report shall include the complete name, address, date of birth, eye color and sex of the person and shall indicate the first and last day of the suspension or postponement period imposed by the court pursuant to this section. The court shall inform the person orally and in writing that if the person is convicted of personally operating a motor vehicle or a vessel, whichever is appropriate, during the period of license suspension or postponement imposed pursuant to this section, the person shall, upon conviction, be subject to the penalties set forth in the license suspension statute. A person shall be required to acknowledge receipt of the written notice in writing. Failure to receive a written notice or failure to acknowledge in writing the receipt of a written notice shall not be a defense to a subsequent charge of violation of the license suspension statute. If the person is the holder of a driver's or vessel operator's license from another jurisdiction, the court shall not collect the license but shall notify the director, who shall notify the appropriate officials in the licensing jurisdiction. The court shall, however, in accordance with the provisions of this section, revoke the person's non-resident driving or vessel operating privileges, whichever is appropriate, in this State.

For the purposes of this subsection, it shall be a rebuttable presumption that the owner of a vehicle or vessel was the operator of the vehicle or vessel at the time of the offense.

PRACTICAL APPLICATION OF STATUTE

Resisting Arrest

Per the provisions of 16-2a., Cecilia Swan is guilty of resisting arrest for her attempt to prevent Balsam County Police Officer Wil Frietag from effecting her arrest. In this case, Swan is guilty of a third degree felony.

Normally, resisting arrest is a misdemeanor A (see subsection a.(1)), but it is elevated to a fourth degree felony where an actor's flight prevents a law enforcement officer from effecting an arrest (see a.(2)). Resisting arrest becomes a third degree offense if an actor uses or threatens physical force (see a.(3)(a)) or creates any other kind of substantial risk of physical injury by his resisting actions (see a.(3)(b)). It is important to note that the actor must "purposely" prevent or attempt to prevent the arrest in order to be guilty of this offense.

Cecilia Swan was a fugitive from justice, having fled Ocean County where she faced criminal charges. Once away from the shoreside area, she committed a multitude of other criminal offenses in the Balsam County town of Hillsdale, which resulted in a massive law enforcement search for her whereabouts. Officer Frietag located the fugitive at a trailer home owned by Peter Pumpcano. There, Frietag's canine partner, Clementine, chased Swan until the two tangled in a violent squabble wherein Swan viciously bit the dog. Frietag, in full police uniform, attempted to effectuate an arrest of Swan, announcing the same; however, he was kicked by the woman in an attempt to prevent the arrest from being executed. Finally, Frietag was able to control Swan's resisting and handcuffed her.

Cecilia Swan knew that she was a fugitive from justice and that police were actively searching for her. Moreover, she was confronted by Wil Frietag, a fully uniformed police officer, who announced that she was under arrest. Still, she "purposely" resisted his attempts to arrest her. Swan's resisting, however, was not limited to argument or even simple flight—she battled with the officer, using physical force in an attempt to prevent the arrest. Accordingly, Swan is guilty of a third degree resisting arrest offense, per subsection a.(3)(a), as she used force against the officer during his attempt to arrest her.

Eluding While Operating a Motor Vehicle

Any person who "knowingly" flees from a law enforcement officer—in a motor vehicle—after having received a signal to stop is guilty of eluding. This is a third degree felony; it is elevated to a second degree felony if the eluding "creates a risk of death or injury to any person."

Cecilia Swan is guilty of second degree eluding. As a fugitive from Ocean County and an individual who had just committed a burglary in Balsam County, Swan fled in her automobile when she noted that Hillsdale police officers wanted to speak to her. The officers activated the overhead lights and sirens of their cruisers, clearly signaling Swan to stop. Swan ignored their commands and continued to flee—she was therefore "knowingly" eluding the officers.

As Swan fled, the Hillsdale officers trailed her at a safe distance. Still, she raced through the town's narrow streets, running stop signs and red lights, and eventually plowed into another moving motor vehicle. Given this type of reckless driving and the ultimate car crash, Swan obviously created a "risk of death or injury" to other individuals. Under these circumstances, she is guilty of a second degree eluding offense per 16-2b.

16-3.   **Hindering apprehension or prosecution**

a. A person commits an offense if, with purpose to hinder the detention, apprehension, investigation, prosecution, conviction or punishment of another for an offense or violation of the State motor vehicle statutes, he:

  (1) Harbors or conceals the other;

  (2) Provides or aids in providing a weapon, money, transportation, disguise or other means of avoiding discovery or apprehension or effecting escape;

  (3) Suppresses, by way of concealment or destruction, any evidence of the felony or tampers with a witness, informant, document or other source of information,

regardless of its admissibility in evidence, which might aid in the discovery or apprehension of such person or in the lodging of a charge against him;

(4) Warns the other of impending discovery or apprehension, except that this paragraph does not apply to a warning given in connection with an effort to bring another into compliance with law;

(5) Prevents or obstructs, by means of force, intimidation or deception, anyone from performing an act which might aid in the discovery or apprehension of such person or in the lodging of a charge against him;

(6) Aids such person to protect or expeditiously profit from an advantage derived from such felony; or

(7) Gives false information to a law enforcement officer or a civil State investigator assigned to the Office of the Insurance Fraud Prosecutor.

The offense is a felony of the third degree if the conduct which the actor knows has been charged or is liable to be charged against the person aided would constitute a felony of the second degree or greater, unless the actor is a spouse, parent or child of the person aided, in which case the offense is a felony of the fourth degree. The offense is a felony of the fourth degree if such conduct would constitute a felony of the third degree. Otherwise it is a misdemeanor A.

b. A person commits an offense if, with purpose to hinder his own detention, apprehension, investigation, prosecution, conviction or punishment for an offense or violation of the State motor vehicle statutes, he:

(1) Suppresses, by way of concealment or destruction, any evidence of the felony or tampers with a document or other source of information, regardless of its admissibility in evidence, which might aid in his discovery or apprehension or in the lodging of a charge against him;

(2) Prevents or obstructs by means of force or intimidation anyone from performing an act which might aid in his discovery or apprehension or in the lodging of a charge against him;

(3) Prevents or obstructs by means of force, intimidation or deception any witness or informant from providing testimony or information, regardless of its admissibility, which might aid in his discovery or apprehension or in the lodging of a charge against him; or

(4) Gives false information to a law enforcement officer or a civil State investigator assigned to the Office of the Insurance Fraud Prosecutor.

The offense is a felony of the third degree if the conduct which the actor knows has been charged or is liable to be charged against him would constitute a felony of the second degree or greater. The offense is a felony of the fourth degree if such conduct would constitute a felony of the third degree. Otherwise it is a misdemeanor A.

PRACTICAL APPLICATION OF STATUTE

Hindering Another's Apprehension

Peter Pumpcano is guilty of hindering apprehension for harboring and concealing Cecilia Swan in his trailer home. His offense falls under subsection a. of the statute; this subsection covers hindering *another's* apprehension or prosecution.

Subsections 16-3a.(1) through a.(7) set forth seven types of actions where a person can be convicted for hindering another's apprehension. These actions range from harboring/concealing someone to providing disguises or money to a fugitive to giving false information to a law enforcement officer. In all seven scenarios, the person can only be convicted if he is hindering the apprehension of another who is facing a criminal offense or other charges such as misdemeanor As or motor vehicle offenses.

Balsam County Police Officer Wil Frietag and his canine partner, Clementine, located fugitive Cecilia Swan at Peter Pumpcano's trailer home. The law enforcement team, however, did not find Swan via Pumpcano's cooperation; in fact, Pumpcano denied knowing Swan. The fugitive was only apprehended after a wildly barking Clementine broke from Officer Frietag's grasp and hunted down Swan in the trailer. The woman was ultimately arrested after a struggle. A subsequent search of Pumpcano's home revealed a bag that contained a blond wig, black lipstick, a handgun and $5,000 cash. The bag was marked with a note that read "For my love, Cecilia."

Here, Peter Pumpcano is guilty of hindering apprehension under 16-3a.(1), which prohibits the harboring or concealing of another. He is also guilty of this offense under 16-3a.(2), which prohibits providing items such as disguises, money and weapons to individuals sought by law enforcement. Cecilia Swan was a fugitive from justice who was facing charges in Ocean County, and she had absconded from parole and had just committed several felonies (including burglary and eluding) in Hillsdale. Pumpcano was obviously aware of her flight from the law, yet he chose to lie to Officer Frietag about Swan's whereabouts and conceal her in his trailer home. This concealing of Swan warrants a charge under subsection a.(1) of the statute. Pumpcano's gift bag of disguises (the blond wig and black lipstick), handgun and money subjects him to a charge under subsection a.(2) of the statute.

It is very important to note that the grading of a hindering apprehension charge under subsection a. depends on two matters—the seriousness of the underlying offense that the "other" is trying to avoid and the relationship between the "aider" and the "other." The "aider" must also "know" the type of offense the "other" is facing.

If the aider "knows" that he is hindering the apprehension of another who is facing a first or second degree felony, then the aider is guilty of a third degree hindering apprehension. There is one caveat, though: If the aider is a "spouse," "parent" or "child" of the "other," then it is a fourth degree hindering apprehension.

If the aider "knows" that he is hindering the apprehension of another who is facing a third degree felony, then the aider is guilty of a fourth degree hindering apprehension. All other matters are misdemeanor As.

In Pumpcano's case, his charge should probably be a third degree hindering apprehension. Cecilia Swan had committed several felonies, including a second degree eluding. If Pumpcano "knew" she had committed this serious felony, then he is guilty of a third degree hindering apprehension. Since Cecilia Swan was not Pumpcano's spouse, parent or child, his charge should not be lowered to a fourth degree offense.

Hindering One's Own Apprehension

For hindering his own apprehension, Peter Pumpcano should be charged with an offense under subsection b. of 16-3. This charge arises out of Pumpcano's provision of a false name and driver's license to a Balsam County police officer.

Per subsection b.(4), a person is guilty of an offense when he "gives false information to a law enforcement officer" in an effort to hinder his own apprehension or prosecution. Peter Pumpcano was facing charges for hindering Cecilia Swan's apprehension. In an effort to avoid his own ultimate prosecution, he told the Balsam County police officer that his name was Peter Pumpcano, and he provided him with a state driver's license that stated the same. Police later searched Pumpcano's home and found a birth certificate and another state driver's license that named him as "Peter Jasowitz." For providing the law enforcement officer with the false name and driver's license, Pumpcano/Jasowitz should be charged with hindering his own apprehension.

The grading of an offense under subsection b. depends on the underlying offense that the actor knows he has been charged with—or with which he is likely to be charged. If he is trying to avoid the prosecution of a first or second degree offense, he is guilty of a third degree hindering apprehension. If he is trying to avoid the prosecution of a third degree offense, he is guilty of a fourth degree hindering apprehension. All other matters are misdemeanor As.

With reference to Pumpcano's hindering his own apprehension, he should be charged with a fourth degree offense. Why? Pumpcano presented the false name in an attempt to avoid prosecution for hindering Cecilia Swan's apprehension. That underlying offense was a third degree felony. Accordingly, since he was trying to avoid the prosecution of a third degree felony, Pumpcano here should be charged with a fourth degree hindering apprehension.

16-3.1.   **Animal owned, used by law enforcement agency, search and rescue dog, infliction of harm upon, interference with officer, degree of felony, penalties**

Any person who purposely kills a dog, horse or other animal owned or used by a law enforcement agency or a search and rescue dog shall be guilty of a felony of the third degree. Any person who purposely maims or otherwise inflicts harm upon a dog, horse or other animal owned or used by a law enforcement agency or a search and rescue dog shall be guilty of a felony of the fourth degree. Any person who interferes with any law enforcement officer using an animal in the performance of his official duties commits a misdemeanor A, subject to a sentence of six months' imprisonment, some or all of which may be community service, restitution and a $1,000 fine.

As used in this section, "search and rescue dog" means any dog trained or being trained for the purpose of search and rescue that is owned by an independent handler or member of a search and rescue team and used in conjunction with local law enforcement or emergency services organizations for the purpose of locating missing persons or evidence of arson.

PRACTICAL APPLICATION OF STATUTE

In addition to all of her other offenses, Cecilia Swan is guilty of violating section 16-3.1 for viciously biting the Balsam County Canine Unit dog, Clementine. In her case, this is a fourth degree felony.

Per this statute, any person who kills a dog or any other animal used by law enforcement—or any search and rescue dog (which is defined in the second paragraph of the statute)—is guilty of a third degree offense. Any person who maims or otherwise inflicts harm on any of these animals is guilty of a fourth degree offense. Cecilia Swan, a fugitive from justice who was the subject of a Balsam County manhunt, was located by Clementine, a police dog. Either in an effort to thwart the dog's efforts or just to harm the innocent animal, Swan viciously bit Clementine's neck. The dog survived her attack after his partner, Officer Wil Frietag, interceded. Accordingly, Swan is guilty of a fourth degree felony.

16-4.   **Compounding**

A person commits a felony if he accepts or agrees to accept any pecuniary benefit in consideration of refraining from reporting to law enforcement authorities the commission or suspected commission of any offense or information relating to an offense or from seeking prosecution of an offense. A person commits a felony if he confers or agrees to confer any pecuniary benefit in consideration of the other person agreeing to refrain from any such reporting or seeking prosecution. It is an affirmative defense to prosecution under this section that the pecuniary benefit did not exceed an amount which the actor reasonably believed to be due as restitution or indemnification for harm caused by the offense. An offense proscribed by this section is a felony of the second degree. If the thing of value accepted, agreed to be accepted, conferred or agreed to be conferred is any benefit of $200 or less, an offense proscribed by this section is a felony of the third degree.

PRACTICAL APPLICATION OF STATUTE

Compounding is a rarely invoked statute that makes it a felony for a person to accept money for refraining from reporting an offense to law enforcement. The statute also makes it a felony to offer money to another in exchange for agreeing to not report an offense. Strom Milton, a Hillsdale resident, is guilty of compounding, which is a second degree felony; Cecilia Swan, likewise, is guilty of this felony.

Cecilia Swan committed a burglary in the small Balsam County town of Hillsdale. In an effort to avoid being caught for her felony, she offered to pay Milton $1,000—Milton, a neighbor of the burglarized home, had witnessed the felony. Milton accepted her payment. This payoff situation renders both Milton and Swan guilty of second degree compounding. Their charge could only be one of the third degree if the monetary benefit involved was $200 or less.

16-5.   **Escape**

    a. Escape. A person commits an offense if he, without lawful authority, removes himself from official detention or fails to return to official detention following temporary leave granted for a specific purpose or limited period. "Official detention" means arrest, detention in any facility for custody of persons under charge or conviction of a felony or offense or alleged or found to be delinquent, detention for extradition or deportation or any other detention for law enforcement purposes; but "official detention" does not include supervision of probation or parole or constraint incidental to release on bail.

    b. Absconding from parole. A person subject to parole commits a felony of the third degree if the person goes into hiding or leaves the State with a purpose of avoiding supervision. As used in this subsection, "parole" includes participation in the Intensive Supervision Program (ISP) established pursuant to the Rules Governing the Courts of this State. Abandoning a place of residence without the prior permission of or notice to the appropriate supervising authority shall constitute *prima facie* evidence that the person intended to avoid such supervision.

    c. Permitting or facilitating escape. A public servant concerned in detention commits an offense if he knowingly or recklessly permits an escape. Any person who knowingly causes or facilitates an escape commits an offense.

    d. Effect of legal irregularity in detention. Irregularity in bringing about or maintaining detention, or lack of jurisdiction of the committing or detaining authority, shall not be a defense to prosecution under this section if the escape is from a prison or other custodial facility or from detention pursuant to commitment by official proceedings. In the case of other detentions, irregularity or lack of jurisdiction shall be a defense only if:

(1) The escape involved no substantial risk of harm to the person or property of anyone other than the detainee; or

(2) The detaining authority did not act in good faith under color of law.

e. Grading of offenses. An offense under subsection a. or c. of this section is a felony of the second degree where the actor employs force, threat, deadly weapon or other dangerous instrumentality to effect the escape. Otherwise it is a felony of the third degree.

PRACTICAL APPLICATION OF STATUTE

Escape

Herman Diaz should be charged with escape. In his case, he is ripe for a second degree conviction. Simply stated, a person is guilty of escape if he leaves an "official detention" (e.g., prison, jail, holding cell or custodial arrest) or if he fails to return to official detention after being granted a temporary leave. If the escape involved "force, threat, deadly weapon or other dangerous instrumentality," it is a second degree felony; otherwise, it is a third degree offense.

Former Seaside Grove Superintendent of Schools Herman Diaz was standing trial in Ocean County. During the trial, Diaz's wife baked a cake and had it delivered to him in his courtroom holding cell. Inside the dessert, wrapped in a plastic bag, was a powerful knock-out chemical. Diaz slipped this drug into the blue raspberry fruit punch that was being enjoyed by his sheriff's officer jailers. As they passed out, the prisoner was able to snatch their cell keys and escape. Diaz, though, was later captured by a brave courtroom stenographer who tripped him with an umbrella and restrained him in a grappling hold.

Here, Diaz was in "official detention"—a courtroom holding cell. He unlawfully left the cell by stealing the cell's keys from the sheriff's officers who were watching over him. His escape involved the employment of "dangerous instrumentality," a powerful knockout chemical which was slipped into the officers' beverage. Accordingly, Diaz is guilty of second degree escape as provided for in subsection a. of the statute.

Facilitating Escape

Pursuant to subsection c. of the escape statute, Herman Diaz's wife is guilty of facilitating an escape. This is a second degree felony for the same reason that her husband's escape is a second degree felony.

One who facilitates or permits an escape is just as criminally liable as the individual who actually escapes. A public official, such as a sheriff's officer or corrections officer, who aids or permits an escape is guilty of a felony under 16-5c. Similarly, any person at all who facilitates an escape is guilty of a felony under 16-5c. It is important to note that where a public official "knowingly" or "recklessly" facilitates the escape, he is guilty of this offense. Any other person is guilty of this offense *only* if he "knowingly" facilitates the escape.

The above-mentioned "facilitators'" offenses are just as serious as the escapee's, meaning that if "force, threat, deadly weapon or other dangerous instrumentality" is employed in the escape, then the people are guilty of a second degree felony. Therefore, since Diaz's wife "knowingly" facilitated his escape by providing him the cake packed with the powerful knockout chemical—a "dangerous instrumentality"—she is guilty of a second degree felony per subsection c. of 16-5.

Absconding from Parole

Cecilia Swan is guilty of absconding from parole, a felony which is defined in subsection b. of 16-5. This third degree offense occurs where a parolee either "goes into hiding" or "leaves the State" with a "purpose of avoiding supervision."

Cecilia Swan was on parole for a prior drug distribution conviction when she was arrested in Ocean County for her involvement in a real estate scam with her brother-in-law, Herman Diaz. With a purpose of avoiding her parole supervision (and her pending charges in Ocean County), Swan went "into hiding," trekking 85 miles to Hillsdale and concealing herself in the trailer home of Peter Pumpcano. This constitutes a violation of 16-5b. for absconding from parole.

16-6. **Implements for escape; other contraband**

    a. Escape implements.

        (1) A person commits an offense if he knowingly and unlawfully introduces within an institution for commitment of persons by reason of insanity or a detention facility or knowingly and unlawfully provides an inmate with any weapon, tool, instrument, document or other thing which may be useful for escape. The offense is a felony of the second degree and shall be punished by a minimum term of imprisonment, which shall be fixed at no less than three years if the item is a weapon as defined by 24-1(r). Otherwise it is a felony of the third degree.

        (2) An inmate of an institution or facility defined by paragraph (1) of subsection a. of this section commits an offense if he knowingly and unlawfully procures, makes or otherwise provides himself with, or has in his possession, any such implement of escape. The offense is a felony of the second degree and shall be punished by a minimum term of imprisonment, which shall be fixed at no less than three years if the item is a weapon as defined by 24-1(r). Otherwise it is a felony of the third degree.

            "Unlawfully" means surreptitiously or contrary to law, regulation or order of the detaining authority.

    b. Other contraband. A person commits a misdemeanor B if he provides an inmate with any other thing which the actor knows or should know is unlawful for the inmate to possess.

PRACTICAL APPLICATION OF STATUTE

Escape Implements

Herman Diaz's wife is guilty of introducing an implement for escape into his detention facility. Her felony should be graded as a second degree offense.

Herman Diaz was incarcerated in a courtroom holding cell during his trial. While waiting there, Diaz's wife had a cake delivered to him; baked inside the cake was a powerful knockout chemical wrapped in a plastic bag. Diaz's wife planted the chemicals in the cake to assist her husband in escaping. Since subsection a. of the statute makes it illegal for anyone to "knowingly and unlawfully" provide an inmate with any item—such as a weapon, tool or document—to aid in escape, she is guilty of violating this statute.

It is important to note that this is only a felony of the second degree where the escape implement involved is a "weapon as defined by 24-1(r)." Weapons as defined by 24-1(r) include "anything readily capable of lethal use or of inflicting serious bodily injury." Given that a powerful knockout chemical could likely inflict "serious bodily injury," Diaz's wife should be charged with a second degree felony under 16-6a.(1). Otherwise, where the escape implement is not a weapon, this is a third degree felony.

Please also note that Herman Diaz should be charged with a second degree felony for possessing the knockout chemical. As an inmate, his offense is pursuant to a violation of subsection a.(2) of the statute.

Providing Inmate with Other Contraband

Where an individual provides an inmate with contraband other than escape implements, he is guilty of a misdemeanor B. In order for a conviction, though, the actor must "know" or "should know" that it is unlawful for an inmate to possess the contraband. For example, one who provides an inmate with a six-pack of beer should know that it is unlawful for the inmate to possess alcoholic beverages; therefore, this person would probably be convicted of a misdemeanor B per subsection b. of 16-6.

16-7. **Bail jumping; default in required appearance**

A person set at liberty by court order, with or without bail, or who has been issued a summons, upon condition that he will subsequently appear at a specified time and place in connection with any offense or any violation of law punishable by a period of incarceration, commits an offense if, without lawful excuse, he fails to appear at that time and place. It is an affirmative defense for the defendant to prove, by a preponderance of evidence, that he did not knowingly fail to appear. The offense constitutes a felony of the third degree where the required appearance was to answer to a charge of a felony of the third degree or greater, or for disposition of any such charge, and the actor took flight or went into hiding to avoid apprehension, trial or punishment. The offense constitutes a felony of the fourth degree where the required appearance was otherwise to answer to a charge of felony or for disposition of such charge. The offense constitutes a misdemeanor A or a misdemeanor B, respectively, when the required appearance was to answer a charge of such an offense or for disposition of any such charge. Where the bail imposed or summons issued is in connection with any other violation of law, the failure to appear shall be a misdemeanor A.

This section does not apply to obligations to appear incident to release under suspended sentence or on probation or parole. Nothing herein shall interfere with or prevent the exercise by any court of this State of its power to punish for contempt.

PRACTICAL APPLICATION OF STATUTE

Bail jumping is an offense that can range from a misdemeanor B to a third degree felony. The degree of bail jumping depends on the underlying offense that the actor is trying to avoid. If the underlying offense is a third degree felony (or greater), a person who jumps bail is guilty of a third degree felony. Where the underlying offense is a fourth degree felony, the bail jumping is a felony of the fourth degree. A person who jumps bail on a misdemeanor A is guilty of a bail jumping misdemeanor A; in the same vein, where a person jumps bail on a misdemeanor B, the bail jumping is a misdemeanor B.

Mark Garner is guilty of the most serious bail jumping offense—a third degree felony. Garner, a Seaside Grove police officer, was arrested for committing a number of offenses, including official misconduct, a second degree felony. The police officer then jumped bail. Since one of his underlying offenses was a third degree felony (or greater), Garner is guilty of a third degree bail jumping.

16-8.   **Corrupting or influencing a jury**

Any person who, directly or indirectly, corrupts, influences or attempts to corrupt or influence a jury or juror to be more favorable to the one side than to the other by promises, persuasions, entreaties, threats, letters, money, entertainment or other sinister means or any person who employs any unfair or fraudulent practice, art or contrivance to obtain a verdict or attempts to instruct a jury or juror beforehand at any place or time, or in any manner or way, except in open court at the trial of the cause, by the strength of the evidence, the arguments of the parties or their counsel or the opinion or charge of the court is guilty of a felony. Corrupting or influencing a jury is a felony of the second degree if it is committed by means of violence or the threat of violence. Otherwise, it is a felony of the third degree, provided, however, that the presumption of nonimprisonment for persons who have not previously been convicted of an offense shall not apply.

PRACTICAL APPLICATION OF STATUTE

Mark Garner's girlfriend, Dr. Sharise Witherspoon, is guilty of attempting to influence a juror. In her case, it is a felony of the third degree.

In situations where a person attempts to influence a juror's decision by violence, the person is guilty of a second degree felony. If a person attempts to influence a juror by any other means, he is guilty of a third degree felony.

Mark Garner was on trial for committing a number of felonies. Dr. Witherspoon, Garner's girlfriend, attempted to influence a juror to acquit Garner by providing the juror with $20,000 in cash. Her influence attempt did not involve violence; accordingly, she is guilty of a third degree felony.

16-8.1.   **Prohibited juror contract**

   a. Any person impaneled as a petit or grand juror in any criminal action in this State who, before the rendering of a verdict, entry of a plea, or the termination of service as a grand juror, solicits, negotiates, accepts, or agrees to accept a contract for a movie, book, magazine article, other literary expression, recording, radio or television presentation, or live entertainment or presentation of any kind which would depict his service as a juror is guilty of a felony of the fourth degree.

   b. Any person who offers, negotiates, confers or agrees to confer a contract for a movie, book, magazine article, other literary expression, recording, radio or television presentation, live entertainment or presentation of any kind which would depict the juror's service to any person impaneled as a petit or grand juror in any criminal action in this State, during the term of service of the juror, is guilty of a felony of the fourth degree.

PRACTICAL APPLICATION OF STATUTE

During Mark Garner's trial, a juror attempted to contract with a film production company to sell her knowledge of Garner's case. This is illegal per the provisions of 16-8.1.

Any juror who solicits, or agrees to accept, a contract for any entertainment deal—such as a movie or book—during his service as a juror is guilty of a fourth degree felony; similarly, one who offers such a contract to a juror is guilty of a fourth degree felony.

The juror in Garner's case attempted to contract with a film production company concerning her knowledge of the case. Since she attempted this deal during the course of the trial, she is guilty of a fourth degree felony.

16-9. **Contempt**

a. A person is guilty of a felony of the fourth degree if he purposely or knowingly disobeys a judicial order or hinders, obstructs or impedes the effectuation of a judicial order or the exercise of jurisdiction over any person, thing or controversy by a court, administrative body or investigative entity.

b. Except as provided below, a person is guilty of a felony of the fourth degree if that person purposely or knowingly violates any provision in an order entered under the provisions of the "Prevention of Domestic Violence Act" or an order entered under the provisions of a substantially similar statute under the laws of another state or the United States when the conduct which constitutes the violation could also constitute a felony or a misdemeanor A. In all other cases a person is guilty of a misdemeanor A if that person knowingly violates an order entered under the provisions of this act or an order entered under the provisions of a substantially similar statute under the laws of another state or the United States.

As used in this subsection, "state" means a state of the United States, the District of Columbia, Puerto Rico, the United States Virgin Islands or any territory or insular possession subject to the jurisdiction of the United States. The term includes an Indian tribe or band or Alaskan native village, which is recognized by a federal law or formally acknowledged by a state.

PRACTICAL APPLICATION OF STATUTE

Contempt—Fourth Degree Felony

For ignoring a court order forbidding him to have contact with his ex-wife, Mark Garner is guilty of contempt. Garner's contempt is a fourth degree felony.

Generally, any person who "purposely" or "knowingly" disobeys a judicial order is guilty of a fourth degree offense. This is per the language of subsection a. of 16-9. Pursuant to the language of subsection b. of the statute, any person who "purposely" or "knowingly" violates a judicial order entered under the provisions of the "Prevention of Domestic Violence Act" (or a "substantially similar" statute of another state) is guilty of a fourth degree felony—as long as "the conduct which constitutes the violation could also constitute a felony or misdemeanor A." What does this mean? Mark Garner's case can explain it.

Seaside Grove Police Sergeant Mark Garner suffered a toothache. To remedy his discomfort, he decided to visit his dentist. A wise decision, it would seem. The problem, though, was that Garner's dentist was his ex-wife, Cybil Carrington. The woman had a restraining order against him—an order that was entered under the provisions of the "Prevention of Domestic Violence Act." Still, Garner "purposely" violated this judicial order by driving to Carrington's house.

The police officer's conduct became even more violative of the law when he slapped his ex-wife in the face because she ordered him to leave. Here, the conduct that "constituted the violation"—not only having contact with his wife, but slapping her in the face—also "constitutes a felony or a misdemeanor A." By slapping Carrington in the face, Garner committed a simple assault, which is a misdemeanor A; accordingly, Garner is guilty of a fourth degree contempt of court.

Contempt—Misdemeanor A

It is important to note that even if Mark Garner did not commit what would "constitute a felony or misdemeanor A" when he violated his restraining order, he would still be guilty of a misdemeanor A. If he simply showed up at his ex-wife's house—or "purposely" or "knowingly" made any contact with her whatsoever—Garner would still be guilty of contempt for violating the restraining order's general "no contact" provision. In this case, where no "felony or misdemeanor A" (such as aggravated assault or simple assault) occurred in addition to the prohibited contact, Garner would be guilty of a misdemeanor A for his contempt.

END OF CHAPTER REVIEW

Multiple-Choice Questions

The following fact pattern pertains to questions 1–2.

Cecelia Swan, a fugitive, sped past a Hillsdale police officer in her Chevy dump truck. The officer activated the overhead lights and siren of his police cruiser, clearly signaling Swan to stop. Swan ignored the commands and continued to flee. Eventually, after running a red light and two stop signs, Swan plowed into another moving motor vehicle.

1. The *best* offense to charge Swan with for her refusal to stop her vehicle when signaled to do so by Hillsdale police is:
    a. hindering apprehension
    b. eluding
    c. resisting arrest
    d. obstruction of justice
    e. disorderly conduct

2. The degree of Cecelia Swan's above offense is:
    a. second degree
    b. third degree
    c. fourth degree
    d. misdemeanor A
    e. misdemeanor B

3. A person under official detention can be charged with escape when:
    a. he leaves a jail without lawful authority
    b. he leaves a prison without lawful authority
    c. he fails to return to prison after being granted a temporary leave
    d. all of the above
    e. a and b only

4. Which of the following statements is true?

  a. A person who absconds parole by leaving the state with the purpose of avoiding supervision is liable for administrative repercussions but has not committed a criminal offense.

  b. "Absconding parole" means that the defendant has complied with all supervisory mandates and has completed his parole requirements.

  c. A person who has absconded parole by going into hiding with the purpose of avoiding supervision has committed a third degree felony.

  d. "Absconding parole" means that the defendant has violated his probation status and is now being placed on parole.

  e. None of the above are true.

5. Which of the following actions constitutes hindering apprehension?

  a. Peter knows that the police are seeking to arrest Cecelia for burglary. He purposely hides her in his closet when the police come to his house looking for her.

  b. Archie knows Lois has skipped bail on drug charges. He gives Lois a blond wig, nose ring and collagen for her lips in order for her to disguise her appearance.

  c. Morris gives Frankie $1,000 for airfare to help Morris get out of the country so that he can avoid conviction in his upcoming sexual assault trial.

  d. All of the above constitute hindering apprehension.

  e. None of the above apply because a person can't be convicted of hindering another's apprehension.

6. Tomas is being chased by police officers with trained canines. To avoid being captured, Tomas viciously kills one of the dogs. For killing the dog, Tomas is guilty of:

  a. a first degree felony

  b. although it should be a first degree felony, a third degree felony

  c. although it should be a first degree felony, a misdemeanor A

  d. as ridiculous as it sounds, he is only liable in a civil matter

  e. *res ipsa loquitor*

7. A juror in the criminal trial of Mark Garner attempts to sell her knowledge of Garner's case to a film production company. Which of the following statements is true?

  a. The juror is guilty of a fourth degree felony if she attempted to make the sale during the trial.

  b. The juror is guilty of a fourth degree felony if she attempted to make the sale after the trial concluded but before the jury rendered the verdict.

  c. The juror is guilty of no offense at all if she attempted to make the sale after her service as a juror was terminated.

  d. All of the above are true.

  e. Only a and c are true.

Essay Questions

1. Lucy refused to allow a Yale police officer to effectuate a lawful arrest by clinging to a pole. Axel ran from a Harvard Town police officer as she was trying to lawfully arrest him for burglary. Jamaal threatens to stab a Brownsville Heights police officer and flails his arms, all in an effort to prevent the officer from lawfully arresting him on theft charges. Lucy, Axel and Jamaal have all committed acts of resisting arrest under section 16-2. For each defendant, identify what degree of resisting arrest that he or she has committed—and explain why. Be sure to cite the exact subsections of the statute in your answers.

2. Quick Mick had a restraining order issued against him under the "Prevention of Domestic Violence Act"; the order was issued by a Superior Court judge in an effort to keep him away from his ex-boyfriend, Bernard. A week after the order was issued, Quick Mick stopped by Bernard's workplace, a bakery, and gave Bernard a basket of assorted cheeses. Bernard was rude to Quick Mick and told him to leave. The following week, Quick Mick showed up at Bernard's house and shot him in the arm. In either case, is Quick Mick guilty of contempt? If so, what degree of contempt and why?

17

MISCONDUCT IN OFFICE;
ABUSE OF OFFICE

17-1.

Official misconduct

A public servant is guilty of official misconduct when, with purpose to obtain a benefit for himself or another or to injure or to deprive another of a benefit:

a. He commits an act relating to his office but constituting an unauthorized exercise of his official functions, knowing that such act is unauthorized or he is committing such act in an unauthorized manner; or

b. He knowingly refrains from performing a duty which is imposed upon him by law or is clearly inherent in the nature of his office.

Official misconduct is a felony of the second degree. If the benefit obtained or sought to be obtained, or of which another is deprived or sought to be deprived, is of a value of $200 or less, the offense of official misconduct is a felony of the third degree.

PRACTICAL APPLICATION OF STATUTE

Seaside Grove Police Sergeant Mark Garner entered the evidence locker of his police department and stole 50 pounds of seized marijuana. This illicit behavior is violative of section 17-1, as it amounts to official misconduct. This is a felony of the second degree.

Official misconduct is a felony that only applies to public servants. Those in such positions of trust (e.g., elected officials, judges, police officers) who commit acts within their positions that they know are "unauthorized"—in exchange for a "benefit"—can be convicted of official misconduct. This is per subsection a. of the statute. Likewise, under subsection b., where a public servant "refrains from performing a duty" in exchange for a benefit, he is guilty of official misconduct. This statute also applies to those public servants who act illicitly in order "to injure another or deprive another of a benefit."

Mark Garner's felony of official misconduct falls under the provisions set forth in subsection a. of 17-1. The Seaside Grove police officer was desperate to remedy the physical pain of a toothache and the mental anguish he was suffering due to his ex-wife's refusal to see him. Garner's despair was exacerbated because he knew that he had just violated a restraining order, which would affect his job. The sum total of his woes led Garner to a local drug dealer, where he inquired about a cocaine purchase. The dealer advised that he would indeed provide the aching officer with $1,000 worth of coke—and

$10,000 in cash—if Garner did the following: utilize his position as a Seaside Grove police officer to enter the department's evidence locker and heist 50 pounds of marijuana that had just been confiscated from a rival dealer. Garner agreed, performed the act and was caught.

As a Seaside Grove police officer, Mark Garner was a public servant. With a purpose to benefit himself (obtaining cocaine and cash), Garner performed an "unauthorized" exercise of his official function as a police officer—he took marijuana from the evidence locker with the intent to turn it over to a drug dealer. Garner obviously knew that his heist was not only unauthorized, but also illegal. Accordingly, the Seaside Grove police officer is guilty of official misconduct, per the provisions of subsection a. of the statute. In this case, the official misconduct is a second degree felony, given that the value of the cocaine and cash was greater than $200. In situations where the "benefit" sought—or where the item "deprived"—is of a "value of $200 or less," the official misconduct is a third degree felony.

17-2.

Speculating or wagering on official action or information

A person commits a felony if, in contemplation of official action by himself or by a governmental unit with which he is or has been associated, or in reliance on information to which he has or has had access in an official capacity and which has not been made public, he:

a. Acquires a pecuniary interest in any property, transaction or enterprise which may be affected by such information or official action;

b. Speculates or wagers on the basis of such information or official action; or

c. Aids another to do any of the foregoing, while in office or after leaving office with a purpose of using such information.

An offense proscribed by this section is a felony of the second degree. If the benefit acquired or sought to be acquired is of a value of $200 or less, an offense proscribed by this section is a felony of the third degree.

PRACTICAL APPLICATION OF STATUTE

Section 17-2 is a statute that basically prohibits public servants from utilizing "inside information" in order to acquire a pecuniary interest in a property or otherwise obtain monetary gain. Herman Diaz did just this, using his position with the Seaside Grove Board of Education to manipulate a real estate purchase that netted him a sizable pecuniary profit. Similar to official misconduct, this is a second degree felony. It would only be lowered to a felony of the third degree if the value involved was $200 or less. In Diaz's case, though, the amount of money involved far exceeded a few hundred dollars.

In addition to acquiring a pecuniary interest, two elements are necessary for a conviction under section 17-2: The person "contemplates" official action by himself or a governmental unit that he is associated with *and* the information involved "has not been made public." So how is Herman Diaz guilty of a felony under this statute?

Diaz was the Seaside Grove Superintendent of Schools, and prior to this post, he was the president of the town's board of education. At that time, Diaz privately pushed for Seaside Grove's purchase of a stretch of land that was to be dedicated to the high school as a new sports stadium; in fact, he initiated a purchase price—$1,000,000—for the land. In contemplation of this $1,000,000 purchase by Seaside Grove, Diaz secretly formed a corporation, which then bought the land from its owner for $500,000. Thereafter, Diaz's corporation sold the land to Seaside Grove for the $1,000,000 prize, resulting in a $500,000 profit to his corporation. Diaz owned 90% of the corporation's shares.

Here, all the elements of the offense have been met. Diaz acquired a "pecuniary interest" in a property "in contemplation" of an official action (the land purchase) by a governmental unit (the board of education) with which he had been associated. The information about the land's pending purchase was not public at the time Diaz's corporation bought it from its original owner. The ultimate benefit he obtained was hundreds of thousands of dollars. Thus, he is guilty of a second degree felony under section 17-2.

17-3.   Disbursing moneys, incurring obligations in excess of appropriations

A person or member of a board or body charged with or having the control of a State office, division, department or institution or a member of a county or municipal governing body or a member of a board of education commits a felony of the fourth degree if he purposely and knowingly:

a. Disburses, orders or votes for the disbursement of public moneys, in excess of the appropriation for that office, division, department, institution, board or body; or

b. Incurs obligations in excess of the appropriation and limit of expenditure provided by law for that office, division, department, institution, board or body.

Nothing contained in this section shall be construed to prevent a board of education from keeping open the public schools.

Practical Application of Statute

Seaside Grove Superintendent of Schools Herman Diaz is guilty of violating section 17-3 for ordering monetary disbursements by the board of education that he knew exceeded the board's budget. This is a fourth degree felony.

Simply put, this statute prohibits those having control over governing bodies—such as courts, freeholder boards, municipal governments, boards of education—from disbursing public moneys "in excess of the appropriation" for that body. Herman Diaz did just this.

In an effort to hire more teachers (some were his own family members) and to obtain high-tech computer hardware and upgraded athletic equipment, Diaz ordered monetary disbursements that he knew exceeded the board of education's budget. This improper commitment of public moneys renders Diaz guilty of a fourth degree felony.

17-4.   Felony of official deprivation of civil rights

a. A public servant acting or purporting to act in an official capacity commits the felony of official deprivation of civil rights if, knowing that his conduct is unlawful and acting with the purpose to intimidate or discriminate against an individual or group of individuals because of race, color, religion, gender, handicap, sexual orientation or ethnicity, the public servant:

(1) Subjects another to unlawful arrest or detention, including, but not limited to, motor vehicle investigative stops, search, seizure, dispossession, assessment, lien or other infringement of personal or property rights; or

(2) Denies or impedes another in the lawful exercise or enjoyment of any right, privilege, power or immunity.

b. (1) Except as provided in paragraphs (2) and (3) of this subsection, a public servant who violates the provisions of subsection a. of this section is guilty of a felony of the third degree.

    (2) If bodily injury results from depriving a person of a right or privilege in violation of subsection a. of this section, the public servant is guilty of a felony of the second degree.

    (3) If, during the course of violating the provisions of this section, a public servant commits or attempts or conspires to commit murder, manslaughter, kidnapping or aggravated sexual assault against a person who is being deprived of a right or privilege in violation of subsection a. of this section, the public servant is guilty of a felony of the first degree.

c. A conviction of official deprivation of civil rights under this section shall not merge with a conviction of any other criminal offense, nor shall such other conviction merge with a conviction under this section, and the court shall impose separate sentences upon each violation of this section and any other criminal offense.

d. Proof that a public servant made a false statement or prepared a false report, or if the agency that employs the public servant, the Attorney General or the county prosecutor having supervisory authority over the agency required a report to be prepared failed to prepare a report concerning the conduct that is the subject of the prosecution, shall give rise to an inference that the actor knew his conduct was unlawful.

e. For purposes of this section, an act is unlawful if it violates the Constitution of the United States or the Constitution of this State or if it constitutes a criminal offense under the laws of this State.

PRACTICAL APPLICATION OF STATUTE

Section 17-4 was enacted in an effort to prevent public servants from utilizing their authority to unlawfully discriminate against others based on "race, color, religion, gender, handicap, sexual orientation or ethnicity." In order for a public servant to be convicted under this statute, two threshold prongs must first be met:

1. The public servant must "know" that his conduct is unlawful; and
2. He must act "with the purpose to intimidate or discriminate" against an individual(s) because of his status in one of the protected classes (e.g., race, religion).

With the above state of mind established, the public servant can be prosecuted under 17-4 if he:

1. Subjects the victim(s) to an unlawful arrest or detention such as a motor vehicle stop or search; or
2. Denies or impedes the victim(s) in the lawful exercise or enjoyment of any right, privilege, power or immunity.

How does that work practically? Let's say Clint the Cop, during patrol, watches nine cars pass him by; some are speeding, and others are driving within the speed limit. Clint does nothing but smile, wave and play a handheld video game. A tenth car approaches, moving five miles per hour under the speed limit. At the wheel is Nicola Coppola; a bumper sticker on the back of his automobile reads "The Italian

Prince." Clint puts down his video game, activates his overhead lights and sirens and speeds after "The Italian Prince."

Coppola immediately pulls over. Clint orders Coppola out of the automobile and proceeds to search Coppola's person and vehicle. After coming up with no contraband, Clint issues Coppola a speeding ticket. When Coppola asks Clint why he was pulled over, searched and issued a summons, Clint replies, "Why? Because you're an I-talian. A mobster. A sure criminal."

Here, Clint has committed the felony of official deprivation of civil rights, as all the elements of section 17-4 have been met. First, Clint, a police officer, is a "public servant." As a police officer, he surely "knew" that his "conduct" was "unlawful": He pulled Coppola over and searched him, knowing that he had no probable cause for the stop and the subsequent search; then he issued a speeding summons when he knew that the man wasn't speeding. Next, Clint's unlawful conduct was obviously instituted "with the purpose" to "discriminate" against Coppola on the basis of his Italian "ethnicity." He told Coppola that he stopped, searched and ticketed him "Because you're an I-talian. A mobster. A sure criminal." Finally, Clint's discriminatory practice manifested itself in the form of an "unlawful detention," a motor vehicle stop and search. With all these factors present, Clint is guilty of violating 17-4, a third degree felony.

It is important to note that had Clint pulled over Coppola not because he was Italian but because he was a Red Sox fan or because he was a lawyer, Clint would not be guilty of an offense under section 17-4. The police officer's stop, search and speeding ticket would all still be unlawful and invalid, but they would not constitute the felony of "official deprivation of civil rights." A conviction of this offense can only occur if the unlawful conduct is rooted in a purpose to "discriminate" on the basis of "race, color, religion, gender, handicap, sexual orientation or ethnicity." Whereas "ethnicity" is one of the aforementioned protected classes, a Red Sox fan or a lawyer is not.

Grading of Offense Elevated in Certain Circumstances

Generally, a violation of 17-4 is a third degree felony; however, per subsection b.(2), it is elevated to a felony of the second degree where "bodily injury results from depriving a person of a right or privilege." Per subsection b.(3), the offense becomes a felony of the first degree where the "public servant commits or attempts or conspires to commit" felonies such as murder and kidnapping while violating the provisions of the statute.

17-5.   **Felony of pattern of official misconduct**

a. A person commits the felony of pattern of official misconduct if he commits two or more acts that violate the provisions of 17-1 or 17-4. It shall not be a defense that the violations were not part of a common plan or scheme or did not have similar methods of commission.

b. Pattern of official misconduct is a felony of the second degree if one of the acts committed by the defendant is a first or second degree felony; otherwise, it is a felony of the third degree, provided, however, that the presumption of nonimprisonment set forth for persons who have not previously been convicted of an offense shall not apply. A conviction of pattern of official misconduct shall not merge with a conviction of official misconduct, official deprivation of civil rights or any other criminal offense, nor shall such other conviction merge with a conviction under this section, and the court shall impose separate sentences upon each violation of 17-1, 17-4 and 17-5.

PRACTICAL APPLICATION OF STATUTE

Section 17-5 is basically an extension of the "official misconduct" statute (17-1). That statute's Practical Application section explains the elements of "official misconduct" and how a public servant can be convicted of that offense.

Per 17-5, a "pattern of official misconduct" has been committed where a public servant "commits two or more acts that violate the provisions of 17-1." So where does this apply?

Really, it pertains any time a public servant commits more than one act of official misconduct. For example, Sheriff's Officer Penelope smuggles ten pounds of cocaine into the jail where she works in an effort to sell it to the jail population. In a separate incident, as an act of revenge, she falsely charges an inmate with prostitution. Here, even though these acts were completely unrelated and not part of a common plan or scheme, Officer Penelope is guilty of a "pattern of official misconduct."

Subsection b. of 17-5 sets forth the grading of this offense. If one of the acts of official misconduct is a first or second degree felony, then a second degree offense has been committed under 17-5. In all other cases, a "pattern of official misconduct" is a third degree felony.

END OF CHAPTER REVIEW

Multiple-Choice Questions

1. Official misconduct is an offense that applies to:
   a. state assemblymen
   b. police officers
   c. judges
   d. firemen
   e. all of the above

2. Seaside Grove Police Sergeant Mark Garner entered the evidence locker of his department and stole 50 pounds of seized marijuana. Garner then sold the marijuana to a drug dealer for $10,000 cash and $1,000 worth of cocaine. The *best* offense to charge Garner with is:
   a. contempt
   b. bribery
   c. official deprivation of civil rights
   d. official misconduct
   e. obstruction of justice

3. Clint the Cop, during patrol, watches nine cars pass him by; some are speeding, and others are driving within the speed limit. Clint does nothing but smile, wave

and play a handheld video game. A tenth car approaches, which Clint pulls over; he issues the driver a ticket for speeding. Clint has committed the felony of official deprivation of civil rights in which of the following circumstances?

   a. Clint issued the speeding ticket only because the driver was Italian and not because he was actually speeding.

   b. Although the driver was speeding, Clint would not have issued the speeding ticket. He did issue the ticket, though, because the driver, a male, had long hair and looked like a hippie to Clint.

   c. Clint pulled the driver over and issued him a ticket, although the driver was not speeding, because "the driver was clearly gay."

   d. All of the above are official deprivations of civil rights.

   e. Only a and c are official deprivations of civil rights.

4. Sheriff's Officer Penelope smuggles ten pounds of cocaine into the jail where she works in an effort to sell it to the jail population. In a separate incident, as an act of revenge, she falsely charges an inmate with prostitution. Is Sheriff's Officer Penelope guilty of the felony of "pattern of official misconduct"?

   a. no, because sheriff's officers are exempt from the public servant requirement of the statute

   b. no, because in order to be convicted of the felony of a "pattern of official misconduct," the criminal acts must be part of a common scheme—not separate or different types of acts

   c. no, because of the doctrine of merger

   d. yes, because she committed at least two acts of official misconduct

   e. yes, because sheriff's officers may carry a gun

Essay Question

1. State Attorney General Carolina Moon totally disliked Jared Bamlish, a U.S. senator; additionally, Moon wanted to take Bamlish's seat. In an effort to damage the reputation of Bamlish, Moon fabricated charges that Senator Bamlish smoked crack at a city bathhouse. The day before Bamlish was set to be tried, Moon's case fell apart and she was exposed for creating the fraudulent charges. What offense in Chapter 17 has Moon committed and why? Be sure to explain the elements of the offense in detail. What offense would she be guilty of violating if she falsified the charges against Bamlish because he was Caucasian and not because she wanted his U.S. Senate seat? Here, just name the offense and the statute number.

18

RIOT, DISORDERLY CONDUCT AND RELATED OFFENSES

FACT PATTERN (PERTAINING TO CHAPTERS 18 AND 19)

Milo, Smiles, Bertha, Camille, Bambie and Horatio formed the state's toughest gang, The Bean-Bag Mean Team. Each gang member was required to wear a chili bean pin on the lapel of his or her shirt; during the commission of felonies, the pin was to be placed on the inside of the shirt. The gang initially was ruthless and did in fact commit numerous hard-core felonies, including over 50 carjackings in the previous two years. They also engaged in numerous robberies, burglaries and aggravated assaults.

The Bean-Bag Mean Team, though, recently determined to change its course of business and social activities. After the gang had increased its state membership to over 1,000 members, it solicited one final member, Ned "The Brainiac" Shipman. The Brainiac was courted primarily by Bertha, who sought his induction into the gang with the purpose that he would plan and aid the carrying out of their future criminal events. The Brainiac was receptive and agreed that if he was indeed admitted to be a member, he would actively plot and engage in fresh criminal activities.

In order to become a member of The Bean-Bag Mean Team, the founding members demanded that each new recruit perform multiple acts to prove their dedication and worthiness. Even though The Brainiac was highly sought after, he was still required to conform to the leadership's demands. Accordingly, he completed the following acts:

Smiles owned a 1986 Chevy Cavalier, which he no longer wanted. Since he knew that The Brainiac was a licensed used-car dealer, he ordered The Brainiac to sell the automobile. There was a catch, though—the car had to be sold on a Sunday. The Brainiac complied and sold the Cavalier at his dealership in Camfort on an early Sunday morning.

On the same day, Camille provided The Brainiac with a laundry list of tasks to complete by the end of the week. They included going to North Nestor's most renowned drug distribution area and purchasing a $10 bag of marijuana; calling the Kaine Fire Department and reporting that an explosion was about to occur at the library even though he knew such was false, with a goal to cause an evacuation at the library; anonymously calling Camille's ex-boyfriend at 2 a.m. and screaming and cursing at him; lying down on a busy one-way street in North Nestor, thereby preventing cars from passing; showing up at a Halsey Library Board of Trustees meeting and locking them out of the library; going to "the rock" in Glendale and cutting out a piece of it with an electric saw; painting a swastika on the front door of a Jacinta City Councilman's home and writing "You're dead, pal" on the same; removing the doors from a Salmon Creek church and spray painting "Kill you" on the wall; smoking on a public bus in Packton; after exiting the bus, throwing eggs at it as it drove away; ripping down a railroad crossing safety gate in Glendale; and bringing a bottle of whiskey to Westwood High School and drinking the entire bottle with two students. The Brainiac diligently completed all of the afore-mentioned matters within three days of their order.

At this point, Milo presented The Brainiac with his final demonstration of wor-thiness. The Brainiac was instructed to gather with nine members of The Bean-Bag Mean Team at the Willowstone Mall in Waddington. Once there, The Brainiac and the others were to herd over 30 cows and bulls into the mall. As the animals paraded through the building, the group would scream and yell and pick fights with the mall's patrons. The purpose of the chaos was to distract mall security and merchants while The Brainiac snuck into an upscale jewelry store and heisted $50,000 in gold and silver.

The following day, The Brainiac performed as directed; he turned over the precious gems to Milo and became a *bona fide* member of The Bean-Bag Mean Team. The mall incident, though, resulted in four members of the gang being arrested for refusing to disperse from the scene when ordered to do so by police.

To celebrate his induction, The Brainiac went on a date with Bertha. Their first stop was at the Wood Chop Candy Shop in Birchwood, where The Brainiac sought to purchase green olives and seltzer water. As he impatiently waited in line, The Brainiac watched the clerk sell cigarettes to a 12-year-old boy. The clerk then turned to The Brainiac and said, "What brand would you like?" The Brainiac, now completely annoyed, responded by jumping on the counter, knocking over all the items on it and screaming, "I don't smoke! I don't smoke! It's just olives and seltzer I want." He then smashed the bottle of olives against the wall. Before leaving, he picked up a few of the pimentos and threw them at the clerk.

Bertha, who had been waiting in the car, closely listened to a police radio call system. She frantically waved The Brainiac back to the automobile as she heard infor-mation that particularly interested her. A Birchwood police dispatcher advised all units that an alleged heroin transaction was occurring directly across the street from where they were currently located. Realizing that the dealers would probably have significant amounts of cash and drugs on them, Bertha suggested that they run across the street and rob them. The pair then did just that. Bertha was correct—they left the site with nearly $5,000 in cash and heroin with a street value of about $10,000. As they drove away giggling, they monitored the police radio so as to avoid any law enforcement that may have been attempting to track them.

The two gang members next arrived at Stu's House of Chow where they intended to enjoy a hearty meal. Although the restaurant had no liquor license, the owner permitted The Brainiac and Bertha to drink scotch at a regular dining table. The owner usually charged diners with a "corkage fee" to consume alcohol in his restaurant but waived the fee for his gang member customers.

After dinner, The Brainiac had a special surprise for Bertha—he brought her to two businesses that he had developed for The Bean-Bag Mean Team. The first, Mack Daddy's, was located in Pacorro. Mack Daddy's was a private 24-hour club purporting to hold an exclusive membership of checkers and jacks players. In reality, it was a house of prostitution where patrons paid adult women and men to have sex with them. Mack Daddy's was owned and managed by The Brainiac. On a daily basis, he oversaw and encouraged the individuals who worked there to have sexual relations with the club's many eager clients; more than 30 employees accepted cash in exchange for their services.

Not far down the highway from Mack Daddy's was The Brainiac's second entrepreneurial effort: Piper's Home of Love. This storefront business offered live performances where women danced in G-strings and bikini tops and routinely fondled themselves in the genital and breast areas; they also engaged in simulated acts of masturbation. Piper's Home of Love offered the use of enclosed booths to its patrons where "lap dances" were performed. Sexual activity occurred many times during these sessions.

After observing and engaging in a few lap dances, The Brainiac and Bertha proceeded to the building attached to Piper's Home of Love, which was known as The Annex. There, they thumbed through multiple magazines, looking at hundreds of erotic and sexually explicit pictures. The couple looked on as an employee at The Annex sold two such magazines to a 14-year-old boy and five magazines to a 33-year-old woman. The Brainiac noted that the magazines were easily accessible to the customers, as they all were displayed on shelves less than five feet in height and without any blinders or coverings on them.

Once The Brainiac ended his tour of The Bean-Bag Mean Team's new businesses, he and Bertha headed to a cottage in La Verne where they intended to spend the remainder of the evening. They stopped, though, in North Nestor and began roaming the streets, asking several different people where they could find a prostitute, as they wanted to "speak to one." Unfortunately for the gang members, however, an undercover police officer heard their discourse and arrested them on the spot.

The Brainiac and Bertha smirked at the arresting officer, minimizing what they considered an inconsequential matter. At headquarters, though, their tone changed when they learned that there were multiple outstanding arrest warrants arising out of The Brainiac's previous days' rampage. Someone had "dropped dime" and multiple charges were being levied.

18-1.   **Riot, failure to disperse**

   a. Riot. A person is guilty of riot if he participates with four or more others in a course of disorderly conduct as defined in section 18-2a:

   (1) With the purpose to commit or facilitate the commission of a felony;

   (2) With the purpose to prevent or coerce official action; or

   (3) When he or any other participant known to him uses or plans to use a firearm or other deadly weapon.

   Riot, if committed under circumstances set forth in paragraph (3), is a felony of the third degree. Otherwise riot is a felony of the fourth degree.

   b. Failure of disorderly persons to disperse upon official order. Where five or more persons are participating in a course of disorderly conduct as defined in section 18-2a. likely to cause substantial harm, a peace officer or other public servant engaged in executing or enforcing the law may order the participants and others in the immediate vicinity to disperse. A person who refuses or knowingly fails to obey such an order commits a misdemeanor A.

PRACTICAL APPLICATION OF STATUTE

Riot

Engaging in a riot can be a felony of the third degree or a fourth degree pursuant to 18-1a. The Brainiac is guilty of fourth degree riot for his actions at the Willowstone Mall in Waddington.

Riot is an interesting felony in that it encompasses a whole other offense—disorderly conduct as defined in 18-2a.—as one of its elements. In other words, in order for an individual to be guilty of riot, he must have committed an act of disorderly conduct first. But there is more. To be convicted of riot, his disorderly conduct must be joined by at least four others who are also engaging in disorderly conduct; then this entire group's course of disorderly conduct has to be accompanied by one of the following circumstances: the purpose to commit or facilitate a felony, the purpose to prevent or coerce official action or the purpose to carry on while a participant "known" to him uses or plans to use a firearm or other deadly weapon. Got all that? Well, The Brainiac's antics at the Willowstone Mall can help to make it understandable.

The Brainiac and nine members of the ruthless street gang, The Bean-Bag Mean Team, met at the Willowstone Mall. Once there, they herded over 30 cows and bulls into the large shopping facility. As the animals paraded through the building, the group screamed and yelled wildly and picked fights with the mall's patrons. The purpose of this chaos was to distract mall security and merchants while The Brainiac snuck into an upscale jewelry store and heisted $50,000 in gold and silver.

In this case, all of the elements of riot have been met. First, The Brainiac was joined by nine other people in engaging in a course of disorderly conduct—the group engaged in the tumultuous and violent behavior of picking fights with mall patrons, screaming and yelling and letting loose over 30 cows and bulls into the mall. Next, the purpose of the chaos was to facilitate the commission of a felony, namely the theft of the gold and silver. Accordingly, The Brainiac is guilty of riot. His offense is a fourth degree felony; it would only be elevated to a felony of the third degree if he or one of the participants "known" to him used or planned to use a firearm or other deadly weapon.

It is important to note that the nine other gang members who participated in the mall event with The Brainiac also could be convicted of riot. Even though they didn't actually carry out the heist, their purpose was to facilitate it; therefore, they are equally as culpable.

Failure to Disperse

Four of The Brainiac's counterparts at the Willowstone Mall riot are guilty of failure to disperse. Per subsection b. of 18-1, this is a misdemeanor A.

In order to be convicted of failure of disperse, four elements must be met: Five or more people must be participating in a course of disorderly conduct, the said conduct must be "likely to cause substantial harm," a peace officer or public servant must order them to disperse from the vicinity and the defendant must refuse or knowingly fail to leave.

The four gang members engaged in a course of disorderly conduct at the Willowstone Mall—the group engaged in the tumultuous and violent behavior of picking fights with mall patrons, screaming and yelling and letting loose over 30 cows and bulls into the shopping facility. For obvious reasons, this behavior was "likely to cause substantial harm." Upon observing this chaos, police officers ordered them to disperse from the scene. They refused to do so. With all these elements in place, the four gang members are guilty of the misdemeanor A failure to disperse.

18-2.   **Disorderly conduct**

    a. Improper behavior. A person is guilty of a misdemeanor B if, with the purpose to cause public inconvenience, annoyance or alarm or recklessly creating a risk thereof, he:

      (1) Engages in fighting or threatening or in violent or tumultuous behavior; or

      (2) Creates a hazardous or physically dangerous condition by any act which serves no legitimate purpose of the actor.

    b. Offensive language. A person is guilty of a misdemeanor B if, in a public place and with the purpose to offend the sensibilities of a hearer or in reckless disregard of the probability of so doing, he addresses unreasonably loud and offensively coarse or abusive language, given the circumstances of the person present and the setting of the utterance, to any person present.

      "Public" means affecting or likely to affect persons in a place to which the public or a substantial group has access; among the places included are highways, transport facilities, schools, prisons, apartment houses, places of business or amusement or any neighborhood.

PRACTICAL APPLICATION OF STATUTE

Whether "improper behavior" or "offensive language," disorderly conduct is a misdemeanor B. The Brainiac is guilty of "improper behavior" per subsection a. of the disorderly conduct statute. The Wood Chop Candy Shop in Birchwood was the venue of his most salient offense.

A conviction for "improper behavior" requires a two-prong test to be met: The defendant must engage in matters such as a fight, a violent act or tumultuous behavior or the creation of a dangerous condition that serves no legitimate purpose, *and* this behavior has to be performed with an illicit purpose (e.g., to cause public inconvenience, annoyance or alarm).

At the Wood Chop Candy Shop in Birchwood, The Brainiac impatiently waited in line for the store clerk to finish with a prior customer. Upon the clerk asking The Brainiac a question he apparently didn't like, The Brainiac jumped on the counter, knocking over all the items on it, and screamed, "I don't smoke! I don't smoke! It's just olives and seltzer I want." He then smashed a bottle of olives against the wall. Before leaving the store, he picked out a few pimentos and threw them at the clerk.

Here, The Brainiac violated subsection a. of the disorderly conduct statute by acting with "improper behavior." By screaming, jumping on the counter, knocking over all the items, throwing a bottle against the wall and throwing parts of olives at the store clerk, The Brainiac has acted tumultuously and violently. This behavior was certainly performed with the purpose to cause annoyance and alarm to the public—this was a place of business where several members of the public could be affected by his antics. Accordingly, The Brainiac is guilty of disorderly conduct, a misdemeanor B.

Offensive Language

Watch for First Amendment free speech issues. Subsection b. of 18-2 provides for a misdemeanor B where an individual speaks, in a public place, with "unreasonably loud and offensively coarse or abusive language." The subsection clearly sets out that the speech must be performed "with the purpose to offend the sensibilities" of the person hearing it, and the circumstances of the hearer and the setting are taken into account. Inevitably, however, free speech issues are likely to be evaluated by courts hearing "offensive language" cases—and the constitutional right to speak many times will override another's offended sensibilities.

18-2.1.   **"Public place" defined; loitering to obtain or distribute controlled dangerous substance is a misdemeanor A**

    a. As used in this section:

        "Public place" means any place to which the public has access, including but not limited to a public street, road, thoroughfare, sidewalk, bridge, alley, plaza, park, recreation or shopping area, public transportation facility, vehicle used for public transportation, parking lot, public library or any other public building, structure or area.

    b. A person, whether on foot or in a motor vehicle, commits a misdemeanor A if he:

        (1) Wanders, remains or prowls in a public place with the purpose of unlawfully obtaining or distributing a controlled dangerous substance or controlled substance analog; and

        (2) Engages in conduct that, under the circumstances, manifests the purpose to obtain or distribute a controlled dangerous substance or controlled substance analog.

    c. Conduct that may, where warranted under the circumstances, be deemed adequate to manifest a purpose to obtain or distribute a controlled dangerous substance or controlled substance analog includes, but is not limited to, conduct such as the following:

        (1) Repeatedly beckoning to or stopping pedestrians or motorists in a public place;

        (2) Repeatedly passing objects to or receiving objects from pedestrians or motorists in a public place; or

        (3) Repeatedly circling in a public place in a motor vehicle and on one or more occasions passing any object to or receiving any object from a person in a public place.

    d. The element of the offense described in paragraph (1) of subsection b. of this section may not be established solely by proof that the actor engaged in the conduct that is used to satisfy the element described in paragraph (2) of subsection b. of this section.

PRACTICAL APPLICATION OF STATUTE

As part of Camille's laundry list of gang initiation tasks, The Brainiac was required to purchase a $10 bag of marijuana in North Nestor's most renowned drug distribution area. His search to obtain the controlled dangerous substance could cause him to face a misdemeanor A under 18-2.1.

    This statute, in a quick summary, prohibits a person from "remaining" or "wandering" in public in an effort to obtain or distribute controlled dangerous substances. But how is it possible to prove that someone is "remaining" or "wandering" in a public place for the purpose of carrying out one of these illicit activities?

Section 18-2.1 provides that the defendant's "conduct" is the dispositive factor. Subsection c. goes as far as defining what "conduct" will "be deemed adequate to manifest a purpose to obtain or distribute a controlled dangerous substance." This "conduct" includes, but is not limited to, repeatedly stopping pedestrians or motorists, repeatedly passing objects to or receiving objects from pedestrians and motorists and repeatedly circling in a motor vehicle and (on one or more occasions) passing any object to or receiving any object from a person.

Nothing in the statute requires that any actual evidence of the use, possession, purchase or sale of any controlled dangerous substance be presented in order for a conviction under 18-2.1 to occur. However, subsection d., when dissected, does set out that the above-described "conduct" *alone* cannot solely establish that the defendant acted "with the purpose" to obtain or distribute a controlled dangerous substance (CDS). This implies that some other evidence—such as the odor of a drug or witness testimony identifying something that appeared to be CDS—is necessary for a conviction.

Now what does all this mean for The Brainiac's North Nestor marijuana purchase? It means that even if law enforcement didn't apprehend him with marijuana, he could still be convicted of loitering for the purpose of possessing a controlled dangerous substance. If his "conduct" in the well-known drug distribution area manifested "a purpose to obtain" CDS (e.g., he drove around in circles and then passed an object and received another), then the prosecution has the basis for a case under 18-2.1. But remember, this "conduct" alone is not enough—the prosecution must present something additional such as witness testimony that he received a bag with a vegetation-like substance in it. If this evidence was put forward against The Brainiac, he could actually be convicted of a misdemeanor A for loitering for the purpose of obtaining a controlled dangerous substance.

18-3.   **False public alarms**

a. Except as provided in subsection b. or c. of this section, a person is guilty of a felony of the third degree if he initiates or circulates a report or warning of an impending fire, explosion, bombing, felony, catastrophe or emergency knowing that the report or warning is false or baseless and that it is likely to cause evacuation of a building, place of assembly or facility of public transport or to cause public inconvenience or alarm. A person is guilty of a felony of the third degree if he knowingly causes such false alarm to be transmitted to or within any organization, official or volunteer, for dealing with emergencies involving danger to life or property.

b. A person is guilty of a felony of the second degree if in addition to the report or warning initiated, circulated or transmitted under subsection a. of this section, he places or causes to be placed any false or facsimile bomb in a building, place of assembly or facility of public transport or in a place likely to cause public inconvenience or alarm. A violation of this subsection is a felony of the first degree if it occurs during a declared period of national, State or county emergency.

c. A person is guilty of a felony of the second degree if a violation of subsection a. of this section in fact results in serious bodily injury to another person or occurs during a declared period of national, State or county emergency. A person is guilty of a felony of the first degree if a violation of subsection a. of this section in fact results in death.

d. For the purposes of this section, "in fact" means that strict liability is imposed. It shall not be a defense that the death or serious bodily injury was not a foreseeable consequence of the person's acts or that the death or serious bodily injury was caused by the actions of another person or by circumstances beyond the control of the actor. The actor shall be strictly liable upon proof that the felony occurred during a declared period of national, State or county emergency. It shall not be a defense that the actor did not know that there was a declared period of emergency at the time the felony occurred.

e. A person is guilty of a felony of the fourth degree if the person knowingly places a call to a 911 emergency telephone system without purpose of reporting the need for 911 service.

PRACTICAL APPLICATION OF STATUTE

False Report of Public Alarms

The Brainiac called the Kaine Fire Department and reported that an explosion was about to occur at the town's library, even though he knew the information was false. This false report warrants a charge for a third degree felony.

In order to be convicted of a felony under 18-3a., two elements need to be met. First, the defendant must initiate or circulate "a report or warning of an impending fire, explosion, bombing, felony, catastrophe or emergency." Second, he must "know" that the report is false and that it is likely to cause evacuation of places such as buildings or is likely to cause public inconvenience or alarm. Generally, this is a felony of the third degree. Per subsection c., however, if "serious bodily injury" of another person or "death" does in fact occur, then it is a second degree felony.

In The Brainiac's case, he reported to the Kaine Fire Department that an explosion was about to occur at the town's library. He "knew" that the report was false—and made the report with the purpose to cause the library to be evacuated. With these two elements met, he should be charged with a third degree felony. But how could this be elevated to a first or second degree felony? Let's say that in the ensuing frenzy, a person was trampled to death trying to exit the library; this would render The Brainiac guilty of a first degree felony. Similarly, if a fire truck crashed on the way to the library, causing serious bodily injury to a firefighter, this would give rise to a second degree offense.

False Bombs/Unnecessary 911 Calls

It should be noted that per subsection b. of 18-3, a person is guilty of a third degree felony if—in addition to a false emergency report (e.g., a bombing or explosion)—he places a fake bomb in a structure such as a building. Also, where a person places a 911 call "without purpose of reporting the need for 911 service," he is guilty of a misdemeanor A under subsection e. of this statute.

18-4.   **Harassment**

Except as provided in subsection e., a person commits a misdemeanor B if, with purpose to harass another, he:

a. Makes, or causes to be made, a communication or communications anonymously or at extremely inconvenient hours, in offensively coarse language or in any other manner likely to cause annoyance or alarm;

b. Subjects another to striking, kicking, shoving or other offensive touching or threatens to do so; or

c. Engages in any other course of alarming conduct or of repeatedly committed acts with purpose to alarm or seriously annoy such other person.

A communication under subsection a. may be deemed to have been made either at the place where it originated or at the place where it was received.

d. A person commits a felony of the fourth degree if, in committing an offense under this section, he was serving a term of imprisonment or was on parole or probation as the result of a conviction of any indictable offense under the laws of this State, any other state or the United States.

PRACTICAL APPLICATION OF STATUTE

The Brainiac is guilty of harassment for anonymously calling Bean-Bag Mean Team gang member Camille's ex-boyfriend and screaming and cursing at him. This is a misdemeanor B.

Pursuant to section 18-4, a person commits a misdemeanor B if, "with purpose to harass another," he engages in one of three types of activities. These activities are found in subsections a. through c. of the statute and include making anonymous communications, communicating at extremely inconvenient hours or communicating with offensively coarse language (see subsection a.); subjecting another to offensive touching, such as striking or kicking (see subsection b.); and repeatedly committing acts with the purpose of alarming or seriously annoying another (see subsection c.).

A conviction under this statute hinges on the language "with the purpose to harass." In other words, a simple late-night call does not necessarily rise to the level of harassment; the Brainiac's phone call, however, does.

Gang member Camille had an estranged relationship with her former boyfriend. In an effort to get back at him, she ordered The Brainiac to call him as part of his pledging duties to become a member of the gang. This was not a normal phone call, however. The Brainiac called the ex-lover at the extremely inconvenient hour of 2 a.m, and his entire telephone dialogue consisted of screaming and cursing at the man. Here, this call was made "with the purpose to harass," and accordingly, The Brainiac is guilty of a misdemeanor B under 18-4.

Per subsection d., the offense could become a felony of the fourth degree, however. This would be the case if The Brainiac was "serving a term of imprisonment or was on parole or probation as the result of a conviction of any indictable offense" when the act of harassment was committed.

18-5.

Obstructing highways and other public passages

a. A person who, having no legal privilege to do so, purposely or recklessly obstructs any highway or other public passage, whether alone or with others, commits a misdemeanor B. "Obstructs" means renders impassable without unreasonable inconvenience or hazard. No person shall be deemed guilty of recklessly obstructing in violation of this subsection solely because of a gathering of persons to hear him speak or otherwise communicate or solely because of being a member of such a gathering.

b. A person in a gathering commits a misdemeanor B if he refuses to obey a reasonable official request or order to move:

(1) To prevent obstruction of a highway or other public passage; or

(2) To maintain public safety by dispersing those gathered in dangerous proximity to a fire or other hazard.

An order to move, addressed to a person whose speech or other lawful behavior attracts an obstructing audience, shall not be deemed reasonable if the obstruction can be readily remedied by police control of the size or location of the gathering.

PRACTICAL APPLICATION OF STATUTE

In order to become a member of the ruthless gang named The Bean-Bag Mean Team, The Brainiac was provided a laundry list of "tasks" to complete. One of the "tasks" was to lie down on a busy one-way street in North Nestor, thereby preventing automobiles from passing. This is an example of a misdemeanor B as defined in section 18-5.

18-6.   **Disrupting meetings and processions**

A person commits a misdemeanor A if, with purpose to prevent or disrupt a lawful meeting, procession or gathering, he does an act tending to obstruct or interfere with it physically.

PRACTICAL APPLICATION OF STATUTE

The Brainiac showed up at a Halsey Library Board of Trustees meeting and locked the members out of the building. Here, The Brainiac committed a misdemeanor A under section 18-6 for purposely disrupting and preventing this lawful meeting.

18-7.   **Desecration of venerated objects**

A person commits a misdemeanor A if he purposely desecrates any public monument, insignia, symbol or structure or place of worship or burial. "Desecrate" means defacing, damaging or polluting.

PRACTICAL APPLICATION OF STATUTE

Arriving in the town of Glendale with a special electric saw, The Brainiac cut out a piece of the town's "rock." For this desecration of the town's defining monument, The Brainiac should face a misdemeanor A per the provisions of section 18-7.

18-8.   **Causing fear of unlawful bodily violence, felony of third degree; act of graffiti, additional penalty**

A person is guilty of a felony of the third degree if he purposely, knowingly or recklessly puts or attempts to put another in fear of bodily violence by placing on private property of another a symbol, an object, a characterization, an appellation or graffiti that exposes another to threats of violence. A person shall not be guilty of an attempt unless his actions cause a serious and imminent likelihood of causing fear of unlawful bodily violence.

A person convicted of an offense under this section that involves an act of graffiti may, in addition to any other penalty imposed by the court, be required either to pay to the owner of the damaged property monetary restitution in the amount of the pecuniary damage caused by the act of graffiti or to perform community service, which shall include removing the graffiti from the property, if appropriate. If community service is ordered, it shall be for either not less than 20 days or not less than the number of days necessary to remove the graffiti from the property.

PRACTICAL APPLICATION OF STATUTE

In Jacinta City, The Brainiac painted a swastika on the front door of a councilman's home. He also inscribed the words "You're dead, pal" on the house. This constitutes a felony of the third degree.

Section 18-8 provides that a person who "purposely, knowingly or recklessly puts or attempts to put another in fear of bodily violence" by placing items such as symbols or graffiti on private property is guilty of a third degree felony. Anyone who writes "You're dead, pal" and paints a swastika on the door of another's home knows that he is going to put that other person "in fear of bodily violence." The Brainiac, therefore, is guilty of violating 18-8 for his acts of graffiti at the Jacinta City councilman's home.

18-9.

Defacement of private property, felony of fourth degree; act of graffiti, additional penalty

A person is guilty of a felony of the fourth degree if he purposely defaces or damages, without authorization of the owner or tenant, any private premises or property primarily used for religious, educational, residential, memorial, charitable or cemetery purposes or for assembly by persons for the purpose of exercising any right guaranteed by law or by the Constitution of this State or of the United States by placing thereon a symbol, an object, a characterization, an appellation or graffiti that exposes another to threat of violence.

A person convicted of an offense under this section that involves an act of graffiti may, in addition to any other penalty imposed by the court, be required either to pay to the owner of the damaged property monetary restitution in the amount of pecuniary damage caused by the act of graffiti or to perform community service, which shall include removing the graffiti from the property, if appropriate. If community service is ordered, it shall be for either not less than 20 days or not less than the number of days necessary to remove the graffiti from the property.

PRACTICAL APPLICATION OF STATUTE

Without authorization, The Brainiac removed the doors from a Salmon Creek church and spray painted the words "Kill you" on the wall. This is a violation of section 18-9, which sets out special prohibitions against defacing or damaging any private property primarily used for matters such as religious, educational or cemetery purposes. If the defacement "exposes another to threat of violence," the actor is guilty of a fourth degree felony.

The Brainiac's damage to the church doors and graffiti verbiage "Kill you" certainly would expose the congregation to a threat of violence. Accordingly, per the dictates of 18-9, The Brainiac is guilty of a fourth degree felony.

18-9.1.

Certain actions relevant to evictions, misdemeanor A

a. A person commits a misdemeanor A if, after being warned by a law enforcement or other public official of the illegality of that action, the person (1) takes possession of residential real property or effectuates a forcible entry or detainer of residential real property without lawful execution of a warrant for possession or without the consent of the occupant solely in possession of the residential real property or (2) refuses to restore immediately to exclusive possession and occupancy any such occupant so displaced. Legal occupants unlawfully displaced shall be entitled without delay to reenter and reoccupy the premises and shall not be considered trespassers or chargeable with any offense, provided that a law enforcement officer is present at the time of reentry. It shall be the duty of such officer to prevent the landlord or any other persons from obstructing or hindering the reentry and reoccupancy of the dwelling by the displaced occupant.

As used in this section, "forcible entry and detainer" means to enter upon or into any real property and detain and hold that property by:

(1) Any kind of violence including threatening to kill or injure the party in possession;

(2) Words, circumstances or actions which have a clear intention to incite fear or apprehension or danger in the party in possession;

(3) Putting outside of the residential premises the personal effects or furniture of the party in possession;

(4) Entering peaceably and then, by force or threats, turning the party out of possession;

(5) Padlocking or otherwise changing locks to the property;

(6) Shutting off, or causing to be shut off, vital services such as, but not limited to, heat, electricity or water in an effort to regain possession; or

(7) Any means other than compliance with lawful eviction procedures, as established through possession of a lawfully prepared and valid "Execution of Warrant."

b. A person who is convicted of an offense under this section more than once within a five-year period is guilty of a felony of the fourth degree.

PRACTICAL APPLICATION OF STATUTE

This statute seeks to prevent landlords from improperly taking over premises from tenants who have not been legally evicted. A landlord, or anyone acting on his behalf, commits a misdemeanor A if he "takes possession" or "effectuates a forcible entry" of "residential real property" (e.g., an apartment or house) without having obtained a legal eviction or the consent of the legal occupant (e.g., tenant). Similarly, the actor is guilty of a misdemeanor A if he "refuses to restore immediately to exclusive possession and occupancy" the tenant that he displaced by his takeover.

It is interesting to note that apparently a person can only be convicted under this statute if his actions occurred "after being warned by a law enforcement or other public official of the illegality of that action." The first thing taught in law school is that ignorance of the law is no defense. Apparently, under 18-9.1 it is a defense.

18-10.   Maintaining a nuisance

A person is guilty of maintaining a nuisance when:

a. By conduct either unlawful in itself or unreasonable under all the circumstances, he knowingly or recklessly creates or maintains a condition which endangers the safety or health of a considerable number of persons;

b. He knowingly conducts or maintains any premises, place or resort where persons gather for purposes of engaging in unlawful conduct; or

c. He knowingly conducts or maintains any premises, place or resort as a house of prostitution or as a place where obscene material, as defined in 19-2 and 19-3, is sold, photographed, manufactured, exhibited or otherwise prepared or shown, in violation of 19-2, 19-3 and 19-4.

A person is guilty of a misdemeanor A if the person is convicted under subsection a. or b. of this section. A person is guilty of a felony of the fourth degree if the person is convicted under subsection c. of this section.

PRACTICAL APPLICATION OF STATUTE

The Brainiac is guilty of maintaining a nuisance for the "house of prostitution" he conducted at Mack Daddy's in Pacorro. This is a fourth degree felony.

Per 18-10, an individual can be convicted of maintaining a nuisance for maintaining a condition that endangers the safety of a considerable number of persons (see subsection a.), maintaining premises where persons gather to engage in unlawful conduct (see subsection b.) or maintaining a "house of prostitution" or other place where "obscene material" is sold, photographed, manufactured or exhibited (see subsection c.). A violation of subsection c. renders a defendant guilty of a fourth degree felony; a violation of the other two subsections is a misdemeanor A.

The Brainiac maintained and operated Mack Daddy's, a private club purporting to hold an exclusive membership of checkers and jacks players. In reality, it was a club where patrons paid adult women and men to have sex with them. Accordingly, The Brainiac violated subsection c. of the statute for maintaining a "house of prostitution" and is guilty of a fourth degree felony.

18-10.1.   **Sexually oriented business, nuisance; felony**

a. As used in this act:

(1) "Sexually oriented business" means:

(a) A commercial establishment which as one of its principal business purposes offers for sale, rental or display any of the following: Books, magazines, periodicals or other printed material or photographs, films, motion pictures, video cassettes, slides or other visual representations which depict or describe a "specified sexual activity" or "specified anatomical area"; or still or motion picture machines, projectors or other image-producing devices which show images to one person per machine at any one time and where the images so displayed are characterized by the depiction of a "specified sexual activity" or "specified anatomical area"; or instruments, devices or paraphernalia which are designed for use in connection with a "specified sexual activity"; or

(b) A commercial establishment which regularly features live performances characterized by the exposure of a "specified anatomical area" or by a "specified sexual activity" or which regularly shows films, motion pictures, video cassettes, slides or other photographic representations which depict or describe a "specified sexual activity" or "specified anatomical area."

(2) "Person" means an individual, proprietorship, partnership, corporation, association or other legal entity.

(3) "Specified anatomical area" means:

(a) Less than completely and opaquely covered human genitals, pubic region, buttock or female breasts below a point immediately above the top of the areola; or

(b) Human male genitals in a discernibly turgid state, even if covered.

    (4) "Specified sexual activity" means:

        (a) The fondling or other erotic touching of covered or uncovered human genitals, pubic region, buttock or female breast; or

        (b) Any actual or simulated act of human masturbation, sexual intercourse or deviate sexual intercourse.

b. In addition to any activities proscribed by the provisions of 18-10, a person is guilty of maintaining a nuisance when the person owns or operates a sexually oriented business which offers for public use booths, screens, enclosures or other devices which facilitate sexual activity by patrons.

c. Notwithstanding any other provision of law, a municipality shall have the power to determine restrictions, if any, on the hours of operation of sexually oriented businesses.

d. A person who violates this act is guilty of a felony of the fourth degree.

PRACTICAL APPLICATION OF STATUTE

The Brainiac is guilty of violating 18-10.1 for offering patrons the use of enclosed booths at his "sexually oriented business," Piper's Home of Love. This is a fourth degree felony.

Any person who owns or operates a "sexually oriented business" that "offers for public use booths, screens, enclosures or other devices which facilitate sexual activity by patrons" is guilty of a fourth degree felony. "Sexually oriented business" is just what it sounds like—a business that sells items such as books, magazines or films that depict sexual activity or a business that provides live nude or quasi-nude performances. The complete definition of "sexually oriented business" can be found in subsection a. of 18-10.1.

Piper's Home of Love was a commercial establishment owned and operated by The Brainiac. This storefront business provided live performances where women danced in G-strings and bikini tops and routinely fondled themselves in the breast and genital areas; they also engaged in simulated acts of masturbation. Accordingly, Piper's Home of Love was a "sexually oriented business."

The Brainiac is guilty of violating 18-10.1 not for simply operating this business, however. His offense arises out of the fact that this "sexually oriented business" offered patrons the use of enclosed booths where "lap dances" occurred; sexual activity resulted many times during these sessions. Given that the enclosed booths in Piper's Home of Love "facilitated sexual activity by patrons," The Brainiac is guilty of a fourth degree felony under 18-10.1.

18-11.   **Smoking in public**

a. Any person who smokes or carries lighted tobacco in or upon any bus or other public conveyance, except group charter buses, specially marked railroad smoking cars, limousines or livery services, and when the driver is the only person in the vehicle, auto or cab, is guilty of a misdemeanor B. For the purposes of this section, "bus" includes school buses and other vehicles owned or contracted for by the governing body, board or individual of a nonpublic school, a public or private college, university, or professional training school or by a board of education of a school district that are used to transport students to and from school and school-related activities; and the prohibition on smoking or carrying lighted tobacco shall apply even if students are not present in the vehicle.

b. Any person who smokes or carries lighted tobacco in any public place, including but not limited to places of public accommodation, where such smoking is prohibited by municipal ordinance or by the owner or person responsible for the operation of the public place, and when adequate notice of such prohibition has been conspicuously posted, is guilty of a misdemeanor B. The maximum fine which can be imposed for violation of this section is $200.

c. The provisions of this section shall supersede any other statute and any rule or regulation adopted pursuant to law.

PRACTICAL APPLICATION OF STATUTE

The Brainiac smoked a cigarette on a public bus in Packton. This is an example of a misdemeanor B as defined in section 18-11.

If a cab driver with no passengers in his vehicle smokes a cigarette in the cab, this is an example where the statute does not apply. However, if the cab carries even one passenger, the driver is guilty of a misdemeanor B for his smoking.

18-11.1.   **Sale of cigarettes to persons under age 19, misdemeanor B**

a. A person who sells or gives to a person under 19 years of age any cigarettes made of tobacco or of any other matter or substance which can be smoked, or any cigarette paper or tobacco in any form, including smokeless tobacco, including an employee of a retail dealer licensee who actually sells or otherwise provides a tobacco product to a person under 19 years of age, shall be punished by a fine as provided for a misdemeanor B. A person who has been previously punished under this section and who commits another offense under it may be punishable by a fine of twice that provided for a misdemeanor B.

b. The establishment of all of the following shall constitute a defense to any prosecution brought pursuant to subsection a. of this section:

   (1) That the purchaser or recipient of the tobacco product falsely represented, by producing either a driver's license or non-driver identification card issued by the Motor Vehicle Commission, a similar card issued pursuant to the laws of another state or the federal government of Canada or a photographic identification card issued by a county clerk, that the purchaser or recipient was of legal age to purchase or receive the tobacco product;

   (2) That the appearance of the purchaser or recipient of the tobacco product was such that an ordinary prudent person would believe the purchaser or recipient to be of legal age to purchase or receive the tobacco product; and

   (3) That the sale or distribution of the tobacco product was made in good faith, relying upon the production of the identification set forth in paragraph (1) of this subsection, the appearance of the purchaser or recipient and the reasonable belief that the purchaser or recipient was of legal age to purchase or receive the tobacco product.

c. A penalty imposed pursuant to this section shall be in addition to any penalty that may be imposed.

PRACTICAL APPLICATION OF STATUTE

An example of this statute's misdemeanor B is the clerk's sale of cigarettes to a 12-year-old boy at the Wood Chop Candy Shop in Birchwood. Although subsection b. of 18-11.1 provides an affirmative defense, it is unlikely to work in this case as one of the elements the defendant needs to establish is that the purchaser's appearance "was such that an ordinary person would believe the purchaser or recipient to be of legal age" to purchase tobacco. What 12-year-old boy looks like he is 19 or older?

Legal Age Is 19, Not 18

It is now illegal to sell or give cigarettes to an 18-year-old man or woman in some states. The pertinent language formerly read "under 18 years of age"; for some jurisdictions, it now reads "under 19 years of age." Accordingly, in certain states, an 18-year-old man can fight in a war for the United States, but he can't buy cigarettes in his home state.

18-12.   **Interference with transportation**

   a. A person is guilty of interference with transportation if the person purposely or knowingly:

   (1) Casts, shoots or throws anything at, against or into any vehicle, railroad car, trolley car, subway car, ferry, airplane or other facility of transportation;

   (2) Casts, shoots, throws or otherwise places any stick, stone, object or other substance upon any street, railway track, trolley track or railroad track;

   (3) Endangers or obstructs the safe operation of motor vehicles by casting, shooting, throwing or otherwise placing any stick, stone, object or other substance upon any highway or roadway;

   (4) Unlawfully climbs into or upon any railroad car, either in motion or standing on the track of any railroad company in this State;

   (5) Unlawfully disrupts, delays or prevents the operation of any train, bus, jitney, trolley, subway, airplane or any other facility of transportation. The term "unlawfully disrupts, delays or prevents the operation of" does not include non-violent conduct growing out of a labor dispute; or

   (6) Endangers or obstructs the safe operation of motor vehicles by using a traffic control preemption device to interfere with or impair the operation of a traffic control signal.

   As used in this subsection, "traffic control preemption device" means an infrared transmitter or other device which transmits an infrared beam, radio wave or other signal designed to change, alter or disrupt in any manner the normal operation of a traffic control signal.

   b. Interference with transportation is a misdemeanor A.

   c. Interference with transportation is a felony of the fourth degree if the person purposely, knowingly or recklessly causes bodily injury to another person or causes pecuniary loss in excess of $500 but less than $2,000.

   d. Interference with transportation is a felony of the third degree if the person purposely, knowingly or recklessly causes significant bodily injury to another person or causes pecuniary loss of $2,000 or more or if the person purposely or knowingly creates a risk of significant bodily injury to another person.

   e. Interference with transportation is a felony of the second degree if the person purposely, knowingly or recklessly causes serious bodily injury to another person.

PRACTICAL APPLICATION OF STATUTE

The Brainiac threw eggs at a moving bus in Packton. This is an example of an offense as defined in section 18-12. Under these circumstances, where no one was injured and no property damage occurred, this is a misdemeanor A.

If "bodily injury" had occurred or if "pecuniary loss in excess of $500 but less than $2,000" had occurred, then the offense would be a fourth degree felony. The offense is elevated to a third degree felony if "pecuniary loss of $2,000 or more" had resulted or if the defendant caused "significant bodily injury" to another—or even if he "purposely or knowingly" created a risk of "significant bodily injury" to another. Finally, The Braniac would be guilty of a second degree felony if "serious bodily injury" had resulted from his reckless egg-throwing actions.

18-12.1. **Vandalizing railroad crossing devices, property; grading of offenses; graffiti**

a. Any person who purposely, knowingly or recklessly defaces, damages, obstructs, removes or otherwise impairs the operation of any railroad crossing warning signal or protection device, including but not limited to safety gates, electric bell, electric sign or any other alarm or protection system authorized by the Commissioner of Transportation, which is required, or any other railroad property or equipment, other than administrative buildings, offices or equipment, shall, for a first offense, be guilty of a felony of the fourth degree; however, if the defacement, damage, obstruction, removal or impediment of the crossing warning signal or protection device, property or equipment recklessly causes bodily injury or pecuniary loss of $2,000 or more, the actor is guilty of a felony of the third degree, or if it recklessly causes a death or serious bodily injury, the actor is guilty of a felony of the second degree.

b. A person convicted of a violation of this section that involves an act of graffiti may, in addition to any other penalty imposed by the court, be required to pay to the owner of the damaged property monetary restitution in the amount of the pecuniary damage caused by the act of graffiti and to perform community service, which shall include removing the graffiti from the property, if appropriate. If community service is ordered, it shall be for either not less than 20 days or not less than the number of days necessary to remove the graffiti from the property. As used in this section, "act of graffiti" means the drawing, painting or making of any mark or inscription on public or private real or personal property without the permission of the owner.

PRACTICAL APPLICATION OF STATUTE

In Glendale, The Braniac ripped down a railroad crossing safety gate. This is a fourth degree felony per 18-12.1.

If this act had "recklessly" caused "bodily injury or pecuniary loss of $2,000 or more," then a third degree felony has been committed. If it recklessly caused "death or serious bodily injury," the offense is elevated to a felony of the second degree.

18-13. **Possession, consumption of alcoholic beverages by person under legal age; penalty**

a. Any person under the legal age to purchase alcoholic beverages who knowingly possesses without legal authority or who knowingly consumes any alcoholic beverage in any school, public conveyance, public place or place of public assembly or motor vehicle is guilty of a misdemeanor A and shall be fined not less than $500.

b. Whenever this offense is committed in a motor vehicle, the court shall, in addition to the sentence authorized for the offense, suspend or postpone for six months the driving privilege of the defendant. Upon the conviction of any person under this section, the court shall forward a report to the Division of Motor Vehicles stating the first and last day of the suspension or postponement period imposed by the court pursuant to this section. If a person at the time of the imposition of a sentence is less than 17 years of age, the period of license postponement, including a suspension or postponement of the privilege of operating a motorized bicycle, shall commence on the day the sentence is imposed and shall run for a period of six months after the person reaches the age of 17 years.

If a person at the time of the imposition of a sentence has a valid driver's license issued by this State, the court shall immediately collect the license and forward it to the division along with the report. If for any reason the license cannot be collected, the court shall include in the report the complete name, address, date of birth, eye color and sex of the person as well as the first and last date of the license suspension period imposed by the court.

The court shall inform the person orally and in writing that if the person is convicted of operating a motor vehicle during the period of license suspension or postponement, the person shall be subject to the penalties set forth in the motor vehicles statute, driving on the revoked list. A person shall be required to acknowledge receipt of the written notice in writing.

c. In addition to the general penalty prescribed for a misdemeanor A, the court may require any person who violates this act to participate in an alcohol education or treatment program, authorized by the Department of Health and Senior Services, for a period not to exceed the maximum period of confinement prescribed by law for the offense for which the individual has been convicted.

d. Nothing in this act shall apply to possession of alcoholic beverages by any such person while actually engaged in the performance of employment pursuant to an employment permit issued by the Director of the Division of Alcoholic Beverage Control, or for a *bona fide* hotel or restaurant, or while actively engaged in the preparation of food while enrolled in a culinary arts or hotel management program at a county vocational school or post secondary educational institution.

PRACTICAL APPLICATION OF STATUTE

The Brainiac shared a bottle of whiskey with two students at Westwood High School. The students, both under 21 years of age, are guilty of a misdemeanor A per section 18-13.

Those under age 21 commit a misdemeanor A if they "knowingly" possess or consume alcohol in locations such as a school, motor vehicle or any public place. An exception to this rule is set forth in subsection d. of 18-13—bartenders, cooks and waitresses under the legal age can legally possess alcohol while performing their jobs or training for such occupations in schools.

The Westwood High School students are not exempt from the prohibitions set out in this statute. Accordingly, their "underage" consumption of whiskey on school property renders them guilty of a misdemeanor A.

18-14.   **Alcoholic beverages; bringing or possession on school property by person of legal age; penalty**

Any person of legal age to purchase alcoholic beverages who, knowingly and without the express written permission of the school board, its delegated authority or any school principal, brings or possesses any alcoholic beverages on any property used for school purposes which is owned by any school or school board is guilty of a misdemeanor A.

Practical Application of Statute

The Brainiac is guilty of a misdemeanor A for "knowingly" bringing a bottle of whiskey onto the Westwood High School property. He is guilty of this offense as all the elements of 18-14 were met in his case: He was of legal age to purchase alcohol, he "knowingly" brought the alcohol onto school property and he did not have any appropriate school authority's written permission to do so.

18-15.   **Availability of alcoholic beverages to underaged, offenses**

   a. Anyone who purposely or knowingly offers or serves or makes available an alcoholic beverage to a person under the legal age for consuming alcoholic beverages or entices or encourages that person to drink an alcoholic beverage is guilty of a misdemeanor A.

   This subsection shall not apply to a parent or guardian of the person under legal age for consuming alcoholic beverages if the parent or guardian is of the legal age to consume alcoholic beverages or to a religious observance, ceremony or rite. This subsection shall also not apply to any person in his home who is of the legal age to consume alcoholic beverages who offers or serves or makes available an alcoholic beverage to a person under the legal age for consuming alcoholic beverages or entices that person to drink an alcoholic beverage in the presence of and with the permission of the parent or guardian of the person under the legal age for consuming alcoholic beverages if the parent or guardian is of the legal age to consume alcoholic beverages.

   b. A person who makes real property owned, leased or managed by him available to, or leaves that property in the care of, another person with the purpose that alcoholic beverages will be made available for consumption by, or will be consumed by, persons who are under the legal age for consuming alcoholic beverages is guilty of a misdemeanor A.

   This subsection shall not apply if:

   (1) The real property is licensed or required to be licensed by the Division of Alcoholic Beverage Control;

   (2) The person making the property available, or leaving it in the care of another person, is of the legal age to consume alcoholic beverages and is the parent or guardian of the person who consumes alcoholic beverages while under the legal age for consuming alcoholic beverages; or

   (3) The alcoholic beverages are consumed by a person under the legal age for consuming alcoholic beverages during a religious observance, ceremony or rite.

Practical Application of Statute

For offering whiskey to the Westwood High School students, The Brainiac is guilty of a misdemeanor A. Why? Section 18-15 makes it an offense to "purposely or knowingly" offer, serve, make available or encourage anyone under 21 to drink an alcoholic beverage.

It is interesting to note, however, that this statute does not apply to parents or guardians of those "under the legal age." The statute also does not apply to any person who, "in his home," offers alcohol to someone under 21—as long as the "under the legal age" person's parent/guardian is present and gives permission to do so. In all these circumstances, the person making the alcohol offering (and the parent/guardian) must be "of the legal age to consume alcoholic beverages." Finally, this statute does not apply to a "religious observance, ceremony or rite."

18-16.   **Possession of remotely activated paging devices on school property, misdemeanor A; exemptions**

No person enrolled as a student of an elementary or secondary school, knowingly and without the express written permission of the school board, its delegated authority or any school principal, shall bring or possess any remotely activated paging device on any property used for school purposes at any time and regardless of whether school is in session or other persons are present. A violation of this section shall be a misdemeanor A. No permission to bring or possess any remotely activated paging device on school property shall be granted unless and until a student shall have established to the satisfaction of the school authorities a reasonable basis for the possession of the device on school property.

This section shall not apply to any student who is an active member in good standing of a volunteer fire company or first aid, ambulance or rescue squad provided that (1) the student is required to respond to an emergency and (2) a copy of the statement by the chief executive officer of the volunteer fire company or first aid, ambulance or rescue squad authorizing the possession of the paging device is in the possession of the student at all times while that student is in possession of the remotely activated paging device.

PRACTICAL APPLICATION OF STATUTE

Students cannot bring a pager on school property unless they have the written permission of an appropriate school authority. A violation of section 18-16 is a misdemeanor A—really, that's what this statute provides.

Section 18-16 does set forth an exception for individuals who serve as members of a "volunteer fire company or first aid, ambulance or rescue squad." They still need to present proof of their said membership; a written statement of the "chief executive officer" of the relevant squad is a necessity.

18-17.   **Use of remotely activated paging device during commission of certain felonies is a felony of fourth degree**

A person is guilty of a felony of the fourth degree if he uses a remotely activated paging device while engaged in the commission of or an attempt to commit, or flight after committing or attempting to commit, any felony or offense enumerated in chapter 20 or 21 of this Criminal Code.

PRACTICAL APPLICATION OF STATUTE

Bob the Drug Dealer provides cocaine to Ted the Addict. During this sale, Bob calls a pager to notify his partner, Mike the Money Man, that the transaction has been completed. Mike then meets up with Ted to collect the money owed for the cocaine. The use of the pager device, under these circumstances, renders both Bob and Mike guilty of a fourth degree felony under section 18-17.

18-18.   **Interception or use of official communications**

Any person who intercepts any message or transmission made on or over any police, fire or emergency medical communications system, or any person who is the recipient of information so intercepted, and who uses the information obtained thereby to facilitate the commission of or the attempt to commit a felony or a violation of any law of this State, or uses the same in a manner which interferes with the discharge of police or firefighting operations or provision of medical services by first aid, rescue or ambulance squad personnel, shall be guilty of a felony of the fourth degree.

PRACTICAL APPLICATION OF STATUTE

Bean-Bag Mean Team gang member Bertha closely listened to a police radio system while she waited in an automobile for the new gang member, The Brainiac. She heard a Birchwood police dispatcher advise all units that an alleged heroin transaction was occurring directly across the street from where their car was currently located.

Realizing that the drug dealers would probably have significant amounts of cash and drugs on them, Bertha frantically waved The Brainiac back to their car. Immediately upon his arrival, she suggested that they run across the street and rob the drug dealers. The pair then did just that. Bertha was correct—they left the site with nearly $5,000 in cash and heroin with a street value of about $10,000.

Bertha used the information she intercepted from the "police communication system" to facilitate a felony—the robbery of the drug dealers. This misuse of information constitutes a fourth degree felony under 18-18.

18-19. ## Possession of emergency communications receiver

Any person who, while in the course of committing or attempting to commit a felony, including the immediate flight therefrom, possesses or controls a radio capable of receiving any message or transmission made on or over any police, fire or emergency medical communications system shall be guilty of a felony of the fourth degree.

PRACTICAL APPLICATION OF STATUTE

As Bertha and The Brainiac drove away from their robbery of drug dealers, they monitored a "police radio system" so as to avoid any law enforcement that might be attempting to track them. This is an example of a fourth degree felony as set out in section 18-19.

18-20. ## License required for certain radio transmissions

A person shall not:

a. Make, or cause to be made, a radio transmission of energy in this State unless the person obtains a license, or an exemption from licensure, from the Federal Communications Commission or other applicable federal law or regulation; or

b. Do any act to cause an unlicensed radio transmission of energy or interference with a public or commercial radio station licensed by the Federal Communications Commission or to enable the radio transmission of energy or interference to occur.

A person who violates the provisions of this act is guilty of a felony of the fourth degree.

PRACTICAL APPLICATION OF STATUTE

This statute basically makes it illegal to make a radio transmission in the state without obtaining the appropriate license or exemption from licensure. Under the statute, it is also illegal to "do any act to cause" an interference with a public or commercial radio station licensed by the Federal Communications Commission (FCC). Per subsection c., any violation of 18-20 is a fourth degree felony.

Here's an example. Jermaine wants to produce and host his own radio show, but no one is interested in his services. Technologically advanced and savvy to FCC regulations, Jermaine makes a radio transmission, interrupting a local radio station in this state. For 30 minutes, he takes over the airwaves, telling jokes and singing songs. Jermaine did not have the appropriate license (or exemption from licensure) in order to make a legal radio transmission, and he purposely interrupted an FCC-licensed radio station in this state. Accordingly, he is guilty of a fourth degree felony.

18-21.   **Definitions**

As used in this chapter:

a. "Act of graffiti" means the drawing, painting or making any mark or inscription on public or private real or personal property without the permission of the owner.

b. "Spray paint" means any paint or pigmented substance that is in an aerosol or similar spray container.

18-22.   **Warning sign required for sale of spray paint; violations, penalties**

No person shall knowingly sell or offer for sale to the general public any spray paint unless a sign is exhibited, either where the product is displayed or where it is paid for, warning that in this State an act of graffiti committed by a juvenile may carry a penalty of a one-year driver's license suspension for a first offense and a two-year suspension for a second offense and that an act of graffiti committed by either an adult or a juvenile may carry a penalty of restitution or 20 days' community service.

A person who knowingly violates this section shall be fined $50 for the first offense and $100 for a second or subsequent offense.

PRACTICAL APPLICATION OF STATUTE

This statute is rarely invoked, but in a nutshell, it provides that merchants selling spray paint must exhibit warning signs outlining penalties for using the spray paint to commit acts of graffiti. Failure to exhibit the signs required under this statute shall subject a violator to conviction of a misdemeanor B.

18-23.   **Sale of motor vehicle on Sunday; exception**

A person who engages in the business of buying, selling or exchanging motor vehicles or who opens a place of business and attempts to engage in such conduct on a Sunday commits a misdemeanor A. The first offense is punishable by a fine not to exceed $100 or imprisonment for a period of not more than ten days or both; the second offense is punishable by a fine not to exceed $500 or imprisonment for a period of not more than 30 days or both; the third or each subsequent offense is punishable by a fine of $750 or imprisonment for a period of six months or both. If the person is a licensed dealer in new or used motor vehicles in this State, the person shall also be subject to suspension or revocation of his dealer's license to engage in the business of buying, selling or exchanging motor vehicles in this State for violation of this statute. Nothing contained in this section shall be construed to prohibit a person from accepting a deposit to secure the sale of a recreational vehicle, at an off-site sale, on a Sunday.

PRACTICAL APPLICATION OF STATUTE

The Brainiac, a licensed used-car dealer, sold a 1986 Chevy Cavalier on a Sunday. Believe it or not, this Sunday car sale constitutes a misdemeanor A under section 18-23.

18-24.   **Consumption of alcohol in restaurants**

    a. No person who owns or operates a restaurant, dining room or other public place where food or liquid refreshments are sold or served to the general public, and for which premises a license or permit authorizing the sale of alcoholic beverages for on-premises consumption has not been issued:

        (1) Shall allow the consumption of alcoholic beverages, other than wine or a malt alcoholic beverage, in a portion of the premises which is open to the public;

        (2) Shall charge any admission fee or cover, corkage or service charge or advertise inside or outside of such premises that patrons may bring and consume their own wine or malt alcoholic beverages in a portion of the premises which is open to the public; or

        (3) Shall allow the consumption of wine or malt alcoholic beverages at times or by persons to whom the service or consumption or alcoholic beverages on licensed premises is prohibited by State or municipal law or regulation.

    b. Nothing in this act shall restrict the right of a municipality or an owner or operator of a restaurant, dining room or other public place where food or liquid refreshments are sold or served to the general public from prohibiting the consumption of alcoholic beverages on those premises.

    c. A person who violates any provision of this act is guilty of a misdemeanor A, and the court, in addition to the sentence imposed for the misdemeanor A violation, may by its judgment bar the owner or operator from allowing consumption of wine or malt alcoholic beverages in his premises as authorized by this act.

PRACTICAL APPLICATION OF STATUTE

Bean-Bag Mean Team gang members Bertha and The Brainiac enjoyed a hearty meal at Stu's House of Chow. Although the restaurant had no liquor license, the owner permitted the gang members to drink scotch at a regular dining table.

    Section 18-24a.(1) prohibits a restaurant owner (who does not have a liquor license) from allowing "the consumption of alcoholic beverages other than wine or a malt alcoholic beverage, in a portion of the premises which is open to the public." A violation of this provision constitutes a misdemeanor A.

    Scotch is not "wine" or a "malt beverage." Bertha and The Brainiac drank this liquor at a regular dining table—a table located in a portion of the restaurant that was open to the public. Accordingly, the owner of Stu's House of Chow is guilty of a misdemeanor A for allowing Bertha and The Brainiac to drink scotch at this table.

18-25.   **Solicitation, recruitment to join criminal street gang; felony, degrees**

    a. An actor who solicits or recruits another to join or actively participate in a criminal street gang with the knowledge or purpose that the person who is solicited or recruited will promote, further, assist, plan, aid, agree or attempt to aid in the commission of criminal conduct by a member of a criminal street gang commits a felony of the fourth degree. For purposes of this section, the actor shall have the requisite knowledge or purpose if he knows that the person who is solicited or recruited will engage in some form, though not necessarily which form, of criminal activity.

b. An actor who, in the course of violating subsection a. of this section, threatens another with bodily injury on two or more separate occasions within a 30-day period commits a felony of the third degree.

c. An actor who, in the course of violating subsection a. of this section, inflicts significant bodily injury upon another commits a felony of the second degree.

d. Any defendant convicted of soliciting, recruiting, coercing or threatening a person under 18 years of age in violation of subsection a., b. or c. of this section shall be sentenced by the court to an extended term of imprisonment. A conviction arising under this section shall not merge with a conviction for any criminal offense that the actor committed while involved in criminal street gang related activity, nor shall the conviction for any such offense merge with a conviction pursuant to this section and the sentence imposed upon a violation of this section shall be ordered to be served consecutively to that imposed upon any other such conviction.

PRACTICAL APPLICATION OF STATUTE

Bertha recruited The Brainiac to join the "criminal street gang," The Bean-Bag Mean Team. This is a felony of the fourth degree.

Section 18-25 sets forth the provisions that make it a felony to solicit or recruit another to join a "criminal street gang." Primarily, a "criminal street gang" exists where two prongs are met. First, three or more people must be "associated in fact" (e.g., having a common group name or identifying symbol, tattoo or sign). Second, within the preceding three years, gang members need to have committed "two or more offenses" of felonies such as carjacking, robbery, burglary, aggravated assault and kidnapping.

Where the aforesaid solicitation or recruiting occurs "with the knowledge or purpose that the person who is solicited" will promote, assist or otherwise aid a gang member in the commission of criminal conduct, the actor engaging in the recruitment is guilty of a fourth degree felony.

The offense is elevated to a third degree felony where, during the course of the recruiting, others are threatened with bodily injury "on two or more occasions within a 30-day period." It becomes a second degree felony if the actor violating this statute "inflicts significant bodily injury upon another."

The Bean-Bag Mean Team is a "criminal street gang." Milo, Smiles, Bertha, Camille, Bambie and Horatio formed The Bean-Bag Mean Team. Each member was required to wear a chili bean pin on the lapel of his or her shirt; during the commission of felonies, the pin was to be placed on the inside of the shirt. The gang initially was ruthless and did in fact commit numerous hard-core felonies, including over 50 carjackings in the previous two years, and they also engaged in numerous robberies, burglaries and aggravated assaults. Recently, the membership had reached over 1,000 individuals. Given the number of gang members, the gang-signifying chili bean pin and the quantity of carjackings committed by gang members in the preceding three years, The Bean-Bag Mean Team qualifies as a "criminal street gang."

Bertha solicited The Brainiac to be the gang's final member. She sought his induction into the gang with the purpose that he would plan and aid the carrying out of their future criminal events. The Brainiac was receptive to her advances and agreed that if he was indeed admitted to be a member, he would actively plot and engage in fresh criminal activities.

Since Bertha recruited The Brainiac to be part of her "criminal street gang" with the knowledge that The Brainiac would assist and aid in the gang's criminal conduct, she is guilty of a felony under 18-25. Her felony would only be one of the fourth degree if neither threats of bodily injury nor actual significant bodily injury occurred in the course of her violating this statute. With "significant bodily injury" occurring, it would be elevated to a second degree felony.

END OF CHAPTER REVIEW

Multiple-Choice Questions

1. The felony of riot encompasses what separate offense as one of its elements?
   a. simple assault
   b. disorderly conduct
   c. harassment
   d. terroristic threats
   e. none of the above

2. The Brainiac wandered through the streets of Pokonke City. On foot, he repeatedly stopped pedestrians and spoke to them. In his pickup truck, he repeatedly circled a two-block area, twice stopping. On each occasion when he stopped, he passed and received something from the person he was speaking with. All of the Brainiac's above-described activities were witnessed by Pokonke City Police Sergeant Michael Stallone. Which of the following statements is true?
   a. Based on the totality of the circumstances, Sergeant Stallone can charge The Brainiac with the misdemeanor A of loitering to obtain CDS—but only because he personally witnessed all of the activities described above.
   b. Based on the totality of the circumstances, Sergeant Stallone can charge The Brainiac with the misdemeanor A of loitering to obtain CDS—even if he did not personally witness all of the activities described above.
   c. Sergeant Stallone cannot charge The Brainiac with the misdemeanor A of loitering to obtain CDS based solely on The Brainiac's activities as described above.
   d. Loitering to obtain CDS is not a misdemeanor A. It's a felony of the first degree.
   e. There is no such offense known as loitering to obtain CDS.

3. The Brainiac called his girlfriend at 4 a.m., waking her up, just to talk. Annoyed, she hung up the phone on him. What is the *best* offense to charge The Brainiac with?
   a. disorderly conduct
   b. harassment
   c. terroristic threats
   d. stalking
   e. no offense to charge him with

4. A person can be convicted of maintaining a nuisance under which of the following circumstances?

    a. by creating a condition which endangers the safety or health of a considerable number of persons

    b. by maintaining premises where persons gather to engage in unlawful conduct

    c. by maintaining a house of prostitution

    d. all of the above

    e. a and b only

5. The Brainiac threw eggs at a moving bus in South Sacramente City. What is he guilty of?

    a. a misdemeanor A if no one was injured and no property damage occurred

    b. a fourth degree felony if bodily injury occurred

    c. a fourth degree felony if there was pecuniary loss in excess of $500 but less than $2,000

    d. a second degree felony if serious bodily injury occurred

    e. all of the above

6. Knucklehead, age 40, brings a liter of vodka into a public elementary school in Parsippany. Which of the following statements is true?

    a. Knucklehead is guilty of no offense at all if he obtained written permission by the Parsippany School Board of Education to bring the vodka into the elementary school.

    b. Knucklehead is guilty of no offense if he obtained written permission by the elementary school principal to bring the vodka into the elementary school.

    c. Knucklehead is guilty of no offense if he obtained written permission by the Parsippany School Board's attorney, under the authority of the school board, to bring the vodka into the elementary school.

    d. Knucklehead is guilty of a misdemeanor A regardless of who gave him written permission to bring the vodka into the elementary school.

    e. All of the above *except d* are true.

7. The Brainiac called the Kaine Fire Department and reported that an explosion was about to occur at the town's library. What is The Brainiac guilty of?

    a. a third degree felony

    b. a third degree felony only if he knew that his report was false

    c. a misdemeanor B

    d. a misdemeanor B only if he knew that his report was false

    e. a fifth degree felony

Essay Questions

1. At Mingelino's Restaurant & Bar, Juice becomes angry at Parsons and shoves Parsons backwards. Parsons is not injured in any way but yells at Juice, "I'm going to get you in a bad way." Parsons then rushes behind his bar where he begins wildly banging pots and pans and screaming nonsensical words at the top

of his lungs, disrupting all patrons' dinners. The entire event was witnessed by a Lyndhurst police officer, who grabbed Parsons at the back of the bar. A gun was not recovered. What is the *best* offense for the Lyndhurst police officer to charge Juice with? Cite the statute and the specific subsection in your answer, and explain why it is applicable. Also, what is the degree of this offense? What is the *best* offense for the Lyndhurst police officer to charge Parsons with? Cite the statute and the specific subsection in your answer, and explain why it is applicable. Also, what is the degree of this offense?

2. The Brainiac smoked a cigarette on a public bus in Paterson. Is he guilty of an offense under Chapter 18? If so, what offense and what is its degree? Bob the Drug Dealer provides cocaine to Ted the Addict. During this sale, Bob calls a pager to notify his partner, Mike the Money Man, that the transaction has been completed. Does the use of the pager device under these circumstances render Bob the Drug Dealer guilty of an offense in Chapter 18? If so, what offense and what degree? Costello, age 45, consumed two glasses of wine in an Italian restaurant on a Sunday. Costello is guilty of what degree offense? Is Costello guilty of an offense under Chapter 18? If so, what offense and what is its degree?

19

PUBLIC INDECENCY

19-1.   **Prostitution and related offenses**

    a. As used in this section:

       (1) "Prostitution" is sexual activity with another person in exchange for something of economic value or the offer or acceptance of an offer to engage in sexual activity in exchange for something of economic value.

       (2) "Sexual activity" includes, but is not limited to, sexual intercourse, including genital-genital, oral-genital, anal-genital and oral-anal contact, whether between persons of the same or opposite sex; masturbation; touching of the genitals, buttocks or female breasts; sadistic or masochistic abuse; and other deviate sexual relations.

       (3) "House of prostitution" is any place where prostitution or promotion of prostitution is regularly carried on by one person under the control, management or supervision of another.

       (4) "Promoting prostitution" is:

         (a) Owning, controlling, managing, supervising or otherwise keeping, alone or in association with another, a house of prostitution or a prostitution business;

         (b) Procuring an inmate for a house of prostitution or place in a house of prostitution for one who would be an inmate;

         (c) Encouraging, inducing or otherwise purposely causing another to become or remain a prostitute;

         (d) Soliciting a person to patronize a prostitute;

         (e) Procuring a prostitute for a patron;

         (f) Transporting a person into or within this State with the purpose to promote that person's engaging in prostitution or procuring or paying for transportation with that purpose; or

         (g) Knowingly leasing or otherwise permitting a place controlled by the actor, alone or in association with others, to be regularly used for prostitution or promotion of prostitution, or failing to make a reasonable effort to abate such use by ejecting the tenant, notifying law enforcement authorities or using other legally available means.

    b. A person commits an offense if:

       (1) The actor engages in prostitution;

       (2) The actor promotes prostitution;

       (3) The actor knowingly promotes prostitution of a child under 18 whether or not the actor mistakenly believed that the child was 18 years of age or older, even if such mistaken belief was reasonable;

(4) The actor knowingly promotes prostitution of the actor's child, ward or any other person for whose care the actor is responsible;

(5) The actor compels another to engage in or promote prostitution;

(6) The actor promotes prostitution of the actor's spouse; or

(7) The actor knowingly engages in prostitution with a person under the age of 18, or if the actor enters into or remains in a house of prostitution for the purpose of engaging in sexual activity with a child under the age of 18 or if the actor solicits or requests a child under the age of 18 to engage in sexual activity. It shall be no defense to a prosecution under this paragraph that the actor mistakenly believed that the child was 18 years of age or older, even if such mistaken belief was reasonable.

c. Grading of offenses under subsection b:

(1) An offense under subsection b. constitutes a felony of the second degree if the offense falls within paragraph (3) or (4) of that subsection.

(2) An offense under subsection b. constitutes a felony of the third degree if the offense falls within paragraph (5), (6) or (7) of that subsection.

(3) An offense under paragraph (2) of subsection b. constitutes a felony of the third degree if the conduct falls within subparagraph (a), (b) or (c) of paragraph (4) of subsection a. Otherwise the offense is a felony of the fourth degree.

(4) An offense under subsection b. constitutes a misdemeanor A if the offense falls within paragraph (1) of that subsection except that a second or subsequent conviction for such an offense constitutes a felony of the fourth degree. In addition, where a motor vehicle was used in the commission of any offense under paragraph (1) of subsection b., the court shall suspend for six months the driving privilege of any such offender who has a valid driver's license issued by this State. Upon conviction, the court shall immediately collect the offender's driver's license and shall forward it, along with a report stating the first and last day of the suspension imposed pursuant to this paragraph, to the Motor Vehicle Commission.

d. Presumption from living off prostitutes. A person, other than the prostitute or the prostitute's minor child or other legal dependent incapable of self-support, who is supported in whole or substantial part by the proceeds of prostitution is presumed to be knowingly promoting prostitution.

e. It is an affirmative defense to prosecution for a violation of this section that, during the time of the alleged commission of the offense, the defendant was a victim of human trafficking pursuant to 3-8.

PRACTICAL APPLICATION OF STATUTE

Promoting Prostitution

The Brainiac is guilty of promoting prostitution for his ownership and management activities at Mack Daddy's in Pacorro. In his case, it is a third degree felony.

Per 19-1, a person can be convicted of an offense for engaging in prostitution or promoting prostitution. The offenses are graded in subsection c. of the statute. Promoting prostitution can be a second, third or fourth degree felony depending on the circumstances. Per subsection c.(1), promoting prostitution is a second degree felony where "the offense falls within paragraph (3) or (4)" of subsection b.

This means it is a second degree felony in circumstances such as where the actor knowingly promotes prostitution of the actor's own child (see b.(4)) and where the actor knowingly promotes prostitution of a child under 18 years of age (see b.(3)). It is interesting to note that per b.(3), it doesn't matter whether the actor "mistakenly believed" the child was 18 or older—in other words, even if the mistaken belief was reasonable, he could still be convicted of a second degree felony.

Subsection c.(3) states "an offense under paragraph (2) of subsection b. constitutes a felony of the third degree if the conduct falls within subparagraph (a), (b) or (c) of paragraph (4) of subsection a. Otherwise the offense is a felony of the fourth degree." Huh?! What?! This is clear, right? The case of The Brainiac will help to explain what this means.

After The Brainiac's celebration dinner with his gang member date, Bertha, The Brainiac brought Bertha to his Pacorro business, Mack Daddy's. This was a private 24-hour club purporting to hold an exclusive membership of checkers and jacks players. In reality, Mack Daddy's was a "house of prostitution" where patrons paid adult women and men to have sex with them.

Mack Daddy's was owned and managed by The Brainiac on a daily basis. He oversaw and encouraged the individuals who worked there to have sexual relations with the club's many eager clients, and more than 30 employees accepted cash in exchange for their services.

Now let's revisit the language of subsection c.(3): "an offense under paragraph (2) of subsection b. constitutes a felony of the third degree if the conduct falls within subparagraph (a), (b) or (c) of paragraph (4) of subsection a. Otherwise the offense is a felony of the fourth degree." Now let's break down this language.

"Paragraph (2) of subsection b." provides that a person commits an offense if the actor promotes prostitution. But how does a person "promote prostitution"? This is defined in "subsection a.(4)"—which is further divided into subparagraphs (a) through (g). Persons who promote prostitution via actions defined in "subparagraphs (a), (b) and (c)" are those guilty of third degree felonies; otherwise, those who promote prostitution via actions defined in the remaining subparagraphs ((d) through (g)) are guilty of a fourth degree felony.

The Brainiac is guilty of a third degree promotion of prostitution offense. Why? Because he violated both subparagraphs (a) and (c) of subsection a.(4)—he owned and managed a "house of prostitution," which violates a.(4)(a), and he "encouraged" others to remain prostitutes, which violates a.(4)(c).

It is important to note that subsection d. drops in a special provision that makes it an offense to promote prostitution in situations where people are "living off prostitutes." The subsection provides that a person is "presumed" to be knowingly promoting prostitution where he is "supported in whole or substantial part by the proceeds of prostitution." Difficult to prove? Perhaps—but this is ultimately a matter to be decided in the courts.

Engaging in Prostitution

The prostitutes who worked for The Brainiac at Mack Daddy's—and the "johns" who utilized their services—are guilty of "engaging in prostitution." This can be a third or fourth degree felony or a misdemeanor A, depending on the circumstances.

As 19-1c.(2) states, "engaging in prostitution" is a third degree felony where it falls within subsections b.(5) and b.(7) of 19-1. This means that it is a third degree felony where the actor "compels another to engage" in prostitution (see b.(5)) or where the actor "engages in prostitution with a person under the age of 18" (see b.(7)). The latter subsection is similarly violated if the actor remains in a house of prostitution with the purpose of engaging in sexual activity with a person under 18 or solicits/requests a child under 18 to have sexual relations with him. Under all these circumstances, it is no defense where the actor mistakenly believed that the child was 18 or older—even if the mistaken belief was reasonable.

"Engaging in prostitution," however, is generally a misdemeanor A as per subsection c.(4). This means that two consenting adults who decide to engage in prostitution are both guilty of a misdemeanor A and not a third degree felony. For example, in the case where John, age 40, goes to Mack Daddy's and pays Wilma, age 21, $50 to have sex with him, they are both guilty of a misdemeanor A. Their offense can be elevated to a fourth degree felony, though, if they have been previously convicted of engaging in prostitution.

Affirmative Defense

An affirmative defense was added to the prostitution statute. It was added as a counterpart to the newly enacted human trafficking statute, 3-8. Simply stated, it is an affirmative defense to a prostitution prosecution if "during the time of the alleged commission of the offenses, the defendant was a victim of human trafficking." For a further explanation of why this is so, see the human trafficking Practical Application section.

19-1.1.   **Loitering for the purpose of engaging in prostitution**

a. As used in this section, "public place" means any place to which the public has access, including but not limited to any public street, sidewalk, bridge, alley, plaza, park, boardwalk, driveway, parking lot or transportation facility, public library or the doorways and entranceways to any building which fronts on any of the aforesaid places or a motor vehicle in or on any such place.

b. A person commits a misdemeanor A if he:

   (1) Wanders, remains or prowls in a public place with the purpose of engaging in prostitution or promoting prostitution as defined in 19-1; and

   (2) Engages in conduct that, under the circumstances, manifests the purpose to engage in prostitution or promoting prostitution as defined in 19-1.

c. Conduct that may, where warranted under the circumstances, be deemed adequate to manifest the purpose to engage in prostitution or promoting prostitution includes, but is not limited to, conduct such as the following:

   (1) Repeatedly beckoning to or stopping pedestrians or motorists in a public place;

   (2) Repeatedly attempting to stop or repeatedly attempting to engage passersby in conversation; or

   (3) Repeatedly stopping or attempting to stop motor vehicles.

d. The element described in paragraph (1) of subsection b. of this section may not be established solely by proof that the actor engaged in the conduct that is used to satisfy the element described in paragraph (2) of subsection b. of this section.

PRACTICAL APPLICATION OF STATUTE

Section 19-1.1 makes it illegal for individuals to loiter for the "purpose of engaging in prostitution or promoting prostitution." The case of The Brainiac provides an example of how loiterers can be convicted of this misdemeanor A.

This statute is nearly identical, in language and form, to 18-2.1 (loitering for the purpose of illegally using, possessing or selling a controlled dangerous substance [CDS]). Accordingly, it will be explained in the same manner. Section 19-1.1, in a quick summary, prohibits a person from "wandering" or "remaining" in public with the purpose to engage in or promote prostitution. But how is it possible to prove that someone is "wandering" or "remaining" in a public place for the purpose of carrying out one of these illicit activities?

Section 19-1.1 provides that the defendant's "conduct" is the dispositive factor. Subsection c. goes as far as defining what "conduct" will be "deemed adequate to manifest the purpose to engage in prostitution or promoting prostitution." This conduct includes, but is not limited to, repeatedly stopping pedestrians or motorists and repeatedly engaging passersby in conversations.

Nothing in this statute requires that any actual evidence of "promoting prostitution" or "engaging in prostitution" be presented in order for a conviction under 19-1.1 to occur. However, subsection d., when dissected, does set out that the above-described "conduct" *alone* cannot establish that the defendant acted "with the purpose" to "promote prostitution" or "engage in prostitution." This implies that some other evidence (e.g., statements by the defendants) is necessary for a conviction.

Now how does The Brainiac's case help explain the practical use of this statute? After celebrating his induction into the ruthless gang named The Bean-Bag Mean Team, The Brainiac took fellow gang member Bertha on a date. Their last stop of the evening was in North Nestor, where they roamed the streets, asking several different people where they could find a prostitute because they wanted to "speak to one."

Here, the "conduct" of The Brainiac and Bertha could "be deemed adequate to manifest the purpose to engage in prostitution"—they repeatedly stopped several pedestrians and passersby, engaging them in conversations. But remember, this "conduct" alone is not enough; the prosecution must present something additional for a conviction to occur. In The Brainiac's case, there is that something—he and Bertha asked the individuals they stopped where they could find a prostitute. Accordingly, with these combined factors, The Brainiac and Bertha could be convicted of "loitering for the purpose of engaging in prostitution."

19-2.   **Obscenity for persons 18 years of age or older**

    a. Definitions for the purpose of this section:

        (1) "Obscene material" means any description, narrative account, display or depiction of sexual activity or anatomical area contained in, or consisting of, a picture or other representation, publication, sound recording, live performance or film, which by means of posing, composition, format or animated sensual details:

            (a) Depicts or describes, in a patently offensive way, ultimate sexual acts, normal or perverted, actual or simulated; masturbation; excretory functions; or lewd exhibition of the genitals;

            (b) Lacks serious literary, artistic, political or scientific value, when taken as a whole; and

    (c) Is a part of a work which, to the average person applying contemporary community standards, has a dominant theme, taken as a whole, which appeals to the prurient interest.

  (2) "Exhibit" means the sale of admission to view obscene material.

b. A person who sells, distributes, rents or exhibits obscene material to a person 18 years of age or older commits a felony of the fourth degree. Sale of obscene material shall be deemed to include any form of transaction which results in the admission to a display or depiction of obscene material or temporary or permanent access to any obscene material.

Nothing contained herein or in 19-7 shall be construed to prohibit a municipality from adopting as a part of its zoning ordinances an ordinance permitting the sale, distribution, rental or exhibition of obscene material in which event such sale, distribution, rental or exhibition shall be deemed legal.

PRACTICAL APPLICATION OF STATUTE

At a store known as The Annex, Bean-Bag Mean Team members The Brainiac and Bertha thumbed through multiple magazines, looking at hundreds of erotic and sexually explicit pictures. They watched as the store clerk sold five of the magazines to a 33-year-old woman. For this sale, could the clerk be convicted of selling "obscene material"—which is a fourth degree felony per 19-2?

Subsection a. of this statute provides a definition for "obscene material." Basically, any magazine, video, etc., containing sexual activity or nudity—in any description, narrative account, display or depiction—could be stretched to fall under this definition. Pursuant to subsection b., any person who "sells, distributes, rents or exhibits" any of this "obscene material" to any person 18 years of age or older commits a fourth degree felony.

Okay, so The Annex clerk technically could be convicted of a fourth degree felony for selling sexually explicit magazines to the 33-year-old woman. Does this sound right, though? If this is the case, how are the hundreds (if not thousands) of stores across the state selling sexually explicit magazines and videos? Well, according to the final paragraph of the statute, any municipality can adopt a municipal ordinance to legally permit the "sale, distribution, rental or exhibition of obscene material" to persons 18 or older. In the event that such an ordinance is adopted, the sale, etc., of "obscene material" to persons 18 or older is "deemed legal."

19-3. **Obscenity for persons under 18**

a. Definitions for purposes of this section:

  (1) "Obscene material" means any description, narrative account, display, depiction of a specified anatomical area or specified sexual activity contained in, or consisting of, a picture or other representation, publication, sound recording, live performance or film, which by means of posing, composition, format or animated sensual details emits sensuality with sufficient impact to concentrate prurient interest on the area or activity.

  (2) "Obscene film" means any motion picture film or preview or trailer to a film, not including newsreels portraying actual current events or pictorial news of the day, in which a scene, taken by itself:

    (a) Depicts a specified anatomical area or specified sexual activity, the simulation of a specified sexual activity or the verbalization concerning a specified sexual activity; and

(b) Emits sensuality sufficient, in terms of the duration and impact of the depiction, to appeal to prurient interest.

(3) "Specified anatomical area" means:

(a) Less than completely and opaquely covered human genitals, pubic region, buttock or female breasts below a point immediately above the top of the areola; or

(b) Human male genitals in a discernibly turgid state, even if covered.

(4) "Specified sexual activity" means:

(a) Human genitals in a state of sexual stimulation or arousal;

(b) Any act of human masturbation, sexual intercourse or deviate sexual intercourse; or

(c) Fondling or other erotic touching of covered or uncovered human genitals, pubic region, buttock or female breast.

(5) "Knowingly" means:

(a) Having knowledge of the character and content of the material or film described herein; or

(b) Having failed to exercise reasonable inspection which would disclose its character and content.

(6) "Exhibit" means the sale of admission to view obscene material.

(7) "Show" means cause or allow to be seen.

b. Promoting obscene material.

(1) A person who knowingly sells, distributes, rents or exhibits to a person under 18 years of age obscene material is guilty of a felony of the third degree.

(2) A person who knowingly shows obscene material to a person under 18 years of age with the knowledge or purpose to arouse, gratify or stimulate himself or another is guilty of a felony of the third degree if the person showing the obscene material is at least four years older than the person under 18 years of age viewing the material.

c. Admitting to exhibition of obscene film.

(1) Any person who knowingly admits a person under 18 years of age to a theatre then exhibiting an obscene film is guilty of a felony of the third degree.

(2) A person who knowingly shows an obscene film to a person under 18 years of age with the knowledge or purpose to arouse, gratify or stimulate himself or another is guilty of a felony of the third degree if the person showing the obscene film is at least four years older than the person under 18 years of age viewing the film.

d. Presumption of knowledge and age. The requisite knowledge with regard to the character and content of the film or material and of the age of the person is presumed in the case of an actor who sells, distributes, rents, exhibits or shows obscene material to a person under 18 years of age or admits to a film obscene for a person under 18 years of age a person who is under 18 years of age.

e. Defenses.

(1) It is an affirmative defense to a prosecution under subsections b. and c. which the defendant must prove by a preponderance of evidence that:

(a) The person under age 18 falsely represented in or by writing that he was age 18 or over;

(b) The person's appearance was such that an individual of ordinary prudence would believe him to be age 18 or over; and

(c) The sale, distribution, rental, showing or exhibition to or admission of the person was made in good faith relying upon such written representation and appearance and in the reasonable belief that he was actually age 18 or over.

(2) It is an affirmative defense to a prosecution under subsection c. that the defendant is an employee in a motion picture theatre who has no financial interest in that motion picture theatre other than his wages and has no decision-making authority or responsibility with respect to the selection of the motion picture show which is exhibited.

PRACTICAL APPLICATION OF STATUTE

The clerk of The Annex sold two sexually explicit magazines to a 14-year-old boy. This is a felony of the third degree.

While 19-2 allows for municipalities to adopt an ordinance that permits the sale, etc., of "obscene material" to persons 18 or older, 19-3 has no such provision. Why is this important? Section 19-3 is the statute that governs the sale, distribution, rental or exhibition of "obscene material" to persons *under* 18 years of age.

The definitions pertinent to "obscenity" for persons under 18 are set forth in subsection a. of the statute. The definition of "obscene material" in 19-3 is even more narrow than the definition in its counterpart statute, 19-2. Also, a person who violates the provisions of 19-3 is guilty of a third degree felony, while a violator of 19-2 is guilty of a felony of the fourth degree.

Not only is it a third degree felony to sell, etc., "obscene material" to persons under 18, it is also a third degree felony to "show" such material to minors. Subsection b.(2) sets out caveats to the latter prohibition, however. In order to be convicted of an offense for "*showing* obscene material" to someone under 18, the person must do it with the knowledge or purpose "to arouse, gratify or stimulate himself or another"; in addition, for a conviction to occur here, the person "showing" the "obscene material" must be "at least four years older than the person under 18 years of age viewing the material."

The clerk at The Annex sold two sexually explicit magazines, containing pictures which are considered "obscene material" under 19-3, to a 14-year-old boy. Accordingly, he is guilty of a third degree felony.

"Knowingly" Requirement

It is important to note that 19-3 provides that an individual such as the clerk must "knowingly" sell, etc., "obscene material" to a person under 18. "Knowingly," in a nutshell, means that he has knowledge that "obscene material" is within the items he is selling or that he failed to make a reasonable inspection of the material that would disclose its content. Obviously, The Annex clerk knew what he was selling to the 14-year-old—the entire product line in his store was erotic and sexually explicit material.

Affirmative Defenses

It is also important to note that subsection e. of the statute provides affirmative defenses to the offenses in 19-3. One of the defenses is that the juvenile falsely represented "in or by writing" that he was 18 or over. For this defense to succeed, however, the juvenile must appear 18 or older to an ordinary prudent person, and the defendant must rely in good faith on this appearance and written representation, thereby actually believing the juvenile was over 18.

The Annex clerk is unlikely to prevail with this defense concerning his sale to the 14-year-old boy. No written representation was presented—and how many 14-year-old boys look 18 or older?

Obscene Films

As explained above, section 19-3 provides prohibitions against the sale, etc., of "obscene material" to persons under 18 years of age. The statute, via subsection c., also provides prohibitions against admitting persons under 18 to a theatre exhibiting an "obscene film" and "showing" an "obscene film" to persons under 18 years of age. Both of these offenses are felonies of the third degree.

19-3.1.   **Retailer defined**

"Retailer," as used in this act, means any person who operates a store, newsstand, booth, concession or similar business with unimpeded access for persons under 18 years old who is in the business of making sales of periodicals or other publications at retail containing pictures, drawings or photographs.

19-3.2.   **Display of obscene material**

A municipality may enact an ordinance making it a misdemeanor B for a retailer to display or permit to be displayed at his business premises any obscene material, as defined in 19-3, at a height of less than five feet or without a blinder or other covering placed or printed on the front of the material displayed. Any such ordinance shall contain a provision stating that public display of the obscene material shall constitute presumptive evidence that the retailer knowingly made or permitted the display.

PRACTICAL APPLICATION OF STATUTE

The owner of The Annex may be guilty of a misdemeanor B for displaying "obscene material" (magazines) on shelves "at a height less than five feet" and without blinders or coverings on the front of the material.

The Annex owner, however, may be able to evade conviction under 19-3.2. Why? The statute is only in effect in municipalities that have enacted an ordinance providing for the aforesaid provisions, so if The Annex is located in a municipality that has failed to enact such an ordinance, the owner cannot be convicted of the misdemeanor B defined in 19-3.2.

19-4.   **Public communication of obscenity**

a. "Publicly communicate" means to display, post, exhibit, give away or vocalize material in such a way that its character and content may be readily and distinctly perceived by the public by normal unaided vision or hearing when viewing or hearing it in, on or from a public street, road, thoroughfare, recreation or shopping center or area, public transportation facility or vehicle used for public transportation.

b. A person who knowingly publicly communicates obscene material, as defined in section 19-3, or causes or permits it to be publicly communicated on property he owns or leases or operates is guilty of a felony of the fourth degree.

c. Public communication of obscene material shall constitute presumptive evidence that the defendant made the communication or caused or permitted it to be made knowingly.

PRACTICAL APPLICATION OF STATUTE

Land owners, lessees and operators of property cannot "publicly communicate . . . obscenity," meaning "obscene material" as defined in section 19-3. Doing so constitutes a felony of the fourth degree.

But what does "publicly communicate" mean? Can a person talking in an obscene manner on his front porch be convicted of 19-4's fourth degree felony? Probably not, as First Amendment rights would likely prevent a conviction. If a person puts up a theatrical screen on his front lawn and shows a pornographic movie, would he be convicted of "publicly communicating" obscenity? In this case, the answer is probably yes.

"Publicly communicate" is defined in subsection a. of the statute. The definition primarily provides that "publicly communicate" means the exhibition or vocalization of "obscene material" that a person could readily and distinctly hear or see from areas such as public streets and shopping centers. Accordingly, in the case of the man exhibiting a pornographic movie on his front lawn, he is ripe for a fourth degree felony conviction in a situation where a passerby or motorist could see or hear the film.

19-5. **Diseased person committing an act of sexual penetration**

a. A person is guilty of a felony of the fourth degree who, knowing that he or she is infected with a venereal disease such as chancroid, gonorrhea, syphilis, herpes virus or any of the varieties or stages of such diseases, commits an act of sexual penetration without the informed consent of the other person.

b. A person is guilty of a felony of the third degree who, knowing that he or she is infected with human immune deficiency virus (HIV) or any other related virus identified as a probable causative agent of acquired immune deficiency syndrome (AIDS), commits an act of sexual penetration without the informed consent of the other person.

PRACTICAL APPLICATION OF STATUTE

Per subsection a. of 19-5, anyone who commits an act of sexual penetration while "knowing" that he is infected with a venereal disease is guilty of a fourth degree felony. Pursuant to subsection b., anyone who commits an act of sexual penetration while "knowing" that he is infected with HIV or AIDS is guilty of a third degree felony. There is one caveat, though—a person cannot be convicted under this statute if he has the "informed consent" of the person with whom he is having sex. In other words, if Bob's partner knows that Bob has AIDS or the venereal disease herpes and still consents to the act of penetration, Bob cannot be convicted of an offense under 19-5.

19-6. **Definitions**

As used in sections 19-7 of this chapter:

a. "Sexually oriented business" means:

(1) A commercial establishment which as one of its principal business purposes offers for sale, rental or display any of the following: Books, magazines, periodicals or

other printed material or photographs, films, motion pictures, video cassettes, slides or other visual representations which depict or describe a "specified sexual activity" or "specified anatomical area"; still or motion picture machines, projectors or other image-producing devices which show images to one person per machine at any one time and where the images so displayed are characterized by the depiction of a "specified sexual activity" or "specified anatomical area"; or instruments, devices or paraphernalia which are designed for use in connection with a "specified sexual activity"; or

    (2) A commercial establishment which regularly features live performances characterized by the exposure of a "specified anatomical area" or by a "specified sexual activity" or which regularly shows films, motion pictures, video cassettes, slides or other photographic representations which depict or describe a "specified sexual activity" or "specified anatomical area."

b. "Person" means an individual, proprietorship, partnership, corporation, association or other legal entity.

c. "Specified anatomical area" means:

    (1) Less than completely and opaquely covered human genitals, pubic region, buttock or female breasts below a point immediately above the top of the areola; or

    (2) Human male genitals in a discernibly turgid state, even if covered.

d. "Specified sexual activity" means:

    (1) The fondling or other erotic touching of covered or uncovered human genitals, pubic region, buttock or female breast; or

    (2) Any actual or simulated act of human masturbation, sexual intercourse or deviate sexual intercourse.

19-7.   **Sexually oriented business; location; building requirements; penalty**

a. Except as provided in a municipal zoning ordinance adopted pursuant to 19-2, no person shall operate a sexually oriented business within 1,000 feet of any existing sexually oriented business, or any church, synagogue, temple or other place of public worship, or any elementary or secondary school or any school bus stop, or any municipal or county playground or place of public resort and recreation, or any hospital or any child care center or within 1,000 feet of any area zoned for residential use. This subsection shall not apply to a sexually oriented business already lawfully operating on the effective date of this act where another sexually oriented business, an elementary or secondary school or school bus stop, or any municipal or county playground or place of public resort and recreation, or any hospital or any child care center is subsequently established within 1,000 feet or a residential district or residential lot is subsequently established within 1,000 feet.

b. Every sexually oriented business shall be surrounded by a perimeter buffer of at least 50 feet in width with plantings, fence or other physical divider along the outside of the perimeter sufficient to impede the view of the interior of the premises in which the business is located. The municipality may, by ordinance, require the perimeter buffer to meet additional requirements or standards. This subsection shall not apply to a sexually oriented business already lawfully operating on the effective date of this act.

c. No sexually oriented business shall display more than two exterior signs, consisting of one identification sign and one sign giving notice that the premises are off limits to minors. The identification sign shall be no more than 40 square feet in size.

d. A person who violates this section is guilty of a felony of the fourth degree.

PRACTICAL APPLICATION OF STATUTE

Section 19-7 provides a number of requirements that "sexually oriented businesses" must meet. For example, subsection a. sets out that no person shall operate a "sexually oriented business" within 1,000 feet of a number of locations such as churches, schools, school bus stops, hospitals and other existing sexually oriented businesses. There are exceptions to this provision, though—for instance, if a municipal zoning ordinance provides otherwise. A violation of this subsection, or any subsection of 19-7, constitutes a fourth degree felony. "Sexually oriented business," by the way, is defined in the previous statute, 19-6.

END OF CHAPTER REVIEW

Multiple-Choice Questions

1. The clerk of a store known as The Annex sold two sexually explicit magazines to Arthur, age 17. What is the clerk guilty of?
   a. a third degree felony if he "knew" the magazines he was selling to Arthur had "obscene material" in them
   b. a third degree felony regardless if he "knew" the magazines he was selling to Arthur had "obscene material" in them
   c. a first degree felony if he was related to Arthur
   d. a and c
   e. b and c

2. The clerk in the above question would have an affirmative defense and be guilty of no offense at all if:
   a. Arthur falsely represented "in or by writing" that he was 18
   b. Arthur appeared 18 or older to an ordinary prudent person
   c. the clerk relied in good faith on Arthur's 18+ appearance and written representation, thereby actually believing he was 18 or over
   d. all of the above factors are necessary for an affirmative defense
   e. there is no affirmative defense to selling "obscene material" to a juvenile

3. Rinaldo pays Mona $50 to comb his hair and whisper sexual words to him while she combs away. The event really turned on Rinaldo. Which of the following statements is true?
   a. Mona is guilty of engaging in prostitution because she was paid to engage in a physical encounter that involved sexual dialogue for the purpose of gratifying Rinaldo.
   b. Rinaldo is guilty of engaging in prostitution because he paid Mona to engage in a physical encounter that involved sexual dialogue for the purpose of gratifying himself.
   c. Rinaldo is guilty of promoting prostitution.
   d. Neither Rinaldo nor Mona is guilty of any act of prostitution.
   e. Only a and b are true.

4. Babs owns a convenience store in Parker County. At her store she sells various magazines that contain "obscene material" (standard nudity magazines). An undercover police officer watched Babs sell one of the magazines to a 33-year-old woman. What should Babs be charged with?

   a. nothing because there are thousands of stores across the state that sell "obscene material" to adults

   b. nothing if the town has adopted a municipal ordinance to legally permit the sale of "obscene material"

   c. a fourth degree felony if the town has not adopted a municipal ordinance to legally permit the sale of "obscene material"

   d. b and c

   e. none of the above

Essay Question

1. Madame Luci owns and manages a house of prostitution. There, she knowingly promotes the prostitution of her 14-year-old daughter, Jennifer. She also knowingly promotes the prostitution of her daughter's 14-year-old friend Janice, who is not related to Madame Luci in any way. Madame Luci was presented what appeared to be a valid driver's license by Janice, indicating that she was 20 years old. By all accounts, Janice appeared 18 or older to an ordinary prudent person. In addition, Madame Luci knowingly promotes the prostitution of 48 women who are over the age of 18; all of the females consent to their acts of prostitution. Is Madame Luci guilty of promoting prostitution for Jennifer? Janice? The 48 adult women? If so, what degree offense has she committed in each case? Does she have any defenses (regarding age) available to her in the matters of her daughter and/or Janice? Why or why not? Cite the specific subsections of the statute relative to all parts of this question.

20

CONTROLLED DANGEROUS SUBSTANCES

FACT PATTERN (PERTAINING TO CHAPTERS 20 AND 21)

Hawthorne was the site of the year's largest drug bust. The event was sparked by an unlikely perceptive operative, the borough's mayor, Frank Castelleti. The ultimate seizure, however, was the result of careful planning and brave, raw police work carried out by Hawthorne's finest. The department's chief, Seamus Mallorin, orchestrated the monumental law enforcement maneuver with the head of his detective bureau, Captain Ryan O'Dashing.

Mayor Castelleti and his wife, Betty, finished an early supper at one of Hawthorne's quaint Italian eateries, Lancellotti's. As he prepared to pay the $100 bill plus his usual 25% gratuity, Castelleti overheard two out-of-towners discussing an unusual topic—a drug deal. The first man, who stood approximately six feet tall and sported a red beard, advised the other, "Step out to my pickup, and I'll drop you the eight-ball." The second man responded with, "How about a bunch of eight-balls." The red-bearded fellow nodded and said, "Fine."

Castelleti, understanding some drug lingo, knew that the red-bearded gentleman was referring to cocaine. Annoyed with this illegal intrusion in Hawthorne, Castelleti immediately phoned the borough's police department and spoke directly to Captain O'Dashing.

A patrol unit, followed by O'Dashing in a detective vehicle, was at Lancellotti's within minutes, where they captured the two men in the middle of their parking lot controlled dangerous substance (CDS) transfer—cash was being exchanged for several packages of cocaine. A headquarters interrogation of the red-bearded man that followed not only caused O'Dashing to call his chief in from home but resulted in the creation of "Project Red Beard."

In the meantime, Red Beard's car was towed to the Hawthorne Police Department headquarters. There, a routine inventory search of the automobile revealed the following: 29 individually wrapped packages of cocaine marked with the logo "Tuned-Up," which totaled 11 ounces in weight; 25 grams of marijuana in a plastic container; a pipe ordinarily used for smoking marijuana; a hypodermic needle; and $2,400 in cash.

Captain O'Dashing, Chief Mallorin and two Hawthorne detectives positioned themselves in chairs circling Red Beard, who was handcuffed to a pole in the center of the department's detective bureau. There, after *Miranda* warnings were read for a second time since the arrest, a flurry of questions were fired at the drug dealer. Where did he live? Where did he work? Was cocaine distribution his only business? Where did he obtain his cocaine? How about the marijuana? Who did he work with or for? How often did he deal in Hawthorne? Was this his main venue of operation, or was he just passing through?

Red Beard was initially unfazed by the officers' questions, only advising that he did not reside in Hawthorne; however, his demeanor changed when Captain O'Dashing slapped a copy of the man's state driver's license against the pole. "Where did you get that?" Red Beard demanded. "I don't carry any ID."

O'Dashing replied with a slight smile and then looked at Chief Mallorin, who unleashed a 20-page rap sheet. As the document unraveled from the top of the pole to the floor, Red Beard mumbled, "Okay, I'll talk."

Chief Mallorin responded with a third *Miranda* reading and inquired, "Are you sure you don't want an attorney present?" Red Beard looked at him and the rap sheet and answered, "Just get a prosecutor down here so we can cut a deal. I know I'm looking at a lot of time without a deal." An assistant prosecutor was then summoned from the County Prosecutor's Office. After her arrival, the cocaine dealer was promised a plea agreement that provided for a reduced prison sentence in exchange for specifics about what Red Beard termed "a monumental drug bust." And yes, a monumental drug bust it would be.

Red Beard rolled—and rolled hard—on a close friend, Charlie Chaplowitz. Ironically, although the two men were both in the business of selling drugs, they kept their business dealings separate. Red Beard, currently a resident of Halford County, was actually in Hawthorne on the day of his arrest to meet with Chaplowitz. The two had been friends since childhood and still shared each other's company to discuss their various business ventures and to play chess.

According to Red Beard, the men were quite different in their affairs and personalities. Chaplowitz was a quiet, well-dressed restaurateur who never used drugs; he also had never been arrested and was never suspected by law enforcement of any illegal activities whatsoever. Chaplowitz was a ten-year resident of Hawthorne.

Red Beard, on the other hand, was a traveler, never living in any one town for more than two years. He was a career drug dealer and hardly put up a front that he was involved in any legitimate businesses. He also regularly smoked marijuana and dabbled in other, more serious controlled dangerous substances such as heroin. That drug was one of the reasons why Red Beard liked to meet with Chaplowitz—because Chaplowitz provided him with his personal stash of heroin. Many times, though, Red Beard won his little packages of junk when he was the victor of their chess matches; Chaplowitz simply gave heroin to him. As the assistant prosecutor and the Hawthorne officers learned, Charlie Chaplowitz had plenty of heroin to spare.

Approximately one-half mile from Lancellotti's was another thriving Hawthorne restaurant, The Fire Down Under. Serving a variety of spicy entrees and unusual pasta dishes, The Fire Down Under also doubled as an upscale dance club on Friday and Saturday nights. Unusual about the restaurant was that although the building had a large lower level, it was never utilized for dining or dancing. Chaplowitz, the apparent owner of The Fire Down Under, held out that the space was reserved for "future plans." No one ever had a reason to suspect anything illicit about Chaplowitz, the restaurant or the empty space, so his assertion about "future plans" went unquestioned. Chaplowitz's plans, however, were quite current—and the space was far from empty.

Located on the lower level of The Fire Down Under was a carefully plotted and controlled heroin manufacturing and distribution hub. Ten employees, working directly under Chaplowitz's command, prepared and packaged large quantities of heroin that were disseminated to multiple street dealers across the state. Four other silent partners joined Chaplowitz as financiers of the network. The drug was never sold in small quantities, and it was never distributed in the restaurant. Buyers were strictly dealers who appeared in person at various highway locations to pick up weekly supplies of heroin. It was a cash-and-carry business.

Chief Mallorin assessed the situation with Captain O'Dashing and the assistant prosecutor. His first thought was to simply procure a search warrant based on Red Beard's information; however, O'Dashing, who had been searching tax records, advised that the restaurant and property were actually owned by a corporation whose principals did not include Chaplowitz. Without this direct ownership link to The Fire Down Under, he thought problems might arise when trying to legally tie Chaplowitz to the restaurant and its lower level.

Mallorin needed a different plan to ensure an airtight case against Chaplowitz. The chief wanted to act quickly because he feared that as more time passed, it would become more likely that Chaplowitz would learn of Red Beard's arrest. With this in mind, he arranged for Red Beard to phone Chaplowitz and advise that he was delayed in reaching Hawthorne. Mallorin then made a tactical but risky decision.

Red Beard was suited with a wire and told to meet Chaplowitz at The Fire Down Under, as they had agreed in their phone conversation. Joining Red Beard, however, would be the newest addition to Hawthorne's police department, Cole Morrison. Although a recent arrival, Morrison was a ten-year law enforcement veteran, having transferred from the Edholm County Sheriff's Department. He was a street-smart officer and personally physically equipped, as he bench-pressed well over 400 pounds. Chief Mallorin was confident in Morrison's abilities but knew that Chaplowitz would be wary of Morrison's presence.

To counteract Chaplowitz's likely suspicions, Mallorin and O'Dashing formed a simple but important plan in an attempt to make the drug kingpin comfortable with Morrison—comfortable with his company and comfortable enough to show him his heroin manufacturing center.

The story would be that Red Beard and Morrison were cousins and that Morrison was new to the state, having arrived from Canada a month prior. In Canada, Morrison dealt in heroin, although in only small amounts. Since Red Beard limited his dealing to cocaine, Morrison would be a perfect street partner for him—someone he knew and trusted, and someone who was accustomed to dealing that substance. With this plan in place, Morrison was quickly schooled in Red Beard's background—his age, his mother's and sister's names, the circumstances of his father's death, his delight in smoking marijuana, his chess abilities and his vehicle. Then the men were off to meet with Charlie Chaplowitz.

An hour later, a conversation unfolded where Morrison talked in passing about Aunt Carol and joked, much to Red Beard's chagrin, about how cousin Cindy was "hot." The authenticity of their personal bantering was an instant sale. Chaplowitz, never suspecting that Red Beard would roll on him, invited the pair down to the lower level to play chess and to inspect the operation and sample the product. Within minutes, half of the Hawthorne Police Department, accompanied by several Prosecutor's Office narcotics investigators, descended into the bowels of The Fire Down Under. There, they arrested Charlie Chaplowitz and seven of his employees and confiscated over 500 pounds of pure heroin.

A subsequent thorough search of the manufacturing center revealed that there was only one entrance/exit door to the lower level. The door was made of solid thick steel and surrounded by an intricate but cleverly hidden alarm device. The alarm, it was later learned, only notified Chaplowitz and his direct underlings if it was activated. After the steel door was a hallway, which led to a similar steel door and alarm device. This door required not only two keys for entrance but also a computerized security card. Once through this door, those entering would come into a large, dark empty room. There a flashlight was procured to lead the entering individuals to a special unmarked brick located in the center of a brick-walled fireplace. Upon pushing the brick, a secret passage opened up that led the individuals down a flight of stairs and into the manufacturing center. Law enforcement personnel were not going to find Chaplowitz's operation unless he, or someone involved with him, led them to it. Unfortunately for him, he was duped by a disloyal friend and a few crafty, gutsy police officers.

20-1.   ### Definitions

As used in this chapter:

a. "Administer" means the direct application of a controlled dangerous substance or controlled substance analog, whether by injection, inhalation, ingestion or any other means, to the body of a patient or research subject by (1) a practitioner S(or, in his presence, by his lawfully authorized agent), or (2) the patient or research subject at the lawful direction and in the presence of the practitioner.

b. "Agent" means an authorized person who acts on behalf of or at the direction of a manufacturer, distributor or dispenser but does not include a common or contract carrier, public warehouseman or employee thereof.

c. "Controlled dangerous substance" means a drug, substance or immediate precursor in Schedules I through V, any substance the distribution of which is specifically prohibited in 20-2, 20-4.1 or in 20-4.2 and any drug or substance which, when ingested, is metabolized or otherwise becomes a controlled dangerous substance in the human body. When any statute refers to controlled dangerous substances, or to a specific controlled dangerous substance, it shall also be deemed to refer to any drug or substance which, when ingested, is metabolized or otherwise becomes a controlled dangerous substance or the specific controlled dangerous substance, and to any substance that is an immediate precursor of a controlled dangerous substance or the specific controlled dangerous substance. The term shall not include distilled spirits, wine, malt beverages or tobacco and tobacco products. The term, wherever it appears in any law or administrative regulation of this State, shall include controlled substance analogs.

d. "Controlled substance analog" means a substance that has a chemical structure substantially similar to that of a controlled dangerous substance and that was specifically designed to produce an effect substantially similar to that of a controlled dangerous substance. The term shall not include a substance manufactured or distributed in conformance with the provisions of an approved new drug application or an exemption for investigational use within the meaning of section 505 of the "Federal Food, Drug and Cosmetic Act."

e. "Counterfeit substance" means a controlled dangerous substance or controlled substance analog which, or the container or labeling of which, without authorization, bears the trademark, trade name or other identifying mark, imprint, number or device, or any likeness thereof, of a manufacturer, distributor or dispenser other than the person or persons who in fact manufactured, distributed or dispensed such substance and which thereby falsely purports or is represented to be the product of, or to have been distributed by, such other manufacturer, distributor or dispenser.

f. "Deliver" or "delivery" means the actual, constructive or attempted transfer from one person to another of a controlled dangerous substance or controlled substance analog, whether or not there is an agency relationship.

g. "Dispense" means to deliver a controlled dangerous substance or controlled substance analog to an ultimate user or research subject by or pursuant to the lawful order of a practitioner, including the prescribing, administering, packaging, labeling or compounding necessary to prepare the substance for that delivery. "Dispenser" means a practitioner who dispenses.

h. "Distribute" means to deliver other than by administering or dispensing a controlled dangerous substance or controlled substance analog. "Distributor" means a person who distributes.

i. "Drugs" means (a) substances recognized in the official United States Pharmacopoeia, official Homeopathic Pharmacopoeia of the United States or official National Formulary, or any supplement to any of them; and (b) substances intended for use in the diagnosis, cure, mitigation, treatment or prevention of disease in man or other animals; and (c) substances (other than food) intended to affect the structure or any function of the body of man or other animals; and (d) substances intended for use as a component of any article specified in subsections (a), (b) and (c) of this section but does not include devices or their components, parts or accessories.

j. "Drug or alcohol dependent person" means a person who, as a result of using a controlled dangerous substance or controlled substance analog or alcohol, has been in a state of psychic or physical dependence, or both, arising from the use of that controlled dangerous substance or controlled substance analog or alcohol on a continuous or repetitive basis. Drug or alcohol dependence is characterized by behavioral and other responses, including but not limited to a strong compulsion to take the substance on a recurring basis in order to experience its psychic effects or to avoid the discomfort of its absence.

k. "Hashish" means the resin extracted from any part of the plant Genus *Cannabis L.* and any compound, manufacture, salt, derivative, mixture or preparation of such resin.

l. "Manufacture" means the production, preparation, propagation, compounding, conversion or processing of a controlled dangerous substance or controlled substance analog, either directly or by extraction from substances of natural origin, or independently by means of chemical synthesis or by a combination of extraction and chemical synthesis, and includes any packaging or repackaging of the substance or labeling or relabeling of its container, except that this term does not include the preparation or compounding of a controlled dangerous substance or controlled substance analog by an individual for his own use or the preparation, compounding, packaging or labeling of a controlled dangerous substance (1) by a practitioner as an incident to his administering or dispensing of a controlled dangerous substance or controlled substance analog in the course of his professional practice, or (2) by a practitioner (or someone under his supervision) for the purpose of, or as an incident to, research, teaching or chemical analysis and not for sale.

m. "Marijuana" means all parts of the plant Genus *Cannabis L.,* whether growing or not, the seeds thereof and every compound, manufacture, salt, derivative, mixture or preparation of such plant or its seeds, except those containing resin extracted from such plant, but shall not include the mature stalks of such plant, fiber produced from such stalks, oil or cake made from the seeds of such plant or any other compound, manufacture, salt, derivative, mixture or preparation of such mature stalks, fiber, oil or cake or the sterilized seed of such plant which is incapable of germination.

n. "Narcotic drug" means any of the following, whether produced directly or indirectly by extraction from substances of vegetable origin, or independently by means of chemical synthesis or by a combination of extraction and chemical synthesis:

   (1) Opium, coca leaves and opiates;

   (2) A compound, manufacture, salt, derivative or preparation of opium, coca leaves or opiates;

   (3) A substance (and any compound, manufacture, salt, derivative or preparation thereof) which is chemically identical with any of the substances referred to in subsections (a) and (b), except that the words "narcotic drug" as used in this act shall not include decocainized coca leaves or extracts of coca leaves, which extracts do not contain cocaine or ecogine.

o. "Opiate" means any dangerous substance having an addiction-forming or addiction-sustaining liability similar to morphine or being capable of conversion into a drug having such addiction-forming or addiction-sustaining liability. It does not include, unless specifically designated as controlled, the dextrorotatory isomer of 3-methoxy-n-methylmorphinan and its salts (dextromethorphan). It does include its racemic and levorotatory forms.

p. "Opium poppy" means the plant of the species *Papaver somniferum L.,* except the seeds thereof.

q. "Person" means any corporation, association, partnership, trust, other institution or entity or one or more individuals.

r. "Plant" means an organism having leaves and a readily observable root formation, including, but not limited to, a cutting having roots, a root-ball or root hairs.

s. "Poppy straw" means all parts, except the seeds, of the opium poppy, after mowing.

t. "Practitioner" means a physician, dentist, veterinarian, scientific investigator, laboratory, pharmacy, hospital or other person licensed, registered or otherwise permitted to distribute, dispense, conduct research with respect to or administer a controlled dangerous substance or controlled substance analog in the course of professional practice or research in this State:

   (1) "Physician" means a physician authorized by law to practice medicine in this or any other state and any other person authorized by law to treat sick and injured human beings in this or any other state.

   (2) "Veterinarian" means a veterinarian authorized by law to practice veterinary medicine in this State.

   (3) "Dentist" means a dentist authorized by law to practice dentistry in this State.

   (4) "Hospital" means any federal institution, or any institution for the care and treatment of the sick and injured, operated or approved by the appropriate State department as proper to be entrusted with the custody and professional use of controlled dangerous substances or controlled substance analogs.

   (5) "Laboratory" means a laboratory to be entrusted with the custody of narcotic drugs and the use of controlled dangerous substances or controlled substance analogs for scientific, experimental and medical purposes and for purposes of instruction approved by the State Department of Health and Senior Services.

u. "Production" includes the manufacture, planting, cultivation, growing or harvesting of a controlled dangerous substance or controlled substance analog.

v. "Immediate precursor" means a substance which the State Department of Health and Senior Services has found to be and by regulation designates as being the principal compound commonly used or produced primarily for use and which is an immediate chemical intermediary used or likely to be used in the manufacture of a controlled dangerous substance or controlled substance analog, the control of which is necessary to prevent, curtail or limit such manufacture.

w. "Residential treatment facility" means any facility licensed and approved by the Department of Health and Senior Services and which is approved by any county probation department for the inpatient treatment and rehabilitation of drug or alcohol dependent persons.

x. "Schedules I, II, III, IV and V" are the schedules set forth in sections 5 through 8 of "The Comprehensive Controlled Dangerous Substance Prohibition Act" and as modified by any regulations issued by the Commissioner of Health and Senior Services.

y. "State" means this State.

z. "Ultimate user" means a person who lawfully possesses a controlled dangerous substance or controlled substance analog for his own use or for the use of a member of his household or for administration to an animal owned by him or by a member of his household.

aa. "Prescription legend drug" means any drug which under federal or State law requires dispensing by prescription or order of a licensed physician, veterinarian or dentist and is required to bear the statement "Rx only" or similar wording indicating that such drug may be sold or dispensed only upon the prescription of a licensed medical practitioner and is not a controlled dangerous substance or stramonium preparation.

bb. "Stramonium preparation" means a substance prepared from any part of the stramonium plant in the form of a powder, pipe mixture, cigarette or any other form with or without other ingredients.

cc. "Stramonium plant" means the plant *Datura Stramonium Linne,* including *Datura Tatula Linne.*

20-2.   Leader of narcotics trafficking network

As used in this section:

"Financier" means a person who, with the intent to derive a profit, provides money or credit or other thing of value in order to purchase a controlled dangerous substance or an immediate precursor or otherwise to finance the operations of a drug trafficking network.

A person is a leader of a narcotics trafficking network if he conspires with two or more other persons in a scheme or course of conduct to unlawfully manufacture, distribute, dispense, bring into or transport in this State methamphetamine, lysergic acid diethylamide, phencyclidine, gamma hydroxybutyrate, flunitrazepam or any controlled dangerous substance classified in Schedule I or II or any controlled substance analog thereof as a financier or as an organizer, supervisor or manager of at least one other person.

Leader of narcotics trafficking network is a felony of the first degree and upon conviction thereof, except as may be provided by 20-12, a person shall be sentenced to an ordinary term of life imprisonment during which the person must serve 25 years before being eligible for parole. The court may also impose a fine not to exceed $750,000 or five times the street value of the controlled dangerous substance, controlled substance analog, gamma hydroxybutyrate or flunitrazepam involved, whichever is greater.

It shall not be necessary in any prosecution under this section for the prosecution to prove that any intended profit was actually realized. The trier of fact may infer that a particular scheme or course of conduct was undertaken for profit from all of the attendant circumstances, including but not limited to the number of persons involved in the scheme or course of conduct, the actor's net worth and his expenditures in relation to his legitimate sources of income, the amount or purity of the specified controlled dangerous substance, controlled substance analog, gamma hydroxybutyrate or flunitrazepam involved or the amount of cash or currency involved.

It shall not be a defense to a prosecution under this section that such controlled dangerous substance, controlled substance analog, gamma hydroxybutyrate or flunitrazepam was brought into or transported in this State solely for ultimate distribution or dispensing in another jurisdiction; nor shall it be a defense that any profit was intended to be made in another jurisdiction.

It shall not be a defense that the defendant was subject to the supervision or management of another, nor that another person or persons were also leaders of the narcotics trafficking network.

PRACTICAL APPLICATION OF STATUTE

Charlie Chaplowitz should be prosecuted as a leader of a narcotics trafficking network for his operation headquartered at The Fire Down Under restaurant in Hawthorne. This is a felony of the first degree as stated in section 20-2.

A person is a leader of a narcotics trafficking network if two elements are met: (1) He conspires with two or more other persons in a scheme or course of conduct to unlawfully manufacture, distribute, dispense or bring into the state one of a number of drugs; and (2) he has some sort of leadership position in the conspiracy, such as a financier or manager of at least one other person. A person can only be charged under this statute if he is the leader of a drug-dealing scheme that involves methamphetamine (speed), lysergic acid diethylamide (LSD), phencyclidine (PCP), gamma hydroxybutyrate (GHB), flunitrazepam (roofies) or any controlled dangerous substance classified in Schedule I or II. In other words, while the manufacture/distribution of a multitude of substances can result in a charge under 20-4, there are several others (specifically, those classified in Schedules III, IV and V) that do not warrant a charge. Please note here that a detailed discussion of the different substances found in Schedules I, II, III, IV and V will be provided in the Practical Application section for 20-4.

Charlie Chaplowitz ran The Fire Down Under restaurant in Hawthorne. However, while his patrons were dining and dancing in the upper level of the establishment, Chaplowitz was cooking up and packaging hundreds of pounds of heroin in the restaurant's lower level. Pursuant to a plan devised by Hawthorne top police brass—Chief Seamus Mallorin and Detective Captain Ryan O'Dashing—an undercover officer, aided by an informant, infiltrated the facility. Chaplowitz and several coconspirators were then quickly arrested; coinciding with the arrests was the seizure of over 500 pounds of heroin.

Hawthorne police uncovered a massive drug-dealing scheme that stretched across the entire Garden State. Charlie Chaplowitz, an unassuming restaurateur, headed a carefully plotted and controlled heroin manufacturing and distribution hub. Ten employees, working directly under Chaplowitz's command, prepared and packaged large quantities of heroin that were disseminated to multiple street dealers across the state. The network was financed by Chaplowitz and four other silent partners.

Here, Chaplowitz should be charged as a leader of a narcotics trafficking network as all the elements of the offense have been met. First, Chaplowitz conspired with several individuals to manufacture and distribute heroin, a controlled dangerous substance classified in Schedule I. His coconspirators included four silent partners who financed the scheme with him and the several employees who worked under his command. Chaplowitz's managerial role in the business and his position as a financier ensure that the offense's second element has been met. Accordingly, Chaplowitz should be charged as the leader of a narcotics trafficking network.

No Defense That Under Management of Another or That Another Is Charged with the Offense

It is important to note that other members of Chaplowitz's narcotics trafficking scheme could also be charged under 20-2. The statute provides that it shall not be a defense that a defendant was subject to the management of another or that "another person or persons were also leaders of the narcotics trafficking network." In other words, if all the elements of the offense are met—the conspiracy, the financier/management component and the right kind of drugs—then a number of individuals could conceivably be charged as a leader of one particular narcotics trafficking network. In Chaplowitz's case, it is very likely that his silent partners, as well as some of the employees who worked under him, would face this charge.

20-3.   **Maintaining or operating a controlled dangerous substance facility**

Any person who knowingly maintains or operates any premises, place or facility used for the manufacture of methamphetamine, lysergic acid diethylamide, phencyclidine, gamma hydroxybutyrate, flunitrazepam, marijuana in an amount greater than five pounds or ten plants or any substance listed in Schedule I or II, or the analog of any such substance, or any person who knowingly aids, promotes, finances or otherwise participates in the maintenance or operations of such premises, place or facility, is guilty of a felony of the first degree and shall, except as provided in 20-12, be sentenced to a term of imprisonment which shall include the imposition of a minimum term which shall be fixed at, or between, one-third and one-half of the sentence imposed, during which the defendant shall be ineligible for parole. The court may also impose a fine not to exceed $750,000 or five times the street value of all controlled dangerous substances, controlled substance analogs, gamma hydroxybutyrate or flunitrazepam at any time manufactured or stored at such premises, place or facility, whichever is greater.

PRACTICAL APPLICATION OF STATUTE

Maintaining or operating a controlled dangerous substance production facility is a felony of the first degree. Charlie Chaplowitz is guilty of this offense.

Anyone who maintains/operates—or who aids, promotes or finances—a facility used for the manufacture of serious controlled dangerous substances such as heroin, LSD, GHB and methamphetamine is guilty of violating section 20-3. Other drugs that can give rise to a charge under this statute are PCP, flunitrazepam, marijuana (where the amount involved is greater than five pounds or ten plants) and any substance listed in Schedule I or II.

Charlie Chaplowitz is guilty of violating 20-3 as he maintained and operated a facility that manufactured the Schedule I substance heroin. This facility, located on the lower level of his restaurant, The Fire Down Under, served as a major manufacturing and distribution center for this illegal drug; at the time it was infiltrated by police, in fact, 500 pounds of the substance were confiscated. Since Chaplowitz was the mastermind behind this huge drug-dealing operation who actively maintained and operated the facility at The Fire Down Under, he is guilty of violating 20-3.

20-3.1.   **Booby traps in manufacturing or distribution facilities: fortified premises**

a. As used in this section:

(1) "Booby trap" means any concealed or camouflaged device designed or reasonably likely to cause bodily injury when triggered by the action of a person entering a property or building or any portion thereof, or moving on the property or in the building, or by the action of another person. The term includes, but is not limited to, firearms, ammunition or destructive devices activated by a trip wire or other triggering mechanism, sharpened stakes, traps and lines or wires with hooks, weights or other objects attached.

(2) "Structure" means any building, room, ship, vessel or airplane and also means any place adapted for overnight accommodation of persons, or for carrying on business therein, whether or not the person is actually present.

b. Any person who knowingly assembles, maintains, places or causes to be placed a booby trap on property used for the manufacture, distribution, dispensing or possession or control with intent to manufacture, distribute or dispense controlled dangerous substances in violation of this chapter shall be guilty of a felony of the second degree. If the booby trap causes bodily injury to any person, the defendant shall be guilty of a felony of the first degree.

It shall not be a defense that the device was inoperable or was not actually triggered or that its existence or location was known to a law enforcement officer or another person.

c. Any person who fortifies or maintains in a fortified condition a structure for the manufacture, distribution, dispensing or possession or control with intent to manufacture, distribute or dispense controlled dangerous substances, or who violates section 3, 4, 5, 6 or 7 of chapter 20 in a structure which he owns, leases, occupies or controls and which has been fortified, is guilty of a felony of the third degree. A structure has been fortified if steel doors, wooden planking, cross bars, alarm systems, dogs, lookouts or any other means are employed to prevent, impede, delay or provide warning of the entry into a structure or any part of a structure by law enforcement officers.

d. A booby trap or fortification is maintained if it remains on property or in a structure while the property or structure is owned, occupied, controlled or used by the defendant.

Practical Application of Statute

Booby Traps

If Charlie Chaplowitz had set up booby traps in his heroin manufacturing facility, he would have been guilty of a second degree felony. Booby traps are basically any "concealed or camouflaged" devices that are erected in an effort to cause bodily injury to any unwanted persons who enter a drug manufacturing house. Chaplowitz, however, did not utilize booby traps at his facility at The Fire Down Under, but he did fortify the structure.

Fortified Premises

One who "fortifies" a drug manufacturing facility is guilty of a third degree felony. A structure is considered to be fortified if items such as steel doors, wooden planking or alarm systems are put in place in order to prevent, impede or provide warning of the entrance by law enforcement officers into the facility. The use of dogs or lookouts is also prohibited under the statute.

Charlie Chaplowitz maintained a massive heroin manufacturing center in the lower level of his restaurant, The Fire Down Under. In an effort to prevent law enforcement officers (or any other uninvited guests) from entering the facility, Chaplowitz fortified the premises with two solid, thick steel doors, a computerized security card system and a hidden alarm system. But his preventive measures didn't end there—after clearing the steel doors and security card and alarm systems, those entering had to find a special unmarked brick located in the center of a brick-walled fireplace. Upon pushing the brick, a secret passage opened up that led the individuals down a flight of stairs and into the manufacturing center. This intricate fortification of his facility renders Chaplowitz guilty of a third degree felony.

20-4.   **Manufacturing, distributing or dispensing**

    a. It shall be unlawful for any person knowingly or purposely:

        (1) To manufacture, distribute or dispense, or to possess, or have under his control with intent to manufacture, distribute or dispense, a controlled dangerous substance or controlled substance analog; or

        (2) To create, distribute or possess, or have under his control with intent to distribute, a counterfeit controlled dangerous substance.

    b. Any person who violates subsection a. with respect to:

        (1) Heroin, or its analog, or coca leaves and any salt, compound, derivative or preparation of coca leaves, and any salt, compound, derivative or preparation thereof which is chemically equivalent or identical with any of these substances, or analogs, except that the substances shall not include decocainized coca leaves or extractions which do not contain cocaine or ecogine, or or 3,4-methylenedioxymethamphetamine or 3,4-methylenedioxyamphetamine, in a quantity of five ounces or more, including any adulterants or dilutants, is guilty of a felony of the first degree. The defendant shall, except as provided in 20-12, be sentenced to a term of imprisonment by the court. The term of imprisonment shall include the imposition of a minimum term which shall be fixed at, or between, one-third and one-half of the sentence imposed, during which the defendant shall be ineligible for parole. A fine of up to $500,000 may be imposed;

        (2) A substance referred to in paragraph (1) of this subsection, in a quantity of one-half ounce or more but less than five ounces, including any adulterants or dilutants, is guilty of a felony of the second degree;

        (3) A substance referred to paragraph (1) of this subsection in a quantity less than one-half ounce, including any adulterants or dilutants, is guilty of a felony of the third degree except that a fine of up to $75,000 may be imposed;

        (4) A substance classified as a narcotic drug in Schedule I or II other than those specifically covered in this section, or the analog of any such substance, in a quantity of one ounce or more, including any adulterants or dilutants, is guilty of a felony of the second degree;

(5) A substance classified as a narcotic drug in Schedule I or II other than those specifically covered in this section, or the analog of any such substance, in a quantity of less than one ounce, including any adulterants or dilutants, is guilty of a felony of the third degree except that a fine of up to $75,000 may be imposed;

(6) Lysergic acid diethylamide, or its analog, in a quantity of 100 milligrams or more, including any adulterants or dilutants, or phencyclidine, or its analog, in a quantity of ten grams or more, including any adulterants or dilutants, is guilty of a felony of the first degree. Except as provided in 20-12, the court shall impose a term of imprisonment which shall include the imposition of a minimum term, fixed at, or between, one-third and one-half of the sentence imposed by the court, during which the defendant shall be ineligible for parole. A fine of up to $500,000 may be imposed;

(7) Lysergic acid diethylamide, or its analog, in a quantity of less than 100 milligrams, including any adulterants or dilutants, or where the amount is undetermined, or phencyclidine, or its analog, in a quantity of less than ten grams, including any adulterants or dilutants, or where the amount is undetermined is guilty of a felony of the second degree;

(8) Methamphetamine, or its analog, or phenyl-2-propanone (P2P), in a quantity of five ounces or more, including any adulterants or dilutants, is guilty of a felony of the first degree. A fine of up to $300,000 may be imposed;

(9) (a) Methamphetamine, or its analog, or phenyl-2-propanone (P2P), in a quantity of one-half ounce or more but less than five ounces, including any adulterants or dilutants, is guilty of a felony of the second degree;

(b) Methamphetamine, or its analog, or phenyl-2-propanone (P2P), in a quantity of less than one-half ounce, including any adulterants or dilutants, is guilty of a felony of the third degree. A fine of up to $75,000 may be imposed.

(10) (a) Marijuana in a quantity of 25 pounds or more, including any adulterants or dilutants, or 50 or more marijuana plants, regardless of weight, or hashish in a quantity of five pounds or more, including any adulterants or dilutants, is guilty of a felony of the first degree. A fine of up to $300,000 may be imposed;

(b) Marijuana in a quantity of five pounds or more but less than 25 pounds, including any adulterants or dilutants, or ten or more but fewer than 50 marijuana plants, regardless of weight, or hashish in a quantity of one pound or more but less than five pounds, including any adulterants and dilutants, is guilty of a felony of the second degree.

(11) Marijuana in a quantity of one ounce or more but less than five pounds, including any adulterants or dilutants, or hashish in a quantity of five grams or more but less than one pound, including any adulterants or dilutants, is guilty of a felony of the third degree. A fine of up to $25,000 may be imposed;

(12) Marijuana in a quantity of less than one ounce, including any adulterants or dilutants, or hashish in a quantity of less than five grams, including any adulterants or dilutants, is guilty of a felony of the fourth degree;

(13) Any other controlled dangerous substance classified in Schedule I, II, III or IV, or its analog, is guilty of a felony of the third degree. A fine of up to $25,000 may be imposed; or

(14) Any Schedule V substance, or its analog, is guilty of a felony of the fourth degree. A fine of up to $25,000 may be imposed.

c. Where the degree of the offense for violation of this section depends on the quantity of the substance, the quantity involved shall be determined by the trier of fact. Where the indictment or accusation so provides, the quantity involved in individual acts of manufacturing, distribution, dispensing or possessing with intent to distribute may be aggregated in determining the grade of the offense, whether distribution or dispensing is to the same person or several persons, provided that each individual act of manufacturing, distribution, dispensing or possession with intent to distribute was committed within the applicable statute of limitations.

PRACTICAL APPLICATION OF STATUTE

Schedule I, II, III, IV and V Substances—Unlawful Distribution Prohibited

Section 20-4 is the statute that prohibits the unlawful manufacturing, distributing and dispensing of all substances (or their analogs) classified in Schedules I, II, III, IV and V. The only exceptions for the manufacturing, dispensing or distributing of these substances (e.g., by medical doctors) are found in "The Comprehensive Controlled Dangerous Substance Prohibition Act." Please note that one who "intends" to manufacture, distribute or dispense any of these substances is equally culpable under 20-4.

But what exactly are Schedule I, II, III, IV and V substances? Pursuant to the definitions found in 20-1, the schedules are set forth in sections 5 through 8 of "The Comprehensive Controlled Dangerous Substance Prohibition Act." Okay, now what are these substances?!

A Schedule I substance is a substance that "(1) has high potential for abuse; and (2) has no accepted medical use in treatment in the United States or lacks accepted safety for use in treatment under medical supervision." They include opiates, narcotics and hallucinogenic substances. Examples of Schedule I opiates are acetylmethadol, betameprodine, ketobemidone and trimeperidine. Heroin, morphine methylbromide and codeine-n-oxide are some of the narcotics found in Schedule I. Hallucinogens listed in this schedule include LSD, mescaline and peyote.

A Schedule II substance is defined as a substance that "(1) has high abuse potential; (2) has currently accepted medical use in treatment in the United States or currently accepted medical use with severe restrictions; and (3) abuse may lead to severe psychological or physical dependence." Schedule II substances include cocaine, anileridine and piminodine.

A Schedule III substance is one that "(1) has a potential for abuse less than the substances listed in Schedules I and II; (2) has currently accepted medical use in treatment in the United States; and (3) abuse may lead to moderate or low physical dependence or high psychological dependence." Examples of Schedule III substances are amphetamine, chlorhexadol and sulfunethylmethone.

A substance is classified in Schedule IV if it "(1) has low potential for abuse relative to the substances listed in Schedule III; (2) has currently accepted medical use in treatment in the United States; and (3) may lead to limited physical dependence or psychological dependence relative to the substances listed in Schedule III." Schedule IV substances include barbitol, chloral betaine and methohexitol.

Finally, a Schedule V substance is defined as a substance that "(1) has low potential for abuse relative to the substances listed in Schedule IV; (2) has currently accepted medical use treatment in the United States; and (3) has limited physical dependence or psychological dependence liability relative to substances listed in Schedule IV."

Schedule V substances are primarily compounds or mixtures that contain limited quantities of narcotic drugs within them, but these mixtures contain "one or more non-narcotic active medicinal ingredients in sufficient proportion to confer upon the mixture valuable medicinal qualities other than those possessed by the narcotic drug alone." An example of a Schedule V substance is one that contains "not more than 200 milligrams of codeine or any of its salts per 100 milliliters or per 100 grams."

Specific Drugs Itemized; Quantity of CDS Determines Degree of Offense in Many Categories

While section 20-4 prohibits the manufacturing, distributing and dispensing of all substances classified in Schedules I, II, III, IV and V, it sets forth specific subsections for heroin, cocaine, LSD, marijuana, hashish and methamphetamine.

These subsections generally define the degree of the offense based on the *quantity* of the substance involved. For example, 20-4b.(10)(a) provides that a person who distributes marijuana in a "quantity of 25 pounds or more" is guilty of a first degree felony; 20-4b.(10)(b), on the other hand, provides that a second degree felony has been committed where a person distributes marijuana in a quantity of "five pounds or more but less than 25 pounds."

It is interesting to note that the weight of all substances discussed in 20-4 includes "any adulterants or dilutants." However, at the end of the day, as subsection c. of the statute states, the ultimate quantity involved "shall be determined by the trier of fact." This means the jury or judge.

Heroin and Cocaine Distribution

Red Beard should be charged with a first degree felony for possession of cocaine with the intent to distribute it. Likewise, Charlie Chaplowitz should be charged with a first degree CDS distribution offense arising out of his intent to sell heroin. In both cases, these men face the most serious degree offense—one of the first degree—based on the quantity of drugs that they had in their control and possession.

Per 20-4b.(1), the distribution of heroin in a quantity of five ounces or more is a first degree felony; the distribution of powder or crack cocaine (products of coca leaves) in a quantity of five ounces or more is also a first degree felony. If the weight of the heroin/cocaine distributed is more than one-half ounce but less than five ounces, the appropriate charge is a second degree felony (see b.(2)). Where the amount involved is less than one-half ounce, a third degree felony has been committed (see b.(3)). Please remember that one can be convicted of all of the above (or for violating any of the subsections found in 20-4) for manufacturing, distributing, dispensing or *possessing with intent* to manufacture, distribute or dispense these prohibited drugs. To make things simple, these various activities will be collectively referred to as "distributing" in this Practical Application section.

Mayor Frank Castelleti overheard Red Beard engaging in conversation about a pending cocaine drug deal. In an effort to thwart it, he contacted the Hawthorne Police Department, which immediately responded to the scene. There, Red Beard was captured in the process of effecting a cocaine sale. He was arrested with various drugs in his possession, including 11 ounces of cocaine which had been divided into 29 individually wrapped packages marked with the logo "Tuned-Up."

Clearly, Red Beard was in the business of selling cocaine—the 29 individual packages were not for his personal use; additionally, he was caught in a transaction, actually distributing the illicit substance for a cash payment. The facts accordingly merit a drug distribution charge rather than simple possession. Given that the ultimate weight of the cocaine confiscated was 11 ounces, exceeding the five-ounce minimum necessary for a first degree charge, Red Beard is guilty of a first degree cocaine distribution offense.

Charlie Chaplowitz, the drug kingpin handed to Hawthorne Police by Red Beard, similarly is guilty of a first degree drug distribution offense. Simply stated, Chaplowitz was caught at his CDS manufacturing warehouse with over 500 pounds of heroin, all of which was being prepared and packaged for the purpose of being distributed to buyers. Therefore, Chaplowitz is guilty of first degree heroin distribution.

Distribution of LSD and PCP

Had Red Beard been caught distributing lysergic acid diethylamide, commonly known as "LSD," in an amount of 100 milligrams or more, he would be guilty of a first degree felony pursuant to 20-4b.(6). This same subsection similarly makes it a first degree felony to distribute "ten grams or more" of phencyclidine, which is better known as "PCP" or "angel dust."

Per subsection b.(7), if a person distributes LSD in a quantity of less than 100 milligrams—or where the amount is undetermined—he is guilty of a second degree felony. Likewise, where a person distributes PCP in a quantity of less than ten grams, or where it is undetermined, he is guilty of a second degree offense.

Marijuana Distribution

Marijuana distribution offenses are graded according to pounds and ounces—and sometimes the number of plants involved. Under 20-4b.(10)(a), where an individual distributes marijuana in a "quantity of 25 pounds or more," he is guilty of a first degree felony. He is also guilty of a first degree felony if he is busted with 50 or more marijuana plants, possessed for the purpose of distribution; here, weight is not a factor.

Per subsection b.(10)(b), the distributor is guilty of a second degree felony where the quantity of marijuana is "five pounds or more but less than 25 pounds." A second degree felony has also been committed if he is caught with between ten and 50 marijuana plants, possessed for the purpose of distribution—again, weight is not a factor.

Per subsection b.(11), a person is guilty of a third degree felony if he distributes marijuana in a "quantity of one ounce or more but less than five pounds." Finally, under subsection b.(12), he is guilty of a fourth degree felony where he distributes less than one ounce of marijuana.

Hashish, Speed, Ecstasy and Other CDS Distribution

The terms defining the gradation of hashish distribution offenses are found in the same subsections for marijuana distribution—subsections b.(1) through b.(12). Methamphetamine, commonly known as "speed," and P2P distribution offenses are set forth in b.(8) and b.(9). Included within the heroin and cocaine subsections (b.(1) through b.(3)) are the provisions outlawing distribution of 3,4-methylenedioxymethamphetamine and 3,4-methylenedioxyamphetamine, best known as "ecstasy."

Subsections b.(4) and b.(5) provide the different gradations of offenses for distributing any narcotic drug in Schedule I or II "other than those specifically covered" in 20-4. Subsection b.(13) sets forth that distribution of "any other controlled dangerous substance classified in Schedule I, II, III or IV" is a third degree offense—this means any CDS in those schedules other than those specifically itemized in the previous subsections. And finally, b.(14) provides that distributing "any Schedule V substance" will result in conviction of a fourth degree felony.

Distribution of Counterfeit Controlled Dangerous Substances

Pursuant to 20-4a.(2), it is equally illegal to distribute a "counterfeit" version of all the controlled dangerous substances referred to in the statute. A counterfeit controlled dangerous substance is basically CDS that is distributed via false representation that it is legal. For example, a dealer may package a drug, without authorization, in a container that bears a legitimate manufacturer's trademark or trade name, thereby purporting the substance to be distributed by that legitimate company. This, however, is illegal drug distribution to the same extent as any other drug distribution that is prohibited by 20-4.

20-4.1.   ### Manufacturing, etc. gamma hydroxybutyrate; penalties

a. It shall be a felony of the second degree for any person knowingly or purposely to manufacture, distribute or dispense, or to possess or have under his control with intent to manufacture, distribute or dispense, gamma hydroxybutyrate.

b. A fine of up to $150,000 may be imposed upon a person who violates this section.

PRACTICAL APPLICATION OF STATUTE

It is a felony of the second degree for any individual to manufacture, distribute or possess with the intent to distribute gamma hydroxybutyrate, commonly known as GHB. The statute apparently does not differentiate among quantities of GHB. Accordingly, had Red Beard attempted to sell packages of GHB rather than cocaine, he would be guilty of a second degree felony—regardless of the amount of GHB that he was intending to distribute.

20-4.2.   ### Manufacturing, etc., flunitrazepam; penalties

a. It is unlawful for any person knowingly or purposely to manufacture, distribute or dispense, or to possess or have under his control with intent to manufacture, distribute or dispense, flunitrazepam.

b. A person who violates subsection a. of this section with respect to flunitrazepam in a quantity of one gram or more is guilty of a felony of the first degree and a fine of up to $250,000 may be imposed upon the person.

c. A person who violates subsection a. of this section with respect to flunitrazepam in a quantity of less than one gram is guilty of a felony of the second degree and a fine of up to $150,000 may be imposed upon the person.

PRACTICAL APPLICATION OF STATUTE

Flunitrazepam is known on the streets as "roofies." Per subsection b. of the statute, anyone who distributes this drug in a "quantity of one gram or more" is guilty of a first degree felony. Under subsection c., a person has committed a felony of the second degree if he distributes "less than one gram" of this substance.

20-5. **Employing a juvenile in a drug distribution scheme**

Any person being at least 18 years of age who knowingly uses, solicits, directs, hires or employs a person 17 years of age or younger to violate 20-3 or subsection a. of 20-4 is guilty of a felony of the second degree and shall, except as provided in 20-12, be sentenced to a term of imprisonment which shall include the imposition of a minimum term which shall be fixed at, or between, one-third and one-half of the sentence imposed, or five years, whichever is greater, during which the defendant shall be ineligible for parole. The court may also impose a fine not to exceed $500,000 or five times the street value of the controlled dangerous substance or controlled substance analog involved, whichever is greater.

It shall be no defense to a prosecution under this section that the actor mistakenly believed that the person which the actor used, solicited, directed, hired or employed was 18 years of age or older, even if such mistaken belief was reasonable.

Nothing in this section shall be construed to preclude or limit a prosecution or conviction for a violation of any offense defined in this chapter or any other provision of law governing an actor's liability for the conduct of another, and a conviction arising under this section shall not merge with a conviction for a violation of 20-2 (leader of narcotics trafficking network), 20-3 (maintaining or operating a CDS production facility), 20-4 (manufacturing, distributing or dispensing) or 20-7 (strict liability for drug induced death).

Practical Application of Statute

If any one of Charlie Chaplowitz's employees at his heroin manufacturing center was 17 years old or younger, he would be guilty of a second degree felony under 20-5. This is basically a strict liability offense.

Section 20-5 provides that anyone at least 18 years of age who solicits or employs a juvenile (someone 17 or younger) to violate 20-3 (maintain/operate a drug manufacturing center) or 20-4 (distribute CDS) is guilty of a second degree felony. The statute also provides that it is not a defense if the defendant mistakenly believed that the individual he solicited or employed was 18 or older. Accordingly, Chaplowitz would be strictly liable for violating 20-5 if any of the individuals he employed in his drug distribution operation were under 18 years of age.

20-6. **Distribution on or within 1,000 feet of school property**

Any person who violates subsection a. of 20-4 by distributing, dispensing or possessing with intent to distribute a controlled dangerous substance or controlled substance analog while on any school property used for school purposes which is owned by or leased to any elementary or secondary school or school board, or within 1,000 feet of such school property or a school bus or while on any school bus is guilty of a felony of the third degree and shall, except as provided in 20-12, be sentenced by the court to a term of imprisonment. Where the violation involves less than one ounce of marijuana, the term of imprisonment shall include the imposition of a minimum term which shall be fixed at, or between, one-third and one-half of the sentence imposed, or one year, whichever is greater, during which the defendant shall be ineligible for parole. In all other cases, the term of imprisonment shall include the imposition of a minimum term which shall be fixed at, or between, one-third and one-half of the sentence imposed, or three years, whichever is greater, during which the defendant shall be ineligible for parole. A fine of up to $150,000 may also be imposed upon any conviction for a violation of this section.

A conviction arising under this section shall not merge with a conviction for a violation of subsection a. of 20-4 (manufacturing, distributing or dispensing) or 20-5 (employing a juvenile in a drug distribution scheme).

It shall be no defense to a prosecution for a violation of this section that the actor was unaware that the prohibited conduct took place while on or within 1,000 feet of any school property. Nor shall it be a defense to a prosecution under this section, or under any other provision of this title, that no juveniles were present on the school property at the time of the offense or that the school was not in session.

It is an affirmative defense to prosecution for a violation of this section that the prohibited conduct took place entirely within a private residence, that no person 17 years of age or younger was present in such private residence at any time during the commission of the offense and that the prohibited conduct did not involve distributing, dispensing or possessing with the intent to distribute or dispense any controlled dangerous substance or controlled substance analog for profit. The affirmative defense established in this section shall be proved by the defendant by a preponderance of the evidence. Nothing herein shall be construed to establish an affirmative defense with respect to a prosecution for an offense defined in any other section of this chapter.

In a prosecution under this section, a map produced or reproduced by any municipal or county engineer for the purpose of depicting the location and boundaries of the area on or within 1,000 feet of any property used for school purposes which is owned by or leased to any elementary or secondary school or school board, or a true copy of such a map, shall, upon proper authentication, be admissible and shall constitute *prima facie* evidence of the location and boundaries of those areas, provided that the governing body of the municipality or county has adopted a resolution or ordinance approving the map as official finding and record of the location and boundaries of the area or areas on or within 1,000 feet of the school property. Any map approved pursuant to this section may be changed from time to time by the governing body of the municipality or county. The original of every map approved or revised pursuant to this section, or a true copy thereof, shall be filed with the clerk of the municipality or county and shall be maintained as an official record of the municipality or county. Nothing in this section shall be construed to preclude the prosecution from introducing or relying upon any other evidence or testimony to establish any element of this offense, nor shall this section be construed to preclude the use or admissibility of any map or diagram other than one which has been approved by the governing body of a municipality or county, provided that the map or diagram is otherwise admissible pursuant to the Rules of Evidence of this State.

PRACTICAL APPLICATION OF STATUTE

A drug dealer who distributes a controlled dangerous substance (or its analog) or a counterfeit controlled dangerous substance within 1,000 feet of school property or a school bus is guilty of a third degree felony. School property is defined as "any school property used for school purposes which is owned by or leased to any elementary or secondary school or school board." Accordingly, this would include any public or private grammar school or high school, but not any colleges or universities.

A "1,000 feet" offense is in addition to any offense the dealer has committed under 20-4 (manufacturing, distributing or dispensing CDS). A survey of Red Beard's case can serve as an example of how this statute works.

Red Beard exited the Italian restaurant Lancellotti's with another man. They walked directly to his pickup truck where the man handed Red Beard cash in exchange for several packages of cocaine. On a tip from Hawthorne's mayor, police immediately responded to the scene, arrested Red Beard and confiscated 11 ounces of cocaine from him.

Here, Red Beard is guilty of violating 20-4 for distributing cocaine. Since the quantity of cocaine seized from him was over five ounces, he is guilty of a first degree felony under that statute. However, he may also be guilty of an additional third degree felony pursuant to the provisions of 20-6, that is, if his drug distribution was within 1,000 feet of school property or a school bus.

It should be noted that a drug dealer has no defense that he was unaware that his distribution occurred within 1,000 feet of school property or a school bus. Also, it is no defense that "no juveniles were present on the school property at the time of the offense or that the school was not in session."

20-6.1.   **Violations of 20-4, certain locations; degree of felony; terms defined**

a. Any person who violates subsection a. of 20-4 by distributing, dispensing or possessing with intent to distribute a controlled dangerous substance or controlled substance analog while in, on or within 500 feet of the real property comprising a public housing facility, a public park or a public building is guilty of a felony of the second degree, except that it is a felony of the third degree if the violation involved less than one ounce of marijuana.

b. It shall be no defense to a prosecution for violation of this section that the actor was unaware that the prohibited conduct took place while on or within 500 feet of a public housing facility, a public park or a public building.

c. A conviction arising under this section shall not merge with a conviction for a violation of subsection a. of 20-4 (manufacturing, distributing or dispensing) or 20-5 (employing a juvenile in a drug distribution scheme). Nothing in this section shall be construed to preclude or limit a prosecution or conviction for a violation of 20-6 or any other offense defined in this chapter.

d. It is an affirmative defense to prosecution for a violation of this section that the prohibited conduct did not involve distributing, dispensing or possessing with the intent to distribute or dispense any controlled dangerous substance or controlled substance analog for profit and that the prohibited conduct did not involve distribution to a person 17 years of age or younger. The affirmative defense established in this section shall be proved by the defendant by a preponderance of the evidence. Nothing herein shall be construed to establish an affirmative defense with respect to a prosecution for an offense defined in any other section of this chapter.

e. In a prosecution under this section, a map produced or reproduced by any municipal or county engineer for the purpose of depicting the location and boundaries of the area on or within 500 feet of a public housing facility which is owned by or leased to a housing authority according to the "Local Redevelopment and Housing Law," the area in or within 500 feet of a public park or the area in or within 500 feet of a public building, or a true copy of such a map, shall, upon proper authentication, be admissible and shall constitute *prima facie* evidence of the location and boundaries of those areas, provided that the governing body of the municipality or county has adopted a resolution or ordinance approving the map as official finding and record of the location and boundaries of the area or areas on or within 500 feet of a public housing facility, a public park or a public building. Any map approved pursuant to this section may be changed from time to time by the governing body of the municipality or county. The original of every map approved or revised pursuant to this section, or a true copy thereof, shall be filed with the clerk of the municipality or county and shall be maintained as an official record of the municipality or county. Nothing in this section shall be construed to preclude the prosecution from introducing or relying upon any other evidence or testimony to establish any element of this offense, nor shall this section be construed to preclude the use or admissibility of any map or diagram other than one which has been approved by the governing body of a municipality or county, provided that the map or diagram is otherwise admissible pursuant to the Rules of Evidence.

f. As used in this act:

(1) "Public housing facility" means any dwelling, complex of dwellings, accommodation, building, structure or facility and real property of any nature appurtenant thereto, and used in connection therewith, which is owned by or leased to a local housing authority in accordance with the "Local Redevelopment and Housing Law," for the purpose of providing living accommodations to persons of low income.

(2) "Public park" means a park, recreation facility or area or playground owned or controlled by a State, county or local government unit.

(3) "Public building" means any publicly owned or leased library or museum.

PRACTICAL APPLICATION OF STATUTE

Similar to the language of 20-6 (the "1,000 feet" offense), 20-6.1 provides that an additional felony has been committed when drug distribution has occurred "on or within 500 feet" of a public housing facility, public park or public building. Like the "1,000 feet" statute, there is no defense available where the actor was unaware that he was within 500 feet of these public areas. A "500 feet" offense is a felony of the second degree—except if the violation involved "less than one ounce of marijuana"; in that case, it is a third degree felony.

Accordingly, had Red Beard's cocaine distribution occurred within 500 feet of a public housing facility, a public park or a public building, he would be guilty of a second degree felony under 20-6.1. This would be in addition to his drug distribution charge under 20-4.

While the statute's definitions of "public housing facility" and "public park" are quite broad, its definition of "public building" is rather narrow. It is confined to any publicly owned or leased "library or museum." "Public housing facility" includes any property "owned or leased to a local housing authority," and "public park" means any "park, recreation facility or area or playground controlled by a state, county or local government unit."

20-7.   **Strict liability for drug-induced deaths**

a. Any person who manufactures, distributes or dispenses methamphetamine, lysergic acid diethylamide, phencyclidine or any other controlled dangerous substance classified in Schedule I or II, or any controlled substance analog thereof, in violation of subsection a. of 20-4 is strictly liable for a death which results from the injection, inhalation or ingestion of that substance and is guilty of a felony of the first degree.

b. The provisions of which governing the causal relationship between conduct and result shall not apply in a prosecution under this section. For purposes of this offense, the defendant's act of manufacturing, distributing or dispensing a substance is the cause of a death when:

(1) The injection, inhalation or ingestion of the substance is an antecedent but for which the death would not have occurred; and

(2) The death was not:

(a) Too remote in its occurrence as to have a just bearing on the defendant's liability; or

(b) Too dependent upon conduct of another person which was unrelated to the injection, inhalation or ingestion of the substance or its effect as to have a just bearing on the defendant's liability.

c. It shall not be a defense to a prosecution under this section that the decedent contributed to his own death by his purposeful, knowing, reckless or negligent injection, inhalation or ingestion of the substance or by his consenting to the administration of the substance by another.

d. Nothing in this section shall be construed to preclude or limit any prosecution for homicide. A conviction arising under this section shall not merge with a conviction for leader of narcotics trafficking network, maintaining or operating a controlled dangerous substance production facility or unlawfully manufacturing, distributing, dispensing or possessing with intent to manufacture, distribute or dispense the controlled dangerous substance or controlled substance analog which resulted in the death.

PRACTICAL APPLICATION OF STATUTE

Technically, 20-7 is not a homicide statute, although its provisions basically amount to one. The elements of this offense are rather confusing, but in sum, they primarily provide that an individual who distributes certain drugs to another is "strictly liable" for that person's death if that other person dies from using the drugs. Let's look at Red Beard's case for a detailed explanation.

Red Beard attempted to sell cocaine to another man in a restaurant parking lot in Hawthorne. His drug-dealing efforts, though, were thwarted when Hawthorne police arrested him. But what if the deal had been consummated, and the buyer went on his jolly way with the cocaine—and then snorted it all and died? Well, then Red Beard would most likely be liable for his purchaser's death under 20-7 and face a first degree felony.

Subsection a. of the statute enumerates the drugs whose distribution can give rise to a strict liability death charge. They include methamphetamine, LSD, PCP and all CDS classified in Schedules I and II. If a person manufactures one of these substances and then another injects, inhales or ingests it—and dies—that manufacturer is guilty of a first degree felony. If a person distributes one of these substances to another, who in turn takes it and dies, then that distributor is guilty of a first degree felony. If a person dispenses one of these substances to another and that other individual dies after taking it, then the one who dispensed it is guilty of a first degree felony. Please keep in mind that the manufacturer, distributor or dispenser is only liable if he performs these activities illegally, in violation of 20-4.

Subsection b. specifically sets forth that the provisions that govern the causal relationship between conduct and result "shall not apply in a prosecution under this section." The subsection then goes on to set forth exactly when a manufacturer/distributor/dispenser's actions will be considered the "cause" of someone's death. Per b.(1), a death is deemed to be caused if the person would not have died "but for" the taking of the drug. However, pursuant to b.(2), the taking of the drug will *not* be considered the cause of death if the death was "too remote" in time from the taking of the drug or if the death was "too dependent upon the conduct of another person which was unrelated" to the taking of the drug (see b.(2)(b)). So what does all this mean? Let's go back to Red Beard.

Red Beard's buyer inhales the massive quantities of cocaine dealt to him and then dies. If the man had never taken the illegal substance, he would not have died; in other words, "but for" his use of the cocaine, his death would not have occurred. Accordingly,

Red Beard's cocaine distribution is deemed to be the "cause" of the man's death under 20-7. Now, what about if he took all the cocaine and then died 18 months later? Are Red Beard's distribution activities the cause of the man's death? Not according subsection b.(2)(a) because his death would be "too remote" in its occurrence to have a just bearing on the defendant's liability. What exactly is "too remote" is a matter of law to be decided in the courts.

What about if the man snorted the cocaine and then went to a bar, got into a fistfight and was killed during the fight? Does the fact that the man inhaled Red Beard's cocaine directly before his death make Red Beard liable for his demise? No, per subsection b.(2)(b), because the man's death was "too dependent" on another's conduct (the other fighter) to have a just bearing on Red Beard's liability.

Even though the statute carves out the above-mentioned situations where a person's drug-dealing actions will not be deemed the "cause" of a user's death, in most scenarios the dealer will be held strictly liable. Accordingly, if Red Beard's purchaser inhaled the cocaine (a Schedule II substance), laid down in his bed and then died as the result of the drug's intake, Red Beard would be held strictly liable for the man's death. And Red Beard cannot escape conviction of this first degree felony even if the user is found to have contributed to his own death through his purposeful, knowing, reckless or negligent taking of the illegal drug.

20-8.   **Possession, use or being under the influence, or failure to make lawful disposition**

a. It is unlawful for any person, knowingly or purposely, to obtain or to possess, actually or constructively, a controlled dangerous substance or controlled substance analog, unless the substance was obtained directly or pursuant to a valid prescription or order form from a practitioner while acting in the course of his professional practice. Any person who violates this section with respect to:

   (1) A controlled dangerous substance, or its analog, classified in Schedule I, II, III or IV, other than those specifically covered in this section, is guilty of a felony of the third degree. A fine of up to $35,000 may be imposed;

   (2) Any controlled dangerous substance, or its analog, classified in Schedule V is guilty of a felony of the fourth degree. A fine of up to $15,000 may be imposed;

   (3) Possession of more than 50 grams of marijuana, including any adulterants or dilutants, or more than five grams of hashish is guilty of a felony of the fourth degree. A fine of up to $25,000 may be imposed; or

   (4) Possession of 50 grams or less of marijuana, including any adulterants or dilutants, or five grams or less of hashish is guilty of a misdemeanor A.

   Any person who commits any offense defined in this section while on any property used for school purposes which is owned by or leased to any elementary or secondary school or school board, or within 1,000 feet of any such school property or a school bus or while on any school bus, and who is not sentenced to a term of imprisonment shall, in addition to any other sentence which the court may impose, be required to perform not less than 100 hours of community service.

b. Any person who uses or who is under the influence of any controlled dangerous substance, or its analog, for a purpose other than the treatment of sickness or injury as lawfully prescribed or administered by a physician is guilty of a misdemeanor A.

   In a prosecution under this subsection, it shall not be necessary for the State to prove that the accused did use or was under the influence of any specific drug, but it shall be sufficient for a conviction under this subsection for the State to prove that the accused did use or was under the influence of some controlled dangerous substance, counterfeit controlled dangerous substance or controlled substance analog by proving that the accused did manifest physical and physiological symptoms or reactions caused by the use of any controlled dangerous substance or controlled substance analog.

c. Any person who knowingly obtains or possesses a controlled dangerous substance or controlled substance analog in violation of subsection a. of this section and who fails to voluntarily deliver the substance to the nearest law enforcement officer is guilty of a misdemeanor A. Nothing in this subsection shall be construed to preclude a prosecution or conviction for any other offense defined in this title or any other statute.

Practical Application of Statute

Possession of CDS

Red Beard is guilty of violating section 20-8 for possessing marijuana. Given that the quantity he was caught with was less than 50 grams, he is guilty of a misdemeanor A.

A person has not committed an offense if he possesses a controlled dangerous substance pursuant to a valid prescription from a practitioner who is acting in his professional capacity. However, generally, the possession of these substances is a third degree felony. Subsection a.(1) of the statute states that when a person possesses a "controlled dangerous substance, or its analog, classified in Schedule I, II, III or IV, other than those specifically covered in this section," he is guilty of a felony of the third degree. Subsection a.(2) through a.(4) set forth the specific cases where CDS possession is a fourth degree felony or a misdemeanor A. Per a.(2), a person is guilty of a fourth degree felony where he possesses any CDS or its analog classified in Schedule V. Similarly, under a.(3), a fourth degree felony has been committed where a person possesses "more than 50 grams of marijuana, including any adulterants or dilutants, or more than five grams of hashish." Please note, however, that an individual who possesses significant quantities of marijuana (or any CDS, for that matter) very likely will be charged under 20-4 for possessing it "with intent to distribute" rather than just for simply possessing the substance.

Subsection a.(4) lowers CDS possession to a misdemeanor A—but only in circumstances where the defendant possesses 50 grams or less of marijuana or five grams or less of hashish. Since Red Beard possessed only 25 grams of marijuana, he is guilty of a misdemeanor A.

Under the Influence of CDS

Simply stated, per 20-8b., one who "uses" or is "under the influence" of any controlled dangerous substance (or its analog) is guilty of a misdemeanor A. The only exception is if the use of the CDS was for treatment of sickness or injury as lawfully prescribed or administered by a physician.

Not so simple, though, is the statutory language of this subsection that provides that the state need not prove that a defendant was under the influence of any specific drug. Additionally, the subsection provides that a conviction can be sustained "by proving that the accused did manifest physical and psychological symptoms or reactions caused by the use of any controlled dangerous substance." What does this mean? It basically means that someone can be convicted of a misdemeanor A if he appears to be under the influence of any illegal drug.

However, in order for the state to prove, beyond a reasonable doubt, that a person was actually under the influence of CDS, expert testimony is necessary. In any case, it is a matter that ultimately must be decided in the courts by the trier of fact.

Failure to Make Proper Disposition

Red Beard could be convicted of a misdemeanor A under 20-8c. for failing to "voluntarily" turn over his 25 grams of marijuana to a law enforcement officer. This conviction could be in addition to a CDS possession conviction under subsection a. of the statute.

Subsection c. of 20-8 makes it a misdemeanor A where a person fails to voluntarily turn over, to the "nearest law enforcement officer," any controlled dangerous substances he illegally possesses. This means that if a person buys marijuana or cocaine, he should immediately go to the nearest police officer and give it to him or he can be charged with an offense under this subsection—and this charge can be in addition to a CDS possession charge or any other appropriate charges. Accordingly, since Red Beard did not voluntarily turn over his stash of marijuana to any law enforcement officer, he is guilty of violating 20-8c.

20-8.1.   **Possession, etc. of gamma hydroxybutyrate; penalties**

    a. It is a felony of the third degree for any person, knowingly or purposely, to obtain, or to possess, gamma hydroxybutyrate unless the substance was obtained directly or pursuant to a valid prescription or order form from a practitioner while acting in the course of his professional practice.

    b. A fine of up to $100,000 may be imposed upon a person who violates this section.

Practical Application of Statute

Simple possession of GHB—without a valid prescription—is a felony of the third degree. Accordingly, if Red Beard had a personal stash of GHB rather than marijuana, he would be guilty of a third degree felony.

20-8.2.   **Possession, etc., of flunitrazepam; penalties**

    a. It is a felony of the third degree for any person, knowingly or purposely, to obtain, or to possess, flunitrazepam, unless the substance was obtained directly or pursuant to a valid prescription or order form from a practitioner while acting in the course of his professional practice.

    b. A fine of up to $100,000 may be imposed upon a person who violates this section.

Practical Application of Statute

Like possession of GHB, possession of flunitrazepam ("roofies") is a third degree felony. As per the other CDS possession statutes, a felony has not been committed if possession of the substance was pursuant to a valid prescription.

20-8.3. **Toxic chemicals**

a. As used in this section, the term "toxic chemical" means any chemical having the property of releasing toxic fumes and includes the following chemicals: acetone, acetate, benzene, butyl alcohol, ethyl alcohol, ethylene dichloride, isopropyl alcohol, methyl alcohol, methyl ethyl ketone, pentachlorophenol, petroleum ether, toluol or toluene.

b. A person commits a misdemeanor A if the person:

(1) Inhales the fumes of any toxic chemical for the purpose of causing a condition of intoxication; or

(2) Possesses any toxic chemical for the purpose of causing a condition of intoxication.

c. A person commits a fourth degree offense if the person sells, or offers to sell, any substance containing a toxic chemical knowing that the intended use of the product is to cause a condition of intoxication or knowing that the product does not include an additive required by the Commissioner of the State Department of Health and Senior Services to discourage the inhalation of vapors of toxic chemicals for the purpose of causing a condition of intoxication. This subsection does not apply to adhesives manufactured only for industrial application.

PRACTICAL APPLICATION OF STATUTE

Per 20-8.3, one who inhales (see subsection b.(1)) or possesses (see subsection b.(2)) any "toxic chemical" is guilty of a misdemeanor A. Pursuant to subsection c., a person who sells any "toxic chemical" is guilty of a fourth degree felony. What constitutes a "toxic chemical" can be easily found in subsection a. of this statute.

20-8.4. **Prescription legend drugs**

a. A person who knowingly:

(1) Distributes a prescription legend drug or stramonium preparation in an amount of four or fewer dosage units unless lawfully prescribed or administered by a licensed physician, veterinarian, dentist or other practitioner authorized by law to prescribe medication is guilty of a misdemeanor A;

(2) Distributes for pecuniary gain or possesses or has under his control with intent to distribute for pecuniary gain a prescription legend drug or stramonium preparation in an amount of four or fewer dosage units unless lawfully prescribed or administered by a licensed physician, veterinarian, dentist or other practitioner authorized by law to prescribe medication is guilty of a felony of the fourth degree;

(3) Distributes or possesses or has under his control with intent to distribute a prescription legend drug or stramonium preparation in an amount of at least five but fewer than 100 dosage units unless lawfully prescribed or administered by a licensed physician, veterinarian, dentist or other practitioner authorized by law to prescribe medication is guilty of a felony of the third degree. A fine of up to $200,000 may be imposed; or

(4) Distributes or possesses or has under his control with intent to distribute a prescription legend drug or stramonium preparation in an amount of 100 or more dosage units unless lawfully prescribed or administered by a licensed physician, veterinarian, dentist or other practitioner authorized by law to prescribe medication is guilty of a felony of the second degree. A fine of up to $300,000 may be imposed.

Notwithstanding the above, a violation of paragraph (1) or (3) of this subsection shall be deemed a *de minimis* infraction subject to dismissal if the person demonstrates that the conduct involved no more than six dosage units distributed within a 24-hour period, that the prescription legend drug or stramonium preparation was lawfully prescribed for or administered to that person by a licensed physician, veterinarian, dentist or other practitioner authorized by law to prescribe medication and that the person intended for the amount he distributed to be solely for the recipient's personal use.

b. A person who uses any prescription legend drug or stramonium preparation for a purpose other than treatment of sickness or injury as lawfully prescribed or administered by a licensed physician, veterinarian, dentist or other practitioner authorized by law to prescribe medication is guilty of a misdemeanor A.

c. A defendant may be convicted for a violation of subsection b. if the prosecution proves that the defendant manifested symptoms or reactions caused by the use of prescription legend drugs or stramonium preparation. The prosecution need not prove which specific prescription legend drug or stramonium preparation the defendant used.

d. A person who obtains or attempts to obtain possession of a prescription legend drug or stramonium preparation by forgery or deception is guilty of a felony of the fourth degree. Nothing in this section shall be deemed to preclude or limit a prosecution for theft as defined in chapter 9 of this Criminal Code.

e. A person who knowingly possesses, actually or constructively:

   (1) A prescription legend drug or stramonium preparation in an amount of four or fewer dosage units unless lawfully prescribed or administered by a licensed physician, veterinarian, dentist or other practitioner authorized by law to prescribe medication is guilty of a misdemeanor A; or

   (2) A prescription legend drug or stramonium preparation in an amount of five or more dosage units unless lawfully prescribed or administered by a licensed physician, veterinarian, dentist or other practitioner authorized by law to prescribe medication is guilty of a felony of the fourth degree.

   Notwithstanding the above, a violation of this subsection shall be deemed a *de minimis* infraction subject to dismissal if the person demonstrates that he unlawfully received no more than six dosage units within a 24-hour period, that the prescription legend drug or stramonium preparation was lawfully prescribed for or administered to the person from whom he had received it and that the person possessed the prescription legend drug or stramonium preparation solely for his personal use.

f. Where the degree of the offense for violation of this section depends on the number of dosage units of the prescription legend drug or stramonium preparation, the number of dosage units involved shall be determined by the trier of fact. Where the indictment or accusation so provides, the number of dosage units involved in individual acts of distribution or possession with intent to distribute may be aggregated in determining the grade of the offense, whether distribution is to the same person or several persons, provided that each individual act of distribution or possession with intent to distribute was committed within the applicable statute of limitations.

g. Subsections a. and e. of this section shall not apply to a licensed pharmacy, licensed pharmacist, researcher, wholesaler, distributor, manufacturer, warehouseman or his representative acting within the line and scope of his employment; a physician, veterinarian, dentist or other practitioner authorized by law to prescribe medication; a nurse acting under the direction of a physician; or a common carrier or messenger when transporting such prescription legend drug or stramonium preparation in the same unbroken package in which the prescription legend drug or stramonium preparation was delivered to him for transportation.

PRACTICAL APPLICATION OF STATUTE

Drugs Generally

This statute enumerates offenses for possessing, distributing and being under the influence of "prescription legend" drugs and "stramonium preparation." Per the definitions set forth in 20-1, "prescription legend" drugs include steroids, cough syrup with codeine and any other "drug which under federal or State law requires dispensing by prescription or order of a licensed physician, veterinarian, or dentist and is required to bear the statement 'Rx only' or similar wording indicating that such drug may be sold or dispensed only upon the prescription of a licensed medical practitioner."

Also, a "prescription legend" drug is not a controlled dangerous substance or stramonium preparation. "Stramonium preparation" is defined as "a substance prepared from any part of the stramonium plant in the form of a powder, pipe mixture, cigarette or any other form with or without other ingredients."

Distribution

A person who unlawfully distributes a prescription legend drug or stramonium preparation can be convicted of a misdemeanor A or fourth, third or second degree felony. Subsections a.(1) through a.(4) itemize the circumstances that control the degree of offense.

Primarily, the degree becomes greater as the amount of doses increases; however, there is a caveat in determining whether a misdemeanor A or a fourth degree felony has been committed. A person can be convicted of a misdemeanor A or a fourth degree felony where he distributes a prescription legend drug or stramonium preparation "in an amount of four or fewer dosage units." The offense is only elevated to a fourth degree felony, though, when the actor distributes "for pecuniary gain."

Distribution of a prescription legend drug or stramonium preparation is only legal where it is "lawfully prescribed or administered by a licensed physician, veterinarian, dentist, or other practitioner authorized by law to prescribe medication."

Possession/Use/Under the Influence

Per subsection e., one who possesses a prescription legend drug or stramonium preparation—unless it is lawfully prescribed—is guilty of a misdemeanor A or fourth degree felony. A misdemeanor A has occurred if the amount involved is "four or fewer dosage units"; "five or more dosage units" makes it a fourth degree felony.

Subsection b. makes the "use" of a prescription legend drug or stramonium preparation a misdemeanor A—unless, of course, it is used lawfully. Subsection c. of 20-8.4, in a vein similar to the provisions of the CDS "under the influence" statute (20-8b.), sets out how a person can be convicted of unlawfully using a prescription legend drug or stramonium preparation. The state need only prove that the "defendant manifested symptoms or reactions caused by the use of prescription legend drugs or stramonium preparation." The state, though, does not need to prove which specific substance the defendant used.

Obtaining by Forgery

Subsection d. of this statute makes it a separate offense to obtain a prescription legend drug or stramonium preparation by forgery or deception. For instance, if a person created a false prescription and brought it to a pharmacist, he could be convicted of a fourth degree felony pursuant to 20-8.4d. Similarly, if he lifted a prescription pad from a medical doctor and thereafter used one of the pages to obtain a drug, he is ripe for a charge under this subsection—not to mention a charge of theft under 9-3.

De Minimis Infractions to Be Dismissed

Please note that subsections a. and e. provide for "*de minimis* infractions," which are subject to dismissal. Basically, if the defendant distributes or possesses "no more than six dosage units within a 24-hour period," the offense should be dismissed. Two caveats exist, however. First, in the case of the "distributor," the item must have been lawfully prescribed to him; for the possessor, the item must have been lawfully prescribed to the person who gave it to him. Second, the distributor must have intended that the item he distributed was "solely for the recipient's personal use"; the possessor must have possessed it "solely for his personal use."

20-9.   **Imitation controlled dangerous substances; distribution, possession, manufacture, etc.; penalties**

    a. It is unlawful for any person to distribute or to possess or have under his control with intent to distribute any substance which is not a controlled dangerous substance or controlled substance analog:

        (1) Upon the express or implied representation to the recipient that the substance is a controlled dangerous substance or controlled substance analog;

        (2) Upon the express or implied representation to the recipient that the substance is of such nature, appearance or effect that the recipient will be able to distribute or use the substance as a controlled dangerous substance or controlled substance analog; or

        (3) Under circumstances which would lead a reasonable person to believe that the substance is a controlled dangerous substance or controlled substance analog.

            Any of the following shall constitute *prima facie* evidence of such circumstances:

            (a) The substance was packaged in a manner normally used for the unlawful distribution of controlled dangerous substances or controlled substance analogs;

            (b) The distribution or attempted distribution of the substance was accompanied by an exchange of or demand for money or other thing as consideration for the substance, and the value of the consideration exceeded the reasonable value of the substance; or

            (c) The physical appearance of the substance is substantially the same as that of a specific controlled dangerous substance or controlled substance analog.

    b. It is unlawful for any person to manufacture, compound, encapsulate, package or imprint any substance which is not a controlled dangerous substance, controlled substance analog or any combination of such substances, other than a prescription drug, with the purpose that it resemble or duplicate the physical appearance of the finished form, package, label or imprint of a controlled dangerous substance or controlled substance analog.

c. In any prosecution under this section, it shall not be a defense that the defendant mistakenly believed a substance to be a controlled dangerous substance or controlled substance analog.

d. A violation of this section is a felony of the third degree. A fine of up to $200,000 may be imposed.

e. The provisions of this section shall not be applicable to (1) practitioners or agents or servants and employees of practitioners dispensing or administering noncontrolled substances to patients on behalf of practitioners in the normal course of their business or professional practice; and (2) persons who manufacture, process, package, distribute or sell noncontrolled substances to practitioners for use as placebos in the normal course of their business, professional practice or research or for use in Federal Food and Drug Administration investigational new drug trials.

PRACTICAL APPLICATION OF STATUTE

Not only is the sale of controlled dangerous substances illegal, but the sale of imitation controlled dangerous substances is also illegal. Remember the case of Red Beard? He was caught selling cocaine to a man in a restaurant parking lot. If this substance had turned out to be flour, however, he still would be guilty of a felony. The violation is distributing imitation cocaine, which is a third degree offense.

Section 20-9, in a nutshell, makes it a felony for someone to represent to another that a substance (which he is selling) is CDS. This representation may be expressed or implied. The statute, in fact, enumerates three types of circumstances where a person's actions constitute "*prima facie*" evidence of attempting to hold out a phony product as actual CDS. These actions include when the substance is "packaged in a manner normally used for the unlawful distribution" of CDS (see subsection a.(3)(a)); where the distribution is accompanied by an exchange of money and the amount of money "exceeded the reasonable value of the substance" (see subsection a.(3)(b)); and "the physical appearance of the substance is substantially the same as that of a specific" CDS (see subsection a.(3)(c)).

Subsection c. of the statute provides that it is not a defense that the defendant mistakenly believed the substance he was distributing was actually a controlled dangerous substance. The statute also does not utilize weight to differentiate among degrees of felonies. Simply put, per subsection d., a violation of the statute is a third degree felony.

Now, go back to Red Beard in the restaurant parking lot, where Hawthorne police caught him with 29 individually wrapped packages of cocaine marked with the logo "Tuned-Up," which totaled 11 ounces in weight. Prior to the sale, Hawthorne Mayor Frank Castelleti overheard Red Beard tell his potential buyer, "Step out to my pickup, and I'll drop you the eight-ball." This statement constituted an express representation by Red Beard that he was offering to sell cocaine, as "eight-ball" is street lingo for cocaine. In addition, there is separate *prima facie* evidence that he was representing the substance to be cocaine—it was wrapped in 29 individual packages and marked with the logo "Tuned-Up." This type of packaging is consistent with the packaging of CDS that is unlawfully distributed. Accordingly, even if the substance turned out to be flour rather than cocaine, Red Beard would still be guilty of a third degree felony. As noted earlier, the quantity involved does not affect the degree of the felony under 20-9. Thus, Red Beard would face a third degree charge whether he attempted to sell one ounce, three ounces, 11 ounces or 75 ounces of the substance.

It is interesting to note, though, that with the substance *actually* being cocaine, Red Beard would be guilty of a first degree distribution offense under 20-4. Pursuant to that statute, distribution of cocaine in the amount of "five ounces or more" is a first degree felony. This means that since the quantity of cocaine involved was 11 ounces—exceeding five ounces—Red Beard would face a first degree charge for distribution of the real McCoy.

20-10.   Obtaining by fraud

It shall be unlawful for any person to acquire or obtain possession of a controlled dangerous substance or controlled substance analog by misrepresentation, fraud, forgery, deception or subterfuge. It shall be unlawful for any person to acquire or obtain possession of a forged or fraudulent certificate of destruction required pursuant to 20-9. A violation of this section shall be a felony of the third degree except that a fine of up to $50,000 may be imposed. Nothing in this section shall be deemed to preclude or limit a prosecution for theft as defined in chapter 9 of this Criminal Code.

PRACTICAL APPLICATION OF STATUTE

A person can be convicted of a third degree felony under 20-10 for obtaining CDS by deceptive matters such as fraud or misrepresentation. Also, per this statute, a person can be convicted of a third degree felony for obtaining "possession of a forged or fraudulent certificate of destruction required pursuant to 20-9." What does that mean?

Section 20-9 sets forth what is required in order for forensic laboratories to destroy controlled dangerous substances. Specifically, that statute provides that the laboratory "shall file with the court a certificate under oath attesting to the date on which the substance was destroyed, the quantity of the substance destroyed and the method used to destroy the substance."

So under what circumstances can a person face a charge under 20-10? Let's say that after Red Beard's 11 ounces of cocaine were seized by Hawthorne police, the state sought to have it destroyed. Thereafter, a colleague of Red Beard's, who worked in a state forensic laboratory, filed a "certificate of destruction" attesting to the date and method of destruction of the cocaine. The lab tech, however, never actually destroyed the drug but instead returned it to Red Beard, who was out on bail. In this case, the lab tech would have presented a fraudulent "certificate of destruction" to the court and is therefore guilty of a third degree felony under 20-10. Also, if Red Beard was part of this scheme, he similarly would be guilty of a third degree felony, as he would have reobtained his cocaine via a deceptive act.

20-11.   Possession of certain prescription drugs

A person who possesses a controlled dangerous substance that was prescribed or dispensed lawfully may possess it only in the container in which it was dispensed, except that the person may possess no more than a ten-day supply in other than the original container if the person produces, upon the request of a law enforcement officer, the name and address of the practitioner who prescribed the substance or the pharmacist who dispensed it. A person who violates this section is guilty of a misdemeanor A.

PRACTICAL APPLICATION OF STATUTE

At times, an individual may lawfully possess a controlled dangerous substance. This legal possession of CDS can only occur via a valid prescription from a practitioner such as a medical doctor.

Per 20-11, an individual who lawfully possesses a controlled dangerous substance must keep it in the container in which it was originally dispensed. The only exception to this rule is that the person "may possess no more than a ten-day supply" in a different container. If a person violates the provisions of this statute, he is guilty of a misdemeanor A.

20-12.   **Sale restrictions for ephedrine products; misdemeanor A**

    a. Except as provided in subsection c. of this section, no person shall sell, offer for sale or purchase in any single retail transaction more than:

      (1) Three packages, or any number of packages that contain a total of nine grams, of any drug containing a sole active ingredient of ephedrine, pseudoephedrine, phenylpropanolamine or any of their salts, optical isomers or salts of optical isomers; or

      (2) Three packages of any combination drug containing, as one of its active ingredients, ephedrine, pseudoephedrine, phenylpropanolamine or any of their salts, optical isomers or salts of optical isomers or any number of packages of such combination drugs that contain a total of nine grams of ephedrine, pseudoephedrine, phenylpropanolamine or any of their salts, optical isomers or salts of optical isomers.

    b. A violation of this section is a misdemeanor A.

    c. This act shall not apply to a drug lawfully prescribed or administered by a licensed physician, veterinarian or dentist.

PRACTICAL APPLICATION OF STATUTE

Section 20-12 deals with illicit transactions of the drug ephedrine and related products and defines what will make an ephedrine transaction a misdemeanor A. The following fact pattern provides an example of an offense under this statute.

In a single transaction, a convenience store owner sells five packages of "Epho-Lox," a drug containing a sole active ingredient of ephedrine, to Stuart. Here, both the store owner and Stuart are guilty of a misdemeanor A. Why? Because subsection a.(1) makes it illegal to sell (or purchase)—"in any single retail transaction" either "three packages" or "any number of packages that contain a total of nine grams of any drug containing a sole active ingredient of ephedrine."

Please note that under subsection a.(1), it is equally illegal if the sole active ingredient is "pseudoephedrine" or "phenylpropanolamine." Also equally illegal, per subsection a.(2), are "combination drugs," which contain any one of the aforementioned active ingredients.

The enactment of this statute is the reason why consumers now cannot find their favorite cold medicines on the shelves of a pharmacy or supermarket and instead must request the medicine from the pharmacist. Consumers are now limited to a minimum of three bottles of medicine (which contain the active ingredients detailed in 20-12) in a single retail purchase—and they must sign for it.

20-13.   **Unlawful possession of precursors; manufacturing methamphetamine; felony of second degree**

    a. A person is guilty of the felony of unlawful possession of a precursor if the person knowingly or purposely possesses anhydrous ammonia with intent to unlawfully manufacture methamphetamine or any of its analogs.

    b. A person is guilty of the felony of unlawful possession of a precursor if the person knowingly or purposely possesses phenylalanine with intent to unlawfully manufacture methamphetamine or amphetamine or any of their analogs.

    c. A person is guilty of the felony of unlawful possession of a precursor if the person knowingly or purposely possesses, with intent to manufacture a controlled dangerous substance or controlled substance analog, any of the following:

        (1) Carbamide (urea) and propanedioc and malonic acid or its derivatives;

        (2) Ergot or an ergot derivative and diethylamine or dimethyl-formamide or diethylamide;

        (3) Phenylacetone (1-phenyl-2 propanone);

        (4) Pentazocine and methyliodid;

        (5) Phenylacetonitrile and dichlorodiethyl methylamine or dichlorodiethyl benzylamine;

        (6) Diephenylacetonitrile and dimethylaminoisopropyl chloride;

        (7) Piperidine and cyclohexanone and bromobenzene and lithium or magnesium; or

        (8) 2, 5-dimethoxy benzaldehyde and nitroethane and a reducing agent.

    d. (1) A person is guilty of the felony of unlawful possession of a precursor if the person, with intent to unlawfully manufacture methamphetamine, knowingly or purposely possesses ephedrine (including its salts, isomers or salts of isomers), norpseudoephedrine (including its salts, isomers or salts of isomers), n-methylephedrine (including its salts, isomers or salts of isomers), n-methylpseudoephedrine (including its salts, isomers or salts of isomers) or pseudoephedrine (including its salts, isomers or salts of isomers).

        (2) Proof that a person in possession of any of the substances enumerated in paragraph (1) of this subsection at the same time also possesses any of the following substances shall give rise to a permissive inference by the trier of fact that the person acted with intent to unlawfully manufacture methamphetamine:

            (a) Amorphous (red) phosphorus or white phosphorus;

            (b) Hydroiodic acid;

            (c) Anhydrous ammonia;

            (d) Sodium; or

            (e) Lithium.

    Unlawful possession of a precursor in violation of this section is a felony of the second degree.

Practical Application of Statute

Section 20-13 has defined the felony of unlawful possession of a precursor. A "precursor" is an ingredient of some sort that is utilized to make more dangerous illicit substances. Possession of the precursor substance becomes a second degree felony under 20-13 if "the person knowingly or purposely possesses" it "with intent to unlawfully manufacture" another substance such as methamphetamine or any controlled dangerous substance.

Lucy, an aging hippie academic living in Hadwyn, wants to impress a group of younger scientists. She goes out and procures anhydrous ammonia. Her intent is to use this precursor substance to unlawfully manufacture methamphetamine. Before she could actually make the drug, however, one of the young scientists contacts Detective Captain Antonio, who in turn arrests Lucy at her home. Lucy provides a full confession. Because she "purposely possessed" the "anhydrous ammonia" with the "intent to unlawfully manufacture" the methamphetamine, Lucy is guilty of the second degree felony of unlawful possession of a precursor.

END OF CHAPTER REVIEW

Multiple-Choice Questions

The following fact pattern pertains to questions 1–3.

Charlie Chaplowitz maintained a massive heroin distribution center in the lower level of his restaurant, The Fire Down Under, in Hawthorne. In an effort to prevent law enforcement officers (or any other uninvited guests) from entering the facility, Chaplowitz erected two solid, thick steel doors, a computerized security card system and a hidden alarm system. Hawthorne police raided his facility, confiscating over 500 pounds of heroin, all of which was being prepared and packaged for the purpose of being distributed to buyers.

1. For the 500 pounds of heroin, Hawthorne police should charge Chaplowitz with what offense?
    a. a fourth degree possession of heroin
    b. first degree possession of heroin with intent to distribute it
    c. third degree possession of heroin with intent to distribute it
    d. all of the above, depending on the packaging
    e. none of the above

2. For erecting the steel doors, computerized security system and hidden alarm system at his distribution center, Chaplowitz is guilty of what offense?
    a. a third degree felony of heroin possession
    b. a misdemeanor A of fortifying a drug distribution center
    c. a third degree felony of fortifying a drug distribution center
    d. a second degree felony of prescription legend drug housing
    e. no offense at all because steel doors and alarms are not illegal

3. If Chaplowitz had booby traps at his drug distribution center, he would be guilty of:
    a. a second degree felony
    b. a third degree felony
    c. a misdemeanor A
    d. all of the above, depending on the type of booby trap
    e. no offense that defines or categorizes booby traps

4. Imitation CDS is:
    a. the same as counterfeit CDS
    b. oregano purporting to be marijuana
    c. flour purporting to be cocaine
    d. all of the above
    e. b and c only

5. Snooty snorts a whole bundle of cocaine and then dies. Which of the following is true?
    a. A dealer who distributed the cocaine to Snooty could be held strictly liable for his death and convicted of a first degree felony.
    b. A friend who dispensed the cocaine to Snooty could be held strictly liable for his death and convicted of a first degree felony.
    c. A dealer who distributed the cocaine to Snooty could not be held strictly liable for his death and convicted of a first degree felony if Snooty died a year later after Snooty had inhaled cocaine from several other dealers.
    d. All of the above are true.
    e. Only a and c are true.

6. Red Beard was caught by Hawthorne police with a dime bag of marijuana—under 50 grams. What is Red Beard guilty of?
    a. a capital offense
    b. a first degree felony
    c. a third degree felony because he had under 50 grams of marijuana and that is the lowest degree offense for CDS possession
    d. a misdemeanor A because he had under 50 grams of marijuana and that is the lowest degree offense for CDS possession
    e. no offense if he had a note from his principal

7. Simple possession of GHB, without a valid prescription, constitutes:
    a. a first degree felony
    b. a third degree felony
    c. a misdemeanor A
    d. a misdemeanor B
    e. none of the above

Essay Questions

1. Red Beard was arrested after undercover police officers observed him selling 11 ounces of cocaine to buyer Dumb Head. The cocaine was divided into 29 individually wrapped packages marked with the logo "Tuned-Up." For this CDS sale, Red Beard is guilty of what degree offense and why? State the specific statute and subsection in your answer. If Red Beard conducted his cocaine transaction 750 feet away from a public elementary school, should he be charged with an additional offense? Why or why not? If so, what are the specific statute and the degree of the offense? If Red Beard conducted his cocaine transaction 750 feet away from a public park,

should he be charged with an additional offense? Why or why not? If so, what is the specific statute and the degree of the offense?

2. Schwartz has been under surveillance by Cold River police for six months. Finally, detectives arrange an undercover buy at his home; there, they purchase 75 marijuana plants from him. They also purchased 15 pounds of oregano from Schwartz, which he falsely claimed to be marijuana. Once busted, Schwartz rolls on Leroy, arranging a buy of 250 milligrams of LSD. Leroy ultimately sold that amount of LSD to the same detectives. When Leroy was busted, police found eight ounces of heroin on his person; he admitted that he intended to sell it to his friend Barbara. The heroin, however, was only two ounces of pure heroin and six ounces of dilutants. For the sale of the 75 marijuana plants, Schwartz is guilty of what degree offense and why? For Schwartz's sale of the 15 pounds of oregano, he is guilty of what degree offense and why? For the sale of the 250 milligrams of LSD, Leroy is guilty of what degree offense and why? For the heroin that Leroy intended to sell to Barbara, Leroy is guilty of what degree offense and why? Does the six ounces of dilutants lower the degree of his offense? Be sure to cite the relevant statutes and subsections in your answers.

21

DRUG PARAPHERNALIA

21-1.   **Drug paraphernalia; defined; determination**

As used in this act, "drug paraphernalia" means all equipment, products and materials of any kind which are used or intended for use in planting, propagating, cultivating, growing, harvesting, manufacturing, compounding, converting, producing, processing, preparing, testing, analyzing, packaging, repackaging, storing, containing, concealing, ingesting, inhaling or otherwise introducing into the human body a controlled dangerous substance or controlled substance analog in violation of the provisions of chapter 20 of this Criminal Code. It shall include, but not be limited to:

a. Kits used or intended for use in planting, propagating, cultivating, growing or harvesting of any species of plant which is a controlled dangerous substance or from which a controlled dangerous substance can be derived;

b. Kits used or intended for use in manufacturing, compounding, converting, producing, processing, or preparing controlled dangerous substances or controlled substance analogs;

c. Isomerization devices used or intended for use in increasing the potency of any species of plant which is a controlled dangerous substance;

d. Testing equipment used or intended for use in identifying or in analyzing the strength, effectiveness or purity of controlled dangerous substances or controlled substance analogs;

e. Scales and balances used or intended for use in weighing or measuring controlled dangerous substances or controlled substance analogs;

f. Dilutants and adulterants, such as quinine hydrochloride, mannitol, mannite, dextrose and lactose, used or intended for use in cutting controlled dangerous substances or controlled substance analogs;

g. Separation gins and sifters used or intended for use in removing twigs and seeds from, or in otherwise cleaning or refining, marijuana;

h. Blenders, bowls, containers, spoons and mixing devices used or intended for use in compounding controlled dangerous substances or controlled substance analogs;

i. Capsules, balloons, envelopes and other containers used or intended for use in packaging small quantities of controlled dangerous substances or controlled substance analogs;

j. Containers and other objects used or intended for use in storing or concealing controlled dangerous substances or controlled substance analogs;

k. Objects used or intended for use in ingesting, inhaling or otherwise introducing marijuana, cocaine, hashish or hashish oil into the human body, such as:

(1) Metal, wooden, acrylic, glass, stone, plastic or ceramic pipes with or without screens, permanent screens, hashish heads or punctured metal bowls;

(2) Water pipes;

(3) Carburetion tubes and devices;

(4) Smoking and carburetion masks;

(5) Roach clips, meaning objects used to hold burning material, such as a marijuana cigarette, that has become too small or too short to be held in the hand;

(6) Miniature cocaine spoons and cocaine vials;

(7) Chamber pipes;

(8) Carburetor pipes;

(9) Electric pipes;

(10) Air-driven pipes;

(11) Chillums;

(12) Bongs; and

(13) Ice pipes or chillers.

In determining whether or not an object is drug paraphernalia, the trier of fact, in addition to or as part of the proofs, may consider the following factors:

(a) Statements by an owner or by anyone in control of the object concerning its use;

(b) The proximity of the object of illegally possessed controlled dangerous substances or controlled substance analogs;

(c) The existence of any residue of illegally possessed controlled dangerous substances or controlled substance analogs on the object;

(d) Direct or circumstantial evidence of the intent of an owner, or of anyone in control of the object, to deliver it to persons whom he knows intend to use the object to facilitate a violation of this act; the innocence of an owner, or of anyone in control of the object, as to a direct violation of this act shall not prevent a finding that the object is intended for use as drug paraphernalia;

(e) Instructions, oral or written, provided with the object concerning its use;

(f) Descriptive materials accompanying the object which explain or depict its use;

(g) National or local advertising whose purpose the person knows or should know is to promote the sale of objects intended for use as drug paraphernalia;

(h) The manner in which the object is displayed for sale;

(i) The existence and scope of legitimate uses for the object in the community; and

(j) Expert testimony concerning its use.

21-2.   **Use or possession with intent to use; misdemeanor A**

It shall be unlawful for any person to use, or to possess with intent to use, drug paraphernalia to plant, propagate, cultivate, grow, harvest, manufacture, compound, convert, produce, process, prepare, test, analyze, pack, repack, store, contain, conceal, ingest, inhale or otherwise introduce into the human body a controlled dangerous substance or controlled substance analog in violation of the provisions of chapter 20 of this Criminal Code. Any person who violates this section is guilty of a misdemeanor A.

PRACTICAL APPLICATION OF STATUTE

Red Beard is guilty of violating 21-2 for possessing a pipe ordinarily used for smoking marijuana. This is a misdemeanor A.

Section 21-2 is the statute that prohibits the possession or use of any drug paraphernalia. Drug paraphernalia are not just items like pipes, bongs and straws that are used for intake of controlled dangerous substances into the human body. Prohibited paraphernalia also include objects like indoor gardening lamps and devices that are used for planting and cultivating CDS. In addition, possession of "cow patties" and tropinine are violative of the statute, as they are used to manufacture psychedelic mushrooms and cocaine, respectively. Glass containers, bags and vials can be considered drug paraphernalia as well because drugs are often packaged and contained in them. In sum, this statute makes it illegal to possess a wide range of items—basically, anything that is connected to the manufacture, distribution and use of CDS.

Red Beard was caught by the Hawthorne police amid a rather large illegal cocaine transaction. At the time of his arrest, cocaine and marijuana were confiscated from his person and automobile. Also confiscated was a pipe ordinarily used for smoking marijuana. Red Beard's possession of this item of drug paraphernalia renders him guilty of a misdemeanor A under 21-2.

21-3.   **Distribute, dispense or possession with intent to distribute or manufacture; felony of fourth degree**

It shall be unlawful for any person to distribute or dispense, possess with intent to distribute or dispense or manufacture with intent to distribute or dispense drug paraphernalia, knowing that it will be used to plant, propagate, cultivate, grow, harvest, manufacture, compound, convert, produce, process, prepare, test, analyze, pack, repack, store, contain, conceal, ingest, inhale or otherwise introduce into the human body a controlled dangerous substance or controlled substance analog in violation of the provisions of chapter 20 of this Criminal Code. Any person who violates this section commits a felony of the fourth degree.

PRACTICAL APPLICATION OF STATUTE

While it is a misdemeanor A to use or possess drug paraphernalia, it is a fourth degree felony to distribute it. Here, the mental state of "knowledge" is key. One must "know" that the items he is distributing to another will be used as drug paraphernalia (e.g, to cultivate, grow, manufacture, package, ingest, etc., CDS).

21-4.   **Advertising to promote sale; felony of fourth degree**

It shall be unlawful for any person to place in any newspaper, magazine, handbill or other publication any advertisement, knowing that the purpose of the advertisement, in whole or in part, is to promote the sale of objects intended for use as drug paraphernalia. Any person who violates this section commits a felony of the fourth degree.

PRACTICAL APPLICATION OF STATUTE

It is a fourth degree felony to advertise, in any publication, the sale of any objects intended for use as drug paraphernalia. Again, "knowledge" is important—the defendant must "know" that the purpose of the ad is to promote the sale of drug paraphernalia. In other words, a person cannot be convicted under this statute if his total purpose of advertising a particular object was to promote the sale of the object for a lawful use (e.g., advertising in a medical magazine the sale of vials to hold blood).

21-5.   **Delivering drug paraphernalia to person under 18 years of age; felony of third degree**

Any person 18 years of age or over who violates section 21-3 by delivering drug paraphernalia to a person under 18 years of age commits a felony of the third degree.

PRACTICAL APPLICATION OF STATUTE

This statute is an offshoot of 21-3. Simply, a person who distributes drug paraphernalia to a minor is guilty of a third degree felony rather than a fourth degree felony.

21-6.   **Possession or distribution of hypodermic syringe or needle**

a. Except as authorized by subsection b., c. or other law, it shall be unlawful for a person to have under his control or possess with intent to use a hypodermic syringe, hypodermic needle or any other instrument adapted for the use of a controlled dangerous substance or a controlled substance analog as defined in chapter 20 of this Criminal Code or to sell, furnish or give to any person such syringe, needle or instrument. Any person who violates this section is guilty of a misdemeanor A.

b. A person is authorized to possess and use a hypodermic needle or hypodermic syringe if the person obtains the hypodermic syringe or hypodermic needle by a valid prescription issued by a licensed physician, dentist or veterinarian and uses it for its authorized purpose.

      No prescription for a hypodermic syringe, hypodermic needle or any other instrument adapted for the use of controlled dangerous substances by subcutaneous injections shall be valid for more than one year from the date of issuance.

c. Subsection a. does not apply to a duly licensed physician, dentist, veterinarian, undertaker, nurse, podiatrist, or registered pharmacist; a hospital, sanitarium, clinical laboratory or any other medical institution; a state or a governmental agency; a regular dealer in medical, dental or surgical supplies; or a resident physician or intern of a hospital, sanitarium or other medical institution.

PRACTICAL APPLICATION OF STATUTE

Generally, any person who possesses a hypodermic needle or syringe is guilty of a misdemeanor A. Following Red Beard's arrest for cocaine distribution, he was caught with a hypodermic syringe and should be convicted under this statute.

      Subsections b. and c. provide exceptions where individuals may lawfully possess hypodermic needles and syringes. Examples include licensed physicians, dentists, veterinarians, undertakers, nurses (see subsection c.) and individuals who are validly prescribed the objects by licensed physicians, dentists and veterinarians (see subsection b.). Since Red Beard does not fall within any of these categories, he should be convicted of a misdemeanor A under 21-6. He had a hypodermic needle under his control—but had no lawful reason for the same.

21-6.1.   **Discarding hypodermic needle or syringe**

    a. A person commits a misdemeanor B if:

        (1) The person discards, in a place accessible to other persons, a hypodermic needle or syringe without destroying the hypodermic needle or syringe; or

        (2) He is the owner, lessee or person in control of real property and, knowing that needles and syringes in an intact condition have been discarded or abandoned on his real property, allows them to remain.

    b. A hypodermic needle is destroyed if the needle is broken from the hub or mangled. A syringe is destroyed if the nipple of the barrel is broken from the barrel, or the plunger and barrel are melted. Alternatively, a hypodermic needle or syringe is destroyed if it is discarded as a single unit, without recapping, into a rigid container and the container is destroyed by grinding or crushing in a compactor, or by burning in an incinerator approved by the Department of Environmental Protection or by another method approved by the Department of Health and Senior Services.

PRACTICAL APPLICATION OF STATUTE

Per 21-6.1a.(1), a person who discards a hypodermic needle or syringe without destroying it is guilty of a misdemeanor B—unless it is in a place not accessible to other persons. Likewise, under 21-6.1a.(2), a person in control of real estate property (e.g., owner, lessee) who "knowingly" permits discarded—and not destroyed—hypodermic needles to remain on the property is guilty of a misdemeanor B. Subsection b. of the statute defines what constitutes "destroyed" needles and syringes.

END OF CHAPTER REVIEW

Multiple-Choice Questions

    1. The following group of items can be considered drug paraphernalia:

        a. pipes, bongs, straws

        b. shoes, sneakers, crumb buns

        c. glass containers, vials, indoor gardening lamps

        d. all of the above

        e. a and c only

    2. Possession of drug paraphernalia under section 21-2 is:

        a. a felony of the first degree

        b. a felony of the third degree

        c. a misdemeanor A

        d. all of the above, depending on the type of paraphernalia

        e. none of the above

    3. One who distributes a hash pipe is guilty of:

        a. a felony of the first degree

        b. a felony of the fourth degree

    c. a misdemeanor A

    d. *modus operandi* only

    e. *res ipsa loquitor* under the doctrine of conniptions

4. The following persons may legally possess a hypodermic needle:

    a. podiatrists

    b. veterinarians

    c. sharpshooters

    d. all of the above

    e. a and b only

Essay Question

1. Horace, a heroin-addicted craps dealer, used a hypodermic needle to shoot the illicit substance into his arm. Afterward, he discarded the implement on the floor in the casino bathroom where he performed his injection. Several gamblers saw the entire incident; one of them reported it to an off-duty police officer. As the officer approached Horace, he observed Horace sell a marijuana bong to Nipsy, a 15-year-old boy. Explain three offenses that Horace has committed under Chapter 21. Be sure to detail the degree of each offense and cite the statute numbers in your answers.

22

GAMBLING OFFENSES

FACT PATTERN

Every Wednesday evening for as long as he could remember, Earl "The Smart Man" Jackey held a poker game in his modest three-bedroom Masontown home. Invited to the game were Bobby "Small Teeth" Smith, James "The Hyena" Lamonti and Stan "Knuckles" Malfowitz. Usually, The Smart Man's games lasted through the middle of the night and sometimes to early the next morning. The stakes were high—the gentlemen bet with the various vegetables that they cultivated in their respective home gardens. Small Teeth might lay out a few hundred tomatoes a night, while Knuckles was known to drop dozens upon dozens of eggplants. The Hyena's favorite betting vegetable was the carrot, and The Smart Man was partial to corn on the cob; indeed, both men, without fail, came to the table with baskets of each.

Now just because each player had his preferred stock, it didn't mean that other vegetables weren't part of the mix. String beans, parsley, cabbage, lettuce, zucchini and squash were always valued commodities thrown out in a confident bet, daring bluff or calculated gamble. Yes, the homegrown vegetables tossed around at The Smart Man's Wednesday night games were always interesting—always interesting to a Mason County law enforcement task force that had been monitoring the games for nearly six months. Why? Because The Smart Man, Small Teeth, The Hyena and Knuckles were the heads of the largest gambling ring ever operated in Mason County. The men felt comfortable in The Smart Man's house, which was often swept for bugs—and they gambled and talked and gambled and talked through the late night and early morning hours. Unfortunately for these crime bosses, however, The Smart Man's countersurveillance tactics were not smart enough. The task force, through multiple hidden mini-microphones, captured each and every word they said. Aside from various meatless recipes, this is what they uncovered.

Small Teeth was the lowest man on the totem pole. He acquired the various locations where the group's bookmaking activities occurred, and he solicited clients who placed bets with the group. Most recently, the task force recorded him bragging that his work "netted over 500 bets in the last week that totaled more than a million dollars."

Knuckles was the chief enforcer. He went out to personally collect money from losers who didn't come to him. On a weekly basis, he would receive seven figures in cash pursuant to the bettors' understanding that they had to pay up when they lost.

The Hyena actually manned the facilities where incoming bets were laid. Working under him were several other persons who answered phone calls, recording the code names and monetary figures of all those betting. The Hyena also ran a separate "after-hours" club, The Purple Mule, where gamblers played illegal games of poker, black-jack, craps and roulette. On a nightly basis, The Hyena received significant amounts of cash and sometimes other items of substantial value, such as jewelry, automobiles and property deeds—all from people who lost in their respective games.

The Smart Man oversaw the entire operation. At the end of each business day, all proceeds were personally turned over to him; later, he divvied them up among the group. He also held all pertinent records in his possession.

Pursuant to the information learned by the Mason County task force, search warrants were procured. Members of the Mason County Prosecutor's Office, the Mason County Sheriff's Department and the Masontown Police Department raided the various locations where bets were placed as well as the personal homes of the gang and The Purple Mule.

At the betting locations, numerous phones and computers were confiscated. Also found in these offices were thousands of blank sheets of "water soluble" paper. Coincidentally, the same "water soluble" paper was found in the basement of The Smart Man's home—except there, the paper recovered contained over a thousand different coded bets valued in excess of $3 million. The task force estimated that several million dollars of additional bets were recorded on other such paper, but when they arrived at The Smart Man's home, he was in the process of spraying a fire hose all over his basement floor. Also confiscated from The Smart Man's bedroom was nearly $5 million in cash, which was stuffed in corn husks, green peppers and hollowed-out large eggplants.

Upon executing the search warrant of The Purple Mule, law enforcement person-nel confiscated five roulette boards, dozens of decks of playing cards, three crap tables and various other objects related to the club's gambling activities. Other than cash, nothing else was seized at the personal homes of The Hyena, Small Teeth and Knuckles. All three men, however, were arrested along with The Smart Man. They were charged accordingly.

22-1. **Definitions**

The following definitions apply to this chapter:

a. "Contest of chance" means any contest, game, pool, gaming scheme or gaming device in which the outcome depends in a material degree upon an element of chance, notwith-standing that skill of the contestants or some other persons may also be a factor therein.

b. "Gambling" means staking or risking something of value upon the outcome of a contest of chance or a future contingent event not under the actor's control or influence, upon an agreement or understanding that he will receive something of value in the event of a certain outcome.

c. "Player" means a person who engages in any form of gambling solely as a contestant or bettor, without receiving or becoming entitled to receive any profit therefrom other than personal gambling winnings and without otherwise rendering any material assistance to the establishment, conduct or operation of the particular gambling activity. A person who gambles at a social game of chance on equal terms with the other participants therein does not thereby render material assistance to the establishment, conduct or operation of such game if he performs, without fee or remuneration, acts directed toward the arrangement or facilitation of the game, such as inviting persons to play, permitting the use of premises therefor or supplying cards or other equipment used therein. A person who engages in "bookmaking" as defined in this section is not a "player."

d. "Something of value" means any money or property, any token, object or article exchangeable for money or property, or any form of credit or promise directly or indirectly contemplating transfer of money or property or of any interest therein or involving extension of a service, entertainment or a privilege of playing at a game or scheme without charge. This definition, however, does not include any form of promise involving extension of a privilege of playing at a game without charge on a mechanical or electronic amusement device other than a slot machine as an award for the attainment of a certain score on that device.

e. "Gambling device" means any device, machine, paraphernalia or equipment which is used or usable in the playing phases of any gambling activity, whether such activity consists of gambling between persons or gambling by a person involving the playing of a machine. Notwithstanding the foregoing, lottery tickets, policy slips and other items used in the playing phases of lottery and policy schemes are not gambling devices.

f. "Slot machine" means any mechanical, electrical or other device, contrivance or machine which, upon insertion of a coin, token or similar object therein, or upon payment of any consideration whatsoever, is available to play or operate, the play or operation of which, whether by reason of the skill of the operator or application of the element of chance, or both, may deliver or entitle the person playing or operating the machine to receive cash or tokens to be exchanged for cash, whether the payoff is made automatically from the machine or in any other manner whatsoever. A device so constructed, or readily adaptable or convertible to such use, is no less a slot machine because it is not in working order or because some mechanical act of manipulation or repair is required to accomplish its adaptation, conversion or workability.

g. "Bookmaking" means advancing gambling activity by unlawfully accepting bets from members of the public upon the outcome of future contingent events as a business.

h. "Lottery" means an unlawful gambling scheme in which:
    (1) The players pay or agree to pay something of value for chances, represented and differentiated by numbers or by combinations of numbers or by some other media, one or more of which chances are to be designated the winning ones;
    (2) The winning chances are to be determined by a drawing or by some other method based upon the element of chance; and
    (3) The holders of the winning chances are to receive something of value.

i. "Policy" or "the numbers game" means a form of lottery in which the winning chances or plays are not determined upon the basis of a drawing or other act on the part of persons conducting or connected with the scheme but upon the basis of the outcome or outcomes of a future contingent event or events otherwise unrelated to the particular scheme.

j. "Gambling resort" means a place to which persons may resort for engaging in gambling activity.

k. "Unlawful" means not specifically authorized by law.

22-2.   Promoting gambling

a. Promoting gambling defined. A person is guilty of promoting gambling when he knowingly:
    (1) Accepts or receives money or other property, pursuant to an agreement or understanding with any person whereby he participates or will participate in the proceeds of gambling activity; or
    (2) Engages in conduct, which materially aids any form of gambling activity. Such conduct includes but is not limited to conduct directed toward the creation or establishment

of the particular game, contest, scheme, device or activity involved, toward the acquisition or maintenance of premises, paraphernalia, equipment or apparatus therefor, toward the solicitation or inducement of persons to participate therein, toward the actual conduct of the playing phases thereof, toward the arrangement of any of its financial or recording phases or toward any other phase of its operation.

b. Grading. A person who violates the provisions of subsection a. by:

(1) Engaging in bookmaking to the extent he receives or accepts in any one day more than five bets totaling more than $1,000; or

(2) Receiving, in connection with a lottery or policy scheme or enterprise money or written records from a person other than a player whose chances or plays are represented by such money or records or more than $100 in any one day of money played in such scheme or enterprise, is guilty of a felony of the third degree and shall be subject to a fine of not more than $35,000 and any other appropriate disposition.

A person who violates the provisions of subsection a. by engaging in bookmaking to the extent he receives or accepts three or more bets in any two-week period is guilty of a felony of the fourth degree and shall be subject to a fine of not more than $25,000 and any other appropriate disposition. Otherwise, promoting gambling is a misdemeanor A and shall be subject to a fine of not more than $10,000 and any other appropriate disposition.

c. It is a defense to a prosecution under subsection a. that the person participated only as a player. It shall be the burden of the defendant to prove by clear and convincing evidence his status as such player.

PRACTICAL APPLICATION OF STATUTE

All members of The Smart Man's gang are guilty of promoting gambling per the provisions of section 22-2. As particular examples, Knuckles is guilty of violating subsection a.(1) for his weekly collection work, and Small Teeth is guilty of violating subsection a.(2) for acquiring the various locations where the group's bookmaking activities occurred and for soliciting clients who placed bets.

Promoting Gambling Under Subsection a.(1)

In a nutshell, per 22-2a.(1), a person who accepts or receives money (or other property), pursuant to gambling activity, is guilty of promoting gambling. To be convicted, the person must "participate in the proceeds of the gambling activity." Per subsection b. of the statute, this is a third degree felony where "he receives or accepts in any one day more than five bets totaling more than $1,000." It is a fourth degree felony where "he receives or accepts three or more bets in any two-week period." Otherwise, it is a misdemeanor A.

Knuckles was the chief enforcer of the gang. He went out to personally collect money from losers who didn't come to him. On a weekly basis, he would receive seven figures in cash pursuant to the bettors' understanding that they had to pay up when they lost. Knuckles personally profited from the proceeds of this gambling activity; accordingly, his actions render him guilty of promoting gambling under subsection a.(1) of the statute. His offense is a third degree felony, given that his weekly seven figures collection obviously involved "more than five bets totaling more than $1,000" in any one day.

Promoting Gambling Under Subsection a.(2)

A person is guilty of promoting gambling under subsection a.(2) where he "engages in conduct which materially aids any form of gambling activity." Such conduct ranges from acquiring premises to obtaining gambling paraphernalia to soliciting gamblers. The grading of an offense under a.(2) is the same as it is under subsection a.(1).

Small Teeth acquired the various locations where the group's bookmaking activities occurred, and he solicited clients who placed bets with them. The Mason County task force investigating the gang actually recorded him bragging that his work "netted over 500 bets in the last week that totaled more than a million dollars." Small Teeth's conduct in acquiring locations and bringing in gamblers clearly materially aided the gang's gambling activity, so he is guilty of promoting gambling per the provisions of subsection a.(2) of the statute. This is a third degree felony—over 500 bets totaling more than a million dollars in a week surely exceeds the five bets/$1,000 in a day requirement necessary for this statute's highest degree offense.

Player Defense

As is common throughout the gambling offenses, section 22-2 provides a defense for the bettors. Subsection c. of the statute states that a person has a defense to prosecution where he "participated only as a player."

22-3.   **Possession of gambling records**

   a. A person is guilty of possession of gambling records when, with knowledge of the contents thereof, he possesses any writing, paper, instrument or article:

      (1) Of a kind commonly used in the operation or promotion of a bookmaking scheme or enterprise, including any paper or paper product in sheet form chemically converted to nitrocellulose having explosive characteristics as well as any water soluble paper or paper derivative in sheet form; or

      (2) Of a kind commonly used in the operation, promotion or playing of a lottery or policy scheme or enterprise.

   b. Defenses.

      (1) It is a defense to a prosecution under subsection a.(2) which must be proven by the defendant by clear and convincing evidence that the writing, paper, instrument or article possessed by the defendant constituted, reflected or represented plays, bets or chances of the defendant himself in a number not exceeding ten.

      (2) It is a defense to a prosecution under subsection a. which must be proven by the defendant by clear and convincing evidence that the writing, paper, instrument or article possessed by the defendant was neither used nor intended to be used in the operation or promotion of a bookmaking scheme or enterprise or in the operation, promotion or playing of a lottery or policy scheme or enterprise.

   c. Grading. Possession of gambling records is a felony of the third degree and shall be subject to a fine of not more than $35,000 and any other appropriate disposition when the writing, paper, instrument or article:

      (1) In a bookmaking scheme or enterprise constitutes, reflects or represents more than five bets totaling more than $1,000; or

      (2) In the case of a lottery or policy scheme or enterprise constitutes, reflects or represents more than 100 plays or chances therein.

      Otherwise, possession of gambling records is a misdemeanor A and shall be subject to a fine of not more than $20,000 and any other appropriate disposition.

PRACTICAL APPLICATION OF STATUTE

The Smart Man is guilty of possessing gambling records. In his case, it is a felony of the third degree.

A person who possesses items such as papers or instruments that are commonly used in promoting gambling activities may be convicted of an offense under 22-3. However, as subsection a. of the statute provides, he must have "knowledge" that the items he possesses are actually records of gambling activities.

The Smart Man's personal home was raided by a Mason County task force armed with a search warrant. There, they found The Smart Man spraying a fire hose all over his basement floor. He was attempting to destroy thousands of sheets of "water soluble" paper that contained thousands of coded bets valued in the millions of dollars. The task force, however, was able to thwart The Smart Man's efforts to the extent that they recovered sheets that contained over a thousand different bets valued in excess of $3 million.

"Water soluble" paper is commonly used in gambling activities for the obvious reason that it is easy to destroy. This particular "water soluble" paper supply contained thousands of coded bets that were worth millions of dollars—thus, the sheets of paper are gambling records as defined in 22-3. The question is, though, did The Smart Man have "knowledge" of the paper's illicit contents? Of course he did. The Smart Man was the individual who oversaw the gang's entire operation. The task force had evidence that, at the end of each business day, all gambling proceeds were turned over to him— not to mention that he was furiously spraying water all over the paper in an effort to destroy it. The Smart Man, accordingly, is guilty of possessing gambling records.

Subsection c. of 22-3 sets forth the grading for possession of gambling records. With reference to a bookmaking scheme, it is a third degree offense where the records "represent more than five bets totaling more than $1,000"; otherwise, it is a misdemeanor A. Since The Smart Man's confiscated "water soluble" paper contained over a thousand bets valued in excess of $3 million, he is guilty of a third degree gambling records offense.

Defenses

Subsection b. creates defenses to prosecution under the statute. Of particular note is the language of b.(2) that allows a defendant to avoid prosecution where his records represent "plays, bets or chances of the defendant himself in a number not exceeding ten." This again is a provision that protects players. In other words, if a gambler jots down on a piece of paper $500 on the Yankees, $500 on the Braves, $250 on the Cardinals and $250 on the Mariners, he cannot be convicted of possessing gambling records.

22-4.

Maintenance of a gambling resort

a. A person is guilty of a felony of the fourth degree if, having substantial proprietary or other authoritative control over premises which are being used with his knowledge for purposes of activities prohibited by 22-2 and 22-3, he permits such to occur or continue or makes no effort to prevent its occurrence or continuation and he accepts or receives money or other property pursuant to an agreement or understanding with any person whereby he participates or will participate in the proceeds of such gambling activity on such premises and shall be subject to a fine of not more than $25,000 and any other appropriate disposition.

b. A person is guilty of a felony of the fourth degree if, having substantial proprietary or other authoritative control over premises open to the general public which are being used with his knowledge for purposes of gambling activity, he permits such to occur or continue or makes no effort to prevent its occurrence or continuation and shall be subject to a fine of not more than $25,000 and any other appropriate disposition.

PRACTICAL APPLICATION OF STATUTE

The Hyena is guilty of maintaining a gambling resort for running The Purple Mule, an "after-hours" club where patrons gambled on a nightly basis. This is a felony of the fourth degree.

Basically, a person is guilty of maintaining a gambling resort where he permits gambling to occur on premises that he owns or has authoritative control over. In order to be convicted of this offense, the person must "know" that the gambling is happening. He also must accept or receive something of value (e.g., money) pursuant to an agreement (e.g., a bet), and he must "participate in the proceeds of such gambling activity."

The Hyena had authoritative control over the "after-hours" club, The Purple Mule—he ran it. At this club, people played illegal games of poker, blackjack, craps and roulette. The Hyena not only "knew" that the illicit gambling was happening at The Purple Mule, he encouraged it to continue and participated in it. At the end of each evening, he received significant amounts of cash and sometimes other items of substantial monetary value, such as jewelry, automobiles and property deeds—all from people who lost in their respective games. And The Hyena personally profited from the proceeds of the gambling at The Purple Mule, as the profits were split up among his partners and him. With all of the aforesaid elements occurring, The Hyena is guilty of the fourth degree felony of maintaining a gambling resort.

22-4.1.   **Shipboard gambling; felony; grading; exception**

a. A person is guilty of shipboard gambling when the person:
  (1) Knowingly causes, engages in or permits any gambling activity prohibited under 22-2, 22-3 or 22-4 to be conducted on a vessel that embarks from any point within the State, and disembarks at the same or another point within the State, whether the gambling activity is conducted within or without the waters of the State; or
  (2) Manages, supervises, controls, operates or owns any vessel that embarks from any point within the State, and disembarks at the same or another point within the State, during which time the person knowingly causes or permits any gambling activity prohibited under this chapter, whether the gambling activity is conducted within or without the waters of the State.

b. Any person who violates the provisions of subsection a. of this section is guilty of a felony of the same degree as the most serious felony that was committed in violation of 22-2, 22-3 or 22-4, as appropriate.

c. This section shall not apply to gambling activity conducted on United States-flagged or foreign-flagged vessels during travel from a foreign nation or another state or possession of the United States up to the point of first entry into this State's waters or during travel to a foreign nation or another state or possession of the United States from the point of departure from this State's waters, provided that nothing herein shall preclude prosecution for any other offense under this chapter.

PRACTICAL APPLICATION OF STATUTE

This statute primarily prohibits any illegal gambling—as defined in 22-2 (promoting gambling), 22-3 (possessing gambling records) and 22-4 (maintaining a gambling resort) from occurring on a ship. A person is only guilty of an offense under this statute if the ship both embarks from a point in the state and disembarks at a point within the state. If these factors are met, it is irrelevant "whether the gambling activity is conducted within or without the waters" of this state.

Follow this example. A ship leaves Port Vertas in this state and travels to waters in the *next* state wherein an illegal blackjack game is commenced by the ship's personnel. The personnel act as dealers while guests on the ship place bets. The gambling stops before the ship leaves the waters of the other state. The ship then turns around and heads to Port Vertas, where it eventually docks. The ship personnel who "promoted gambling" as defined in 22-2 are guilty of an offense under 22-4.1—even though the actual gambling occurred in the waters of *another state*. Why? Because the ship both embarked and disembarked at points in this state.

Subsection b. provides that any person who violates this statute "is guilty of a felony of the same degree as the most serious felony that was committed in violation of 22-2, 22-3 or 22-4." Accordingly, if the shipboard gambling offenses included actions that would constitute a fourth degree maintenance of a gambling resort offense and a third degree promoting gambling offense, then the person would be guilty of a third degree felony under 22-4.1 because the third degree promoting gambling offense was the most serious offense committed.

22-5.   ## Possession of a gambling device

A person except a player is guilty of possession of a gambling device when, with knowledge of the character thereof, he manufactures, sells, transports, places or possesses or conducts or negotiates any transaction affecting or designed to affect ownership, custody or use of:

  a. A slot machine; or
  b. Any other gambling device, believing that the same is to be used in the advancement of unlawful gambling activity.

Possession of a gambling device other than under such circumstances as would constitute a violation of the "Casino Control Act" is a misdemeanor A; provided, however, that possession of not more than one gambling device other than a slot machine for social use within the home shall not be an offense under this section; and provided further, however, that possession of one or more antique slot machines shall not be an offense under this section or under the "Casino Control Act." As used in this section, "antique slot machine" means a slot machine which was manufactured prior to 1941. Nothing herein contained shall be construed to authorize the use of an antique slot machine for any unlawful purpose or for gaming.

PRACTICAL APPLICATION OF STATUTE

Members of the Mason County task force confiscated five roulette boards, dozens of decks of playing cards and three crap tables at The Purple Mule. Pursuant to this seizure, The Hyena is guilty of possessing gambling devices, which is a misdemeanor A.

A person—except a player—is guilty of possessing a gambling device if he "believes that the same is to be used in the advancement of unlawful gambling activity." If the aforementioned elements are met, a person can be convicted of possessing a gambling device whether he simply possesses it, manufactures it, sells it or even transports it.

The Hyena ran the "after-hours" club The Purple Mule, where gamblers played illegal games of poker, blackjack, craps and roulette. He knew the gambling devices involved—the roulette boards, crap tables and playing cards—were "used in the advancement of unlawful gambling activity." Accordingly, he has violated the provisions of 22-5.

It is interesting to note that "possession of not more than one gambling device" does not constitute a violation of the statute. Also, a person can apparently possess any number of slot machines "for social use within the home" and not be guilty of an offense under 22-5. Similarly, possession of "antique slot machines" is not unlawful— obviously, as long as they are not used for unlawful gambling purposes.

END OF CHAPTER REVIEW

Multiple-Choice Questions

1. Which of the following statements is true about a person who participates in an illegal card game only as a player?
   a. He is guilty of only a misdemeanor B.
   b. He is guilty of a fourth degree felony under all circumstances.
   c. He is guilty of an offense one degree less than the actor guilty of promoting the card game.
   d. He is guilty of an offense of the same degree as the actor guilty of promoting the card game.
   e. He has an affirmative defense.

2. Knuckles collects money from losing bettors for an illegal gambling operation. Last week, he received over $150,000 from losers who made hundreds of bets, pursuant to their understanding that they had to pay up when they lost. Knuckles, a partner in the gambling operation, personally profited from these funds. Knuckles is guilty of what offense for receiving these funds?
   a. nothing, if he was a player himself
   b. a misdemeanor A because all gambling offenses are now a misdemeanor A
   c. a fourth degree felony of shipboard gambling because of the collection activities
   d. a third degree felony of promoting gambling, given that his one-week $150,000 collection on hundreds of bets exceeded more than five bets totaling more than $1,000 on any given day
   e. a first degree felony of promoting gambling, given that his one-week $150,000 collection on hundreds of bets exceeded more than 50 bets totaling more than $10,000 in any one week

3. Which of the following is *not* an element of the offense in promoting gambling?
   a. The bookmaking must be controlled by organized crime.
   b. The bookmaking must be performed in a centralized location.
   c. The actor must "knowingly engage" in promoting the gambling activities.
   d. All of the above are *not* elements of the offense of promoting gambling.
   e. Only a and b are *not* elements of the offense of promoting gambling.

4. Possessing gambling records is:
   a. a felony of the third degree when the instrument used in a bookmaking scheme reflects more than five bets totaling more than $1,000
   b. a felony of the third degree when the instrument in a lottery scheme reflects more than one 100 bets
   c. a misdemeanor A in all matters other than those described in a and b
   d. all of the above
   e. none of the above because it is always a misdemeanor A

Essay Question

1. The Hyena had authoritative control over the "after-hours" club The Purple Mule— he ran it. At this club, people played games of poker, blackjack, craps and roulette. The Hyena encouraged the gambling to continue, participated in it and profited from all the players by charging a "playing fee" and by taking in all their monetary losses. What offense, if any, is The Hyena guilty of for running The Purple Mule? Explain your answer, applying the elements of the offense to the facts. Also, note the degree of the offense, if you believe he is indeed guilty.

23

TERRORISM

FACT PATTERN (PERTAINING TO CHAPTERS 23–26)

State Police Captain Manny Tamro arrested brothers George and Alex Evile after a daring, and often grotesque, trek through Jefferson City's underground sewer system. The Evile brothers had been the subject of a two-year arson and terrorism investigation that ended when George detonated a briefcase bomb at the Sharpese Hotel in New Bainbridge.

George Evile was the founder and pastor of MIFA, a radical religious cult that consistently disrupted political activities through various disorderly behaviors. Several of the cult's members also had previously been arrested for an array of violent felonies. George, in an effort to instantly put MIFA on the national map, plotted and carried out the cult's ultimate act of infamy.

Posing as a lobbyist for a prestigious firm, George arrived at the Sharpese Hotel on an otherwise uncelebrated Friday evening. He entered the hotel's lobby carrying an oversized briefcase, his destination being a convention of political lobbyists who were assembled to hear one of the industry's top personnel speak on multiple domestic and international issues. George sat with the other lobbyists, mixing in with the men and women; thereafter, he left his briefcase in the middle of the meeting room. The briefcase, however, did not include the usual materials retained by a lobbyist—it held a massive exploding device that contained the nerve agent sarin. The bomb exploded five minutes after George's departure from the hotel, with 14 people killed and another 75 injured by the explosion.

George Evile stated that his reason for the murders was "to exact revenge for the state's unfair policies toward MIFA." He was specifically upset that the government required MIFA members to pay past-due state income taxes. He also demanded that the state turn over Jefferson City to MIFA, wherein the cult would run it as its own separate state. Evile warned that more devastation would occur if his demands were not met.

One week to the day of the bombing, Captain Tamro, off duty, spotted an individual who appeared to be George Evile. Although the man was wearing a hard hat and sunglasses, the state police captain recognized the unmistakable cleft chin and unibrow that marked the master criminal's face. As Tamro approached, the suspect was descending into a manhole on a busy Jefferson City street. Tamro drew his off-duty pistol and ordered the man to "freeze"; instead, the man scurried down the manhole, and Tamro heard him yell, "Alex, move! It's 5-0!" Tamro immediately followed—and the rat race commenced.

Thundering down the manhole ladder, Tamro could make out two shadowy figures streaming into the Jefferson City sewer system. A former Olympic qualifier in the 1,500 meters, Tamro utilized his long strides to catch up to the men within moments. He tackled the individual who was closer to him, forcing the man's nostrils and mouth into the sewer mush located on the ground beneath their feet—it was Alex Evile.

Tamro immediately knocked Alex unconscious and proceeded after George, who had left his younger brother in the dust. The former track star turned up the heat, accelerating to a speed that most could only accomplish in an automobile. Soon another human being was in his path. This time, it was George Evile. Tamro again ordered the man to stop. Suddenly George did, but instead of surrendering, he fired two quick rounds at his law enforcement pursuer. Unharmed, Tamro fired back, striking George in the leg and arm. The terrorist crumbled to the ground, crying and whimpering in pain. Backup soon arrived, and the Evile brothers were carted away to jail.

Subsequent to their arrests, both brothers, with the presence of legal counsel, provided statements to the state police. Their own words confirmed most of Captain Tamro's suspicions—the men brazenly admitted to committing a variety of felonies.

Alex Evile was the president of a supposedly legitimate charitable organization, The Lady Dove Society, which purported to raise and distribute funds for a selection of endangered bird species. Alex, though, admitted that The Lady Dove Society was actually a front for MIFA. The majority of the funds raised via Alex's efforts were diverted to support the terrorist activities of MIFA; specifically, Alex Evile transferred over $500,000 to MIFA so that his brother could carry out the bombing at the Sharpese Hotel.

In a separate MIFA fund-raising campaign, George Evile engaged in a multitude of activities involving firearms and other dangerous weapons. As his first order of business, George set up a machine gun manufacturing shop in Jefferson City where he produced and sold in excess of 1,000 machine guns; over 200 distinct transactions to nearly 150 separate buyers occurred over an eight-year period, the first occurring in 1995.

At this shop, George also routinely defaced firearms, such as automatic rifles and handguns, because by removing these weapons' serial numbers, he could more readily sell them. George closely monitored his firearms shop, visiting the establishment on a daily basis and barking orders and directives to the dozens of employees who worked for him. When George couldn't make it to the shop, his brother, Alex, operated the business in his stead.

Outside of the gun manufacturing shop, George Evile also personally committed a number of felonies where he employed the use of his firearms. Wielding an automatic rifle, he held up a candy shop in Walcott; there he sported a body vest and shot the clerk in the leg just before fleeing the store. In Holbrooke, George sold a kilogram of cocaine to a pawnbroker. To protect himself during the deal, George carried a machine gun and a .22-caliber pistol. During this same transaction, he sold the pawnbroker five handguns and ten daggers, which the pawnbroker resold to a college student later that day. The pawnbroker's business day was completed by the sale of three pairs of handcuffs and a combat knife with an eight-inch blade to a 15-year-old high school freshman. George's day ended when he appeared at the pawnbroker's home and personally instructed the man on how to manufacture machine guns in exchange for a $20,000 cash payment. George did this knowing that the pawnbroker was intending to manufacture machine guns, not to engage in his usual sale activities but to use them in the commission of a string of planned armored car robberies.

Subsequent to the Evile brothers' confessions, Captain Tamro procured a search warrant to search their homes and businesses. At the machine gun shop, nearly 300 machine guns were seized along with several automatic rifles. At George Evile's home, the police confiscated a .22-caliber handgun and a handgun silencer. The search of Alex Evile's house netted a sawed-off shotgun, a 12-inch switchblade and 500 hollow nose bullets. This search also resulted in the arrest of Alice B. Mackerel. The reason? When the police arrived, she put up her hands and said, "Okay. You got me. I hid Alex's brother, George, in my basement after he bombed the Sharpese Hotel. I'm sorry . . . Does anyone have a cigarette?"

Back at the trooper barracks, Captain Tamro signed the complaints for the numerous charges filed against the Evile brothers, Alice B. Mackerel and the pawnbroker, who was picked up on an arrest warrant. Criminal case histories were secured on each individual, and two had prior records. Alex Evile was convicted of arson when he was 33 years old; at 21, he also had faced a charge resulting from his paddling of three young men who were pledging his college fraternity.

The pawnbroker, though, boasted a lengthy rap sheet. He once was convicted of an offense for maintaining an uncovered abandoned cesspool on his property; in the same year, he was arrested at a supermarket for opening a package of cupcakes, spitting on the baked goods and resealing the package. Two years after that incident, he was arrested for taking down a stop sign that was located at a busy Union City intersection. On the same day that he removed the sign, an unassuming motorist crossed through the intersection without stopping and crashed into another motor vehicle, and a passenger in one of the cars was killed.

In the most bizarre case, investigators from a joint task force of the Union City Police Department, the Magno County Sheriff's Department and the Magno County Prosecutor's Office learned that the pawnbroker drew blood from his sister just prior to her dying. Following a lead connected to this medical procedure, investigators ransacked a home laboratory in neighboring Sterling County. There, they found a futuristic incubator system and certain "growths" accruing in them. Though not human, the growths were mammal forms.

In adjoining setups, the investigators discovered the woman's blood distributed among several test tubes and mixed with various chemicals and hormones, and an embryo appeared to be developing in the largest test tube. Plans attached to the test tubes described the cloning of the pawnbroker's sister. Arrested at the home lab was Dr. Cornelius Monteforte, a chiropractor-turned-scientist. These offenses concluded the pawnbroker's criminal history.

23-1. **Short title**

This act shall be known and may be cited as the "September 11th, 2001 Anti-Terrorism Act."

23-2. **Felony of terrorism; definitions**

    a. A person is guilty of the felony of terrorism if he commits or attempts, conspires or threatens to commit any felony enumerated in subsection c. of this section with the purpose:

        (1) To promote an act of terror;

        (2) To terrorize five or more persons;

      (3) To influence the policy or affect the conduct of government by terror; or

      (4) To cause by an act of terror the impairment or interruption of public communications, public transportation, public or private buildings, common carriers, public utilities or other public services.

b. Terrorism is a felony of the first degree.

      (1) Notwithstanding any other provision of law to the contrary, any person convicted under this section shall be sentenced to a term of 30 years, during which the person shall not be eligible for parole, or to a specific term of years which shall be between 30 years and life imprisonment, of which the person shall serve not less than 30 years before being eligible for parole.

      (2) If a violation of this section results in death, the person shall be sentenced to a term of life imprisonment, during which time the person shall not be eligible for parole.

c. The felonies encompassed by this section are murder; aggravated manslaughter or manslaughter; vehicular homicide; aggravated assault; disarming a law enforcement officer; kidnapping; criminal restraint; robbery; carjacking; aggravated arson or arson; causing or risking widespread injury or damage; damage to nuclear plant with the purpose to cause or threat to cause release of radiation; damage to nuclear plant resulting in death by radiation; damage to nuclear plant resulting in injury by radiation; producing or possessing chemical weapons, biological agents or nuclear or radiological devices pursuant; burglary; possession of prohibited weapons and devices; possession of weapons for unlawful purposes; unlawful possession of weapons; weapons training for illegal activities; racketeering; and any other felony involving a risk of death or serious bodily injury to any person.

d. Definitions. For the purposes of this section:

      (1) "Government" means the United States, any state, county, municipality or other political unit, or any department, agency or subdivision of any of the foregoing, or any corporation or other association carrying out the functions of government.

      (2) "Serious bodily injury" means bodily injury which creates a substantial risk of death or which causes serious, permanent disfigurement or protracted loss or impairment of the function of any bodily member or organ.

      (3) "Terror" means the menace or fear of death or serious bodily injury.

      (4) "Terrorize" means to convey the menace or fear of death or serious bodily injury by words or actions.

e. A prosecution pursuant to this section may be brought by the Attorney General, his assistants and deputies within the Division of Criminal Justice or a county prosecutor or a designated assistant prosecutor if the county prosecutor is expressly authorized in writing by the Attorney General to prosecute a violation of this section.

f. A conviction of terrorism under this section shall not merge with a conviction of any other offense, nor shall such other conviction merge with a conviction under this section, and the court shall impose separate sentences upon each violation of this section and any other offense.

g. Nothing contained in this section shall be deemed to preclude, if the evidence so warrants, an indictment and conviction for murder under the provisions of 1-3 or any other offense.

PRACTICAL APPLICATION OF STATUTE

George Evile is guilty of terrorism for murdering 14 individuals at the Sharpese Hotel. This is a felony of the first degree, and it is in addition to the separate offenses of murder that he is guilty of committing.

In order for a person to be convicted of terrorism, he must commit, attempt, conspire or threaten to commit one of several offenses enumerated in subsection c. of 23-2. The offenses found in subsection c. range from murder to aggravated assault to carjacking to racketeering to arson and include a number of others. In addition to being involved in one of these felonies, a defendant must act with the purpose "to promote an act of terror," "to terrorize five or more persons" or "to influence the policy or affect the conduct of government by terror." A defendant can also be convicted of terrorism if, in addition to being involved in one of the enumerated felonies, he causes "by an act of terror" the impairment of matters such as public transportation, public or private buildings or public utilities.

"Terror" is defined in subsection d. of the statute as "the menace or fear of death or serious bodily injury." "Terrorize," per subsection d., means "to convey the menace or fear of death or serious bodily injury by words or actions."

George Evile entered the Sharpese Hotel carrying an oversized briefcase. His destination was a convention of political lobbyists who were assembled to hear one of the industry's top personnel speak on various domestic and international issues. George sat with the lobbyists, mixing in with the men and women; thereafter, he left his briefcase in the middle of the meeting room. The briefcase, however, did not contain the usual materials retained by a lobbyist—it held a massive explosive device containing the nerve agent sarin. The bomb exploded five minutes after George's departure from the hotel, with 14 people killed and another 75 injured by the explosion.

George Evile stated that his reason for the murders was "to exact revenge for the state's unfair policies toward MIFA," his religious group, which failed to pay state taxes. He demanded that the government not only agree to relieve MIFA of their past-due taxes but also provide them Jefferson City, where they would set up a separate state. He warned that more devastation would occur if his demands were not met.

George Evile is guilty of terrorism under 23-2, as all of the elements of the statute were met through his mass murder at the Sharpese Hotel. First, George committed one of the felonies enumerated in subsection c.—he murdered 14 people and injured 75 others. He murdered these innocent people with the purpose "to influence the policy or affect the conduct of the government" because his goal was to avoid tax payments for his religious group, MIFA, and to obtain Jefferson City as their own separate state. With these elements met, George Evile has committed the first degree felony of terrorism; he also has committed murder and aggravated assault and should be convicted under those statutes as well.

23-3.   **Producing or possessing chemical weapons, biological agents or nuclear or radiological devices; definitions**

a. A person who, purposely or knowingly, unlawfully develops, produces, otherwise acquires, transfers, receives, stockpiles, retains, owns, possesses or uses, or threatens to use, any chemical weapon, biological agent, toxin, vector or delivery system for use as a weapon, or nuclear or radiological device commits a felony of the first degree, except that:

(1) Notwithstanding any other provision of law to the contrary, any person convicted under this subsection shall be sentenced to a term of 30 years, during which the person shall not be eligible for parole, or to a specific term of years which shall be between 30 years and life imprisonment, of which the person shall serve not less than 30 years before being eligible for parole.

    (2) If a violation of this section results in death, the person shall be sentenced to a term of life imprisonment, during which time the person shall not be eligible for parole.

b. Any manufacturer, distributor, transferor, possessor or user of any toxic chemical, biological agent, toxin or vector, or radioactive material that is related to a lawful industrial, agricultural, research, medical, pharmaceutical or other activity, who recklessly allows an unauthorized individual to obtain access to the toxic chemical or biological agent, toxin or vector or radioactive material commits a felony of the second degree and shall be subject to a fine of up to $250,000 for each violation.

c. For the purposes of this section:

    (1) "Chemical weapon" means:

        (a) A toxic chemical and its precursors, except where intended for a lawful purpose as long as the type and quantity are consistent with such a purpose. "Chemical weapon" shall include but not be limited to:

           (i) Nerve agents, including GA (Tabun) cyanide irreversible inhibitor, Sarin (GB), GB (Soman) fluorine, reversible "slow aging," GF and VX sulfur, irreversible;

           (ii) Choking agents, including Phosgene (CG) and Diphosgene (DP);

           (iii) Blood agents, including Hydrogen Cyanide (AC), Cyanogen Chloride (CK) and Arsine (SA);

           (iv) Blister agents, including mustards (H, HD [sulfur mustard], HN-1, HN-2, HN-3 [nitrogen mustard]), arsenicals such as Lewisite (L), and urticants, including CX; and

           (v) Incapacitating agents, including BZ; or

        (b) A munition or device specifically designed to cause death or other harm through the toxic properties of those chemical weapons defined in subparagraph (a) of paragraph (1) of subsection c. of this section, which would be released as a result of the employment of such munition or device; or

        (c) Any equipment specifically designed for use directly in connection with the employment of munitions or devices specified in subparagraph (b) of paragraph (1) of subsection c. of this section.

    (2) "Biological agent" means any microorganism, virus, bacteria, rickettsiae, fungi, toxin, infectious substance or biological product that may be engineered as a result of biotechnology, or any naturally occurring or bioengineered component of any such microorganism, virus, bacteria, rickettsiae, fungi, infectious substance or biological product, capable of causing:

        (a) Death, disease or other biological malfunction in a human, an animal, a plant or another living organism;

        (b) Deterioration of food, water, equipment, supplies or material of any kind; or

        (c) Deleterious alteration of the environment.

        "Biological agent" shall include, but not be limited to, viruses, including Felonyan-Congo hemorrhagic fever virus, eastern equine encephalitis virus, ebola viruses, equine morbilli virus, lassa fever virus, Marburg virus, Rift Valley fever virus, South American hemorrhagic fever viruses (Junin, Machupo, Sabia, Flexal, Guanarito), tick-borne encephalitis complex viruses, variola major virus (smallpox virus), Venezuelan equine encephalitis virus, viruses causing hantavirus pulmonary syndrome and yellow fever virus; bacteria, including Bacillus anthracis (commonly known as anthrax), Brucella abortus, Brucella melitensis, Brucella suis, Burkholderia (pseudomonas) mallei, Burkholderia (pseudomonas) pseudomallei, Clostridium botulinum, Francisella tularensis, Yersinia pestis (commonly known as plague); rickettsiae, including Coxiella burnetii, Rickettsia prowazekii and Rickettsia rickettsii; Coccidioides immitis fungus; and abrin, aflatoxins, Botulinus toxins, Clostridium perringes epsilon toxin, conotoxins, diacetoxyscirpenol, ricin, saxitoxin, shiga toxin, Staphylococcal enterotoxins, tetrodotoxins and T-2 toxin.

(3) "Toxin" means the toxic material of plants, animals, microorganisms, viruses, fungi or infectious substances or a recombinant molecule, whatever its origin or method of production, including:

   (a) Any poisonous substance or biological product that may be engineered as a result of biotechnology or produced by a living organism; or

   (b) Any poisonous isomer or biological product, homolog or derivative of such a substance.

(4) "Vector" means a living organism or molecule, including a recombinant molecule, or biological product that may be engineered as a result of biotechnology, capable of carrying a biological agent or toxin to a host.

(5) "Nuclear or radiological device" includes:

   (a) Any nuclear device which is an explosive device designed to cause a nuclear yield;

   (b) A radiological dispersal device which is an explosive device used to spread radioactive material; or

   (c) A simple radiological dispersal device which is any act, container or any other device used to release radiological material for use as a weapon.

(6) "Delivery system" means any apparatus, equipment, device or means of delivery specifically designed to deliver or disseminate a biological agent, toxin or vector.

(7) "For use as a weapon" means all situations in which the circumstances indicate that the person intended to employ an item's ready capacity of lethal use or of inflicting serious bodily injury.

d. This section shall not apply to the development, production, acquisition, transfer, receipt, possession or use of any toxic chemical, biological agent, toxin or vector that is related to a lawful industrial, agricultural, research, medical, pharmaceutical or other activity.

e. This section shall not apply to any device whose possession is otherwise lawful pursuant to 24-6.

f. Nothing contained in this section shall be deemed to preclude, if the evidence so warrants, an indictment and conviction for murder under the provisions of 1-3 or any other offense.

PRACTICAL APPLICATION OF STATUTE

Section 23-3 provides that it is a first degree felony to possess any chemical weapons, biological agents or nuclear or radiological devices. George Evile utilized the nerve agent sarin in his deadly bombing at the Sharpese Hotel and therefore is guilty of violating this statute.

Chemical weapons include nerve agents (e.g., sarin), choking agents (e.g., phosgene), blood agents (e.g., hydrogen cyanide), blistering agents (e.g., sulfur mustard) and incapacitating agents (e.g., BZ). Biological agents are matters such as microorganisms, viruses, bacteria and toxins that can cause death or disease to living organisms or deteriorate necessities such as food and water. Examples of biological agents that can be used as weapons are the smallpox virus, the plague, anthrax and T-2 toxin.

Per subsection a. of the statute, it is not only an offense to possess a chemical weapon, biological agent or nuclear or radiological device but also a felony for developing, acquiring, transferring and using the items. The person is even guilty of a first degree felony if he threatens to use any of them as a weapon.

George Evile did actually use the nerve agent sarin as a chemical weapon. He left a briefcase in the middle of a conference room, filled with political lobbyists, at the Sharpese Hotel. This briefcase, however, did not include the usual materials retained by a lobbyist; instead, it held a massive explosive device that contained sarin. After George departed the room, the briefcase exploded, killing 14 people. For George's possession of the nerve agent sarin, which he used as a chemical weapon, he is guilty of a first degree felony under 23-3.

Manufacturer/Distributor Recklessly Allowing Access to Chemical/Biological Agents, Radioactive Material

Even those who are permitted by law to manufacture, possess and transfer materials such as toxic chemicals, biological agents and radioactive material may be guilty of a felony. In certain circumstances, it is lawful to possess the aforementioned deadly items, for example, in agricultural research or medical activities. However, if someone involved in any of these activities (e.g., a manufacturer or distributor) "recklessly" allows an unauthorized individual to obtain access to any of the deadly materials, then that person is guilty of a second degree felony.

Here's an example. Jarrod Mashington is an employee of a medical research facility that is currently performing research on anthrax. Marty Ponroe approaches Mashington and advises that he will pay Mashington $5,000 to sneak him into the building. Ponroe tells Mashington that he wants to get into the building because the facility's president has a safe with over $100,000 cash stored in it; he further tells Mashington that he will provide him with an additional $15,000 once the money heist has been completed. Believing all this, Mashington sneaks Ponroe into the facility, and Ponroe steals quantities of anthrax, his true target.

Jarrod Mashington should be convicted of a second degree felony under subsection b. of 23-3. Although he didn't "purposely" or "knowingly" permit Ponroe, an unauthorized individual, access to the anthrax, he certainly did so "recklessly." His greed to obtain a cash reward in exchange for Ponroe's improper entrance into the facility more than carelessly opened the gateway for Ponroe to steal the deadly biological agent. Accordingly, Mashington is guilty of this second degree offense.

23-4. **Hindering apprehension or prosecution for terrorism**

    a. A person commits a felony if, with the purpose to hinder the detention, apprehension, investigation, prosecution, conviction or punishment of another for the felony of terrorism, he:

        (1) Harbors or conceals the other;

        (2) Provides or aids in providing a weapon, money, transportation, disguise or other means of avoiding discovery or apprehension or effecting escape;

(3) Suppresses, by way of concealment or destruction, any evidence of the felony or tampers with a witness, informant, document or other source of information, regardless of its admissibility in evidence, which might aid in the discovery or apprehension of such person or in the lodging of a charge against him;

(4) Warns the other of impending discovery or apprehension, except that this paragraph does not apply to a warning given in connection with an effort to bring another into compliance with law;

(5) Prevents or obstructs, by means of force, intimidation or deception, anyone from performing an act which might aid in the discovery or apprehension of such person or in the lodging of a charge against him;

(6) Aids such person to protect or expeditiously profit from an advantage derived from such felony; or

(7) Gives false information to a law enforcement officer.

b. A violation of subsection a. of this section is a felony of the first degree if the felony of terrorism resulted in death. Otherwise, it is a felony of the second degree.

PRACTICAL APPLICATION OF STATUTE

Alice B. Mackerel is guilty of violating the special hindering apprehension offense set forth in section 23-4. In her case, this is a felony of the first degree.

Normally, a person who hinders the apprehension of another will be charged under section 16-3; however, with the introduction of Chapter 23, which covers activities involving terrorism, 23-4 was created to specifically address those who hinder the apprehension of terrorists. Subsections a.(1) through a.(7) delineate the various manners in which a person can illegally hinder the apprehension of a terrorist suspect, and these range from harboring the suspect to providing a disguise or transportation to him to giving false information to a law enforcement officer.

When the state police conducted the search of Alex Evile's home, Alice B. Mackerel approached them and proclaimed, "Okay. You got me. I hid Alex's brother, George, in my basement after he bombed the Sharpese Hotel. I'm sorry . . . Does anyone have a cigarette?" Since Mackerel harbored the terrorist suspect George Evile, she is guilty of an offense under 23-4. Her felony is one of the first degree because death had resulted from George's terrorist bombing. If death had not occurred, Mackerel would instead be guilty of a second degree offense under this statute.

23-5.   **Soliciting or providing material support or resources for terrorism; definitions**

a. As used in this section:

"Charitable organization" means:

(1) Any person determined by the federal Internal Revenue Service to be a tax exempt organization pursuant to section 501(c)(3) of the Internal Revenue Code; or

(2) Any person who is, or holds himself out to be, established for any benevolent, philanthropic, humane, social welfare, public health or other eleemosynary purpose, or for the benefit of law enforcement personnel, firefighters or other persons who protect the public safety, or any person who in any manner employs a charitable appeal as the basis of any solicitation or an appeal which has a tendency to suggest there is a charitable purpose to any such solicitation.

"Charitable purpose" means:

(1) Any purpose described in section 501 (c)(3)of the Internal Revenue Code; or

(2) Any benevolent, philanthropic, humane, social welfare, public health or other eleemosynary objective or an objective that benefits law enforcement personnel, firefighters or other persons who protect the public safety

"Material support or resources" means:

(1) Services or assistance with knowledge or purpose that the services or assistance will be used in preparing for or carrying out an act of terrorism in violation of 23-2;

(2) Currency, financial securities or other monetary instruments, financial services, lodging, training, safe houses, false documentation or identification, communications equipment, facilities, weapons, lethal substances, explosives, personnel, transportation and other physical assets or anything of value; or

(3) Any chemical weapon, or any biological agent, toxin, vector or delivery system for use as a weapon, or any nuclear or radiological device, as defined in subsection c. of 23-3.

"Professional fund raiser" means any person who for compensation performs for a charitable organization any service in connection with which contributions are or will be solicited in this State by that compensated person or by any compensated person he employs, procures or engages, directly or indirectly, to solicit contributions. A *bona fide* salaried officer, employee or volunteer of a charitable organization shall not be deemed to be a professional fund raiser. No attorney, accountant or banker who advises a person to make a charitable contribution during the course of rendering professional services to that person shall be deemed, as a result of that advice, to be a professional fund raiser.

b. (1) It shall be unlawful for any person, charitable organization or professional fund raiser to solicit, transport or otherwise provide material support or resources with the purpose or knowledge that such material support or resources will be used, in whole or in part, to aid, plan, prepare or carry out an act of terrorism in violation of 23-2 or with the purpose or knowledge that such material support or resources are to be given, in whole or in part, to a person or an organization that has committed or has the purpose to commit or has threatened to commit an act of terrorism in violation of 23-2.

(2) It shall be unlawful for any person, charitable organization or professional fund raiser to solicit, transport or otherwise provide material support or resources to or on behalf of a person or an organization that is designated as a foreign terrorist organization by the United States Secretary of State. It shall not be a defense to a prosecution for a violation of this section that the actor did not know that the person or organization is designated as a foreign terrorist organization.

c. A person who violates the provisions of subsection b. of this section shall be guilty of a felony of the first degree if the act of terrorism in violation of 23-2 results in death. Otherwise, it is a felony of the second degree.

PRACTICAL APPLICATION OF STATUTE

Alex Evile's solicitation of funds for his supposedly legitimate charitable organization, The Lady Dove Society, violated section 23-5. His fund-raising activities render him guilty of a first degree felony. Why? His efforts were designed not to actually raise money for a charitable purpose but to divert the funds to his brother's terrorist organization, MIFA.

In a nutshell, 23-5 makes it unlawful for any charitable organization or professional fund-raiser—or any person whatsoever—to raise funds or provide material support or resources to any individual or organization that is involved in terrorist activities. It is irrelevant if the funds raised or the resources provided will be used "in whole" or "in part" for terrorist activities. However, in order for a conviction to be substantiated under the statute, the defendant must have at least "knowledge" that his funds or resources will be used in the advancement of terrorist activities.

Alex Evile was the president of a supposedly legitimate charitable organization, The Lady Dove Society, which purported to raise and distribute funds for a selection of endangered bird species, but Alex admitted that The Lady Dove Society was actually a front for MIFA. The majority of the funds raised via Alex's efforts were diverted to support the terrorist activities of MIFA. Specifically, Alex Evile transferred over $500,000 to MIFA so that his brother could carry out the bombing at the Sharpese Hotel, which resulted in the death of 14 innocent people.

Given that Alex Evile "knew" his fund-raising efforts were performed to materially support the terrorist activities, he is guilty of violating 23-5. Per subsection c. of the statute, a defendant has committed a first degree felony if the act of terrorism results in death; otherwise, it is a felony of the second degree. Since the beneficiary of Alex Evile's fund-raising efforts—MIFA—carried out terrorist activities that resulted in death (i.e., the Sharpese Hotel bombing), Alex Evile is guilty of a first degree felony.

END OF CHAPTER REVIEW

Multiple-Choice Questions

1. Which of the following felonies is *not* a felony that can trigger a conviction of terrorism under section 23-2?
    a. kidnapping
    b. murder
    c. criminal restraint
    d. disarming a law enforcement officer
    e. none of the above because all of these offenses can trigger a conviction of terrorism

2. George Evile entered a New Bainbridge hotel with a briefcase, placing it in a meeting room with hundreds of political lobbyists. Inside the briefcase was a massive explosive device containing the nerve agent sarin. The bomb exploded five minutes after George's departure from the hotel; 14 people were killed by the explosion, and another 75 were injured. Can George be convicted of the felony of terrorism in addition to murder?
    a. no, he can be convicted of either murder or terrorism, but not both
    b. no, if Evile is an American citizen
    c. yes, if he conducted his mass killing to influence the policy of the government by his act of terror
    d. yes, but only if he is an American citizen
    e. c and d

3. Jarrod Mashington is an employee of a medical research facility that is legally performing research on anthrax. Marty Ponroe pays Mashington $5,000 to sneak him into the building because he "wants to steal $100,000 cash stored in the president's safe." Believing all this, Mashington sneaks Ponroe into the facility, where Ponroe steals quantities of anthrax, his true target. Is Mashington guilty of an offense under a statute in Chapter 23?

    a. no, but he is guilty of theft and burglary offenses as a coconspirator

    b. no, because he did not act "purposely" or with "knowledge" that Ponroe was stealing a deadly biological agent

    c. no, because the facility lawfully possessed the anthrax, Mashington was an employee of the facility in lawful possession of the anthrax and he did not actually steal the anthrax or conspire to do so

    d. yes, because he acted "recklessly" in permitting Ponroe, an unauthorized individual, to access the anthrax

    e. a and b

4. Which of the following is a first degree offense?

    a. unlawfully manufacturing the biological agent Marburg virus

    b. unlawfully possessing a recombinant molecule vector

    c. threatening to use the biological agent *Brucella abortus*

    d. all of the above

    e. none of the above because none of these items exist

Essay Question

1. Scott Zero drove a car bomb into a supermarket, jumping out of the vehicle just before impact. Fortunately, no one was killed, but several people were injured. His reason for the bombing was because he wanted the state to change its welfare policy and give more money to people who do not work. After the car bombing, Zero fled to the home of Sunshine, where she hid him in her basement. Although Sunshine did not condone Zero's car bombing, she nonetheless was aware that he had committed the act and still hid him. Police, suspecting that Zero was at Sunshine's house, stopped by to talk to her. Sunshine lied and said that she hadn't seen Zero in weeks; however, the police heard Zero singing in the basement shower. Ultimately, both Zero and Sunshine were arrested. Is Zero guilty of terrorism? Why or why not? Can he avoid the charge since no one was killed? Why or why not? Use the elements of the statute to explain your answers. Can Sunshine be convicted of any offense found in Chapter 23? If so, what is the statute, and what is the degree of her offense—and why?

24

FIREARMS, OTHER DANGEROUS WEAPONS AND INSTRUMENTS OF CRIME

24-1.   **Definitions**

Definitions. The following definitions apply to this chapter:

a. "Antique firearm" means any rifle or shotgun and "antique cannon" means a destructive device defined in paragraph (3) of subsection c. of this section, if the rifle, shotgun or destructive device, as the case may be, is incapable of being fired or discharged or which does not fire fixed ammunition, regardless of date of manufacture, or was manufactured before 1898, for which cartridge ammunition is not commercially available, and is possessed as a curiosity or ornament or for its historical significance or value.

b. "Deface" means to remove, deface, cover, alter or destroy the name of the maker, model designation, manufacturer's serial number or any other distinguishing identification mark or number on any firearm.

c. "Destructive device" means any device, instrument or object designed to explode or produce uncontrolled combustion, including:

    (1) Any explosive or incendiary bomb, mine or grenade;

    (2) Any rocket having a propellant charge of more than four ounces or any missile having an explosive or incendiary charge of more than one-quarter of an ounce;

    (3) Any weapon capable of firing a projectile of a caliber greater than 60 caliber, except a shotgun or shotgun ammunition generally recognized as suitable for sporting purposes; or

    (4) Any Molotov cocktail or other device consisting of a breakable container containing flammable liquid and having a wick or similar device capable of being ignited. The term does not include any device manufactured for the purpose of illumination, distress signaling, line-throwing, safety or similar purposes.

d. "Dispose of" means to give, give away, lease, loan, keep for sale, offer, offer for sale, sell, transfer or otherwise transfer possession.

e. "Explosive" means any chemical compound or mixture that is commonly used or is possessed for the purpose of producing an explosion and which contains any oxidizing and combustible materials or other ingredients in such proportions, quantities or packing that an ignition by fire, by friction, by concussion or by detonation of any part of the compound or mixture may cause such a sudden generation of highly heated gases that the resultant gaseous pressures are capable of producing destructive effects on contiguous objects. The term shall not include small arms ammunition or explosives in the form prescribed by the official United States Pharmacopoeia.

f. "Firearm" means any handgun, rifle, shotgun, machine gun, automatic or semi-automatic rifle or any gun, device or instrument in the nature of a weapon from which may be fired or ejected any solid projectable ball, slug, pellet, missile or bullet, or any gas, vapor or other noxious thing, by means of a cartridge or shell or by the action of an explosive or the igniting of flammable or explosive substances. It shall also include, without limitation, any firearm which is in the nature of an air gun, spring gun or pistol or other weapon of a similar nature in which the propelling force is a spring, elastic band, carbon dioxide, compressed or other gas or vapor, air or compressed air, or is ignited by compressed air, and ejecting a bullet or missile smaller than three-eighths of an inch in diameter, with sufficient force to injure a person.

g. "Firearm silencer" means any instrument, attachment, weapon or appliance for causing the firing of any gun, revolver, pistol or other firearm to be silent or intended to lessen or muffle the noise of the firing of any gun, revolver, pistol or other firearm.

h. "Gravity knife" means any knife which has a blade which is released from the handle or sheath thereof by the force of gravity or the application of centrifugal force.

i. "Machine gun" means any firearm, mechanism or instrument not requiring that the trigger be pressed for each shot and having a reservoir, belt or other means of storing and carrying ammunition which can be loaded into the firearm, mechanism or instrument and fired therefrom.

j. "Manufacturer" means any person who receives or obtains raw materials or parts and processes them into firearms or finished parts of firearms, except a person who exclusively processes grips, stocks and other nonmetal parts of firearms. The term does not include a person who repairs existing firearms or receives new and used raw materials or parts solely for the repair of existing firearms.

k. "Handgun" means any pistol, revolver or other firearm originally designed or manufactured to be fired by the use of a single hand.

l. "Retail dealer" means any person including a gunsmith, except a manufacturer or a wholesale dealer, who sells, transfers or assigns for a fee or profit any firearm or parts of firearms or ammunition which he has purchased or obtained with the intention, or for the purpose, of reselling or reassigning to persons who are reasonably understood to be the ultimate consumers and includes any person who is engaged in the business of repairing firearms or who sells any firearm to satisfy a debt secured by the pledge of a firearm.

m. "Rifle" means any firearm designed to be fired from the shoulder and using the energy of the explosive in a fixed metallic cartridge to fire a single projectile through a rifled bore for each single pull of the trigger.

n. "Shotgun" means any firearm designed to be fired from the shoulder and using the energy of the explosive in a fixed shotgun shell to fire through a smooth bore either a number of ball shots or a single projectile for each pull of the trigger or any firearm designed to be fired from the shoulder which does not fire fixed ammunition.

o. "Sawed-off shotgun" means any shotgun having a barrel or barrels of less than 18 inches in length measured from the breech to the muzzle, or a rifle having a barrel or barrels of less than 16 inches in length measured from the breech to the muzzle or any firearm made from a rifle or a shotgun, whether by alteration or otherwise, if such firearm as modified has an overall length of less than 26 inches.

p. "Switchblade knife" means any knife or similar device which has a blade which opens automatically by hand pressure applied to a button, spring or other device in the handle of the knife.

q. "Superintendent" means the Superintendent of the State Police.

r. "Weapon" means anything readily capable of lethal use or of inflicting serious bodily injury. The term includes, but is not limited to:

(1) Firearms, even though not loaded or lacking a clip or other component to render them immediately operable;

(2) Components which can be readily assembled into a weapon;

(3) Gravity knives, switchblade knives, daggers, dirks, stilettos or other dangerous knives, billies, blackjacks, bludgeons, metal knuckles, sandclubs, slingshots, cesti or similar leather bands studded with metal filings or razor blades embedded in wood; and

(4) Stun guns and any weapon or other device which projects, releases or emits tear gas or any other substance intended to produce temporary physical discomfort or permanent injury through being vaporized or otherwise dispensed in the air.

s. "Wholesale dealer" means any person, except a manufacturer, who sells, transfers or assigns firearms, or parts of firearms, to persons who are reasonably understood not to be the ultimate consumers and includes persons who receive finished parts of firearms and assemble them into completed or partially completed firearms, in furtherance of such purpose, except that it shall not include those persons dealing exclusively in grips, stocks and other nonmetal parts of firearms.

t. "Stun gun" means any weapon or other device which emits an electrical charge or current intended to temporarily or permanently disable a person.

u. "Ballistic knife" means any weapon or other device capable of lethal use and which can propel a knife blade.

v. "Imitation firearm" means an object or device reasonably capable of being mistaken for a firearm.

w. (1) "Assault firearm" means the following firearms:

Algimec AGM1 type
Any shotgun with a revolving cylinder such as the "Street Sweeper" or "Striker 12"
Armalite AR-180 type
Australian Automatic Arms SAR
Avtomat Kalashnikov type semi-automatic firearms
Beretta AR-70 and BM59 semi-automatic firearms
Bushmaster Assault Rifle
Calico M-900 Assault carbine and M-900
CETME G3
Chartered Industries of Singapore SR-88 type
Colt AR-15 and CAR-15 series
Daewoo K-1, K-2, Max 1 and Max 2, AR 100 types
Demro TAC-1 carbine type
Encom MP-9 and MP-45 carbine types
FAMAS MAS223 type
FN-FAL, FN-LAR or FN-FNC type semi-automatic firearms
Franchi SPAS 12 and LAW 12 shotguns
G3SA type
Galil type Heckler and Koch HK91, HK93, HK94, MP5, PSG-1
Intratec TEC 9 and 22 semi-automatic firearms
M1 carbine type

M14S type
MAC 10, MAC 11, MAC 11-9mm carbine type firearms
PJK M-68 carbine type
Plainfield Machine Company Carbine
Ruger K-Mini-14/5F and Mini-14/5RF
SIG AMT, SIG 550SP, SIG 551SP, SIG PE-57 types
SKS with detachable magazine type
Spectre Auto carbine type
Springfield Armory BM59 and SAR-48 types
Sterling MK-6, MK-7 and SAR types
Steyr A.U.G. semi-automatic firearms
USAS 12 semi-automatic type shotgun
Uzi type semi-automatic firearms
Valmet M62, M71S, M76 or M78 type semi-automatic firearms
Weaver Arm Nighthawk

(2) Any firearm manufactured under any designation which is substantially identical to any of the firearms listed above;

(3) A semi-automatic shotgun with either a magazine capacity exceeding six rounds, a pistol grip or a folding stock;

(4) A semi-automatic rifle with a fixed magazine capacity exceeding 15 rounds; or

(5) A part or combination of parts designed or intended to convert a firearm into an assault firearm or any combination of parts from which an assault firearm may be readily assembled if those parts are in the possession or under the control of the same person.

x. "Semi-automatic" means a firearm which fires a single projectile for each single pull of the trigger and is self-reloading or automatically chambers a round, cartridge or bullet.

y. "Large capacity ammunition magazine" means a box, drum, tube or other container which is capable of holding more than 15 rounds of ammunition to be fed continuously and directly therefrom into a semi-automatic firearm.

z. "Pistol grip" means a well-defined handle, similar to that found on a handgun, that protrudes conspicuously beneath the action of the weapon and which permits the shotgun to be held and fired with one hand.

aa. "Antique handgun" means a handgun manufactured before 1898, or a replica thereof, which is recognized as being historical in nature or of historical significance and either (1) utilizes a match, friction, flint or percussion ignition or utilizes a pin-fire cartridge in which the pin is part of the cartridge or (2) does not fire fixed ammunition or for which cartridge ammunition is not commercially available.

bb. "Trigger lock" means a commercially available device approved by the Superintendent of State Police which is operated with a key or combination lock that prevents a firearm from being discharged while the device is attached to the firearm. It may include, but need not be limited to, devices that obstruct the barrel or cylinder of the firearm, as well as devices that immobilize the trigger.

cc. "Trigger locking device" means a device that, if installed on a firearm and secured by means of a key or mechanically, electronically or electromechanically operated combination lock, prevents the firearm from being discharged without first deactivating or removing the device by means of a key or mechanically, electronically or electromechanically operated combination lock.

dd. "Personalized handgun" means a handgun which incorporates within its design, and as part of its original manufacture, technology which automatically limits its operational use and which cannot be readily deactivated, so that it may only be fired by an authorized or recognized user. The technology limiting the handgun's operational use may include, but not be limited to, radio frequency tagging, touch memory, remote control, fingerprint, magnetic encoding and other automatic user identification systems utilizing biometric, mechanical or electronic systems. No make or model of a handgun shall be deemed to be a "personalized handgun" unless the Attorney General has determined, through testing or other reasonable means, that the handgun meets any reliability standards that the manufacturer may require for its commercially available handguns that are not personalized or, if the manufacturer has no such reliability standards, the handgun meets the reliability standards generally used in the industry for commercially available handguns.

24-2. **Presumptions**

a. Possession of firearms, weapons, destructive devices, silencers or explosives in a vehicle. When a firearm, weapon, destructive device, silencer or explosive described in this chapter is found in a vehicle, it is presumed to be in the possession of the occupant if there is but one. If there is more than one occupant in the vehicle, it shall be presumed to be in the possession of all, except under the following circumstances:

    (1) When it is found upon the person of one of the occupants, it shall be presumed to be in the possession of that occupant alone;

    (2) When the vehicle is not a stolen one and the weapon or other instrument is found out of view in a glove compartment, trunk or other enclosed customary depository, it shall be presumed to be in the possession of the occupant or occupants who own or have authority to operate the vehicle; and

    (3) When the vehicle is a taxicab and a weapon or other instrument is found in the passenger's portion of the vehicle, it shall be presumed to be in the possession of all the passengers, if there are any, and if not, in the possession of the driver.

b. Licenses and permits. When the legality of a person's conduct under this chapter depends on his possession of a license or permit or on his having registered with or given notice to a particular person or agency, it shall be presumed that he does not possess such a license or permit or has not registered or given the required notice, until he establishes the contrary.

24-3. **Prohibited weapons and devices**

a. Destructive devices. Any person who knowingly has in his possession any destructive device is guilty of a felony of the third degree.

b. Sawed-off shotguns. Any person who knowingly has in his possession any sawed-off shotgun is guilty of a felony of the third degree.

c. Silencers. Any person who knowingly has in his possession any firearm silencer is guilty of a felony of the fourth degree.

d. Defaced firearms. Any person who knowingly has in his possession any firearm which has been defaced, except an antique firearm or an antique handgun, is guilty of a felony of the fourth degree.

e. Certain weapons. Any person who knowingly has in his possession any gravity knife, switchblade knife, dagger, dirk, stiletto, billy, blackjack, metal knuckle, sandclub, slingshot, cestus or similar leather band studded with metal filings or razor blades embedded in wood or ballistic knife, without any explainable lawful purpose, is guilty of a felony of the fourth degree.

f. Dum-dum or body armor penetrating bullets. (1) Any person, other than a law enforcement officer or persons engaged in activities pursuant to subsection f. of 24-6, who knowingly has in his possession any hollow nose or dum-dum bullet or (2) any person, other than a collector of firearms or ammunition as curios or relics as defined in Title 18, United States Code, section 921 (a) (13) and has in his possession a valid Collector of Curios and Relics License issued by the Bureau of Alcohol, Tobacco and Firearms, who knowingly has in his possession any body armor breaching or penetrating ammunition, which means (a) ammunition primarily designed for use in a handgun and (b) which is comprised of a bullet whose core or jacket, if the jacket is thicker than .025 of an inch, is made of tungsten carbide, or hard bronze or other material which is harder than a rating of 72 or greater on the Rockwell B. Hardness Scale and (c) is therefore capable of breaching or penetrating body armor, is guilty of a felony of the fourth degree. For purposes of this section, a collector may possess not more than three examples of each distinctive variation of the ammunition described above. A distinctive variation includes a different head stamp, composition, design or color.

g. Exceptions.

(1) Nothing in subsection a., b., c., d., e., f., j. or k. of this section shall apply to any member of the Armed Forces of the United States or the National Guard, or except as otherwise provided, to any law enforcement officer while actually on duty or traveling to or from an authorized place of duty, provided that his possession of the prohibited weapon or device has been duly authorized under the applicable laws, regulations or military or law enforcement orders. Nothing in subsection h. of this section shall apply to any law enforcement officer who is exempted from the provisions of that subsection by the Attorney General. Nothing in this section shall apply to the possession of any weapon or device by a law enforcement officer who has confiscated, seized or otherwise taken possession of said weapon or device as evidence of the commission of a felony or because he believed it to be possessed illegally by the person from whom it was taken, provided that said law enforcement officer promptly notifies his superiors of his possession of such prohibited weapon or device.

(2) (a) Nothing in subsection f.(1) shall be construed to prevent a person from keeping such ammunition at his dwelling, premises or other land owned or possessed by him, or from carrying such ammunition from the place of purchase to said dwelling or land, nor shall subsection f.(1) be construed to prevent any licensed retail or wholesale firearms dealer from possessing such ammunition at its licensed premises, provided that the seller of any such ammunition shall maintain a record of the name, age and place of residence of any purchaser who is not a licensed dealer, together with the date of sale and quantity of ammunition sold.

(b) Nothing in subsection f.(1) shall be construed to prevent a designated employee or designated licensed agent for a nuclear power plant under the license of the Nuclear Regulatory Commission from possessing hollow nose ammunition while in the actual performance of his official duties if the federal licensee certifies that the designated employee or designated licensed agent is assigned to perform site protection, guard, armed response or armed escort duties and is appropriately trained and qualified, as prescribed by federal regulation, to perform those duties.

(3) Nothing in paragraph (2) of subsection f. or in subsection j. shall be construed to prevent any licensed retail or wholesale firearms dealer from possessing that ammunition or large capacity ammunition magazine at its licensed premises for sale or disposition to another licensed dealer, the Armed Forces of the United States or the National Guard or to a law enforcement agency, provided that the seller maintains a record of any sale or disposition to a law enforcement agency. The record shall include the name of the purchasing agency, together with written authorization of

the chief of police or highest ranking official of the agency, the name and rank of the purchasing law enforcement officer, if applicable, and the date, time and amount of ammunition sold or otherwise disposed. A copy of this record shall be forwarded by the seller to the Superintendent of the Division of State Police within 48 hours of the sale or disposition.

(4) Nothing in subsection a. of this section shall be construed to apply to antique cannons as exempted in subsection d. of 24-6.

(5) Nothing in subsection c. of this section shall be construed to apply to any person who is specifically identified in a special deer management permit issued by the Division of Fish and Wildlife to utilize a firearm silencer as part of an alternative deer control method implemented in accordance with a special deer management permit issued pursuant to the "Fish and Wildlife Act" while the person is in the actual performance of the permitted alternative deer control method and while going to and from the place where the permitted alternative deer control method is being utilized. This exception shall not, however, otherwise apply to any person to authorize the purchase or possession of a firearm silencer.

h. Stun guns. Any person who knowingly has in his possession any stun gun is guilty of a felony of the fourth degree.

i. Nothing in subsection e. of this section shall be construed to prevent any guard in the employ of a private security company, who is licensed to carry a firearm, from the possession of a nightstick when in the actual performance of his official duties, provided that he has satisfactorily completed a training course approved by the Police Training Commission in the use of a nightstick.

j. Any person who knowingly has in his possession a large capacity ammunition magazine is guilty of a felony of the fourth degree unless the person has registered an assault firearm pursuant to the "State Firearms and Ammunitions Act" and the magazine is maintained and used in connection with participation in competitive shooting matches sanctioned by the Director of Civilian Marksmanship of the United States Department of the Army.

k. Handcuffs. Any person who knowingly has in his possession handcuffs as defined in 24-8.2, under circumstances not manifestly appropriate for such lawful uses as handcuffs may have, is guilty of a misdemeanor A. A law enforcement officer shall confiscate handcuffs possessed in violation of the law.

PRACTICAL APPLICATION OF STATUTE

Alex Evile is guilty of a third degree felony for his possession of a sawed-off shotgun; he is also guilty of a fourth degree felony for possessing a 12-inch switchblade and a fourth degree felony for possessing hollow nose bullets. Alex's brother, George, is guilty of a felony of the fourth degree as he possessed a handgun silencer. All of these offenses fall under the prohibitions set forth in section 24-3.

This statute provides that it is illegal for unauthorized persons to possess weapons ranging from sawed-off shotguns (see subsection b.) to defaced firearms (see subsection d.) to gravity knives, switchblades, blackjacks, metal knuckles and slingshots (see subsection e.). Per subsection c., firearm silencers are prohibited. Subsection f. prohibits the possession of dum-dum, hollow nose and body armor–penetrating bullets. Subsections h., j. and k. set out the prohibitions surrounding the possession of stun guns, large capacity ammunition magazines and handcuffs, respectively. Finally, subsection a. makes it illegal to possess any "destructive device"—this is any device designed to explode or produce uncontrolled combustion. Each subsection clearly defines what degree of offense has occurred when the subsection's particular weapons or devices are possessed.

Accordingly, since subsection b. provides that it is a third degree felony to possess a sawed-off shotgun, Alex Evile is guilty of a third degree felony for the sawed-off shotgun that the state police confiscated at his home. In the same vein, he is guilty of fourth degree felonies for his possession of a switchblade and hollow nose bullets, as they are defined offenses in subsections e. and f., respectively. Possessing a firearm silencer is deemed a fourth degree felony per the tenets of subsection c.; therefore, George Evile is guilty of this degree offense for the silencer found in his home.

It is extremely important to note that 24-3 sets forth a number of exceptions to the prohibited possession of weapons and devices, as defined in the statute. For example, subsection g. begins by stating that "nothing in subsections a., b., c., d., e., f., j. or k. of this section shall apply to any member of the Armed Forces of the United States or the National Guard." Other exceptions are obviously provided for as well. Although a trier of fact may ultimately determine if a particular defendant was legally authorized to possess a weapon or device prohibited under 24-3, it is important to consider the exceptions carved out in the statute.

24-4.   **Possession of weapons for unlawful purposes**

   a. Firearms. Any person who has in his possession any firearm with a purpose to use it unlawfully against the person or property of another is guilty of a felony of the second degree.

   b. Explosives. Any person who has in his possession or carries any explosive substance with a purpose to use it unlawfully against the person or property of another is guilty of a felony of the second degree.

   c. Destructive devices. Any person who has in his possession any destructive device with a purpose to use it unlawfully against the person or property of another is guilty of a felony of the second degree.

   d. Other weapons. Any person who has in his possession any weapon, except a firearm, with a purpose to use it unlawfully against the person or property of another is guilty of a felony of the third degree.

   e. Imitation firearms. Any person who has in his possession an imitation firearm under circumstances that would lead an observer to reasonably believe that it is possessed for an unlawful purpose is guilty of a felony of the fourth degree.

PRACTICAL APPLICATION OF STATUTE

Any person who possesses firearms, explosives or destructive devices for an unlawful purpose is guilty of a second degree felony. A person who possesses any weapon—other than a firearm—for an unlawful purpose is guilty of a third degree felony, and a person who possesses an imitation firearm for an unlawful purpose is guilty of a fourth degree felony. But what is an "unlawful purpose"? How can a person get convicted under this statute? A case involving George Evile can help to answer these questions.

Wielding an automatic rifle, George held up a candy shop in Walcott. During the stickup, he shot the store's clerk in the leg. Here, George is not just guilty of simple unlawful possession of the automatic rifle—he is guilty of unlawfully possessing this firearm for an "unlawful purpose." George's "unlawful purpose" was to utilize the firearm "against the person and property of another" in the commission of the felonies of robbery and aggravated assault. Accordingly, George Evile is guilty of a second degree felony under 24-4.

24-4.1.   **Weapons; controlled dangerous substances and other offenses, penalties**

a. Any person who has in his possession any firearm while in the course of committing, attempting to commit or conspiring to commit a violation of any offense found in chapter 20 of this Criminal Code is guilty of a felony of the second degree.

b. Any person who has in his possession any weapon, except a firearm, with a purpose to use such weapon unlawfully against the person or property of another while in the course of committing, attempting to commit or conspiring to commit a violation of any offense found in chapter 20 of this Criminal Code is guilty of a felony of the second degree.

c. Any person who has in his possession any weapon, except a firearm, under circumstances not manifestly appropriate for such lawful uses as the weapon may have while in the course of committing, attempting to commit or conspiring to commit a violation of any offense found in chapter 20 of this Criminal Code is guilty of a felony of the second degree.

PRACTICAL APPLICATION OF STATUTE

In Holbrooke, George Evile sold a kilogram of cocaine to a pawnbroker. During the drug deal, George carried a .22-caliber pistol and a machine gun. For simply possessing these weapons during this controlled dangerous substance (CDS) transaction, George is guilty of a second degree felony.

Section 24-4.1 is basically an extension of 24-4. This statute, in subsection a., specifically provides that it is a second degree felony to possess a firearm while "committing, attempting to commit or conspiring to commit" any one of a number of drug offenses "found in chapter 20 of this Criminal Code" (e.g., distributing CDS per 20-4, maintaining a CDS production facility per 20-3, leading a narcotics trafficking network per 20-2).

The firearm need not be possessed with a purpose to use it unlawfully against a person or property in order for a conviction to be sustained under this statute—simple possession during the commission of any of the drug offenses is enough. Accordingly, since George possessed a .22-caliber pistol and a machine gun during his cocaine transaction with the pawnbroker, he is guilty of a second degree offense as set forth in 24-4.1.

Please note that 24-4.1 also makes it a second degree felony for a person to possess any weapon—other than a firearm—during the enumerated drug offenses; however, simple possession of these "other" weapons will not be enough for a conviction under 24-4.1. A conviction can only be sustained if the person possesses the weapon "with a purpose to use such weapon unlawfully against the person or property of another" (see subsection b.) or if the person possesses the weapon "under circumstances not manifestly appropriate for such lawful uses as the weapon may have" (see subsection c.). The moral of the story: Very often a person will face a higher degree felony if he possesses a weapon during the commission of a drug offense than if he simply possessed the weapon in other circumstances.

24-5.   **Unlawful possession of weapons**

a. Machine guns. Any person who knowingly has in his possession a machine gun or any instrument or device adaptable for use as a machine gun, without being licensed to do so as provided in the "State Firearms and Ammunitions Act," is guilty of a felony of the third degree.

b. Handguns. Any person who knowingly has in his possession any handgun, including any antique handgun, without first having obtained a permit to carry the same as provided in "State Firearms and Ammunitions Act" is guilty of a felony of the third degree.

c. Rifles and shotguns.

    (1) Any person who knowingly has in his possession any rifle or shotgun without having first obtained a firearms purchaser identification card in accordance with the provisions of the "State Firearms and Ammunitions Act" is guilty of a felony of the third degree.

    (2) Unless otherwise permitted by law, any person who knowingly has in his possession any loaded rifle or shotgun is guilty of a felony of the third degree.

d. Other weapons. Any person who knowingly has in his possession any other weapon under circumstances not manifestly appropriate for such lawful uses as it may have is guilty of a felony of the fourth degree.

e. Firearms or other weapons in educational institutions.

    (1) Any person who knowingly has in his possession any firearm in or upon any part of the buildings or grounds of any school, college, university or other educational institution, without the written authorization of the governing officer of the institution, is guilty of a felony of the third degree, irrespective of whether he possesses a valid permit to carry the firearm or a valid firearms purchaser identification card.

    (2) Any person who knowingly possesses any weapon enumerated in paragraphs (3) and (4) of subsection r. of 24-1, or any components which can readily be assembled into a firearm or other weapon enumerated in subsection r. of 24-1 or any other weapon under circumstances not manifestly appropriate for such lawful use as it may have while in or upon any part of the buildings or grounds of any school, college, university or other educational institution without the written authorization of the governing officer of the institution is guilty of a felony of the fourth degree.

    (3) Any person who knowingly has in his possession any imitation firearm in or upon any part of the buildings or grounds of any school, college, university or other educational institution, without the written authorization of the governing officer of the institution, or while on any school bus is guilty of a misdemeanor A, irrespective of whether he possesses a valid permit to carry a firearm or a valid firearms purchaser identification card.

f. Assault firearms. Any person who knowingly has in his possession an assault firearm is guilty of a felony of the third degree except if the assault firearm is licensed pursuant to the "State Firearms and Ammunitions Act," registered pursuant to the "State Firearms and Ammunitions Act" or rendered inoperable pursuant to the "State Firearms and Ammunitions Act."

g. (1) The temporary possession of a handgun, rifle or shotgun by a person receiving, possessing, carrying or using the handgun, rifle or shotgun under the provisions of the "State Firearms and Ammunitions Act" shall not be considered unlawful possession under the provisions of subsection b. or c. of this section.

    (2) The temporary possession of a firearm by a person receiving, possessing, carrying or using the firearm under the provisions of the "State Firearms and Ammunitions Act" shall not be considered unlawful possession under the provisions of this section.

PRACTICAL APPLICATION OF STATUTE

Similar to section 24-3, 24-5 makes it illegal for individuals to simply possess certain weapons. Pursuant to this statute, it is an offense to possess weapons such as machine guns, handguns, rifles and shotguns—these felonies are all of the third degree and are found in subsections a. through c. Under subsection f., a person is guilty of a third degree felony for unlawfully possessing an assault firearm. Pursuant to subsection d., it is a fourth degree felony to possess "any other weapon under circumstances not manifestly appropriate for such lawful uses as it may have" (e.g., possessing a steak knife or a baseball bat "just in case a fight breaks out").

George Evile is guilty of a third degree felony under 24-5 for the .22-caliber handgun confiscated at his home. This offense should be differentiated from his use of the .22-caliber gun during the Walcott candy store robbery; pursuant to that incident, he should appropriately face the greater second degree charge of possession of a firearm for an unlawful purpose.

It is important to note that there are multiple exceptions and exemptions to the unlawful possession of weapons offenses located in 24-5. For example, subsection g. of this statute provides exceptions to the unlawful possession of handguns, rifles and shotguns. The entirety of 24-6 sets forth exemptions where 24-5 does not apply to individuals. When charging individuals under 24-5, law enforcement should take special note of these exemptions.

Weapons in Educational Institutions

Subsection e. of 24-5 provides special provisions for individuals who possess weapons in educational institutions. For instance, under e.(1), a person is guilty of a third degree felony if he possesses a firearm "in or upon any part of the buildings or grounds of any educational institution." A defendant is guilty of this offense even if "he possesses a valid permit" or a "valid firearms purchaser identification card"—unless he has "written authorization of the governing offices of the institution." In other words, if a private detective licensed to carry a handgun enters an academic building of Fairmount University carrying his pistol, he can be convicted of a third degree felony under subsection e. of 24-5—unless the president of Fairmount gave him written authorization to carry the gun in the building.

24-6.   **Exemptions**

   a. Provided a person complies with the requirements of subsection j. of this section, 24-5 does not apply to:

   (1) Members of the Armed Forces of the United States or of the National Guard while actually on duty or while traveling between places of duty and carrying authorized weapons in the manner prescribed by the appropriate military authorities;

   (2) Federal law enforcement officers and any other federal officers and employees required to carry firearms in the performance of their official duties;

   (3) Members of the State Police and, under conditions prescribed by the superintendent, members of the Marine Law Enforcement Bureau of the Division of State Police;

   (4) A sheriff, undersheriff, sheriff's officer, county prosecutor, assistant prosecutor, prosecutor's detective or investigator, deputy attorney general or State investigator employed by the Division of Criminal Justice of the Department of Law and Public

Safety, investigator employed by the State Commission of Investigation, inspector of the Alcoholic Beverage Control Enforcement Bureau of the Division of State Police in the Department of Law and Public Safety authorized to carry such weapons by the Superintendent of State Police, State park police officer or State conservation officer;

(5) A prison or jail warden of any penal institution in this State or his deputies, or an employee of the Department of Corrections engaged in the interstate transportation of convicted offenders, while in the performance of his duties and when required to possess the weapon by his superior officer, or a correction officer or keeper of a penal institution in this State at all times while in this State, provided he annually passes an examination approved by the superintendent testing his proficiency in the handling of firearms;

(6) A civilian employee of the United States Government under the supervision of the commanding officer of any post, camp, station, base or other military or naval installation located in this State who is required, in the performance of his official duties, to carry firearms and who is authorized to carry such firearms by said commanding officer while in the actual performance of his official duties;

(7) (a) A regularly employed member, including a detective, of the police department of any county or municipality or of any state, interstate, municipal or county park police force or boulevard police force at all times while in this State;

(b) A special law enforcement officer authorized to carry a weapon as provided in the "State Firearms and Ammunitions Act";

(c) An airport security officer or a special law enforcement officer appointed by the governing body of any county or municipality, except as provided in subsection (b) of this section, or by the commission, board or other body having control of a county park or airport or boulevard police force, while engaged in the actual performance of his official duties and when specifically authorized by the governing body to carry weapons;

(8) A full-time, paid member of a paid or part-paid fire department or force of any municipality who is assigned full-time or part-time to an arson investigation unit or to the county arson investigation unit in the county prosecutor's office while either engaged in the actual performance of arson investigation duties or while actually on call to perform arson investigation duties and when specifically authorized by the governing body or the county prosecutor, as the case may be, to carry weapons. Prior to being permitted to carry a firearm, such a member shall take and successfully complete a firearms training course administered by the Police Training Commission and shall annually qualify in the use of a revolver or similar weapon prior to being permitted to carry a firearm;

(9) A juvenile corrections officer in the employment of the Juvenile Justice Commission;

(10) A designated employee or designated licensed agent for a nuclear power plant under license of the Nuclear Regulatory Commission while in the actual performance of his official duties, if the federal licensee certifies that the designated employee or designated licensed agent is assigned to perform site protection, guard, armed response or armed escort duties and is appropriately trained and qualified, as prescribed by federal regulation, to perform those duties. Any firearm utilized by an employee or agent for a nuclear power plant pursuant to this paragraph shall be returned each day at the end of the employee's or agent's authorized official duties to the employee's or agent's supervisor. All firearms returned each day pursuant to this paragraph shall be stored in locked containers located in a secure area.

b. Subsections a., b. and c. of 24-5 do not apply to:

   (1) A law enforcement officer employed by a governmental agency outside of this State while actually engaged in his official duties, provided, however, that he has first notified the superintendent or the chief law enforcement officer of the municipality or the prosecutor of the county in which he is engaged; or

   (2) A licensed dealer in firearms and his registered employees during the course of their normal business while traveling to and from their place of business and other places for the purpose of demonstration, exhibition or delivery in connection with a sale, provided, however, that the weapon is carried in the manner specified in subsection g. of this section.

c. Provided a person complies with the requirements of subsection j. of this section, subsections b. and c. of 24-5 do not apply to:

   (1) A special agent of the Division of Taxation who has passed an examination in an approved police training program testing proficiency in the handling of any firearm which he may be required to carry while in the actual performance of his official duties and while going to or from his place of duty, or any other police officer while in the actual performance of his official duties;

   (2) A State deputy conservation officer or a full-time employee of the Division of Parks and Forestry having the power of arrest and authorized to carry weapons while in the actual performance of his official duties;

   (3) A State Ranger;

   (4) A court attendant serving as such under appointment by the sheriff of the county or by the judge of any municipal court or other court of this State while in the actual performance of his official duties;

   (5) A guard in the employ of any railway express company, banking or building and loan or savings and loan institution of this State while in the actual performance of his official duties;

   (6) A member of a legally recognized military organization while actually under orders or while going to or from the prescribed place of meeting and carrying the weapons prescribed for drill, exercise or parade;

   (7) A humane law enforcement officer of the State's Society for the Prevention of Cruelty to Animals or of a county society for the prevention of cruelty to animals while in the actual performance of his duties;

   (8) An employee of a public utilities corporation actually engaged in the transportation of explosives;

   (9) A railway policeman, except a transit police officer of this State's Transit Police Department, at all times while in this State, provided the officer has satisfied the training requirements of the Police Training Commission;

   (10) A State university campus police officer, at all times while in this State, provided the officer has satisfied the training requirements of the Police Training Commission;

   (11) A private university campus police officer where such university is located in this State, at all times while in this State, provided the officer has satisfied the training requirements of the Police Training Commission;

   (12) A transit police officer of this State's Transit Police Department, at all times while in this State, provided the officer has satisfied the training requirements of the Police Training Commission;

   (13) A parole officer employed by the State Parole Board at all times. Prior to being permitted to carry a firearm, a parole officer shall take and successfully complete a

basic course for regular police officer training administered by the Police Training Commission;

(14) A Human Services police officer, at all times while in this State, as authorized by the Commissioner of Human Services;

(15) A person or employee of any person who, pursuant to and as required by a contract with a governmental entity, supervises or transports persons charged with or convicted of an offense;

(16) A housing authority police officer, at all times while in this State, provided the officer has satisfied the training requirements of the Police Training Commission; or

(17) A probation officer assigned to the "Probation Officer Community Safety Unit" while in the actual performance of the probation officer's official duties. Prior to being permitted to carry a firearm, a probation officer shall take and successfully complete a basic course for regular police officer training administered by the Police Training Commission.

d. (1) Subsections c. and d. of 24-5 do not apply to antique firearms, provided that such antique firearms are unloaded or are being fired for the purposes of exhibition or demonstration at an authorized target range or in such other manner as has been approved in writing by the chief law enforcement officer of the municipality in which the exhibition or demonstration is held, or if not held on property under the control of a particular municipality, the superintendent.

(2) Subsection a. of 24-3 and subsection d. of 24-5 do not apply to an antique cannon that is capable of being fired but that is unloaded and immobile, provided that the antique cannon is possessed by:

(a) A scholastic institution, a museum, a municipality, a county or the State; or

(b) A person who obtained a firearms purchaser identification card as specified in the "State Firearms and Ammunitions Act."

(3) Subsection a. of 24-3 and subsection d. of 24-5 do not apply to an unloaded antique cannon that is being transported by one eligible to possess it, in compliance with regulations the superintendent may promulgate, between its permanent location and place of purchase or repair.

(4) Subsection a. of 24-3 and subsection d. of 24-5 do not apply to antique cannons that are being loaded or fired by one eligible to possess an antique cannon for purposes of exhibition or demonstration at an authorized target range or in the manner as has been approved in writing by the chief law enforcement officer of the municipality in which the exhibition or demonstration is held, or if not held on property under the control of a particular municipality, the superintendent, provided that performer has given at least 30 days' notice to the superintendent.

(5) Subsection a. of 24-3 and subsection d. of 24-5 do not apply to the transportation of unloaded antique cannons directly to or from exhibitions or demonstrations authorized under paragraph (4) of subsection d. of this section, provided that the transportation is in compliance with safety regulations the superintendent may promulgate. Nor do those subsections apply to transportation directly to or from exhibitions or demonstrations authorized under the law of another jurisdiction, provided that the superintendent has been given 30 days' notice and that the transportation is in compliance with safety regulations the superintendent may promulgate.

e. Nothing in subsections b., c. and d. of 24-5 shall be construed to prevent a person keeping or carrying about his place of business, residence, premises or other land owned or possessed by him any firearm or from carrying the same, in the manner specified in subsection g. of this section, from any place of purchase to his residence or place of business, between his dwelling and his place of business, between one place of business or residence and another when moving or between his dwelling or place of business and place where such firearms are repaired for the purpose of repair. For the purposes of this section, a place of business shall be deemed to be a fixed location.

f. Nothing in subsections b., c. and d. of 24-5 shall be construed to prevent:

(1) A member of any rifle or pistol club, organized in accordance with the rules prescribed by the National Board for the Promotion of Rifle Practice, in going to or from a place of target practice carrying such firearms as are necessary for said target practice, provided that the club has filed a copy of its charter with the superintendent and annually submits a list of its members to the superintendent and provided further that the firearms are carried in the manner specified in subsection g. of this section;

(2) A person carrying a firearm or knife in the woods or fields or upon the waters of this State for the purpose of hunting, target practice or fishing, provided that the firearm or knife is legal and appropriate for hunting or fishing purposes in this State and he has in his possession a valid hunting license or, with respect to fresh water fishing, a valid fishing license;

(3) A person transporting any firearm or knife while traveling:

(a) Directly to or from any place for the purpose of hunting or fishing, provided the person has in his possession a valid hunting or fishing license;

(b) Directly to or from any target range or other authorized place for the purpose of practice, match, target, trap or skeet shooting exhibitions, provided in all cases that during the course of the travel all firearms are carried in the manner specified in subsection g. of this section and the person has complied with all the provisions and requirements of the "State Firearms and Ammunitions Act"; or

(c) In the case of a firearm, directly to or from any exhibition or display of firearms which is sponsored by any law enforcement agency, any rifle or pistol club or any firearms collectors club for the purpose of displaying the firearms to the public or to the members of the organization or club, provided, however, that not less than 30 days prior to the exhibition or display, notice of the exhibition or display shall be given to the Superintendent of the State Police by the sponsoring organization or club, and the sponsor has complied with such reasonable safety regulations as the superintendent may promulgate. Any firearms transported pursuant to this section shall be transported in the manner specified in subsection g. of this section.

(4) A person from keeping or carrying about a private or commercial aircraft or any boat, or from transporting to or from such vessel for the purpose of installation or repair, a visual distress signaling device approved by the United States Coast Guard.

g. All weapons being transported under paragraph (2) of subsection b., subsection e. or paragraph (1) or (3) of subsection f. of this section shall be carried unloaded and contained in a closed and fastened case, gun box or securely tied package, or locked in the trunk of the automobile in which it is being transported, and in the course of travel shall include only such deviations as are reasonably necessary under the circumstances.

h. Nothing in subsection d. of 24-5 shall be construed to prevent any employee of a public utility doing business in this State or any United States Postal Service employee, while in the actual performance of duties which specifically require regular and frequent visits to private premises, from possessing, carrying or using any device which projects, releases or emits any substance specified as being noninjurious to canines or other animals by the

Commissioner of Health and Senior Services and which immobilizes only on a temporary basis and produces only temporary physical discomfort through being vaporized or otherwise dispensed in the air for the sole purpose of repelling canine or other animal attacks.

The device shall be used solely to repel only those canine or other animal attacks when the canines or other animals are not restrained in a fashion sufficient to allow the employee to properly perform his duties.

Any device used pursuant to this act shall be selected from a list of products, which consist of active and inert ingredients, permitted by the Commissioner of Health and Senior Services.

i. Nothing in 24-5 shall be construed to prevent any person who is 18 years of age or older and who has not been convicted of a felony from possession for the purpose of personal self-defense of one pocket-sized device which contains and releases not more than three-quarters of an ounce of chemical substance not ordinarily capable of lethal use or of inflicting serious bodily injury but rather is intended to produce temporary physical discomfort or disability through being vaporized or otherwise dispensed in the air. Any person in possession of any device in violation of this subsection shall be deemed and adjudged to be guilty of a misdemeanor A and, upon conviction thereof, shall be punished by a fine of not less than $100.

j. A person shall qualify for an exemption from the provisions of 24-5, as specified under subsections a. and c. of this section, if the person has satisfactorily completed a firearms training course approved by the Police Training Commission.

Such exempt person shall not possess or carry a firearm until the person has satisfactorily completed a firearms training course and shall annually qualify in the use of a revolver or similar weapon. For purposes of this subsection, a "firearms training course" means a course of instruction in the safe use, maintenance and storage of firearms which is approved by the Police Training Commission. A person who is specified in paragraph (1), (2), (3) or (6) of subsection a. of this section shall be exempt from the requirements of this subsection.

k. Nothing in subsection d. of 24-5 shall be construed to prevent any financial institution, or any duly authorized personnel of the institution, from possessing, carrying or using for the protection of money or property any device which projects, releases or emits tear gas or other substances intended to produce temporary physical discomfort or temporary identification.

l. Nothing in subsection b. of 24-5 shall be construed to prevent a law enforcement officer who retired in good standing, including a retirement because of a disability, provided the officer was a regularly employed full-time law enforcement officer for an aggregate of five or more years prior to his disability retirement and further provided that the disability which constituted the basis for the officer's retirement did not involve a certification that the officer was mentally incapacitated for the performance of his usual law enforcement duties and any other available duty in the department which his employer was willing to assign to him or does not subject that retired officer to any of the disabilities set forth in the "State Firearms and Ammunitions Act" which would disqualify the retired officer from possessing or carrying a firearm, who semi-annually qualifies in the use of the handgun he is permitted to carry in accordance with the requirements and procedures established by the Attorney General pursuant to subsection j. of this section and pays the actual costs associated with those semi-annual qualifications, who is less than 70 years of age and who was regularly employed as a full-time member of the State Police, a full-time member of an interstate police force, a full-time member of a county or municipal police department in this State, a full-time member of a State law enforcement agency, a full-time sheriff, under-sheriff or sheriff's officer of a county of this State, a full-time State or county corrections officer, a full-time county park police officer, a full-time county prosecutor's detective or investigator or a full-time federal law enforcement officer from carrying a handgun in the same manner as law enforcement officers exempted under paragraph (7) of subsection a. of this section under the conditions provided herein:

(1) The retired law enforcement officer, within six months after retirement, shall make application in writing to the Superintendent of State Police for approval to carry a handgun for one year. An application for annual renewal shall be submitted in the same manner.

(2) Upon receipt of the written application of the retired law enforcement officer, the superintendent shall request a verification of service from the chief law enforcement officer of the organization in which the retired officer was last regularly employed as a full-time law enforcement officer prior to retiring. The verification of service shall include:

    (a) The name and address of the retired officer;

    (b) The date that the retired officer was hired and the date that the officer retired;

    (c) A list of all handguns known to be registered to that officer;

    (d) A statement that, to the reasonable knowledge of the chief law enforcement officer, the retired officer is not subject to any of the restrictions set forth in the "State Firearms and Ammunitions Act"; and

    (e) A statement that the officer retired in good standing.

(3) If the superintendent approves a retired officer's application or reapplication to carry a handgun pursuant to the provisions of this subsection, the superintendent shall notify in writing the chief law enforcement officer of the municipality wherein that retired officer resides. In the event the retired officer resides in a municipality which has no chief law enforcement officer or law enforcement agency, the superintendent shall maintain a record of the approval.

(4) The superintendent shall issue to an approved retired officer an identification card permitting the retired officer to carry a handgun pursuant to this subsection. This identification card shall be valid for one year from the date of issuance and shall be valid throughout this State. The identification card shall not be transferable to any other person. The identification card shall be carried at all times on the person of the retired officer while the retired officer is carrying a handgun. The retired officer shall produce the identification card for review on the demand of any law enforcement officer or authority.

(5) Any person aggrieved by the denial of the superintendent of approval for a permit to carry a handgun pursuant to this subsection may request a hearing in the Superior Court of this State in the county in which he resides by filing a written request for such a hearing within 30 days of the denial. Copies of the request shall be served upon the superintendent and the county prosecutor. The hearing shall be held within 30 days of the filing of the request, and no formal pleading or filing fee shall be required. Appeals from the determination of such a hearing shall be in accordance with law and the rules governing the courts of this State.

(6) A judge of the Superior Court may revoke a retired officer's privilege to carry a handgun pursuant to this subsection for good cause shown on the application of any interested person. A person who becomes subject to any of the disabilities set forth in the "State Firearms and Ammunitions Act" shall surrender, as prescribed by the superintendent, his identification card issued under paragraph (4) of this subsection to the chief law enforcement officer of the municipality wherein he resides or the superintendent and shall be permanently disqualified to carry a handgun under this subsection.

(7) The superintendent may charge a reasonable application fee to retired officers to offset any costs associated with administering the application process set forth in this subsection.

m. Nothing in subsection d. of 24-5 shall be construed to prevent duly authorized personnel of the Division of Fish and Wildlife, while in the actual performance of duties, from possessing, transporting or using any device that projects, releases or emits any substance specified as being non-injurious to wildlife by the Director of the Division of Animal Health in the Department of Agriculture and which may immobilize wildlife and produces only temporary physical discomfort through being vaporized or otherwise dispensed in the air for the purpose of repelling bear or other animal attacks or for the aversive conditioning of wildlife.

n. Nothing in subsection b., c., d. or e. of 24-5 shall be construed to prevent duly authorized personnel of the Division of Fish and Wildlife, while in the actual performance of duties, from possessing, transporting or using handheld pistol-like devices, rifles or shotguns that launch pyrotechnic missiles for the sole purpose of frightening, hazing or aversive conditioning of nuisance or depredating wildlife; from possessing, transporting or using rifles, pistols or similar devices for the sole purpose of chemically immobilizing wild or non-domestic animals; or provided the duly authorized person complies with the requirements of subsection j. of this section, from possessing, transporting or using rifles or shotguns, upon completion of a Police Training Commission approved training course, in order to dispatch injured or dangerous animals or for non-lethal use for the purpose of frightening, hazing or aversive conditioning of nuisance or depredating wildlife.

24-7. Certain persons not to have weapons

a. Except as provided in subsection b. of this section, any person having been convicted in this State or elsewhere of the felony of aggravated assault, arson, burglary, escape, extortion, homicide, kidnapping, robbery, aggravated sexual assault, sexual assault, bias intimidation or endangering the welfare of a child, whether or not armed with or having in his possession any weapon enumerated in subsection r. of 24-1, or any person convicted of a felony pursuant to the provisions of 24-3, 24-4 or 24-8, or any person who has ever been committed for a mental disorder to any hospital, mental institution or sanitarium, unless he possesses a certificate of a medical doctor or psychiatrist licensed to practice in this State or other satisfactory proof that he is no longer suffering from a mental disorder which interferes with or handicaps him in the handling of a firearm, or any person who has been convicted of other than a misdemeanor A or misdemeanor B for the unlawful use, possession or sale of a controlled dangerous substance as defined in 20-1 who purchases, owns, possesses or controls any of the said weapons is guilty of a felony of the fourth degree.

b. (1) A person having been convicted in this State or elsewhere of the felony of aggravated assault, arson, burglary, escape, extortion, homicide, kidnapping, robbery, aggravated sexual assault, sexual assault, bias intimidation, endangering the welfare of a child or a felony involving domestic violence, whether or not armed with or having in his possession a weapon enumerated in subsection r. of 24-1, or a person having been convicted of a felony pursuant to any of the offenses found in chapter 20 of this Criminal Code who purchases, owns, possesses or controls a firearm is guilty of a felony of the second degree.

(2) A person having been convicted in this State or elsewhere of a misdemeanor A involving domestic violence, whether or not armed with or having in his possession a weapon enumerated in subsection r. of 24-1, who purchases, owns, possesses or controls a firearm is guilty of a felony of the third degree.

(3) A person whose firearm is seized pursuant to the "Prevention of Domestic Violence Act" and whose firearm has not been returned or who is subject to a court order prohibiting the possession of firearms issued pursuant to the "Prevention of Domestic Violence Act" who purchases, owns, possesses or controls a firearm is guilty of a felony of the third degree, except that the provisions of this paragraph shall not apply to any law enforcement officer while actually on duty or to any member of the Armed Forces of the United States or member of the National Guard while actually on duty or traveling to or from an authorized place of duty.

c. Whenever any person shall have been convicted in another state, territory, commonwealth or other jurisdiction of the United States or any country in the world, in a court of competent jurisdiction, of a felony which in said other jurisdiction or country is comparable to one of the felonies enumerated in subsection a. or b. of this section, then that person shall be subject to the provisions of this section.

PRACTICAL APPLICATION OF STATUTE

Section 24-7a., in a lot of language, provides that certain persons who possess any weapons (these are the weapons found in subsection r. of 24-1) are guilty of a fourth degree felony. This is in addition to any other applicable weapons offenses. Who are these certain persons, though? They range from people who have been "committed for a mental disorder" to people previously convicted of felonies such as homicide, kidnapping, burglary, arson, possession of a weapon for an unlawful purpose and CDS distribution.

Subsection b. elaborates on subsection a. by making it a second degree felony—for persons convicted of the enumerated felonies only—for possessing a firearm. Interestingly, as subsection c. clarifies, a charge under 24-7 is valid for any person who has been convicted anywhere in the United States (or anywhere in the world) "of a felony which in said other jurisdiction or country is comparable to one of the felonies enumerated in subsection a. or b. of this section." Subsection b., as of 2004, also makes it a third degree felony if a person who has been convicted in this state (or elsewhere) of a misdemeanor A involving domestic violence "purchases, owns, possesses or controls a firearm."

Alex Evile is guilty of a second degree felony under 24-7b. and a fourth degree felony under 24-7a. Why? A sawed-off shotgun (i.e., a firearm) was found in his home, so this constitutes the second degree charge under subsection b. of the statute. Also found in his home was a switchblade, and this weapon possession renders him guilty of a fourth degree felony per subsection a. of the statute.

24-8.   **Manufacture, transport, disposition and defacement of weapons and dangerous instruments and appliances**

a. Machine guns. Any person who manufactures, causes to be manufactured, transports, ships, sells or disposes of any machine gun without being registered or licensed to do so is guilty of a felony of the third degree.

b. Sawed-off shotguns. Any person who manufactures, causes to be manufactured, transports, ships, sells or disposes of any sawed-off shotgun is guilty of a felony of the third degree.

c. Firearm silencers. Any person who manufactures, causes to be manufactured, transports, ships, sells or disposes of any firearm silencer is guilty of a felony of the fourth degree.

d. Weapons. Any person who manufactures, causes to be manufactured, transports, ships, sells or disposes of any weapon, including gravity knives, switchblade knives, ballistic knives, daggers, dirks, stilettos, billies, blackjacks, metal knuckles, sandclubs, slingshots, cesti or similar leather bands studded with metal filings, or in the case of firearms if he is not licensed or registered to do so as provided in the "State Firearms and Ammunitions Act," is guilty of a felony of the fourth degree. Any person who manufactures, causes to be manufactured, transports, ships, sells or disposes of any weapon or other device which projects, releases or emits tear gas or other substances intended to produce temporary physical discomfort or permanent injury through being vaporized or otherwise dispensed in the air, which is intended to be used for any purpose other than for authorized military or law enforcement purposes by duly authorized military or law enforcement personnel or the device is for the purpose of personal self-defense, is pocket-sized and contains not more than three-quarters of an ounce of chemical substance not ordinarily capable of lethal use or of inflicting serious bodily injury, or other than to be used by any person permitted to possess such weapon or device under the provisions of subsection d. of 24-5, which is intended for use by financial and other business institutions as part of an integrated security system, placed at fixed locations, for the protection of money and property by the duly authorized personnel of those institutions, is guilty of a felony of the fourth degree.

e. Defaced firearms. Any person who defaces any firearm is guilty of a felony of the third degree. Any person who knowingly buys, receives, disposes of or conceals a defaced firearm, except an antique firearm or an antique handgun, is guilty of a felony of the fourth degree.

f. (1) Any person who manufactures, causes to be manufactured, transports, ships, sells, or disposes of any bullet, which is primarily designed for use in a handgun and which is comprised of a bullet whose core or jacket, if the jacket is thicker than .025 of an inch, is made of tungsten carbide, or hard bronze or other material which is harder than a rating of 72 or greater on the Rockwell B. Hardness Scale and is therefore capable of breaching or penetrating body armor and which is intended to be used for any purpose other than for authorized military or law enforcement purposes by duly authorized military or law enforcement personnel, is guilty of a felony of the fourth degree.

(2) Nothing in this subsection shall be construed to prevent a licensed collector of ammunition as defined in paragraph (2) of subsection f. of 24-3 from transporting the bullets defined in paragraph (1) of this subsection from any licensed retail or wholesale firearms dealer's place of business to the collector's dwelling, premises or other land owned or possessed by him, or to or from the collector's dwelling, premises or other land owned or possessed by him to any gun show for the purposes of display, sale, trade or transfer between collectors or to or from the collector's dwelling, premises or other land owned or possessed by him to any rifle or pistol club organized in accordance with the rules prescribed by the National Board for the Promotion of Rifle Practice, provided that the club has filed a copy of its charter with the Superintendent of the State Police and annually submits a list of its members to the superintendent and provided further that the ammunition being transported shall be carried not loaded in any firearm and contained in a closed and fastened case or gun box, or locked in the trunk of the automobile in which it is being transported, and the course of travel shall include only such deviations as are reasonably necessary under the circumstances.

g. Assault firearms. Any person who manufactures, causes to be manufactured, transports, ships, sells or disposes of an assault firearm without being registered or licensed to do so pursuant to the "State Firearms and Ammunitions Act" is guilty of a felony of the third degree.

h. Large capacity ammunition magazines. Any person who manufactures, causes to be manufactured, transports, ships, sells or disposes of a large capacity ammunition magazine which is intended to be used for any purpose other than for authorized military or law enforcement purposes by duly authorized military or law enforcement personnel is guilty of a felony of the fourth degree.

PRACTICAL APPLICATION OF STATUTE

George Evile is guilty of a third degree felony for manufacturing machine guns at his shop in Jefferson City. He is also guilty of a third degree felony for defacing automatic rifles and handguns at this same location.

Pursuant to the tenets of 24-8, it is a third degree felony to "manufacture, cause to be manufactured, transport, ship, sell or dispose of" (herein, collectively "manufacture") machine guns (subsection a.), sawed-off shotguns (subsection b.) and assault firearms (subsection g.). Any person who manufactures bullets (subsection f.), firearm silencers (subsection c.) or large capacity ammunition magazines (subsection h.) is guilty of a fourth degree felony.

Per subsection e. of the statute, a person who defaces any firearm is guilty of a third degree offense, while a person who "knowingly buys, receives, disposes of or conceals" a defaced firearm—other than an antique unit—is guilty of a fourth degree offense.

Subsection d. handles the statute's prohibitions against manufacturing weapons such as gravity knives, switchblades, billies and blackjacks. It is a fourth degree offense to manufacture any of these items. This subsection also provides that it is a fourth degree offense to manufacture weapons or devices that emit tear gas or other injurious substances dispensed through the air, such as mace. Obviously, anyone who is legally authorized to manufacture any of the weapons or items prohibited in 24-8 is exempt from prosecution.

George Evile was not a licensed manufacturer of machine guns, and he would never be legally permitted to deface automatic rifles and handguns. Accordingly, he is guilty of third degree felonies for manufacturing machine guns (subsection a.) and defacing firearms (subsection e.) at his Jefferson City shop.

24-8.1.

Sale of knives to minors; felony of the fourth degree; exceptions

A person who sells any hunting, fishing, combat or survival knife having a blade length of five inches or more or an overall length of ten inches or more to a person under 18 years of age commits a felony of the fourth degree, except that the establishment by a preponderance of the evidence of all of the following facts by a person making the sale shall constitute an affirmative defense to any prosecution therefor:

a. That the purchaser falsely represented his age by producing a driver's license bearing a photograph of the licensee, by producing a photographic State motor vehicles license or by producing a card purporting to be a valid identification card indicating that he was 18 years of age or older;

b. That the appearance of the purchaser was such that an ordinary prudent person would believe him to be 18 years of age or older; and

c. That the sale was made in good faith relying upon the indicators of age listed in a. and b. above.

PRACTICAL APPLICATION OF STATUTE

The pawnbroker sold a combat knife with an eight-inch blade to a 15-year-old high school freshman. This is a fourth degree felony.

Section 24-8.1 provides that it is illegal to sell any hunting, fishing, combat or survival knife to anyone under 18 years of age. The knife, though, must have a blade of five inches or more or have an overall length of ten inches.

Certain circumstances will afford a seller an affirmative defense to prosecution under 24-8.1. If the seller can show that the minor provided him a card, such as a driver's license, that purported to be a valid identification card, he has met the first element to an affirmative defense. If he further can show that the appearance of the purchaser "was such that an ordinary person would believe him to be 18 years of age or older" and that the sale was made in good faith based on the indicators of age, then the seller has his affirmative defense.

The pawnbroker sold a combat knife to a 15-year-old high school student, the blade exceeded five inches in length (it was eight inches) and the student never presented any identification whatsoever to the pawnbroker indicating that he was 18 or older. Given all these facts, the pawnbroker is guilty of a fourth degree felony.

24-8.2.   **Sale of handcuffs to minors, penalties**

A person who sells handcuffs to a person under 18 years of age is guilty of a misdemeanor A. A law enforcement officer shall confiscate handcuffs sold in violation of the law. As used in this section, "handcuffs" means a device, conventionally used for law enforcement purposes, that can be tightened and locked about the wrists for the purpose of restraining a person's movement.

PRACTICAL APPLICATION OF STATUTE

The pawnbroker sold three pairs of handcuffs to a 15-year-old high school freshman. Simply stated, under section 24-8.2, he is guilty of a misdemeanor A for this act.

24-9.   **Pawnbrokers; loaning on firearms**

a. Any pawnbroker who sells or offers to sell or to lend or to give away any weapon, destructive device or explosive is guilty of a felony of the third degree.

b. Any person who loans money, the security for which is any handgun, rifle or shotgun, is guilty of a misdemeanor A.

PRACTICAL APPLICATION OF STATUTE

The pawnbroker is guilty of a third degree felony under 24-9. Under subsection a. of this statute, a pawnbroker who sells—or even gives away—any weapon, destructive device or explosive is guilty of a felony of the third degree.

George Evile sold the pawnbroker cocaine and weapons. After their deal was completed, the pawnbroker resold a number of the items to a college student; specifically, he sold the handguns and ten daggers to the young man. This illegal transaction renders the pawnbroker guilty of a third degree felony under 24-9.

24-10.   **Unlawful use of body vests**

A person is guilty of a felony if he uses or wears a body vest while engaged in the commission of or an attempt to commit, or flight after committing or attempting to commit, murder, manslaughter, robbery, sexual assault, burglary, kidnapping, criminal escape or aggravated assault. Use or wearing a body vest while engaged in the commission of or an attempt to commit, or flight after committing or attempting to commit, a felony of the first degree is a felony of the second degree. Otherwise it is a felony of the third degree.

As used in this section, "body vest" means bullet-resistant body armor which is intended to provide ballistic and trauma protection.

Practical Application of Statute

George Evile wore a body vest when he robbed a candy store in Walcott. This act warrants a second degree charge pursuant to section 24-10.

In addition to other appropriate charges, a person will face either a second or third degree charge if he wears a body vest during the commission or flight from one of a number of serious felonies. The felonies that act as a springboard for the body vest charge under 24-10 include offenses such as burglary, robbery, sexual assault and murder. If the underlying offense is a felony of the first degree, the body vest charge will be one of the second degree; otherwise, it will be a third degree felony.

Wielding an automatic rifle, George Evile held up a candy store in Walcott. There, he sported a body vest and shot the clerk in the leg just before fleeing the store. Robbery and aggravated assault are among the felonies George committed at the candy store—in this case, the robbery is a felony of the first degree. Given the first degree nature of this underlying offense, George is guilty of a second degree felony for wearing a body vest during the commission of the crime.

24-11.   **Training, practice or instruction in use, application of making of firearms or explosive devices**

a. Any person who teaches or demonstrates to any other person the use, application or making of any firearm, explosive or destructive device or technique capable of causing injury or death to a person knowing or having reason to know or intending that it will be employed for use in, or in furtherance of, an illegal activity is guilty of a felony of the second degree.

b. Any person who assembles with one or more persons for the purpose of training with, practicing with or being instructed in the use of any firearm, explosive or destructive device or technique capable of causing injury or death to a person intending to unlawfully employ it for use in, or in furtherance of, an illegal activity is guilty of a felony of the second degree.

Practical Application of Statute

For teaching the pawnbroker how to manufacture machine guns, George Evile is guilty of a second degree felony. George's "knowledge" that the pawnbroker was planning to utilize the machine guns for future robberies is the linchpin for a conviction under this statute.

Per subsection a. of 24-11, a person who teaches another how to make "any firearm, explosive or destructive device or technique capable of causing injury or death" can be convicted of a felony of the second degree. The statute further provides, though, that the teacher must perform the instruction "knowing or having reason to know or intending" that the devices or techniques will be "employed for use in, or in furtherance of, an illegal activity."

George Evile's instruction meets all of the elements of this offense. George appeared at the pawnbroker's home and personally instructed him in how to manufacture firearms—specifically, machine guns. George did this "knowing" that the pawnbroker was intending to manufacture the guns for use in the "illegal activity" of armored car robberies. Accordingly, George Evile should be convicted of a second degree felony as provided for in 24-11.

24-12. Gun advertising requirement

Any person who offers to sell a machine gun, semi-automatic rifle or assault firearm by means of an advertisement published in a newspaper circulating within this State, which advertisement does not specify that the purchaser shall hold a valid license to purchase and possess a machine gun or assault firearm or a valid firearms identification card to purchase and possess an automatic or semi-automatic rifle, is guilty of a misdemeanor A.

PRACTICAL APPLICATION OF STATUTE

Licensed dealers may advertise, in newspapers, the sale of machine guns, semi-automatic rifles or assault firearms. However, dealers can be convicted of a misdemeanor A per 24-12 if their advertisements fail to specify certain language. In the case of machine guns and assault firearms, the advertisements must state that the purchaser must "hold a valid license" to purchase and possess such items; in the case of automatic and semi-automatic rifles, the ad must specify that the purchaser must possess "a valid firearms identification card."

24-13. "Leader of a firearms trafficking network" defined; first degree felony; fines; sentencing

A person is a leader of a firearms trafficking network if he conspires with others as an organizer, supervisor, financier or manager to engage for profit in a scheme or course of conduct to unlawfully manufacture, transport, ship, sell or dispose of any firearm. Leader of firearms trafficking network is a felony of the first degree.

As used in this section, "leader of a firearms trafficking network" means a person who occupies a position of authority or control over other persons in a scheme or organization of illegal firearms manufacturing, transporting, shipping or selling and who exercises that authority or control over others involved in the scheme or organization.

It shall not be necessary in any prosecution under this section for the prosecution to prove that any intended profit was actually realized. The trier of fact may infer that a particular scheme or course of conduct was undertaken for profit from all of the attendant circumstances, including but not limited to the number of persons involved in the scheme or course of conduct, the actor's net worth and his expenditures in relation to his legitimate sources of income, the amount of firearms involved or the amount of cash or currency involved.

It shall not be a defense to a prosecution under this section that the firearms were brought into or transported in this State solely for ultimate distribution or dispensing in another jurisdiction, nor shall it be a defense that any profit was intended to be made in another jurisdiction.

PRACTICAL APPLICATION OF STATUTE

George Evile is guilty of being the leader of a firearms trafficking network. This is a felony of the first degree.

In order to be convicted of being the leader of a firearms trafficking network, the defendant must "conspire with others" to "unlawfully manufacture, transport, ship, sell or dispose of any firearm." The work of the network must be performed in order to earn "profit," and the defendant must be an "organizer, supervisor, financier or manager" of the scheme.

George Evile set up a machine gun manufacturing shop in Jefferson City where he produced and sold in excess of 1,000 machine guns. The shop was created by George for the purpose of raising funds for his terrorist group, MIFA. George closely monitored the manufacturing shop, visiting the establishment on a daily basis and barking orders and directives to the dozens of employees who worked for him.

In this case, George "conspired with others" to "unlawfully manufacture" machine guns—several people worked under him and they did not have a license to produce the firearms; the work of the group was performed in order to earn a "profit"—they were raising money for Evile's terrorist conglomerate, MIFA. George was the "organizer" and "supervisor" of the operation—he set up the shop in Jefferson City and barked orders and directives to his dozens of employees on a daily basis. With all of the afore-mentioned elements met, George Evile is guilty of being a leader of a firearms trafficking network. Pursuant to 24-13, this is a first degree felony.

END OF CHAPTER REVIEW

Multiple-Choice Questions

1. Jermaine, age 23, sold handcuffs to Michael, age 15. What offense is Jermaine guilty of?
    a. a first degree weapons trafficking
    b. a third degree weapons distribution
    c. a misdemeanor A for selling handcuffs to a minor
    d. a civil offense only, to be adjudicated in juvenile court
    e. no offense at all

The following fact pattern pertains to questions 2–3.

Officer Bolognese of the Walcott Police Department overhears Trumpet tell Sax that he "always carries a baseball bat" in his trunk "just in case a fight breaks out." A couple of months later, Officer Bolognese reports to a dispute by the waterfront. As he's arriving, he sees Trumpet arguing with Woodwin. Trumpet then runs toward his car, popping the trunk with his electronic key. Just as the trunk flies open, Woodwin shoots Trumpet in the leg.

2. Of the following, what is the *best* offense for Officer Bolognese to charge Trumpet with?
    a. no offense at all, because it is not unlawful to possess a baseball bat
    b. no offense at all, because Trumpet was a victim in the matter and was shot in the leg as he was about to defend himself

    c. second degree possession of a weapon for unlawful purposes

    d. fifth degree possession of a weapon for unlawful purposes

    e. fourth degree unlawful possession of a weapon

3. Of the following, what is the *best* offense for Officer Bolognese to charge Woodwin with?

    a. second degree possession of a weapon for unlawful purposes

    b. fifth degree possession of a weapon for unlawful purposes

    c. fourth degree unlawful possession of a weapon

    d. a misdemeanor A if Officer Bolognese learned that Woodwin was an off-duty police officer

    e. no offense at all if Officer Bolognese learned that Trumpet started the dispute

4. Which of the following statements is true?

    a. Possession of a firearm silencer is a fourth degree felony.

    b. Possession of a stun gun is a felony of the fourth degree.

    c. Possession of dum-dum bullets is a felony of the fourth degree.

    d. All of the above are misdemeanor As.

    e. Only a, b and c are true.

5. Mike Woodland is an officer in the U.S. Army currently stationed at Fort McMartin. After drills one evening, Woodland is notified that he is to report, with several other officers of the U.S. Armed Forces, to Washington, D.C., on a special mission. Woodland, pursuant to the orders, loads up an Army vehicle with multiple machine guns and body armor–penetrating bullets; joining him in the vehicle were 25 other soldiers. En route to Washington, D.C., the Army vehicle breaks down, and a state trooper comes to the scene to assist. The state trooper, upon seeing the machine guns and bullets, should charge Woodland with what offense(s)?

    a. unlawful possession of weapons for the machine guns

    b. unlawful possession of body armor–penetrating bullets

    c. possession of a weapon for unlawful purposes

    d. a and b

    e. none of the above because he is exempt from being charged with these offenses

6. In Holbrooke, George Evile sold a kilogram of cocaine to a pawnbroker, and during the drug deal, George carried a .22-caliber pistol. Which of the following offenses should George be charged with?

    a. a first degree felony for possession of a weapon for unlawful purposes

    b. a third degree felony for unlawful possession of a weapon

    c. a second degree felony for possession of a firearm during a drug distribution deal

    d. a and c

    e. b and c

7. Sally, angry at her lover, Suave, for cheating on her with an attorney, shows up at Suave's house with a dagger and attempts to stab him in the neck. Suave wrestles

the dagger away from Sally, thwarting her effort. Which of the following offenses could Sally be charged with?

    a. a fourth degree felony for unlawfully possessing the dagger

    b. a third degree felony for possession of a weapon for unlawful purposes

    c. attempted murder

    d. all of the above

    e. none of the above

Essay Questions

1. Scorpion had previously been convicted of kidnapping but was "maxed out" and released from prison a completely unsupervised man. Marlboro police responded to an armed offense in progress at a diner. There, they apprehended Scorpion, who was wielding a machine gun at the cashier and patrons as he took all of their cash. He was screaming, "I'll kill you! I'll shoot your heads off!" Name three offenses that Scorpion should be charged with in Chapter 24, including the exact statute numbers and subsections. What are the degrees of these offenses?

2. In order to be convicted of being a leader of a firearms trafficking network, what elements must be present? What degree felony is this offense? Also, in a few sentences, provide an example of someone acting as a leader of a firearms trafficking network.

25

HAZING, CLONING AND OTHER OFFENSES RELATING TO PUBLIC SAFETY

25-1.   **Creating a hazard**

A person is guilty of a misdemeanor A when:

    a. He maintains, stores or displays unattended in a place other than a permanently enclosed building or discards in any public or private place, including any junkyard, where it might attract children, a container which has a compartment of more than one and one-half cubic feet capacity and a door or lid which locks or fastens automatically when closed and which cannot easily be opened from the inside and he fails to remove the door, lid or locking or fastening device;

    b. Being the owner or otherwise having possession of property upon which an abandoned well or cesspool is located, he fails to cover the same with suitable protective construction; or

    c. He discards or abandons in any public or private place accessible to children, whether or not such children are trespassers, any intact television picture tube, or being the owner, lessee or manager of such place, he knowingly permits such abandoned or discarded television picture tube to remain there in such condition.

PRACTICAL APPLICATION OF STATUTE

Pursuant to 25-1, a person can be convicted of a misdemeanor A for manufacturing items such as inoperable refrigerators (see subsection a.), abandoned cesspools (see subsection b.) and abandoned television picture tubes (see subsection c.). These items are potentially hazardous to children who may come upon them. For example, a child who climbs into a discarded refrigerator may have the door shut on him and thereby faces peril.

    The pawnbroker was once convicted under this statute. Why? He kept an abandoned cesspool on property he owned. As long as the pawnbroker failed to "cover the same with suitable protective construction," as subsection b. provides, his misdemeanor A conviction was proper.

25-2.   **Refusing to yield a party line**

A person is guilty of a misdemeanor A when, being informed that a party line is needed for an emergency call, he refuses immediately to relinquish such line.

"Party line" means a subscriber's line telephone circuit consisting of two or more main telephone stations connected therewith, each station with a distinctive ring or telephone number.

"Emergency call" means a telephone call to a police or fire department or for medical aid or ambulance service, necessitated by a situation in which human life or property is in jeopardy and prompt summoning of aid is essential.

PRACTICAL APPLICATION OF STATUTE

Hang up the phone or be convicted of a misdemeanor A—is that possible? Under 25-2 it is. Here's an example.

Jack is on the phone, in his own house, with his girlfriend, Melanie. The doorbell rings; Jack answers the door, holding his phone, and is met by a frantic man he does not know. The man tells him that he just got into an automobile accident and the driver of the other vehicle is bleeding from his head. The man tells Jack, "Please give me your phone to call the police!" Jack, however, slams the door and continues speaking to Melanie.

Here, Jack is guilty of a misdemeanor A. Section 25-2 requires a person to give up a "party line"—the phone—if he is informed that the line is needed for an "emergency call." An "emergency call" is defined in the statute as meaning calls to "a police or fire department or for medical or ambulance service" for situations where "human life or property is in jeopardy and prompt summoning of aid is essential." Jack was advised that an automobile accident had occurred and that a human being was bleeding from the head. His failure to relinquish the telephone in that emergency circumstance renders him guilty of a misdemeanor A per the tenets of 25-2.

25-3. ### Hazing; aggravated hazing

    a. A person is guilty of hazing, a misdemeanor A, if, in connection with initiation of applicants to or members of a student or fraternal organization, he knowingly or recklessly organizes, promotes, facilitates or engages in any conduct, other than competitive athletic events, which places or may place another person in danger of bodily injury.

    b. A person is guilty of aggravated hazing, a felony of the fourth degree, if he commits an act prohibited in subsection a. which results in serious bodily injury to another person.

PRACTICAL APPLICATION OF STATUTE

Delta Delta Delta fraternity, located at a state college, organized its final spring semester event for its newest pledge class. At the completion of this day's activities, each pledge would become a *bona fide* brother in the fraternity.

The majority of the morning and most of the afternoon were marked by the pledges cleaning the fraternity house—mopping floors, washing dishes, vacuuming, dusting and scrubbing the bathroom to a sparkling finish. During the twilight hours, the young men were ordered to take tests on fraternity history and to repeatedly enunciate and spell each brother's full name.

The evening, though, yielded a different chain of events, specifically two separate and distinct activities. First, every pledge was slapped ten times on his backside by Delta Delta Delta brothers Sam Concord and Michael Diaz. Next, brothers Tony

Tangemi and Leroy Manning led the pledges to the fourth floor, which was otherwise known as "the office." Once there, the pledges were ordered to climb out a window and onto the house's roof and were then told to jump from the roof into an in-ground pool that waited below. All the pledges complied; they all landed safely except for pledge Karl, who broke his leg in three places.

In this case, Delta Delta Delta brothers Sam Concord and Michael Diaz are guilty of hazing, a misdemeanor A as provided for in subsection a. of 25-3. Fraternity brothers Tony Tangemi and Leroy Manning are guilty of aggravated hazing under subsection b. of the statute, aggravated hazing being a fourth degree felony.

For a person to be convicted of hazing, he must "knowingly" or "recklessly" organize, promote or facilitate an activity that places (or may place) another in danger of "bodily injury." However, there is an additional provision—this activity must be in connection with the initiation of applicants, such as pledges, in becoming members of a student or fraternal organization. Hazing is elevated to aggravated hazing if the said activity "results in serious bodily injury" to another.

The Delta Delta Delta fraternity is a fraternal organization located at a state college. In an organized ritual to allow their pledges to become brothers in the fraternity, they paddled the pledges and had them jump from a fourth-story roof into a pool. The fraternity brothers involved in these initiation practices at least "recklessly," if not "knowingly," promoted activities that placed the pledges in danger of bodily injury. Paddling someone certainly subjects that person to personal "bodily injuries" such as bruises and abrasions. Accordingly, Sam Concord and Michael Diaz are guilty of hazing under subsection a. of the statute. Given that one of the pledges suffered the "serious bodily injury" of a broken leg when he jumped from the fraternity house roof, Delta Delta Delta brothers Tony Tangemi and Leroy Manning are guilty of the fourth degree felony of aggravated hazing for their roles in that dangerous event.

It is important to note that a person (e.g., a fraternity member) cannot be prosecuted under section 25-3 in circumstances where he has pledges engage in competitive athletic events. Also interesting, per 25-4, a pledge's "consent" to involve himself in any type of hazing activity shall not be a defense to prosecution under 25-3.

25-4. **Consent not available as defense to hazing**

Notwithstanding any other provision of this Criminal Code to the contrary, consent shall not be available as a defense to a prosecution under this act.

25-5. **Definitions**

As used in this act:

a. "Cosmetic" means any substance or other device which is used for the treatment of the skin, hair or nails.

b. "Drug" means any over-the-counter or prescribed medicine.

c. "Food product" means anything sold for human consumption and includes tobacco products.

d. "Tamper" means to adulterate a cosmetic, drug or food product by adding any poisonous, deleterious or noxious substance which may be injurious or detrimental to a person's health.

25-6.   **Fourth degree felony**

A person who tampers with a cosmetic, drug or food product is guilty of a felony of the fourth degree, except that nothing herein shall be deemed to preclude a charge for a greater felony under any other provision of this Criminal Code.

PRACTICAL APPLICATION OF STATUTE

The pawnbroker was arrested at a supermarket for opening a package of cupcakes, spitting on the baked goods and resealing the package. This is a fourth degree felony under 25-6, as this statute prohibits a person from tampering with a "cosmetic, drug or food."

25-7.   **Violation of law intended to protect public health and safety; grading**

   a. A person is guilty of a felony of the second degree if the person knowingly violates a law intended to protect the public health and safety or knowingly fails to perform a duty imposed by a law intended to protect the public health and safety and recklessly causes death.

   b. A person is guilty of a felony of the third degree if the person knowingly violates a law intended to protect the public health and safety or knowingly fails to perform a duty imposed by a law intended to protect the public health and safety and recklessly causes serious bodily injury.

   c. A person is guilty of a felony of the fourth degree if the person knowingly violates a law intended to protect the public health and safety or knowingly fails to perform a duty imposed by a law intended to protect the public health and safety and recklessly causes significant bodily injury.

PRACTICAL APPLICATION OF STATUTE

Section 25-7a. makes it a second degree felony where a person "knowingly" violates a law (or fails to perform a duty) intended to protect the public health and safety and "recklessly" causes "death." Under subsection b., this same type of behavior is a third degree felony where it "recklessly" causes "serious bodily injury"; per subsection c., it is a fourth degree felony if it "recklessly" causes "significant bodily injury." But where is this statute applicable? A review of another incident involving the pawnbroker can answer this question.

For some reason, the pawnbroker decided to remove a stop sign at a busy Union City intersection. On the same day, an unassuming motorist crossed through the intersection, without stopping, and crashed into another motor vehicle, and a passenger in one of the cars was killed. Here, the pawnbroker "knowingly" violated a law intended to protect the public health and safety: He committed an act of criminal mischief by taking down a stop sign. The stop sign was obviously in place to prevent the ill that did in fact occur—a motor vehicle accident. His action was certainly "reckless" in that any person could reasonably foresee that a motor vehicle accident could occur as a result of removing a stop sign at a busy intersection. Since his unlawful act "recklessly" resulted in death, the pawnbroker is guilty of a second degree felony as provided in subsection a. of 25-7.

25-8.   **Consumer products; unauthorized writing; offense**

a. Except as provided in subsection b. of this section, any person who stamps, prints, places or inserts any writing in or on a consumer product offered for sale or the box, package or other container containing the product is guilty of a misdemeanor A.

b. This act shall not apply in any case where the owner or manager of the premises where the product is stored or sold, the product manufacturer, the authorized distributor or the retailer of the product consents to the placing or inserting of the writing.

c. As used in this act:

(1) "Writing" means any form of representation or communication, including handbills, notices or advertising, that contains letters, words or pictorial representations.

(2) "Consumer product" includes but is not limited to any cosmetic, drug or food product or any article, product or commodity which is customarily produced or distributed for use by individuals.

PRACTICAL APPLICATION OF STATUTE

Manuk, a car dealer, enters a supermarket and stamps the following on every box of pasta in the store: "For the best car deals, come to Manuk's, in Freehold." This act renders Manuk guilty of a misdemeanor A under 25-8. Why? This statute makes it illegal to stamp, print, place or insert any writing (e.g., advertisements, notices) "on a consumer product offered for sale or the box, package or other container containing the product." In the case where any authorized person (such as the store owner or the product manufacturer) consents to the placing or inserting of the writing, this statute does not apply.

25-9.   **Use of certain cable, wire devices; fourth degree felony**

A person who uses any type of device, including but not limited to wire or cable, that is not a fence but is installed at a height under ten feet from the ground to indicate boundary lines or otherwise to divide, partition or segregate portions of real property, if the device is not readily visible or marked in such a way as to make it readily visible to persons who are pedestrians, equestrians, bicyclists or drivers of off-the-road vehicles and poses a risk of causing significant bodily injury to such persons, shall be guilty of a felony of the fourth degree. However, this section is not intended to apply to markers set by a licensed land surveyor, pursuant to existing statute.

PRACTICAL APPLICATION OF STATUTE

Perry encircles his Johnson Township ranch with a clear heavyweight cable. The cable is approximately five feet from the ground, and at night it is nearly impossible to see it; even during daylight hours, it is difficult to see it. On a late weekend evening, Marty decided to cut through Perry's yard in an effort to more quickly reach a home located behind Perry's house. Unfortunately for Marty, he was "clotheslined" by the cable as his neck ran directly into it. Marty hit the ground with considerable force and broke his arm.

In the aforementioned matter, Perry is guilty of a fourth degree felony pursuant to the provisions laid out in section 25-9. This statute makes it such an offense where a person uses any type of device, such as cable or wire, that is "installed at a height under ten feet from the ground" in order to indicate boundary lines or to otherwise separate portions of real property. However, in order for a conviction to occur under this statute, the device must not be readily visible and it must pose "a risk of causing significant bodily injury."

Perry's cable was five feet off the ground, and it was not readily visible to people coming upon it. It obviously posed "a risk of causing significant bodily injury"—Marty could not see it, was "clotheslined," crashed to the ground and broke his arm. Accordingly, the danger imposed by Perry renders him guilty of a fourth degree felony under 25-9.

25-10.   ### Cloning of human being, first degree felony; definition

A person who knowingly engages or assists, directly or indirectly, in the cloning of a human being is guilty of a felony of the first degree.

As used in this section, "cloning of a human being" means the replication of a human individual by cultivating a cell with genetic material through the egg, embryo, fetal and newborn stages into a new human individual.

PRACTICAL APPLICATION OF STATUTE

Dr. Cornelius Monteforte, the chiropractor-turned-scientist, is guilty of cloning under section 25-10. The pawnbroker would also likely be convicted of this first degree offense for "assisting" the doctor in his attempts to subvert God in human creation.

This cloning statute simply provides that a person is guilty of a first degree felony where he "knowingly" engages or assists "in the cloning of a human being." The term "cloning of a human being" is defined in the second paragraph of the statute.

Dr. Monteforte obtained the blood of the recently deceased sister of the pawnbroker. In a home laboratory, the chiropractic physician had transcended from cracking backs to attempting to replicate various mammals, including human beings. The woman's blood was part of this scheme.

In one setup, her blood was distributed among several test tubes and mixed with various chemicals and hormones. An embryo appeared to be developing in the largest test tube, and the plans attached to the test tubes described the cloning of the pawnbroker's sister.

Dr. Monteforte obviously "knowingly" engaged in "the cloning of a human being" given the use of the blood of the pawnbroker's sister in his home laboratory setup, the plans revealing his intent. Accordingly, he should be convicted of cloning under 25-10.

The pawnbroker also could be convicted of violating this statute for "assisting" Dr. Monteforte in his cloning activities; he provided the doctor with his sister's blood. To ultimately secure a guilty verdict, however, the prosecution would need to prove that the pawnbroker "knew" his provision of the blood to Dr. Monteforte would (or could) aid in the chiropractor's cloning efforts.

Cloning Versus Attempting to Clone

An interesting question arising from a charge under this statute is whether Dr. Monteforte and the pawnbroker would be convicted of a *first degree* felony for "the cloning of a human being" or a *second degree* felony for *attempting* "the cloning of a human being." The second paragraph of the statute, in defining "the cloning of a human being," apparently provides that a human cell must be cultivated "into a new human individual."

The definitional language is as follows: "the replication of a human individual by cultivating a cell with genetic material through the egg, embryo, fetal and newborn stages *into* a *new human individual* [italics added]." This seems to indicate that in order to be convicted of cloning—a first degree felony—a new cloned human individual actually must be created by the perpetrator.

The finding of a cloned human egg or embryo—not yet born into the world—may only substantiate an "attempt" to clone under 25-10. Accordingly, per 27-21 (grading of criminal attempt), Dr. Monteforte and the pawnbroker would only be guilty of second degree felonies, as an "attempt" to commit a first degree felony (such as cloning) constitutes a second degree offense. Under 27-21, an "attempt" to commit any first degree felony is a second degree offense (except murder and terrorism, where "attempts" to commit those offenses still amount to first degree felonies).

END OF CHAPTER REVIEW

Multiple-Choice Questions

1. Delta Delta Delta fraternity brothers Sam Concord and Michael Diaz slapped each fraternity pledge with a paddle on his backside. The pledges consented to the slapping and received bruises and slight lacerations to their backsides. Concord and Diaz are guilty of which of the following offenses?

    a. third degree aggravated assault

    b. a misdemeanor A of simple assault

    c. a misdemeanor A of hazing

    d. a fourth degree felony of aggravated hazing

    e. no offense at all because the bodily harm consented to was not serious

2. Fraternity brother Diaz smacked a paddle against the head of one of the fraternity's pledges, knocking him unconscious and causing him to receive 30 stitches. The pledge consented to the head beating. Diaz could be convicted of what offense(s)?

    a. second degree aggravated assault and fourth degree aggravated hazing

    b. second degree aggravated assault and a misdemeanor A of hazing

    c. a misdemeanor A of hazing, but no assault charge at all because the pledge consented to the head beating

    d. a fourth degree aggravated hazing, but no assault charge at all because the pledge consented to the head beating

    e. aggravated assault only

3. The pawnbroker went to a supermarket, opened a package of cupcakes, spit on the baked goods and resealed the package. The pawnbroker is guilty of what offense?

    a. a felony of the first degree

    b. a felony of the fourth degree

    c. a misdemeanor B

    d. any of the above, depending on the value of the cupcakes

    e. none of the above

4. For some reason a pawnbroker decided to remove a stop sign at a busy Union City intersection. On the same day, an unassuming motorist crossed through the intersection without stopping and crashed into another motor vehicle. A passenger in one of the cars was killed. Which of the following statements is accurate?

   a. The driver who passed through the intersection should be charged with vehicular homicide.

   b. The driver who passed through the intersection should not be charged with vehicular homicide but should be charged with a fourth degree negligent homicide if it was proved that he had previously passed through that intersection.

   c. The pawnbroker should be charged with a felony of the second degree.

   d. Only a and c are accurate.

   e. Only b and c are accurate.

Essay Question

1. Maximus Larabelle, a filmmaker who has directed over 25 horror movies, decided that he wanted to have the most human-like monster/robot in the history of cinema—but he didn't want to use a human actor. Instead, he set out to create his own monster. To effectuate his goal, Larabelle procured the skeleton of an ape. He stuffed the skeleton with various synthetic materials that mimicked human organs in texture and weight. He used the same method to fabricate human skin. After all the bells and whistles were completed, Larabelle had created Bombisto—a nine-foot-tall monster whose features closely resembled those of a deformed, maniacal-looking human being. Through advanced technology, Larabelle was able to make Bombisto walk and grunt. In creating Bombisto, is Larabelle guilty of the criminal offense of cloning? Why or why not?

26

RACKETEERING

26-1.   **Definitions**

For purposes of this section and 26-2 through 26-6:

a. "Racketeering activity" means:

   (1) Any of the following felonies which are felonies under the laws of this State or are equivalent felonies under the laws of any other jurisdiction:

     (a) Murder.

     (b) Kidnapping.

     (c) Gambling.

     (d) Promoting prostitution.

     (e) Obscenity.

     (f) Robbery.

     (g) Bribery.

     (h) Extortion.

     (i) Criminal usury.

     (j) Violations of chapter 18 of this Criminal Code.

     (k) Violation of 25-10, cloning.

     (l) Arson.

    (m) Burglary.

     (n) Theft and all felonies defined in chapter 9 of this Criminal Code.

     (o) Forgery and fraudulent practices and all felonies defined in chapter 10 of this Criminal Code.

     (p) Fraud in the offering, sale or purchase of securities.

     (q) Alteration of motor vehicle identification numbers.

     (r) Unlawful manufacture, purchase, use or transfer of firearms.

     (s) Unlawful possession or use of destructive devices or explosives.

     (t) Violation of sections 112 through 116 inclusive of the "Casino Control Act."

     (u) Violation of 20-4, 20-5 or 20-6 and all felonies involving illegal distribution of a controlled dangerous substance or controlled substance analog, except possession of less than one ounce of marijuana.

     (v) Violation of subsection b. of 12-4 except for subparagraph (b) of paragraph (5) of subsection b.

     (w) Violation of 24-16, leader of firearms trafficking network.

     (x) Violation of 24-14, weapons training for illegal activities.

(y) Violation of section 23-2, terrorism.

(z) Violation of 3-8, human trafficking.

(2) Any conduct defined as "racketeering activity."

b. "Person" includes any individual or entity or enterprise as defined herein holding or capable of holding a legal or beneficial interest in property.

c. "Enterprise" includes any individual, sole proprietorship, partnership, corporation, business or charitable trust, association or other legal entity, any union or group of individuals associated in fact, although not a legal entity, and illicit as well as licit enterprises and governmental as well as other entities.

d. "Pattern of racketeering activity" requires:

(1) Engaging in at least two incidents of racketeering conduct, one of which shall have occurred after the effective date of this act and the last of which shall have occurred within ten years (excluding any period of imprisonment) after a prior incident of racketeering activity; and

(2) A showing that the incidents of racketeering activity embrace criminal conduct that has either the same or similar purposes, results, participants or victims or methods of commission or are otherwise interrelated by distinguishing characteristics and are not isolated incidents.

e. "Unlawful debt" means a debt:

(1) Which was incurred or contracted in gambling activity which was in violation of the law of the United States, a state or political subdivision thereof; or

(2) Which is unenforceable under State or federal law in whole or in part as to principal or interest because of the laws relating to usury.

f. "Documentary material" includes any book, paper, document, writing, drawing, graph, chart, photograph, phonograph record, magnetic or recording or video tape, computer printout or other data compilation from which information can be obtained or from which information can be translated into useable form or other tangible item.

g. "Attorney General" includes the State Attorney General, his assistants and deputies. The term shall also include a county prosecutor or his designated assistant prosecutor if a county prosecutor is expressly authorized in writing by the Attorney General to carry out the powers conferred on the Attorney General by this chapter.

h. "Trade or commerce" shall include all economic activity involving or relating to any commodity or service.

26-2.   Prohibited activities

a. It shall be unlawful for any person who has received any income derived, directly or indirectly, from a pattern of racketeering activity or through collection of an unlawful debt in which he has participated as a principal to use or invest, directly or indirectly, any part of the income, or the proceeds of the income, in acquisition of any interest in or the establishment or operation of any enterprise which is engaged in or the activities of which affect trade or commerce. A purchase of securities on the open market for purposes of investment, and without the intention of controlling or participating in the control of the issuer or of assisting another to do so, shall not be unlawful under this section, provided that the sum total of the securities of the issuer held by the purchaser, the members of his family and his or their accomplices in any pattern of racketeering activity or in the collection of an unlawful debt does not amount in the aggregate to 1% of the outstanding securities of any one class or does not, either in law or in fact, empower the holders thereof to elect one or more directors of the issuer, provided further that if, in any proceeding involving an alleged investment in violation of this section, it is established that over half of the defendant's aggregate income for a period of two or more years immediately preceding the investment was derived from a pattern of racketeering activity, a rebuttable presumption shall arise that the investment included income derived from a pattern of racketeering activity.

b. It shall be unlawful for any person through a pattern of racketeering activity or through collection of an unlawful debt to acquire or maintain, directly or indirectly, any interest in or control of any enterprise which is engaged in or activities of which affect trade or commerce.

c. It shall be unlawful for any person employed by or associated with any enterprise engaged in or activities of which affect trade or commerce to conduct or participate, directly or indirectly, in the conduct of the enterprise's affairs through a pattern of racketeering activity or collection of unlawful debt.

d. It shall be unlawful for any person to conspire to violate any of the provisions of this section.

PRACTICAL APPLICATION OF STATUTE

George and Alex Evile could be convicted of a first degree felony for violating section 26-2 by engaging in a "pattern of racketeering activity" in manufacturing machine guns. But what exactly is "racketeering"? What really constitutes an offense under 26-2? Let's evaluate subsection a. to better understand this statute.

In a quick summary, 26-2a. makes it unlawful for a person to use or invest any income that he derived from a "pattern of racketeering activity" (or from the collection of an "unlawful debt") to acquire any interest in an "enterprise" whose activities "affect trade or commerce." Okay, now what does that mean?

First, what is "racketeering activity"? "Racketeering activity" and all the definitions pertinent to 26-2 are defined in 26-1. "Racketeering activity" basically means engaging in any one of numerous serious felonies, including but not limited to murder, kidnapping, gambling, unlawful manufacture of firearms and usury.

A "pattern of racketeering activity" requires two elements: that the person engage in at least two incidents of racketeering within a specified time period, and that the racketeering incidents embrace a pattern of criminal conduct, including matters such as similar purposes, results, participants, victims or methods of commission.

The "specified time period" means that the first incident of racketeering must have occurred "after the effective date of this act"—which is June 15, 1981. The last incident "shall have occurred within ten years (excluding any period of imprisonment) after a prior incident of racketeering." Accordingly, if there are only two incidents of racketeering and the first incident happened in 1992, the last incident must happen by 2002 in order for a "pattern of racketeering activity" to occur.

How about an "unlawful debt"—what's that? It's a debt that was incurred through unlawful gambling activity or a debt that is unenforceable because of laws related to usury.

Now let's revisit what section 26-2a. provides: Any income derived from a "pattern of racketeering activity" or the collection of an "unlawful debt" violates the statute when it is used to acquire any interest in an "enterprise" whose activities "affect trade or commerce." Let's keep going by explaining these terms.

What constitutes "enterprise" is simple—basically it's any business or entity, whether illicit or licit. But how does one know if an enterprise's activities "affect trade or commerce"? Section 26-1 provides that "trade or commerce" shall include "all economic activity involving or relating to any commodity or service." Well, what business activities don't affect trade or commerce? For example, a shipping company has trucks and planes that carry packages across the country. Money is exchanged for the shipment of the packages; trucks and planes travel across roadways and the air. Accordingly, trade and commerce are affected by the enterprise's existence. Another example is a pizza parlor. Money is exchanged for the pizza, strombolis and sodas. Food supplies, napkins and cups are delivered to the pizza place; the delivery of these supplies requires trucks to travel to and from the restaurant. Accordingly, the existence of this pizza parlor "affects trade and commerce."

The Evile Brothers—Guilty of Racketeering

George Evile set up an unlawful machine gun manufacturing shop in Jefferson City where he provided and sold in excess of 1,000 machine guns. George's purpose in creating the shop was to sell the machine guns in order to raise funds for his terrorist group, MIFA.

Over 200 distinct transactions to nearly 150 separate buyers occurred over an eight-year period, the first occurring in 1995. George closely monitored his firearms shop, visiting the establishment on a daily basis and barking orders and directives to the dozens of employees who worked for him. When George couldn't make it to the shop, his brother, Alex, operated the business in his stead. The Evile brothers are obviously guilty of illegally manufacturing machine guns—but how can they be convicted of a "racketeering" offense under 26-2a.?

First, they did in fact engage in "racketeering activity." The unlawful manufacturing of firearms is one of the many felonies that are considered "racketeering activity" as defined in 26-1.

The men engaged in a "pattern of racketeering activity" given that both elements of that term have been met. First, they engaged in not just two incidents of racketeering but over 200—remember, they engaged in over 200 distinct machine gun transactions to nearly 150 separate buyers. The incidents began in 1995, and all happened within eight years of each other, thereby occurring within the required time period outlined in 26-1's definition of "pattern of racketeering activity."

The second element was met in that the racketeering incidents embraced a pattern of conduct that had similar purposes, participants and methods of commission. The similar "purpose" was that each machine gun manufactured and sold was executed in an effort to raise funds for the Evile brothers' terrorist group, MIFA. The "participants" were similar—George Evile, Alex Evile, a consistent employee base and repeat buyers. The "method of commission" was similar in that the machine guns were manufactured in a uniform manner and then sold to waiting buyers.

Engaging in a "pattern of racketeering activity" alone, however, is not sufficient for a conviction under 26-2a. The Evile brothers must use or invest income derived from the "pattern of racketeering activity" to acquire an interest in an "enterprise" whose activities "affect trade or commerce."

Let's say George and Alex Evile pull $100,000 from the proceeds of their machine gun sales to purchase and take over a fruit stand in Holbrooke. Here, they have used income derived from their "pattern of racketeering activity" to acquire an "enterprise," the fruit stand. The activities of this "enterprise"—just like nearly all others—"affect trade or commerce." The fruit is purchased and delivered to the stand; money is paid to the "enterprise" when consumers buy the fruit.

With all of the aforementioned elements present, George and Alex Evile can be convicted of a "racketeering" offense under 26-2a. In their case, it is a felony of the first degree. Why? Section 26-3 provides that anyone who violates 26-2 "in connection with a pattern of racketeering activity which involves a felony of violence, a felony of the first degree or the use of firearms" shall be guilty of a first degree felony. All other violations of 26-2 are second degree felonies.

The Evile brothers' offense was in connection with a "pattern of racketeering activity" that involved firearms and at least one felony of the first degree. As leaders of a firearms trafficking network, they committed a first degree felony. Accordingly, their offense under 26-2a. is a felony of the first degree.

End of Chapter Review

Multiple-Choice Questions

1. Which of the following "pattern of racketeering" activities can elevate a charge of racketeering to a first degree felony?
    a. activities that involve a felony of violence
    b. activities that involve a felony of the first degree
    c. activities that involve firearms
    d. all of the above
    e. a and b only

2. "Racketeering activity" does not include which of the following offenses?
    a. criminal usury
    b. criminal restraint
    c. extortion
    d. burglary
    e. bribery

The following fact pattern pertains to questions 3–4.

George Evile set up an unlawful machine gun manufacturing shop in Jefferson City, where he provided and sold in excess of 1,000 machine guns. George's purpose in creating the shop was to sell the machine guns in order to raise funds for his terrorist group, MIFA. Over 200 distinct transactions to nearly 150 separate buyers occurred over an eight-year period, the first occurring in 1995. George closely monitored his firearms shop, visiting the establishment on a daily basis and barking orders and directives to the dozens of employees who worked for him. When George couldn't make it to the shop, his brother, Alex, operated the business in his stead.

3. Which of the following facts helps establish that the Evile brothers engaged in a "pattern of racketeering"?
    a. They engaged in more than two incidents of racketeering—over 200, to be specific.

b. The incidents began in 1995, and all happened within eight years of each other.

c. Their racketeering incidents provided a pattern of conduct that had similar purposes, participants and methods of commission.

d. All of the above help to establish a "pattern of racketeering."

e. Only b and c help to establish a "pattern of racketeering."

4. In order to ultimately be convicted of racketeering, the Evile brothers must:

a. engage in a pattern of racketeering activity

b. be principals in the pattern of racketeering activity

c. use or invest income derived from the pattern of racketeering to acquire an interest in an enterprise whose activities affect trade or commerce

d. all of the above

e. a and b only

27

GENERAL PRINCIPLES OF LIABILITY AND JUSTIFICATION; DEFENSES; INCHOATE FELONIES

FACT PATTERN

Over an 18-month period, 30 separate armed robberies involving a masked assailant had occurred on numerous state highways. Similarities in each case ended with the unifying factor of the perpetrator's mask—a white handkerchief. Race and ethnicity varied; ages were different, as was hair color. Some perpetrators were men, others women. The English language (as well as Spanish, Hebrew, Arabic and Italian) was used. The weapon in each case was different; sometimes a gun was used, and at other times a knife or baseball bat was wielded. The robberies spanned the Parkway, the Turnpike and several of their intersecting state roadways. Getaway cars ranged from domestic models to Japanese and German imports. The accompanying felonies in each case were distinct from one another, almost to the point of being bizarre.

Initially law enforcement officials entertained a theory that a string of copycat masked robberies had occurred; however, that idea was quickly disbanded when five of the suspected felons were arrested—all of whom ultimately admitted under interrogation that they were part of a single intricate, organized felony outfit headed by one mastermind operative. Learning the identity of this criminal chieftain was the subject of a series of meetings convened by State Police Colonel Frank Winters. Winters formed a council of several high-ranking law enforcement officers hailing from municipalities stretching from Cape City to Northwood. Together, these men and women determined to locate the group's leader and ascertain the purpose and goals of these criminal activities.

The first order of business was for each officer to recount the felonies that occurred in his or her jurisdiction. The borough of Carlton Heights was the site of the first robbery, a venture that netted masked gunman Michael Westmont almost $100,000. Carlton Heights Police Chief Andrew Beaumont explained the unusual circumstances as the other panel members listened intently.

On Route 505 North, less than one mile from the Meadowlands Sports Complex, two intoxicated football players argued furiously inside the 505 Diner. They knocked a plate of spaghetti and marinara sauce on the floor and tossed their respective drinks at each other. Their cursing was so loud that it could be heard outside the restaurant's entrance doors. In an effort to satisfy the diner's other customers and end the argument, management called the Carlton Heights police. Their arrival and presence, however, were not sufficient to quell the argument, as it actually swelled into a fistfight when one of the players slapped the other in the face. As the fight ensued and the patrol officers attempted to break it up, the situation took a strange turn of events. A dark-haired Caucasian male, draping a white handkerchief across his face, entered the establishment. He brandished a sawed-off shotgun and fired a few shots into the air. In English, the man ordered everyone to lie facedown on the floor. Everyone, including the police officers, complied—they had no other recourse because their backs were to the gunman. The assailant then proceeded to the now-docile football players and reached into the front pocket of the leather jacket belonging to one of the men, removed the man's car keys and exited the 505 Diner as quickly as he had entered. The assailant then sped off in the athlete's brand-new Mercedes. It was later learned that a suitcase containing $95,000 in U.S. currency was hidden in the vehicle's trunk.

The two football players were arrested at the scene for violating state statutes related to their tumultuous behavior in the diner. The patrol officers, suspicious of the evening's events, probed the two men about the nature of their fight and the source of the large amount of cash in the one gentleman's automobile. The quick arrival of the athletes' defense attorneys thwarted the police questioning, however, but not their follow-up investigation. Was either of the players involved in the robbery, and if so, for what reason?

The Carlton Heights police chief summed up what had happened. Rodney Crawson, the player whose car was stolen, had owed Bill McNichol, the other player, $200,000 in gambling debts. Crawson had placed bets with McNichol and lost; McNichol was attempting to collect the funds the evening of the argument. Although he was aware that Crawson had a portion of the debt in cash in his Mercedes, McNichol feared Crawson would not turn the money over. This fear resulted in McNichol contacting an underworld friend, who arranged for the robbery of Crawson's car and cash. McNichol was going to allow the masked assailant to retain the proceeds related to the stolen automobile, but the cash was to be split between them.

In order to obtain a more lenient plea deal, McNichol cooperated with authorities and advised that Michael Westmont was the man wearing the white handkerchief but that Westmont was not the person responsible for planning the robbery—Westmont, of course, was still arrested. Both men refused to identify the name of the man who put them together.

Following standard protocol, the Carlton Heights police fingerprinted McNichol and Westmont and ran a National Crime Information Center (NCIC) report to ascertain their respective criminal histories. While the cumulative results of the NCIC searches resulted in no criminal convictions, Chief Beaumont reported that Michael Westmont's fingerprints matched those of an individual sought for a 35-year-old murder of a nursing student.

In the southwest part of the state, West Deal police officers recently arrested Jacques Vandermeit, charging him with armed robbery, aggravated assault and other related offenses. West Deal Chief of Police M. P. Ironstone explained the circumstances that led to Vandermeit's arrest—an arrest he personally performed.

While traveling to headquarters on an early Thursday morning, Ironstone bypassed his daily stop at his favorite highway coffee shop because his attention had been diverted by the strange appearances of two men in a jewelry store parking lot across the highway. One man was wearing a white handkerchief over his face and the other was shirtless and barefoot, only sporting blue jeans. Ironstone immediately notified his on-duty patrol officers and headed to the closest U-turn, which was about two miles south of his current location. As he looked in his rearview mirror, Ironstone saw the men enter the jewelry establishment. Minutes later, he arrived alone at the store, witnessing a violent chain of events.

As he approached, Ironstone saw the masked man pull the jewelry clerk over a glass countertop and begin beating him on the upper body and face with a baseball bat. The half-naked man looked on, chanting and screaming for the masked man to "Knock the dude out!" He then stuffed a handful of diamonds into the masked man's coat pocket. At this, Ironstone burst through the door, gun drawn, and ordered the assailants to hit the floor with arms and legs outstretched. The masked man seemingly complied with the chief's directive, dropping the baseball bat and falling to the ground. As he did so, however, his shirtless companion tripped over him and fell directly into Ironstone. The felon and police officer simultaneously crashed to the ground, allowing the masked man to escape through a back exit. Ironstone immediately ascertained that the jewelry clerk, although injured, was not in a life-threatening condition, so Ironstone handcuffed the one robbery suspect and then chased after the other.

A 20-minute foot pursuit followed where Ironstone tracked the assailant across the highway, through wooded areas, into residential backyards and finally into a supermarket. Once inside the grocery store, Ironstone tackled the fleeing felon before any more danger could occur. Backup officers arrived moments later, and the suspect, who was later identified as Jacques Vandermeit, was transported to the West Deal police headquarters. There, $500,000 in diamonds, rubies and emeralds was confiscated from his person.

Vandermeit's accomplice, however, never made it to the police station. Ironstone advised that the jewelry clerk had shot and killed the man before police made it to the gem store. Apparently, although the shirtless man was handcuffed, he was able to reach into his pants where he was attempting to remove a solid black instrument. The clerk, frightened and believing it was a gun, grabbed a pistol he kept stashed behind the counter. The gun accidentally went off as the clerk pointed it at the handcuffed man in an attempt to prevent his reaching. The solid black instrument turned out to be a hairbrush. The dead man's family subsequently argued that the clerk should be charged with manslaughter, but the West Deal Police Department and the Wayne County Prosecutor's Office denied their request. Ironstone also noted that an autopsy of the shirtless man showed that he had high levels of both PCP and alcohol in his bloodstream.

In Paris City, Spartan County Prosecutor Francine Colongero recently successfully indicted Jillian Peterson for armed robbery and attempted murder. She described to her group of colleagues the circumstances that led to this indictment.

The Paris City police received a late afternoon report that a red Mercedes was traveling in excess of 100 mph on Route 70, a busy commuter highway. Several independent witnesses verified that the vehicle's lone occupant was a woman whose face was masked with a white handkerchief. Two patrol cars were dispatched to the stretch of roadway where the vehicle was traveling. One of the units located the Mercedes but did not find it violating any motor vehicle statutes. To the contrary, the vehicle was parked at a local car dealership, and the suspect driver was not visible from the patrol officer's highway purview.

Aware of the reports that the Mercedes driver was masked, the officer was naturally cautious and drove past the dealership and parked in the lot of an adjoining business. Moments later, he heard screaming and two loud thuds. Following the sounds of this violent eruption, the officer raced to the dealership's showroom. There, he found the masked woman alone. Two machetes were lodged in a wall leading down a staircase; the woman stood motionless, holding a black leather suitcase. The officer ordered her to freeze, pointing his pistol at her. She responded by saying, "Queen Elizabeth told me to steal this cash. I am flying to the moon with her tomorrow to start a cheese factory." Upon the completion of her statements, she reached inside her overcoat and produced a hand grenade. As she was about to pull the explosive device's pin, the police officer lunged at her, knocking the grenade from her hand and allowing it to fall harmlessly to the floor. The woman, who was later identified as Jillian Peterson, was arrested on the spot.

A subsequent investigation revealed that Peterson was a martial arts enthusiast with particular expertise in sword and knife fighting. She had employed those skills in her failed robbery attempt of the car dealership. Wielding two machetes, she had ordered the business's general manager to turn over the company's $500,000 cash reserve, which she advised she knew was hidden in a safe in the back office. The manager had complied and had immediately led her to the money. When they returned to the showroom, Peterson had waved the machetes and had told the manager, "Thanks for the cash. I'm going to kill you with these machetes anyway." The manager, who was so close to Peterson that the knives could touch him, had quickly dropped to the floor, rolling through an open doorway and down a staircase. As he was doing this, Peterson had whipped the knives at him, narrowly missing the man's head. Though the man had fled, she had stayed in place, staring at the knives stuck in the wall. She later told the police that she was so distraught about missing the general manager that she was initially unable to move. Peterson provided no further statements, and the Spartan County Prosecutor's Office prepared to succeed in proving their various felony charges against her.

27-1.   **General definitions**

In this Criminal Code, unless a different meaning plainly is required:

   a. "Statute" includes the Constitution, laws enacted by the State legislature and a local law or ordinance of a political subdivision of the State.
   b. "Act" or "action" means a bodily movement whether voluntary or involuntary.
   c. "Omission" means a failure to act.
   d. "Conduct" means an action or omission and its accompanying state of mind, or, where relevant, a series of acts and omissions.
   e. "Actor" includes, where relevant, a person guilty of an omission.
   f. "Acted" includes, where relevant, "omitted to act."
   g. "Person," "he" and "actor" include any natural person and, where relevant, a corporation or an unincorporated association.
   h. "Element of an offense" means:
      (1) Such conduct;
      (2) Such attendant circumstances; or

    (3) Such a result of conduct as:

        (a) Is included in the description of the forbidden conduct in the definition of the offense;

        (b) Establishes the required kind of culpability;

        (c) Negates an excuse or justification for such conduct;

        (d) Negates a defense under the statute of limitations; or

        (e) Establishes jurisdiction or venue.

i. "Material element of an offense" means an element that does not relate exclusively to the statute of limitations, jurisdiction, venue or to any other matter similarly unconnected with:

    (1) The harm or evil, incident to conduct, sought to be prevented by the law defining the offense; or

    (2) The existence of a justification or excuse for such conduct.

j. "Reasonably believes" or "reasonable belief" designates a belief the holding of which does not make the actor reckless or criminally negligent.

k. "Offense" means a felony, a misdemeanor A or a misdemeanor B unless a particular section in this Criminal Code is intended to apply to less than all three.

l. "Amount involved," "benefit" and other terms of value. Where it is necessary in this act to determine value, for purposes of fixing the degree of an offense, that value shall be the fair market value at the time and place of the operative act.

m. "Motor vehicle" shall have the meaning provided in the "State Motor Vehicles Act."

n. "Research facility" means any building, laboratory, institution, organization, school or person engaged in research, testing, educational or experimental activities or any commercial or academic enterprise that uses warm-blooded or cold-blooded animals for food or fiber production, agriculture, research, testing, experimentation or education. A research facility includes, but is not limited to, any enclosure, separately secured yard, pad, pond, vehicle, building structure or premises or separately secured portion thereof.

o. "Communication" means any form of communication made by any means, including, but not limited to, any verbal or written communication and communications conveyed by any electronic communication device, which includes but is not limited to a wire, radio, electromagnetic, photoelectric or photo-optical system, telephone, including a cordless, cellular or digital telephone, computer, video recorder, fax machine, pager or any other means of transmitting voice or data and communications made by sign or gesture.

27-2.   General requirements of culpability

a. Minimum requirements of culpability. Except as provided in subsection c.(3) of this section, a person is not guilty of an offense unless he acted purposely, knowingly, recklessly or negligently, as the law may require, with respect to each material element of the offense.

b. Kinds of culpability defined.

    (1) Purposely. A person acts purposely with respect to the nature of his conduct or a result thereof if it is his conscious object to engage in conduct of that nature or to cause such a result. A person acts purposely with respect to attendant circumstances if he is aware of the existence of such circumstances or he believes or hopes that they exist. "With purpose," "designed," "with design" or equivalent terms have the same meaning.

    (2) Knowingly. A person acts knowingly with respect to the nature of his conduct or the attendant circumstances if he is aware that his conduct is of that nature, or that such circumstances exist, or he is aware of a high probability of their existence. A person

acts knowingly with respect to a result of his conduct if he is aware that it is practically certain that his conduct will cause such a result. "Knowing," "with knowledge" or equivalent terms have the same meaning.

(3) Recklessly. A person acts recklessly with respect to a material element of an offense when he consciously disregards a substantial and unjustifiable risk that the material element exists or will result from his conduct. The risk must be of such a nature and degree that, considering the nature and purpose of the actor's conduct and the circumstances known to him, its disregard involves a gross deviation from the standard of conduct that a reasonable person would observe in the actor's situation. "Recklessness," "with recklessness" or equivalent terms have the same meaning.

(4) Negligently. A person acts negligently with respect to a material element of an offense when he should be aware of a substantial and unjustifiable risk that the material element exists or will result from his conduct. The risk must be of such a nature and degree that the actor's failure to perceive it, considering the nature and purpose of his conduct and the circumstances known to him, involves a gross deviation from the standard of care that a reasonable person would observe in the actor's situation. "Negligently" or "negligence," when used in this Code, shall refer to the standard set forth in this section and not to the standards applied in civil cases.

c. Construction of statutes with respect to culpability requirements.

(1) Prescribed culpability requirement applied to all material elements. When the law defining an offense prescribes the kind of culpability that is sufficient for the commission of an offense, without distinguishing among the material elements thereof, such provision shall apply to all the material elements of the offense, unless a contrary purpose plainly appears.

(2) Substitutes for kinds of culpability. When the law provides that a particular kind of culpability suffices to establish an element of an offense, such element is also established if a person acts with higher kind of culpability.

(3) Construction of statutes not stating culpability requirement. Although no culpable mental state is expressly designated in a statute defining an offense, a culpable mental state may nevertheless be required for the commission of such offense, or with respect to some or all of the material elements thereof, if the proscribed conduct necessarily involves such culpable mental state. A statute defining a felony, unless clearly indicating a legislative intent to impose strict liability, should be construed as defining a felony with the culpability defined in paragraph b.(2) of this section. This provision applies to offenses defined both within and outside of this Code.

d. Culpability as to illegality of conduct. Neither knowledge nor recklessness nor negligence as to whether conduct constitutes an offense or as to the existence, meaning or application of the law determining the elements of an offense is an element of such offense, unless the definition of the offense or the Code so provides.

e. Culpability as determinant of grade of offense. When the grade or degree of an offense depends on whether the offense is committed purposely, knowingly, recklessly or criminally negligently, its grade or degree shall be the lowest for which the determinative kind of culpability is established with respect to any material element of the offense.

27-3.   **Classes of offenses; sentencing**

a. An offense defined by this Criminal Code or by any other statute of this State, for which a sentence of imprisonment in excess of six months is authorized, constitutes a felony within the meaning of the Constitution of this State. Felonies are designated in this Code as being of the first, second, third or fourth degree.

    b. Except as otherwise provided in the "State Sentencing Act" where extended terms of imprisonment are defined, including life imprisonment and death sentences, a person who has been convicted of a felony may be sentenced to imprisonment, as follows:

        (1) In the case of a felony of the first degree, for a specific term of years which shall be fixed by the court and shall be between ten years and 20 years;

        (2) In the case of a felony of the second degree, for a specific term of years which shall be fixed by the court and shall be between five years and ten years;

        (3) In the case of a felony of the third degree, for a specific term of years which shall be fixed by the court and shall be between three years and five years;

        (4) In the case of a felony of the fourth degree, for a specific term which shall be fixed by the court and shall not exceed 18 months.

    c. An offense is a misdemeanor A if it is so designated in this Criminal Code or in a statute other than this Criminal Code. An offense is a misdemeanor B if it is so designated in this Code or in a statute other than this Code. Misdemeanor A's and misdemeanor B's are petty offenses and are not felonies within the meaning of the Constitution of this State. There shall be no right to indictment by a grand jury nor any right to trial by jury on such offenses. Conviction of such offenses shall not give rise to any disability or legal disadvantage based on conviction of a felony.

    d. A person who has been convicted of a misdemeanor A or a misdemeanor B may be sentenced to imprisonment for a definite term which shall be fixed by the court and shall not exceed six months in the case of a misdemeanor A or 30 days in the case of a misdemeanor B.

PRACTICAL APPLICATION OF STATUTE

Throughout this Criminal Code, an offense is classified as a felony, a misdemeanor A or a misdemeanor B. The primary differentiating factors among these classifications are the penalties that each category can yield and the different rights attached to the same.

For example, an individual charged with a felony such as murder, armed robbery or theft is entitled to an indictment by a grand jury and a jury trial. A person charged with simple assault, a misdemeanor A, however, has no such rights, and this defendant will simply be served a complaint and then face a singular judge as his trier of fact.

The penalty for a misdemeanor A cannot exceed six months of imprisonment; 30 days is the maximum prison term for a conviction of a misdemeanor B. The rationale behind this light sentencing structure is simple—the offenses are considered less serious in nature. Examples of misdemeanor As and misdemeanor Bs are harassment, shoplifting, disorderly conduct and simple assault. The football players' various antics in the diner would be misdemeanor As, while the subsequent armed robbery would be a felony.

Offenses become felonies when the potential prison sentence attached to the offense exceeds six months. Sentences for the most serious felonies in this state may reach 25 years in prison, life in prison or even the death penalty. Subsection b. of 27-3 sets forth the ordinary terms of imprisonment for first, second, third and fourth degree felonies; the "State Sentencing Act" sets out the provisions for extended terms and capital punishment.

Felonies are gradated according to their degree. First degree felonies, such as murder, kidnapping and aggravated sexual assault, are the most serious offenses and carry the greatest possible prison terms. Fourth degree felonies (e.g., reckless endangerment, certain theft offenses, certain forgery offenses) are the least serious, and although a prison term up to 18 months may be imposed, individuals convicted of these offenses often will escape prison sentences.

27-4.   ### Time limitations

   a. A prosecution for any offense set forth in 1-3, 1-4, 4-2 or sections 1 through 5 of chapter 23 of this Criminal Code may be commenced at any time.

   b. Except as otherwise provided in this section, prosecutions for other offenses are subject to the following periods of limitations:

   (1) A prosecution for a felony must be commenced within five years after it is committed;

   (2) A prosecution for a misdemeanor A or misdemeanor B must be commenced within one year after it is committed;

   (3) A prosecution for any offense set forth in 14-2, 14-4, 16-4, 17-1 or 17-2, or any attempt or conspiracy to commit such an offense, must be commenced within seven years after the commission of the offense; and

   (4) A prosecution for an offense set forth in 4-3 or 12-2, when the victim at the time of the offense is below the age of 18 years, must be commenced within five years of the victim's attaining the age of 18 or within two years of the discovery of the offense by the victim, whichever is later.

   c. An offense is committed either when every element occurs or, if a legislative purpose to prohibit a continuing course of conduct plainly appears, at the time when the course of conduct or the defendant's complicity therein is terminated. Time starts to run on the day after the offense is committed, except that when the prosecution is supported by physical evidence that identifies the actor by means of DNA testing or fingerprint analysis, time does not start to run until the State is in possession of both the physical evidence and the DNA or fingerprint evidence necessary to establish the identification of the actor by means of comparison to the physical evidence.

   d. A prosecution is commenced for a felony when an indictment is found and for a nonindictable offense when a warrant or other process is issued, provided that such warrant or process is executed without unreasonable delay. Nothing contained in this section, however, shall be deemed to prohibit the downgrading of an offense at any time if the prosecution of the greater offense was commenced within the statute of limitations applicable to the greater offense.

   e. The period of limitation does not run during any time when a prosecution against the accused for the same conduct is pending in this State.

   f. The limitations in this section shall not apply to any person fleeing from justice.

   g. Except as otherwise provided in this Code, no civil action shall be brought pursuant to this Code more than five years after such action accrues.

PRACTICAL APPLICATION OF STATUTE

Section 27-4a. provides that there is no time limitation to prosecute individuals who have committed murder (1-3), aggravated manslaughter or manslaughter (1-4) or sexual assault (4-2). In other words, a person can be charged with murder, manslaughter or sexual assault even if the criminal offense occurred ten years ago, 25 years ago or 100 years ago. Accordingly, with receipt of Michael Westmont's matching fingerprints, law enforcement authorities may appropriately charge him with the 35-year-old murder of a nursing student; they are not barred by any statute of limitations provision.

If Westmont, however, had merely punched the nursing student in the face, thereby committing a simple assault, or stabbed the nursing student in the arm, committing an aggravated assault, authorities would be barred from prosecuting him at this time. Under 27-4b.(1), prosecutions for felonies must be commenced within five years of their commission. Since aggravated assault is defined as a felony under the Code, authorities would not be able to charge Westmont for an aggravated assault that is 35 years old.

Similarly, Westmont could not be charged currently for a 35-year-old simple assault. The time limitation to commence prosecution of simple assault, a misdemeanor A, is even shorter than for a felony: Section 27-4b.(2) provides that a prosecution for a misdemeanor A or misdemeanor B must be commenced within one year after it is committed. While Westmont cannot get away with murder, he could certainly get away with committing other violent felonies such as aggravated assault and simple assault if enough time passes.

Please note that there are a few felonies where the statute of limitations is extended to seven years (see subsection b.(3)). Also, per subsection b.(4), there are a few felonies where prosecution "must be commenced within five years of the victim's attaining the age of 18 or within two years of the discovery of the offense by the victim, whichever is later."

It is also important to note that the statutory limitations on prosecutions as stated in 27-4 only act as bars to the *initiation* or *commencement* of prosecutions. In other words, if in 1975 an indictment had been handed down against Michael Westmont for an aggravated assault or a warrant had been issued charging him with simple assault, Westmont would not be able to escape facing either of these charges if he had fled and become a fugitive of justice. Currently, the state would still be able to prosecute him for those already-charged offenses.

27-5.   **Requirement of voluntary act; omission as basis of liability; possession as an act**

a. A person is not guilty of an offense unless his liability is based on conduct which includes a voluntary act or the omission to perform an act of which he is physically capable. A bodily movement that is not a product of the effort or determination of the actor, either conscious or habitual, is not a voluntary act within the meaning of this section.

b. Liability for the commission of an offense may not be based on an omission unaccompanied by action unless:

   (1) The omission is expressly made sufficient by the law defining the offense; or

   (2) A duty to perform the omitted act is otherwise imposed by law, including but not limited to laws such as the "Uniform Fire Safety Act," the "State Uniform Construction Code Act" or any other law intended to protect the public safety or any rule or regulation promulgated thereunder.

c. Possession is an act, within the meaning of this section, if the possessor knowingly procured or received the thing possessed or was aware of his control thereof for a sufficient period to have been able to terminate his possession.

PRACTICAL APPLICATION OF STATUTE

One football player slapping the other is a voluntary act and therefore makes him culpable for simple assault. However, if the facts were modified wherein the ballplayer's striking conduct was the result of an epileptic seizure, his bodily movement would not be considered legally voluntary, so it would be inappropriate to charge him with simple assault.

27-6.   ### Ignorance or mistake

    a. Ignorance or mistake as to a matter of fact or law is a defense if the defendant reasonably arrived at the conclusion underlying the mistake and:

        (1) It negates the culpable mental state required to establish the offense; or

        (2) The law provides that the state of mind established by such ignorance or mistake constitutes a defense.

    b. Although ignorance or mistake would otherwise afford a defense to the offense charged, the defense is not available if the defendant would be guilty of another offense had the situation been as he supposed. In such case, however, the ignorance or mistake of the defendant shall reduce the grade and degree of the offense of which he may be convicted to those of the offense of which he would be guilty had the situation been as he supposed.

    c. A belief that conduct does not legally constitute an offense is a defense to a prosecution for that offense based upon such conduct when:

        (1) The statute defining the offense is not known to the actor and has not been published or otherwise reasonably made available prior to the conduct alleged;

        (2) The actor acts in reasonable reliance upon an official statement of the law, afterward determined to be invalid or erroneous, contained in:

            (a) A statute;

            (b) A judicial decision, opinion, judgment or rule;

            (c) An administrative order or grant of permission; or

            (d) An official interpretation of the public officer or body charged by law with responsibility for the interpretation, administration or enforcement of the law defining the offense; or

        (3) The actor otherwise diligently pursues all means available to ascertain the meaning and application of the offense to his conduct and honestly and in good faith concludes his conduct is not an offense in circumstances in which a law-abiding and prudent person would also so conclude.

           The defendant must prove a defense arising under subsection c. of this section by clear and convincing evidence.

PRACTICAL APPLICATION OF STATUTE

The West Deal Police Department and the Wayne County Prosecutor's Office were correct in their decision in declining to prosecute the jewelry clerk for manslaughter after he had shot and killed the shirtless man handcuffed in his store. The sound rationale to decline prosecution is based on the fact that the clerk would be successful in a defense of mistake. Section 27-6 provides that a mistake as to a matter of fact is a defense if an individual "reasonably arrived at the conclusion underlying the mistake" and such mistake negates an offense's required mental state.

    Manslaughter and aggravated manslaughter require an individual to manifest a mental state of "recklessness" in order to be convicted of either of these offenses. In other words, a person must act recklessly in causing another's death.

    A review of the circumstances that led to the shirtless man's death shows that the jewelry clerk did not act recklessly in grabbing a gun to protect himself. The clerk had just been robbed by an armed assailant who had repeatedly struck him with a baseball bat. The shirtless man clearly was involved in the robbery, egging the masked man on and screaming for him to "Knock the dude out!" Even though the half-clothed man was handcuffed, he reached for an item that reasonably could appear to be a gun. Unfortunately, the item turned out to be a hairbrush, and the clerk's gun accidentally fired.

The jewelry clerk's *mistake of fact*—that the robbery suspect was actually reaching for a brush and not a gun—was reasonable under the totality of the circumstances. It gave rise to his appropriately grabbing a gun to protect himself because he feared for his life. This reasonable conclusion negates manslaughter's required culpable mental state of recklessness. Under state law, recklessness and mistake of fact have a mirror relationship: Where a person makes a reasonable mistake, he cannot act recklessly. Accordingly, while defenses are generally raised at trial to ward off a state-sought conviction, it would be fundamentally unfair to even charge the jewelry clerk in this case given the reasonableness of his mistake.

As a special note, generally courts will find that a mistake of law, or ignorance of the law, is no defense. Special exceptions will occur, however, in circumstances where a defendant has relied on an erroneous statute or judicial opinion of an official interpretation of the law by a sanctioned body. For example, if a state attorney general or a county prosecutor specifically advised a pharmacist that it was legal to prescribe cocaine to individuals suffering from depression, then the state would be hard-pressed to charge that pharmacist with illegal drug distribution (found in Chapter 20) if he did indeed fulfill a prescription for cocaine for a depressed patient.

In most cases, however, individuals are responsible for knowing the criminal laws that govern in the state. Arguments that lack of knowledge or insufficient notice of the law is present almost always will be rejected. Rarely, if ever, should law enforcement officers not charge an individual with an offense because a defendant or his attorney claims ignorance of the law; if such a defense exists, it is a matter for the courts to determine.

27-7.   **Liability for conduct of another; complicity**

     a. A person is guilty of an offense if it is committed by his own conduct or by the conduct of another person for which he is legally accountable, or both.

     b. A person is legally accountable for the conduct of another person when:

         (1) Acting with the kind of culpability that is sufficient for the commission of the offense, he causes an innocent or irresponsible person to engage in such conduct;

         (2) He is made accountable for the conduct of such other person by this Criminal Code or by the law defining the offense;

         (3) He is an accomplice of such other person in the commission of an offense; or

         (4) He is engaged in a conspiracy with such other person.

     c. A person is an accomplice of another person in the commission of an offense if:

         (1) With the purpose of promoting or facilitating the commission of the offense, he:

             (a) Solicits such other person to commit it;

             (b) Aids or agrees or attempts to aid such other person in planning or committing it; or

             (c) Having a legal duty to prevent the commission of the offense, fails to make proper effort so to do; or

         (2) His conduct is expressly declared by law to establish his complicity.

     d. A person who is legally incapable of committing a particular offense himself may be guilty thereof if it is committed by another person for whose conduct he is legally accountable, unless such liability is inconsistent with the purpose of the provision establishing his incapacity.

e. Unless otherwise provided by this Criminal Code or by the law defining the offense, a person is not an accomplice in an offense committed by another person if:

   (1) He is a victim of that offense;

   (2) The offense is so defined that his conduct is inevitably incident to its commission; or

   (3) He terminates his complicity under circumstances manifesting a complete and voluntary renunciation prior to the commission of the offense. Termination by renunciation is an affirmative defense which the defendant must prove by a preponderance of the evidence.

f. An accomplice may be convicted on proof of the commission of the offense and of his complicity therein, though the person claiming to have committed the offense has not been prosecuted or convicted or has been convicted of a different offense or degree of offense or has an immunity to prosecution or conviction or has been acquitted.

PRACTICAL APPLICATION OF STATUTE

Accountable as an Accomplice—Soliciting an Offense

Bill McNichol should be charged with the armed robbery of his football player teammate Rodney Crawson. While McNichol did not actually tote the gun or physically steal the cash from Crawson's automobile, under 27-7c.(1)(a), McNichol is an accomplice to the robbery because he solicited Michael Westmont to commit the offense.

Section 27-7b.(3) provides that a "person is legally accountable for the conduct of another person when he is an accomplice of such other person in the commission of an offense." McNichol is an accomplice to the armed robbery due to his solicitation of Westmont's criminal activities, as aforementioned. Accordingly, McNichol's status as an accomplice makes him legally accountable for the armed robbery to the same extent as Westmont.

Accountable as an Accomplice—Aiding an Offense

In the same vein, had the shirtless man lived, he would have been appropriately charged for armed robbery even though Jacques Vandermeit brandished the weapon and took the gems. What makes the shirtless man an accomplice to the offense is not that he solicited Vandermeit to commit the felony but that he aided Vandermeit in the commission of it.

Section 27-7c.(1)(b) states that a "person is an accomplice of another person in the commission of an offense if . . . he aids or agrees or attempts to aid such other person in planning or committing it." The shirtless man drove to the felony location with Vandermeit. He accompanied him into the jewelry store and urged Vandermeit to knock the victim out during the baseball bat beating, and he stuffed a handful of diamonds in his masked partner's pocket. The sum total of these actions demonstrates that the shirtless man aided Vandermeit in committing the armed robbery of the jewelry store. Accordingly, he would be an accomplice to the offense and legally accountable for Vandermeit's armed robbery conduct. But would the shirtless man be held legally accountable for the separate offense of aggravated assault for Vandermeit's beating of the jewelry clerk? The answer is probably yes.

While the shirtless man did not physically partake in hitting the clerk with the baseball bat, he actively urged Vandermeit to strike him. The shirtless man screamed for him to "Knock the dude out!" Although case law is a bit gray in this area, state courts have routinely found this kind of conduct to amount to complicity, making an individual an accomplice to the offense. As such, the shirtless man would have been appropriately charged with aggravated assault had he not been later killed by the jewelry clerk.

Accountable Due to Conspiracy

In both the football player heist and the jewelry store robbery, the criminal mastermind sought by state and local police would be legally accountable for the armed robberies as a conspirator. Section 27-7b.(4) sets forth that a person is legally accountable for the conduct of another person if "he is engaged in a conspiracy with such other person." The elements necessary to charge someone with conspiracy will be discussed later in this chapter. However, simply stated, the mastermind's planning and arrangement with Michael Westmont (in the football player case) and Jacques Vandermeit (in the jewelry store case) to commit the respective armed robberies make him a coconspirator in those offenses. Being culpable in this manner, the mastermind is legally accountable for both armed robberies to the same extent as Westmont and Vandermeit. He would be appropriately charged with both felonies.

27-8.   **Intoxication**

     a. Except as provided in subsection d. of this section, intoxication of the actor is not a defense unless it negates an element of the offense.

     b. When recklessness establishes an element of the offense, if the actor, due to self-induced intoxication, is unaware of a risk of which he would have been aware had he been sober, such unawareness is immaterial.

     c. Intoxication does not, in itself, constitute mental disease within the meaning of chapter 4.

     d. Intoxication which (1) is not self-induced or (2) is pathological is an affirmative defense if by reason of such intoxication the actor at the time of his conduct did not know the nature and quality of the act he was doing, or if he did know it, that he did not know what he was doing was wrong. Intoxication under this subsection must be proved by clear and convincing evidence.

     e. Definitions. In this section unless a different meaning plainly is required:

         (1) "Intoxication" means a disturbance of mental or physical capacities resulting from the introduction of substances into the body;

         (2) "Self-induced intoxication" means intoxication caused by substances which the actor knowingly introduces into his body, the tendency of which to cause intoxication he knows or ought to know, unless he introduces them pursuant to medical advice or under such circumstances as would afford a defense to a charge of felony;

         (3) "Pathological intoxication" means intoxication grossly excessive in degree, given the amount of the intoxicant, to which the actor does not know he is susceptible.

PRACTICAL APPLICATION OF STATUTE

When charging an individual with offenses, law enforcement officers may want to take intoxication into consideration. However, this is a defense and, as such, really is a matter for the trier of fact to determine at the time of trial. In any case, had the shirtless man survived the aftermath of the jewelry store robbery, intoxication may have been a valid defense for the offenses he was involved with that day. Autopsy results showed he had high levels of PCP and alcohol in his blood.

In order to prevail in this defense, the shirtless man would need to show either that his intoxication was not self-induced or that it was pathological, meaning that it was "grossly excessive in degree." Furthermore, subsection d. of the statute provides that he would need to demonstrate that this intoxication resulted in an inability to know the nature and quality of his actions, or if he did know it, he did not know what he was doing was wrong.

Was the shirtless man's intoxication not self-induced, meaning that the masked man, Jacques Vandermeit, injected PCP into the shirtless man's system and forced him to consume alcohol? Evidence at trial could show that. If his intoxication was self-induced, was it grossly excessive in degree? An expert at trial could testify to this. Self-induced or not, grossly excessive or not, did the intoxication cause the shirtless man to not know the nature and quality of his acts or to not know that what he was doing was wrong? Again, an expert at trial may be able to convince a jury of this. Get the picture?

Although the West Deal Police Department and Wayne County Prosecutor's Office certainly would want to take into consideration the shirtless man's intoxication for evidentiary purposes, they shouldn't avoid charging him (or anyone for that matter) because of their findings of intoxication. Intoxication, as a defense, should be left to the court system for determination.

As a special note, intoxication can be a defense to murder, reducing the offense to the lesser homicide statute of manslaughter. Courts have concluded that intoxication can negate the necessary mental states of murder, "purposeful" or "knowledge." However, intoxication cannot be a defense to manslaughter, as it cannot negate one of manslaughter's crucial elements—an actor's "reckless" mental state. So while a defendant may be able to use the intoxication defense to lower his charge from murder to manslaughter, he cannot escape a homicide conviction altogether because he was drunk or high.

27-9. **Duress**

a. Subject to subsection b. of this section, it is an affirmative defense that the actor engaged in the conduct charged to constitute an offense because he was coerced to do so by the use of, or a threat to use, unlawful force against his person or the person of another, which a person of reasonable firmness in his situation would have been unable to resist.

b. The defense provided by this section is unavailable if the actor recklessly placed himself in a situation in which it was probable that he would be subjected to duress. The defense is also unavailable if he was criminally negligent in placing himself in such a situation, whenever criminal negligence suffices to establish culpability for the offense charged. In a prosecution for murder, the defense is only available to reduce the degree of the felony to manslaughter.

c. It is not a defense that a woman acted on the command of her husband, unless she acted under such coercion as would establish a defense under this section. The presumption that a woman, acting in the presence of her husband, is coerced is abolished.

PRACTICAL APPLICATION OF STATUTE

Whether duress is a defense in a given case is a matter for the courts to determine. A modification of the facts involving the shirtless man, however, can exemplify where this defense may be applicable.

If Jacques Vandermeit, the masked criminal, had stripped the shirtless man of his clothing and forced him by gunpoint to be part of the jewelry store heist, then the shirtless man probably would be successful in a defense of duress. Section 27-9a. provides that duress is an affirmative defense where an individual is coerced by the use or threat to use unlawful force to commit a felony "which a person of reasonable firmness in his situation would have been unable to resist." Here, again, the Code sets forth a reasonableness requirement. Certainly, a person of reasonable firmness would have accompanied Vandermeit into the jewelry store if forced to do so by gunpoint. Therefore, under these circumstances, duress would be an affirmative defense for the shirtless man. Would duress be an affirmative defense, however, if the shirtless man was aware that the masked man was about to commit the robbery and actively sought to drive with him to the jewelry store and thereafter the masked man forced him at gunpoint to join him in the robbery? It's unlikely that the defense would be available here.

Section 27-9b. provides that the defense of duress is "unavailable if the actor recklessly placed himself in a situation in which it was probable that he would be subjected to duress." Under the aforementioned fact pattern, the shirtless man's own decision to travel with the masked man to a robbery location likely would be found to be reckless. Accordingly, he would lose any defense of duress.

27-10.   Consent

a. In general. The consent of the victim to conduct charged to constitute an offense or to the result thereof is a defense if such consent negates an element of the offense or precludes the infliction of the harm or evil sought to be prevented by the law defining the offense.

b. Consent to bodily harm. When conduct is charged to constitute an offense because it causes or threatens bodily harm, consent to such conduct or to the infliction of such harm is a defense if:

   (1) The bodily harm consented to or threatened by the conduct consented to is not serious;

   (2) The conduct and the harm are reasonably foreseeable hazards of joint participation in a concerted activity of a kind not forbidden by law; or

   (3) The consent establishes a justification for the conduct under chapter 3 of the Code.

c. Ineffective consent. Unless otherwise provided by the Code or by the law defining the offense, assent does not constitute consent if:

   (1) It is given by a person who is legally incompetent to authorize the conduct charged to constitute the offense;

   (2) It is given by a person who by reason of youth, mental disease or defect or intoxication is manifestly unable or known by the actor to be unable to make a reasonable judgment as to the nature of harmfulness of the conduct charged to constitute an offense; or

   (3) It is induced by force, duress or deception of a kind sought to be prevented by the law defining the offense.

PRACTICAL APPLICATION OF STATUTE

The West Deal Police Department would be correct in charging Jacques Vandermeit with aggravated assault even if they learned that the jewelry clerk consented to Vandermeit's baseball bat beating of the clerk. While 27-10b.(1) provides a defense for the infliction of bodily injury that is consented to, it permits it only under circumstances where "the bodily harm consented to . . . is not serious." Given that the jewelry clerk was struck multiple times with the baseball bat, the bodily harm likely would be quite serious. Accordingly, in this situation, consent would not be a defense.

A person, however, probably could prevail through a consent defense if another had consented to a slap in the face or a punch to the arm. Interestingly, the statute provides language in subsection b.(2) for a consent defense in circumstances of "joint participation in a concerted activity of a kind not forbidden by law." This is why people are not prosecuted for participating in a boxing or wrestling match—the opponent's consent to his beating is a valid defense in those situations.

27-11.   **Entrapment**

    a. A public law enforcement official or a person engaged in cooperation with such an official or one acting as an agent of a public law enforcement official perpetrates an entrapment if for the purpose of obtaining evidence of the commission of an offense, he induces or encourages and, as a direct result, causes another person to engage in conduct constituting such offense by either:

        (1) Making knowingly false representations designed to induce the belief that such conduct is not prohibited; or

        (2) Employing methods of persuasion or inducement which create a substantial risk that such an offense will be committed by persons other than those who are ready to commit it.

    b. Except as provided in subsection c. of this section, a person prosecuted for an offense shall be acquitted if he proves by a preponderance of evidence that his conduct occurred in response to an entrapment. The issue of entrapment shall be tried by the trier of fact.

    c. The defense afforded by this section is unavailable when causing or threatening bodily injury is an element of the offense charged and the prosecution is based on conduct causing or threatening such injury to a person other than the person perpetrating the entrapment.

PRACTICAL APPLICATION OF THE STATUTE

Entrapment is a defense that is rarely successful in its imposition. However, it is a legally viable mechanism for an accused individual to avoid conviction, so it is important to understand the narrow circumstances that allow it to be invoked.

As subsection c. of the statute provides, the defense is unavailable when an element of the charged offense involves "causing or threatening bodily injury." With this being the case, none of the accused armed robbers—Michael Westmont, Jacques Vandermeit or Jillian Peterson—could avail himself/herself of the defense because bodily injury was caused or threatened in all of their incidents. But what if the facts were modified in one of their cases? For instance, what if Westmont merely snuck into Rodney Crawson's car and stole his cash and he was solicited to commit this nonviolent theft, not by professional football star Bill McNichol but by an undercover police officer? Could Westmont claim entrapment? Perhaps.

For an entrapment defense to prevail, the statute necessitates that the underlying felony must be "induced or encouraged" by a "public law enforcement official." This inducement must directly cause an individual to commit the felony. Even more so, for the entrapment defense to work, the defendant must prove that the law enforcement officer made "knowingly false representations" that the conduct constituting the offense is not prohibited or employed methods of inducement that created a "substantial risk" that a person not ready to commit the offense would thereafter commit it.

Based on the aforesaid, Westmont could not succeed in an entrapment defense merely because an undercover officer solicited his thievery conduct, but he could be victorious via the defense if he proved that the undercover cop purposely lied to him, advising that taking Crawson's cash was not illegal because the money had been abandoned and belonged to no one. Westmont could also be victorious if he were able to prove that he would have never normally been predisposed to commit the theft but that the undercover officer's methods of persuasion were so severe that they changed his perspective, thereby causing him to steal Crawson's cash. As one can see, the burden of proof here is on the defendant, and it is a very difficult burden to meet. This is why the defense is rarely invoked and also why triers of fact rarely accept it. Still, law enforcement officers should be wary of engaging in certain felony-inducing activities; otherwise, their charges may not stick.

27-12.   **Use of force in self-protection**

a. Use of force justifiable for protection of the person. Subject to the provisions of this section and of section 27-17, the use of force upon or toward another person is justifiable when the actor reasonably believes that such force is immediately necessary for the purpose of protecting himself against the use of unlawful force by such other person on the present occasion.

b. Limitations on justifying necessity for use of force.

   (1) The use of force is not justifiable under this section:

       (a) To resist an arrest which the actor knows is being made by a peace officer in the performance of his duties, although the arrest is unlawful, unless the peace officer employs unlawful force to effect such arrest; or

       (b) To resist force used by the occupier or possessor of property or by another person on his behalf, where the actor knows that the person using the force is doing so under a claim of right to protect the property, except that this limitation shall not apply if:

           (i) The actor is a public officer acting in the performance of his duties or a person lawfully assisting him therein or a person making or assisting in a lawful arrest;

           (ii) The actor has been unlawfully dispossessed of the property and is making a reentry or recapture justified by section 27-14; or

           (iii) The actor reasonably believes that such force is necessary to protect himself against death or serious bodily harm.

   (2) The use of deadly force is not justifiable under this section unless the actor reasonably believes that such force is necessary to protect himself against death or serious bodily harm; nor is it justifiable if:

       (a) The actor, with the purpose of causing death or serious bodily harm, provoked the use of force against himself in the same encounter; or

       (b) The actor knows that he can avoid the necessity of using such force with complete safety by retreating or by surrendering possession of a thing to a person asserting a claim of right thereto or by complying with a demand that he abstain from any action which he has no duty to take, except that:

           (i) The actor is not obliged to retreat from his dwelling, unless he was the initial aggressor; and

        (ii) A public officer justified in using force in the performance of his duties or a person justified in using force in his assistance or a person justified in using force in making an arrest or preventing an escape is not obliged to desist from efforts to perform such duty, effect such arrest or prevent such escape because of resistance or threatened resistance by or on behalf of the person against whom such action is directed.

    (3) Except as required by paragraphs (1) and (2) of this subsection, a person employing protective force may estimate the necessity of using force when the force is used, without retreating, surrendering possession, doing any other act which he has no legal duty to do or abstaining from any lawful action.

c. (1) Notwithstanding the provisions of this section, the use of force or deadly force upon or toward an intruder who is unlawfully in a dwelling is justifiable when the actor reasonably believes that the force is immediately necessary for the purpose of protecting himself or other persons in the dwelling against the use of unlawful force by the intruder on the present occasion.

    (2) A reasonable belief exists when the actor, to protect himself or a third person, was in his own dwelling at the time of the offense or was privileged to be thereon and the encounter between the actor and intruder was sudden and unexpected, compelling the actor to act instantly and:

        (a) The actor reasonably believed that the intruder would inflict personal injury upon the actor or others in the dwelling; or

        (b) The actor demanded that the intruder disarm, surrender or withdraw, and the intruder refused to do so.

    (3) An actor employing protective force may estimate the necessity of using force when the force is used, without retreating, surrendering possession, withdrawing or doing any other act which he has no legal duty to do or abstaining from any lawful action.

PRACTICAL APPLICATION OF STATUTE

The car dealership manager would have been justified in using force—even deadly force—to protect himself from machete-wielding Jillian Peterson. The Spartan County Prosecutor Francine Colongero would be in error if she tried to indict the manager for homicide if he had shot Peterson after she threatened to kill him with the machetes.

The Code, in 27-12a., provides that an individual is justified in using force against another when the "actor reasonably believes that such force is immediately necessary" to protect himself against the use of unlawful force by another. To use deadly force, the person must reasonably believe it is necessary to protect himself against death or serious bodily harm. The courts have clarified this part of the statute by determining that the defense of deadly force can be used only when a threat of death is imminent. Also, one cannot justify his use of such force unless he can show that the only way to preserve his life was by killing his assailant.

Certainly, the dealership manager would have manifested a reasonable belief that force was immediately necessary to protect his own life. First, Peterson had just completed the theft of thousands of dollars, giving her a potent motive to not be identified. Next, she was waving two deadly weapons at the man, and she actually told him that she was going to kill him. Under these circumstances, death would appear imminent to any reasonable person, providing justification to utilize deadly force as the only means to save his life. Had the dealership manager shot and killed Peterson instead of fleeing, it is almost definite that no law enforcement agency would charge him for murder or any homicide statute at all. Deadly force, in that situation, would have been justified.

Deadly Force Not Justified If Person Can Retreat

It is important to note, however, that under 27-12b.(2)(b), the use of deadly force is not justifiable if an individual knows that he can retreat with complete safety. For example, if the dealership manager was not only next to a doorway but 100 feet from Peterson, he probably would not be able to avail himself of a self-defense argument. Why? Under those circumstances, he most likely could have avoided shooting Peterson and retreated with complete safety. However, because the actual facts have Peterson right next to the manager—where the machetes were so close they could actually touch him—Peterson had no obligation to retreat. The fact that he actually did was just fortuitous for Peterson.

No Requirement to Retreat from Dwelling

The requirement to retreat instead of using deadly force changes when the person threatened with violence is in his own dwelling or "privileged to be in someone else's dwelling." Per 27-12b.(2)(b)(i), an "actor is not obliged to retreat from his dwelling, unless he was the initial aggressor." Under subsection c. of the statute, an actor may use force or deadly force against an intruder in his dwelling if he "reasonably believes that the force is immediately necessary for the purpose of protecting himself or other persons in the dwelling against the use of unlawful force." In other words, even if the dwelling occupant can retreat safely, he can use force or deadly force to ward off an intruder if he reasonably believes the intruder would inflict personal injury on an occupant in the home.

What is a reasonable belief and when a person should retreat, however, are to be measured by an objective standard, not by what a particular actor finds reasonable. These are questions to be resolved by a jury.

27-13. **Use of force for the protection of other persons**

a. Subject to the provisions of this section and of section 27-17, the use of force upon or toward the person of another is justifiable to protect a third person when:

  (1) The actor would be justified under section 27-12 in using such force to protect himself against the injury he believes to be threatened to the person whom he seeks to protect;

  (2) Under the circumstances as the actor reasonably believes them to be, the person whom he seeks to protect would be justified in using such protective force; and

  (3) The actor reasonably believes that his intervention is necessary for the protection of such other person.

b. Notwithstanding subsection a. of this section:

  (1) When the actor would be obliged under section 27-12 b.(2)(b) to retreat or take other action, he is not obliged to do so before using force for the protection of another person, unless he knows that he can thereby secure the complete safety of such other person;

  (2) When the person whom the actor seeks to protect would be obliged under section 27-12 b.(2)(b) to retreat or take similar action if he knew that he could obtain complete safety by so doing, the actor is obliged to try to cause him to do so before using

force in his protection if the actor knows that he can obtain complete safety in that way; and

(3) Neither the actor nor the person whom he seeks to protect is obliged to retreat when in the other's dwelling to any greater extent than in his own.

PRACTICAL APPLICATION OF STATUTE

An individual may use force to protect others for the same reasons he can use force to protect himself as defined in 27-12. A caveat to this, however, is that that individual must also reasonably believe that his force "is necessary for the protection of such other person" and that the other person must be justified himself "in using such protective force." A modification of the facts of the car dealership robbery can exemplify this.

The dealership manager is still right next to Jillian Peterson and her machetes, and salesperson Sarah Sunshine is 100 feet away from them. Although she can safely retreat, Sunshine fires a pistol at Peterson, killing her immediately. Here, Sunshine is justified in her use of deadly force against Peterson; objectively speaking, Sunshine's force was necessary to protect the manager's life. In the same vein, the manager himself would have been justified in using the same protective force. With these two prongs met, Sunshine's shooting of Peterson is justifiable deadly force. As this statute provides in subsection b., Sunshine was not obligated to retreat because she could not reasonably know that she could secure the manager's complete safety without using force.

27-14.   **Use of force in defense of premises or personal property**

   a. Use of force in defense of premises. Subject to the provisions of this section and of section 27-17, the use of force upon or toward the person of another is justifiable when the actor is in possession or control of premises or is licensed or privileged to be thereon and he reasonably believes such force necessary to prevent or terminate what he reasonably believes to be the commission or attempted commission of a criminal trespass by such other person in or upon such premises.

   b. Limitations on justifiable use of force in defense of premises.

   (1) Request to desist. The use of force is justifiable under this section only if the actor first requests the person against whom such force is used to desist from his interference with the property, unless the actor reasonably believes that

      (a) Such request would be useless;

      (b) It would be dangerous to himself or another person to make the request; or

      (c) Substantial harm will be done to the physical condition of the property which is sought to be protected before the request can effectively be made.

   (2) Exclusion of trespasser. The use of force is not justifiable under this section if the actor knows that the exclusion of the trespasser will expose him to substantial danger of serious bodily harm.

   (3) Use of deadly force. The use of deadly force is not justifiable under subsection a. of this section unless the actor reasonably believes that:

      (a) The person against whom the force is used is attempting to dispossess him of his dwelling otherwise than under a claim of right to its possession; or

      (b) The person against whom the force is used is attempting to commit or consummate arson, burglary, robbery or other criminal theft or property destruction; except that

    (c) Deadly force does not become justifiable under subparagraphs (a) and (b) of this subsection unless the actor reasonably believes that:

        (i) The person against whom it is employed has employed or threatened deadly force against or in the presence of the actor; or

        (ii) The use of force other than deadly force to terminate or prevent the commission or the consummation of the felony would expose the actor or another in his presence to substantial danger of bodily harm. An actor within a dwelling shall be presumed to have a reasonable belief in the existence of the danger. The State must rebut this presumption by proof beyond a reasonable doubt.

c. Use of force in defense of personal property. Subject to the provisions of subsection d. of this section and of section 27-17, the use of force upon or toward the person of another is justifiable when the actor reasonably believes it necessary to prevent what he reasonably believes to be an attempt by such other person to commit theft, criminal mischief or other criminal interference with personal property in his possession or in the possession of another for whose protection he acts.

d. Limitations on justifiable use of force in defense of personal property.

    (1) Request to desist and exclusion of trespasser. The limitations of subsection b.(1) and (2) of this section apply to subsection c. of this section.

    (2) Use of deadly force. The use of deadly force in defense of personal property is not justified unless justified under another provision of this chapter.

PRACTICAL APPLICATION OF STATUTE

When an individual has the legal right to use force in defense of property is quite subjective and depends on the peculiar circumstances of his case. The statute governing these matters permits an actor to employ force when "he reasonably believes such force is necessary to prevent or terminate what he reasonably believes to be the commission" of a criminal trespass on premises that he controls or possesses. However, subsection b. of the statute requires that the person must first request that the trespasser "desist from his interference with the property." Exceptions to the desist requirement are enumerated later in the subsection. For instance, per 27-14b.(1)(b), a property owner does not have to request that the trespasser desist if the owner reasonably believes that "it would be dangerous to himself or another person to make the request." Masked assailant Jillian Peterson's case, modified, sheds light on how this statute functions.

Let's say that Peterson arrives at the car dealership unarmed, surreptitiously entering through the back door; once inside, she is discovered by the manager. The manager notes that she is without weaponry but nonetheless wants her to vacate the premises because it is after hours. Here, the manager would not be justified if he employed force without first requesting that Peterson desist and immediately vacate the store. If, however, Peterson did not leave after a request for her to do so, then the manager would be permitted to use force under the statute.

The manager would not be required to make the desist request if Peterson visibly carried a knife. Under that scenario, it would be dangerous for the manager to stop and make such a request, so he would be justified in simply reacting with force to stop her from trespassing on the premises that he controlled. Similarly, if the manager stumbled upon Peterson smashing an automobile with a hammer, he would be justified in using force against her without first asking her to stop her criminal activities. Section 27-14b.(1)(c) eliminates the desist request where an individual reasonably believes that substantial harm will be done to the physical property sought to be protected before a desist request can effectively be made.

The manager surely would have a reasonable belief that substantial physical harm would occur to the car if he didn't immediately act with force to stop her hammering on it. Accordingly, he would not be required to ask her to desist before using force in that situation. But could the manager use deadly force to protect his property in this situation? No way.

Deadly Force in Defense of Property

While 27-14b.(3) provides that deadly force may be used to defend property, in practice, deadly force may *not* be employed in these cases. More specifically, in the defense of property alone, deadly force is not justifiable. The statute only permits lethal action where deadly force has been "employed or threatened" against the actor or in his presence (27-14b.(3)(c)(i)) or where the use of force other than deadly force will expose the actor or another to "substantial danger of bodily harm" (27-14b.(3)(c)(ii)). In other words, deadly force may only be used to protect oneself or another—not the property.

27-15.   **Use of force in law enforcement**

a. Use of force justifiable to effect an arrest. Subject to the provisions of this section and of section 27-17, the use of force upon or toward the person of another is justifiable when the actor is making or assisting in making an arrest and the actor reasonably believes that such force is immediately necessary to effect a lawful arrest.

b. Limitations on the use of force.

(1) The use of force is not justifiable under this section unless:

(a) The actor makes known the purpose of the arrest or reasonably believes that it is otherwise known by or cannot reasonably be made known to the person to be arrested; and

(b) When the arrest is made under a warrant, the warrant is valid or reasonably believed by the actor to be valid.

(2) The use of deadly force is not justifiable under this section unless:

(a) The actor effecting the arrest is authorized to act as a peace officer or has been summoned by and is assisting a person whom he reasonably believes to be authorized to act as a peace officer;

(b) The actor reasonably believes that the force employed creates no substantial risk of injury to innocent persons;

(c) The actor reasonably believes that the felony for which the arrest is made was homicide, kidnapping, an offense under 4-2 or 4-3, arson, robbery, burglary of a dwelling or an attempt to commit one of these felonies; and

(d) The actor reasonably believes:

(i) There is an imminent threat of deadly force to himself or a third party;

(ii) The use of deadly force is necessary to thwart the commission of a felony as set forth in subparagraph (c) of this paragraph; or

(iii) The use of deadly force is necessary to prevent an escape.

c. Use of force to prevent escape from custody. The use of force to prevent the escape of an arrested person from custody is justifiable when the force could, under subsections a. and b. of this section, have been employed to effect the arrest under which the person is in custody. A corrections officer or other person authorized to act as a peace officer is, however, justified in using any force, including deadly force, which he reasonably believes to be immediately necessary to prevent the escape of a person committed to a jail, prison or other institution for the detention of persons charged with or convicted of an offense so long as the actor believes that the force employed creates no substantial risk of injury to innocent persons.

d. Use of force by private person assisting an unlawful arrest.

   (1) A private person who is summoned by a peace officer to assist in effecting an unlawful arrest is justified in using any force which he would be justified in using if the arrest were lawful, provided that he does not believe the arrest is unlawful.

   (2) A private person who assists another private person in effecting an unlawful arrest, or who, not being summoned, assists a peace officer in effecting an unlawful arrest, is justified in using any force which he would be justified in using if the arrest were lawful, provided that:

      (a) He reasonably believes the arrest is lawful; and

      (b) The arrest would be lawful if the facts were as he believes them to be and such belief is reasonable.

e. Use of force to prevent suicide or the commission of a felony. The use of force upon or toward the person of another is justifiable when the actor reasonably believes that such force is immediately necessary to prevent such other person from committing suicide, inflicting serious bodily harm upon himself, committing or consummating the commission of a felony involving or threatening bodily harm, damage to or loss of property or a breach of the peace, except that:

   (1) Any limitations imposed by the other provisions of this chapter on the justifiable use of force in self-protection, for the protection of others, the protection of property, the effectuation of an arrest or the prevention of an escape from custody shall apply notwithstanding the criminality of the conduct against which such force is used; and

   (2) The use of deadly force is not in any event justifiable under this subsection unless the actor reasonably believes that it is likely that the person whom he seeks to prevent from committing a felony will endanger human life or inflict serious bodily harm upon another unless the commission or the consummation of the felony is prevented and that the use of such force presents no substantial risk of injury to innocent persons.

PRACTICAL APPLICATION OF STATUTE

Chief M. P. Ironstone was justified in using force against Jacques Vandermeit when arresting him for his armed robbery and aggravated assault of the jewelry store clerk. Under subsection a. of 27-15, a law enforcement officer may use force in making an arrest when he "reasonably believes that such force is immediately necessary to effect a lawful arrest."

When Chief Ironstone finally caught up to Vandermeit after chasing him for several minutes, force was objectively necessary to effectuate the arrest. Ironstone held a reasonable belief that tackling Vandermeit was the only means available to finally arrest him; therefore, his use of force was justifiable. But would he have been justified to employ deadly force against Vandermeit? The answer is probably yes.

Use of Deadly Force in Law Enforcement

Law enforcement officers, and others assisting law enforcement officers, should be careful in using deadly force; however, there are many circumstances where such force is necessary and justifiable. Under the provisions of section 27-15, Chief Ironstone would have been justified in using deadly force against Vandermeit for a few reasons.

The statute specifically enumerates the necessary factors that need to exist in order for deadly force to be justifiable in law enforcement. First, the actor must be a law enforcement officer or an individual authorized to assist an officer (27-15b.(2)(a)). Second, the actor must reasonably believe that the force employed creates no substantial risk of injury to innocent persons (27-15b.(2)(b)). Next, the felony involved must be homicide, kidnapping, sexual assault, criminal sexual assault, arson, robbery or burglary of a dwelling, although an attempt of any of these felonies will also suffice (27-15b.(2)(c)). The actor must also have a reasonable belief that one of the following situations exists: There is an imminent threat of deadly force to himself or a third party, the use of deadly force is necessary to thwart any of the aforementioned felonies or deadly force is necessary to prevent an escape (27-15b.(2)(d)(i), d(ii) and d(iii)).

After reviewing the above-listed elements, it appears that Chief Ironstone would have been within the boundaries of the law if he had employed deadly force against Vandermeit. Ironstone is a law enforcement officer who witnessed a robbery in progress and thereafter chased a fleeing felon who was escaping an arrest. Vandermeit also was violently beating the jewelry clerk with a baseball bat, which reasonably could have been construed as an attempted murder. It is quite likely that at multiple times during the incident—inside the jewelry store and during the ensuing chase—Ironstone held a reasonable belief that employing deadly force created no substantial risk of injury to innocent persons. Chief Ironstone could have shot Vandermeit without putting the jewelry clerk or any passersby at risk. A shooting by the chief likely would ultimately be considered justified because he held a reasonable belief for all three prongs of subsection b.(2)(d) of the statute: There was an imminent threat of deadly force against the jewelry clerk, his use of deadly force was necessary to thwart Vandermeit's armed robbery and attempted murder and it may have been necessary to prevent his escape.

While it appears accurate that Chief Ironstone could have legally utilized deadly force to thwart Vandermeit's criminal activities and preserve the safety of innocent victim(s), such use of force is truly reserved for only the most grave and serious situations. In other words, though the statute seems to permit the use of deadly force to thwart a burglary of a dwelling, a law enforcement officer may want to strongly consider other options before shooting, or otherwise killing, the suspect burglar. Without an imminent threat of deadly force to the officer himself or to a third party, or without the presence of a violent felony such as sexual assault or kidnapping, courts may find that deadly force was not justifiable—and then a law enforcement officer finds himself charged with a felony.

27-16.   **Use of force by persons with special responsibility for care, discipline or safety of others**

The use of force upon or toward the person of another is justifiable as permitted by law or as would be a defense in a civil action based thereon where the actor has been vested or entrusted with special responsibility for the care, supervision, discipline or safety of another or of others and the force is used for the purpose of and, subject to section 27-17(b), to the extent necessary to further that responsibility, unless:

a. This Criminal Code or the law defining the offense deals with the specific situation involved;

b. A legislative purpose to exclude the justification claimed otherwise plainly appears; or

c. Deadly force is used, in which case such force must be otherwise justifiable under the provisions of this chapter.

27-17.   **Mistake of law as to unlawfulness of force or legality of arrest; reckless or negligent use of excessive but otherwise justifiable force; reckless or negligent injury or risk of injury to innocent persons**

a. The justification afforded by sections 27-12 to 27-15 is unavailable when:

(1) The actor's belief in the unlawfulness of the force or conduct against which he employs protective force or his belief in the lawfulness of an arrest which he endeavors to effect by force is erroneous; and

(2) His error is due to ignorance or mistake as to the provisions of the Code, any other provisions of the criminal law or the law governing the legality of an arrest or search.

b. When the actor is justified under sections 27-12 to 27-16 in using force upon or toward the person of another but he recklessly or negligently injures or creates a risk of injury to innocent persons, the justification afforded by those sections is unavailable in a prosecution for such recklessness or negligence toward innocent persons.

27-18.   **Insanity defense**

A person is not criminally responsible for conduct if at the time of such conduct he was laboring under such a defect of reason, from disease of the mind, as not to know the nature and quality of the act he was doing, or if he did know it, that he did not know what he was doing was wrong. Insanity is an affirmative defense which must be proved by a preponderance of the evidence.

PRACTICAL APPLICATION OF STATUTE

Jillian Peterson perhaps could succeed in an insanity defense. This woman attempted to rob a car dealership while wearing a white handkerchief and manipulating two sharp machetes. Upon her failed attempt to strike her intended victim with the heavy knives, she stood motionless, incapable of movement because she was so distraught. Then she advised law enforcement officers that "Queen Elizabeth told me to steal this cash. I am flying to the moon with her tomorrow to start a cheese factory." While she sounds nuts, was she legally insane at the time of her felonies?

Section 27-18 provides that a person is not criminally responsible for his conduct due to insanity if he did not "know the nature and quality of the act he was doing" or "if he did know it, that he did not know what he was doing was wrong." This is clearly a question for a jury to decide. However, did Peterson understand what she was doing—the nature and quality of her act? Probably. She told the car dealership manager that she was going to kill him and then immediately threw machetes at him, attempting to complete that task. She also actively sought to heist cash from the business, even having knowledge about where the money was stored. This seems to add up to a person knowing the nature and quality of her actions to rob and murder. But did she know that her criminal activities were wrong? Maybe not—she did mention that Queen Elizabeth told her to steal the cash and that she was flying to the moon with her to start a cheese factory. This may be enough for her to prove by a preponderance of the evidence that she was legally insane. Ultimately, though, psychiatric expert witnesses would duel this out in the courtroom; thereafter, a jury would decide the fate of Peterson's insanity defense.

27-19.   **Criminal attempt**

    a. Definition of attempt. A person is guilty of an attempt to commit a felony if, acting with the kind of culpability otherwise required for commission of the felony, he:

        (1) Purposely engages in conduct which would constitute the felony if the attendant circumstances were as a reasonable person would believe them to be;

        (2) When causing a particular result is an element of the felony, does or omits to do anything with the purpose of causing such result without further conduct on his part; or

        (3) Purposely does or omits to do anything which, under the circumstances as a reasonable person would believe them to be, is an act or omission constituting a substantial step in a course of conduct planned to culminate in his commission of the felony.

    b. Conduct which may be held a substantial step under subsection a.(3). Conduct shall not be held to constitute a substantial step under subsection a.(3) of this section unless it is strongly corroborative of the actor's criminal purpose.

    c. Conduct designed to aid another in commission of a felony. A person who engages in conduct designed to aid another to commit a felony which would establish his complicity under section 27-7 if the felony were committed by such other person is guilty of an attempt to commit the felony, although the felony is not committed or attempted by such other person.

    d. Renunciation of criminal purpose. When the actor's conduct would otherwise constitute an attempt under subsection a.(2) or (3) of this section, it is an affirmative defense which he must prove by a preponderance of the evidence that he abandoned his effort to commit the felony or otherwise prevented its commission, under circumstances manifesting a complete and voluntary renunciation of his criminal purpose. The establishment of such defense does not, however, affect the liability of an accomplice who did not join in such abandonment or prevention.

        Within the meaning of this chapter, renunciation of criminal purpose is not voluntary if it is motivated, in whole or in part, by circumstances not present or apparent at the inception of the actor's course of conduct which increase the probability of detection or apprehension or which make more difficult the accomplishment of the criminal purpose. Renunciation is not complete if it is motivated by a decision to postpone the criminal conduct until a more advantageous time or to transfer the criminal effort to another but similar objective or victim. Renunciation is also not complete if mere abandonment is insufficient to accomplish avoidance of the offense in which case the defendant must have taken further and affirmative steps that prevented the commission thereof.

PRACTICAL APPLICATION OF STATUTE

Criminal Attempt

The Spartan County Prosecutor Francine Colongero would be correct in charging Jillian Peterson with attempted murder. Section 27-19 sets forth the elements necessary for a person to be charged, and ultimately convicted, for attempting to commit an offense. This statute, under subsection a.(3), specifically provides that a "substantial step" must be taken by an individual in his planned course of criminal conduct in order for him to be guilty of a criminal attempt. Subsection b. further clarifies the "substantial step" require-ment by adding that it must be "strongly corroborative of the actor's criminal purpose."

Peterson did not kill the car dealership manager; however, she intended to cause his death. She not only advised the manager that she was going to kill him but also threw two large machetes at him, narrowly missing him. Peterson also had a motive to kill the man—to escape being caught for her armed robbery of the dealership.

Peterson identified her criminal intent and purpose by telling the manager that she was going to kill him. She took a substantial step in reaching this goal by whipping the machetes at him—this action is certainly "strongly corroborative" of her criminal pur-pose to kill him. Accordingly, Peterson should be charged for her attempt to murder the car dealership manager. What if Peterson had an accomplice with her? A cohort waiting in a getaway car? Should this accomplice also be charged with attempted murder? The answer is probably yes.

Conduct Designed to Aid Another in Commission of a Felony

Section 27-19c. is the component of the criminal attempt statute that addresses the cul-pability of accomplices. Basically, the subsection determines that if a person solicits or aids another in the planning or commission of a felony, he "is guilty of an attempt to commit the felony, although the felony is not committed or attempted by such other person." With this being the case, a companion of Peterson's likely would be charged with attempted murder.

For example, if Peterson and another individual, George, arrived at the car deal-ership together, planning to rob it and to kill the manager, George would be guilty of attempted murder just the same as Peterson. Why? George is an accomplice—someone who aided Peterson in planning and carrying out the felony.

It is interesting to note here that George probably would be convicted of attempted murder even if he did not actively plan with Peterson to kill the manager due to the pro-visions of 1-3a.(3), which outlines the elements for a felony murder conviction. As will be discussed in more detail later, a person is guilty of murder if he is engaged in one of several different felonies (including robbery) and a death occurs during the commission or flight from one of these felonies. If the person at least knows that another participant is armed with a deadly weapon, he can be convicted of murder if death occurs during one of the enumerated felonies. Accordingly, had Peterson succeeded in killing the manager, George could be charged with murder. Following this, per the language of 27-19c., he could be charged with attempted murder if he at least knew that Peterson was armed with the machetes.

Renunciation—Affirmative Defense

George could escape an attempted murder charge if he abandoned his efforts to commit the criminal activities with Peterson or if he outright prevented the felonies. Section 27-19d. sets forth the necessary elements to allow a defendant to succeed in this defense, but it is a decision that ultimately should be determined by a jury; however, law enforcement agencies could consider renunciation evidence when deciding to charge a person with criminal attempt.

For instance, if ample evidence were presented that showed that George refused to drive with Peterson to the car dealership but thereafter arrived and physically stopped her from throwing the machetes at the manager, he should not be charged or indicted for attempted murder. Similarly, if evidence showed that although he initially intended to be a participant of the robbery, he completely and voluntarily removed himself from the felony, then he likely should not be charged. Specifically, if George contacted Peterson and told her, in no uncertain terms, that he was not going to participate in the robbery, then he likely would succeed in a renunciation defense and avoid an attempted murder conviction. Once again, while this may be best left for a jury to determine, the police or prosecutor's office certainly may take such renunciation evidence into consideration when deciding what charges to institute or when seeking an indictment.

27-20.   **Conspiracy**

a. Definition of conspiracy. A person is guilty of conspiracy with another person or persons to commit a felony if with the purpose of promoting or facilitating its commission he:

   (1) Agrees with such other person or persons that they or one or more of them will engage in conduct which constitutes such felony or an attempt or solicitation to commit such felony; or

   (2) Agrees to aid such other person or persons in the planning or commission of such felony or of an attempt or solicitation to commit such felony.

b. Scope of conspiratorial relationship. If a person guilty of conspiracy, as defined by subsection a. of this section, knows that a person with whom he conspires to commit a felony has conspired with another person or persons to commit the same felony, he is guilty of conspiring with such other person or persons, whether or not he knows their identity, to commit such felony.

c. Conspiracy with multiple objectives. If a person conspires to commit a number of felonies, he is guilty of only one conspiracy so long as such multiple felonies are the object of the same agreement or continuous conspiratorial relationship. It shall not be a defense to a charge under this section that one or more of the objectives of the conspiracy were not criminal, provided that one or more of its objectives or the means of promoting or facilitating an objective of the conspiracy are criminal.

d. Overt act. No person may be convicted of conspiracy to commit a felony other than a felony of the first or second degree or distribution or possession with intent to distribute a controlled dangerous substance or controlled substance analog as defined in chapter 35 of this title, unless an overt act in pursuance of such conspiracy is proved to have been done by him or by a person with whom he conspired.

e. Renunciation of purpose. It is an affirmative defense which the actor must prove by a preponderance of the evidence that he, after conspiring to commit a felony, informed the authority of the existence of the conspiracy and his participation therein and thwarted or caused to be thwarted the commission of any offense in furtherance of the conspiracy, under circumstances manifesting a complete and voluntary renunciation of criminal purpose as defined in 27-19d., provided, however, that an attempt as defined in 27-19 shall not be considered an offense for purposes of renunciation under this subsection.

f. Duration of conspiracy. For the purposes of 27-3d.:

   (1) Conspiracy is a continuing course of conduct which terminates when the felony or felonies which are its object are committed or the agreement that they be committed is abandoned by the defendant and by those with whom he conspired;

(2) Such abandonment is presumed with respect to a felony other than one of the first or second degree if neither the defendant nor anyone with whom he conspired does any overt act in pursuance of the conspiracy during the applicable period of limitation; and

(3) If an individual abandons the agreement, the conspiracy is terminated as to him only if and when he advises those with whom he conspired of his abandonment or he informs the law enforcement authorities of the existence of the conspiracy and of his participation therein.

g. Leader of organized crime. A person is a leader of organized crime if he purposefully conspires with others as an organizer, supervisor, manager or financier to commit a continuing series of felonies which constitute a pattern of racketeering activity under the provisions of 26-1. As used in this section, "financier" means a person who provides money, credit or a thing of value with the purpose or knowledge that it will be used to finance or support the operations of a conspiracy to commit a series of felonies which constitute a pattern of racketeering activity, including but not limited to the purchase of materials to be used in the commission of felonies, buying or renting housing or vehicles, purchasing transportation for members of the conspiracy or otherwise facilitating the commission of felonies which constitute a pattern of racketeering activity.

PRACTICAL APPLICATION OF STATUTE

Conspiracy

The criminal mastermind sought by State Police Colonel Frank Winters and all of the individuals involved in the string of masked robberies (Michael Westmont, Bill McNichol, Jacques Vandermeit, Jillian Peterson) should be charged under the conspiracy statute. Section 27-20 provides that a person is guilty of conspiracy when he agrees with other person(s) to commit a felony or aids other person(s) in committing a felony. A person also may be convicted of conspiracy for soliciting or attempting a felony.

Per subsection b. of the statute, an individual can be found guilty of conspiracy with one or more persons even if he does not know their identities provided that he conspired with one or more individuals who had conspired with the unknown person(s) to commit the same felony. Confusing? Let's use an example.

Remember the case of the two football players arguing in the diner? Bill McNichol hired Michael Westmont to rob his football player friend, Rodney Crawson. Westmont, sporting a white handkerchief over his face and armed with a sawed-off shotgun, heisted Crawson's car keys and then stole his automobile, which held almost $100,000 cash in the trunk. Before the actual robbery, McNichol had never met Westmont; they were put together by the mysterious underworld mastermind sought by the state's top law enforcement bosses.

In this case, each of the men—McNichol, Westmont and the mastermind— could be charged with robbery, and they also all could be charged with conspiring with one another. McNichol solicited the mastermind to aid him in his theft of Crawson; the mastermind solicited Westmont to carry out the actual robbery. Even though McNichol did not know the identity of Westmont until after the robbery, he is still guilty of conspiring with this masked gunman. Under the statute, McNichol would be guilty of conspiring with Westmont even if he had never learned the identity of Westmont. Simply put, since McNichol conspired to commit the robbery with the mastermind, who in turn conspired with Westmont to commit the same felony, all three are guilty of conspiring with each other.

Following the above rationale, it is also true that Jacques Vandermeit (jewelry store robbery) and Jillian Peterson (car dealership robbery) could be charged with conspiring with Westmont, McNichol, and the mastermind because they were all engaged in a continuing course of criminal conduct under one organized felony outfit. Remember Colonel Frank Winters' goal of locating the group's leader and ascertaining the purpose and goals of their criminal activities? While law enforcement officials did not know the criminals' exact goal, they did know that all these individuals were working together to raise money for a particular purpose. Accordingly, under the statute, the criminals all could be charged with conspiring with each other—even though they did not know each other and even though they committed separate, distinct robberies.

One Charge of Conspiracy When Continuous Conspiratorial Relationship Exists

It is likely that the mastermind and his gang would only each be charged with one count of conspiracy. Subsection c. of the conspiracy statute states: "If a person conspires to commit a number of felonies, he is guilty of only one conspiracy so long as such multiple felonies are the object of the same agreement or continuous conspiratorial relationship." Since the bandits' individual robberies were the object of a singular continuous conspiratorial relationship—a string of felonies arranged by the mastermind to net money for their organized felony outfit—each conspirator should be charged with only one count of conspiracy.

Overt Act

The conspiracy statute sets forth an "overt act" requirement in order for a defendant to be found guilty of conspiracy. However, there is a caveat to this requirement—an overt act, in furtherance of the conspiracy, is not a necessary element for conspiracies involving felonies of the first or second degree or for conspiracies to commit drug distribution offenses.

First, what is an "overt act," and where does it apply? An overt act is some kind of behavior, by either the accused or a coconspirator, that furthers the felony they have agreed to commit—and it may not even be an action that is directly related to the actual commission of the felony.

A modification of the car dealership facts demonstrates this point. Let's say that prior to the dealership robbery, Jillian Peterson had discussed her plan with a man named Bart Sampson. Sampson, sympathetic to her cause, agrees with her that he is interested in assisting her in the robbery. For weeks, he does nothing about the pending felony, but two days before the robbery, he purchases two machetes and provides them to Peterson. Sampson's discussion with Peterson about aiding her in the robbery, standing alone, does not constitute an overt act in furtherance of the conspiracy; however, his provision of the machetes to her clearly is an overt act that furthered the felony. But what if Sampson had purchased the machetes for Peterson but was unable to get them to her before she carried out the robbery or if Peterson was arrested before she was able to actually commit the felony? Could Sampson still be found guilty of conspiracy?

Sampson's purchase alone should satisfy the overt act requirement because it was an action that openly and clearly was taken to further their conspiracy. Interestingly, though, in this case, Sampson could be charged with conspiracy even if he had not committed an overt act at all. As aforementioned, conspiracies involving felonies of the first or second degree do not require an "overt act" for a person to be found guilty of conspiracy. Accordingly, with armed robbery being a felony of the first degree, Sampson's simple agreement with Peterson to assist her in the felony would suffice for him to be guilty of conspiracy. The only way for him to avoid conviction would be if he had completely and voluntarily renounced his involvement in the felony as per subsection e. of the statute.

Leader of Organized Crime

As per 27-20g., the individual who arranged the masked robberies should be charged as a "leader of organized crime." The mastermind purposely organized and conspired with Westmont, Vandermeit, and Peterson to perform their respective robberies. Law enforcement similarly suspects him of supervising and leading numerous other illegal activities. This series of continuing organized criminal events could constitute a pattern of racketeering activity under 26-1. Accordingly, the mastermind, if he eventually is identified, would appropriately be charged with being a "leader of organized crime," which is a separate and distinct criminal offense.

27-21.   **Grading of criminal attempt and conspiracy; mitigation in cases of lesser danger**

a. Grading. Except as provided in subsections c. and d., an attempt or conspiracy to commit a felony of the first degree is a felony of the second degree, except that an attempt or conspiracy to commit murder or terrorism is a felony of the first degree. Otherwise an attempt is a felony of the same degree as the most serious felony which is attempted, and conspiracy is a felony of the same degree as the most serious felony which is the object of the conspiracy, provided that, leader of organized crime is a felony of the second degree.

b. Mitigation. The court may impose sentence for a felony of a lower grade or degree if neither the particular conduct charged nor the defendant presents a public danger warranting the grading provided for such felony under subsection a. because:

   (1) The criminal attempt or conspiracy charged is so inherently unlikely to result or culminate in the commission of a felony; or

   (2) The conspiracy, as to the particular defendant charged, is so peripherally related to the main unlawful enterprise.

PRACTICAL APPLICATION OF STATUTE

Attempt/Conspiracy to Commit First Degree Felony Is a Second Degree Felony—Murder and Terrorism Are Exceptions

Michael Westmont wielded a shotgun at diner patrons and police officers and then fled the scene after stealing nearly $100,000 from a professional football player's automobile. This theft was also the product of a conspiracy. Jillian Peterson conspired to heist cash from a car dealership, and in the process, she attempted to kill the dealership manager by whipping machetes at him. So how should Westmont and Peterson be charged? Were their conspiracies felonies of the first degree or second degree—or even lower?

Michael Westmont should be charged with first degree robbery and second degree conspiracy for his offenses at the diner. Jillian Peterson should be charged with first degree robbery and first degree attempted murder but second degree conspiracy for her robbery of the car dealership. Why are their conspiracy charges lower degree felonies than their robberies? Why is Peterson's attempted murder charge a first degree offense?

Section 27-21 provides for grading of criminal attempt and conspiracy offenses. In part, this section states that "an attempt or conspiracy to commit a felony of the first degree is a felony of the second degree." Under that language, Peterson's attempt to kill the dealership manager would only be a second degree felony even though murder is a first degree felony. However, the statute provides two singular exceptions to that rule— "an attempt or conspiracy to commit murder or terrorism is a felony of the first degree." Accordingly, Peterson's attempted murder of the dealership manager is a first degree offense. Similarly, if she conspired to commit murder, then her conspiracy charge would be one of the first degree.

Now let's look at the robbery conspiracies. As stated above, the statute generally provides that a conspiracy to commit a felony of the first degree is a felony of the second degree. Therefore, Westmont's and Peterson's conspiracies to commit first degree felonies—robbery in each of their cases—are appropriately graded as second degree conspiracy offenses.

All Other Degree Felonies—Attempt/Conspiracy Same Degree as Underlying Felony

One should note, however, that for all other degree offenses, "an attempt is a felony of the same degree as the most serious felony which is attempted" and a "conspiracy is a felony of the same degree as the most serious felony which is the object of the conspiracy." For example, if an individual conspires with others to commit a third degree burglary, then he should be charged with third degree conspiracy to commit burglary; if he attempts to commit a third degree burglary but is caught, he should be charged with third degree attempted burglary.

27-22.   **Burglar's tools**

    a. Any person who manufactures or possesses any engine, machine, tool or implement adapted, designed or commonly used for committing or facilitating any offense in chapter 20 of this Criminal Code or offenses involving forcible entry into premises:

        (1) Knowing the same to be so adapted or designed or commonly used; and

        (2) With either a purpose so to use or employ it, or with a purpose to provide it to some person who he knows has such a purpose to use or employ it, is guilty of an offense.

    b. Any person who publishes plans or instructions dealing with the manufacture or use of any burglar tools as defined above with the intent that such publication be used for committing or facilitating any offense in chapter 9 of this Criminal Code or offenses involving forcible entry into premises is guilty of an offense.

The offense under a. or b. of this section is a felony of the fourth degree if the defendant manufactured such instruments or implements or published such plans or instructions; otherwise it is a misdemeanor A.

PRACTICAL APPLICATION OF STATUTE

Section 27-22 makes the possession or manufacture of burglar's tools an illegal offense. Specifically, if a person manufactures burglar's tools, implements them during a burglary/theft or publishes plans or instructions detailing how to manufacture burglar's tools, he is guilty of a fourth degree felony. It should be noted, however, that the manufacture of such tools or publication of plans alone technically is not an offense. The individual must know that the tools are commonly used for burglary/theft purposes and must have an intent to use these tools, or provide them to others, for use in a burglary/theft offense. Similarly, an individual publishing plans or instructions on the manufacturing of burglar's tools must intend for said plans to be used to aid others in a burglary/theft in order to be convicted under this statute.

A person who merely possesses burglar's tools but hasn't manufactured or implemented them is guilty of a misdemeanor A. Again, possession alone is not sufficient for a conviction; it must also be proved that the person knew the tools were commonly used for illegal activity and that he intended to use them at some point. This isn't an easy task.

A modification of the facts involving Jacques Vandermeit and the jewelry store robbery will exemplify the above. Instead of Chief M. P. Ironstone arriving at the store during the robbery, he pulls over Vandermeit's car for speeding. Vandermeit is alone and not wearing a handkerchief. Laying on the passenger seat, however, is an oddly sharpened screwdriver, a device commonly used in the illegal entry of dwellings and other structures. Based on this observation alone, should Ironstone arrest and charge Vandermeit? Maybe or maybe not.

A crucial element of this offense is proof of intent to use the tool in the commission of a burglary/theft. If Ironstone elicited or found corroborating evidence that demonstrated Vandermeit's intent to use the screwdriver in a theft-type activity, then it is likely that Vandermeit would be convicted of a burglar's tools offense. Without such corroboration, however, a guilty verdict is unlikely, and an arrest may be futile.

END OF CHAPTER REVIEW

Multiple-Choice Questions

1. Where is consent to bodily harm *not* a defense?
    a. in a boxing match
    b. if the bodily harm inflicted is serious, such as in a stabbing
    c. if the bodily harm inflicted causes a bruised bicep
    d. in a wrestling match
    e. consent to bodily harm is never a defense

2. When may a law enforcement officer use deadly force?
    a. to thwart a kidnapping
    b. to stop an aggravated sexual assault in progress
    c. to stop the theft of a bicycle
    d. a and b only
    e. none of the above

The following fact pattern pertains to questions 3–4.

Phantom X conspired with Paul, Frank, Mark and ten others to commit 13 separate robberies. Phantom X organized the group and financed their individual robberies, paying for the weapons and other necessary materials. The state attorney general determined that this series of continuing organized criminal events constituted a pattern of racketeering activity.

3. Phantom X could be charged with:
    a. maintaining a controlled dangerous substance (CDS) manufacturing outfit
    b. cleaning, under the Clean Hands doctrine
    c. being a leader of organized crime
    d. being a leader of a contemptuous illegal facility
    e. committing attempted contempt

4. Let's say Paul never actually met Phantom X or any of the other individuals who committed robberies for Phantom X's organization. Given this situation, which of the following is true?
    a. Paul could not be charged with conspiracy because he never actually met Phantom X or the others who conspired to commit the robberies.
    b. Paul could not be charged with conspiracy because he did not organize the group.
    c. Paul could not be charged with conspiracy because of the "$100,000 requirement."
    d. Paul could be charged with conspiracy even though he never actually met Phantom X or the others who conspired to commit the robberies.
    e. Only a, b and c are true.

The following fact pattern pertains to questions 5–6.

A man masked in a white handkerchief beat a jewelry store clerk with a baseball bat. A shirtless barefoot man accompanied the masked man and repeatedly screamed, "Knock the dude out!" The shirtless man then stuffed a handful of diamonds into the masked man's pocket. The jewelry clerk, severely beaten, suffered a fractured skull and a broken nose.

5. Should the shirtless man be charged with the armed robbery of the jewelry store?
    a. no, because he never struck the jewelry clerk
    b. no, because he was obviously insane
    c. yes, because he was an accomplice to the offense as he aided the masked man in committing it
    d. yes, because robbery is a first degree felony
    e. c and d only

6. Which of the following defenses could relieve the shirtless man of culpability for the beating of the jewelry clerk?
    a. consent—if the jewelry clerk had agreed to the beating
    b. mistake of law—if the shirtless man mistakenly believed that the beating was legal

c. intoxication—if the shirtless man had been injected with PCP and it was not self-induced and that resulted in his inability to know the nature and quality of his actions

d. all of the above

e. none of the above

7. There is no statute of limitations for which of the following offenses?

a. murder

b. aggravated manslaughter

c. manslaughter

d. all of the above

e. none of the above

Essay Questions

1. Walter Muscrat enters a law office holding two hand grenades. He orders the only attorney in the office to turn over the firm's checkbook. The attorney complies with his demands and turns over the checkbook to Muscrat. The armed assailant then orders the lawyer to the floor; the lawyer complies and drops down next to his desk. Unbeknownst to Muscrat, the attorney reaches under the desk where he has a pistol hidden. Muscrat, high on crack, suddenly pulls the pin of one of the grenades and tosses it to floor, right at his victim's head. The grenade doesn't detonate. Muscrat, annoyed, attempts to pull the pin from the second grenade. Before he could accomplish this, the lawyer fires a perfect shot at Muscrat's head, instantly killing him. Was the lawyer justified in using deadly force against Muscrat? Did the lawyer have a duty to retreat since the first grenade didn't detonate? Explain your answers. Also, cite the appropriate statute number in your answer.

2. Oscar, Felix, Gilligan and Ginger conspire to murder J.R. They succeed by having him thrown off a bridge. Mickey, Pops and Horatio conspire to steal $50,000 cash, a third degree felony, from Kong; the heist goes off as planned. What degree conspiracy should Oscar, Felix, Gilligan and Ginger be charged with and why? What degree conspiracy should Mickey, Pops and Horatio be charged with and why?

ANSWER GUIDE

Below are the answers to the multiple choice and essay questions for each chapter. Bullet points in the essay question section serve as a guide for answers to the essay questions.

CHAPTER 1

Multiple-Choice Questions

1. c	2. a
3. a	4. c
5. e	6. c
7. b	

Essay Questions

1. • Under the felony murder component of the murder statute, Beef is guilty of murder (for the death of the patron) because the death of the patron occurred while Beef was involved in committing a robbery. He is culpable for the death of the patron even though his partner shot the person and even though he did not intend for the patron to be killed or have any knowledge that his partner was going to shoot him.
   • Robbery is one of the enumerated crimes that invoke a felony murder charge.
   • See 1-3a.(3).
   • See the Practical Application section for murder (1-3).
   • Beef is not guilty of murder for the death of his partner, Elliot. The "accomplice exception" of the felony murder statute relieves Beef of culpability for the deaths of other participants in a crime.
   • See 1-3a.(3).
   • See the Practical Application section for murder (1-3).

2. • Aggravated manslaughter is the most appropriate offense to charge Big Ed with.
   • When an actor causes the death of another person while eluding police, he is guilty of aggravated manslaughter.
   • This is a first degree felony.
   • See 1-4a.(2).
   • See the Practical Application section for aggravated manslaughter (1-4).
   • Death by auto (vehicular homicide) is the best offense to charge Big Ed with for killing the pedestrian while driving while intoxicated.

- This is a second degree felony.
- See 1-5a. and 1-5b.
- See the Practical Application section for death by auto (1-5).

CHAPTER 2

Multiple-Choice Questions

1. c	2. d
3. d	4. e
5. e	6. b
7. a	

Essay Questions

1. • Police should not charge Sara with stalking.
   - Although there is a repeated course of conduct, Sara's acts would not cause a reasonable person to fear bodily injury to himself or a member of his immediate family.
   - See 2-4 and its Practical Application section.

2. • Beef is guilty of terroristic threats for threatening to kill Carl. Beef's purpose was to put Carl in "imminent fear of death"; Carl would "reasonably believe the immediacy of the threat" and that it would "likely be carried out."
   - This is a third degree felony.
   - See 2-3 and its Practical Application section.
   - For pointing a pistol at Officer Geronimo, Beef is guilty of aggravated assault.
   - This is a third degree felony.
   - See 2-1b.(9).
   - See the Practical Application section for aggravated assault (2-1).
   - For shattering Officer Geronimo's kneecap with a baseball bat, Beef is guilty of aggravated assault.
   - Per 2-1b.(1), he "knowingly" (if not "purposely") caused the officer "serious bodily injury." Here, this is a second degree felony.
   - Although Beef could be charged under 2-1b.(2) for "purposely" or "knowingly" causing "bodily injury" to another with a "deadly weapon" (a third degree felony), the second degree offense under 2-1b.(1) is the more appropriate charge because of the gravity of the injury.
   - See the Practical Application section for aggravated assault (2-1).
   - For pointing a pistol at Charles (the neighbor), Beef is guilty of aggravated assault.
   - This is a fourth degree felony.
   - See 2-1b.(4).
   - See the Practical Application section for aggravated assault (2-1).

- Punching McMichael in the face, causing his lip to bleed, is a simple assault; similarly, punching Charles in the face, causing him a black eye, is a simple assault. By these acts, Beef purposely caused "bodily injury" to others.
- Simple assault is a misdemeanor A.
- See 2-1a.(1).
- See the Practical Application section for simple assault (2-1).

CHAPTER 3

Multiple-Choice Questions

1. b	2. a
3. e	4. a
5. c	6. d
7. e	

Essay Questions

1. • Anderson is guilty of kidnapping because (a) he unlawfully removed Wesley from her car; (b) he unlawfully confined Wesley in the East Pinedale apartment; (c) he demanded a $50,000 ransom.
    - See 3-1a.
    - See the Practical Application section for kidnapping (3-1).
    - This is a second degree kidnapping because Anderson released Wesley unharmed and in a safe place prior to apprehension.
    - See 3-1c.
    - See the Practical Application section for kidnapping (3-1).
2. • Lucy is guilty of luring a child for enticing Alex into an alley with the purpose of committing a criminal offense (a sexual assault) against the child.
    - This is a second degree felony.
    - See 3-6 and its Practical Application section.
    - If Alex were age 65 instead of age 8, Lucy would be guilty of luring an adult.
    - This is a third degree felony.
    - See 3-7 and its Practical Application section.

CHAPTER 4

Multiple-Choice Questions

1. c	2. b
3. e	4. d
5. d	6. b
7. e	

Essay Questions

1. • Martin should be charged with aggravated sexual assault because non-consensual sexual intercourse occurred during a kidnapping—a specific enumerated felony that elevates this otherwise sexual assault to aggravated sexual assault.
   • This is a first degree felony.
   • See 4-2a.(3).
   • See the Practical Application section for aggravated sexual assault (4-2).
   • For the "date rape," Martin should be charged with sexual assault because Kerry did not suffer severe personal injury and because no other necessary factor existed that would elevate the offense to aggravated sexual assault.
   • This is a first degree felony.
   • See 4-2c.(1).
   • See the Practical Application section for sexual assault and aggravated sexual assault (4-2).

2. • Grandpa is guilty of no offense at all because he did not rub his grandson's groin to sexually gratify himself or to humiliate the boy. Thus, the act does not constitute a criminal sexual contact.
   • See definitions under 4-1.
   • See the Practical Application section for criminal sexual contact (4-3).
   • Grandpa is not guilty of lewdness for urinating in the alley because he did not expose his genitals "for the purpose of arousing or gratifying the sexual desire" of anyone else or to gratify his own sexual desire.
   • See 4-4 and its Practical Application section.

CHAPTER 5

Multiple-Choice Questions

1. d   2. e
3. d   4. c

Essay Question

1. • Tubby has committed a robbery because he threatened to immediately commit a "felony of the first or second degree" (rape) during the course of a theft.
   • This is a second degree robbery because Tubby didn't commit any of the aggravating factors that would elevate the offense to a first degree felony (e.g., he wasn't armed with and didn't threaten to use a deadly weapon, he didn't threaten to kill anyone, nor did he inflict or attempt to inflict serious bodily injury).
   • See 5-1 and its Practical Application section.

CHAPTER 6

Multiple-Choice Questions

1. d	2. c
3. e	4. a

CHAPTER 7

Multiple-Choice Questions

1. c	2. a
3. e	4. b
5. a	6. d
7. d	

Essay Questions

1. • Maria is guilty of arson rather than aggravated arson. She is guilty of arson because she "purposely started a fire" that "recklessly" placed her brother in danger of death or bodily injury. Because she didn't know her brother was in the tree house, Maria didn't "purposely" or "knowingly" place him in danger of death or bodily injury, which would elevate the offense to aggravated arson.
   • See 7-1b.(1).
   • See the Practical Application section for arson and aggravated arson (7-1).
   • It is extremely unlikely that a tree house would be considered a "structure," which is defined in section 8-1. However, as explained above, Maria did not need to recklessly place a structure in danger of damage or destruction in order to be convicted of arson—recklessly placing another person (her brother) in danger of death or bodily injury certainly suffices for an arson conviction in her case.
   • Maria also could be convicted of criminal mischief for purposely destroying the baseball cards.
   • See 7-3 and its Practical Application section.

2. • Arson for hire (e.g., paying someone to burn down a house) elevates aggravated arson from a second degree felony to a first degree felony.
   • See 7-1d.
   • If the target of the aggravated arson is a place of worship, such as a church or synagogue, the actor is guilty of first degree aggravated arson rather than a second degree offense.
   • See 7-1g.
   • See the Practical Application section for arson and aggravated arson (7-1).

CHAPTER 8

Multiple-Choice Questions

1. b   2. c

3. a   4. e

Essay Question

1. • Fidel has committed a burglary because he entered a "structure" (a house) "with the purpose to commit an offense therein" (sexual assault). The purpose to commit any offense—felony or misdemeanor—is sufficient. The actor therefore does not need to commit a theft to be convicted of burglary.

   • See 8-2 and its Practical Application section.

   • Burglary is elevated from a third degree felony to a second degree felony where the actor purposely, knowingly or recklessly inflicts, attempts to inflict or threatens to inflict bodily injury on anyone or is armed with or displays what appears to be explosives or a deadly weapon.

   • See 8-2b.(1) and b.(2), grading of burglary.

   • See 8-2 and its Practical Application section.

CHAPTER 9

Multiple-Choice Questions

1. b   2. d

3. e   4. d

5. b   6. b

7. d

Essay Questions

1. • Sol is guilty of theft by extortion for threatening to inflict bodily injury on Julie if Julie didn't sign over the title of her car to him. This is a second degree offense, as all thefts by extortion are second degree offenses.

   • See 9-5 and its Practical Application section.

   • Sol again is guilty of theft by extortion for threatening to testify against Jim if Jim did not give Sol the motorcycle in his garage. This is a second degree offense, as all thefts by extortion are second degree offenses.

   • See 9-5 and its Practical Application section.

2. • Paul Canapa is guilty of theft of property delivered by mistake for depositing Francisco Maxgoose's $100,000 money order into his account. Key elements that make Canapa guilty of this felony are the following: (a) He knew that the money order was delivered to him by mistake; (b) he knew

the identity of the person who was supposed to receive the money order; (c) he converted the funds to his own use by depositing the money order into his own bank account; (d) he did this with the purpose to deprive Maxgoose of the funds.

- See 9-6 and its Practical Application section.
- This is a second degree felony because the amount of money involved in the theft is "$75,000 or more."
- See 9-2b.(1)(a).

CHAPTER 10

Multiple-Choice Questions

1. b	2. e
3. b	4. b
5. d	6. b
7. a	

Essay Questions

1. • Jameson is guilty of issuing a bad check under 10-5b. if he knew there were insufficient funds in his account at the time he issued the check. He is also guilty of issuing a bad check under 10-5a. if he knew the bank account, on which the check was written, was closed when he issued the check.
   - See 10-5a. and 10-5b. and the Practical Application section for this statute.
   - Jameson's bad check charge is a felony of the third degree because the amount of the bad check ($15,000) is "$1,000 or more but is less than $75,000."
   - See 10-5c. and the Practical Application section for this statute.

2. • Premium Loan is guilty of usury for lending $5,000 to Bob, an individual, at an interest rate of 75% per annum because the yearly interest rate exceeded 30%—which is the maximum interest rate on a loan to an individual.
   - See 10-19 and its Practical Application section.
   - Premium Loan is guilty of usury for lending $500,000 to Smack Hack's Bar and Restaurant, a limited liability company, at an interest rate of 75% per annum because the yearly interest rate exceeded 50%—which is the maximum interest rate on a loan to a corporation.
   - See 10-19 and its Practical Application section.
   - Marty is not guilty of usury for lending $10,000 to his friend's company, Jose Shoes, Inc., at an interest rate of 45% per annum because the yearly interest rate did not exceed 50%—which is the maximum interest rate on a loan to a corporation.
   - See 10-19 and its Practical Application section.

CHAPTER 11

Multiple-Choice Question

1. e

CHAPTER 12

Multiple-Choice Questions

1. a   2. b
3. d   4. a

Essay Question

1. • Senator Chavez would be guilty of a fourth degree crime if he stayed at the party and watched the child pornography tape.
   • See 12-2b.(4)(b) and the statute's Practical Application section.
   • Senator Chavez would be guilty of a second degree crime if he took the child porn tape and sold it to a friend.
   • See 12-2b.(4)(a) and the statute's Practical Application section.

CHAPTER 13

Multiple-Choice Questions

1. c   2. a
3. c   4. d

Essay Question

1. • Both Mr. and Mrs. McMoose are potential victims protected under the Prevention of Domestic Violence Act because they are spouses.
   • See 13-1d. and the Practical Application section for 13-2.
   • Officer Simon *must* arrest Mrs. McMoose because there is probable cause to believe that she struck Mr. McMoose and Mr. McMoose has visible signs of injuries.
   • See 13-2a.(1) and the statute's Practical Application section.
   • Officer Simon should not arrest Mr. McMoose because nothing in the fact pattern shows that he would have probable cause that Mr. McMoose committed any act of domestic violence. However, per 13-2b., a law enforcement officer *may* arrest a person if he has probable cause to believe the person committed an act of domestic violence—even in matters where there are no

visible signs of injuries or any of the other factors as described in subsection a. of the statute.

- See 13-2b. and the statute's Practical Application section.
- If Officer Simon had found that Mrs. McMoose had caused the scratch to her husband by using "reasonable force" to protect herself, then the officer should *not* arrest her.
- See 13-2c.(3) and the statute's Practical Application section.

CHAPTER 14

Multiple-Choice Questions

1. b   2. a
3. d   4. c

Essay Question

1. • Seaver is not guilty of bribery or any other offense in Chapter 14 because a public servant or party official was not involved in the matter.
   - See definitions in 14-1.
   - See 14-2 and its Practical Application section.
   - Both Kingman and Mayor Koosman are guilty of second degree bribery for Kingman's payment of $7,500 to Mayor Koosman.
   - See 14-2 and its Practical Application section.

CHAPTER 15

Multiple-Choice Questions

1. d   2. d
3. d   4. c
5. e   6. c
7. a

Essay Questions

1. • Horowitz's false statement providing Simeone with an alibi is "material" because it could affect the outcome of the trial (e.g., whether or not Simeone is convicted).
   - "Materiality" is an element of perjury.
   - See 15-1 and its Practical Application section.
   - Horowitz is guilty of no offense at all because the proof of his false statement rested on one witness's contradictory testimony; there is no corroboration.
   - See 15-1e.
   - See the Practical Application section for perjury (15-1).

2. • Skip should be charged with witness tampering because he knowingly attempted to cause a witness to withhold testimony.

   • See 15-5a. and the statute's Practical Application section.

   • Skip is guilty of a second degree felony of tampering with a witness because he threatened to use force to prevent the testimony.

   • See 15-5a. and the statute's Practical Application section.

CHAPTER 16

Multiple-Choice Questions

1.	b	2.	a
3.	d	4.	c
5.	d	6.	b
7.	d		

Essay Questions

1. • Lucy has committed a misdemeanor A resisting arrest for refusing to allow a Yale police officer to effectuate a lawful arrest by clinging to a pole. This is because she simply refused to allow the officer to arrest her, and there were no aggravating factors (as listed in the statute).

   • See 16-2a.(1) and the statute's Practical Application section.

   • Axel is guilty of a fourth degree resisting arrest for running from a Harvard Town police officer as she was trying to lawfully arrest him for burglary. This is because he used flight to purposely prevent a law enforcement officer from effectuating an arrest.

   • See 16-2a.(2) and the statute's Practical Application section.

   • Jamaal is guilty of a third degree resisting arrest for threatening to stab a Brownsville Heights police officer and flailing his arms, all in an effort to prevent the officer from lawfully arresting him on theft charges. This is because he threatened physical violence against the police office while resisting the arrest.

   • See 16-2a.(3)(a) and the statute's Practical Application section.

2. • In the first case, where Quick Mick stopped by the bakery and gave Bernard a basket of assorted cheeses, he is guilty of a misdemeanor A contempt because he violated the restraining order but did not commit an act that would "constitute a felony or misdemeanor A" while violating it.

   • See 16-9b. and the statute's Practical Application section.

   • In the second case, where Quick Mick showed up at Bernard's house and shot him in the arm, he is guilty of a fourth degree felony of contempt because his conduct while violating the restraining order would "constitute a felony or misdemeanor A" (here, an act of aggravated assault).

   • See 16-9b. and the statute's Practical Application section.

CHAPTER 17

Multiple-Choice Questions

1. e   2. d
3. e   4. d

Essay Question

1. • Attorney General Moon is guilty of official misconduct for fabricating charges against U.S. Senator Jared Bamlish—all in an effort to disparage the man's reputation and to take his U.S. Senate seat. She is guilty of this offense because the following elements are present: (a) She is a "public servant" (the attorney general); (b) she had the "purpose to benefit herself" and/or "injure another" (obtain a U.S. Senate seat and destroy Bamlish's reputation); (c) she committed an act relating to her office (filed criminal charges); (d) she knew that she was committing an unauthorized exercise of her official functions (knowing the criminal charges were fabricated).

   • See 17-1a. and the statute's Practical Application section.

   • If Moon falsified the charges against Bamlish because he was Caucasian and not because she wanted his U.S. Senate seat, she is guilty of official deprivation of civil rights.

   • See 17-4 and the statute's Practical Application section.

CHAPTER 18

Multiple-Choice Questions

1. b   2. c
3. e   4. d
5. e   6. e
7. b

Essay Questions

1. • The *best* offense for the Lyndhurst police officer to charge Juice with is harassment; this is more appropriate than simple assault because harassment has its "offensive touching" component, which has specific language prohibiting "shoving."

   • This is a misdemeanor B.

   • See 18-4b. and the statute's Practical Application section.

   • The *best* offense for the Lyndhurst police officer to charge Parsons with is disorderly conduct because he engaged in "threatening" and "tumultuous" behavior by saying "I'm going to get you in a bad way" and rushing behind the bar and wildly banging pots and pans, screaming nonsensical words (which disrupted customers' dinners).

- This is a misdemeanor B.
- See 18-2a.(1) and the statute's Practical Application section.

2. • The Brainiac smoked a cigarette on a public bus in Paterson and therefore is guilty of a petty disorderly person's offense for smoking in public.
- See 18-11 and the statute's Practical Application section.
- Bob the Drug Dealer is guilty of a fourth degree crime for using a pager during a drug deal.
- See 18-17 and the statute's Practical Application section.
- Costello, age 45, consumed two glasses of wine in an Italian restaurant on a Sunday. He is guilty of no offense under this Criminal Code.

CHAPTER 19

Multiple-Choice Questions

1. a   2. d
3. d   4. d

Essay Question

1. • In knowingly promoting the prostitution of her 14-year-old daughter, Jennifer, Madame Luci is guilty of a second degree felony.
- She has no defenses available to her because Jennifer is her child.
- See 19-1b.(4) and 19-1c.(1) and the Practical Application section for this statute.
- In knowingly promoting the prostitution of her daughter's 14-year-old friend Janice, Madame Luci is guilty of a second degree felony.
- She has no defenses available to her per the statute's specific language that an offense is committed "whether or not the actor mistakenly believed that the child was 18 years of age or older, even if such mistaken belief was reasonable."
- See 19-1b.(3) and 19-1c.(1) and the Practical Application section for this statute.
- In knowingly promoting the prostitution of the 48 adult women, Madame Luci is guilty of a third degree felony on each count.
- See 19-1b.(2), 19-1c.(1) and 19-1a.(4)(a) and the Practical Application section for this statute.

CHAPTER 20

Multiple-Choice Questions

1. b   2. c
3. a   4. e
5. d   6. d
7. b

Essay Questions

1. • For selling 11 ounces of cocaine to buyer Dumb Head, Red Beard is guilty of first degree distribution of CDS. This is because the quantity of cocaine exceeded 5 ounces.
   • See 20-4b.(1) and the statute's Practical Application section.
   • If Red Beard conducted his cocaine transaction 750 feet away from a public elementary school, he should be charged with an additional offense under 20-6. This is because he dealt CDS "within 1,000 feet of school property."
   • See 20-6 and its Practical Application section.
   • If Red Beard conducted his cocaine transaction 750 feet away from a public park, he should *not* be charged with an additional offense. Under 20-6.1, there is an additional offense for distributing CDS near public parks, housing facilities, etc.; however, the distribution must be "on or within *500* feet" of such property.
   • See 20-6.1 and its Practical Application section.

2. • For the sale of the 75 marijuana plants, Schwartz is guilty of first degree distribution of marijuana. This is because he sold them "50 or more marijuana plants."
   • See 20-4b.(10)(a) and the statute's Practical Application section.
   • For Schwartz's sale of the 15 pounds of oregano, he is guilty of a third degree felony for selling "imitation CDS." The weight of the imitation CDS is irrelevant to grading.
   • See 20-9 and the statute's Practical Application section.
   • For the sale of the 250 milligrams of LSD, Leroy is guilty of a first degree felony of distributing LSD because he sold detectives "100 milligrams or more" of LSD.
   • See 20-4b.(6) and the statute's Practical Application section.
   • For possessing the eight ounces of heroin with the intent to distribute it, Leroy is guilty of a first degree felony. This is because the quantity of heroin exceeded five ounces. It is irrelevant that six of the eight ounces constituted "dilutants" as the statute specifically provides the language "including any adulterants or dilutants." Accordingly, the degree of Leroy's offense is not lowered because of the dilutants mixed in with the pure heroin.
   • See 20-4b.(1) and the statute's Practical Application section.

CHAPTER 21

Multiple-Choice Questions

1. e   2. c
3. b   4. e

Essay Question

1. • For possessing and using the hypodermic needle, Horace is guilty of a misdemeanor A.
   • See 21-6 and the statute's Practical Application section.

- For discarding the needle on the floor in the casino bathroom, Horace is guilty of a misdemeanor B.
- See 21-6.1 and the statute's Practical Application section.
- For selling a marijuana bong to Nipsy, a 15-year-old boy, Horace is guilty of third degree felony.
- See 21-5 and the statute's Practical Application section.

CHAPTER 22

Multiple-Choice Questions

1. e   2. d
3. e   4. d

Essay Question

1. • The Hyena is guilty of maintaining a gambling resort. This is because he actively ran the resort, accepted a "playing fee" in exchange for allowing individuals to engage in the illegal games and profited from their losses.
   - This is a fourth degree felony.
   - See 22-4 and the statute's Practical Application section.

CHAPTER 23

Multiple-Choice Questions

1. e   2. c
3. d   4. d

Essay Question

1. • For driving a car bomb into a supermarket, Scott Zero is guilty of terrorism. The reasons he is guilty of this offense are as follows: (a) He attempted to commit murder or at least aggravated assault, an offense necessary to trigger a terrorism charge, and (b) his purpose in committing this criminal act was to influence a policy of the government (he wanted the state to change its welfare policy and give more money to people who do not work).
   - See 23-2 and the statute's Practical Application section.
   - The fact that no one was killed does not relieve Zero from culpability—the statute enumerates several predicate crimes, many of which do not involve death.
   - See 23-2c. and the statute's Practical Application section.
   - Sunshine is guilty of hindering the apprehension of a terrorist for harboring Scott Zero in her basement with the purpose of hindering his apprehension.
   - See 23-4a.(1) and the statute's Practical Application section.

- This is a second degree felony because no one was killed during the terrorist act committed by Zero.
- See 23-4b. and the statute's Practical Application section.

CHAPTER 24

Multiple-Choice Questions

1. c   2. e
3. a   4. e
5. e   6. e
7. d

Essay Questions

1. • Scorpion should be charged with possession of a weapon for unlawful purposes. This is a second degree felony because the weapon was a firearm.
   - See 24-4a. and the statute's Practical Application section.
   - Scorpion can also be charged with possession of a firearm by a convicted felon because he was previously convicted of kidnapping. This is a second degree felony.
   - See 24-7b. and the statute's Practical Application section.
   - Finally, Scorpion can be charged with unlawful possession of a weapon. This is a third degree felony because the weapon was a firearm.
   - See 24-5a. and the statute's Practical Application section.

2. • In order to be convicted of being a leader of a firearms trafficking network, the following elements must be present: (a) The defendant must unlawfully manufacture, transport, ship, sell or dispose of any firearm; (b) the defendant must conspire with others; (c) the network must exist to earn a profit.
   - This is a felony of the first degree.
   - See 24-13 and the statute's Practical Application section.

CHAPTER 25

Multiple-Choice Questions

1. c   2. a
3. b   4. c

Essay Question

1. • Maximus Larabelle is not guilty of cloning because he did not replicate or attempt to replicate a human being by "cultivating a cell" with human genetic material. Simply creating a dummy or robot that may resemble a human

being by using synthetic materials and even animal skeletons does not meet the elements of the cloning statute.

- See 25-10 and the statute's Practical Application section.

CHAPTER 26

Multiple-Choice Questions

1. d	2. b
3. d	4. d

CHAPTER 27

Multiple-Choice Questions

1. b	2. d
3. c	4. d
5. c	6. c
7. d	

Essay Questions

1. • The lawyer was justified in using deadly force against Walter Muscrat because, under the circumstances, he would have a reasonable belief that deadly force was necessary to protect his own life.

   • The lawyer did not have a duty to retreat because the first grenade did not detonate. Muscrat still possessed a second grenade, which the lawyer had every reason to believe he would attempt to use. This was not a situation where the lawyer would know that he could retreat with complete safety; accordingly, he did not have a duty to retreat.

   • See 27-12 and the statute's Practical Application section.

2. • Oscar, Felix, Gilligan and Ginger should be charged with a first degree conspiracy because a conspiracy to commit murder is always a first degree offense.

   • Mickey, Pops and Horatio should be charged with a third degree conspiracy because the underlying theft offense is a third degree felony.

   • Generally, those who conspire to commit a first degree felony are guilty of a second degree conspiracy, except in cases of murder and terrorism where it is a first degree conspiracy. For all other felonies, a "conspiracy is a felony of the same degree as the most serious felony which is the object of the conspiracy."

   • See 27-21 and the statute's Practical Application section.

Index